Classic Shell Scripting

Arnold Robbins and Nelson H. F. Beebe

O'REILLY®

Beijing · Cambridge · Farnham · Köln · Paris · Sebastopol · Taipei · Tokyo

Classic Shell Scripting
by Arnold Robbins and Nelson H. F. Beebe

Published by O'Reilly Media, Inc., 1005 Gravenstein Highway North, Sebastopol, CA 95472.

O'Reilly books may be purchased for educational, business, or sales promotional use. Online editions are also available for most titles (*safari.oreilly.com*). For more information, contact our corporate/institutional sales department: (800) 998-9938 or *corporate@oreilly.com*.

Editors:	Tatiana Apandi
	Allison Randal
Production Editor:	Adam Witwer
Cover Designer:	Emma Colby
Interior Designer:	David Futato

Printing History:

May 2005:	First Edition.

 This book uses RepKover, a durable and flexible lay-flat binding.

ISBN: 0-596-00595-4
[M]

Table of Contents

Foreword ix

Preface xi

1. Background **1**
   1.1 Unix History   1
   1.2 Software Tools Principles   4
   1.3 Summary   6

2. Getting Started **8**
   2.1 Scripting Languages Versus Compiled Languages   8
   2.2 Why Use a Shell Script?   9
   2.3 A Simple Script   9
   2.4 Self-Contained Scripts: The #! First Line   10
   2.5 Basic Shell Constructs   12
   2.6 Accessing Shell Script Arguments   23
   2.7 Simple Execution Tracing   24
   2.8 Internationalization and Localization   25
   2.9 Summary   28

3. Searching and Substitutions **30**
   3.1 Searching for Text   30
   3.2 Regular Expressions   31
   3.3 Working with Fields   56
   3.4 Summary   65

4. Text Processing Tools **67**
    4.1 Sorting Text   67
    4.2 Removing Duplicates   75
    4.3 Reformatting Paragraphs   76
    4.4 Counting Lines, Words, and Characters   77
    4.5 Printing   78
    4.6 Extracting the First and Last Lines   83
    4.7 Summary   86

5. Pipelines Can Do Amazing Things **87**
    5.1 Extracting Data from Structured Text Files   87
    5.2 Structured Data for the Web   94
    5.3 Cheating at Word Puzzles   100
    5.4 Word Lists   102
    5.5 Tag Lists   105
    5.6 Summary   107

6. Variables, Making Decisions, and Repeating Actions **109**
    6.1 Variables and Arithmetic   109
    6.2 Exit Statuses   120
    6.3 The case Statement   129
    6.4 Looping   130
    6.5 Functions   135
    6.6 Summary   138

7. Input and Output, Files, and Command Evaluation **140**
    7.1 Standard Input, Output, and Error   140
    7.2 Reading Lines with read   140
    7.3 More About Redirections   143
    7.4 The Full Story on printf   147
    7.5 Tilde Expansion and Wildcards   152
    7.6 Command Substitution   155
    7.7 Quoting   161
    7.8 Evaluation Order and eval   162
    7.9 Built-in Commands   168
    7.10 Summary   175

8. Production Scripts **177**

    8.1 Path Searching   177

    8.2 Automating Software Builds   192

    8.3 Summary   222

9. Enough awk to Be Dangerous **223**

    9.1 The awk Command Line   224

    9.2 The awk Programming Model   225

    9.3 Program Elements   226

    9.4 Records and Fields   236

    9.5 Patterns and Actions   238

    9.6 One-Line Programs in awk   240

    9.7 Statements   244

    9.8 User-Defined Functions   252

    9.9 String Functions   255

    9.10 Numeric Functions   264

    9.11 Summary   266

10. Working with Files **267**

    10.1 Listing Files   267

    10.2 Updating Modification Times with touch   273

    10.3 Creating and Using Temporary Files   274

    10.4 Finding Files   279

    10.5 Running Commands: xargs   293

    10.6 Filesystem Space Information   295

    10.7 Comparing Files   299

    10.8 Summary   307

11. Extended Example: Merging User Databases **308**

    11.1 The Problem   308

    11.2 The Password Files   309

    11.3 Merging Password Files   310

    11.4 Changing File Ownership   317

    11.5 Other Real-World Issues   321

    11.6 Summary   323

12. Spellchecking **325**

    12.1 The spell Program   325

    12.2 The Original Unix Spellchecking Prototype   326

    12.3 Improving ispell and aspell   327

    12.4 A Spellchecker in awk   331

    12.5 Summary   350

13. Processes **352**

    13.1 Process Creation   353

    13.2 Process Listing   354

    13.3 Process Control and Deletion   360

    13.4 Process System-Call Tracing   368

    13.5 Process Accounting   372

    13.6 Delayed Scheduling of Processes   373

    13.7 The /proc Filesystem   378

    13.8 Summary   379

14. Shell Portability Issues and Extensions **381**

    14.1 Gotchas   381

    14.2 The bash shopt Command   385

    14.3 Common Extensions   389

    14.4 Download Information   402

    14.5 Other Extended Bourne-Style Shells   405

    14.6 Shell Versions   405

    14.7 Shell Initialization and Termination   406

    14.8 Summary   412

15. Secure Shell Scripts: Getting Started **413**

    15.1 Tips for Secure Shell Scripts   413

    15.2 Restricted Shell   416

    15.3 Trojan Horses   418

    15.4 Setuid Shell Scripts: A Bad Idea   419

    15.5 ksh93 and Privileged Mode   421

    15.6 Summary   422

A. Writing Manual Pages 423

B. Files and Filesystems 437

C. Important Unix Commands 473

Bibliography 478

Glossary 484

Index 509

Foreword

Surely I haven't been doing shell scripting for 30 years?!? Well, now that I think about it, I suppose I have, although it was only in a small way at first. (The early Unix shells, before the Bourne shell, were very primitive by modern standards, and writing substantial scripts was difficult. Fortunately, things quickly got better.)

In recent years, the shell has been neglected and underappreciated as a scripting language. But even though it was Unix's first scripting language, it's still one of the best. Its combination of extensibility and efficiency remains unique, and the improvements made to it over the years have kept it highly competitive with other scripting languages that have gotten a lot more hype. GUIs are more fashionable than command-line shells as user interfaces these days, but scripting languages often provide most of the underpinnings for the fancy screen graphics, and the shell continues to excel in that role.

The shell's dependence on other programs to do most of the work is arguably a defect, but also inarguably a strength: you get the concise notation of a scripting language plus the speed and efficiency of programs written in C (etc.). Using a common, general-purpose data representation—lines of text—in a large (and extensible) set of tools lets the scripting language plug the tools together in endless combinations. The result is far more flexibility and power than any monolithic software package with a built-in menu item for (supposedly) everything you might want. The early success of the shell in taking this approach reinforced the developing Unix philosophy of building specialized, single-purpose tools and plugging them together to do the job. The philosophy in turn encouraged improvements in the shell to allow doing more jobs that way.

Shell scripts also have an advantage over C programs—and over some of the other scripting languages too (naming no names!)—of generally being fairly easy to read and modify. Even people who are not C programmers, like a good many system administrators these days, typically feel comfortable with shell scripts. This makes shell scripting very important for extending user environments and for customizing software packages.

Indeed, there's a "wheel of reincarnation" here, which I've seen on several software projects. The project puts simple shell scripts in key places, to make it easy for users to customize aspects of the software. However, it's so much easier for the *project* to solve problems by working in those shell scripts than in the surrounding C code, that the scripts steadily get more complicated. Eventually they are too complicated for the users to cope with easily (some of the scripts we wrote in the C News project were notorious as stress tests for shells, never mind users!), and a new set of scripts has to be provided for user customization...

For a long time, there's been a conspicuous lack of a good book on shell scripting. Books on the Unix programming environment have touched on it, but only briefly, as one of several topics, and the better books are long out-of-date. There's reference documentation for the various shells, but what's wanted is a novice-friendly tutorial, covering the tools as well as the shell, introducing the concepts gently, offering advice on how to get the best results, and paying attention to practical issues like readability. Preferably, it should also discuss how the various shells differ, instead of trying to pretend that only one exists.

This book delivers all that, and more. Here, at last, is an up-to-date and painless introduction to the first and best of the Unix scripting languages. It's illustrated with realistic examples that make useful tools in their own right. It covers the standard Unix tools well enough to get people started with them (and to make a useful reference for those who find the manual pages a bit forbidding). I'm particularly pleased to see it including basic coverage of awk, a highly useful and unfairly neglected tool which excels in bridging gaps between other tools and in doing small programming jobs easily and concisely.

I recommend this book to anyone doing shell scripting or administering Unix-derived systems. I learned things from it; I think you will too.

—Henry Spencer
SP Systems

Preface

The user or programmer new to Unix[*] is suddenly faced with a bewildering variety of programs, each of which often has multiple options. Questions such as "What purpose do they serve?" and "How do I use them?" spring to mind.

This book's job is to answer those questions. It teaches you how to combine the Unix tools, together with the standard shell, to get your job done. This is the art of *shell scripting*. Shell scripting requires not just a knowledge of the shell language, but also a knowledge of the individual Unix programs: why each one is there, and how to use them by themselves and in combination with the other programs.

Why should you learn shell scripting? Because often, medium-size to large problems can be decomposed into smaller pieces, each of which is amenable to being solved with one of the Unix tools. A shell script, when done well, can often solve a problem in a mere fraction of the time it would take to solve the same problem using a conventional programming language such as C or C++. It is also possible to make shell scripts *portable*—i.e., usable across a range of Unix and POSIX-compliant systems, with little or no modification.

When talking about Unix programs, we use the term *tools* deliberately. The Unix *toolbox approach* to problem solving has long been known as the "Software Tools" philosophy.[†]

A long-standing analogy summarizes this approach to problem solving. A Swiss Army knife is a useful thing to carry around in one's pocket. It has several blades, a screwdriver, a can opener, a toothpick, and so on. Larger models include more tools, such as a corkscrew or magnifying glass. However, there's only so much you can do with a Swiss Army knife. While it might be great for whittling or simple carving, you

---

[*] Throughout this book, we use the term *Unix* to mean not only commercial variants of the original Unix system, such as Solaris, Mac OS X, and HP-UX, but also the freely available workalike systems, such as GNU/Linux and the various BSD systems: BSD/OS, NetBSD, FreeBSD, and OpenBSD.

[†] This approach was popularized by the book *Software Tools* (Addison-Wesley).

wouldn't use it, for example, to build a dog house or bird feeder. Instead, you would move on to using *specialized* tools, such as a hammer, saw, clamp, or planer. So too, when solving programming problems, it's better to use specialized software tools.

Intended Audience

This book is intended for computer users and software developers who find themselves in a Unix environment, with a need to write shell scripts. For example, you may be a computer science student, with your first account on your school's Unix system, and you want to learn about the things you can do under Unix that your Windows PC just can't handle. (In such a case, it's likely you'll write multiple scripts to customize your environment.) Or, you may be a new system administrator, with the need to write specialized programs for your company or school. (Log management and billing and accounting come to mind.) You may even be an experienced Mac OS developer moving into the brave new world of Mac OS X, where installation programs are written as shell scripts. Whoever you are, if you want to learn about shell scripting, this book is for you. In this book, you will learn:

Software tool design concepts and principles
> A number of principles guide the design and implementation of good software tools. We'll explain those principles to you and show them to you in use throughout the book.

What the Unix tools are
> A core set of Unix tools are used over and over again when shell scripting. We cover the basics of the shell and regular expressions, and present each core tool within the context of a particular kind of problem. Besides covering what the tools do, for each tool we show you *why* it exists and why it has particular options.

> *Learning Unix* is an introduction to Unix systems, serving as a primer to bring someone with no Unix experience up to speed as a basic user. By contrast, *Unix in a Nutshell* covers the broad swath of Unix utilities, with little or no guidance as to when and how to use a particular tool. Our goal is to bridge the gap between these two books: we teach you how to exploit the facilities your Unix system offers you to get your job done quickly, effectively, and (we hope) elegantly.

How to combine the tools to get your job done
> In shell scripting, it really is true that "the whole is greater than the sum of its parts." By using the shell as "glue" to combine individual tools, you can accomplish some amazing things, with little effort.

About popular extensions to standard tools
> If you are using a GNU/Linux or BSD-derived system, it is quite likely that your tools have additional, useful features and/or options. We cover those as well.

About indispensable nonstandard tools

> Some programs are not "standard" on most traditional Unix systems, but are nevertheless too useful to do without. Where appropriate, these are covered as well, including information about where to get them.

For longtime Unix developers and administrators, the software tools philosophy is nothing new. However, the books that popularized it, while still being worthwhile reading, are all on the order of 20 years old, or older! Unix systems have changed since these books were written, in a variety of ways. Thus, we felt it was time for an updated presentation of these ideas, using modern versions of the tools and current systems for our examples. Here are the highlights of our approach:

- Our presentation is POSIX-based. "POSIX" is the short name for a series of formal standards describing a portable operating system environment, at the programmatic level (C, C++, Ada, Fortran) and at the level of the shell and utilities. The POSIX standards have been largely successful at giving developers a fighting chance at making both their programs and their shell scripts portable across a range of systems from different vendors. We present the shell language, and each tool and its most useful options, as described in the most recent POSIX standard.

    The official name for the standard is IEEE Std. 1003.1–2001.* This standard includes several optional parts, the most important of which are the *X/Open System Interface* (XSI) specifications. These features document a fuller range of historical Unix system behaviors. Where it's important, we'll note changes between the current standard and the earlier 1992 standard, and also mention XSI-related features. A good starting place for Unix-related standards is *http://www.unix.org/*.†

    The home page for the Single UNIX Specification is *http://www.unix.org/version3/*. Online access to the current standard is available, but requires registration at *http://www.unix.org/version3/online.html*.

    Occasionally, the standard leaves a particular behavior as "unspecified." This is done on purpose, to allow vendors to support historical behavior as *extensions*, i.e., additional features above and beyond those documented within the standard itself.

- Besides just telling you how to run a particular program, we place an emphasis on *why* the program exists and on what problem it solves. Knowing why a program was written helps you better understand when and how to use it.

- Many Unix programs have a bewildering array of options. Usually, some of these options are more useful for day-to-day problem solving than others are. For each

---

* A 2004 edition of the standard was published after this book's text was finalized. For purposes of learning about shell scripting, the differences between the 2001 and 2004 standard don't matter.

† A technical frequently asked questions (FAQ) file about IEEE Std. 1003.1–2001 may be found at *http://www.opengroup.org/austin/papers/posix_faq.html*. Some background on the standard is at *http://www.opengroup.org/austin/papers/backgrounder.html*.

program, we tell you which options are the most useful. In fact, we typically do not cover all the options that individual programs have, leaving that task to the program's manual page, or to other reference books, such as *Unix in a Nutshell* (O'Reilly) and *Linux in a Nutshell* (O'Reilly).

By the time you've finished this book, you should not only understand the Unix toolset, but also have internalized the Unix mindset and the Software Tools philosophy.

What You Should Already Know

You should already know the following things:

- How to log in to your Unix system
- How to run programs at the command line
- How to make simple pipelines of commands and use simple I/O redirectors, such as ‹ and ›
- How to put jobs in the background with &
- How to create and edit files
- How to make scripts executable, using chmod

Furthermore, if you're trying to work the examples here by typing commands at your terminal (or, more likely, terminal emulator) we recommend the use of a POSIX-compliant shell such as a recent version of ksh93, or the current version of bash. In particular, /bin/sh on commercial Unix systems may not be fully POSIX-compliant.

Chapter 14 provides Internet download URLs for ksh93, bash, and zsh.

Chapter Summary

We recommend reading the book in order, as each chapter builds upon the concepts and material covered in the chapters preceding it. Here is a chapter-by-chapter summary:

Chapter 1, *Background*
Here we provide a brief history of Unix. In particular, the computing environment at Bell Labs where Unix was developed motivated much of the Software Tools philosophy. This chapter also presents the principles for good Software Tools that are then expanded upon throughout the rest of the book.

Chapter 2, *Getting Started*
This chapter starts off the discussion. It begins by describing compiled languages and scripting languages, and the tradeoffs between them. Then it moves on, covering the very basics of shell scripting with two simple but useful shell scripts. The coverage includes commands, options, arguments, shell variables,

output with echo and printf, basic I/O redirection, command searching, accessing arguments from within a script, and execution tracing. It closes with a look at internationalization and localization; issues that are increasingly important in today's "global village."

Chapter 3, *Searching and Substitutions*

Here we introduce text searching (or "matching") with regular expressions. We also cover making changes and extracting text. These are fundamental operations that form the basis of much shell scripting.

Chapter 4, *Text Processing Tools*

In this chapter we describe a number of the text processing software tools that are used over and over again when shell scripting. Two of the most important tools presented here are sort and uniq, which serve as powerful ways to organize and reduce data. This chapter also looks at reformatting paragraphs, counting text units, printing files, and retrieving the first or last lines of a file.

Chapter 5, *Pipelines Can Do Amazing Things*

This chapter shows several small scripts that demonstrate combining simple Unix utilities to make more powerful, and importantly, more flexible tools. This chapter is largely a cookbook of problem statements and solutions, whose common theme is that all the solutions are composed of linear pipelines.

Chapter 6, *Variables, Making Decisions, and Repeating Actions*

This is the first of two chapters that cover the rest of the essentials of the shell language. This chapter looks at shell variables and arithmetic, the important concept of an exit status, and how decision making and loops are done in the shell. It rounds off with a discussion of shell functions.

Chapter 7, *Input and Output, Files, and Command Evaluation*

This chapter completes the description of the shell, focusing on input/output, the various substitutions that the shell performs, quoting, command-line evaluation order, and shell built-in commands.

Chapter 8, *Production Scripts*

Here we demonstrate combinations of Unix tools to carry out more complex text processing jobs. The programs in this chapter are larger than those in Chapter 5, but they are still short enough to digest in a few minutes. Yet they accomplish tasks that are quite hard to do in conventional programming languages such as C, C++, or Java™.

Chapter 9, *Enough awk to Be Dangerous*

This chapter describes the essentials of the awk language. awk is a powerful language in its own right. However, simple, and sometimes, not so simple, awk programs can be used with other programs in the software toolbox for easy data extraction, manipulation, and formatting.

Chapter 10, *Working with Files*

This chapter introduces the primary tools for working with files. It covers listing files, making temporary files, and the all-important `find` command for finding files that meet specific criteria. It looks at two important commands for dealing with disk space utilization, and then discusses different programs for comparing files.

Chapter 11, *Extended Example: Merging User Databases*

Here we tie things together by solving an interesting and moderately challenging task.

Chapter 12, *Spellchecking*

This chapter uses the problem of doing spellchecking to show how it can be solved in different ways. It presents the original Unix shell script pipeline, as well as two small scripts to make the freely available `ispell` and `aspell` commands more usable for batch spellchecking. It closes off with a reasonably sized yet powerful spellchecking program written in `awk`, which nicely demonstrates the elegance of that language.

Chapter 13, *Processes*

This chapter moves out of the realm of text processing and into the realm of job and system management. There are a small number of essential utilities for managing processes. In addition, this chapter covers the `sleep` command, which is useful in scripts for waiting for something to happen, as well as other standard tools for delayed or fixed-time-of-day command processing. Importantly, the chapter also covers the `trap` command, which gives shell scripts control over Unix signals.

Chapter 14, *Shell Portability Issues and Extensions*

Here we describe some of the more useful extensions available in both `ksh` and `bash` that aren't in POSIX. In many cases, you can safely use these extensions in your scripts. The chapter also looks at a number of "gotchas" waiting to trap the unwary shell script author. It covers issues involved when writing scripts, and possible implementation variances. Furthermore, it covers download and build information for `ksh` and `bash`. It finishes up by discussing shell initialization and termination, which differ among different shell implementations.

Chapter 15, *Secure Shell Scripts: Getting Started*

In this chapter we provide a cursory introduction to shell scripting security issues.

Appendix A, *Writing Manual Pages*

This chapter describes how to write a manual page. This necessary skill is usually neglected in typical Unix books.

Appendix B, *Files and Filesystems*

Here we describe the Unix byte-stream filesystem model, contrasting it with more complex historical filesystems and explaining why this simplicity is a virtue.

Appendix C, *Important Unix Commands*

This chapter provides several lists of Unix commands. We recommend that you learn these commands and what they do to improve your skills as a Unix developer.

Bibliography

Here we list further sources of information about shell scripting with Unix.

Glossary

The Glossary provides definitions for the important terms and concepts introduced in this book.

Conventions Used in This Book

We leave it as understood that, when you enter a shell command, you press Enter at the end. Enter is labeled Return on some keyboards.

Characters called Ctrl-*X*, where *X* is any letter, are entered by holding down the Ctrl (or Ctl, or Control) key and then pressing that letter. Although we give the letter in uppercase, you can press the letter without the Shift key.

Other special characters are newline (which is the same as Ctrl-J), Backspace (the same as Ctrl-H), Esc, Tab, and Del (sometimes labeled Delete or Rubout).

This book uses the following font conventions:

Italic

Italic is used in the text for emphasis, to highlight special terms the first time they are defined, for electronic mail addresses and Internet URLs, and in manual page citations. It is also used when discussing dummy parameters that should be replaced with an actual value, and to provide commentary in examples.

`Constant Width`

This is used when discussing Unix filenames, external and built-in commands, and command options. It is also used for variable names and shell keywords, options, and functions; for filename suffixes; and in examples to show the contents of files or the output from commands, as well as for command lines or sample input when they are within regular text. In short, anything related to computer usage is in this font.

`Constant Width Bold`

This is used in the text to distinguish regular expressions and shell wildcard patterns from the text to be matched. It is also used in examples to show interaction between the user and the shell; any text the user types in is shown in **`Constant Width Bold`**. For example:

```
$ pwd                          User typed this
/home/tolstoy/novels/w+p        System printed this
$
```

Constant Width Italic

This is used in the text and in example command lines for dummy parameters that should be replaced with an actual value. For example:

```
$ cd directory
```

 This icon indicates a tip, suggestion, or general note.

 This icon indicates a warning or caution.

References to entries in the Unix User's Manual are written using the standard style: *name*(N), where *name* is the command name and N is the section number (usually 1) where the information is to be found. For example, *grep*(1) means the manpage for grep in section 1. The reference documentation is referred to as the "man page," or just "manpage" for short.

We refer both to Unix system calls and C library functions like this: open( ), printf( ). You can see the manpage for either kind of call by using the man command:

```
$ man open             Look at open(2) manpage
$ man printf           Look at printf(3) manpage
```

When programs are introduced, a sidebar, such as shown nearby, describes the tool as well as its significant options, usage, and purpose.

Example

Usage

whizprog [*options* ...] [*arguments* ...]

This section shows how to run the command, here named whizprog.

Purpose

This section describes *why* the program exists.

Major options

This section lists the options that are important for everyday use of the program under discussion.

Behavior

This section summarizes what the program does.

Caveats

If there's anything to be careful of, it's mentioned here.

Code Examples

This book is full of examples of shell commands and programs that are designed to be useful in your everyday life as a user or programmer, not just to illustrate the feature being explained. We especially encourage you to modify and enhance them yourself.

The code in this book is published under the terms of the GNU General Public License (GPL), which allows copying, reuse, and modification of the programs. See the file COPYING included with the examples for the exact terms of the license.

The code is available from this book's web site: *http://www.oreilly.com/catalog/shellsrptg/index.html*.

We appreciate, but do not require, attribution. An attribution usually includes the title, author, publisher, and ISBN. For example: "*Classic Shell Scripting*, by Arnold Robbins and Nelson H.F. Beebe. Copyright 2005 O'Reilly Media, Inc., 0-596-00595-4."

Unix Tools for Windows Systems

Many programmers who got their initial experience on Unix systems and subsequently crossed over into the PC world wished for a nice Unix-like environment (especially when faced with the horrors of the MS-DOS command line!), so it's not surprising that several Unix shell-style interfaces to small-computer operating systems have appeared.

In the past several years, we've seen not just shell clones, but also entire Unix environments. Two of them use bash and ksh93. Another provides its own shell reimplementation. This section describes each environment in turn (in alphabetical order), along with contact and Internet download information.

Cygwin

Cygnus Consulting (now Red Hat) created the cygwin environment. First creating cgywin.dll, a shared library that provides Unix system call emulation, the company ported a large number of GNU utilities to various versions of Microsoft Windows. The emulation includes TCP/IP networking with the Berkeley socket API. The greatest functionality comes under Windows/NT, Windows 2000, and Windows XP, although the environment can and does work under Windows 95/98/ME, as well.

The cygwin environment uses bash for its shell, GCC for its C compiler, and the rest of the GNU utilities for its Unix toolset. A sophisticated mount command provides a mapping of the Windows C:\path notation to Unix filenames.

The starting point for the cygwin project is *http://www.cygwin.com/*. The first thing to download is an installer program. Upon running it, you choose what additional packages you wish to install. Installation is entirely Internet-based; there are no official cygwin CDs, at least not from the project maintainers.

DJGPP

The DJGPP suite provides 32-bit GNU tools for the MS-DOS environment. To quote the web page:

> DJGPP is a complete 32-bit C/C++ development system for Intel 80386 (and higher) PCs running MS-DOS. It includes ports of many GNU development utilities. The development tools require an 80386 or newer computer to run, as do the programs they produce. In most cases, the programs it produces can be sold commercially without license or royalties.

The name comes from the initials of D.J. Delorie, who ported the GNU C++ compiler, g++, to MS-DOS, and the text initials of g++, GPP. It grew into essentially a full Unix environment on top of MS-DOS, with all the GNU tools and bash as its shell. Unlike cygwin or UWIN (see further on), you don't need a version of Windows, just a full 32-bit processor and MS-DOS. (Although, of course, you can use DJGPP from within a Windows MS-DOS window.) The web site is *http://www.delorie.com/djgpp/*.

MKS Toolkit

Perhaps the most established Unix environment for the PC world is the MKS Toolkit from Mortice Kern Systems:

> MKS Canada – Corporate Headquarters
> 410 Albert Street
> Waterloo, ON
> Canada N2L 3V3
> 1-519-884-2251
> 1-519-884-8861 (FAX)
> 1-800-265-2797 (Sales)
> *http://www.mks.com/*

The MKS Toolkit comes in various versions, depending on the development environment and the number of developers who will be using it. It includes a shell that is POSIX-compliant, along with just about all the features of the 1988 Korn shell, as well as more than 300 utilities, such as awk, perl, vi, make, and so on. The MKS library supports more than 1500 Unix APIs, making it extremely complete and easing porting to the Windows environment.

AT&T UWIN

The UWIN package is a project by David Korn and his colleagues to make a Unix environment available under Microsoft Windows. It is similar in structure to cygwin, discussed earlier. A shared library, `posix.dll`, provides emulation of the Unix system call APIs. The system call emulation is quite complete. An interesting twist is that the Windows registry can be accessed as a filesystem under `/reg`. On top of the Unix API emulation, ksh93 and more than 200 Unix utilities (or rather, reimplementations) have been compiled and run. The UWIN environment relies on the native Microsoft Visual C/C++ compiler, although the GNU development tools are available for download and use with UWIN.

http://www.research.att.com/sw/tools/uwin/ is the web page for the project. It describes what is available, with links for downloading binaries, as well as information on commercial licensing of the UWIN package. Also included are links to various papers on UWIN, additional useful software, and links to other, similar packages.

The most notable advantage to the UWIN package is that its shell *is* the authentic ksh93. Thus, compatibility with the Unix version of ksh93 isn't an issue.

Safari Enabled

 When you see a Safari® Enabled icon on the cover of your favorite technology book, it means the book is available online through the O'Reilly Network Safari Bookshelf.

Safari offers a solution that's better than e-books. It's a virtual library that lets you easily search thousands of top technology books, cut and paste code samples, download chapters, and find quick answers when you need the most accurate, current information. Try it for free at *http://safari.oreilly.com*.

We'd Like to Hear from You

We have tested and verified all of the information in this book to the best of our ability, but you may find that features have changed (or even that we have made mistakes!). Please let us know about any errors you find, as well as your suggestions for future editions, by writing:

> O'Reilly Media, Inc.
> 1005 Gravenstein Highway North
> Sebastopol, CA 95472
> 1-800-998-9938 (in the U.S. or Canada)
> 1-707-829-0515 (international/local)
> 1-707-829-0104 (FAX)

You can also send us messages electronically. To be put on the mailing list or request a catalog, send email to:

> *info@oreilly.com*

To ask technical questions or comment on the book, send email to:

bookquestions@oreilly.com

We have a web site for the book where we provide access to the examples, errata, and any plans for future editions. You can access these resources at:

http://www.oreilly.com/catalog/shellsrptg/index.html

Acknowledgments

Each of us would like to acknowledge the other for his efforts. Considering that we've never met in person, the co-operation worked out quite well. Each of us also expresses our warmest thanks and love to our wives for their contributions, patience, love, and support during the writing of this book.

Chet Ramey, bash's maintainer, answered innumerable questions about the finer points of the POSIX shell. Glenn Fowler and David Korn of AT&T Research, and Jim Meyering of the GNU Project, also answered several questions. In alphabetical order, Keith Bostic, George Coulouris, Mary Ann Horton, Bill Joy, Rob Pike, Hugh Redelmeier (with help from Henry Spencer), and Dennis Ritchie answered several Unix history questions. Nat Torkington, Allison Randall, and Tatiana Diaz at O'Reilly Media shepherded the book from conception to completion. Robert Romano at O'Reilly did a great job producing figures from our original ASCII art and pic sketches. Angela Howard produced a comprehensive index for the book that should be of great value to our readers.

In alphabetical order, Geoff Collyer, Robert Day, Leroy Eide, John Halleck, and Henry Spencer acted as technical reviewers for the first draft of this book. Sean Burke reviewed the second draft. We thank them all for their valuable and helpful feedback.

Henry Spencer is a Unix Guru's Unix Guru. We thank him for his kind words in the Foreword.

Access to Unix systems at the University of Utah in the Departments of Electrical and Computer Engineering, Mathematics, and Physics, and the Center for High-Performance Computing, as well as guest access kindly provided by IBM and Hewlett-Packard, were essential for the software testing needed for writing this book; we are grateful to all of them.

—Arnold Robbins
—Nelson H.F. Beebe

## CHAPTER 1

Background

This chapter provides a brief history of the development of the Unix system. Understanding where and how Unix developed and the intent behind its design will help you use the tools better. The chapter also introduces the guiding principles of the Software Tools philosophy, which are then demonstrated throughout the rest of the book.

1.1   Unix History

It is likely that you know something about the development of Unix, and many resources are available that provide the full story. Our intent here is to show how the environment that gave birth to Unix influenced the design of the various tools.

Unix was originally developed in the Computing Sciences Research Center at Bell Telephone Laboratories.* The first version was developed in 1970, shortly after Bell Labs withdrew from the Multics project. Many of the ideas that Unix popularized were initially pioneered within the Multics operating system; most notably the concepts of devices as files, and of having a command interpreter (or *shell*) that was intentionally not integrated into the operating system. A well-written history may be found at *http://www.bell-labs.com/history/unix*.

Because Unix was developed within a research-oriented environment, there was no commercial pressure to produce or ship a finished product. This had several advantages:

- The system was developed by its users. They used it to solve real day-to-day computing problems.

- The researchers were free to experiment and to change programs as needed. Because the user base was small, if a program needed to be rewritten from

---

* The name has changed at least once since then. We use the informal name "Bell Labs" from now on.

scratch, that generally wasn't a problem. And because the users were the developers, they were free to fix problems as they were discovered and add enhancements as the need for them arose.

Unix itself went through multiple research versions, informally referred to with the letter "V" and a number: V6, V7, and so on. (The formal name followed the edition number of the published manual: First Edition, Second Edition, and so on. The correspondence between the names is direct: V6 = Sixth Edition, and V7 = Seventh Edition. Like most experienced Unix programmers, we use both nomenclatures.) The most influential Unix system was the Seventh Edition, released in 1979, although earlier ones had been available to educational institutions for several years. In particular, the Seventh Edition system introduced both awk and the Bourne shell, on which the POSIX shell is based. It was also at this time that the first published books about Unix started to appear.

- The researchers at Bell Labs were all highly educated computer scientists. They designed the system for their personal use and the use of their colleagues, who also were computer scientists. This led to a "no nonsense" design approach; programs did what you told them to do, without being chatty and asking lots of "are you sure?" questions.

- Besides just extending the state of the art, there existed a quest for *elegance* in design and problem solving. A lovely definition for elegance is "power cloaked in simplicity."* The freedom of the Bell Labs environment led to an *elegant* system, not just a *functional* one.

Of course, the same freedom had a few disadvantages that became clear as Unix spread beyond its development environment:

- There were many inconsistencies among the utilities. For example, programs would use the same option letter to mean different things, or use different letters for the same task. Also, the regular-expression syntaxes used by different programs were similar, but not identical, leading to confusion that might otherwise have been avoided. (Had their ultimate importance been recognized, regular expression-matching facilities could have been encoded in a standard library.)

- Many utilities had limitations, such as on the length of input lines, or on the number of open files, etc. (Modern systems generally have corrected these deficiencies.)

- Sometimes programs weren't as thoroughly tested as they should have been, making it possible to accidentally kill them. This led to surprising and confusing "core dumps." Thankfully, modern Unix systems rarely suffer from this.

---

* I first heard this definition from Dan Forsyth sometime in the 1980s.

- The system's documentation, while generally complete, was often terse and min-
  imalistic. This made the system more difficult to learn than was really desirable.*

Most of what we present in this book centers around processing and manipulation of
textual, not binary, data. This stems from the strong interest in text processing that
existed during Unix's early growth, but is valuable for other reasons as well (which
we discuss shortly). In fact, the first production use of a Unix system was doing text
processing and formatting in the Bell Labs Patent Department.

The original Unix machines (Digital Equipment Corporation PDP-11s) weren't capable of running large programs. To accomplish a complex task, you had to break it
down into smaller tasks and have a separate program for each smaller task. Certain
common tasks (extracting fields from lines, making substitutions in text, etc.) were
common to many larger projects, so they became standard tools. This was eventually recognized as being a good thing in its own right: the lack of a large address
space led to smaller, simpler, *more focused* programs.

Many people were working semi-independently on Unix, reimplementing each
other's programs. Between version differences and no need to standardize, a lot of
the common tools diverged. For example, grep on one system used -i to mean
"ignore case when searching," and it used -y on another variant to mean the same
thing! This sort of thing happened with multiple utilities, not just a few. The common small utilities were named the same, but shell programs written for the utilities
in one version of Unix probably wouldn't run unchanged on another.

Eventually the need for a common set of standardized tools and options became
clear. The POSIX standards were the result. The current standard, IEEE Std. 1003.1–
2004, encompasses both the C library level, and the shell language and system utilities and their options.

The good news is that the standardization effort paid off. Modern commercial Unix
systems, as well as freely available workalikes such as GNU/Linux and BSD-derived
systems, are all POSIX-compliant. This makes learning Unix easier, and makes it
possible to write portable shell scripts. (However, do take note of Chapter 14.)

Interestingly enough, POSIX wasn't the only Unix standardization effort. In particular, an initially European group of computer manufacturers, named X/Open, produced its own set of standards. The most popular was XPG4 (X/Open Portability
Guide, Fourth Edition), which first appeared in 1988. There was also an XPG5, more

---

* The manual had two components: the reference manual and the user's manual. The latter consisted of tutorial papers on major parts of the system. While it was possible to learn Unix by reading all the documentation, and many people (including the authors) did exactly that, today's systems no longer come with printed
  documentation of this nature.

widely known as the UNIX 98 standard, or as the *"Single UNIX Specification."* XPG5 largely included POSIX as a subset, and was also quite influential.[*]

The XPG standards were perhaps less rigorous in their language, but covered a broader base, formally documenting a wider range of existing practice among Unix systems. (The goal for POSIX was to make a standard formal enough to be used as a guide to implementation from scratch, even on non-Unix platforms. As a result, many features common on Unix systems were initially excluded from the POSIX standards.) The 2001 POSIX standard does double duty as XPG6 by including the *X/Open System Interface Extension* (or XSI, for short). This is a formal extension to the base POSIX standard, which documents attributes that make a system not only POSIX-compliant, but also XSI-compliant. Thus, there is now only one formal standards document that implementors and application writers need refer to. (Not surprisingly, this is called the Single Unix Standard.)

Throughout this book, we focus on the shell language and Unix utilities as defined by the POSIX standard. Where it's important, we'll include features that are XSI-specific as well, since it is likely that you'll be able to use them too.

1.2   Software Tools Principles

Over the course of time, a set of core principles developed for designing and writing software tools. You will see these exemplified in the programs used for problem solving throughout this book. Good software tools should do the following things:

Do one thing well
> In many ways, this is the single most important principle to apply. Programs that do only one thing are easier to design, easier to write, easier to debug, and easier to maintain and document. For example, a program like grep that searches files for lines matching a pattern should *not* also be expected to perform arithmetic.
>
> A natural consequence of this principle is a proliferation of smaller, specialized programs, much as a professional carpenter has a large number of specialized tools in his toolbox.

Process lines of text, not binary
> Lines of text are the universal format in Unix. Datafiles containing text lines are easy to process when writing your own tools, they are easy to edit with any available text editor, and they are portable across networks and multiple machine architectures. Using text files facilitates combining any custom tools with existing Unix programs.

---

[*] The list of X/Open publications is available at *http://www.opengroup.org/publications/catalog/*.

Use regular expressions

Regular expressions are a powerful mechanism for working with text. Understanding how they work and using them properly simplifies your script-writing tasks.

Furthermore, although regular expressions varied across tools and Unix versions over the years, the POSIX standard provides only two kinds of regular expressions, with standardized library routines for regular-expression matching. This makes it possible for you to write your own tools that work with regular expressions identical to those of grep (called *Basic Regular Expressions* or BREs by POSIX), or identical to those of egrep (called *Extended Regular Expressions* or EREs by POSIX).

Default to standard I/O

When not given any explicit filenames upon which to operate, a program should default to reading data from its standard input and writing data to its standard output. Error messages should always go to standard error. (These are discussed in Chapter 2.) Writing programs this way makes it easy to use them as data *filters*—i.e., as components in larger, more complicated pipelines or scripts.

Don't be chatty

Software tools should not be "chatty." No `starting processing`, `almost done`, or `finished processing` kinds of messages should be mixed in with the regular output of a program (or at least, not by default).

When you consider that tools can be strung together in a pipeline, this makes sense:

```
tool_1 < datafile | tool_2 | tool_3 | tool_4 > resultfile
```

If each tool produces "yes I'm working" kinds of messages and sends them down the pipe, the data being manipulated would be hopelessly corrupted. Furthermore, even if each tool sends its messages to standard error, the screen would be full of useless progress messages. When it comes to tools, no news is good news.

This principle has a further implication. In general, Unix tools follow a "you asked for it, you got it" design philosophy. They don't ask "are you sure?" kinds of questions. When a user types `rm somefile`, the Unix designers figured that he knows what he's doing, and `rm` removes the file, no questions asked.[*]

Generate the same output format accepted as input

Specialized tools that expect input to obey a certain format, such as header lines followed by data lines, or lines with certain field separators, and so on, should produce output following the same rules as the input. This makes it easy to

---

[*] For those who are really worried, the -i option to rm forces rm to prompt for confirmation, and in any case rm prompts for confirmation when asked to remove suspicious files, such as those whose permissions disallow writing. As always, there's a balance to be struck between the extremes of never prompting and always prompting.

process the results of one program run through a different program run, perhaps with different options.

For example, the netpbm suite of programs* manipulate image files stored in a Portable BitMap format.† These files contain bitmapped images, described using a well-defined format. Each tool reads PBM files, manipulates the contained image in some fashion, and then writes a PBM format file back out. This makes it easy to construct a simple pipeline to perform complicated image processing, such as scaling an image, then rotating it, and then decreasing the color depth.

Let someone else do the hard part

Often, while there may not be a Unix program that does *exactly* what you need, it is possible to use existing tools to do 90 percent of the job. You can then, if necessary, write a small, specialized program to finish the task. Doing things this way can save a large amount of work when compared to solving each problem fresh from scratch, each time.

Detour to build specialized tools

As just described, when there just isn't an existing program that does what you need, take the time to build a tool to suit your purposes. However, before diving in to code up a quick program that does exactly your specific task, stop and think for a minute. Is the task one that other people are going to need done? Is it possible that your specialized task is a specific case of a more general problem that doesn't have a tool to solve it? If so, think about the general problem, and write a program aimed at solving that. Of course, when you do so, design and write your program so it follows the previous rules! By doing this, you graduate from being a tool user to being a *toolsmith*, someone who creates tools for others!

1.3 Summary

Unix was originally developed at Bell Labs by and for computer scientists. The lack of commercial pressure, combined with the small capacity of the PDP-11 minicomputer, led to a quest for small, elegant programs. The same lack of commercial pressure, though, led to a system that wasn't always consistent, nor easy to learn.

As Unix spread and variant versions developed (notably the System V and BSD variants), portability at the shell script level became difficult. Fortunately, the POSIX standardization effort has borne fruit, and just about all commercial Unix systems and free Unix workalikes are POSIX-compliant.

---

* The programs are not a standard part of the Unix toolset, but are commonly installed on GNU/Linux and BSD systems. The WWW starting point is *http://netpbm.sourceforge.net/*. From there, follow the links to the Sourceforge project page, which in turn has links for downloading the source code.

† There are three different formats; see the *pnm*(5) manpage if netpbm is installed on your system.

The Software Tools principles as we've outlined them provide the guidelines for the development and use of the Unix toolset. Thinking with the Software Tools mindset will help you write clear shell programs that make correct use of the Unix tools.

CHAPTER 2

Getting Started

When you need to get some work done with a computer, it's best to use a tool that's appropriate to the job at hand. You don't use a text editor to balance your checkbook or a calculator to write a proposal. So too, different programming languages meet different needs when it comes time to get some computer-related task done.

Shell scripts are used most often for system administration tasks, or for combining existing programs to accomplish some small, specific job. Once you've figured out how to get the job done, you can bundle up the commands into a separate program, or *script*, which you can then run directly. What's more, if it's useful, other people can make use of the program, treating it as a *black box*, a program that gets a job done, without their having to know *how* it does so.

In this chapter we'll make a brief comparison between different kinds of programming languages, and then get started writing some simple shell scripts.

2.1   Scripting Languages Versus Compiled Languages

Most medium and large-scale programs are written in a *compiled* language, such as Fortran, Ada, Pascal, C, C++, or Java. The programs are translated from their original *source code* into *object code* which is then executed directly by the computer's hardware.*

The benefit of compiled languages is that they're efficient. Their disadvantage is that they usually work at a low level, dealing with bytes, integers, floating-point numbers, and other machine-level kinds of objects. For example, it's difficult in C++ to say something simple like "copy all the files in this directory to that directory over there."

---

* This statement is not quite true for Java, but it's close enough for discussion purposes.

8

So-called scripting languages are usually *interpreted*. A regular compiled program, the *interpreter*, reads the program, translates it into an internal form, and then executes the program.[*]

2.2   Why Use a Shell Script?

The advantage to scripting languages is that they often work at a higher level than compiled languages, being able to deal more easily with objects such as files and directories. The disadvantage is that they are often less efficient than compiled languages. Usually the tradeoff is worthwhile; it can take an hour to write a simple script that would take two days to code in C or C++, and usually the script will run fast enough that performance won't be a problem. Examples of scripting languages include awk, Perl, Python, Ruby, and the shell.

Because the shell is universal among Unix systems, and because the language is standardized by POSIX, shell scripts can be written once and, if written carefully, used across a range of systems. Thus, the reasons to use a shell script are:

Simplicity
> The shell is a high-level language; you can express complex operations clearly and simply using it.

Portability
> By using just POSIX-specified features, you have a good chance of being able to move your script, *unchanged*, to different kinds of systems.

Ease of development
> You can often write a powerful, useful script in little time.

·2.3   A Simple Script

Let's start with a simple script. Suppose that you'd like to know how many users are currently logged in. The who command tells you who is logged in:

```
$ who
george    pts/2     Dec 31 16:39    (valley-forge.example.com)
betsy     pts/3     Dec 27 11:07    (flags-r-us.example.com)
benjamin  dtlocal   Dec 27 17:55    (kites.example.com)
jhancock  pts/5     Dec 27 17:55    (:32)
camus     pts/6     Dec 31 16:22
tolstoy   pts/14    Jan  2 06:42
```

On a large multiuser system, the listing can scroll off the screen before you can count all the users, and doing that every time is painful anyway. This is a perfect

---

[*] See *http://foldoc.doc.ic.ac.uk/foldoc/foldoc.cgi?Ousterhout's+dichotomy* for an attempt to formalize the distinction between compiled and interpreted language. This formalization is not universally agreed upon.

opportunity for automation. What's missing is a way to count the number of users. For that, we use the wc (word count) program, which counts lines, words, and characters. In this instance, we want wc -l, to count just lines:

```
$ who | wc -l                       Count users
        6
```

The | (pipe) symbol creates a pipeline between the two programs: who's output becomes wc's input. The result, printed by wc, is the number of users logged in.

The next step is to make this pipeline into a separate command. You do this by entering the commands into a regular file, and then making the file executable, with chmod, like so:

```
$ cat > nusers                      Create the file, copy terminal input with cat
who | wc -l                         Program text
^D                                  Ctrl-D is end-of-file
$ chmod +x nusers                   Make it executable
$ ./nusers                          Do a test run
        6                           Output is what we expect
```

This shows the typical development cycle for small one- or two-line shell scripts: first, you experiment directly at the command line. Then, once you've figured out the proper incantations to do what you want, you put them into a separate script and make the script executable. You can then use that script directly from now on.

2.4   Self-Contained Scripts: The #! First Line

When the shell runs a program, it asks the Unix kernel to start a new process and run the given program in that process. The kernel knows how to do this for compiled programs. Our nusers shell script isn't a compiled program; when the shell asks the kernel to run it, the kernel will fail to do so, returning a "not executable format file" error. The shell, upon receiving this error, says "Aha, it's not a compiled program, it must be a shell script," and then proceeds to start a new copy of /bin/sh (the standard shell) to run the program.

The "fall back to /bin/sh" mechanism is great when there's only one shell. However, because current Unix systems have multiple shells, there needs to be a way to tell the Unix kernel which shell to use when running a particular shell script. In fact, it helps to have a general mechanism that makes it possible to directly invoke *any* programming language interpreter, not just a command shell. This is done via a special first line in the script file—one that begins with the two characters #!.

When the first two characters of a file are #!, the kernel scans the rest of the line for the full pathname of an interpreter to use to run the program. (Any intervening whitespace is skipped.) The kernel also scans for a *single* option to be passed to that interpreter. The kernel invokes the interpreter with the given option, along with the rest of the command line. For example, assume a csh script* named /usr/ucb/whizprog, with this first line:

```
#! /bin/csh -f
```

Furthermore, assume that /usr/ucb is included in the shell's search path (described later). A user might type the command whizprog -q /dev/tty01. The kernel interprets the #! line and invokes csh as follows:

```
/bin/csh -f /usr/ucb/whizprog -q /dev/tty01
```

This mechanism makes it easy to invoke *any* interpreted language. For example, it is a good way to invoke a standalone awk program:

```
#! /bin/awk -f
awk program here
```

Shell scripts typically start with #! /bin/sh. Use the path to a POSIX-compliant shell if your /bin/sh isn't POSIX compliant. There are also some low-level "gotchas" to watch out for:

- On modern systems, the maximum length of the #! line varies from 63 to 1024 characters. Try to keep it less than 64 characters. (See Table 2-1 for a representative list of different limits.)

- On some systems, the "rest of the command line" that is passed to the interpreter includes the full pathname of the command. On others, it does not; the command line as entered is passed to the program. Thus, scripts that look at the command-line arguments cannot portably depend on the full pathname being present.

- Don't put any trailing whitespace after an option, if present. It will get passed along to the invoked program along with the option.

- You have to know the full pathname to the interpreter to be run. This can prevent cross-vendor portability, since different vendors put things in different places (e.g., /bin/awk versus /usr/bin/awk).

- On antique systems that don't have #! interpretation in the kernel, some shells will do it themselves, and they may be picky about the presence or absence of whitespace characters between the #! and the name of the interpreter.

Table 2-1 lists the different line length limits for the #! line on different Unix systems. (These were discovered via experimentation.) The results are surprising, in that they are often not powers of two.

---

* /bin/csh is the C shell command interpreter, originally developed at the University of California at Berkeley. We don't cover C shell programming in this book for many reasons, the most notable of which are that it's universally regarded as being a poorer shell for scripting, and because it's not standardized by POSIX.

Table 2-1. #! line length limits on different systems

Vendor platform	O/S version	Maximum length
Apple Power Mac	Mac Darwin 7.2 (Mac OS 10.3.2)	512
Compaq/DEC Alpha	OSF/1 4.0	1024
Compaq/DEC/HP Alpha	OSF/1 5.1	1000
GNU/Linux[a]	Red Hat 6, 7, 8, 9; Fedora 1	127
HP PA–RISC and Itanium-2	HP–UX 10, 11	127
IBM RS/6000	AIX 4.2	255
Intel x86	FreeBSD 4.4	64
Intel x86	FreeBSD 4.9, 5.0, 5.1	128
Intel x86	NetBSD 1.6	63
Intel x86	OpenBSD 3.2	63
SGI MIPS	IRIX 6.5	255
Sun SPARC, x86	Solaris 7, 8, 9, 10	1023

[a] All architectures.

The POSIX standard leaves the behavior of #! "unspecified." This is the standardese way of saying that such a feature may be used as an extension while staying POSIX-compliant.

All further scripts in this book start with a #! line. Here's the revised nusers program:

```
$ cat nusers               Show contents
#! /bin/sh -               Magic #! line

who | wc -l                Commands to run
```

The bare option – says that there are no more shell options; this is a security feature to prevent certain kinds of spoofing attacks.

2.5   Basic Shell Constructs

In this section we introduce the basic building blocks used in just about all shell scripts. You will undoubtedly be familiar with some or all of them from your interactive use of the shell.

· 2.5.1   Commands and Arguments

The shell's most basic job is simply to execute commands. This is most obvious when the shell is being used interactively: you type commands one at a time, and the shell executes them, like so:

```
$ cd work ; ls -l whizprog.c
-rw-r--r--    1 tolstoy   devel          30252 Jul  9 22:52 whizprog.c
$ make
...
```

These examples show the basics of the Unix command line. First, the format is simple, with *whitespace* (space and/or tab characters) separating the different components involved in the command.

Second, the command name, rather logically, is the first item on the line. Most typically, options follow, and then any additional arguments to the command follow the options. No gratuitous syntax is involved, such as:

```
COMMAND=CD,ARG=WORK
COMMAND=LISTFILES,MODE=LONG,ARG=WHIZPROG.C
```

Such command languages were typical of the larger systems available when Unix was designed. The free-form syntax of the Unix shell was a real innovation in its time, contributing notably to the readability of shell scripts.

Third, options start with a dash (or minus sign) and consist of a single letter. Options are optional, and may require an argument (such as `cc -o whizprog whizprog.c`). Options that don't require an argument can be grouped together: e.g., `ls -lt whizprog.c` rather than `ls -l -t whizprog.c` (which works, but requires more typing).

Long options are increasingly common, particularly in the GNU variants of the standard utilities, as well as in programs written for the X Window System (X11). For example:

```
$ cd whizprog-1.1
$ patch --verbose --backup -p1 < /tmp/whizprog-1.1-1.2-patch
```

Depending upon the program, long options start with either one dash, or with two (as just shown). (The `< /tmp/whizprog-1.1-1.2-patch` is an I/O redirection. It causes `patch` to read from the file `/tmp/whizprog-1.1-1.2-patch` instead of from the keyboard. I/O redirection is one of the fundamental topics covered later in the chapter.)

Originally introduced in System V, but formalized in POSIX, is the convention that two dashes (--) should be used to signify the end of options. Any other arguments on the command line that look like options are instead to be treated the same as any other arguments (for example, treated as filenames).

Finally, semicolons separate multiple commands on the same line. The shell executes them sequentially. If you use an ampersand (&) instead of a semicolon, the shell runs the preceding command in the *background*, which simply means that it doesn't wait for the command to finish before continuing to the next command.

The shell recognizes three fundamental kinds of commands: built-in commands, shell functions, and external commands:

- Built-in commands are just that: commands that the shell itself executes. Some commands are built-in from necessity, such as `cd` to change the directory, or `read` to get input from the user (or a file) into a shell variable. Other commands are often built into the shell for efficiency. Most typically, these include the test command (described later in "The test Command" [6.2.4]), which is heavily used in shell scripting, and I/O commands such as echo or printf.

- Shell functions are self-contained chunks of code, written in the shell language, that are invoked in the same way as a command is. We delay discussion of them until "Functions" [6.5]. At this point, it's enough to know that they're invoked, and they act, just like regular commands.

- External commands are those that the shell runs by creating a separate process. The basic steps are:

  a. Create a new process. This process starts out as a copy of the shell.

  b. In the new process, search the directories listed in the PATH variable for the given command. /bin:/usr/bin:/usr/X11R6/bin:/usr/local/bin might be a typical value of PATH. (The path search is skipped when a command name contains a slash character, /.)

  c. In the new process, execute the found program by replacing the running shell program with the new program.

  d. When the program finishes, the original shell continues by reading the next command from the terminal, or by running the next command in the script. This is illustrated in Figure 2-1.

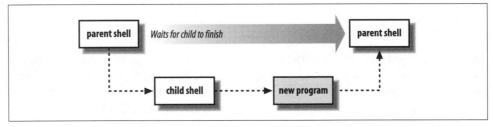

Figure 2-1. Program execution

That's the basic process. Of course, the shell can do many other things for you, such as variable and wildcard expansion, command and arithmetic substitution, and so on. We'll touch on these topics as we progress through the book.

2.5.2 Variables

A *variable* is a name that you give to a particular piece of information, such as first_name or driver_lic_no. All programming languages have variables, and the shell is no exception. Every variable has a *value*, which is the contents or information that you assigned to the variable. In the case of the shell, variable values can be, and often are, empty—that is, they contain no characters. This is legitimate, common, and useful. Empty values are referred to as *null*, and we'll use that term a lot in the rest of the book.

Shell variable names start with a letter or underscore, and may contain any number of following letters, digits, or underscores. There is no limit on the number of characters in a variable name. Shell variables hold string values, and there is also no limit on the number of characters that they may hold. (The Bourne shell was one of the few early Unix programs to follow a "no arbitrary limits" design principle.) For example:

```
$ myvar=this_is_a_long_string_that_does_not_mean_much       Assign a value
$ echo $myvar                                                Print the value
this_is_a_long_string_that_does_not_mean_much
```

As you can see, variables are assigned values by writing the variable name, immediately followed by an = character, and the new value, without any intervening spaces. Shell variable *values* are retrieved by prefixing the variable's name with a $ character. Use quotes when assigning a literal value that contains spaces:

```
first=isaac middle=bashevis last=singer    Multiple assignments allowed on one line
fullname="isaac bashevis singer"           Use quotes for whitespace in value
oldname=$fullname                          Quotes not needed to preserve spaces in value
```

As shown in the previous example, double quotes (discussed later in" "Quoting" [7.7]) aren't necessary around the value of one variable being used as the new value of a second variable. Using them, though, doesn't hurt either, and is necessary when concatenating variables:

```
fullname="$first $middle $last"            Double quotes required here
```

·2.5.3   Simple Output with echo

We just saw the echo command for printing out the value of myvar, and you've probably used it at the command line. echo's job is to produce output, either for prompting or to generate data for further processing.

The original echo command simply printed its arguments back to standard output, with each one separated from the next by a single space and terminated with a newline:

```
$ echo Now is the time for all good men
Now is the time for all good men
$ echo to come to the aid of their country.
to come to the aid of their country.
```

Unfortunately, over time, different versions of echo developed. The BSD version accepted a first argument of -n, which would make it omit the trailing newline. For example (the underscore represents the terminal's cursor):

```
$ echo -n "Enter your name: "              Print prompt
Enter your name: _                         Enter data
```

echo

Usage
> echo [*string* ...]

Purpose
> To produce output from shell scripts.

Major options
> None.

Behavior
> echo prints each argument to standard output, separated by a single space and terminated by a newline. It interprets escape sequences within each string that represent special characters and also control its behavior.

Caveats
> Historical differences in behavior among Unix variants make it difficult to use echo portably for all but the simplest kinds of output.

> Many versions support a -n option. When supplied, echo omits the final newline from its output. This is useful for printing prompts. However, the current POSIX-standard version of echo does not include this option. See the discussion in the text.

The System V version interpreted special escape sequences (explained shortly) within the arguments. For example, \c indicated that echo should not print the final newline:

```
$ echo "Enter your name: \c"          Print prompt
Enter your name: _                    Enter data
```

Escape sequences are a way to represent hard-to-type or hard-to-see characters within a program. When echo sees an escape sequence, it prints the corresponding character. The valid escape sequences are listed in Table 2-2.

Table 2-2. echo escape sequences

Sequence	Description
\a	Alert character, usually the ASCII BEL character.
\b	Backspace.
\c	Suppress the final newline in the output. Furthermore, any characters left in the argument, and any following arguments, are ignored (not printed).
\f	Formfeed.
\n	Newline.
\r	Carriage return.
\t	Horizontal tab.
\v	Vertical tab.

Table 2-2. echo escape sequences (continued)

Sequence	Description
\\	A literal backslash character.
\0*ddd*	Character represented as a 1- to 3-digit octal value.

When shell scripting, the \a sequence is most useful for getting a user's attention. The \0*ddd* sequence is useful for (very) primitive cursor manipulation by sending terminal escape sequences, but we don't recommend this.

Since many systems still default to the BSD behavior for echo, we only use its simplest form throughout this book. We use printf for more complicated output.

2.5.4   Fancier Output with printf

The differences between the two versions of echo led to one of the most infamous of the Unix-variant portability headaches. During the first round of standardization for POSIX, the committee members could not agree on how to standardize echo, so they came up with a compromise. While echo was part of the POSIX standard, the standard didn't specify the behavior if the first argument was –n, or if any argument contained escape sequences. Instead the behavior was left as *implementation-defined*, meaning that each vendor was required to document what its version of echo does.[*] In effect, echo could be used portably only if it was used in the simplest fashion. Instead, they adopted the printf command from the Ninth Edition Research Unix system. This command is more flexible than echo, but at the cost of some added complexity.

The printf command is modeled after the printf( ) library routine from the C library. It closely duplicates the facilities of that function (see the manual pages for *printf*(3)), and it's likely that if you've done any programming in C, C++, awk, Perl, Python, or Tcl, you're familiar with the basics. Of course, there are a few quirks specific to the shell-level version.

The printf command can output a simple string just like the echo command:

```
printf "Hello, world\n"
```

The main difference that you will notice immediately is that, unlike echo, printf does not automatically supply a newline. You must specify it explicitly as \n. The full syntax of the printf command has two parts:

```
printf format-string [arguments ...]
```

---

[*] Interestingly enough, the current version of the standard has echo being essentially the same as the System V version, which processes escape sequences in its arguments and does not treat -n specially.

The first part is a string describing the desired output; this is best supplied as a string constant in quotes. This string is a mixture of characters to be printed literally, and *format specifications*, which are special placeholders that describe how to print each corresponding argument.

The second part is an argument list, such as a list of strings or variable values, that correspond to the format specifications. (If there are more arguments than format specifications, printf cycles through the format specifications in the format string, reusing them in order, until done.) A format specification is preceded by a percent sign (%) and the specifier is one of the characters described later in the book. Two of the main format specifiers are %s for strings and %d for decimal integers.

Within the format string, regular characters are printed verbatim. Escape sequences, similar to those of echo, are interpreted and then output as the corresponding character. Format specifiers, which begin with the character % and end with one of a defined set of letters, control the output of the following corresponding arguments. For example, %s is used for strings:

```
$ printf "The first program always prints '%s, %s!'\n" Hello world
The first program always prints 'Hello, world!'
```

All the details on printf are given in "The Full Story on printf" [7.4].

2.5.5   Basic I/O Redirection

Standard I/O is perhaps the most fundamental concept in the Software Tools philosophy.[*] The idea is that programs should have a data source, a data sink (where data goes), and a place to report problems. These are referred to by the names *standard input*, *standard output*, and *standard error*, respectively. A program should neither know, nor care, what kind of device lies behind its input and outputs: disk files, terminals, tape drives, network connections, or even another running program! A program can expect these standard places to be already open and ready to use when it starts up.

Many, if not most, Unix programs follow this design. By default, they read standard input, write standard output, and send error messages to standard error. Such programs are called *filters*, for reasons that will become clear shortly. The default for standard input, standard output, and standard error is the terminal. This can be seen with cat:

```
$ cat                          With no arguments, read standard input, write standard output
now is the time                Typed by the user
now is the time                Echoed back by cat
for all good men
```

---

[*] "Standard I/O," as used here, should not be confused with the C library's standard I/O library, whose interface is defined in <stdio.h>, although that library's job is to provide this abstraction to C programs.

```
for all good men
to come to the aid of their country
to come to the aid of their country
^D                                    Ctrl-D, End of file
```

You may be wondering, who initializes standard input, output, and error for a running program? After all, *somebody* has to open these files for any given program, even the interactive shell that each user sees at login!

The answer is that when you log in, Unix arranges the default place for standard input, output, and error to be your terminal. *I/O redirection* is the process by which you, at the terminal interactively, or from within a shell script, then arrange to change the places from which input comes or to which output goes.

2.5.5.1   Redirection and pipelines

The shell provides several syntactic notations for specifying how to change the default I/O sources and destinations. We cover the basic ones here; later we'll provide the full story. Moving from simple to complex, these notations are as follows:

Change standard input with <
Use *program* < *file* to make *program*'s standard input be *file*:

```
tr -d '\r' < dos-file.txt ...
```

Change standard output with >
Use *program* > *file* to make *program*'s standard output be *file*:

```
tr -d '\r' < dos-file.txt > unix-file.txt
```

This tr invocation removes *ASCII* carriage-return characters from dos-file.txt, placing the transformed data into unix-file.txt. The original data in dos-file.txt is not changed. (The tr command is discussed in more detail in Chapter 5.)

The > redirector creates the destination file if it doesn't exist. However, if the file does exist, then it is *truncated*; all existing contents are lost.

Append to a file with >>
Use *program* >> *file* to send *program*'s standard output to the end of *file*.

Like >, the >> operator creates the destination file if it doesn't exist. However, if it already exists, instead of truncating the file, any new data generated by the running program is *appended* to the end of the file:

```
for f in dos-file*.txt
do
    tr -d '\r' < $f >> big-unix-file.txt
done
```

(The for loop is described in "Looping" [6.4].)

Create pipelines with |
Use *program1* | *program2* to make the standard output of *program1* become the standard input of *program2*.

Although < and > connect input and output to *files*, a pipeline hooks together two or more running *programs*. The standard output of the first program becomes the standard input of the second one. In favorable cases, pipelines can run as much as ten times faster than similar code using temporary files. Most of this book is about learning how to hook together the various tools into pipelines of increasing complexity and power. For example:

```
tr -d '\r' < dos-file.txt | sort > unix-file.txt
```

This pipeline removes carriage-return characters from the input file, and then sorts the data, sending the resulting output to the destination file.

---

tr

Usage

    tr [*options*] *source-char-list replace-char-list*

Purpose

    To transliterate characters. For example, converting uppercase characters to lowercase. Options let you remove characters and compress runs of identical characters.

Major options

    -c

        Complement the values in *source-char-list*. The characters that tr translates then become those that are *not* in *source-char-list*. This option is usually used with one of -d or -s.

    -C

        Like -c but work on (possibly multibyte) characters, not binary byte values. See *Caveats*.

    -d

        Delete characters in *source-char-list* from the input instead of transliterating them.

    -s

        "Squeeze out" duplicate characters. Each sequence of repeated characters listed in *source-char-list* is replaced with a single instance of that character.

Behavior

    Acts as a filter, reading characters from standard input and writing them to standard output. Each input character in *source-char-list* is replaced with the corresponding character in *replace-char-list*. POSIX-style character and equivalence classes may be used, and tr also supports a notation for repeated characters in *replace-char-list*. See the manual pages for *tr*(1) for the details on your system.

Caveats

    According to POSIX, the -c option operates on the binary byte values, whereas -C operates on characters as specified by the current locale. As of early 2005, many systems don't yet support the -C option.

When working with the Unix tools, it helps to visualize data as being similar to water in a pipeline. Untreated water goes into a water-processing plant and passes through a variety of filters, until the final output is water fit for human consumption.

Similarly, when scripting, you often have raw data in some defined input format, and you need processed data as the result. (Processing may mean any number of things: sorting, summing and averaging, formatting for printing, etc.) You start with the original data, and then construct a pipeline, step by step, where each stage in the pipeline further refines the data.

If you're new to Unix, it may help your visualization if you look at < and > as data "funnels"—data goes into the big end and comes out the small end.

 A final tip: when constructing pipelines, try to write them so that the amount of data is reduced at each stage. In other words, if you have two steps that could be done in either order relative to each other, put the one that will reduce the amount of data first in the pipeline. This improves the overall efficiency of your script, since Unix will have to move less data between programs, and each program in turn will have less work to do.

For example, use grep to choose interesting lines before using sort to sort them; this way sort has less work to do.

2.5.5.2   Special files: /dev/null and /dev/tty

Unix systems provide two special files that are particularly useful in shell programming. The first file, /dev/null, is often known as the "bit bucket." Data sent to this file is thrown away by the system. In other words, a program writing data to this file always believes that it has successfully written the data, but in practice, nothing is done with it. This is useful when you need a command's exit status (described in "Exit Statuses" [6.2]) but not its output. For example, to test if a file contains a pattern:

```
if grep pattern myfile > /dev/null
then
    ...        Pattern is there
else
    ...        Pattern is not there
fi
```

In contrast to writes, reading from /dev/null always returns end-of-file immediately. Reading from /dev/null is rare in shell programming, but it's important to know how the file behaves.

The other special file is /dev/tty. When a program opens this file, Unix automatically redirects it to the real terminal (physical console or serial port, or pseudoterminal for network and windowed logins) associated with the program. This is particularly useful for reading input that *must* come from a human, such as a password. It is also useful, although less so, for generating error messages:

```
printf "Enter new password: "    Prompt for input
stty -echo                       Turn off echoing of typed characters
read pass < /dev/tty             Read password
printf "Enter again: "           Prompt again
read pass2 < /dev/tty            Read again for verification
stty echo                        Don't forget to turn echoing back on
...
```

The stty (set tty) command controls various settings of your terminal (or window).* The –echo option turns off the automatic printing (echoing) of every character you type; stty echo restores it.

2.5.6   Basic Command Searching

Earlier, we mentioned that the shell searches for commands along the search path, $PATH. This is a colon-separated list of directories in which commands are found. Commands may be compiled executables or shell scripts; there's no real distinction from the user's perspective.

The default path varies from system to system. It will contain at least /bin and /usr/bin. It might contain /usr/X11R6/bin for X Windows programs, and it might also contain /usr/local/bin for programs that your local system administrator has installed. For example:

```
$ echo $PATH
/bin:/usr/bin:/usr/X11R6/bin:/usr/local/bin
```

The term "bin" for directories that hold executables is short for binary. However, you can also think of it as having the corresponding English meaning—a place to hold things; in this case, executable programs.

When you write your own scripts, it would be nice to have your own bin in which to place them, and have the shell find them automatically. This is easy to do. Just create your own bin directory and add it to the list in $PATH:

```
$ cd                        Change to home directory
$ mkdir bin                 Make a personal "bin" directory
$ mv nusers bin             Put our script there
$ PATH=$PATH:$HOME/bin      Append our bin directory to PATH
$ nusers                    Test it out
       6                    The shell finds it
```

To make the change permanent, add your bin directory to $PATH in your .profile file, which is read every time you log in, by putting a line like this at the end of it:

```
PATH=$PATH:$HOME/bin
```

---

* stty is possibly the most baroque and complicated Unix command in existence. See the *stty*(1) manpage for the gory details, or *Unix in a Nutshell*.

Empty components in $PATH mean "the current directory." An empty component can be designated by two successive colons in the middle of the path value, or by a leading or trailing colon, which puts the current directory first or last, respectively, in the path search:

```
PATH=:/bin:/usr/bin:/usr/X11R6/bin:/usr/local/bin      Current directory first
PATH=/bin:/usr/bin:/usr/X11R6/bin:/usr/local/bin:      Current directory last
PATH=/bin:/usr/bin:/usr/X11R6/bin::/usr/local/bin      Current directory in middle
```

If you wish to include the current directory in the search path, it is preferable to use an explicit dot in $PATH; this makes it clearer to the reader of your program what's going on.

In our testing, we found two versions of the same system that did not correctly support supplying an empty component at the end of $PATH. Empty components thus represent a minor portability problem.

 In general, you should not have the current directory in your path *at all*. It represents a security problem. (See Chapter 15 for more information.) We describe empty components only so that you understand how path searching works.

2.6   Accessing Shell Script Arguments

The so-called *positional parameters* represent a shell script's command-line arguments. They also represent a function's arguments within shell functions. Individual arguments are named by integer numbers. For historical reasons, you have to enclose the number in braces if it's greater than nine:

```
echo first arg is $1
echo tenth arg is ${10}
```

Special "variables" provide access to the total number of arguments that were passed, and to all the arguments at once. We provide the details later, in "Positional parameters" [6.1.2.2].

Suppose you want to know what terminal a particular user is using. Well, once again, you could use a plain who command and manually scan the output. However, that's difficult and error prone, especially on systems with lots of users. This time what you want to do is search through who's output for a particular user. Well, anytime you want to do searching, that's a job for the grep command, which prints lines matching the pattern given in its first argument. Suppose you're looking for user betsy because you *really* need that flag you ordered from her:

```
$ who | grep betsy                    Where is betsy?
betsy       pts/3        Dec 27 11:07   (flags-r-us.example.com)
```

Now that we know *how* to find a particular user, we can put the commands into a script, with the script's first argument being the username we want to find:

```
$ cat > finduser                          Create new file
#! /bin/sh

# finduser --- see if user named by first argument is logged in

who | grep $1
^D                                        End-of-file

$ chmod +x finduser                       Make it executable

$ ./finduser betsy                        Test it: find betsy
betsy      pts/3      Dec 27 11:07        (flags-r-us.example.com)

$ ./finduser benjamin                     Now look for good old Ben
benjamin   dtlocal    Dec 27 17:55        (kites.example.com)

$ mv finduser $HOME/bin                   Save it in our personal bin
```

The line beginning with # finduser ... is a *comment*. The shell ignores everything from the # to the end of the line. (This is serendipitous; the special #! line described earlier acts as a comment when the shell reads a script.) Commenting your programs is always a good idea. It will help someone else, or you a year from now, to figure out what you were doing and why. Once we see that the program works, we move it to our personal bin directory.

This program isn't perfect. What happens if we don't give it any arguments?

```
$ finduser
Usage: grep [OPTION]... PATTERN [FILE]...
Try 'grep --help' for more information.
```

We will see in "The test Command" [6.2.4], how to test the number of command-line arguments and take appropriate action when the right number isn't supplied.

2.7   Simple Execution Tracing

Because program development is a human activity, there will be times when your script just doesn't do what you want it to do. One way to get some idea of what your program is doing is to turn on *execution tracing*. This causes the shell to print out each command as it's executed, preceded by "+ "—that is, a plus sign followed by a space. (You can change what gets printed by assigning a new value to the PS4 shell variable.) For example:

```
$ sh -x nusers                            Run with tracing on
+ who                                     Traced commands
+ wc -l
        7                                 Actual output
```

You can turn execution tracing on within a script by using the command set -x, and turn it off again with set +x. This is more useful in fancier scripts, but here's a simple program to demonstrate:

```
$ cat > trace1.sh          Create script
#! /bin/sh

set -x                     Turn on tracing
echo 1st echo              Do something

set +x                     Turn off tracing
echo 2nd echo              Do something else
^D                         Terminate with end-of-file

$ chmod +x trace1.sh       Make program executable

$ ./trace1.sh              Run it
+ echo 1st echo            First traced line
1st echo                   Output from command
+ set +x                   Next traced line
2nd echo                   Output from next command
```

When run, the set -x is not traced, since tracing isn't turned on until after that command completes. Similarly, the set +x is traced, since tracing isn't turned off until after it completes. The final echo isn't traced, since tracing is turned off at that point.

2.8 Internationalization and Localization

Writing software for an international audience is a challenging problem. The task is usually divided into two parts: *internationalization* (*i18n* for short, since that long word has 18 letters between the first and last), and *localization* (similarly abbreviated *l10n*).

Internationalization is the process of designing software so that it can be adapted for specific user communities without having to change or recompile the code. At a minimum, this means that all character strings must be wrapped in library calls that handle runtime lookup of suitable translations in message catalogs. Typically, the translations are specified in ordinary text files that accompany the software, and then are compiled by gencat or msgfmt into compact binary files organized for fast lookup. The compiled message catalogs are then installed in a system-specific directory tree, such as the GNU conventional /usr/share/locale and /usr/local/share/locale, or on commercial Unix systems, /usr/lib/nls or /usr/lib/locale. Details can be found in the manual pages for *setlocale*(3), *catgets*(3C), and *gettext*(3C).

Localization is the process of adapting internationalized software for use by specific user communities. This may require translating software documentation, and all text strings output by the software, and possibly changing the formats of currency, dates, numbers, times, units of measurement, and so on, in program output. The character set used for text may also have to be changed, unless the universal *Unicode* character set can be used, and different fonts may be required. For some languages, the writing direction has to be changed as well.

In the Unix world, ISO programming language standards and POSIX have introduced limited support for addressing these problems, but much remains to be done, and progress varies substantially across the various flavors of Unix. For the user, the feature that controls which language or cultural environment is in effect is called the *locale*, and it is set by one or more of the *environment variables* shown in Table 2-3.

Table 2-3. Locale environment variables

Name	Description
LANG	Default value for any LC_xxx variable that is not otherwise set
LC_ALL	Value that overrides all other LC_xxx variables
LC_COLLATE	Locale name for collation (sorting)
LC_CTYPE	Locale name for character types (alphabetic, digit, punctuation, and so on)
LC_MESSAGES	Locale name for affirmative and negative responses and for messages; POSIX only
LC_MONETARY	Locale name for currency formatting
LC_NUMERIC	Locale name for number formatting
LC_TIME	Locale name for date and time formatting

In general, you set LC_ALL to force a single locale, and you set LANG to provide a fallback locale. In most cases, you should avoid setting any of the other LC_xxx variables. For example, although it might appear to be more precise to set LC_COLLATE when you use the sort command, that setting might conflict with a setting of LC_CTYPE, or be ignored entirely if LC_ALL is set.

Only a single standard locale name, C, is prescribed by the ISO C and C++ standards: it selects traditional ASCII-oriented behavior. POSIX specifies one additional locale name, POSIX, which is equivalent to C.

Apart from the names C and POSIX, locale names are not standardized. However, most vendors have adopted similar, but not identical, naming conventions. The locale name encodes a language, a territory, and optionally, a codeset and a modifier. It is normally represented by a lowercase two-letter ISO 639 language code,[*] an underscore, and an uppercase two-letter ISO 3166-1 country code,[†] optionally followed by a dot and the character-set encoding, and an at-sign and a modifier word. Language names are sometimes used as well. You can list all of the recognized locale names on your system like this:

```
$ locale -a                          List all locales
...
français
fr_BE
```

---

[*] Available at *http://www.ics.uci.edu/pub/ietf/http/related/iso639.txt*.

[†] Available at *http://userpage.chemie.fu-berlin.de/diverse/doc/ISO_3166.html*.

```
fr_BE@euro
fr_BE.iso88591
fr_BE.iso885915@euro
fr_BE.utf8
fr_BE.utf8@euro
fr_CA
fr_CA.iso88591
fr_CA.utf8
...
french
...
```

You can query the details of a particular locale variable by defining a locale in the environment (here, as a prefix to the command) and running the `locale` command with the -ck option and an LC_xxx variable. Here is an example from a Sun Solaris system that reports information about the Danish time locale:

```
$ LC_ALL=da locale -ck LC_TIME        Get locale information for Danish time
LC_TIME
d_t_fmt="%a %d %b %Y %T %Z"
d_fmt="%d-%m-%y"
t_fmt="%T"
t_fmt_ampm="%I:%M:%S %p"
am_pm="AM";"PM"
day="søndag";"mandag";"tirsdag";"onsdag";"torsdag";"fredag";"lørdag"
abday="søn";"man";"tir";"ons";"tor";"fre";"lør"
mon="januar";"februar";"marts";"april";"maj";"juni";"juli";"august"; \
    "september";"oktober";"november";"december"
abmon="jan";"feb";"mar";"apr";"maj";"jun";"jul";"aug";"sep";"okt"; \
    "nov";"dec"
era=""
era_d_fmt=""
era_d_t_fmt=""
era_t_fmt=""
alt_digits=""
```

The number of available locales varies widely. A survey of about 20 flavors of Unix found none at all on BSD and Mac OS X systems (they lack the `locale` command), as few as five on some systems, and almost 500 on recent GNU/Linux releases. Locale support may be an installation option at the discretion of the system manager, so even the same operating system release on two similar machines may have differing locale support. We found filesystem requirements for locale support approaching 300MB[*] on some systems.

---

[*] MB = megabyte, approximately 1 million bytes, where one byte is now conventionally eight bits (binary digits), although both larger and smaller byte sizes have been used in the past. Despite the metric prefix, in computer use, M usually means $2^{20} = 1,048,576$.

A handy rule of thumb is that one megabyte is about the amount of text in a book (300 pages × 60 lines/page × 60 characters/line = 1,080,000 characters).

Several GNU packages have been internationalized, and localization support has been added for many locales. For example, in an Italian locale, GNU ls offers help like this:

```
$ LC_ALL=it_IT ls --help          Get help for GNU ls in Italian
Uso: ls [OPZIONE]... [FILE]...
Elenca informazioni sui FILE (predefinito: la directory corrente).
Ordina alfabeticamente le voci se non è usato uno di -cftuSUX oppure --sort.
""
Mandatory arguments to long options are mandatory for short options too.
  -a, --all                 non nasconde le voci che iniziano con .
  -A, --almost-all          non elenca le voci implicite . e ..
      --author              stampa l'autore di ogni file
  -b, --escape              stampa escape ottali per i caratteri non grafici
      --block-size=DIMENS   usa blocchi lunghi DIMENS byte
  ...
```

Notice that when a translation is unavailable (fifth output line), the fallback is to the original language, English. Program names and option names are not translated, because that would destroy software portability.

There is currently little support on most systems for the shell programmer to address the issues of internationalization and localization. However, shell scripts are often affected by locales, notably in collation order, and in bracket-expression character ranges in regular expressions. Although we describe character classes, collating symbols, and equivalence classes in "What Is a Regular Expression?" [3.2.1], it appears to be quite difficult on most Unix systems to determine from locale documentation or tools exactly what characters are members of the character and equivalence classes, and what collating symbols are available. This reflects the immaturity of locale support on current systems.

When the GNU *gettext* package[*] is installed, it is possible to use it to support the internationalization and localization of shell scripts. This is an advanced topic that we do not cover in this book, but you can find the details in the *Preparing Shell Scripts for Internationalization* section of the *gettext* manual.

The wide variations in locale support, and the lack of standardized locale names, make it hard to do much with locales in portable shell scripts, other than force the traditional locale by setting LC_ALL to C. We do that in some of the scripts in this book when locale dependence could otherwise produce unexpected results.

2.9   Summary

The choice of compiled language versus scripting language is usually made based on the need of the application. Scripting languages generally work at a higher level than compiled languages, and the loss in performance is often more than made up for by

---

[*] Available at *ftp://ftp.gnu.org/gnu/gettext/*.

the speed with which development can be done and the ability to work at a higher level.

The shell is one of the most important and widely used scripting languages in the Unix environment. Because it is ubiquitous, and because of the POSIX standard, it is possible to write shell programs that will work on many different vendor platforms. Because the shell functions at a high level, shell programs have a lot of bang for the buck; you can do a lot with relatively little work.

The `#!` first line should be used for all shell scripts; this mechanism provides you with flexibility, and the ability to write scripts in your choice of shell or other language.

The shell is a full programming language. So far we covered the basics of commands, options, arguments, and variables, and basic output with `echo` and `printf`. We also looked at the basic I/O redirection operators, `<`, `>`, `>>`, and `|`, with which we expect you're really already familiar.

The shell looks for commands in each directory in `$PATH`. It's common to have a personal `bin` directory in which to store your own private programs and scripts, and to list it in `PATH` by doing an assignment in your `.profile` file.

We looked at the basics of accessing command-line arguments and simple execution tracing.

Finally, we discussed internationalization and localization, topics that are growing in importance as computer systems are adapted to the computing needs of more of the world's people. While support in this area for shell scripts is still limited, shell programmers need to be aware of the influence of locales on their code.

## CHAPTER 3

Searching and Substitutions

As we discussed in "Software Tools Principles" [1.2], Unix programmers prefer to work on lines of text. Textual data is more flexible than binary data, and Unix systems provide a number of tools that make slicing and dicing text easy.

In this chapter, we look at two fundamental operations that show up repeatedly in shell scripting: text *searching*—looking for specific lines of text—and text *substitution*—changing the text that is found.

While you can accomplish many things by using simple constant text strings, *regular expressions* provide a much more powerful notation for matching many different actual text fragments with a single expression. This chapter introduces the two regular expression "flavors" provided by various Unix programs, and then proceeds to cover the most important tools for text extraction and rearranging.

3.1   Searching for Text

The workhorse program for finding text (or "matching text," in Unix jargon) is grep. On POSIX systems, grep can use either of the two regular expression flavors, or match simple strings.

Traditionally, there were three separate programs for searching through text files:

- grep

    The original text-matching program. It uses Basic Regular Expressions (BREs) as defined by POSIX, and as we describe later in the chapter.

  egrep

    "Extended grep." This program uses Extended Regular Expressions (EREs), which are a more powerful regular expression notation. The cost of EREs is that they can be more computationally expensive to use. On the original PDP-11s this was important; on modern systems, there is little difference.

fgrep

"Fast grep." This variant matches fixed strings instead of regular expressions using an algorithm optimized for fixed-string matching. The original version was also the only variant that could match multiple strings *in parallel*. In other words, grep and egrep could match only a single regular expression, whereas fgrep used a different algorithm that could match multiple strings, effectively testing each input line for a match against all the requested search strings.

The 1992 POSIX standard merged all three variants into one grep program whose behavior is controlled by different options. The POSIX version can match multiple patterns, even for BREs and EREs. Both fgrep and egrep were also available, but they were marked as "deprecated," meaning that they would be removed from a subsequent standard. And indeed, the 2001 POSIX standard only includes the merged grep command. However, in practice, both egrep and fgrep continue to be available on all Unix and Unix-like systems.

3.1.1   Simple grep

The simplest use of grep is with constant strings:

```
$ who                                        Who is logged on
tolstoy   tty1       Feb 26 10:53
tolstoy   pts/0      Feb 29 10:59
tolstoy   pts/1      Feb 29 10:59
tolstoy   pts/2      Feb 29 11:00
tolstoy   pts/3      Feb 29 11:00
tolstoy   pts/4      Feb 29 11:00
austen    pts/5      Feb 29 15:39 (mansfield-park.example.com)
austen    pts/6      Feb 29 15:39 (mansfield-park.example.com)
$ who | grep -F austen                       Where is austen logged on?
austen    pts/5      Feb 29 15:39 (mansfield-park.example.com)
austen    pts/6      Feb 29 15:39 (mansfield-park.example.com)
```

This example used the –F option, to search for the fixed string **austen**. And in fact, as long as your pattern doesn't contain any regular expression metacharacters, grep's default behavior is effectively the same as if you'd used the –F option:

```
$ who | grep austen                          No -F, same result
austen    pts/5      Feb 29 15:39 (mansfield-park.example.com)
austen    pts/6      Feb 29 15:39 (mansfield-park.example.com)
```

3.2   Regular Expressions

This section provides a brief review of regular expression construction and matching. In particular, it describes the POSIX BRE and ERE constructs, which are intended to formalize the two basic "flavors" of regular expressions found among most Unix utilities.

grep

Usage

> grep [*options* ...] *pattern-spec* [*files* ...]

Purpose

> To print lines of text that match one or more patterns. This is often the first stage in a pipeline that does further processing on matched data.

Major options

> -E
>
>> Match using extended regular expressions. grep -E replaces the traditional egrep command.
>
> -F
>
>> Match using fixed strings. grep -F replaces the traditional fgrep command.
>
> -e *pat-list*
>
>> Usually, the first nonoption argument specifies the pattern(s) to match. Multiple patterns can be supplied by quoting them and separating them with newlines. In the case that the pattern starts with a minus sign, grep could get confused and treat it as an option. The -e option specifies that its argument is a pattern, even if it starts with a minus sign.
>
> -f *pat-file*
>
>> Read patterns from the file *pat-file*.
>
> -i
>
>> Ignore lettercase when doing pattern matching.
>
> -l
>
>> List the names of files that match the pattern instead of printing the matching lines.
>
> -q
>
>> Be quiet. Instead of writing lines to standard output, grep exits successfully if it matches the pattern, unsuccessfully otherwise. (We haven't discussed success/nonsuccess yet; see "Exit Statuses" [6.2].)
>
> -s
>
>> Suppress error messages. This is often used together with -q.
>
> -v
>
>> Print lines that *don't* match the pattern.

Behavior

> Read through each file named on the command line. When a line matches the pattern being searched for, print the line. When multiple files are named, grep precedes each line with the filename and a colon. The default is to use BREs.

Caveats

> You can use multiple -e and -f options to build up a list of patterns to search for.

We expect that you've had some exposure to regular expressions and text matching prior to this book. In that case, these subsections summarize how you can expect to use regular expressions for portable shell scripting.

If you've had no exposure at all to regular expressions, the material here may be a little too condensed for you, and you should detour to a more introductory source, such as *Learning the Unix Operating System* (O'Reilly) or *sed & awk* (O'Reilly). Since regular expressions are a fundamental part of the Unix tool-using and tool-building paradigms, any investment you make in learning how to use them, and use them well, will be amply rewarded, multifold, time after time.

If, on the other hand, you've been chopping, slicing, and dicing text with regular expressions for years, you may find our coverage cursory. If such is the case, we recommend that you review the first part, which summarizes POSIX BREs and EREs in tabular form, skip the rest of the section, and move on to a more in-depth source, such as *Mastering Regular Expressions* (O'Reilly).

3.2.1 What Is a Regular Expression?

Regular expressions are a notation that lets you search for text that fits a particular criterion, such as "starts with the letter a." The notation lets you write a single expression that can select, or *match*, multiple data strings.

Above and beyond traditional Unix regular expression notation, POSIX regular expressions let you:

- Write regular expressions that express locale-specific character sequence orderings and equivalences

- Write your regular expressions in a way that does not depend upon the underlying character set of the system

A large number of Unix utilities derive their power from regular expressions of one form or another. A partial list includes the following:

- The grep family of tools for finding matching lines of text: grep and egrep, which are always available, as well as the nonstandard but useful agrep utility[*]

- The sed stream editor, for making changes to an input stream, described later in the chapter

- String processing languages, such as awk, Icon, Perl, Python, Ruby, Tcl, and others

---

[*] The original Unix version from 1992 is at *ftp://ftp.cs.arizona.edu/agrep/agrep-2.04.tar.Z*. A current version for Windows systems is at *http://www.tgries.de/agrep/337/agrep337.zip*. Unlike most downloadable software that we cite in this book, agrep is not freely usable for any arbitrary purpose; see the permissions files that come with the program.

- File viewers (sometimes called pagers), such as more, page, and pg, which are common on commercial Unix systems, and the popular less pager[*]
- Text editors, such as the venerable ed line editor, the standard vi screen editor, and popular add-on editors such as emacs, jed, jove, vile, vim, and others

Because regular expressions are so central to Unix use, it pays to master them, and the earlier you do so, the better off you'll be.

In terms of the nuts and bolts, regular expressions are built from two basic components: *ordinary characters* and *special characters*. An ordinary character is any character that isn't special, as defined in the following table. In some contexts even special characters are treated as ordinary characters. Special characters are often called *metacharacters*, a term that we use throughout the rest of this chapter. Table 3-1 lists the POSIX BRE and ERE metacharacters.

Table 3-1. POSIX BRE and ERE metacharacters

Character	BRE / ERE	Meaning in a pattern
\	Both	Usually, turn off the special meaning of the following character. Occasionally, enable a special meaning for the following character, such as for \(...\) and \{...\}.
.	Both	Match any *single* character except NUL. Individual programs may also disallow matching newline.
*	Both	Match any number (or none) of the single character that immediately precedes it. For EREs, the preceding character can instead be a regular expression. For example, since . (dot) means any character, .* means "match any number of any character." For BREs, * is not special if it's the first character of a regular expression.
^	Both	Match the following regular expression at the beginning of the line or string. BRE: special only at the beginning of a regular expression. ERE: special everywhere.
$	Both	Match the preceding regular expression at the end of the line or string. BRE: special only at the end of a regular expression. ERE: special everywhere.
[...]	Both	Termed a *bracket expression*, this matches any *one* of the enclosed characters. A hyphen (-) indicates a range of consecutive characters. (Caution: ranges are locale-sensitive, and thus not portable.) A circumflex (^) as the first character in the brackets reverses the sense: it matches any one character *not* in the list. A hyphen or close bracket (]) as the first character is treated as a member of the list. All other metacharacters are treated as members of the list (i.e., literally). Bracket expressions may contain collating symbols, equivalence classes, and character classes (described shortly).
\{n,m\}	BRE	Termed an *interval expression*, this matches a range of occurrences of the single character that immediately precedes it. \{n\} matches exactly *n* occurrences, \{n,\} matches at least *n* occurrences, and \{n,m\} matches any number of occurrences between *n* and *m*. *n* and *m* must be between 0 and RE_DUP_MAX (minimum value: 255), inclusive.

[*] So named as a pun on more. See *ftp://ftp.gnu.org/gnu/less/*.

Table 3-1. POSIX BRE and ERE metacharacters (continued)

Character	BRE / ERE	Meaning in a pattern
\(\)	BRE	Save the pattern enclosed between \(and \) in a special *holding space*. Up to nine subpatterns can be saved on a single pattern. The text matched by the subpatterns can be reused later in the same pattern, by the escape sequences \1 to \9. For example, **\(ab\).*\1** matches two occurrences of ab, with any number of characters in between.
\n	BRE	Replay the *n*th subpattern enclosed in \(and \) into the pattern at this point. *n* is a number from 1 to 9, with 1 starting on the left.
{n,m}	ERE	Just like the BRE \{n,m\} earlier, but without the backslashes in front of the braces.
+	ERE	Match one or more instances of the preceding regular expression.
?	ERE	Match zero or one instances of the preceding regular expression.
|	ERE	Match the regular expression specified before or after.
( )	ERE	Apply a match to the enclosed group of regular expressions.

Table 3-2 presents some simple examples.

Table 3-2. Simple regular expression matching examples

Expression	Matches
tolstoy	The seven letters tolstoy, anywhere on a line
^tolstoy	The seven letters tolstoy, at the beginning of a line
tolstoy$	The seven letters tolstoy, at the end of a line
^tolstoy$	A line containing exactly the seven letters tolstoy, and nothing else
[Tt]olstoy	Either the seven letters Tolstoy, or the seven letters tolstoy, anywhere on a line
tol.toy	The three letters tol, any character, and the three letters toy, anywhere on a line
tol.*toy	The three letters tol, any sequence of zero or more characters, and the three letters toy, anywhere on a line (e.g., toltoy, tolstoy, tolWHOtoy, and so on)

3.2.1.1 POSIX bracket expressions

In order to accommodate non-English environments, the POSIX standard enhanced the ability of character set ranges (e.g., **[a-z]**) to match characters not in the English alphabet. For example, the French è is an alphabetic character, but the typical character class **[a-z]** would not match it. Additionally, the standard provides for sequences of characters that should be treated as a single unit when matching and collating (sorting) string data. (For example, there are locales where the two characters ch are treated as a unit, and must be matched and sorted that way.) The growing popularity of the Unicode character set standard adds further complications to the use of simple ranges, making them even less appropriate for modern applications.

POSIX also changed what had been common terminology. What we saw earlier as a range expression is often called a "character class" in the Unix literature. It is now called a bracket expression in the POSIX standard. Within "bracket expressions," besides literal characters such as z, ;, and so on, you can have additional components. These are:

Character classes

A POSIX character class consists of keywords bracketed by [: and :]. The keywords describe different classes of characters such as alphabetic characters, control characters, and so on. See Table 3-3.

Collating symbols

A collating symbol is a multicharacter sequence that should be treated as a unit. It consists of the characters bracketed by [. and .]. Collating symbols are specific to the locale in which they are used.

Equivalence classes

An equivalence class lists a set of characters that should be considered equivalent, such as e and è. It consists of a named element from the locale, bracketed by [= and =].

All three of these constructs *must* appear inside the square brackets of a bracket expression. For example, **[[:alpha:]!]** matches any single alphabetic character or the exclamation mark, and **[[.ch.]]** matches the collating element ch, but does not match just the letter c or the letter h. In a French locale, **[[=e=]]** might match any of e, è, ë, ê, or é. We provide more information on character classes, collating symbols, and equivalence classes shortly.

Table 3-3 describes the POSIX character classes.

Table 3-3. POSIX character classes

Class	Matching characters	Class	Matching characters
[:alnum:]	Alphanumeric characters	[:lower:]	Lowercase characters
[:alpha:]	Alphabetic characters	[:print:]	Printable characters
[:blank:]	Space and tab characters	[:punct:]	Punctuation characters
[:cntrl:]	Control characters	[:space:]	Whitespace characters
[:digit:]	Numeric characters	[:upper:]	Uppercase characters
[:graph:]	Nonspace characters	[:xdigit:]	Hexadecimal digits

BREs and EREs share some common characteristics, but also have some important differences. We'll start by explaining BREs, and then we'll explain the additional metacharacters in EREs, as well as the cases where the same (or similar) metacharacters are used but have different semantics (meaning).

3.2.2 Basic Regular Expressions

BREs are built up of multiple components, starting with several ways to match single characters, and then combining those with additional metacharacters for matching multiple characters.

3.2.2.1 Matching single characters

The first operation is to match a single character. This can be done in several ways: with ordinary characters; with an escaped metacharacter; with the . (dot) metacharacter; or with a bracket expression:

- Ordinary characters are those not listed in Table 3-1. These include all alphanumeric characters, most whitespace characters, and most punctuation characters. Thus, the regular expression **a** matches the character a. We say that ordinary characters stand for themselves, and this usage should be pretty straightforward and obvious. Thus, **shell** matches shell, **WoRd** matches WoRd but not word, and so on.

- If metacharacters don't stand for themselves, how do you match one when you need to? The answer is by *escaping* it. This is done by preceding it with a backslash. Thus, ***** matches a literal *, **** matches a single literal backslash, and **\\[** matches a left bracket. (If you put a backslash in front of an ordinary character, the POSIX standard leaves the behavior as explicitly undefined. Typically, the backslash is ignored, but it's poor practice to do something like that.)

- The . (dot) character means "any single character." Thus, **a.c** matches all of abc, aac, aqc, and so on. The single dot by itself is only occasionally useful. It is much more often used together with other metacharacters that allow the combination to match multiple characters, as described shortly.

- The last way to match a single character is with a *bracket expression*. The simplest form of a bracket expression is to enclose a list of characters between square brackets, such as **[aeiouy]**, which matches any lowercase English vowel. For example, **c[aeiouy]t** matches cat, cot, and cut (as well as cet, cit, and cyt), but won't match cbt.

  Supplying a caret (^) as the first character in the bracket expression complements the set of characters that are matched; such a complemented set matches any character *not* in the bracketed list. Thus, **[^aeiouy]** matches anything that isn't a lowercase vowel, including the uppercase vowels, all consonants, digits, punctuation, and so on.

Matching lots of characters by listing them all gets tedious—for example, **[0123456789]** to match a digit or **[0123456789abcdefABCDEF]** to match a hexadecimal digit. For this reason, bracket expressions may include *ranges* of characters. The previous two expressions can be shortened to **[0-9]** and **[0-9a-fA-F]**, respectively.

Originally, the range notation matched characters based on their numeric values in the machine's character set. Because of character set differences (ASCII versus EBCDIC), this notation was never 100 percent portable, although in practice it was "good enough," since almost all Unix systems used ASCII.

With POSIX locales, things have gotten worse. Ranges now work based on each character's defined position in the locale's collating sequence, which is unrelated to machine character-set numeric values. Therefore, the range notation is portable only for programs running in the "POSIX" locale. The POSIX character class notation, mentioned earlier in the chapter, provides a way to portably express concepts such as "all the digits," or "all alphabetic characters." Thus, ranges in bracket expressions are discouraged in new programs.

Earlier, in "What Is a Regular Expression?" [3.2.1], we briefly mentioned POSIX collating symbols, equivalence classes, and character classes. These are the final components that may appear inside the square brackets of a bracket expression. The following paragraphs explain each of these constructs.

In several non-English languages, certain pairs of characters must be treated, for comparison purposes, as if they were a single character. Such pairs have a defined way of sorting when compared with single letters in the language. For example, in Czech and Spanish, the two characters ch are kept together and are treated as a single unit for comparison purposes.

Collating is the act of giving an ordering to some group or set of items. A POSIX collating element consists of the name of the element in the current locale, enclosed by [. and .]. For the ch just discussed, the locale might use [.ch.]. (We say "might" because each locale defines its own collating elements.) Assuming the existence of [.ch.], the regular expression **[ab[.ch.]de]** matches any of the characters a, b, d, or e, or the pair ch. It does *not* match a standalone c or h character.

An equivalence class is used to represent different characters that should be treated the same when matching. Equivalence classes enclose the name of the class between [= and =]. For example, in a French locale, there might be an [=e=] equivalence class. If it exists, then the regular expression **[a[=e=]iouy]** would match all the lowercase English vowels, as well as the letters è, é, and so on.

As the last special component, character classes represent classes of characters, such as digits, lower- and uppercase letters, punctuation, whitespace, and so on. They are written by enclosing the name of the class in [: and :]. The full list was shown earlier, in Table 3-3. The pre-POSIX range expressions for decimal and hexadecimal digits can (and should) be expressed portably, by using character classes: **[[:digit:]]** and **[[:xdigit:]]**.

Collating elements, equivalence classes, and character classes are only recognized *inside* the square brackets of a bracket expression. Writing a standalone regular expression such as **[:alpha:]** matches the characters a, l, p, h, and :. The correct way to write it is **[[:alpha:]]**.

Within bracket expressions, all other metacharacters lose their special meanings. Thus, **[*\.]** matches a literal asterisk, a literal backslash, or a literal period. To get a] into the set, place it first in the list: **[ ]*\.]** adds the] to the list. To get a minus character into the set, place it first in the list: **[-*\.]**. If you need both a right bracket and a minus, make the right bracket the first character, and make the minus the last one in the list: **[ ]*\.-]**.

Finally, POSIX explicitly states that the NUL character (numeric value zero) need not be matchable. This character is used in the C language to indicate the end of a string, and the POSIX standard wanted to make it straightforward to implement its features using regular C strings. In addition, individual utilities may disallow matching of the newline character by the **.** (dot) metacharacter or by bracket expressions.

3.2.2.2 Backreferences

BREs provide a mechanism, known as *backreferences*, for saying "match whatever an earlier part of the regular expression matched." There are two steps to using backreferences. The first step is to enclose a subexpression in \(and \). There may be up to nine enclosed subexpressions within a single pattern, and they may be nested.

The next step is to use *digit*, where *digit* is a number between 1 and 9, in a later part of the same pattern. Its meaning there is "match whatever was matched by the *n*th earlier parenthesized subexpression." Here are some examples:

Pattern	Matches
\(ab\)\(cd\)[def]*\2\1	abcdcdab, abcdeeecdab, abcdddeeffcdab, …
\(why\).*\1	A line with two occurrences of why
\([[:alpha:]_][[:alnum:]_]*\) = \1;	Simple C/C++ assignment statement

Backreferences are particularly useful for finding duplicated words and matching quotes:

    \(["']\).*\1   *Match single- or double-quoted words, like 'foo' or "bar"*

This way, you don't have to worry about whether a single quote or double quote was found first.

3.2.2.3   Matching multiple characters with one expression

The simplest way to match multiple characters is to list them one after the other (concatenation). Thus, the regular expression **ab** matches the characters ab, **..** (dot dot) matches any two characters, and **[[:upper:]][[:lower:]]** matches any uppercase character followed by any lowercase one. However, listing characters out this way is good only for short regular expressions.

Although the **.** (dot) metacharacter and bracket expressions provide a nice way to match one character at a time, the real power of regular expressions comes into play when using the additional *modifier* metacharacters. These metacharacters come after a single-character regular expression, and they modify the meaning of the regular expression.

The most commonly used modifier is the asterisk or star (*), whose meaning is "match zero or more of the preceding single character." Thus, **ab*c** means "match an a, zero or more b characters, and a c." This regular expression matches ac, abc, abbc, abbbc, and so on.

It is important to understand that "match zero or more of one thing" does *not* mean "match *one* of something else." Thus, given the regular expression **ab*c**, the text aQc does not match, even though there are zero b characters in aQc. Instead, with the text ac, the b* in **ab*c** is said to match the *null string* (the string of zero width) in between the a and the c. (The idea of a zero-width string takes some getting used to if you've never seen it before. Nevertheless, it does come in handy, as will be shown later in the chapter.)

The * modifier is useful, but it is unlimited. You can't use * to say "match three characters but not four," and it's tedious to have to type out a complicated bracket expression multiple times when you want an exact number of matches. *Interval expressions* solve this problem. Like *, they come after a single-character regular expression, and they let you control how many repetitions of that character will be matched. Interval expressions consist of one or two numbers enclosed between \{ and \}. There are three variants, as follows:

\{*n*\}	Exactly *n* occurrences of the preceding regular expression
\{*n*,\}	At least *n* occurrences of the preceding regular expression
\{*n*,*m*\}	Between *n* and *m* occurrences of the preceding regular expression

Given interval expressions, it becomes easy to express things like "exactly five occurrences of a," or "between 10 and 42 instances of q." To wit: **a\{5\}** and **q\{10,42\}**.

The values for *n* and *m* must be between 0 and RE_DUP_MAX, inclusive. RE_DUP_MAX is a symbolic constant defined by POSIX and available via the getconf command. The minimum value for RE_DUP_MAX is 255; some systems allow larger values. On one of our GNU/Linux systems, it's quite large:

```
$ getconf RE_DUP_MAX
32767
```

3.2.2.4 Anchoring text matches

Two additional metacharacters round out our discussion of BREs. These are the caret (^) and the dollar sign ($). These characters are called *anchors* because they restrict the regular expression to matching at the beginning or end, respectively, of the string being matched against. (This use of ^ is entirely separate from the use of ^ to complement the list of characters inside a bracket expression.) Assuming that the text to be matched is abcABCdefDEF, Table 3-4 provides some examples:

Table 3-4. Examples of anchors in regular expressions

Pattern	Matches?	Text matched (in bold) / Reason match fails
ABC	Yes	Characters 4, 5, and 6, in the middle: abc**ABC**defDEF
^ABC	No	Match is restricted to beginning of string
def	Yes	Characters 7, 8, and 9, in the middle: abcABC**def**DEF
def$	No	Match Is restricted to end of string
[[:upper:]]\{3\}	Yes	Characters 4, 5, and 6, in the middle: abc**ABC**defDEF
[[:upper:]]\{3\}$	Yes	Characters 10, 11, and 12, at the end: abcDEFdef**DEF**
^[[:alpha:]]\{3\}	Yes	Characters 1, 2, and 3, at the beginning: **abc**ABCdefDEF

^ and $ may be used together, in which case the enclosed regular expression must match the entire string (or line). It is also useful occasionally to use the simple regular expression ^$, which matches empty strings or lines. Together with the –v option to grep, which prints all lines that *don't* match a pattern, these can be used to filter out empty lines from a file.

For example, it's sometimes useful to look at C source code after it has been processed for #include files and #define macros so that you can see exactly what the C compiler sees. (This is low-level debugging, but sometimes it's what you have to do.) Expanded files often contain many more blank or empty lines than lines of source text: thus it's useful to exclude empty lines:

```
$ cc -E foo.c | grep -v '^$' > foo.out          Preprocess, remove empty lines
```

^ and $ are special only at the beginning or end of a BRE, respectively. In a BRE such as ab^cd, the ^ stands for itself. So too in ef$gh, the $ in this case stands for itself. And, as with any other metacharacter, \^ and \$ may be used, as may [$].[*]

---

[*] The corresponding [^] is not a valid regular expression. Make sure you understand why.

3.2.2.5 BRE operator precedence

As in mathematical expressions, the regular expression operators have a certain defined *precedence*. This means that certain operators are applied before (have higher precedence than) other operators. Table 3-5 provides the precedence for the BRE operators, from highest to lowest.

Table 3-5. BRE operator precedence from highest to lowest

Operator	Meaning
[..] [==] [::]	Bracket symbols for character collation
\metacharacter	Escaped metacharacters
[ ]	Bracket expressions
\(\) \digit	Subexpressions and backreferences
* \{\}	Repetition of the preceding single-character regular expression
no symbol	Concatenation
^ $	Anchors

3.2.3 Extended Regular Expressions

EREs, as the name implies, have more capabilities than do basic regular expressions. Many of the metacharacters and capabilities are identical. However, some of the metacharacters that look similar to their BRE counterparts have different meanings.

3.2.3.1 Matching single characters

When it comes to matching single characters, EREs are essentially the same as BREs. In particular, normal characters, the backslash character for escaping metacharacters, and bracket expressions all behave as described earlier for BREs.

One notable exception is that in awk, \ is special inside bracket expressions. Thus, to match a left bracket, dash, right bracket, or backslash, you could use **[\[\-\]\\]**. Again, this reflects historical practice.

3.2.3.2 Backreferences don't exist

Backreferences don't exist in EREs.[*] Parentheses are special in EREs, but serve a different purpose than they do in BREs (to be described shortly). In an ERE, \(and \) match literal left and right parentheses.

---

[*] This reflects differences in the historical behavior of the grep and egrep commands, not a technical incapability of regular expression matchers. Such is life with Unix.

3.2.3.3 Matching multiple regular expressions with one expression

EREs have the most notable differences from BREs in the area of matching multiple characters. The * does work the same as in BREs.*

Interval expressions are also available in EREs; however, they are written using plain braces, not braces preceded by backslashes. Thus, our previous examples of "exactly five occurrences of a" and "between 10 and 42 instances of q" are written **a{5}** and **q{10,42}**, respectively. Use **\{** and **\}** to match literal brace characters. POSIX purposely leaves the meaning of a { without a matching } in an ERE as "undefined."

EREs have two additional metacharacters for finer-grained matching control, as follows:

?	Match zero or one of the preceding regular expression
+	Match one or more of the preceding regular expression

You can think of the ? character as meaning "optional." In other words, text matching the preceding regular expression is either present or it's not. For example, **ab?c** matches both ac and abc, but nothing else. (Compare this to **ab*c**, which can match any number of intermediate b characters.)

The + character is conceptually similar to the * metacharacter, except that at least one occurrence of text matching the preceding regular expression must be present. Thus, **ab+c** matches abc, abbc, abbbc, and so on, but does *not* match ac. You can always replace a regular expression of the form **ab+c** with **abb*c**; however, the + can save a lot of typing (and the potential for typos!) when the preceding regular expression is complicated.

3.2.3.4 Alternation

Bracket expressions let you easily say "match this character, or that character, or ...." However, they don't let you specify "match this sequence, or that sequence, or ...." You can do this using the *alternation* operator, which is the vertical bar or pipe character (|). Simply write the two sequences of characters, separated by a pipe. For example, **read|write** matches both read and write, **fast|slow** matches both fast and slow, and so on. You may use more than one: **sleep|doze|dream|nod off|slumber** matches all five expressions.

The | character has the lowest precedence of all the ERE operators. Thus, the lefthand side extends all the way to the left of the operator, to either a preceding | character or the beginning of the regular expression. Similarly, the righthand side of the | extends all the way to the right of the operator, to either a succeeding | character or

---

* An exception is that the meaning of a * as the first character of an ERE is "undefined," whereas in a BRE it means "match a literal *."

the end of the whole regular expression. The implications of this are discussed in the next section.

3.2.3.5   Grouping

You may have noticed that for EREs, we've stated that the operators are applied to "the preceding regular expression." The reason is that parentheses ((...)) provide grouping, to which the operators may then be applied. For example, **(why)+** matches one or more occurrences of the word why.

Grouping is particularly valuable (and necessary) when using alternation. It allows you to build complicated and flexible regular expressions. For example, **[Tt]he (CPU|computer) is** matches sentences using either CPU or computer in between The (or the) and is. Note that here the parentheses are metacharacters, not input text to be matched.

Grouping is also often necessary when using a repetition operator together with alternation. **read|write+** matches exactly one occurrence of the word read or an occurrence of the word write, followed by any number of e characters (writee, writeee, and so on). A more useful pattern (and probably what would be meant) is **(read|write)+**, which matches one or more occurrences of either of the words read or write.

Of course, **(read|write)+** makes no allowance for intervening whitespace between words. **((read|white)[[:space:]]*)+** is a more complicated, but more realistic, regular expression. At first glance, this looks rather opaque. However, if you break it down into its component parts, from the outside in, it's not too hard to follow. This is illustrated in Figure 3-1.

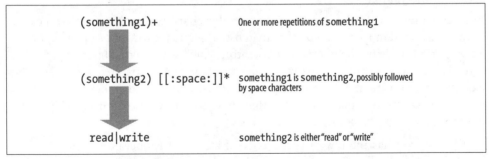

Figure 3-1. Reading a complicated regular expression

The upshot is that this single regular expression matches multiple successive occurrences of either read or write, possibly separated by whitespace characters.

The use of a * after the [[:space:]] is something of a judgment call. By using a * and not a +, the match gets words at the end of a line (or string). However, this opens up the possibility of matching words with no intervening whitespace at all. Crafting regular expressions often requires such judgment calls. How you build your regular expressions will depend on both your input data and what you need to do with that data.

Finally, grouping is helpful when using alternation together with the ^ and $ anchor characters. Because | has the lowest precedence of all the operators, the regular expression **^abcd|efgh$** means "match abcd at the beginning of the string, *or* match efgh at the end of the string." This is different from **^(abcd|efgh)$**, which means "match a string containing exactly abcd or exactly efgh."

3.2.3.6 Anchoring text matches

The ^ and $ have the same meaning as in BREs: anchor the regular expression to the beginning or end of the text string (or line). There is one significant difference, though. In EREs, ^ and $ are *always* metacharacters. Thus, regular expressions such as **ab^cd** and **ef$gh** are valid, but cannot match anything, since the text preceding the ^ and the text following the $ prevent them from matching "the beginning of the string" and "the end of the string," respectively. As with the other metacharacters, they do lose their special meaning inside bracket expressions.

3.2.3.7 ERE operator precedence

Operator precedence applies to EREs as it does to BREs. Table 3-6 provides the precedence for the ERE operators, from highest to lowest.

Table 3-6. ERE operator precedence from highest to lowest

Operator	Meaning
[..] [==] [::]	Bracket symbols for character collation
metacharacter	Escaped metacharacters
[ ]	Bracket expressions
( )	Grouping
* + ? {}	Repetition of the preceding regular expression
no symbol	Concatenation
^ $	Anchors
|	Alternation

3.2.4 Regular Expression Extensions

Many programs provide extensions to regular expression syntax. Typically, such extensions take the form of a backslash followed by an additional character, to create new operators. This is similar to the use of a backslash in \\(...\\) and \\{...\\} in POSIX BREs.

The most common extensions are the operators \< and \>, which match the beginning and end of a "word," respectively. Words are made up of letters, digits, and underscores. We call such characters *word-constituent*.

The beginning of a word occurs at either the beginning of a line or the first word-constituent character following a nonword-constituent character. Similarly, the end of a word occurs at the end of a line, or after the last word-constituent character before a nonword-constituent one.

In practice, word matching is intuitive and straightforward. The regular expression **\<chop** matches use `chopsticks` but does not match eat a `lambchop`. Similarly, the regular expression **chop\>** matches the second string, but does not match the first. Note that **\<chop\>** does not match either string.

Although standardized by POSIX only for the ex editor, word matching is universally supported by the ed, ex, and vi editors that come standard with every commercial Unix system. Word matching is also supported on the "clone" versions of these programs that come with GNU/Linux and BSD systems, as well as in emacs, vim, and vile. Most GNU utilities support it as well. Additional Unix programs that support word matching often include grep and sed, but you should double-check the manpages for the commands on your system.

GNU versions of the standard utilities that deal with regular expressions typically support a number of additional operators. These operators are outlined in Table 3-7.

Table 3-7. Additional GNU regular expression operators

Operator	Meaning
\w	Matches any word-constituent character. Equivalent to `[[:alnum:]_]`.
\W	Matches any nonword-constituent character. Equivalent to `[^[:alnum:]_]`.
\< \>	Matches the beginning and end of a word, as described previously.
\b	Matches the null string found at either the beginning or the end of a word. This is a generalization of the \< and \> operators.
	Note: Because awk uses \b to represent the backspace character, GNU awk (gawk) uses \y.
\B	Matches the null string between two word-constituent characters.
\' \`	Matches the beginning and end of an emacs buffer, respectively. GNU programs (besides emacs) generally treat these as being equivalent to ^ and $.

Finally, although POSIX explicitly states that the NUL character need not be matchable, GNU programs have no such restriction. If a NUL character occurs in input data, it can be matched by the . metacharacter or a bracket expression.

3.2.5   Which Programs Use Which Regular Expressions?

It is a historical artifact that there are two different regular expression flavors. While the existence of egrep-style extended regular expressions was known during the early

Unix development period, Ken Thompson didn't feel that it was necessary to implement such full-blown regular expressions for the ed editor. (Given the PDP-11's small address space, the complexity of extended regular expressions, and the fact that for most editing jobs basic regular expressions are enough, this decision made sense.)

The code for ed then served as the base for grep. (grep is an abbreviation for the ed command g/*re*/p: globally match *re* and print it.) ed's code also served as an initial base for sed.

Somewhere in the pre-V7 timeframe, egrep was created by Al Aho, a Bell Labs researcher who did groundbreaking work in regular expression matching and language parsing. The core matching code from egrep was later reused for regular expressions in awk.

The \< and \> operators originated in a version of ed that was modified at the University of Waterloo by Rob Pike, Tom Duff, Hugh Redelmeier, and David Tilbrook. (Rob Pike was the one who invented those operators.) Bill Joy at UCB adopted it for the ex and vi editors, from whence it became widely used. Interval expressions originated in *Programmer's Workbench Unix*[*] and they filtered out into the commercial Unix world via System III, and later, System V. Table 3-8 lists the various Unix programs and which flavor of regular expression they use.

Table 3-8. Unix programs and their regular expression type

Type	grep	sed	ed	ex/vi	more	egrep	awk	lex
BRE	•	•	•	•	•			
ERE						•	•	•
\< \>	•	•	•	•	•			

lex is a specialized tool, generally used for the construction of lexical analyzers for language processors. Even though it's included in POSIX, we don't discuss it further, since it's not relevant for shell scripting. The less and pg pagers, while not part of POSIX, also support regular expressions. Some systems have a page program, which is essentially the same as more, but clears the screen between each screenful of output.

As we mentioned at the beginning of the chapter, to (attempt to) mitigate the multiple grep problem, POSIX mandates a single grep program. By default, POSIX grep uses BREs. With the –E option, it uses EREs, and with the –F option, it uses the fgrep fixed-string matching algorithm. Thus, truly POSIX-conforming programs use grep -E... instead of egrep.... However, since all Unix systems do have it, and are likely to for many years to come, we continue to use it in our scripts.

---

[*] Programmer's Workbench (PWB) Unix was a variant used within AT&T to support telephone switch software development. It was also made available for commercial use.

A final note is that traditionally, awk did not support interval expressions within its flavor of extended regular expressions. Even as of 2005, support for interval expressions is not universal among different vendor versions of awk. For maximal portability, if you need to match braces from an awk program, you should escape them with a backslash, or enclose them inside a bracket expression.

3.2.6 Making Substitutions in Text Files

Many shell scripting tasks start by extracting interesting text with grep or egrep. The initial results of a regular expression search then become the "raw data" for further processing. Often, at least one step consists of *text substitution*—that is, replacing one bit of text with something else, or removing some part of the matched line.

Most of the time, the right program to use for text substitutions is sed, the Stream Editor. sed is designed to edit files in a batch fashion, rather than interactively. When you know that you have multiple changes to make, whether to one file or to many files, it is much easier to write down the changes in an editing script and apply the script to all the files that need to be changed. sed serves this purpose. (While it is possible to write editing scripts for use with the ed or ex line editors, doing so is more cumbersome, and it is much harder to [remember to] save the original file.)

We have found that for shell scripting, sed's primary use is making simple text substitutions, so we cover that first. We then provide some additional background and explanation of sed's capabilities, but we purposely don't go into a lot of detail. sed in all its glory is described in the book *sed & awk* (O'Reilly), which is cited in the Bibliography.

GNU sed is available at the location *ftp://ftp.gnu.org/gnu/sed/*. It has a number of interesting extensions that are documented in the manual that comes with it. The GNU sed manual also contains some interesting examples, and the distribution includes a test suite with some unusual programs. Perhaps the most amazing is an implementation of the Unix dc arbitrary-precision calculator, written as a sed script!

An excellent source for all things sed is *http://sed.sourceforge.net/*. It includes links to two FAQ documents on sed on the Internet. The first is available from *http://www.dreamwvr.com/sed-info/sed-faq.html*. The second, and older, FAQ is available from *ftp://rtfm.mit.edu/pub/faqs/editor-faq/sed*.

3.2.7 Basic Usage

Most of the time, you'll use sed in the middle of a pipeline to perform a substitution. This is done with the s command, which takes a regular expression to look for, replacement text with which to replace matched text, and optional flags:

```
sed 's/:.*//' /etc/passwd |          Remove everything after the first colon
    sort -u                          Sort list and remove duplicates
```

sed

Usage

    sed [-n] 'editing command' [file ...]

    sed [-n] -e 'editing command' ... [file ...]

    sed [-n] -f script-file ... [file ...]

Purpose

    To edit its input stream, producing results on standard output, instead of modifying files in place the way an interactive editor does. Although sed has many commands and can do complicated things, it is most often used for performing text substitutions on an input stream, usually as part of a pipeline.

Major options

    -e 'editing command'

        Use editing command on the input data. -e must be used when there are multiple commands.

    -f script-file

        Read editing commands from script-file. This is useful when there are many commands to execute.

    -n

        Suppress the normal printing of each final modified line. Instead, lines must be printed explicitly with the p command.

Behavior

    This reads each line of each input file, or standard input if no files. For each line, sed executes every editing command that applies to the input line. The result is written on standard output (by default, or explicitly with the p command and the -n option). With no -e or -f options, sed treats the first argument as the editing command to use.

Here, the / character acts as a *delimiter*, separating the regular expression from the replacement text. In this instance, the replacement text is empty (the infamous null string), which effectively deletes the matched text. Although the / is the most commonly used delimiter, any printable character may be used instead. When working with filenames, it is common to use punctuation characters for the delimiter (such as a semicolon, colon, or comma):

```
find /home/tolstoy -type d -print  |     Find all directories
  sed 's;/home/tolstoy/;/home/lt/;' |     Change name, note use of semicolon delimiter
    sed 's/^/mkdir /'                |     Insert mkdir command
      sh -x                                Execute, with shell tracing
```

This script creates a copy of the directory structure in /home/tolstoy in /home/lt (perhaps in preparation for doing backups). (The find command is described in Chapter 10. Its output in this case is a list of directory names, one per line, of every directory underneath /home/tolstoy.) The script uses the interesting trick of *generating commands* and then feeding the stream of commands as input to the shell. This is a powerful and general technique that is not used as often as it should be.[*]

3.2.7.1   Substitution details

We've already mentioned that any delimiter may be used besides slash. It is also possible to escape the delimiter within the regular expression or the replacement text, but doing so can be much harder to read:

```
sed 's/\/home\/tolstoy//\/home\/lt\//'
```

Earlier, in "Backreferences" [3.2.2.2], when describing POSIX BREs, we mentioned the use of backreferences in regular expressions. sed understands backreferences. Furthermore, they may be used *in the replacement text* to mean "substitute at this point the text matched by the *n*th parenthesized subexpression." This sounds worse than it is:

```
$ echo /home/tolstoy/ | sed 's;\(/home\)/tolstoy/;\1/lt/;'
/home/lt/
```

sed replaces the \1 with the text that matched the **/home** part of the regular expression. In this case, all of the characters are literal ones, but any regular expression can be enclosed between the \(and the \). Up to nine backreferences are allowed.

A few other characters are special in the replacement text as well. We've already mentioned the need to backslash-escape the delimiter character. This is also, not surprisingly, necessary for the backslash character itself. Finally, the & in the replacement text means "substitute at this point the entire text matched by the regular expression." For example, suppose that we work for the Atlanta Chamber of Commerce, and we need to change our description of the city everywhere in our brochure:

```
mv atlga.xml atlga.xml.old
sed 's/Atlanta/&, the capital of the South/' < atlga.xml.old > atlga.xml
```

(Being a modern shop, we use XML for all the possibilities it gives us, instead of an expensive proprietary word processor.) This script saves the original brochure file, as a backup. Doing something like this is *always* a good idea, especially when you're still learning to work with regular expressions and substitutions. It then applies the change with sed.

To get a literal & character in the replacement text, backslash-escape it. For instance, the following small script can be used to turn literal backslashes in DocBook/XML files into the corresponding DocBook \ entity:

```
sed 's/\\/\&bsol;/g'
```

---

[*] This script does have a flaw: it can't handle directories whose names contain spaces. This can be solved using techniques we haven't seen yet; see Chapter 10.

The g suffix on the previous s command stands for *global*. It means "replace *every* occurrence of the regular expression with the replacement text." Without it, sed replaces only the *first* occurrence. Compare the results from these two invocations, with and without the g:

```
$ echo Tolstoy reads well. Tolstoy writes well. > example.txt    Sample input
$ sed 's/Tolstoy/Camus/' < example.txt                           No "g"
Camus reads well. Tolstoy writes well.
$ sed 's/Tolstoy/Camus/g' < example.txt                          With "g"
Camus reads well. Camus writes well.
```

A little-known fact (amaze your friends!) is that you can specify a trailing number to indicate that the *n*th occurrence should be replaced:

```
$ sed 's/Tolstoy/Camus/2' < example.txt           Second occurrence only
Tolstoy reads well. Camus writes well.
```

So far, we've done only one substitution at a time. While you can string multiple instances of sed together in a pipeline, it's easier to give sed multiple commands. On the command line, this is done with the –e option. Each command is provided by using one –e option per editing command:

```
sed -e 's/foo/bar/g' -e 's/chicken/cow/g' myfile.xml > myfile2.xml
```

When you have more than a few edits, though, this form gets tedious. At some point, it's better to put all your edits into a script file, and then run sed using the –f option:

```
$ cat fixup.sed
s/foo/bar/g
s/chicken/cow/g
s/draft animal/horse/g
...
$ sed -f fixup.sed myfile.xml > myfile2.xml
```

You can build up a script by combining the –e and –f options; the script is the concatenation of all editing commands provided by all the options, in the order given. Additionally, POSIX allows you to separate commands on the same line with a semicolon:

```
sed 's/foo/bar/g ; s/chicken/cow/g' myfile.xml > myfile2.xml
```

However, many commercial versions of sed don't (yet) allow this, so it's best to avoid it for absolute portability.

Like its ancestor ed and its cousins ex and vi, sed remembers the last regular expression used at any point in a script. That same regular expression may be reused by specifying an empty regular expression:

```
s/foo/bar/3           Change third foo
s//quux/              Now change first one
```

Consider a straightforward script named `html2xhtml.sed` for making a start at converting HMTL to XHTML. This script converts tags to lowercase, and changes the `<br>` tag into the self-closing form, `<br/>`:

```
s/<H1>/<h1>/g                          Slash delimiter
s/<H2>/<h2>/g
s/<H3>/<h3>/g
s/<H4>/<h4>/g
s/<H5>/<h5>/g
s/<H6>/<h6>/g
s:</H1>:</h1>:g                         Colon delimiter, slash in data
s:</H2>:</h2>:g
s:</H3>:</h3>:g
s:</H4>:</h4>:g
s:</H5>:</h5>:g
s:</H6>:</h6>:g
s/<[Hh][Tt][Mm][LL]>/<html>/g
s:</[Hh][Tt][Mm][LL]>:</html>:g
s:<[Bb][Rr]>:<br/>:g
...
```

Such a script can automate a large part of the task of converting from HTML to XHTML, the standardized XML-based version of HTML.

3.2.8 sed Operation

sed's operation is straightforward. Each file named on the command line is opened and read, in turn. If there are no files, standard input is used, and the filename "`-`" (a single dash) acts as a pseudonym for standard input.

sed reads through each file one line at a time. The line is placed in an area of memory termed the *pattern space*. This is like a variable in a programming language: an area of memory that can be changed as desired under the direction of the editing commands. All editing operations are applied to the contents of the pattern space. When all operations have been completed, sed prints the final contents of the pattern space to standard output, and then goes back to the beginning, reading another line of input.

This operation is shown in Figure 3-2. The script uses two commands to change `The Unix System` into `The UNIX Operating System`.

3.2.8.1 To print or not to print

The `-n` option modifies sed's default behavior. When supplied, sed does *not* print the final contents of the pattern space when it's done. Instead, `p` commands in the script explicitly print the line. For example, one might simulate grep in this way:

```
sed -n '/<HTML>/p' *.html              Only print <HTML> lines
```

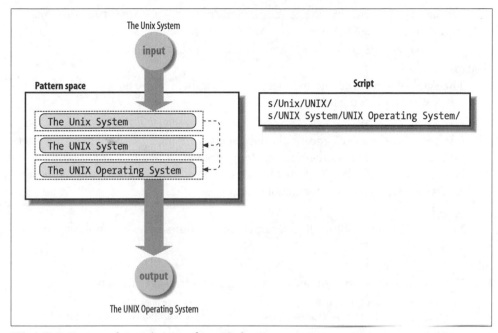

Figure 3-2. Commands in sed scripts changing the pattern space

Although this example seems trivial, this feature is useful in more complicated scripts. If you use a script file, you can enable this feature by using a special first line:

```
#n                              Turn off automatic printing
/<HTML>/p                       Only print <HTML> lines
```

As in the shell and many other Unix scripting languages, the # is a comment. sed comments have to appear on their own lines, since they're syntactically commands; they're just commands that don't do anything. While POSIX indicates that comments may appear anywhere in a script, many older versions of sed allow them only on the first line. GNU sed does not have this limitation.

3.2.9   Matching Specific Lines

As mentioned, by default, sed applies every editing command to every input line. It is possible to restrict the lines to which a command applies by prefixing the command with an *address*. Thus, the full form of a sed command is:

```
address command
```

There are different kinds of addresses:

Regular expressions

Prefixing a command with a pattern limits the command to lines matching the pattern. This can be used with the s command:

```
/oldfunc/ s/$/# XXX: migrate to newfunc/    Annotate some source code
```

An empty pattern in the s command means "use the previous regular expression":

```
/Tolstoy/ s//& and Camus/g                    Talk about both authors
```

The last line

The symbol $ (as in ed and ex) means "the last line." For example, this script is a quick way to print the last line of a file:

```
sed -n '$p' "$1"                              Quoting as shown required!
```

For sed, the "last line" means the last line of the input. Even when processing multiple files, sed views them as one long input stream, and $ applies only to the last line of the last file. (GNU sed has an option to cause addresses to apply separately to each file; see its documentation.)

Line numbers

You can use an absolute line number as an address. An example is provided shortly.

Ranges

You can specify a range of lines by separating addresses with a comma:

```
sed -n '10,42p' foo.xml                       Print only lines 10–42
sed '/foo/,/bar/ s/baz/quux/g'                Make substitution only on range of lines
```

The second command says "starting with lines matching **foo**, and continuing through lines matching **bar**, replace all occurrences of **baz** with quux." (Readers familiar with ed, ex, or the colon command prompt in vi will recognize this usage.)

The use of two regular expressions separated by commas is termed a *range expression*. In sed, it *always* includes at least two lines.

Negated regular expressions

Occasionally it's useful to apply a command to all lines that *don't* match a particular pattern. You specify this by adding an ! character after a regular expression to look for:

```
/used/!s/new/used/g                           Change new to used on lines not matching used
```

The POSIX standard indicates that the behavior when whitespace follows the ! is "unspecified," and recommends that completely portable applications not place any space after it. This is apparently due to some historical versions of sed not allowing it.

Example 3-1 demonstrates the use of absolute line numbers as addresses by presenting a simple version of the head program using sed.

Example 3-1. A version of the head command using sed

```
# head --- print first n lines
#
# usage:   head N file

count=$1
sed ${count}q "$2"
```

When invoked as head 10 foo.xml, sed ends up being invoked as sed 10q foo.xml. The q command causes sed to quit, immediately; no further input is read or commands executed. Later, in "Using sed for the head Command" [7.6.1], we show how to make this script look more like the real head command.

As we've seen so far, sed uses / characters to delimit patterns to search for. However, there is provision for using a different delimiter in patterns. This is done by preceding the character with a backslash:

```
$ grep tolstoy /etc/passwd                          Show original line
tolstoy:x:2076:10:Leo Tolstoy:/home/tolstoy:/bin/bash
$ sed -n '\:tolstoy: s;;Tolstoy;p' /etc/passwd       Make a change
Tolstoy:x:2076:10:Leo Tolstoy:/home/tolstoy:/bin/bash
```

In this example, the colon delimits the pattern to search for, and semicolons act as delimiters for the s command. (The editing operation itself is trivial; our point here is to demonstrate the use of different delimiters, not to make the change for its own sake.)

3.2.10 How Much Text Gets Changed?

One issue we haven't discussed yet is the question "how much text matches?" Really, there are two questions. The second question is "where does the match start?" Indeed, when doing simple text searches, such as with grep or egrep, both questions are irrelevant. All you want to know is whether a line matched, and if so, to see the line. Where in the line the match starts, or to where in the line it extends, doesn't matter.

However, knowing the answer to these questions becomes vitally important when doing text substitution with sed or programs written in awk. (Understanding this is also important for day-to-day use when working inside a text editor, although we don't cover text editing in this book.)

The answer to both questions is that a regular expression matches the *longest, leftmost substring* of the input text that can match the entire expression. In addition, a match of the null string is considered to be longer than no match at all. (Thus, as we explained earlier, given the regular expression **ab*c**, matching the text ac, the b* successfully matches the null string between a and c.) Furthermore, the POSIX standard states: "Consistent with the whole match being the longest of the leftmost matches, each subpattern, from left to right, shall match the longest possible string." (Subpatterns are the parts enclosed in parentheses in an ERE. For this purpose, GNU programs often extend this feature to \(...\) in BREs too.)

If sed is going to be replacing the text matched by a regular expression, it's important to be sure that the regular expression doesn't match too little or too much text. Here's a simple example:

```
$ echo Tolstoy writes well | sed 's/Tolstoy/Camus/'    Use fixed strings
Camus writes well
```

Of course, sed can use full regular expressions. This is where understanding the "longest leftmost" rule becomes important:

```
$ echo Tolstoy is worldly | sed 's/T.*y/Camus/'     Try a regular expression
Camus                                                What happened?
```

The apparent intent was to match just Tolstoy. However, since the match extends over the longest possible amount of text, it went all the way to the y in worldly! What's needed is a more refined regular expression:

```
$ echo Tolstoy is worldly | sed 's/T[[:alpha:]]*y/Camus/'
Camus is worldly
```

In general, and especially if you're still learning the subtleties of regular expressions, when developing scripts that do lots of text slicing and dicing, you'll want to test things very carefully, and verify each step as you write it.

Finally, as we've seen, it's possible to match the null string when doing text searching. This is also true when doing text replacement, allowing you to *insert* text:

```
$ echo abc | sed 's/b*/1/'     Replace first match
1abc
$ echo abc | sed 's/b*/1/g'    Replace all matches
1a1c1
```

Note how **b*** matches the null string at the front and at the end of abc.

3.2.11 Lines Versus Strings

It is important to make a distinction between lines and strings. Most simple programs work on lines of input data. This includes grep and egrep, and 99 percent of the time, sed. In such a case, by definition there won't be any embedded newline characters in the data being matched, and ^ and $ represent the beginning and end of the line, respectively.

However, programming languages that work with regular expressions, such as awk, Perl, and Python, usually work on strings. It may be that each string represents a single input line, in which case ^ and $ still represent the beginning and end of the line. However, these languages allow you to use different ways to specify how input records are delimited, opening up the possibility that a single input "line" (i.e., record) may indeed have embedded newlines. In such a case, ^ and $ do *not* match an embedded newline; they represent only the beginning and end of a *string*. This point is worth bearing in mind when you start using the more programmable software tools.

3.3   Working with Fields

For many applications, it's helpful to view your data as consisting of records and fields. A *record* is a single collection of related information, such as what a business might have for a customer, supplier, or employee, or what a school might have for a student. A *field* is a single component of a record, such as a last name, a first name, or a street address.

3.3.1   Text File Conventions

Because Unix encourages the use of textual data, it's common to store data in a text file, with each line representing a single record. There are two conventions for separating fields within a line from each other. The first is to just use whitespace (spaces or tabs):

```
$ cat myapp.data
# model     units sold    salesperson
xj11        23            jane
rj45        12            joe
cat6        65            chris
...
```

In this example, lines beginning with a # character represent comments, and are ignored. (This is a common convention. The ability to have comment lines is helpful, but it requires that your software be able to ignore such lines.) Each field is separated from the next by an arbitrary number of space or tab characters. The second convention is to use a particular delimiter character to separate fields, such as a colon:

```
$ cat myapp.data
# model:units sold:salesperson
xj11:23:jane
rj45:12:joe
cat6:65:chris
...
```

Each convention has advantages and disadvantages. When whitespace is the separator, it's difficult to have real whitespace within the fields' contents. (If you use a tab as the separator, you can use a space character within a field, but this is visually confusing, since you can't easily tell the difference just by looking at the file.) On the flip side, if you use an explicit delimiter character, it then becomes difficult to include that delimiter within your data. Often, though, it's possible to make a careful choice, so that the need to include the delimiter becomes minimal or nonexistent.

 One important difference between the two approaches has to do with multiple occurrences of the delimiter character(s). When using whitespace, the convention is that multiple successive occurrences of spaces or tabs act as a *single* delimiter. However, when using a special character, *each* occurrence separates a field. Thus, for example, two colon characters in the second version of myapp.data (a "::") delimit an *empty* field.

The prime example of the delimiter-separated field approach is /etc/passwd. There is one line per user of the system, and the fields are colon-separated. We use /etc/passwd for many examples throughout the book, since a large number of system administration tasks involve it. Here is a typical entry:

```
tolstoy:x:2076:10:Leo Tolstoy:/home/tolstoy:/bin/bash
```

The seven fields of a password file entry are:

1. The username.
2. The encrypted password. (This can be an asterisk if the account is disabled, or possibly a different character if encrypted passwords are stored separately in /etc/shadow.)
3. The user ID number.
4. The group ID number.
5. The user's personal name and possibly other relevant data (office number, telephone number, and so on).
6. The home directory.
7. The login shell.

Some Unix tools work better with whitespace-delimited fields, others with delimiter-separated fields, and some utilities are equally adept at working with either kind of file, as we're about to see.

3.3.2   Selecting Fields with cut

The cut command was designed for cutting out data from text files. It can work on either a field basis or a character basis. The latter is useful for cutting out particular columns from a file. Beware, though: a tab character counts as a single character![*]

For example, the following command prints the login name and full name of each user on the system:

```
$ cut -d : -f 1,5 /etc/passwd          Extract fields
root:root                              Administrative accounts
...
tolstoy:Leo Tolstoy                    Real users
austen:Jane Austen
camus:Albert Camus
...
```

By choosing a different field number, we can extract each user's home directory:

```
$ cut -d : -f 6 /etc/passwd            Extract home directory
/root                                  Administrative accounts
...
```

---

[*] This can be worked around with expand and unexpand: see the manual pages for *expand*(1).

cut

Usage

> cut -c *list* [*file* ...]
>
> cut -f *list* [-d *delim*] [*file* ...]

Purpose

> To select one or more fields or groups of characters from an input file, presumably for further processing within a pipeline.

Major options

> -c *list*
>
>> Cut based on characters. *list* is a comma-separated list of character numbers or ranges, such as 1,3,5-12,42.
>
> -d *delim*
>
>> Use *delim* as the delimiter with the -f option. The default delimiter is the tab character.
>
> -f *list*
>
>> Cut based on fields. *list* is a comma-separated list of field numbers or ranges.

Behavior

> Cut out the named fields or ranges of input characters. When processing fields, each delimiter character separates fields. The output fields are separated by the given delimiter character. Read standard input if no *files* are given on the command line. See the text for examples.

Caveats

> On POSIX systems, cut understands multibyte characters. Thus, "character" is not synonymous with "byte." See the manual pages for *cut*(1) for the details.
>
> Some systems have limits on the size of an input line, particularly when multibyte characters are involved.

```
/home/tolstoy                    Real users
/home/austen
/home/camus
...
```

Cutting by character list can occasionally be useful. For example, to pull out just the permissions field from ls -l:

```
$ ls -l | cut -c 1-10
total 2878
-rw-r--r--
drwxr-xr-x
-r--r--r--
-rw-r--r--
...
```

However, this is riskier than using fields, since you're not guaranteed that each field in a line will always have the exact same width in every line. In general, we prefer field-based commands for extracting data.

3.3.3   Joining Fields with join

The `join` command lets you merge files, where the records in each file share a common *key*—that is, the field which is the primary one for the record. Keys are often things such as usernames, personal last names, employee ID numbers, and so on. For example, you might have two files, one which lists how many items a salesperson sold and one which lists the salesperson's quota:

---

join

Usage
> join [*options* ...] *file1 file2*

Purpose
> To merge records in sorted files based on a common key.

Major options
> -1 *field1*
>
> -2 *field2*
>> Specifies the fields on which to join. -1 *field1* specifies *field1* from *file1*, and -2 *field2* specifies *field2* from *file2*. Fields are numbered from one, not from zero.
>
> -o *file.field*
>> Make the output consist of field *field* from file *file*. The common field is not printed unless requested explicitly. Use multiple -o options to print multiple output fields.
>
> -t *separator*
>> Use *separator* as the input field separator instead of whitespace. This character becomes the output field separator as well.

Behavior
> Read *file1* and *file2*, merging records based on a common key. By default, runs of whitespace separate fields. The output consists of the common key, the rest of the record from *file1*, followed by the rest of the record from *file2*. If *file1* is -, join reads standard input. The first field of each file is the default key upon which to join; this can be changed with -1 and -2. Lines without keys in both files are not printed by default. (Options exist to change this; see the manual pages for *join*(1).)

Caveats
> The -1 and -2 options are relatively new. On older systems, you may need to use -j1 *field1* and -j2 *field2*.

```
$ cat sales                              Show sales file
# sales data                             Explanatory comments
# salesperson    amount
joe       100
jane      200
herman    150
chris     300

$ cat quotas                             Show quotas file
# quotas
# salesperson    quota
joe       50
jane      75
herman    80
chris     95
```

Each record has two fields: the salesperson's name and the corresponding amount. In this instance, there are multiple spaces between the columns so that they line up nicely.

In order for join to work correctly, the input files must be *sorted*. The program in Example 3-2, merge-sales.sh, merges the two files using join.

Example 3-2. merge-sales.sh

```
#! /bin/sh

# merge-sales.sh
#
# Combine quota and sales data

# Remove comments and sort datafiles
sed '/^#/d' quotas | sort > quotas.sorted
sed '/^#/d' sales  | sort > sales.sorted

# Combine on first key, results to standard output
join quotas.sorted sales.sorted

# Remove temporary files
rm quotas.sorted sales.sorted
```

The first step is to remove the comment lines with sed, and then to sort each file. The sorted temporary files become the input to the join command, and finally the script removes the temporary files. Here is what happens when it's run:

```
$ ./merge-sales.sh
chris 95 300
herman 80 150
jane 75 200
joe 50 100
```

3.3.4 Rearranging Fields with awk

awk is a useful programming language in its own right. In fact, we devote Chapter 9 to covering the most important parts of the language. Although you can do quite a lot with awk, it was purposely designed to be useful in shell scripting—for doing simple text manipulation, such as field extraction and rearrangement. In this section, we examine the basics of awk so that you can understand such "one-liners" when you see them.

3.3.4.1 Patterns and actions

awk's basic paradigm is different from many programming languages. It is similar in many ways to sed:

```
awk 'program' [ file ... ]
```

awk reads records (lines) one at a time from each file named on the command line (or standard input if none). For each line, it applies the commands as specified by the program to the line. The basic structure of an awk program is:

```
pattern { action }
pattern { action }
...
```

The *pattern* part can be almost any expression, but in one-liners, it's typically an ERE enclosed in slashes. The *action* can be any awk statement, but in one-liners, it's typically a plain print statement. (Examples are coming up.)

Either the *pattern* or the *action* may be omitted (but, of course, not both). A missing *pattern* executes the *action* for *every* input record. A missing *action* is equivalent to { print }, which (as we shall see shortly) prints the entire record. Most one-liners are of the form:

```
... | awk '{ print some-stuff }' | ...
```

For each record, awk tests each *pattern* in the program. If the pattern is true (e.g., the record matches the regular expression, or the general expression evaluates to true), then awk executes the code in the *action*.

3.3.4.2 Fields

awk has fields and records as a central part of its design. awk reads input records (usually just lines) and automatically splits each record into fields. It sets the built-in variable NF to the number of fields in each record.

By default, whitespace separates fields—i.e., runs of spaces and/or tab characters (like join). This is usually what you want, but you have other options. By setting the variable FS to a different value, you can change how awk separates fields. If you use a single character, then each occurrence of that character separates fields (like cut -d).

Or, and here is where awk stands out, you can set it to a full ERE, in which case each occurrence of text that matches that ERE acts as a field separator.

Field values are designated as such with the $ character. Usually $ is followed by a numeric constant. However, it can be followed by an expression; most typically the name of a variable. Here are some examples:

awk '{ print $1 }'	*Print first field (no pattern)*
awk '{ print $2, $5 }'	*Print second and fifth fields (no pattern)*
awk '{ print $1, $NF }'	*Print first and last fields (no pattern)*
awk 'NF > 0 { print $0 }'	*Print nonempty lines (pattern and action)*
awk 'NF > 0'	*Same (no action, default is to print)*

A special case is field number zero, which represents the whole record.

3.3.4.3   Setting the field separators

For simple programs, you can change the field separator with the -F option. For example, to print the username and full name from the /etc/passwd file:

```
$ awk -F: '{ print $1, $5 }' /etc/passwd       Process /etc/passwd
root root                                        Administrative accounts
...
tolstoy Leo Tolstoy                              Real users
austen Jane Austen
camus Albert Camus
...
```

The -F option sets the FS variable automatically. Note how the program does not have to reference FS directly, nor does it have to manage reading records and splitting them into fields; awk does it all automatically.

You may have noticed that each field in the output is separated with a space, even though the input field separator is a colon. Unlike almost all the other tools, awk treats the two separators as distinct from each other. You can change the output field separator by setting the OFS variable. You do this on the command line with the -v option, which sets awk's variables. The value can be any string. For example:

```
$ awk -F: -v 'OFS=**'  '{ print $1, $5 }' /etc/passwd      Process /etc/passwd
root**root                                                   Administrative accounts
...
tolstoy**Leo Tolstoy                                         Real users
austen**Jane Austen
camus**Albert Camus
...
```

We will see shortly that there are other ways to set these variables. They may be more legible, depending on your taste.

3.3.4.4 Printing lines

As we've shown so far, most of the time you just want to print selected fields, or arrange them in a different order. Simple printing is done with the print statement. You supply it a list of fields, variables, or strings to print:

```
$ awk -F: '{ print "User", $1, "is really", $5 }' /etc/passwd
User root is really root
...
User tolstoy is really Leo Tolstoy
User austen is really Jane Austen
User camus is really Albert Camus
...
```

A plain print statement, without any arguments, is equivalent to print $0, which prints the whole record.

For cases like the example just shown, when you want to mix text and values, it is usually clearer to use awk's version of the printf statement. It is similar enough to the shell (and C) version of printf described in "Fancier Output with printf" [2.5.4], that we won't go into the details again. Here is the previous example, using printf:

```
$ awk -F: '{ printf "User %s is really %s\n", $1, $5 }' /etc/passwd
User root is really root
...
User tolstoy is really Leo Tolstoy
User austen is really Jane Austen
User camus is really Albert Camus
...
```

As with the shell-level echo and printf, awk's print statement automatically supplies a final newline, whereas with the printf statement you must supply it yourself, using the \n escape sequence.

 Be sure to separate arguments to print with a comma! Without the comma, awk *concatenates* adjacent values:

```
$ awk -F: '{ print "User" $1 "is really" $5 }' /etc/passwd
Userrootis reallyroot
...
Usertolstoyis reallyLeo Tolstoy
Useraustenis reallyJane Austen
Usercamusis reallyAlbert Camus
...
```

String concatenation of this form is unlikely to be what you want. Omitting the comma is a common, and hard-to-find, mistake.

3.3.4.5 Startup and cleanup actions

Two special "patterns," BEGIN and END, let you provide startup and cleanup actions for your awk programs. It is more common to use them in larger awk programs, usually written in separate files instead of on the command line:

```
BEGIN      { startup code }

pattern1 { action1 }

pattern2 { action2 }

END        { cleanup code }
```

BEGIN and END blocks are optional. If you have them, it is conventional, but not required, to place them at the beginning and end, respectively, of the awk program. You can also have multiple BEGIN and END blocks; awk executes them in the order they're encountered in the program: all the BEGIN blocks once at the beginning, and all the END blocks once at the end. For simple programs, BEGIN is used for setting variables:

```
$ awk 'BEGIN { FS = ":" ; OFS = "**" }      Use BEGIN to set variables
> { print $1, $5 }' /etc/passwd              Quoted program continues on second line
root**root
...
tolstoy**Leo Tolstoy                         Output, as before
austen**Jane Austen
camus**Albert Camus
...
```

The POSIX standard describes the awk language and the options for the awk program. POSIX awk is based on so-called "new awk," first released to the world with System V Release 3.1 in 1987, and modified somewhat for System V Release 4 in 1989.

Alas, as late as 2005, the Solaris /bin/awk is *still* the original V7 version of awk, from 1979! On Solaris systems, you should use /usr/xpg4/bin/awk, or install one of the free versions of awk mentioned in Chapter 9.

3.4 Summary

The grep program is the primary tool for extracting interesting lines of text from input datafiles. POSIX mandates a single version with different options to provide the behavior traditionally obtained from the three grep variants: grep, egrep, and fgrep.

Although you can search for plain string constants, regular expressions provide a more powerful way to describe text to be matched. Most characters match themselves, whereas certain others act as metacharacters, specifying actions such as "match zero or more of," "match exactly 10 of," and so on.

POSIX regular expressions come in two flavors: Basic Regular Expressions (BREs) and Extended Regular Expressions (EREs). Which programs use which regular expression flavor is based upon historical practice, with the POSIX specification reducing the number of regular expression flavors to just two. For the most part, EREs are a superset of BREs, but not completely.

Regular expressions are sensitive to the locale in which the program runs; in particular, ranges within a bracket expression should be avoided in favor of character classes such as [[:alnum:]]. Many GNU programs have additional metacharacters.

sed is the primary tool for making simple string substitutions. Since, in our experience, most shell scripts use sed only for substitutions, we have purposely not covered everything sed can do. The *sed & awk* book listed in the Bibliography provides more information.

The "longest leftmost" rule describes where text matches and for how long the match extends. This is important when doing text substitutions with sed, awk, or an interactive text editor. It is also important to understand when there is a distinction between a line and a string. In some programming languages, a single string may contain multiple lines, in which case ^ and $ usually apply to the beginning and end of the string.

For many operations, it's useful to think of each line in a text file as an individual record, with data in the line consisting of fields. Fields are separated by either whitespace or a special delimiter character, and different Unix tools are available to work with both kinds of data. The cut command cuts out selected ranges of characters or fields, and join is handy for merging files where records share a common key field.

awk is often used for simple one-liners, where it's necessary to just print selected fields, or rearrange the order of fields within a line. Since it's a programming language, you have much more power, flexibility, and control, even in small programs.

## CHAPTER 4

Text Processing Tools

Some operations on text files are so widely applicable that standard tools for those tasks were developed early in the Unix work at Bell Labs. In this chapter, we look at the most important ones.

4.1 Sorting Text

Text files that contain independent records of data are often candidates for sorting. A predictable record order makes life easier for human users: book indexes, dictionaries, parts catalogs, and telephone directories have little value if they are unordered. Sorted records can also make programming easier and more efficient, as we will illustrate with the construction of an office directory in Chapter 5.

Like awk, cut, and join, sort views its input as a stream of records made up of fields of variable width, with records delimited by newline characters and fields delimited by whitespace or a user-specifiable single character.

4.1.1 Sorting by Lines

In the simplest case, when no command-line options are supplied, complete records are sorted according to the order defined by the current locale. In the traditional C locale, that means ASCII order, but you can set an alternate locale as we described in "Internationalization and Localization" [2.8].

A tiny bilingual dictionary in the ISO 8859-1 encoding translates four French words differing only in accents:

```
$ cat french-english                        Show the tiny dictionary
côte    coast
cote    dimension
coté    dimensioned
côté    side
```

sort

Usage

    sort [*options*] [*file(s)*]

Purpose

Sort input lines into an order determined by the key field and datatype options, and the locale.

Major options

    -b

Ignore leading whitespace.

    -c

Check that input is correctly sorted. There is no output, but the exit code is non-zero if the input is not sorted.

    -d

Dictionary order: only alphanumerics and whitespace are significant.

    -g

General numeric value: compare fields as floating-point numbers. This works like -n, except that numbers may have decimal points and exponents (e.g., 6.022e+23). GNU version only.

    -f

Fold letters implicitly to a common lettercase so that sorting is case-insensitive.

    -i

Ignore nonprintable characters.

    -k

Define the sort key field. See "Sorting by Fields", for details.

    -m

Merge already-sorted input files into a sorted output stream.

    -n

Compare fields as integer numbers.

    -o *outfile*

Write output to the specified file instead of to standard output. If the file is one of the input files, sort copies it to a temporary file before sorting and writing the output.

    -r

Reverse the sort order to descending, rather than the default ascending.

    -t *char*

Use the single character *char* as the default field separator, instead of the default of whitespace.

    -u

Unique records only: discard all but the first record in a group with equal keys. Only the key fields matter: other parts of the discarded records may differ.

Behavior

sort reads the specified files, or standard input if no files are given, and writes the sorted data on standard output.

To understand the sorting, use the octal dump tool, od, to display the French words in ASCII and octal:

```
$ cut -f1 french-english | od -a -b        Display French words in octal bytes
0000000    c    t    t    e   nl    c    o    t    e   nl    c    o    t    i   nl    c
          143  364  164  145  012  143  157  164  145  012  143  157  164  351  012  143
0000020    t    t    i   nl
          364  164  351  012
0000024
```

Evidently, with the ASCII option -a, od strips the high-order bit of characters, so the accented letters have been mangled, but we can see their octal values: é is 351_8 and ô is 364_8.

On GNU/Linux systems, you can confirm the character values like this:

```
$ man iso_8859_1                            Check the ISO 8859-1 manual page
...

      Oct   Dec   Hex   Char   Description
      -----------------------------------------------------------------------
...
      351   233   E9    é      LATIN SMALL LETTER E WITH ACUTE
...
      364   244   F4    ô      LATIN SMALL LETTER O WITH CIRCUMFLEX
...
```

First, sort the file in strict byte order:

```
$ LC_ALL=C sort french-english              Sort in traditional ASCII order
cote    dimension
coté    dimensioned
côte    coast
côté    side
```

Notice that e (145_8) sorted before é (351_8), and o (157_8) sorted before ô (364_8), as expected from their numerical values.

Now sort the text in Canadian-French order:

```
$ LC_ALL=fr_CA.iso88591 sort french-english     Sort in Canadian-French locale
côte    coast
cote    dimension
coté    dimensioned
côté    side
```

The output order clearly differs from the traditional ordering by raw byte values.

Sorting conventions are strongly dependent on language, country, and culture, and the rules are sometimes astonishingly complex. Even English, which mostly pretends that accents are irrelevant, can have complex sorting rules: examine your local telephone directory to see how lettercase, digits, spaces, punctuation, and name variants like McKay and Mackay are handled.

4.1.2   Sorting by Fields

For more control over sorting, the -k option allows you to specify the field to sort on, and the -t option lets you choose the field delimiter.

If -t is not specified, then fields are separated by whitespace and leading and trailing whitespace in the record is ignored. With the -t option, the specified character delimits fields, and whitespace is significant. Thus, a three-character record consisting of space-X-space has one field without -t, but three with -t' ' (the first and third fields are empty).

The -k option is followed by a field number, or number pair, optionally separated by whitespace after -k. Each number may be suffixed by a dotted character position, and/or one of the modifier letters shown in Table 4-1.

Table 4-1. Sort key field types

Letter	Description
b	Ignore leading whitespace.
d	Dictionary order.
f	Fold letters implicitly to a common lettercase.
g	Compare as general floating-point numbers. GNU version only.
i	Ignore nonprintable characters.
n	Compare as (integer) numbers.
r	Reverse the sort order.

Fields and characters within fields are numbered starting from one.

If only one field number is specified, the sort key begins at the start of that field, and continues to the end of the record (*not* the end of the field).

If a comma-separated pair of field numbers is given, the sort key starts at the beginning of the first field, and finishes at the end of the second field.

With a dotted character position, comparison begins (first of a number pair) or ends (second of a number pair) at that character position: -k2.4,5.6 compares starting with the fourth character of the second field and ending with the sixth character of the fifth field.

If the start of a sort key falls beyond the end of the record, then the sort key is empty, and empty sort keys sort before all nonempty ones.

When multiple -k options are given, sorting is by the first key field, and then, when records match in that key, by the second key field, and so on.

While the -k option is available on all of the systems that we tested, sort also recognizes an older field specification, now considered obsolete, where fields and character positions are numbered from zero. The key start for character *m* in field *n* is defined by +*n.m*, and the key end by −*n.m*. For example, sort +2.1 -3.2 is equivalent to sort -k3.2,4.3. If the character position is omitted, it defaults to zero. Thus, +4.0nr and +4nr mean the same thing: a numeric key, beginning at the start of the fifth field, to be sorted in reverse (descending) order.

Let's try out these options on a sample password file, sorting it by the username, which is found in the first colon-separated field:

```
$ sort -t: -k1,1 /etc/passwd          Sort by username
bin:x:1:1:bin:/bin:/sbin/nologin
chico:x:12501:1000:Chico Marx:/home/chico:/bin/bash
daemon:x:2:2:daemon:/sbin:/sbin/nologin
groucho:x:12503:2000:Groucho Marx:/home/groucho:/bin/sh
gummo:x:12504:3000:Gummo Marx:/home/gummo:/usr/local/bin/ksh93
harpo:x:12502:1000:Harpo Marx:/home/harpo:/bin/ksh
root:x:0:0:root:/root:/bin/bash
zeppo:x:12505:1000:Zeppo Marx:/home/zeppo:/bin/zsh
```

For more control, add a modifier letter in the field selector to define the type of data in the field and the sorting order. Here's how to sort the password file by descending UID:

```
$ sort -t: -k3nr /etc/passwd          Sort by descending UID
zeppo:x:12505:1000:Zeppo Marx:/home/zeppo:/bin/zsh
gummo:x:12504:3000:Gummo Marx:/home/gummo:/usr/local/bin/ksh93
groucho:x:12503:2000:Groucho Marx:/home/groucho:/bin/sh
harpo:x:12502:1000:Harpo Marx:/home/harpo:/bin/ksh
chico:x:12501:1000:Chico Marx:/home/chico:/bin/bash
daemon:x:2:2:daemon:/sbin:/sbin/nologin
bin:x:1:1:bin:/bin:/sbin/nologin
root:x:0:0:root:/root:/bin/bash
```

A more precise field specification would have been -k3nr,3 (that is, from the start of field three, numerically, in reverse order, to the end of field three), or -k3,3nr, or even -k3,3 n -r, but sort stops collecting a number at the first nondigit, so -k3nr works correctly.

In our password file example, three users have a common GID in field 4, so we could sort first by GID, and then by UID, with:

```
$ sort -t: -k4n -k3n /etc/passwd          Sort by GID and UID
root:x:0:0:root:/root:/bin/bash
bin:x:1:1:bin:/bin:/sbin/nologin
daemon:x:2:2:daemon:/sbin:/sbin/nologin
chico:x:12501:1000:Chico Marx:/home/chico:/bin/bash
harpo:x:12502:1000:Harpo Marx:/home/harpo:/bin/ksh
```

```
zeppo:x:12505:1000:Zeppo Marx:/home/zeppo:/bin/zsh
groucho:x:12503:2000:Groucho Marx:/home/groucho:/bin/sh
gummo:x:12504:3000:Gummo Marx:/home/gummo:/usr/local/bin/ksh93
```

The useful -u option asks sort to output only unique records, where *unique* means that their sort-key fields match, even if there are differences elsewhere. Reusing the password file one last time, we find:

```
$ sort -t: -k4n -u /etc/passwd          Sort by unique GID
root:x:0:0:root:/root:/bin/bash
bin:x:1:1:bin:/bin:/sbin/nologin
daemon:x:2:2:daemon:/sbin:/sbin/nologin
chico:x:12501:1000:Chico Marx:/home/chico:/bin/bash
groucho:x:12503:2000:Groucho Marx:/home/groucho:/bin/sh
gummo:x:12504:3000:Gummo Marx:/home/gummo:/usr/local/bin/ksh93
```

Notice that the output is shorter: three users are in group 1000, but only one of them was output. We show another way to select unique records later in "Removing Duplicates" [4.2].

4.1.3   Sorting Text Blocks

Sometimes you need to sort data composed of multiline records. A good example is an address list, which is conveniently stored with one or more blank lines between addresses. For data like this, there is no constant sort-key position that could be used in a -k option, so you have to help out by supplying some extra markup. Here's a simple example:

```
$ cat my-friends                        Show address file
# SORTKEY: Schloß, Hans Jürgen
Hans Jürgen Schloß
Unter den Linden 78
D-10117 Berlin
Germany

# SORTKEY: Jones, Adrian
Adrian Jones
371 Montgomery Park Road
Henley-on-Thames RG9 4AJ
UK

# SORTKEY: Brown, Kim
Kim Brown
1841 S Main Street
Westchester, NY 10502
USA
```

The sorting trick is to use the ability of awk to handle more-general record separators to recognize paragraph breaks, temporarily replace the line breaks inside each address with an otherwise unused character, such as an unprintable control character, and replace the paragraph break with a newline. sort then sees lines that look like this:

```
# SORTKEY: Schloß, Hans Jürgen^ZHans Jürgen Schloß^ZUnter den Linden 78^Z...
# SORTKEY: Jones, Adrian^ZAdrian Jones^Z371 Montgomery Park Road^Z...
# SORTKEY: Brown, Kim^ZKim Brown^Z1841 S Main Street^Z...
```

Here, ^Z is a Ctrl-Z character. A filter step downstream from sort restores the line breaks and paragraph breaks, and the sort key lines are easily removed, if desired, with grep. The entire pipeline looks like this:

```
cat my-friends |                                    Pipe in address file
  awk -v RS="" { gsub("\n", "^Z"); print }' |       Convert addresses to single lines
    sort -f |                                       Sort address bundles, ignoring case
      awk -v ORS="\n\n" '{ gsub("^Z", "\n"); print }' |  Restore line structure
        grep -v '# SORTKEY'                         Remove markup lines
```

The gsub( ) function performs "global substitutions." It is similar to the s/x/y/g construct in sed. The RS variable is the input Record Separator. Normally, input records are separated by newlines, making each line a separate record. Using RS="" is a special case, whereby records are separated by blank lines; i.e., each block or "paragraph" of text forms a separate record. This is exactly the form of our input data. Finally, ORS is the Output Record Separator; each output record printed with print is terminated with its value. Its default is also normally a single newline; setting it here to "\n\n" preserves the input format with blank lines separating records. (More detail on these constructs may be found in Chapter 9.)

The output of this pipeline on our address file is:

```
Kim Brown
1841 S Main Street
Westchester, NY 10502
USA

Adrian Jones
371 Montgomery Park Road
Henley-on-Thames RG9 4AJ
UK

Hans Jürgen Schloß
Unter den Linden 78
D-10117 Berlin
Germany
```

The beauty of this approach is that we can easily include additional keys in each address that can be used for both sorting and selection: for example, an extra markup line of the form:

```
# COUNTRY: UK
```

in each address, and an additional pipeline stage of grep '# COUNTRY: UK' just before the sort, would let us extract only the UK addresses for further processing.

You could, of course, go overboard and use XML markup to identify the parts of the address in excruciating detail:

```
<address>
  <personalname>Hans Jürgen</personalname>
  <familyname>Schloß</familyname><br/>
  <streetname>Unter den Linden<streetname>
  <streetnumber>78</streetnumber><br/>
  <postalcode>D-10117</postalcode>
  <city>Berlin</city><br/>
  <country>Germany</country>
</address>
```

With fancier data-processing filters, you could then please your post office by pre-sorting your mail by country and postal code, but our minimal markup and simple pipeline are often good enough to get the job done.

4.1.4   Sort Efficiency

The obvious way to sort data requires comparing all pairs of items to see which comes first, and leads to algorithms known as *bubble sort* and *insertion sort*. These quick-and-dirty algorithms are fine for small amounts of data, but they certainly are not quick for large amounts, because their work to sort n records grows like n^2. This is quite different from almost all of the filters that we discuss in this book: they read a record, process it, and output it, so their execution time is directly proportional to the number of records, n.

Fortunately, the sorting problem has had lots of attention in the computing community, and good sorting algorithms are known whose average complexity goes like $n^{3/2}$ (*shellsort*), $n \log n$ (*heapsort*, *mergesort*, and *quicksort*), and for restricted kinds of data, n (*distribution sort*). The Unix sort command implementation has received extensive study and optimization: you can be confident that it will do the job efficiently, and almost certainly better than you can do yourself without learning a lot more about sorting algorithms.

4.1.5   Sort Stability

An important question about sorting algorithms is whether or not they are *stable*: that is, is the input order of equal records preserved in the output? A stable sort may be desirable when records are sorted by multiple keys, or more than once in a pipeline. POSIX does not require that sort be stable, and most implementations are not, as this example shows:

```
$ sort -t_ -k1,1 -k2,2 << EOF          Sort four lines by first two fields
> one_two
> one_two_three
> one_two_four
> one_two_five
> EOF
```

```
one_two
one_two_five
one_two_four
one_two_three
```

The sort fields are identical in each record, but the output differs from the input, so sort is not stable. Fortunately, the GNU implementation in the *coreutils* package[*] remedies that deficiency via the --stable option: its output for this example correctly matches the input.

4.1.6   Sort Wrap-Up

sort certainly ranks in the top ten Unix commands: learn it well because you'll use it often. More details on sort are provided in the sidebar near the start of this chapter, but consult the manual pages for *sort*(1) for the complete story on your system. sort is, of course, standardized by POSIX, so it should be available on every computer that you are likely to use.

4.2   Removing Duplicates

It is sometimes useful to remove consecutive duplicate records from a data stream. We showed in "Sorting by Fields" [4.1.2] that sort -u would do that job, but we also saw that the elimination is based on matching *keys* rather than matching *records*. The uniq command provides another way to filter data: it is frequently used in a pipeline to eliminate duplicate records downstream from a sort operation:

```
sort ... | uniq | ...
```

uniq has three useful options that find frequent application. The -c option prefixes each output line with a count of the number of times that it occurred, and we will use it in the word-frequency filter in Example 5-5 in Chapter 5. The -d option shows only lines that are duplicated, and the -u option shows just the nonduplicate lines. Here are some examples:

```
$ cat latin-numbers                    Show the test file
tres
unus
duo
tres
duo
tres

$ sort latin-numbers | uniq            Show unique sorted records
duo
tres
unus
```

---

[*] Available at *ftp://ftp.gnu.org/gnu/coreutils/*.

```
$ sort latin-numbers | uniq -c        Count unique sorted records
    2 duo
    3 tres
    1 unus

$ sort latin-numbers | uniq -d        Show only duplicate records
duo
tres

$ sort latin-numbers | uniq -u        Show only nonduplicate records
unus
```

uniq is sometimes a useful complement to the diff utility for figuring out the differences between two similar data streams: dictionary word lists, pathnames in mirrored directory trees, telephone books, and so on. Most implementations have other options that you can find described in the manual pages for *uniq*(1), but their use is rare. Like sort, uniq is standardized by POSIX, so you can use it everywhere.

4.3 Reformatting Paragraphs

Most powerful text editors provide commands that make it easy to reformat paragraphs by changing line breaks so that lines do not exceed a width that is comfortable for a human to read; we used such commands a lot in writing this book. Sometimes you need to do this to a data stream in a shell script, or inside an editor that lacks a reformatting command but does have a shell escape. In this case, fmt is what you need. Although POSIX makes no mention of fmt, you can find it on every current flavor of Unix; if you have an older system that lacks fmt, simply install the GNU *coreutils* package.

Although some implementations of fmt have more options, only two find frequent use: -s means split long lines only, but do not join short lines to make longer ones, and -w *n* sets the output line width to *n* characters (default: usually about 75 or so). Here are some examples with chunks of a spelling dictionary that has just one word per line:

```
$ sed -n -e 9991,10010p /usr/dict/words | fmt        Reformat 20 dictionary words
Graff graft graham grail grain grainy grammar grammarian grammatic
granary grand grandchild grandchildren granddaughter grandeur grandfather
grandiloquent grandiose grandma grandmother

$ sed -n -e 9995,10004p /usr/dict/words | fmt -w 30  Reformat 10 words into short lines
grain grainy grammar
grammarian grammatic
granary grand grandchild
grandchildren granddaughter
```

If your system does not have /usr/dict/words, then it probably has an equivalent file named /usr/share/dict/words or /usr/share/lib/dict/words.

The split-only option, -s, is helpful in wrapping long lines while leaving short lines intact, and thus minimizing the differences from the original version:

```
$ fmt -s -w 10 << END_OF_DATA          Reformat long lines only
> one two three four five
> six
> seven
> eight
> END_OF_DATA
one two
three
four five
six
seven
eight
```

 You might expect that you could split an input stream into one word per line with fmt -w 0, or remove line breaks entirely with a large width. Unfortunately, fmt implementations vary in behavior:

- Older versions of fmt lack the -w option; they use –*n* to specify an *n*-character width.

- All reject a zero width, but accept -w 1 or –1.

- All preserve leading space.

- Some preserve lines that look like mail headers.

- Some preserve lines beginning with a dot (troff typesetter commands).

- Most limit the width. We found peculiar upper bounds of 1021 (Solaris), 2048 (HP/UX 11), 4093 (AIX and IRIX), 8189 (OSF/1 4.0), 12285 (OSF/1 5.1), and 2147483647 (largest 32-bit signed integer: FreeBSD, GNU/Linux, and Mac OS).

- The NetBSD and OpenBSD versions of fmt have a different command-line syntax, and apparently allocate a buffer to hold the output line, since they give an out of memory diagnostic for large width values.

- IRIX fmt is found in /usr/sbin, a directory that is unlikely to be in your search path.

- HP/UX before version 11.0 did not have fmt.

These variations make it difficult to use fmt in portable scripts, or for complex reformatting tasks.

4.4 Counting Lines, Words, and Characters

We have used the word-count utility, wc, a few times before. It is probably one of the oldest, and simplest, tools in the Unix toolbox, and POSIX standardizes it. By default, wc outputs a one-line report of the number of lines, words, and bytes:

```
$ echo This is a test of the emergency broadcast system | wc     Report counts
      1       9      49
```

Request a subset of those results with the -c (bytes), -l (lines), and -w (words) options:

```
$ echo Testing one two three | wc -c     Count bytes
22

$ echo Testing one two three | wc -l     Count lines.
1

$ echo Testing one two three | wc -w     Count words
4
```

The -c option originally stood for *character count*, but with multibyte character-set encodings, such as UTF-8, in modern systems, bytes are no longer synonymous with characters, so POSIX introduced the -m option to count multibyte characters. For 8-bit character data, it is the same as -c.

Although wc is most commonly used with input from a pipeline, it also accepts command-line file arguments, producing a one-line report for each, followed by a summary report:

```
$ wc /etc/passwd /etc/group              Count data in two files
   26     68   1631 /etc/passwd
10376  10376 160082 /etc/group
10402  10444 161713 total
```

Modern versions of wc are locale-aware: set the environment variable LC_CTYPE to the desired locale to influence wc's interpretation of byte sequences as characters and word separators.

In Chapter 5, we will develop a related tool, wf, to report the frequency of occurrence of each word.

4.5 Printing

Compared to computers, printers are slow devices, and because they are commonly shared, it is generally undesirable for users to send jobs directly to them. Instead, most operating systems provide commands to send requests to a print *daemon** that queues jobs for printing, and handles printer and queue management. Print commands can be handled quickly because printing is done in the background when the needed resources are available.

Printing support in Unix evolved into two camps with differing commands but equivalent functionality, as summarized in Table 4-2. Commercial Unix systems and GNU/Linux usually support both camps, whereas BSD systems offer only the Berkeley style. POSIX specifies only the lp command.

---

* A daemon (pronounced *dee-mon*) is a long-running process that provides a service, such as accounting, file access, login, network connection, printing, or time of day.

Table 4-2. Printing commands

Berkeley	System V	Purpose
lpr	lp	Send files to print queue
lprm	cancel	Remove files from print queue
lpq	lpstat	Report queue status

Here is an example of their use, first with the Berkeley style:

```
$ lpr -Plcb102 sample.ps              Send PostScript file to print queue lcb102

$ lpq -Plcb102                        Ask for print queue status
lcb102 is ready and printing
Rank    Owner   Job     File(s)    Total Size
active  jones   81352   sample.ps  122888346 bytes

$ lprm -Plcb102 81352                 Stop the presses! Kill that huge job
```

and then with the System V style:

```
$ lp -d lcb102 sample.ps              Send PostScript file to print queue lcb102
request id is lcb102-81355 (1 file(s))

$ lpstat -t lcb102                    Ask for print queue status
printer lcb102 now printing lcb102-81355

$ cancel lcb102-81355                 Whoops! Don't print that job!
```

lp and lpr can, of course, read input from standard input instead of from command-line files, so they are commonly used at the end of a pipeline.

System management can make a particular single queue the system default so that queue names need not be supplied when the default is acceptable. Individual users can set an environment variable, PRINTER (Berkeley) or LPDEST (System V), to select a personal default printer.

Print queue names are site-specific: a small site might just name the queue printer, and make it the default. Larger sites might pick names that reflect location, such as a building abbreviation and room number, or that identify particular printer models or capabilities, such as bw for a black-and-white printer and color for the expensive one.

Unfortunately, with modern networked intelligent printers, the lprm, cancel, lpq, and lpstat commands are much less useful than they once were: print jobs arrive quickly at the printer and appear to the printer daemon to have been printed already and are thus deleted from the print queue, even though the printer may still be holding them in memory or in a filesystem while other print jobs are still being processed. At that point, the only recourse is to use the printer's control panel to cancel an unwanted job.

4.5.1 Evolution of Printing Technology

Printer technology has changed a lot since Unix was first developed. The industry has moved from large impact printers and electric typewriters that formed characters by hammering a ribbon and paper against a metal character shape, to electrostatic, dot-matrix, inkjet, and laser printers that make characters from tiny dots.

Advances in microprocessors allowed the implementation inside the printer of simple command languages like Hewlett-Packard Printer Command Language (PCL) and HP Graphics Language(HPGL), and complete programming languages—notably, Adobe PostScript. Adobe Portable Document Format (PDF) is a descendant of PostScript that is more compact, but not programmable. PDF offers additional features like color transparency, digital signatures, document-access control, encryption, enhanced data compression, and page independence. That last feature allows high-performance printers to rasterize pages in parallel, and PDF viewers to quickly display any requested page.

The newest generation of devices combines printing, copying, and scanning into a single system with a disk filesystem and network access, support for multiple page-description languages and graphics file formats, and, in at least one case, GNU/Linux as the embedded operating system.

Unfortunately, Unix printing software has not adapted rapidly enough to these improvements in printing technology, and command-level support for access to many features of newer printers remains poor. Two notable software projects attempt to remedy this situation: Common UNIX Printing System[*] (*CUPS*), and lpr next generation[†] (*LPRng*). Many large Unix sites have adopted one or the other; both provide familiar Unix printing commands, but with a lot more options. Both fully support printing of PostScript and PDF files: when necessary, they use the Aladdin or GNU *ghostscript* interpreter to convert such files to other formats needed by less-capable printers. CUPS also supports printing of assorted graphics image file formats, and *n*-up printing to place several reduced page images on a single sheet.

4.5.2 Other Printing Software

Despite its name, the venerable pr command does not print files, but rather, filters data in preparation for printing. In the simplest case, pr produces a page header timestamped with the file's modification time, or if input is from a pipe, with the current time, followed by the filename (empty for piped input) and a page number, with a fixed number (66) of lines per page. The intent was that:

```
pr file(s) | lp
```

[*] Available at *http://www.cups.org/* and documented in a book listed in the Bibliography.
[†] Available at *http://www.lprng.org/*.

would print nice listings. However, that simplicity has not worked since the old mechanical printers of the 1970s were retired. Default font sizes and line spacing vary between printers, and multiple paper sizes are in common use.

---

pr

Usage

    pr [*options*] [*file(s)*]

Purpose

    Paginate text files for printing.

Major options

    -cn

        Produce *n*-column output. This option can be abbreviated to *-n* (e.g., -4 instead of -c4).

    -f

        Prefix each page header after the first with an ASCII formfeed character. This option is called -F on FreeBSD, NetBSD, and Mac OS X. OpenBSD recognizes both options. POSIX has both, but assigns them slightly different meanings.

    -h althdr

        Use the string *althdr* to replace the filename in the page header.

    -ln

        Produce *n*-line pages. Some implementations include page header and trailer lines in the count, whereas others do not.

    -on

        Offset output lines with *n* spaces.

    -t

        Suppress page headers.

    -wn

        Produce lines of at most *n* characters. For single-column output, wrap longer lines onto additional lines as needed; otherwise, for multicolumn output, truncate long lines to fit.

Behavior

    pr reads the specified files, or standard input if no files are given, and writes the paginated data on standard output.

Caveats

    pr implementations vary considerably in supported options and output formatting; the GNU *coreutils* version provides a way to get consistent behavior on all systems.

Instead, you generally have to experiment with setting the output page length with the -l option, and often the page width with the -w option and a text offset with the -o option. It is also essential to add the -f option (-F on some systems) to output an ASCII formfeed control character at the start of every page header after the first, to guarantee that each header starts a new page. The reality is that you generally have to use something like this:

```
pr -f -l60 -o10 -w65 file(s) | lp
```

If you use a different printer later, you may need to change those numeric parameters. This makes it hard to use pr reliably in portable shell scripts.

There is one feature of pr that is often convenient: the -cn option requests n-column output. If you combine that with the -t option to omit the page headers, you can produce nice multicolumn listings, such as this example, which formats 26 words into five columns:

```
$ sed -n -e 19000,19025p /usr/dict/words | pr -c5 -t
reproach       repugnant      request        reredos        resemblant
reptile        repulsion      require        rerouted       resemble
reptilian      repulsive      requisite      rerouting      resent
republic       reputation     requisition    rescind        resentful
republican     repute         requited       rescue         reserpine
repudiate
```

If the column width is too small, pr silently truncates data to prevent column overlap. We can format the same 26 words into 10 (truncated) columns like this:

```
$ sed -n -e 19000,19025p /usr/dict/words | pr -c10 -t
reproa republ repugn reputa requir requit rerout rescue resemb resent
reptil republ repuls repute requis reredo rescin resemb resent reserp
reptil repudi repuls reques requis rerout
```

pr has a lot of options, and historically, there was considerable variation among Unix systems in those options, and in the output format and number of lines per page. We recommend using the version from the GNU *coreutils* package, since it gives a uniform interface everywhere, and more options than most other versions. Consult the manual pages for *pr*(1) for the details.

Although some PostScript printers accept plain text, many do not. Typesetting systems like TEX and troff can turn marked-up documents into PostScript and/or PDF page images. If you have just a plain text file, how do you print it? The Unix printing system invokes suitable filters to do the conversion for you, but you then do not have any control over its appearance. The answer is text-to-PostScript filters like a2ps,[*] lptops,[†] or on Sun Solaris only, mp. Use them like this:

```
a2ps file > file.ps          Make a PostScript listing of file
a2ps file | lp               Print a PostScript listing of file
```

---

[*] Available at *ftp://ftp.gnu.org/gnu/a2ps/*.

[†] Available at *http://www.math.utah.edu/pub/lptops/*.

```
lptops file > file.ps          Make a PostScript listing of file
lptops file | lp               Print a PostScript listing of file

mp file > file.ps              Make a PostScript listing of file
mp file | lp                   Print a PostScript listing of file
```

All three have command-line options to choose the font, specify the typesize, supply or suppress page headers, and select multicolumn output.

BSD, IBM AIX, and Sun Solaris systems have vgrind,[*] which filters files in a variety of programming languages, turning them into troff input, with comments in italics, keywords in bold, and the current function noted in the margin; that data is then typeset and output as PostScript. A derivative called tgrind[†] does a similar job, but with more font choices, line numbering, indexing, and support for many more programming languages. tgrind produces TEX input that readily leads to PostScript and PDF output. Figure 4-1 shows a sample of its output. Both programs are easy to use for printing of typeset program listings:

```
$ tgrind -p hello.c                        Typeset and print hello.c

$ tgrind -i 1 -fn Bookman -p hello.c       Print the listing shown in Figure 4-1

$ vgrind hello.c | lp                      Typeset and print hello.c
```

4.6 Extracting the First and Last Lines

It is sometimes useful to extract just a few lines from a text file—most commonly, lines near the beginning or the end. For example, the chapter titles for the XML files for this book are all visible in the first half-dozen lines of each file, and a peek at the end of job-log files provides a summary of recent activity.

Both of these operations are easy. You can display the first *n* records of standard input or each of a list of command-line files with any of these:

```
head -n n       [ file(s) ]

head -n         [ file(s) ]

awk 'FNR <= n'  [ file(s) ]

sed -e nq       [ file(s) ]

sed nq          [ file(s) ]
```

POSIX requires a head option of -n 3 instead of -3, but every implementation that we tested accepts both.

---

[*] Available at *http://www.math.utah.edu/pub/vgrind/*.

[†] Available at *http://www.math.utah.edu/pub/tgrind/*.

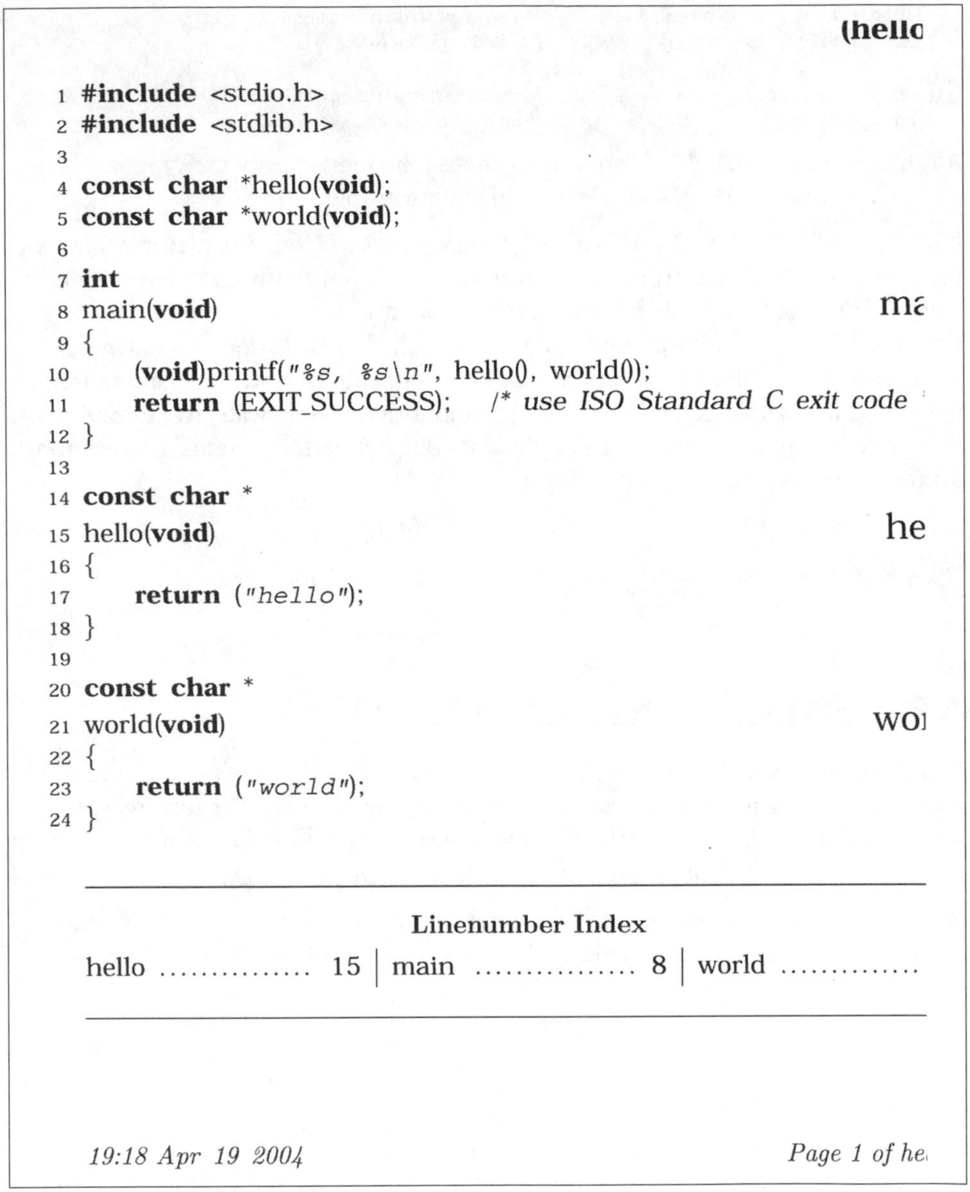

```
 1 #include <stdio.h>
 2 #include <stdlib.h>
 3
 4 const char *hello(void);
 5 const char *world(void);
 6
 7 int
 8 main(void)                                              ma
 9 {
10     (void)printf("%s, %s\n", hello(), world());
11     return (EXIT_SUCCESS);    /* use ISO Standard C exit code
12 }
13
14 const char *
15 hello(void)                                             he
16 {
17     return ("hello");
18 }
19
20 const char *
21 world(void)                                             wo
22 {
23     return ("world");
24 }
```

Linenumber Index

hello .... 15 │ main .... 8 │ world ....

19:18 Apr 19 2004   *Page 1 of he*

Figure 4-1. tgrind typesetting of a famous C program

When there is only a single edit command, sed allows the –e option to be omitted.

It is *not* an error if there are fewer than *n* lines to display.

The last *n* lines can be displayed like this:

```
tail -n n      [ file ]

tail -n         [ file ]
```

As with head, POSIX specifies only the first form, but both are accepted on all of our systems.

Curiously, although head handles multiple files on the command line, traditional and POSIX tail do not. That nuisance is fixed in all modern versions of tail.

In an interactive shell session, it is sometimes desirable to monitor output to a file, such as a log file, while it is still being written. The -f option asks tail to show the specified number of lines at the end of the file, and then to go into an endless loop, sleeping for a second before waking up and checking for more output to display. With -f, tail terminates only when you interrupt it, usually by typing Ctrl-C:

```
$ tail -n 25 -f /var/log/messages        Watch the growth of the system message log
...
^C                                       Ctrl-C stops tail
```

Since tail does not terminate on its own with the -f option, that option is unlikely to be of use in shell scripts.

There are no short and simple alternatives to tail with awk or sed, because the job requires maintaining a history of recent records.

Although we do not illustrate them in detail here, there are a few other commands that we use in small examples throughout the book, and that are worth adding to your toolbox:

- dd copies data in blocks of user-specified size and number. It also has some limited ability to convert between uppercase and lowercase, and between ASCII and EBCDIC. For character-set conversions, however, the modern, and POSIX standard, iconv command for converting files from one code set to another has much more flexibility.

- file matches a few selected leading bytes of the contents of each of its argument files against a pattern database and prints a brief one-line report on standard output of its conclusions for each of them. Most vendor-provided implementations of file recognize 100 or so types of files, but are unable to classify binary executables and object files from other Unix flavors, or files from other operating systems. There is a much better open-source version,[*] however, that has enjoyed the benefits of many contributors: it can recognize more than 1200 file types, including many from non-Unix operating systems.

- od, the octal dump command, prints byte streams in ASCII, octal, and hexadecimal. Command-line options can set the number of bytes read and can select the output format.

- strings searches its input for sequences of four or more printable characters ending with a newline or a NUL, and prints them on standard output. It is often

---

[*] Available at *ftp://ftp.astron.com/pub/file/*.

useful for peeking inside binary files, such as compiled programs or datafiles. Desktop-software, image, and sound files sometimes contain useful textual data near the beginning, and GNU head provides the handy -c option to limit the output to a specified number of characters:

```
$ strings -a horne01.jpg | head -c 256 | fmt -w 65     Examine astronomical image
JFIF Photoshop 3.0 8BIM Comet Hale-Bopp shows delicate
filaments in it's blue ion tail in this exposure made Monday
morning 3/17/97 using  12.5 inch F/4 Newtonian reflecting
telescope. The 15 minute exposure was made on Fujicolor SG-800
Plus film. 8BIM 8BI
```

4.7   Summary

This chapter covered about 30 utilities for processing text files. Collectively, they are a powerful set of tools for writing shell scripts. The most important, and most complex, is sort. The fmt, uniq, and wc commands are often just the tools you need in a pipeline to simplify or summarize data. When you need to get a quick overview of a collection of unfamiliar files, file, head, strings, and tail are often a better choice than visiting each file in turn with a text editor. a2ps, tgrind, and vgrind can make listings of your programs, including shell scripts, easier to read.

## CHAPTER 5

Pipelines Can Do Amazing Things

In this chapter, we solve several relatively simple text processing jobs. What's interesting about all the examples here is that they are scripts built from simple pipelines: chains of one command hooked into another. Yet each one accomplishes a significant task.

When you tackle a text processing problem in Unix, it is important to keep the Unix tool philosophy in mind: ask yourself how the problem can be broken down into simpler jobs, for each of which there is already an existing tool, or for which you can readily supply one with a few lines of a shell program or with a scripting language.

5.1   Extracting Data from Structured Text Files

Most administrative files in Unix are simple flat text files that you can edit, print, and read without any special file-specific tools. Many of them reside in the standard directory, /etc. Common examples are the password and group files (passwd and group), the filesystem mount table (fstab or vfstab), the hosts file (hosts), the default shell startup file (profile), and the system startup and shutdown shell scripts, stored in the subdirectory trees rc0.d, rc1.d, and so on, through rc6.d. (There may be other directories as well.)

File formats are traditionally documented in Section 5 of the Unix manual, so the command man 5 passwd provides information about the structure of /etc/passwd.*

Despite its name, the password file must always be publicly readable. Perhaps it should have been called the user file because it contains basic information about every user account on the system, packed together in one line per account, with fields separated by colons. We described the file's format in "Text File Conventions" [3.3.1]. Here are some typical entries:

```
jones:*:32713:899:Adrian W. Jones/OSD211/555-0123:/home/jones:/bin/ksh
dorothy:*:123:30:Dorothy Gale/KNS321/555-0044:/home/dorothy:/bin/bash
```

---

* On some systems, file formats are in Section 7; thus, you might need to use man 7 passwd instead.

```
toto:*:1027:18:Toto Gale/KNS322/555-0045:/home/toto:/bin/tcsh
ben:*:301:10:Ben Franklin/OSD212/555-0022:/home/ben:/bin/bash
jhancock:*:1457:57:John Hancock/SIG435/555-0099:/home/jhancock:/bin/bash
betsy:*:110:20:Betsy Ross/BMD17/555-0033:/home/betsy:/bin/ksh
tj:*:60:33:Thomas Jefferson/BMD19/555-0095:/home/tj:/bin/bash
george:*:692:42:George Washington/BST999/555-0001:/home/george:/bin/tcsh
```

To review, the seven fields of a password-file entry are:

1. The username
2. The encrypted password, or an indicator that the password is stored in a separate file
3. The numeric user ID
4. The numeric group ID
5. The user's personal name, and possibly other relevant data (office number, telephone number, and so on)
6. The home directory
7. The login shell

All but one of these fields have significance to various Unix programs. The one that does not is the fifth, which conventionally holds user information that is relevant only to local humans. Historically, it was called the gecos field, because it was added in the 1970s at Bell Labs when Unix systems needed to communicate with other computers running the General Electric Comprehensive Operating System, and some extra information about the Unix user was required for that system. Today, most sites use it just to record the personal name, so we simply call it the name field.

For the purposes of this example, we assume that the local site records extra information in the name field: a building and office number identifier (OSD211 in the first sample entry), and a telephone number (555-0123), separated from the personal name by slashes.

One obvious useful thing that we can do with such a file is to write some software to create an office directory. That way, only a single file, /etc/passwd, needs to be kept up-to-date, and derived files can be created when the master file is changed, or more sensibly, by a cron job that runs at suitable intervals. (We will discuss cron in "crontab: Rerun at Specified Times" [13.6.4].)

For our first attempt, we make the office directory a simple text file, with entries like this:

```
Franklin, Ben           •OSD212•555-0022
Gale, Dorothy           •KNS321•555-0044
...
```

where • represents an ASCII tab character. We put the personal name in conventional directory order (family name first), padding the name field with spaces to a convenient fixed length. We prefix the office number and telephone with tab characters to preserve some useful structure that other tools can exploit.

Scripting languages, such as awk, were designed to make such tasks easy because they provide automated input processing and splitting of input records into fields, so we could write the conversion job entirely in such a language. However, we want to show how to achieve the same thing with other Unix tools.

For each password file line, we need to extract field five, split it into three subfields, rearrange the names in the first subfield, and then write an office directory line to a sorting process.

awk and cut are convenient tools for field extraction:

```
... | awk -F: '{ print $5 }' | ...
... | cut -d: -f5 | ...
```

There is a slight complication in that we have two field-processing tasks that we want to keep separate for simplicity, but we need to combine their output to make a directory entry. The join command is just what we need: it expects two input files, each ordered by a common unique key value, and joins lines sharing a common key into a single output line, with user control over which fields are output.

Since our directory entries contain three fields, to use join we need to create three intermediate files containing the colon-separated pairs *key:person*, *key:office*, and *key:telephone*, one pair per line. These can all be temporary files, since they are derived automatically from the password file.

What key do we use? It just needs to be unique, so it could be the record number in the original password file, but in this case it can also be the username, since we know that usernames are unique in the password file and they make more sense to humans than numbers do. Later, if we decide to augment our directory with additional information, such as job title, we can create another nontemporary file with the pair *key: jobtitle* and add it to the processing stages.

Instead of hardcoding input and output filenames into our program, it is more flexible to write the program as a *filter* so that it reads standard input and writes standard output. For commands that are used infrequently, it is advisable to give them descriptive, rather than short and cryptic, names, so we start our shell program like this:

```
#! /bin/sh
# Filter an input stream formatted like /etc/passwd,
# and output an office directory derived from that data.
#
# Usage:
#       passwd-to-directory < /etc/passwd > office-directory-file
#       ypcat passwd | passwd-to-directory > office-directory-file
#       niscat passwd.org_dir | passwd-to-directory > office-directory-file
```

Since the password file is publicly readable, any data derived from it is public as well, so there is no real need to restrict access to our program's intermediate files. However, because all of us at times have to deal with sensitive data, it is good to develop the programming habit of allowing file access only to those users or processes that need it. We therefore reset the umask (see "Default permissions" in Appendix B) as the first action in our program:

```
umask 077                                Restrict temporary file access to just us
```

For accountability and debugging, it is helpful to have some commonality in temporary filenames, and to avoid cluttering the current directory with them: we name them with the prefix /tmp/pd.. To guard against name collisions if multiple instances of our program are running at the same time, we also need the names to be unique: the process number, available in the shell variable $$, provides a distinguishing suffix. (This use of $$ is described in more detail in Chapter 10.) We therefore define these shell variables to represent our temporary files:

```
PERSON=/tmp/pd.key.person.$$             Unique temporary filenames
OFFICE=/tmp/pd.key.office.$$
TELEPHONE=/tmp/pd.key.telephone.$$
USER=/tmp/pd.key.user.$$
```

When the job terminates, either normally or abnormally, we want the temporary files to be deleted, so we use the trap command:

```
trap "exit 1"                            HUP INT PIPE QUIT TERM
trap "rm -f $PERSON $OFFICE $TELEPHONE $USER" EXIT
```

During development, we can just comment out the second trap, preserving temporary files for subsequent examination. (The trap command is described in "Trapping Process Signals" [13.3.2]. For now, it's enough to understand that when the script exits, the trap command arranges to automatically run rm with the given arguments.)

We need fields one and five repeatedly, and once we have them, we don't require the input stream from standard input again, so we begin by extracting them into a temporary file:

```
awk -F: '{ print $1 ":" $5 }' > $USER        This reads standard input
```

We make the *key:person* pair file first, with a two-step sed program followed by a simple line sort; the sort command is discussed in detail in "Sorting Text" [4.1].

```
sed -e 's=/.*==' \
    -e 's=^\([^:]*\):\(.*\) \([^ ]*\)=\1:\3, \2=' <$USER | sort >$PERSON
```

The script uses = as the separator character for sed's s command, since both slashes and colons appear in the data. The first edit strips everything from the first slash to the end of the line, reducing a line like this:

```
jones:Adrian W. Jones/OSD211/555-0123        Input line
```

to this:

```
jones:Adrian W. Jones                    Result of first edit
```

The second edit is more complex, matching three subpatterns in the record. The first part, **\\([^:]*\\)**, matches the username field (e.g., jones). The second part, **\\(.*\\)□**, matches text up to a space (e.g., Adrian□W.□; the □ stands for a space character). The last part, **\\([^□]*\\)**, matches the remaining nonspace text in the record (e.g., Jones). The replacement text reorders the matches, producing something like Jones,□Adrian W. The result of this single sed command is the desired reordering:

```
jones:Jones, Adrian W.                   Printed result of second edit
```

Next, we make the *key:office* pair file:

```
sed -e 's=^\([^:]*\):[^/]*/\([^/]*\)/.*$=\1:\2=' < $USER | sort > $OFFICE
```

The result is a list of users and offices:

```
jones:OSD211
```

The *key:telephone* pair file creation is similar: we just need to adjust the match pattern:

```
sed -e 's=^\([^:]*\):[^/]*/[^/]*/\([^/]*\)=\1:\2=' < $USER | sort > $TELEPHONE
```

At this stage, we have three separate files, each of which is sorted. Each file consists of the key (the username), a colon, and the particular data (personal name, office, telephone number). The $PERSON file's contents look like this:

```
ben:Franklin, Ben
betsy:Ross, Betsy
...
```

The $OFFICE file has username and office data:

```
ben:OSD212
betsy:BMD17
...
```

The $TELEPHONE file records usernames and telephone numbers:

```
ben:555-0022
betsy:555-0033
...
```

By default, join outputs the common key, then the remaining fields of the line from the first file, followed by the remaining fields of the line from the second line. The common key defaults to the first field, but that can be changed by a command-line option: we don't need that feature here. Normally, spaces separate fields for join, but we can change the separator with its −t option: we use it as −t:.

The join operations are done with a five-stage pipeline, as follows:

1. Combine the personal information and the office location:

```
join -t: $PERSON $OFFICE | ...
```

The results of this operation, which become the input to the next stage, look like this:

```
ben:Franklin, Ben:OSD212
betsy:Ross, Betsy:BMD17
...
```

2. Add the telephone number:

```
... | join -t: - $TELEPHONE | ...
```

The results of this operation, which become the input to the next stage, look like this:

```
ben:Franklin, Ben:OSD212:555-0022
betsy:Ross, Betsy:BMD17:555-0033
...
```

3. Remove the key (which is the first field), since it's no longer needed. This is most easily done with cut and a range that says "use fields two through the end," like so:

```
... | cut -d: -f 2- | ...
```

The results of this operation, which become the input to the next stage, look like this:

```
Franklin, Ben:OSD212:555-0022
Ross, Betsy:BMD17:555-0033
...
```

4. Re-sort the data. The data was previously sorted by login name, but now things need to be sorted by personal last name. This is done with sort:

```
... | sort -t: -k1,1 -k2,2 -k3,3 | ...
```

This command uses a colon to separate fields, sorting on fields 1, 2, and 3, in order. The results of this operation, which become the input to the next stage, look like this:

```
Franklin, Ben:OSD212:555-0022
Gale, Dorothy:KNS321:555-0044
...
```

5. Finally, reformat the output, using awk's printf statement to separate each field with tab characters. The command to do this is:

```
... | awk -F: '{ printf("%-39s\t%s\t%s\n", $1, $2, $3) }'
```

For flexibility and ease of maintenance, formatting should always be left until the end. Up to that point, everything is just text strings of arbitrary length.

Here's the complete pipeline:

```
join -t: $PERSON $OFFICE |
    join -t: - $TELEPHONE |
        cut -d: -f 2- |
            sort -t: -k1,1 -k2,2 -k3,3 |
                awk -F: '{ printf("%-39s\t%s\t%s\n", $1, $2, $3) }'
```

The awk `printf` statement used here is similar enough to the shell `printf` command that its meaning should be clear: print the first colon-separated field left-adjusted in a 39-character field, followed by a tab, the second field, another tab, and the third field. Here are the full results:

```
Franklin, Ben                           •OSD212•555-0022
Gale, Dorothy                           •KNS321•555-0044
Gale, Toto                              •KNS322•555-0045
Hancock, John                           •SIG435•555-0099
Jefferson, Thomas                       •BMD19•555-0095
Jones, Adrian W.                        •OSD211•555-0123
Ross, Betsy                             •BMD17•555-0033
Washington, George                      •BST999•555-0001
```

That is all there is to it! Our entire script is slightly more than 20 lines long, excluding comments, with five main processing steps. We collect it together in one place in Example 5-1.

Example 5-1. Creating an office directory

```
#! /bin/sh
# Filter an input stream formatted like /etc/passwd,
# and output an office directory derived from that data.
#
# Usage:
#       passwd-to-directory < /etc/passwd > office-directory-file
#       ypcat passwd | passwd-to-directory > office-directory-file
#       niscat passwd.org_dir | passwd-to-directory > office-directory-file

umask 077

PERSON=/tmp/pd.key.person.$$
OFFICE=/tmp/pd.key.office.$$
TELEPHONE=/tmp/pd.key.telephone.$$
USER=/tmp/pd.key.user.$$

trap "exit 1"                           HUP INT PIPE QUIT TERM
trap "rm -f $PERSON $OFFICE $TELEPHONE $USER" EXIT

awk -F: '{ print $1 ":" $5 }' > $USER

sed -e 's=/.*==' \
    -e 's=^\([^:]*\):\(.*\) \([^ ]*\)=\1:\3, \2=' < $USER | sort > $PERSON

sed -e 's=^\([^:]*\):[^/]*/\([^/]*\)/.*$=\1:\2=' < $USER | sort > $OFFICE

sed -e 's=^\([^:]*\):[^/]*/[^/]*/\([^/]*\)=\1:\2=' < $USER | sort > $TELEPHONE

join -t: $PERSON $OFFICE |
    join -t: - $TELEPHONE |
        cut -d: -f 2- |
            sort -t: -k1,1 -k2,2 -k3,3 |
                awk -F: '{ printf("%-39s\t%s\t%s\n", $1, $2, $3) }'
```

The real power of shell scripting shows itself when we want to modify the script to do a slightly different job, such as insertion of the job title from a separately maintained *key:jobtitle* file. All that we need to do is modify the final pipeline to look something like this:

```
join -t: $PERSON /etc/passwd.job-title |          Extra join with job title
    join -t: - $OFFICE |
        join -t: - $TELEPHONE |
            cut -d: -f 2- |
                sort -t: -k1,1 -k3,3 -k4,4 |       Modify sort command
                    awk -F: '{ printf("%-39s\t%-23s\t%s\t%s\n",
                        $1, $2, $3, $4) }'          And formatting command
```

The total cost for the extra directory field is one more join, a change in the sort fields, and a small tweak in the final awk formatting command.

Because we were careful to preserve special field delimiters in our output, we can trivially prepare useful alternative directories like this:

```
passwd-to-directory < /etc/passwd | sort -t'•' -k2,2 > dir.by-office
passwd-to-directory < /etc/passwd | sort -t'•' -k3,3 > dir.by-telephone
```

As usual, • represents an ASCII tab character.

A critical assumption of our program is that there is a *unique key* for each data record. With that unique key, separate views of the data can be maintained in files as *key:value* pairs. Here, the key was a Unix username, but in larger contexts, it could be a book number (ISBN), credit card number, employee number, national retirement system number, part number, student number, and so on. Now you know why we get so many numbers assigned to us! You can also see that those handles need not be numbers: they just need to be unique text strings.

5.2   Structured Data for the Web

The immense popularity of the World Wide Web makes it desirable to be able to present data like the office directory developed in the last section in a form that is a bit fancier than our simple text file.

Web files are mostly written in a markup language called *HyperText Markup Language (HTML)*. This is a family of languages that are specific instances of the *Standard Generalized Markup Language (SGML)*, which has been defined in several ISO standards since 1986. The manuscript for this book was written in DocBook/XML, which is also a specific instance of SGML. You can find a full description of HTML in *HTML & XHTML: The Definitive Guide* (O'Reilly).[*]

---

[*] In addition to this book (listed in the Bibliography), hundreds of books on SGML and derivatives are listed at *http://www.math.utah.edu/pub/tex/bib/sgml.html* and *http://www.math.utah.edu/pub/tex/bib/sgml2000.html*.

A Digression on Databases

Most commercial databases today are constructed as *relational databases*: data is accessible as *key:value* pairs, and join operations are used to construct multicolumn tables to provide views of selected subsets of the data. Relational databases were first proposed in 1970 by E. F. Codd,[a] who actively promoted them, despite initial database industry opposition that they could not be implemented efficiently. Fortunately, clever programmers soon figured out how to solve the efficiency problem. Codd's work is so important that, in 1981, he was given the prestigious ACM Turing Award, the closest thing in computer science to the Nobel Prize.

Today, there are several ISO standards for the *Structured Query Language (SQL)*, making vendor-independent database access possible, and one of the most important SQL operations is join. Hundreds of books have been published about SQL; to learn more, pick a general one like *SQL in a Nutshell*.[b] Our simple office-directory task thus has an important lesson in it about the central concept of modern relational databases, and Unix software tools can be extremely valuable in preparing input for databases, and in processing their output.

[a] E. F. Codd, *A Relational Model of Data for Large Shared Data Banks*, Communications of the ACM, 13(6) 377–387, June (1970), and *Relational Database: A Practical Foundation for Productivity*, Communications of the ACM, 25(2) 109–117, February (1982) (Turing Award lecture).

[b] By Kevin Kline and Daniel Kline, O'Reilly & Associates, 2000, ISBN 1-56592-744-3. See also *http://www.math.utah.edu/pub/tex/bib/sqlbooks.html* for an extensive list of SQL books.

For the purposes of this section, we need only a tiny subset of HTML, which we present here in a small tutorial. If you are already familiar with HTML, just skim the next page or two.

Here is a minimal standards-conformant HTML file produced by a useful tool written by one of us:[*]

```
$ echo Hello, world. | html-pretty
<!-- -*-html-*- -->
<!-- Prettyprinted by html-pretty flex version 1.01 [25-Aug-2001] -->
<!-- on Wed Jan  8 12:12:42 2003 -->
<!-- for Adrian W. Jones (jones@example.com) -->

<!DOCTYPE HTML PUBLIC "-//IETF//DTD HTML//EN">
<HTML>
    <HEAD>
        <TITLE>
            <!-- Please supply a descriptive title here -->
        </TITLE>
        <!-- Please supply a correct e-mail address here -->
        <LINK REV="made" HREF="mailto:jones@example.com">
```

[*] Available at *http://www.math.utah.edu/pub/sgml/*.

```
    </HEAD>
    <BODY>
        Hello, world.
    </BODY>
</HTML>
```

The points to note in this HTML output are:

- HTML comments are enclosed in `<!--` and `-->`.

- Special processor commands are enclosed in `<!` and `>`: here, the `DOCTYPE` command tells an SGML parser what the document type is and where to find its grammar file.

- Markup is supplied by angle-bracketed words, called *tags*. In HTML, lettercase is *not* significant in tag names: `html-pretty` normally uppercases tag names for better visibility.

- Markup environments consist of a begin tag, `<NAME>`, and an end tag, `</NAME>`, and for many tags, environments can be nested within each other according to rules defined in the HTML grammars.

- An HTML document is structured as an HTML object containing one `HEAD` and one `BODY` object.

- Inside the `HEAD`, a `TITLE` object defines the document title that web browsers display in the window titlebar and in bookmark lists. Also inside the `HEAD`, the `LINK` object generally carries information about the web-page maintainer.

- The visible part of the document that browsers show is the contents of the `BODY`.

- Whitespace is not significant outside of quoted strings, so we can use horizontal and vertical spacing liberally to emphasize the structure, as the HTML prettyprinter does.

- Everything else is just printable ASCII text, with three exceptions. Literal angle brackets must be represented by special encodings, called *entities*, that consist of an ampersand, an identifier, and a semicolon: `&lt;` and `&gt;`. Since ampersand starts entities, it has its own literal *entity* name: `&amp;`. HTML supports a modest repertoire of entities for accented characters that cover most of the languages of Western Europe so that we can write, for example, `caf&eacute;` du bon go`&ucirc;`t to get café du bon goût.

- Although not shown in our minimal example, font style changes are accomplished in HTML with B (bold), EM (emphasis), I (italic), STRONG (extra bold), and TT (typewriter (fixed-width characters)) environments: write `<B>bold phrase</B>` to get **bold phrase**.

To convert our office directory to proper HTML, we need only one more bit of information: how to format a table, since that is what our directory really is and we don't want to force the use of typewriter fonts to get everything to line up in the browser display.

In HTML 3.0 and later, a table consists of a TABLE environment, inside of which are rows, each of them a table row (TR) environment. Inside each row are cells, called table data, each a TD environment. Notice that columns of data receive no special markup: a data column is simply the set of cells taken from the same row position in all of the rows of the table. Happily, we don't need to declare the number of rows and columns in advance. The job of the browser or formatter is to collect all of the cells, determine the widest cell in each column, and then format the table with columns just wide enough to hold those widest cells.

For our office directory example, we need just three columns, so our sample entry could be marked up like this:

```
<TABLE>
    ...
    <TR>
        <TD>
            Jones, Adrian W.
        </TD>
        <TD>
            555-0123
        </TD>
        <TD>
            OSD211
        </TD>
    </TR>
    ...
</TABLE>
```

An equivalent, but compact and hard-to-read, encoding might look like this:

```
<TABLE>
    ...
    <TR><TD>Jones, Adrian W.</TD><TD>555-0123</TD><TD>OSD211</TD></TR>
    ...
</TABLE>
```

Because we chose to preserve special field separators in the text version of the office directory, we have sufficient information to identify the cells in each row. Also, because whitespace is mostly not significant in HTML files (except to humans), we need not be particularly careful about getting tags nicely lined up: if that is needed later, html-pretty can do it perfectly. Our conversion filter then has three steps:

1. Output the leading boilerplate down to the beginning of the document body.

2. Wrap each directory row in table markup.

3. Output the trailing boilerplate.

We have to make one small change from our minimal example: the DOCTYPE command has to be updated to a later grammar level so that it looks like this:

```
<!DOCTYPE HTML PUBLIC "-//IETF//DTD HTML//EN//3.0">
```

You don't have to memorize this: `html-pretty` has options to produce output in any of the standard HTML grammar levels, so you can just copy a suitable `DOCTYPE` command from its output.

Clearly, most of the work is just writing boilerplate, but that is simple since we can just copy text from the minimal HTML example. The only programmatic step required is the middle one, which we could do with only a couple of lines in awk. However, we can achieve it with even less work using a sed stream-editor substitution with two edit commands: one to substitute the embedded tab delimiters with `</TD><TD>`, and a following one to wrap the entire line in `<TR><TD>...</TD></TR>`. We temporarily assume that no accented characters are required in the directory, but we can easily allow for angle brackets and ampersands in the input stream by adding three initial sed steps. We collect the complete program in Example 5-2.

Example 5-2. Converting an office directory to HTML

```
#! /bin/sh
# Convert a tab-separated value file to grammar-conformant HTML.
#
# Usage:
#     tsv-to-html < infile > outfile

cat << EOFILE                          Leading boilerplate
<!DOCTYPE HTML PUBLIC "-//IETF//DTD HTML//EN//3.0">
<HTML>
    <HEAD>
        <TITLE>
            Office directory
        </TITLE>
        <LINK REV="made" HREF="mailto:$USER@`hostname`">
    </HEAD>
    <BODY>
        <TABLE>
EOFILE

sed -e 's=&=\&amp;=g' \                 Convert special characters to entities
    -e 's=<=\&lt;=g' \
    -e 's=>=\&gt;=g' \
    -e 's=\t=</TD><TD>=g' \            And supply table markup
    -e 's=^.*$=          <TR><TD>&</TD></TR>='

cat << EOFILE                          Trailing boilerplate
        </TABLE>
    </BODY>
</HTML>
EOFILE
```

The `<<` notation is called a *here document*. It is explained in more detail in "Additional Redirection Operators" [7.3.1]. Briefly, the shell reads all lines up to the delimiter following the `<<` (EOFILE in this case), does variable and command substitution on the contained lines, and feeds the results as standard input to the command.

There is an important point about the script in Example 5-2: it is independent of the number of columns in the table! This means that it can be used to convert *any* tab-separated value file to HTML. Spreadsheet programs can usually save data in such a format, so our simple tool can produce correct HTML from spreadsheet data.

We were careful in `tsv-to-html` to maintain the spacing structure of the original office directory, because that makes it easy to apply further filters downstream. Indeed, `html-pretty` was written precisely for that reason: standardization of HTML markup layout radically simplifies other HTML tools.

How would we handle conversion of accented characters to HTML entities? We *could* augment the sed command with extra edit steps like -e `'s=é=&eacute;=g'`, but there are about 100 or so entities to cater for, and we are likely to need similar substitutions as we convert other kinds of text files to HTML.

It therefore makes sense to delegate that task to a separate program that we can reuse, either as a pipeline stage following the `sed` command in Example 5-2, or as a filter applied later. (This is the "detour to build specialized tools" principle in action.) Such a program is just a tedious tabulation of substitution commands, and we need one for each of the local text encodings, such as the various ISO 8859-*n* code pages mentioned in "How Are Files Named?" in Appendix B. We don't show such a filter completely here, but a fragment of one in Example 5-3 gives the general flavor. For readers who need it, we include the complete program for handling the common case of Western European characters in the ISO 8859-1 encoding with this book's sample programs. HTML's entity repertoire isn't sufficient for other accented characters, but since the World Wide Web is moving in the direction of Unicode and XML in place of ASCII and HTML, this problem is being solved in a different way, by getting rid of character set limitations.

Example 5-3. Fragment of iso8859-1-to-html program

```
#! /bin/sh
# Convert an input stream containing characters in ISO 8859-1
# encoding from the range 128..255 to HTML equivalents in ASCII.
# Characters 0..127 are preserved as normal ASCII.
#
# Usage:
#       iso8859-1-to-html infile(s) >outfile

sed \
        -e 's= =\ =g' \
        -e 's=¡=\&iexcl;=g' \
        -e 's=¢=\&cent;=g' \
        -e 's=£=\&pound;=g' \
...
        -e 's=ü=\&uuml;=g' \
        -e 's=ý=\&yacute;=g' \
        -e 's=þ=\&thorn;=g' \
        -e 's=ÿ=\&yuml;=g' \
        "$@"
```

Here is a sample of the use of this filter:

```
$ cat danish                            Show sample Danish text in ISO 8859-1 encoding
Øen med åen lå i læ af én halvø,
og én stor ø, langs den græske kyst.

$ iso8859-1-to-html danish              Convert text to HTML entities
Øen med åen lå i lå af én halvø,
og én stor ø, langs den græske kyst.
```

5.3   Cheating at Word Puzzles

Crossword puzzles give you clues about words, but most of us get stuck when we cannot think of, say, a ten-letter word that begins with a b and has either an x or a z in the seventh position.

Regular-expression pattern matching with awk or grep is clearly called for, but what files do we search? One good choice is the Unix spelling dictionary, available as /usr/dict/words, on many systems. (Other popular locations for this file are /usr/share/dict/words and /usr/share/lib/dict/words.) This is a simple text file, with one word per line, sorted in lexicographic order. We can easily create other similar-appearing files from any collection of text files, like this:

```
cat file(s) | tr A-Z a-z | tr -c a-z\' '\n' | sort -u
```

The second pipeline stage converts uppercase to lowercase, the third replaces nonletters by newlines, and the last sorts the result, keeping only unique lines. The third stage treats apostrophes as letters, since they are used in contractions. Every Unix system has collections of text that can be mined in this way—for example, the formatted manual pages in /usr/man/cat*/* and /usr/local/man/cat*/*. On one of our systems, they supplied more than 1 million lines of prose and produced a list of about 44,000 unique words. There are also word lists for dozens of languages in various Internet archives.[*]

Let us assume that we have built up a collection of word lists in this way, and we stored them in a standard place that we can reference from a script. We can then write the program shown in Example 5-4.

Example 5-4. Word puzzle solution helper

```
#! /bin/sh
# Match an egrep(1)-like pattern against a collection of
# word lists.
#
# Usage:
```

---

[*] Available at *ftp://ftp.ox.ac.uk/pub/wordlists/*, *ftp://qiclab.scn.rain.com/pub/wordlists/*, *ftp://ibiblio.org/pub/docs/books/gutenberg/etext96/pgw**, and *http://www.phreak.org/html/wordlists.shtml*. A search for "word list" in any Internet search engine turns up many more.

Example 5-4. Word puzzle solution helper (continued)

```
#        puzzle-help egrep-pattern [word-list-files]

FILES="
        /usr/dict/words
        /usr/share/dict/words
        /usr/share/lib/dict/words
        /usr/local/share/dict/words.biology
        /usr/local/share/dict/words.chemistry
        /usr/local/share/dict/words.general
        /usr/local/share/dict/words.knuth
        /usr/local/share/dict/words.latin
        /usr/local/share/dict/words.manpages
        /usr/local/share/dict/words.mathematics
        /usr/local/share/dict/words.physics
        /usr/local/share/dict/words.roget
        /usr/local/share/dict/words.sciences
        /usr/local/share/dict/words.unix
        /usr/local/share/dict/words.webster
        "
pattern="$1"


egrep -h -i "$pattern" $FILES 2> /dev/null | sort -u -f
```

The FILES variable holds the built-in list of word-list files, customized to the local site. The grep option –h suppresses filenames from the report, the –i option ignores lettercase, and we discard the standard error output with 2> /dev/null, in case any of the word-list files don't exist or they lack the necessary read permission. (This kind of redirection is described in "File Descriptor Manipulation" [7.3.2].) The final sort stage reduces the report to just a list of unique words, ignoring lettercase.

Now we can find the word that we were looking for:

```
$ puzzle-help '^b.....[xz]...$' | fmt
bamboozled Bamboozler bamboozles buDenizens buWheezing Belshazzar
botanizing Brontozoum Bucholzite bulldozing
```

Can you think of an English word with six consonants in a row? Here's some help:

```
$ puzzle-help '[^aeiouy]{6}' /usr/dict/words
Knightsbridge
mightn't
oughtn't
```

If you don't count *y* as a vowel, many more turn up: *encryption, klystron, porphyry, syzygy,* and so on.

We could readily exclude the contractions from the word lists by a final filter step—
egrep -i '^[a-z]+$'—but there is little harm in leaving them in the word lists.

5.4　Word Lists

From 1983 to 1987, Bell Labs researcher Jon Bentley wrote an interesting column in *Communications of the ACM* titled *Programming Pearls*. Some of the columns were later collected, with substantial changes, into two books listed in the Bibliography. In one of the columns, Bentley posed this challenge: write a program to process a text file, and output a list of the *n* most-frequent words, with counts of their frequency of occurrence, sorted by descending count. Noted computer scientists Donald Knuth and David Hanson responded separately with interesting and clever literate programs,* each of which took several hours to write. Bentley's original specification was imprecise, so Hanson rephased it this way: Given a text file and an integer *n*, you are to print the words (and their frequencies of occurrence) whose frequencies of occurrence are among the *n* largest in order of decreasing frequency.

In the first of Bentley's articles, fellow Bell Labs researcher Doug McIlroy reviewed Knuth's program, and offered a six-step Unix solution that took only a couple of minutes to develop and worked correctly the first time. Moreover, unlike the two other programs, McIlroy's is devoid of explicit magic constants that limit the word lengths, the number of unique words, and the input file size. Also, its notion of what constitutes a word is defined entirely by simple patterns given in its first two executable statements, making changes to the word-recognition algorithm easy.

McIlroy's program illustrates the power of the Unix tools approach: break a complex problem into simpler parts that you already know how to handle. To solve the word-frequency problem, McIlroy converted the text file to a list of words, one per line (tr does the job), mapped words to a single lettercase (tr again), sorted the list (sort), reduced it to a list of unique words with counts (uniq), sorted that list by descending counts (sort), and finally, printed the first several entries in the list (sed, though head would work too).

The resulting program is worth being given a name (wf, for word frequency) and wrapped in a shell script with a comment header. We also extend McIlroy's original sed command to make the output list-length argument optional, and we modernize the sort options. We show the complete program in Example 5-5.

Example 5-5. Word-frequency filter

```
#! /bin/sh
# Read a text stream on standard input, and output a list of
# the n (default: 25) most frequently occurring words and
# their frequency counts, in order of descending counts, on
```

---

* *Programming Pearls: A Literate Program: A* WEB program for common words, Comm. ACM **29**(6), 471–483, June (1986), and *Programming Pearls: Literate Programming: Printing Common Words*, **30**(7), 594–599, July (1987). Knuth's paper is also reprinted in his book *Literate Programming*, Stanford University Center for the Study of Language and Information, 1992, ISBN 0-937073-80-6 (paper) and 0-937073-81-4 (cloth).

Example 5-5. Word-frequency filter (continued)

```
# standard output.
#
# Usage:
#       wf [n]

tr -cs A-Za-z\' '\n' |          Replace nonletters with newlines
  tr A-Z a-z |                  Map uppercase to lowercase
    sort |                      Sort the words in ascending order
      uniq -c |                 Eliminate duplicates, showing their counts
        sort -k1,1nr -k2 |      Sort by descending count, and then by ascending word
          sed ${1:-25}q         Print only the first n (default: 25) lines; see Chapter 3
```

POSIX tr supports all of the escape sequences of ISO Standard C. The older X/Open Portability Guide specification only had octal escape sequences, and the original tr had none at all, forcing the newline to be written literally, which was one of the criticisms levied at McIlroy's original program. Fortunately, the tr command on every system that we tested now has the POSIX escape sequences.

A shell pipeline isn't the only way to solve this problem with Unix tools: Bentley gave a six-line awk implementation of this program in an earlier column[*] that is roughly equivalent to the first four stages of McIlroy's pipeline.

Knuth and Hanson discussed the computational complexity of their programs, and Hanson used runtime profiling to investigate several variants of his program to find the fastest one.

The complexity of McIlroy's is easy to identify. All but the sort stages run in a time that is linear in the size of their input, and that size is usually sharply reduced after the uniq stage. Thus, the rate-limiting step is the first sort. A good sorting algorithm based on comparisons, like that in Unix sort, can sort n items in a time proportional to $n \log_2 n$. The logarithm-to-the-base-2 factor is small: for n about 1 million, it is about 20. Thus, in practice, we expect wf to be a few times slower than it would take to just copy its input stream with cat.

Here is an example of applying this script to the text of Shakespeare's most popular play, *Hamlet*,[†] reformatting the output with pr to a four-column display:

```
$ wf 12 < hamlet | pr -c4 -t -w80
   1148 the          6/1 of          550 a          451 in
    970 and          635 i           514 my         419 it
    771 to           554 you         494 hamlet     407 that
```

---

[*] *Programming Pearls: Associative Arrays*, Comm. ACM **28**(6), 570–576, June, (1985). This is an excellent introduction to the power of associative arrays (tables indexed by strings, rather than integers), a common feature of most scripting languages.

[†] Available in the wonderful Project Gutenberg archives at *http://www.gutenberg.net/*.

The results are about as expected for English prose. More interesting, perhaps, is to ask how many unique words there are in the play:

```
$ wf 999999 < hamlet | wc -l
4548
```

and to look at some of the least-frequent words:

```
$ wf 999999 < hamlet | tail -n 12 | pr -c4 -t -w80
      1 yaw             1 yesterday      1 yielding       1 younger
      1 yawn            1 yesternight    1 yon            1 yourselves
      1 yeoman          1 yesty          1 yond           1 zone
```

There is nothing magic about the argument 999999: it just needs to be a number larger than any expected count of unique words, and the keyboard repeat feature makes it easy to type.

We can also ask how many of the 4548 unique words were used just once:

```
$ wf 999999 < hamlet | grep -c '^ *1•'
2634
```

The • following the digit 1 in the grep pattern represents a tab. This result is surprising, and probably atypical of most modern English prose: although the play's vocabulary is large, nearly 58 percent of the words occur only once. And yet, the core vocabulary of frequently occurring words is rather small:

```
$ wf 999999 < hamlet | awk '$1 >= 5' | wc -l
740
```

This is about the number of words that a student might be expected to learn in a semester course on a foreign language, or that a child learns before entering school.

Shakespeare didn't have computers to help analyze his writing,* but we can speculate that part of his genius was in making most of what he wrote understandable to the broadest possible audience of his time.

When we applied wf to the individual texts of Shakespeare's plays, we found that *Hamlet* has the largest vocabulary (4548), whereas *Comedy of Errors* has the smallest (2443). The total number of unique words in the Shakespeare corpus of plays and sonnets is nearly 23,700, which shows that you need exposure to several plays to enjoy the richness of his work. About 36 percent of those words are used only once, and only one word begins with x: Xanthippe, in *Taming of the Shrew*. Clearly, there is plenty of fodder in Shakespeare for word-puzzle enthusiasts and vocabulary analysts!

---

* Indeed, the only word related to the root of "computer" that Shakespeare used is "computation," just once in each of two plays, *Comedy of Errors* and *King Richard III*. "Arithmetic" occurs six times in his plays, "calculate" twice, and "mathematics" thrice.

5.5 Tag Lists

Use of the tr command to obtain lists of words, or more generally, to transform one set of characters to another set, as in Example 5-5 in the preceding section, is a handy Unix tool idiom to remember. It leads naturally to a solution of a problem that we had in writing this book: how do we ensure consistent markup through about 50K lines of manuscript files? For example, a command might be marked up with <command>tr</command> when we talk about it in the running text, but elsewhere, we might give an example of something that you type, indicated by the markup <literal>tr</literal>. A third possibility is a manual-page reference in the form <emphasis>tr</emphasis>(1).

The taglist program in Example 5-6 provides a solution. It finds all begin/end tag pairs written on the same line and outputs a sorted list that associates tag use with input files. Additionally, it flags with an arrow cases where the same word is marked up in more than one way. Here is a fragment of its output from just the file for a version of this chapter:

```
$ taglist ch05.xml
...
        2 cut                       command         ch05.xml
        1 cut                       emphasis        ch05.xml <----
...
        2 uniq                      command         ch05.xml
        1 uniq                      emphasis        ch05.xml <----
        1 vfstab                    filename        ch05.xml
...
```

The tag listing task is reasonably complex, and would be quite hard to do in most conventional programming languages, even ones with large class libraries, such as C++ and Java, and even if you started with the Knuth or Hanson literate programs for the somewhat similar word-frequency problem. Yet, just nine steps in a Unix pipeline with by-now familiar tools suffice.

The word-frequency program did not deal with named files: it just assumed a single data stream. That is not a serious limitation because we can easily feed it multiple input files with cat. Here, however, we need a filename, since it does us no good to report a problem without telling where the problem is. The filename is taglist's single argument, available in the script as $1.

1. We feed the input file into the pipeline with cat. We could, of course, eliminate this step by redirecting the input of the next stage from $1, but we find in complex pipelines that it is clearer to separate *data production* from *data processing*. It also makes it slightly easier to insert yet another stage into the pipeline if the program later evolves.

    ```
    cat "$1" | ...
    ```

2. We apply sed to simplify the otherwise-complex markup needed for web URLs:

```
... | sed -e 's#systemitem *role="url"#URL#g' \
        -e 's#/systemitem#/URL#' | ...
```

This converts tags such as <systemitem role="URL"> and </systemitem> into simpler <URL> and </URL> tags, respectively.

3. The next stage uses tr to replace spaces and paired delimiters by newlines:

```
... | tr ' (){}[]' '\n\n\n\n\n\n\n' | ...
```

4. At this point, the input consists of one "word" per line (or empty lines). Words are either actual text or SGML/XML tags. Using egrep, the next stage selects tag-enclosed words:

```
... | egrep '>[^<>]+</' | ...
```

This regular expression matches tag-enclosed words: a right angle bracket, followed by at least one nonangle bracket, followed by a left angle bracket, followed by a slash (for the closing tag).

5. At this point, the input consists of lines with tags. The first awk stage uses angle brackets as field separators, so the input <literal>tr</literal> is split into four fields: an empty field, followed by literal, tr, and /literal. The filename is passed to awk on the command line, where the -v option sets the awk variable FILE to the filename. That variable is then used in the print statement, which outputs the word, the tag, and the filename:

```
... | awk -F'[<>]' -v FILE="$1" \
        '{ printf("%-31s\t%-15s\t%s\n", $3, $2, FILE) }' | ...
```

6. The sort stage sorts the lines into word order:

```
... | sort | ...
```

7. The uniq command supplies the initial count field. The output is a list of records, where the fields are *count*, *word*, *tag*, *file*:

```
... | uniq -c | ...
```

8. A second sort orders the output by word and tag (the second and third fields):

```
... | sort -k2,2 -k3,3 | ...
```

9. The final stage uses a small awk program to filter successive lines, adding a trailing arrow when it sees the same word as on the previous line. This arrow then clearly indicates instances where words have been marked up differently, and thus deserve closer inspection by the authors, the editors, or the book-production staff:

```
... | awk '{
            print ($2 == Last) ? ($0 " <----") : $0
            Last = $2
        }'
```

The full program is provided in Example 5-6.

Example 5-6. Making an SGML tag list

```
#! /bin/sh -
# Read an HTML/SGML/XML file given on the command
# line containing markup like <tag>word</tag> and output on
# standard output a tab-separated list of
#
#        count word tag filename
#
# sorted by ascending word and tag.
#
# Usage:
#        taglist xml-file

cat "$1" |
  sed -e 's#systemitem *role="url"#URL#g' -e 's#/systemitem#/URL#' |
    tr ' (){}[]' '\n\n\n\n\n\n\n' |
      egrep '>[^<>]+</' |
        awk -F'[<>]' -v FILE="$1" \
            '{ printf("%-31s\t%-15s\t%s\n", $3, $2, FILE) }' |
          sort |
            uniq -c |
              sort -k2,2 -k3,3 |
                awk '{
                        print ($2 == Last) ? ($0 " <    ") : $0
                        Last = $2
                    }'
```

In "Functions" [6.5], we will show how to apply the tag-list operation to multiple files.

5.6   Summary

This chapter has shown how to solve several text processing problems, none of which would be simple to do in most programming languages. The critical lessons of this chapter are:

- Data markup is extremely valuable, although it need not be complex. A unique single character, such as a tab, colon, or comma, often suffices.

- Pipelines of simple Unix tools and short, often inline, programs in a suitable text processing language, such as awk, can exploit data markup to pass multiple pieces of data through a series of processing stages, emerging with a useful report.

- By keeping the data markup simple, the output of our tools can readily become input to new tools, as shown by our little analysis of the output of the word-frequency filter, wf, applied to Shakespeare's texts.

- By preserving some minimal markup in the output, we can later come back and massage that data further, as we did to turn a simple ASCII office directory into a web page. Indeed, it is wise never to consider any form of electronic data as final: there is a growing demand in some quarters for page-description languages, such as PCL, PDF, and PostScript, to preserve the original markup that led to the page formatting. Word processor documents currently are almost devoid of useful logical markup, but that may change in the future. At the time of this writing, one prominent word processor vendor was reported to be considering an XML representation for document storage. The GNU Project's gnumeric spreadsheet, the Linux Documentation Project,[*] and the OpenOffice.org[†] office suite already do that.

- Lines with delimiter-separated fields are a convenient format for exchanging data with more complex software, such as spreadsheets and databases. Although such systems usually offer some sort of report-generation feature, it is often easier to extract the data as a stream of lines of fields, and then to apply filters written in suitable programming languages to manipulate the data further. For example, catalog and directory publishing are often best done this way.

---

[*] See *http://www.tldp.org/*.

[†] See *http://www.openoffice.org/*.

## CHAPTER 6

Variables, Making Decisions, and Repeating Actions

Variables are essential for nontrivial programs. They maintain values useful as data and for managing program state. Since the shell is mostly a string processing language, there are lots of things you can do with the string values of shell variables. However, because mathematical operations are essential too, the POSIX shell also provides a mechanism for doing arithmetic with shell variables.

Control-flow features make a programming language: it's almost impossible to get any real work done if all you have are imperative statements. This chapter covers the shell's facilities for testing results, and making decisions based on those results, as well as looping.

Finally, functions let you group task-related statements in one place, making it easier to perform that task from multiple points within your script.

6.1   Variables and Arithmetic

Shell variables are like variables in any conventional programming language. They hold values until you need them. We described the basics of shell variable names and values in "Variables" [2.5.2]. In addition, shell scripts and functions have *positional parameters*, which is a fancy term for "command-line arguments."

Simple arithmetic operations are common in shell scripts; e.g., adding one to a variable each time around a loop. The POSIX shell provides a notation for inline arithmetic called *arithmetic expansion*. The shell evaluates arithmetic expressions inside $((...)), and places the result back into the text of the command.

6.1.1   Variable Assignment and the Environment

Shell variable assignment and usage were covered in "Variables" [2.5.2]. This section fills in the rest of the details.

Two similar commands provide variable management. The readonly command makes variables read-only; assignments to them become forbidden. This is a good way to create symbolic constants in a shell program:

```
hours_per_day=24 seconds_per_hour=3600 days_per_week=7    Assign values
readonly hours_per_day seconds_per_hour days_per_week     Make read-only
```

---

export, readonly

Usage

    export *name*[=*word*] ...

    export -p

    readonly *name*[=*word*] ...

    readonly -p

Purpose

    export modifies or prints the environment. readonly makes variables unmodifiable.

Major options

    -p

        Print the name of the command and the names and values of all exported (read-only) variables in such a way as to allow the shell to reread the output to re-create the environment (read-only settings).

Behavior

    With the -p option, both commands print their name and all variables and values that are exported or read-only, respectively. Otherwise, they apply the appropriate attribute to the named variables.

Caveats

    The versions of /bin/sh on many commercial Unix systems are (sadly) still not POSIX-compliant. Thus the variable-assignment form of export and readonly don't work. For strictest portability, use:

```
FOO=somevalue
export FOO

BAR=anothervalue
readonly BAR
```

Much more commonly used is the export command, which puts variables into the *environment*. The environment is simply a list of name-value pairs that is available to every running program. New processes inherit the environment from their parent, and are able to modify it before creating new child processes of their own. The export command adds new variables to the environment:

```
PATH=$PATH:/usr/local/bin         Update PATH
export PATH                        Export it
```

The original Bourne shell required you to use a two-step process; i.e., the assignment and the export or readonly are done separately (as we've just shown). The POSIX standard allows you to do the assignment and command together:

```
readonly hours_per_day=24 seconds_per_hour=3600 days_per_week=7

export PATH=$PATH:/usr/local/bin
```

The export command may also be used to print the current environment:

```
$ export -p                              Print current environment
export CDPATH=":/home/tolstoy"
export DISPLAY=":0.0"
export ENV="/home/tolstoy/.kshrc"
export EXINIT="set ai sm"
export FCEDIT="vi"
...
```

Variables may be added to a program's environment without permanently affecting the environment of the shell or subsequent commands. This is done by prefixing the assignment to the command name and arguments:

```
PATH=/bin:/usr/bin awk '...' file1 file2
```

This changes the value of PATH only for execution of the single awk command. Any subsequent commands, however, see the current value of PATH in their environment.

The export command only adds variables to the environment. The env command may be used to remove variables from a program's environment, or to temporarily change environment variable values:

```
env -i PATH=$PATH HOME=$HOME LC_ALL=C awk '...' file1 file2
```

The –i option *initializes* the environment; i.e., throws away any inherited values, passing in to the program only those variables named on the command line.

The unset command removes variables and functions from the running shell. By default it unsets variables, although this can be made explicit with -v:

```
unset full_name                          Remove the full_name variable
unset -v first middle last               Remove the other variables
```

Use unset -f to remove functions:

```
who_is_on () {                           Define a function
    who | awk '{ print $1 }' | sort -u   Generate sorted list of users
}
...
unset -f who_is_on                       Remove the function
```

Early versions of the shell didn't have functions or the unset command. POSIX added the –f option for removing functions, and then added the –v option for symmetry with –f.

env

Usage

    env [-i] [*var=value* ...] [*command_name* [*arguments* ...]]

Purpose

    To provide fine-grained control over the environment inherited by *command_name* when it's run by env.

Major options

    -i

        Ignore the inherited environment, using only the variables and values given on the command line.

Behavior

    With no *command_name*, print the names and values of all variables in the environment. Otherwise, use the variable assignments on the command line to modify the inherited environment, before invoking *command_name*. With the -i option, env ignores the inherited environment completely and uses only the supplied variables and values.

Caveats

    When printing, env does not necessarily quote environment variable values correctly for re-inputting to the shell. Use export -p for that.

unset

Usage

    unset [-v] *variable* ...

    unset -f *function* ...

Purpose

    To remove variables and functions from the current shell.

Major options

    -f

        Unset (remove) the named functions.

    -v

        Unset (remove) the named variables. This is the default action with no options.

Behavior

    With no options, arguments are treated as variable names and said variables are removed. The same occurs with the -v option. With the -f option, arguments are treated as function names and the functions are removed.

The assignment myvar= doesn't remove myvar, it merely sets it to the null string. In contrast, unset myvar removes it completely. This difference comes into play with the various "is the variable set" and "is the variable set but not null" expansions described in the next section.

6.1.2 Parameter Expansion

Parameter expansion is the process by which the shell provides the value of a variable for use in the program; e.g., as the value for a new variable, or as part or all of a command-line argument. The simplest form is undoubtedly familiar:

```
reminder="Time to go to the dentist!"    Save value in reminder
sleep 120                                Wait two hours
echo $reminder                           Print message
```

The shell has more complicated forms that are useful in more specialized situations. All of these forms enclose the variable's name in braces (${variable}), and then add additional syntax telling the shell what to do. Braces by themselves are also useful, should you need to immediately follow a variable name with a character that might otherwise be interpreted as part of the name:

```
reminder="Time to go to the dentist!"    Save value in reminder
sleep 120                                Wait two hours
echo _${reminder}_                       Print message with underscores, for emphasis
```

By default, undefined variables expand to the null (empty) string. Sloppy programming can thus lead to disaster:

```
rm -fr /$MYPROGRAM          If MYPROGRAM isn't set, disaster strikes!
```

It thus pays, as always, to program carefully!

6.1.2.1 Expansion operators

The first group of string-handling operators tests for the existence of variables and allows substitutions of default values under certain conditions. They are listed in Table 6-1.

Table 6-1. Substitution operators

Operator	Substitution
${varname:-word}	If *varname* exists and isn't null, return its value; otherwise, return *word*.
	Purpose: To return a default value if the variable is undefined.
	Example: ${count:-0} evaluates to 0 if count is undefined.
${varname:=word}	If *varname* exists and isn't null, return its value; otherwise, set it to *word* and then return its value.
	Purpose: To set a variable to a default value if it is undefined.
	Example: ${count:=0} sets count to 0 if it is undefined.

Table 6-1. Substitution operators (continued)

Operator	Substitution
${varname:?message}	If *varname* exists and isn't null, return its value; otherwise, print *varname*: *message*, and abort the current command or script. Omitting *message* produces the default message parameter null or not set. Note, however, that interactive shells do not have to abort. (Behavior varies across shells; caveat emptor!)
	Purpose: To catch errors that result from variables being undefined.
	Example: ${count:?"undefined!"} prints count: undefined! and exits if count is undefined.
${varname:+word}	If *varname* exists and isn't null, return *word*; otherwise, return null.
	Purpose: To test for the existence of a variable.
	Example: ${count:+1} returns 1 (which could mean "true") if count is defined.

The colon (:) in each of the operators in Table 6-1 is optional. If the colon is omitted, then change "exists and isn't null" to "exists" in each definition; i.e., the operator tests for existence only.

The operators in Table 6-1 have been part of the Bourne shell for more than 20 years. POSIX standardized additional operators for doing pattern matching and text removal on variable values. The classic use for the new pattern-matching operators is in stripping off components of pathnames, such as directory prefixes and filename suffixes. With that in mind, besides listing the shell's pattern-matching operators, Table 6-2 also has examples showing how all of the operators work. For these examples, assume that the variable path has the value /home/tolstoy/mem/long.file.name.

The patterns used by the operators in Table 6-2 and in other places in the shell, such as the case statement, are all shell "wildcard" patterns. They're described in detail in "Tilde Expansion and Wildcards" [7.5]. However we expect that you're familiar with the basics from your regular everyday use of the shell.

Table 6-2. Pattern-matching operators

Operator	Substitution
${variable#pattern}	If the pattern matches the beginning of the variable's value, delete the shortest part that matches and return the rest.
Example: ${path#/*/}	**Result**: tolstoy/mem/long.file.name
${variable##pattern}	If the pattern matches the beginning of the variable's value, delete the longest part that matches and return the rest.
Example: ${path##/*/}	**Result**: long.file.name
${variable%pattern}	If the pattern matches the end of the variable's value, delete the shortest part that matches and return the rest.
Example: ${path%.*}	**Result**: /home/tolstoy/mem/long.file

Table 6-2. Pattern-matching operators (continued)

Operator	Substitution
${variable%%pattern}	If the pattern matches the end of the variable's value, delete the longest part that matches and return the rest.
Example: ${path%%.*}	**Result**: /home/tolstoy/mem/long

These can be hard to remember, so here's a handy mnemonic device: # matches the front because number signs *precede* numbers; % matches the rear because percent signs *follow* numbers. Another mnemonic comes from the typical placement (in the USA, anyway) of the # and % keys on the keyboard. Relative to each other, the # is on the left, and the % is on the right.

The two patterns used here are **/*/**, which matches anything between two slashes, and **.***, which matches a dot followed by anything.

Finally, POSIX standardized the string-length operator: ${#*variable*} returns the length in characters of the value of $*variable*:

```
$ x=supercalifragilisticexpialidocious    A famous word with amazing properties
$ echo There are ${#x} characters in $x
There are 34 characters in supercalifragilisticexpialidocious
```

6.1.2.2   Positional parameters

The so-called positional parameters represent a shell script's command-line arguments. They also represent a function's arguments within shell functions. Individual arguments are named by integer numbers. For historical reasons, you have to enclose the number in braces if it's greater than nine:

```
echo first arg is $1
echo tenth arg is ${10}
```

You can apply all of the value-testing and pattern-matching operators from the previous section to the positional parameters as well:

```
filename=${1:-/dev/tty}                    Use argument if given, /dev/tty if not
```

Special "variables" provide access to the total number of arguments that were passed, and to all the arguments at once:

$#

> Provides the total number of arguments passed to the shell script or function. It is useful for creating loops (covered later in "Looping" [6.4]) to process options and arguments. For example:
>
> ```
> while [ $# != 0 ]                      $# decremented by shift, loop will terminate
> do
>     case $1 in
>     ...                               Process first argument
>     esac
>     shift                             Shift first argument away (see later in text)
> done
> ```

$*, $@

> Represents all the command-line arguments at once. They can be used to pass the command-line arguments to a program being run by a script or function.

"$*"

> Represents all the command-line arguments as a single string. Equivalent to "$1 $2 ...". The first character of $IFS is used as the separator for the different values to create the string. For example:
>
> ```
> printf "The arguments were %s\n" "$*"
> ```

"$@"

> Represents all the command-line arguments as separate, individual strings. Equivalent to "$1" "$2" .... This is the best way to pass the arguments on to another program, since it preserves any whitespace embedded within each argument. For example:
>
> ```
> lpr "$@"                            Print each file
> ```

The set command serves a number of purposes. (Full information is provided later in "The set Command" [7.9.1].) When invoked without options, it sets the value of the positional parameters, throwing away any previously existing values:

```
set -- hi there how do you do        The -- ends options; "hi" starts new arguments
```

The shift command "lops off" positional parameters from the list, starting at the left. Upon executing shift, the original value of $1 is gone forever, replaced by the old value of $2. The value of $2, in turn, becomes the old value of $3, and so on. The value of $# is decreased by one. shift takes an optional argument, which is a count of how many arguments to shift off the list. Plain shift is the same as shift 1. Here is an annotated example that ties all of these things together:

```
$ set -- hello "hi there" greetings    Set new positional parameters
$ echo there are $# total arguments    Print the count
there are 3 total arguments
$ for i in $*                          Loop over arguments individually
> do   echo i is $i
> done
i is hello                             Note that embedded whitespace was lost
i is hi
i is there
i is greetings
$ for i in $@                          Without quotes, $* and $@ are the same
> do   echo i is $i
> done
i is hello
i is hi
i is there
i is greetings
$ for i in "$*"                        With quotes, $* is one string
> do   echo i is $i
> done
i is hello hi there greetings
```

```
$ for i in "$@"                              With quotes, $@ preserves exact argument values
> do    echo i is $i
> done
i is hello
i is hi there
i is greetings
$ shift                                      Lop off the first argument
$ echo there are now $# arguments            Prove that it's now gone
there are now 2 arguments
$ for i in "$@"
> do    echo i is $i
> done
i is hi there
i is greetings
```

6.1.2.3 Special variables

Besides the special variables we've just seen, such as $# and $*, the shell has a number of additional built-in variables. Some also have single-character, nonalphabetic names. Others have names consisting of all uppercase letters.

Table 6-3 lists the variables that are built into the shell and that affect its behavior. All Bourne-style shells have more variables than listed here that either affect interactive use or have other uses when doing shell programming. However, these are what you can rely upon for portable shell programming.

Table 6-3. POSIX built-in shell variables

Variable	Meaning
#	Number of arguments given to current process.
@	Command-line arguments to current process. Inside double quotes, expands to individual arguments.
*	Command-line arguments to current process. Inside double quotes, expands to a single argument.
- (hyphen)	Options given to shell on invocation.
?	Exit status of previous command.
$	Process ID of shell process.
0 (zero)	The name of the shell program.
!	Process ID of last background command. Use this to save process ID numbers for later use with the wait command.
ENV	Used only by interactive shells upon invocation; the *value* of $ENV is parameter-expanded. The result should be a full pathname for a file to be read and executed at startup. This is an XSI requirement.
HOME	Home (login) directory.
IFS	Internal field separator; i.e., the list of characters that act as word separators. Normally set to space, tab, and newline.
LANG	Default name of current locale; overridden by the other LC_* variables.
LC_ALL	Name of current locale; overrides LANG and the other LC_* variables.
LC_COLLATE	Name of current locale for character collation (sorting) purposes.

Table 6-3. POSIX built-in shell variables (continued)

Variable	Meaning
LC_CTYPE	Name of current locale for character class determination during pattern matching.
LC_MESSAGES	Name of current language for output messages.
LINENO	Line number in script or function of the line that just ran.
NLSPATH	The location of message catalogs for messages in the language given by $LC_MESSAGES (XSI).
PATH	Search path for commands.
PPID	Process ID of parent process.
PS1	Primary command prompt string. Default is "$ ".
PS2	Prompt string for line continuations. Default is "> ".
PS4	Prompt string for execution tracing with set -x. Default is "+ ".
PWD	Current working directory.

The special variable $$ is useful in scripting for creating unique (usually temporary) filenames based on the shell's process ID number. However, systems that have the mktemp command should use that instead. Both of these are discussed in Chapter 10.

6.1.3 Arithmetic Expansion

The shell arithmetic operators are equivalent to their counterparts in the C language. Precedence and associativity are the same as in C. Table 6-4 shows the arithmetic operators that are supported, in order from highest precedence to lowest. Although some of these are (or contain) special characters, there is no need to backslash-escape them, because they are within the $((...)) syntax. This syntax acts like double quotes, except that an embedded double quote need not be escaped (see "Quoting" [7.7]).

Table 6-4. Arithmetic operators

Operator	Meaning	Associativity
++ --	Increment and decrement, prefix and postfix	Left to right
+ - ! ~	Unary plus and minus; logical and bitwise negation	Right to left
* / %	Multiplication, division, and remainder	Left to right
+ -	Addition and subtraction	Left to right
<< >>	Bit-shift left and right	Left to right
< <= > >=	Comparisons	Left to right
== !=	Equal and not equal	Left to right
&	Bitwise AND	Left to right
^	Bitwise Exclusive OR	Left to right
|	Bitwise OR	Left to right
&&	Logical AND (short-circuit)	Left to right
||	Logical OR (short-circuit)	Left to right

Table 6-4. Arithmetic operators (continued)

Operator	Meaning	Associativity
?:	Conditional expression	Right to left
= += -= *= /= %= &= ^= <<= >>= |=	Assignment operators	Right to left

Parentheses can be used to group subexpressions. As in C, the relational operators (<, <=, >, >=, ==, and !=) produce a numeric result that acts as a truth value: 1 for true and 0 for false.

For example, $((3 > 2))$ has the value 1; $(((3 > 2) || (4 <= 1)))$ also has the value 1, since at least one of the two subexpressions is true.

For the logical AND and OR operators, *any* nonzero value functions as true:

```
$ echo $((3 && 4))              Both 3 and 4 are "true"
1
```

This use of nonzero as "true" applies in just about all languages derived from C, such as C++, Java, and awk.

If you're familiar with C, C++, or Java, the operators listed in Table 6-4 will be familiar. If you're not, some of them warrant a little explanation.

The assignment forms of the regular operators are a convenient shorthand for the more conventional way of updating a variable. For example, in many languages you might write x = x + 2 to add 2 to x. The += operator lets you do that more compactly: $((x += 2)) adds 2 to x and stores the result back in x.

Since adding and subtracting one are such frequent operations, the ++ and -- operators provide an even more abbreviated way to do them. As you might guess, ++ adds one, and -- subtracts one. These are unary operators. Let's take a quick look at how they work:

```
$ i=5
$ echo $((i++)) $i
5 6
$ echo $((++i)) $i
7 7
```

What's going on here? In both cases, the value of i is increased by one. However, the value returned by the operator depends upon its placement relative to the variable being operated upon. A *postfix* operator (one that occurs after the variable) returns the variable's *old* value as the result of the expression, and then increments the variable. By contrast, a *prefix* operator, which comes in front of the variable, increments the variable first, and then returns the new value. The -- operator works the same as ++, but it decrements the variable by one, instead of incrementing it.

The ++ and -- operators are optional: conforming implementations do not have to support them. bash and ksh93 do support them.

The standard allows an implementation to support additional operators. All versions of ksh93 support the C comma operator, and recent versions support exponentiation with **. bash also supports both of these.

The standard only describes arithmetic using constant values. When parameter evaluation, such as $i, is done first, the arithmetic evaluator only sees constant values. In practice, all shells that support $((...)) allow you to provide a variable name without prefixing it with $.

According to POSIX, arithmetic is done using C signed long integers. ksh93 supports floating-point arithmetic, but you should not rely on that for portable programs.

6.2   Exit Statuses

Every command—be it built-in, shell function, or external—when it exits, returns a small integer value to the program that invoked it. This is known as the program's *exit status*. There are a number of ways to use a program's exit status when programming with the shell.

6.2.1   Exit Status Values

By convention, an exit status of 0 indicates "success"; i.e., that the program ran and didn't encounter any problems. Any other exit status indicates failure.* (We'll show you shortly how to use the exit status.) The built-in variable ? (accessed as $?) contains the exit value of the last program that the shell ran.

For example, when you type ls, the shell finds and runs the ls program. When ls finishes, the shell recovers ls's exit status. Here's an example:

```
$ ls -l /dev/null                                  ls on an existing file
crw-rw-rw-  1 root  root  1, 3 Aug 30 2001 /dev/null    ls's output
$ echo $?                                          Show exit status
0                                                  Exit status was successful
$ ls foo                                           Now ls a nonexistent file
ls: foo: No such file or directory                 ls's error message
$ echo $?                                          Show exit status
1                                                  Exit status indicates failure
```

The POSIX standard defines the exit statuses and their meanings, as shown in Table 6-5.

---

* C and C++ programmers take note! This is backward from what you're used to, and takes a while to get comfortable with.

Table 6-5. POSIX exit statuses

Value	Meaning
0	Command exited successfully.
> 0	Failure during redirection or word expansion (tilde, variable, command, and arithmetic expansions, as well as word splitting).
1–125	Command exited unsuccessfully. The meanings of particular exit values are defined by each individual command.
126	Command found, but file was not executable.
127	Command not found.
> 128	Command died due to receiving a signal.

Curiously, POSIX leaves exit status 128 unspecified, apart from requiring that it represent some sort of failure. Only the low-order eight bits are returned to the parent process, so an exit status greater than 255 is replaced by the remainder of that value divided by 256.

Your shell script can pass an exit value back to its caller, using the exit command. Simply pass a number to it as the first argument. The script will exit immediately, and the caller receives that number as your script's exit value:

    exit 42   *Return the answer to the ultimate question*

---

exit

Usage
    exit [*exit-value*]

Purpose
    To return an exit status from a shell script to the script's caller.

Major options
    None.

Behavior
    The default exit status used if none is supplied is the exit status of the last command executed. If that is what you want, it is best to do this explicitly in the shell script:

        exit $?

6.2.2   if–elif–else–fi

The most obvious way to use a program's exit status is with the if statement. The general syntax is:

```
if pipeline
   [ pipeline … ]
```

```
then
    statements-if-true-1
[ elif pipeline
  [ pipeline … ]
then
    statements-if-true-2
 … ]
[ else
    statements-if-all-else-fails ]
fi
```

(The square brackets indicate optional parts; they are not typed literally.) The shell's syntax is based loosely on that of Algol 68, which is the language that Steven Bourne, the author of the V7 shell, really admired. It is most notable for the use of opening and closing keywords to bracket statement groups, instead of the begin and end delimiters of Algol 60 and Pascal, or the { and } popularized by C and used almost universally in other programmable Unix tools.

In the case at hand, you can probably guess how this works: the shell runs the first group of statements between the if and the then. If the last statement executed exits successfully, it runs *statements-if-true-1*. Otherwise, if an elif is present, it tries the next group of statements. If the last one exits successfully, it runs *statements-if-true-2*. It continues in this fashion until it encounters a command that exits successfully, running the corresponding group of statements.

If none of the if or elif statements is true, and an else clause is present, it executes *statements-if-all-else-fails*. Otherwise, it does nothing. The exit status of the entire if...fi statement is that of the last command executed following a then or else. If none was executed, the exit status is 0. For example:

```
if grep pattern myfile > /dev/null
then
    ...       Pattern is there
else
    ...       Pattern is not there
fi
```

grep exits with a 0 status if myfile contains *pattern*. It exits with a value of 1 if no line matched the pattern, and with a value greater than 1 if there was an error. Based on grep's exit status, the shell chooses which group of statements to execute.

6.2.3 Logical NOT, AND, and OR

Sometimes it's easier to phrase your tests in the negative: "if John is *not* at home, then ..." The way to do this in the shell is to precede a pipeline with an exclamation mark:

```
if ! grep pattern myfile > /dev/null
then
    ...       Pattern is not there
fi
```

POSIX introduced this notation in the 1992 standard. You will likely see older shell scripts that use the colon (:) command, which does nothing, to handle this kind of case:

```
if grep pattern myfile > /dev/null
then
    :           # do nothing
else
    ...         Pattern is not there
fi
```

Besides just testing the inverse of things with !, you will often want to test multiple subconditions, with AND and OR constructs. ("If John is home, *and* he isn't busy, then ..."). When the operator && separates two commands, the shell executes the first one. If it exits successfully, the shell executes the second one. If that exits successfully too, then the entire group is considered to have succeeded:

```
if grep pattern1 myfile && grep pattern2 myfile
then
    ...         myfile contains both patterns
fi
```

In contrast, the || operator is used when you want to test if one condition or the other is true:

```
if grep pattern1 myfile || grep pattern2 myfile
then
    ...         One or the other is present
fi
```

Both of these are *short-circuit* operators, meaning that the shell stops evaluating commands as soon as it can determine the truth-value of the entire group. For example, in *command1* && *command2*, if *command1* fails, then there is no way the whole thing could be true, so *command2* never executes. Similarly for *command1* || *command2*: if *command1* succeeds, there is no reason to execute *command2*.

Don't try to be overly "terse" and use && and || to replace the if statement. We have little objection to something short and simple, like this:

```
$ who | grep tolstoy > /dev/null && echo tolstoy is logged on
tolstoy is logged on
```

This runs who | grep ..., and if that succeeds it prints the message. However, we have seen vendor shell scripts use constructs like this:

```
some_command && {
    one command
    a second command
    and a third command
}
```

The braces serve to group all the commands together, which are executed only if *some_command* succeeds. This would be much more cleanly written using a simple `if`:

```
if some_command
then
     one command
     a second command
     and a third command
fi
```

6.2.4   The test Command

The aptly named `test` command exists to perform a variety of useful tasks in shell scripts. It produces no regular output, instead being used exclusively for its exit status. `test` accepts a number of different arguments that control what kind of test it performs.

---

test, [...]

Usage
>   test [*expression*]
>   [[*expression*]]

Purpose
> To test conditions in shell scripts, returning results via the exit status. Note that in the second form of the command, the brackets are typed literally, and must be separated from the enclosed *expression* by whitespace.

Major options and expressions
> See Table 6-6 and text.

Behavior
> test tests file attributes, compares strings, and compares numbers.

Caveats
> The expressions mandated by POSIX are a subset of what is often available on real systems. Care is required for full portability. More information is provided in "Extended Test Facility" [14.3.2].

> Except on absolutely ancient Unix systems, test is built into the shell. Since built-in commands are found before external commands, this makes it difficult to write simple test programs that produce an executable named `test`. Such programs must be invoked as `./test` (assuming they're in the current directory).

The test command has a variant form: [...]. It works identically to the `test` command. Thus, these two statements test two strings for equality:

```
if test "$str1" = "$str2"        if [ "$str1" = "$str2" ]
then                             then
    ...                              ...
fi                               fi
```

POSIX describes the arguments to test as "expressions." There are unary and binary expressions. The unary expressions consist of what look likes an option (e.g., -d to test if a file is a directory) with a corresponding operand; typically, but not always, a filename. The binary expressions have two operands with an embedded operator that performs some sort of comparison. Furthermore, when there is only a single argument, test checks to see if it is the null string. The full list is provided in Table 6-6.

Table 6-6. test expressions

Operator	True if ...
string	*string* is not null.
-b *file*	*file* is a block device file.
-c *file*	*file* is a character device file.
-d *file*	*file* is a directory.
-e *file*	*file* exists.
-f *file*	*file* is a regular file.
-g *file*	*file* has its setgid bit set.
-h *file*	*file* is a symbolic link.
-L *file*	*file* is a symbolic link. (Same as –h.)
-n *string*	*string* is non-null.
-p *file*	*file* is a named pipe (*FIFO* file).
-r *file*	*file* is readable.
-S *file*	*file* is a socket.
-s *file*	*file* is not empty.
-t *n*	File descriptor *n* points to a terminal.
-u *file*	*file* has its setuid bit set.
-w *file*	*file* is writable.
-x *file*	*file* is executable, or *file* is a directory that can be searched.
-z *string*	*string* is null.
s1 = *s2*	Strings *s1* and *s2* are the same.
s1 != *s2*	Strings *s1* and *s2* are not the same.
n1 -eq *n2*	Integers *n1* and *n2* are equal.
n1 -ne *n2*	Integers *n1* and *n2* are not equal.
n1 -lt *n2*	*n1* is less than *n2*.
n1 -gt *n2*	*n1* is greater than *n2*.
n1 -le *n2*	*n1* is less than or equal to *n2*.
n1 -ge *n2*	*n1* is greater than or equal to *n2*.

Tests may be negated by preceding them with !. Here are some sample tests in action:

```
if [ -f "$file" ]
then
    echo $file is a regular file
elif [ -d "$file" ]
then
    echo $file is a directory
fi

if [ ! -x "$file" ]
then
    echo $file is NOT executable
fi
```

XSI-conformant systems have a more complicated version of test. Expressions can be combined with -a (for logical AND) and with -o (for logical OR). -a has higher precedence than -o, and = and != have higher precedence than the other binary operators. Parentheses may be used for grouping and to change evaluation order.

There is a difference between using -a and -o, which are test operators, and && and ||, which are shell operators.

if [-n "$str" -a -f "$file"]	*Two conditions, one test command*
if [-n "$str"] && [-f "$file"]	*Two commands, short-circuit evaluation*
if [-n "$str" && -f "$file"]	*Syntax error, see text*

In the first case, test evaluates both conditions. In the second one, the shell runs the first test command, and runs the second one only if the first one was successful. In the last case, && is a shell operator, so it terminates the first test command. This command will complain that there is no terminating] character, and exits with a failure value. Even if test were to exit successfully, the subsequent check would fail, since the shell (most likely) would not find a command named -f.

Both ksh93 and bash support a number of additional tests. More information is available in "Extended Test Facility" [14.3.2].

The POSIX algorithm for test is summarized in Table 6-7.

Table 6-7. POSIX algorithm for test

Arguments	Argument values	Result
0		Exit false (1).
1	If $1 is non-null	Exit true (0).
	If $1 is null	Exit false (1).

Table 6-7. POSIX algorithm for test (continued)

Arguments	Argument values	Result
2	If $1 is !	Negate result of single-argument test, $2.
	If $1 is a unary operator	Result of the operator's test.
	Anything else	Unspecified.
3	If $2 is a binary operator	Result of the operator's test.
	If $1 is !	Negate result of double-argument test, $2 $3.
	If $1 is (and $3 is)	Result of single-argument test, $2 (XSI).
	Anything else	Unspecified.
4	If $1 is !	Negate result of three-argument test, $2 $3 $4.
	If $1 is (and $4 is)	Result of two-argument test, $2 $3 (XSI).
	Anything else	Unspecified.
> 4		Unspecified.

For portability, the POSIX standard recommends the use of shell-level tests for multiple conditions, instead of the -a and -o operators. (We also recommend this.) For example:

```
if [ -f "$file" ] && ! [ -w "$file" ]
then
    # $file exists and is a regular file, but is not writable
    echo $0: $file is not writable, giving up. >&2
    exit 1
fi
```

There are some "Gotchas" associated with test as well:

Arguments are required

For this reason, all shell variable expansions should be quoted so that test receives an argument, even if it turns out to be the null string. For example:

```
if [ -f "$file" ] ...          Correct
if [ -f $file ] ...            Incorrect
```

In the second case, should $file happen to be empty, test receives one less argument than it needs, leading to strange behavior.

String comparisons are tricky

In particular, if a string value is empty, or starts with a minus, test could become confused. This leads to the rather ugly, but widespread convention of prefixing string values with the letter X. (The use of X is arbitrary, but traditional.)

```
if [ "X$answer" = "Xyes" ] ...
```

You will see this used in many shell scripts, and it is in fact used in examples throughout the POSIX standard.

The algorithm just given for test, along with always quoting all arguments, should be enough for a modern version of test, even if the first argument starts with a minus. Thus we don't see a lot of need for the leading X prefix in new programs. However, if maximal portability is more important than readability, you may wish to use it (and we do so, occasionally).

test *can be fooled*

When checking the access of files mounted over a network, it is possible for unusual combinations of mount options and file permissions to "fool" test into thinking that a file is readable, when in fact the operating system won't let you access the file. Thus, although:

```
test -r a_file && cat a_file
```

should always work in principle, it can fail in practice.* About all you can do is add another layer of defensive programming:

```
if test -r a_file && cat a_file
then
    # cat worked, proceed on
else
    # attempt to recover, issue an error message, etc.
fi
```

Numeric tests are integer-only

You cannot do any kind of floating-point arithmetic with test. All numeric tests work only with integers. (ksh93 understands floating-point numbers, but you can't rely on that feature for full portability.)

Example 6-1 presents an improved version of the finduser script presented in "Accessing Shell Script Arguments" [2.6]. This version tests $#, the number of command-line arguments, and prints an error message if exactly one isn't supplied.

Example 6-1. Findusers script, requires a username argument

```
#! /bin/sh

# finduser --- see if user named by first argument is logged in

if [ $# != 1 ]
then
    echo Usage: finduser username >&2
    exit 1
fi

who | grep $1
```

---

* Mike Haertel points out that this has never been completely reliable: a_file could be changed in the interval between running test and running cat.

6.3   The case Statement

If you need to check a variable for one of many values, you could use a cascading series of if and elif tests, together with test:

```
if [ "X$1" = "X-f" ]
then
    ...      Code for –f option
elif [ "X$1" = "X-d" ] || [ "X$1" = "X--directory" ]  # long option allowed
then
    ...      Code for –d option
else
    echo $1: unknown option >&2
    exit 1
fi
```

However, this is awkward to write and difficult to read. (The >&2 in the echo command sends the output to standard error. This is described in "File Descriptor Manipulation" [7.3.2].) Instead, the shell's case construct should be used for pattern matching:

```
case $1 in
-f)
    ...      Code for –f option
    ;;
-d | --directory)  # long option allowed
    ...      Code for –d option
    ;;
*)
    echo $1: unknown option >&2
    exit 1
    # ;; is good form before `esac', but not required
esac
```

As can be seen, the value to be tested appears between case and in. Double-quoting the value, while not necessary, doesn't hurt either. The value is tested against each list of shell patterns in turn. When one matches, the corresponding body of code, up to the ;;, is executed. Multiple patterns may be used, separated by the | character, which in this context means "or." The patterns may contain any shell wildcard characters, and variable, command, and arithmetic substitutions are performed on the value before it is used for pattern matching.

The unbalanced right parenthesis after each pattern list is perhaps surprising; this is the only instance in the shell language of unbalanced delimiters. (In "Miscellaneous Extensions" [14.3.7], we will see that bash and ksh actually allow a leading (in front of the pattern list.)

It is typical, but not required, to use a final pattern of *, which acts as a default case. This is usually where you would print a diagnostic message and exit. As shown previously, the final case does not require the trailing ;;, although it's definitely good form to include it.

6.4 Looping

Besides the if and case statements, the shell's looping constructs are the workhorse facilities for getting things done.

6.4.1 for Loops

The for loop iterates over a list of objects, executing the loop body for each individual object in turn. The objects may be command-line arguments, filenames, or anything else that can be created in list format. In "Substitution details" [3.2.7.1], we showed this two-line script to update an XML brochure file:

```
mv atlga.xml atlga.xml.old
sed 's/Atlanta/&, the capital of the South/' < atlga.xml.old > atlga.xml
```

Now suppose, as is much more likely, that we have a number of XML files that make up our brochure. In this case, we want to make the change in *all* the XML files. The for loop is perfect for this:

```
for i in atlbrochure*.xml
do
    echo $i
    mv $i $i.old
    sed 's/Atlanta/&, the capital of the South/' < $i.old > $i
done
```

This loop moves each original file to a backup copy by appending a .old suffix, and then processing the file with sed to create the new file. It also prints the filename as a sort of running progress indicator, which is helpful when there are many files to process.

The in *list* part of the for loop is optional. When omitted, the shell loops over the command-line arguments. Specifically, it's as if you had typed for i in "$@":

```
for i        # loop over command-line args
do
    case $i in
    -f)  ...
         ;;
    ...
    esac
done
```

6.4.2 while and until Loops

The shell's while and until loops are similar to loops in conventional programming languages. The syntax is:

```
while condition          until condition
do                       do
    statements               statements
done                     done
```

As for the if statement, *condition* may be a simple list of commands, or commands involving && and ||.

The only difference between while and until is how the exit status of *condition* is treated. while continues to loop as long as *condition* exited successfully. until loops as long as *condition* exits unsuccessfully. For example:

```
pattern=...                          pattern controls shortening of string
while [ -n "$string" ]               While string is not empty
do
    process current value of $string
    string=${string%$pattern}        Lop off part of string
done
```

In practice, the until loop is used much less than the while loop, but it can be useful when you need to wait for an event to happen. This is shown in Example 6-2.

Example 6-2. Wait for a user to log in, using until

```
# wait for specified user to log in, check every 30 seconds

printf "Enter username: "
read user
until who | grep "$user" > /dev/null
do
    sleep 30
done
```

It is possible to pipe *into* a while loop, for iterating over each line of input, as shown here:

```
generate data |
    while read name rank serial_no
    do
        ...
    done
```

In such cases, the command used for the while loop's condition is usually the read command. We present a real-life example later in "Additional Redirection Operators" [7.3.1], when discussing here-documents. In "Command Substitution" [7.6], we show that you can also pipe the *output* of a loop into another command.

6.4.3   break and continue

Not everything in the shell came straight from Algol 68. The shell borrowed the break and continue commands from C. They are used to leave a loop, or to skip the rest of the loop body, respectively. The until...do wait-for-a-user script in Example 6-2 can be rewritten more conventionally, as shown here in Example 6-3.

Example 6-3. Wait for a user to log in, using while and break

```
# wait for specified user to log in, check every 30 seconds

printf "Enter username: "
read user
while true
do
    if who | grep "$user" > /dev/null
    then
        break
    fi

    sleep 30
done
```

The true command does nothing but exit successfully. It's used for writing infinite loops—loops that run forever. When you write an infinite loop, you have to place an exit condition in the body of the loop, just as was done here. There is an analogous, but considerably less-used command, false, which does nothing, but it does so unsuccessfully. It would be used in an infinite until false ... loop.

The continue command is used to start the next iteration of a loop early, before reaching the bottom of a loop's body.

Both the break and the continue commands take an optional numeric argument. This indicates how many enclosing loops should be broken out of or continued. (Use $((...)) if the loop count needs to be an expression calculated at runtime.) For example:

```
    while condition1                    Outer loop
    do  ...
        while condition2                Inner loop
        do  ...
            break 2                     Break out of outer loop
        done
    done
    ...                                 Execution continues here after break
```

It is interesting to note that break and continue, particularly with the ability to break or continue multiple loop levels, compensate in a clean fashion for the absence of a goto keyword in the shell language.

6.4.4   shift and Option Processing

We briefly mentioned the shift command earlier, in "Positional parameters" [6.1.2.2]. shift is used when working with command-line arguments. Its job is to move them left by one (or more). After executing shift, the original $1 is lost; it is replaced with the old value of $2. The new value of $2 is the old value of $3, and so on. The value of

$# decreases each time, as well. shift accepts an optional argument, which is the number of places to shift by: the default is 1.

Simple option processing is often done by combining while, case, break, and shift, like so:

```
# set flag vars to empty
file=   verbose=   quiet=   long=

while [ $# -gt 0 ]              Loop until no args left
do
    case $1 in                 Check first arg
    -f)   file=$2
          shift                Shift off "-f" so that shift at end gets value in $2
          ;;
    -v)   verbose=true
          quiet=
          ;;
    -q)   quiet=true
          verbose=
          ;;
    -l)   long=true
          ;;
    --)   shift                By convention, -- ends options
          break
          ;;
    -*)   echo $0: $1: unrecognized option >&2
          ;;
    *)    break                Nonoption argument, break while loop
          ;;
    esac

    shift                      Set up for next iteration
done
```

After this loop has finished, the various flag variables are set, and may be tested using test or case. Any remaining nonoption arguments are still available for further processing in "$@".

The getopts command simplifies option processing. It understands the POSIX option conventions that allow grouping of multiple option letters together, and can be used to loop through command-line arguments one at a time.

The first argument to getopts is a string listing valid option letters. If an option letter is followed by a colon, then that option requires an argument, which must be supplied. Upon encountering such an option, getopts places the argument value into the variable OPTARG. The variable OPTIND contains the index of the next argument to be processed. The shell initializes this variable to 1.

The second argument is a variable name. This variable is updated each time getopts is called; its value is the found option letter. When getopts finds an invalid option, it sets the variable to a question mark character. Here is the previous example, using getopts:

```
# set flag vars to empty
file=   verbose=   quiet=   long=

while getopts f:vql opt
do
    case $opt in          Check option letter
    f)    file=$OPTARG
          ;;
    v)    verbose=true
          quiet=
          ;;
    q)    quiet=true
          verbose=
          ;;
    l)    long=true
          ;;
    esac
done

shift $((OPTIND - 1))          Remove options, leave arguments
```

Three things are immediately noticeable. First, the test in the case is only on the option letter. The leading minus is removed. Second, the case for -- is gone: getopts handles that automatically. Third, also gone is the default case for an invalid option: getopts automatically prints an error message.

Often, though, it's easier to handle errors in the script than to use getopts's default handling. Placing a colon (:) in the option string as the *first* character makes getopts change its behavior in two ways. First, it won't print any error messages. Second, besides setting the variable to a question mark, OPTARG contains the invalid option letter that was provided. Here's the final version of the option processing loop:

```
# set flag vars to empty
file=   verbose=   quiet=   long=

# leading colon is so we do error handling
while getopts :f:vql opt
do
    case $opt in              Check option letter
    f)      file=$OPTARG
            ;;
    v)      verbose=true
            quiet=
            ;;
    q)      quiet=true
            verbose=
            ;;
    l)      long=true
            ;;
    '?')    echo "$0: invalid option -$OPTARG" >&2
            echo "Usage: $0 [-f file] [-vql] [files ...]" >&2
            exit 1
            ;;
    esac
done

shift $((OPTIND - 1))         Remove options, leave arguments
```

 The OPTIND variable is shared between a parent script and any functions it invokes. A function that wishes to use getopts to parse its own arguments should reset OPTIND to 1. Calling such a function from within the parent script's option processing loop is not advisable. (For this reason, ksh93 gives each function its own private copy of OPTIND. Once again, caveat emptor.)

6.5   Functions

As in other languages, a *function* is a separate piece of code that performs some well-defined single task. The function can then be used (called) from multiple places within the larger program.

Functions must be defined before they can be used. This is done either at the beginning of a script, or by having them in a separate file and sourcing them with the "dot" (.) command. (The . command is discussed later on in "Built-in Commands" [7.9].) They are defined as shown in Example 6-4.

Example 6-4. Wait for a user to log in, function version

```
# wait_for_user --- wait for a user to log in
#
# usage: wait_for_user user [ sleeptime ]

wait_for_user () {
    until who | grep "$1" > /dev/null
    do
        sleep ${2:-30}
    done
}
```

Functions are invoked (executed) the same way a command is: by providing its name and any corresponding arguments. The wait_for_user function can be invoked in one of two ways:

> wait_for_user tolstoy   *Wait for tolstoy, check every 30 seconds*
>
> wait_for_user tolstoy 60   *Wait for tolstoy, check every 60 seconds*

Within a function body, the positional parameters ($1, $2, etc., $#, $*, and $@) refer to the *function's* arguments. The parent script's arguments are temporarily *shadowed*, or hidden, by the function's arguments. $0 remains the name of the parent script. When the function finishes, the original command-line arguments are restored.

Within a shell function, the return command serves the same function as exit and works the same way:

```
answer_the_question () {
    ...
    return 42
}
```

Note that using exit in the body of a shell function terminates the entire shell script!

Since the return statement returns an exit value to the caller, you can use functions in if and while statements. For example, instead of using test to compare two strings, you could use the shell's constructs to do so:

```
# equal --- compare two strings

equal () {
    case "$1" in
    "$2")    return 0 ;;   # they match
    esac
```

return

Usage
```
return [ exit-value ]
```

Purpose
To return an exit value from a shell function to the calling script.

Major options
None.

Behavior
The default exit status used if none is supplied is the exit status of the last command executed. If that is what you want, it is best to do this explicitly in the shell function:
```
return $?
```

Caveats
Some shells allow the use of return within a script but outside of a function body to mean the same as exit. This usage isn't recommended, for portability reasons.

```
    return 1             # they don't match
}

if equal "$a" "$b" ...

if ! equal "$c" "$d" ...
```

One item to note here is the use of double quotes in the case pattern list. This forces the value to be treated as a literal string, rather than as a shell pattern. The quotes around $1 don't hurt, but aren't necessary here.

Functions return integer exit status values, just like commands. For functions also, zero means success, nonzero means failure. To return some other value, a function should either set a global shell variable, or print the value, with the parent script capturing it using command substitution (see "Command Substitution" [7.6]):

```
myfunc () {
    ...
}
...
x=$(myfunc "$@")          Call myfunc, save output
```

Example 5-6 in "Tag Lists" [5.5], showed a nine-stage pipeline to produce a sorted list of SGML/XML tags from an input file. It worked only on the one file named on the command line. We can use a for loop for argument processing, and a shell function to encapsulate the pipeline, in order to easily process multiple files. The modified script is shown in Example 6-5.

Example 6-5. Making an SGML tag list from multiple files

```
#! /bin/sh -
# Read one or more HTML/SGML/XML files given on the command
# line containing markup like <tag>word</tag> and output on
# standard output a tab-separated list of
#
#         count word tag filename
#
# sorted by ascending word and tag.
#
# Usage:
#         taglist xml-files

process() {
  cat "$1" |
    sed -e 's#systemitem *role="url"#URL#g' -e 's#/systemitem#/URL#' |
      tr ' (){}[]' '\n\n\n\n\n\n\n' |
        egrep '>[^<>]+</' |
          awk -F'[<>]' -v FILE="$1" \
                '{ printf("%-31s\t%-15s\t%s\n", $3, $2, FILE) }' |
            sort |
              uniq -c |
                sort -k2 -k3 |
                  awk '{
                           print ($2 == Last) ? ($0 " <----") : $0
                           Last = $2
                          }'
}

for f in "$@"
do
    process "$f"
done
```

Functions (at least in the POSIX shell) have no provision for local variables.* Thus, all functions *share* variables with the parent script; this means you have to be careful not to change something that the parent script doesn't expect to be changed, such as PATH. It also means that other state is shared, such as the current directory and traps for signals. (Signals and traps are discussed in "Trapping Process Signals" [13.3.2].)

6.6 Summary

Variables are necessary for any serious programming. Shell variables hold string values, and a large array of operators for use in ${*var...*} lets you control the results of variable substitution.

---

* All of bash, ksh88, ksh93, and zsh do provide for local variables, but not necessarily using the same syntax.

The shell provides a number of special variables (those with nonalphanumeric names, such as $? and $!), that give you access to special information, such as command exit status. The shell also has a number of special variables with predefined meanings, such as PS1, the primary prompt string. The positional parameters and special variables $* and $@ give you access to the arguments used when a script (or function) was invoked. env, export, and readonly give you control over the environment.

Arithmetic expansion with $((...)) provides full arithmetic capabilities, using the same operators and precedence as in C.

A program's exit status is a small integer number that is made available to the invoker when the program is done. Shell scripts use the exit command for this, and shell functions use the return command. A shell script can get the exit status of the last command executed in the special variable $?.

The exit status is used for control-flow with the if, while, and until statements, and the !, && and || operators.

The test command, and its alias [...], test file attributes and string and numeric values, and are useful in if, while, and until statements.

The for loop provides a mechanism for looping over a supplied set of values, be they strings, filenames, or whatever else. while and until provide more conventional looping, with break and continue providing additional loop control. The case statement provides a multiway comparison facility, similar to the switch statement in C and C++.

getopts, shift, and $# provide the tools for processing the command line.

Finally, shell functions let you group related commands together and invoke them as a single unit. They act like a shell script, but the commands are stored in memory, making them more efficient, and they can affect the invoking script's variables and state (such as the current directory).

## CHAPTER 7

Input and Output, Files, and Command Evaluation

This chapter completes the presentation of the shell language. We first look at files, both for I/O and for generating filenames in different ways. Next is command substitution, which lets you use the output of a command as arguments on a command line, and then we continue to focus on the command line by discussing the various kinds of quoting that the shell provides. Finally, we examine evaluation order and discuss those commands that are built into the shell.

7.1   Standard Input, Output, and Error

Standard I/O is perhaps the most fundamental concept in the Software Tools philosophy. The idea is that programs should have a data source, a data sink (where data goes), and a place to report problems. These are referred to by the names *standard input*, *standard output*, and *standard error*, respectively. A program should neither know, nor care, what kind of device lies behind its input and outputs: disk files, terminals, tape drives, network connections, or even another running program! A program can expect these standard places to be already open and ready to use when it starts up.

Many, if not most, Unix programs follow this design. By default, they read standard input, write standard output, and send error messages to standard error. As we saw in Chapter 5, such programs are called *filters* because they "filter" streams of data, each one performing some operation on the data stream and passing it down the pipeline to the next one.

7.2   Reading Lines with read

The read command is one of the most important ways to get information *into* a shell program:

```
$ x=abc ; printf "x is now '%s'. Enter new value: " $x ; read x
x is now 'abc'. Enter new value: PDQ
$ echo $x
PDQ
```

---

read

Usage

   read [-r] *variable* ...

Purpose

   To read information into one or more shell variables.

Major options

   -r

      Raw read. Don't interpret backslash at end-of-line as meaning line continua-
      tion.

Behavior

   Lines are read from standard input and split as via shell field splitting (using $IFS).
   The first word is assigned to the first variable, the second to the second, and so on.
   If there are more words than variables, all the trailing words are assigned to the
   last variable. read exits with a failure value upon encountering end-of-file.

   If an input line ends with a backslash, read discards the backslash and newline,
   and continues reading data from the next line. The -r option forces read to treat
   a final backslash literally.

Caveats

   When read is used in a pipeline, many shells execute it in a separate process. In
   this case, any variables set by read do not retain their values in the parent shell.
   This is also true for loops in the middle of pipelines.

---

read can read values into multiple variables at one time. In this case, characters in
$IFS separate the input line into individual words. For example:

```
printf "Enter name, rank, serial number: "
read name rank serno
```

A typical use is processing the /etc/passwd file. The standard format is seven colon-
separated fields: username, encrypted password, numeric user ID, numeric group ID,
full name, home directory, and login shell. For example:

```
jones:*:32713:899:Adrian W. Jones/OSD211/555-0123:/home/jones:/bin/ksh
```

You can use a simple loop to process /etc/passwd line by line:

```
while IFS=: read user pass uid gid fullname homedir shell
do
    ...         Process each user's line
done < /etc/passwd
```

This loop does *not* say "while IFS is equal to colon, read ..." Rather, the assignment
to IFS causes read to use a colon as the field separator, without affecting the value of
IFS for use in the loop body. It changes the value of IFS *only* in the environment
inherited by read. This was described in "Variable Assignment and the Environment" [6.1.1]. The while loop was described in "Looping" [6.4].

---

read exits with a nonzero exit status when it encounters the end of the input file. This terminates the while loop.

Placing the redirection from /etc/passwd at the end of the loop body looks odd at first. However, it's necessary so that read sees subsequent lines each time around the loop. Had the loop been written this way:

```
# Incorrect use of redirection:
while IFS=: read user pass uid gid fullname homedir shell < /etc/passwd
do
    ...          Process each user's line
done
```

it would never terminate! Each time around the loop, the shell would open /etc/passwd anew, and read would read just the first line of the file!

An alternative to the while read ... do ... done < *file* syntax is to use cat in a pipeline with the loop:

```
# Easier to read, with tiny efficiency loss in using cat:
cat /etc/passwd |
    while IFS=: read user pass uid gid fullname homedir shell
    do
        ...          Process each user's line
    done
```

This is a general technique: *any* command can be used to pipe input into read. This is particularly useful when read is used in a loop. In "Basic Usage" [3.2.7], we presented this simple script for copying a directory tree:

```
find /home/tolstoy -type d -print   |     Find all directories
    sed 's;/home/tolstoy/;/home/lt/;' |     Change name, note use of semicolon delimiter
        sed 's/^/mkdir /'            |     Insert mkdir command
            sh -x                         Execute, with shell tracing
```

However, it can be done easily, and more naturally from a shell programmer's point of view, with a loop:

```
find /home/tolstoy -type d -print   |     Find all directories
    sed 's;/home/tolstoy/;/home/lt/;' |     Change name, note use of semicolon delimiter
        while read newdir                 Read new directory name
        do
            mkdir $newdir                 Make new directory
        done
```

(We note in passing that this script isn't perfect. In particular, it doesn't retain the ownership or permissions of the original directories.)

If there are more input words than variables, the trailing words are assigned to the last variable. Desirable behavior falls out of this rule: using read with a single variable reads an entire input line into that variable.

Since time immemorial, the default behavior of read has been to treat a trailing backslash on an input line as an indicator of *line continuation*. Such a line causes read to discard the backslash-newline combination and continue reading from the next input line:

```
$ printf "Enter name, rank, serial number: " ; read name rank serno
Enter name, rank, serial number: Jones \
> Major \
> 123-45-6789
$ printf "Name: %s, Rank: %s, Serial number: %s\n" $name $rank $serno
Name: Jones, Rank: Major, Serial number: 123-45-6789
```

Occasionally, however, you want to read exactly one line, no matter what it contains. The –r option accomplishes this. (The –r option is a POSIX-ism; many Bourne shells don't have it.) When given –r, read does not treat a trailing backslash as special:

```
$ read -r name rank serno
tolstoy \                                       Only two fields provided
$ echo $name $rank $serno
tolstoy \                                       $serno is empty
```

7.3 More About Redirections

We have already introduced and used the basic I/O redirection operators: <, >, >>, and |. In this section, we look at the rest of the available operators and examine the fundamentally important issue of file-descriptor manipulation.

7.3.1 Additional Redirection Operators

Here are the additional operators that the shell provides:

Use >| with set -C

The POSIX shell has an option that prevents accidental file truncation. Executing the command set -C enables the shell's so-called *noclobber* option. When it's enabled, redirections with plain > to preexisting files fail. The >| operator overrides the noclobber option.

Provide inline input with << *and* <<-

Use *program* << *delimiter* to provide input data within the body of a shell script.

Such data is termed a *here document*. By default, the shell does variable, command, and arithmetic substitutions on the body of the here document:

```
cd /home              Move to top of home directories
du -s *        |      Generate raw disk usage
  sort -nr     |      Sort numerically, highest numbers first
    sed 10q    |      Stop after first 10 lines
      while read amount name
      do
          mail -s "disk usage warning" $name << EOF
Greetings. You are one of the top 10 consumers of disk space
on the system.  Your home directory uses $amount disk blocks.
```

```
    Please clean up unneeded files, as soon as possible.

    Thanks,

    Your friendly neighborhood system administrator.
    EOF
        done
```

This example sends email to the top ten "disk hogs" on the system, asking them to clean up their home directories. (In our experience, such messages are seldom effective, but they do make the system administrator feel better.)

If the delimiter is quoted in any fashion, the shell does no processing on the body of the input:

`$ i=5`	*Set a variable*
`$ cat << 'E'OF`	*Delimiter is quoted*
`> This is the value of i: $i`	*Try a variable reference*
`> Here is a command substitution: $(echo hello, world)`	*Try command substitution*
`> EOF`	
`This is the value of i: $i`	*Text comes out verbatim*
`Here is a command substitution: $(echo hello, world)`	

The second form of the here document redirector has a trailing minus sign. In this case, all leading tab characters are removed from the here document and the closing delimiter before being passed to the program as input. (Note that only leading tab characters are removed, not leading spaces!) This makes shell scripts much easier to read. The revised form letter program is shown in Example 7-1.

Example 7-1. A form letter for disk hogs

`cd /home`	*Move to top of home directories*
`du -s *      |`	*Generate raw disk usage*
`  sort -nr  |`	*Sort numerically, highest numbers first*
`    sed 10q |`	*Stop after first 10 lines*

```
      while read amount name
      do
        mail -s "disk usage warning" $name <<- EOF
          Greetings. You are one of the top 10 consumers
          of disk space on the system.  Your home directory
          uses $amount disk blocks.

          Please clean up unneeded files, as soon as possible.

          Thanks,

          Your friendly neighborhood system administrator.
          EOF
      done
```

Open a file for input and output with <>

Use *program* `<>` *file* to open *file* for both reading and writing. The default is to open *file* on standard input.

Normally, < opens a file read-only, and > opens a file write-only. The <> operator opens the given *file* for both reading and writing. It is up to *program* to be aware of this and take advantage of it; in practice, there's not a lot of need for this operator.

 The <> operator was in the original V7 Bourne shell, but it wasn't documented, and historically there were problems getting it to work correctly in many environments. For this reason it is not widely known or used. Although it was standardized in the 1992 POSIX standard, on many systems /bin/sh doesn't support it. Thus, you should probably avoid it if absolute portability is a requirement.

Similar caveats apply to >|. A feature borrowed from the Korn shell, it has been standardized since 1992, although some systems may not support it.

7.3.2 File Descriptor Manipulation

Internally, Unix represents each process's open files with small integer numbers called *file descriptors*. These numbers start at zero, and go up to some system-defined limit on the number of open files. Historically, the shell allowed you to directly manipulate up to 10 open files: file descriptors 0 through 9. (The POSIX standard leaves it up to the implementation as to whether it is possible to manipulate file descriptors greater than 9. bash lets you, ksh does not.)

File descriptors 0, 1, and 2 correspond to standard input, standard output, and standard error, respectively. As previously mentioned, each program starts out with these file descriptors attached to the terminal (be it a real terminal or a pseudoterminal, such as an X window). By far the most common activity is to change the location of one of these three file descriptors, although it is possible to manipulate others as well. As a first example, consider sending a program's output to one file and its error messages to another:

```
make 1> results 2> ERRS
```

This sends make's[*] standard output (file descriptor 1) to results and its standard error (file descriptor 2) to ERRS. (make never knows the difference: it neither knows nor cares that it isn't sending output or errors to the terminal.) Catching the error messages in a separate file is often useful; this way you can review them with a pager or editor while you fix the problems. Otherwise, a large number of errors would just scroll off the top of your screen. A different take on this is to be cavalier and throw error messages away:

```
make 1> results 2> /dev/null
```

---

[*] The make program is used for controlling recompilation of source files into object files. However, it has many uses. For more information, see *Managing Projects with GNU make* (O'Reilly).

The explicit 1 in 1> results isn't necessary: the default file descriptor for output redirections is standard output: i.e., file descriptor 1. This next example sends both output and error messages to the same file:

```
make > results 2>&1
```

The redirection > results makes file descriptor 1 (standard output) be the file results. The subsequent redirection, 2>&1, has two parts. 2> redirects file descriptor 2; i.e., standard error. The &1 is the shell's notation for "wherever file descriptor 1 is." In this case, file descriptor 1 is the file results, so that's where file descriptor 2 is also attached. Note that the four characters 2>&1 must be kept together on the command line.

Ordering here is significant: the shell processes redirections left to right. Had the example been:

```
make 2>&1 > results
```

the shell would first send standard error to wherever file descriptor 1 is—which is still the terminal—and *then* change file descriptor 1 (standard output) to be results. Furthermore, the shell processes pipelines before file descriptor redirections, making it possible to send both standard output and standard error down the same pipeline:

```
make 2>&1 | ...
```

Finally, the exec command may be used to change the shell's own I/O settings. When used with just I/O redirections and no arguments, exec changes the shell's file descriptors:

```
exec 2> /tmp/$0.log        Redirect shell's own standard error

exec 3< /some/file         Open new file descriptor 3
...
read name rank serno <&3   Read from that file
```

 The first example line that redirects the shell's standard error should be used only in a script. Interactive shells print their prompts on standard error; if you run this command interactively, you won't see a prompt! If you wish to be able to undo a redirection of standard error, save the file descriptor first by copying it to a new one. For example:

```
exec 5>&2           Save original standard error on fd 5
exec 2> /tmp/$0.log Redirect standard error
...                 Stuff here
exec 2>&5           Copy original back to fd 2
excc 5>&-           Close fd 5, no longer needed
```

When used with arguments, exec serves a different purpose, which is to run the named program in place of the current shell. In other words, the shell starts the new program running in its current process. For example, suppose that you wish to do

---

option processing using the shell, but that most of your task is accomplished by some other program. You can do it this way:

```
while [ $# -gt 1 ]                        Loop over arguments
do
    case $1 in                           Process options
    -f)     # code for -f here
            ;;
    -q)     # code for -q here
            ;;
    ...
    *)      break ;;                      Nonoption, break loop
    esac

    shift                                 Move next argument down
done

exec real-app -q "$qargs" -f "$fargs" "$@"    Run the program

echo real-app failed, get help! 1>&2      Emergency message
```

When used this way, exec is a one-way operation. In other words, control never returns to the script. The only exception is if the new program can't be invoked. In that case, you may wish to have "emergency" code that at least prints a message and then does any other possible clean-up tasks.

7.4   The Full Story on printf

We introduced the printf command in "Fancier Output with printf" [2.5.4]. This section completes the description of that command.

As we saw earlier, the full syntax of the printf command has two parts:

```
printf format-string [arguments ...]
```

printf

Usage
```
printf format [ string ... ]
```

Purpose

To produce output from shell scripts. Since printf's behavior is defined by the POSIX standard, scripts that use it can be more portable than those that use echo.

Major options

None.

Behavior

printf uses the *format* string to control the output. Plain characters in the string are printed. Escape sequences as described for echo are interpreted. Format specifiers consisting of % and a letter direct formatting of corresponding argument strings. See text for details.

The first part is a string that describes the format specifications; this is best supplied as a string constant in quotes. The second part is an argument list, such as a list of strings or variable values, that correspond to the format specifications. The format string combines text to be output literally with specifications describing how to format subsequent arguments on the printf command line. Regular characters are printed verbatim. Escape sequences, similar to those of echo, are interpreted and then output as the corresponding character. *Format specifiers*, which begin with the character % and end with one of a defined set of letters, control the output of the following corresponding arguments. printf's escape sequences are described in Table 7-1.

Table 7-1. printf escape sequences

Sequence	Description
\a	Alert character, usually the ASCII BEL character.
\b	Backspace.
\c	Suppress any final newline in the output.[a] Furthermore, any characters left in the argument, any following arguments, and any characters left in the format string are ignored (not printed).
\f	Formfeed.
\n	Newline.
\r	Carriage return.
\t	Horizontal tab.
\v	Vertical tab.
\\	A literal backslash character.
\ddd	Character represented as a 1- to 3-digit octal value. Valid only in the format string.
\0ddd	Character represented as a 1- to 3-digit octal value.

[a] Valid only in argument strings under control of the %b format specifier.

---

printf's handling of escape sequences can be a bit confusing. By default, escape sequences are treated specially only in the format string. Escape sequences appearing in argument strings are not interpreted:

```
$ printf "a string, no processing: <%s>\n" "A\nB"
a string, no processing: <A\nB>
```

When the %b format specifier is used, printf does interpret escape sequences in argument strings:

```
$ printf "a string, with processing: <%b>\n" "A\nB"
a string, with processing: <A
B>
```

As can be seen in Table 7-1, most of the escape sequences are treated identically, whether in the format string, or in argument strings printed with %b. However, \c and \0ddd are only valid for use with %b, and \ddd is only interpreted in the format string. (We have to admit that the occasional wine cooler is a handy accessory to have when first learning some of the Unix utility idiosyncracies.)

As may be surmised, it is the format specifiers that give printf its power and flexibility. The format specification letters are given in Table 7-2.

Table 7-2. printf format specifiers

Item	Description
%b	The corresponding argument is treated as a string containing escape sequences to be processed. See Table 7-1, earlier in this section.
%c	ASCII character. Print the first character of the corresponding argument.
%d, %i	Decimal integer.
%e	Floating-point format ([-]d.precisione[+-]dd).
%E	Floating-point format ([-]d.precisionE[+-]dd).
%f	Floating-point format ([-]ddd.precision).
%g	%e or %f conversion, whichever is shorter, with trailing zeros removed.
%G	%E or %f conversion, whichever is shorter, with trailing zeros removed.
%o	Unsigned octal value.
%s	String.
%u	Unsigned decimal value.
%x	Unsigned hexadecimal number. Use a–f for 10 to 15.
%X	Unsigned hexadecimal number. Use A–F for 10 to 15.
%%	Literal %.

The floating-point formats, %e, %E, %f, %g, and %G, "need not be supported," according to the POSIX standard. This is because awk supports floating-point arithmetic and has its own printf statement. Thus, a shell program needing to do formatted printing of floating-point values can use a small awk program to do so. However, the printf commands built into bash, ksh93, and zsh do support the floating-point formats.

The printf command can be used to specify the width and alignment of output fields. To accomplish this, a format expression can take three optional modifiers following the % and preceding the format specifier:

```
%flags width.precision format-specifier
```

The *width* of the output field is a numeric value. When you specify a field width, the contents of the field are right-justified by default. You must specify a flag of – to get left justification. (The rest of the *flags* are discussed shortly.) Thus, "%-20s" outputs a left-justified string in a field 20 characters wide. If the string is less than 20 characters, the field is padded with spaces to fill. In the following examples, a | is output to indicate the actual width of the field. The first example right-justifies the text:

```
$ printf "|%10s|\n" hello
|     hello|
```

The next example left-justifies the text:

```
$ printf "|%-10s|\n" hello
|hello     |
```

The *precision* modifier is optional. For decimal or floating-point values, it controls the number of digits that appear in the result. For string values, it controls the maximum number of characters from the string that will be printed. The precise meaning varies by format specifier, as shown in Table 7-3.

Table 7-3. Meaning of precision

Conversion	Precision means
%d, %i, %o, %u, %x, %X	The minimum number of digits to print. When the value has fewer digits, it is padded with leading zeros. The default precision is 1.
%e, %E	The minimum number of digits to print. When the value has fewer digits, it is padded with zeros after the decimal point. The default precision is 6. A precision of 0 inhibits printing of the decimal point.
%f	The number of digits to the right of the decimal point.
%g, %G	The maximum number of significant digits.
%s	The maximum number of characters to print.

Here are some quick examples of the precision in action:

```
$ printf "%.5d\n" 15
00015
$ printf "%.10s\n" "a very long string"
a very lon
$ printf "%.2f\n" 123.4567
123.46
```

The C library printf( ) function allows you to specify the width and precision dynamically, via additional values in the argument list. The POSIX standard doesn't supply this, instead recommending the use of shell variable values in the format string.* Here is an example:

```
$ width=5  prec=6  myvar=42.123456
$ printf "|%${width}.${prec}G|\n" $myvar      POSIX
|42.1235|
$ printf "|%*.*G|\n" 5 6 $myvar               ksh93 and bash
|42.1235|
```

Finally, one or more *flags* may precede the field width and the precision. We've already seen the – flag for left justification. The complete set of flags is shown in Table 7-4.

Table 7-4. Flags for printf

Character	Description
–	Left-justify the formatted value within the field.
space	Prefix positive values with a space and negative values with a minus.
+	Always prefix numeric values with a sign, even if the value is positive.
#	Use an alternate form: %o has a preceding 0; %x and %X are prefixed with 0x and 0X, respectively; %e, %E, and %f always have a decimal point in the result; and %g and %G do not have trailing zeros removed.
0	Pad output with zeros, not spaces. This happens only when the field width is wider than the converted result. In the C language, this flag applies to all output formats, even nonnumeric ones. For the printf command, it applies only to the numeric formats.

And again, here are some quick examples:

```
$ printf "|%-10s| |%10s|\n" hello world      Left-, right-justified strings
|hello     | |     world|
$ printf "|% d| |% d|\n" 15 -15              Space flag
| 15| |-15|
$ printf "%+d %+d\n" 15 -15                  + flag
+15 -15
$ printf "%x %#x\n" 15 15                    # flag
f 0xf
$ printf "%05d\n" 15                         0 flag
00015
```

For the %b, %c, and %s conversion specifiers, the corresponding arguments are treated as strings. Otherwise, they're interpreted as C-language numeric constants (leading 0 for octal, and leading 0x or 0X for hexadecimal). Furthermore, if an argument's first

---

* Some versions of printf, such as those built into ksh93 and bash, do support dynamic width and precision specifications.

character is a single or double quote, the corresponding numeric value is the ASCII value of the string's second character:

```
$ printf "%s is %d\n" a "'a"
a is 97
```

When there are more arguments than format specifiers, the format specifiers are reused as needed. This is convenient when the argument list is of unknown length, such as from a wildcard expression. If there are more specifiers left in the *format* string than arguments, the missing values are treated as zero for numeric conversions and as the empty string for string conversions. (This seems to be only marginally useful. It's much better to make sure that you supply the same number of arguments as the format string expects.) If printf cannot perform a format conversion, it returns a nonzero exit status.

7.5   Tilde Expansion and Wildcards

The shell does two different expansions related to filenames. The first is *tilde expansion*, and the second is variously termed *wildcard expansion*, *globbing*, or *pathname expansion*.

7.5.1   Tilde Expansion

The shell performs tilde expansion if the first character of a command-line string is a tilde (~), or if the first character after any unquoted colon in the value of a variable assignment (such as for the PATH or CDPATH variables) is a tilde.

The purpose of tilde expansion is to replace a symbolic representation for a user's home directory with the actual path to that directory. The user may be named either explicitly, or implicitly, in which case it is the current user running the program:

```
$ vi ~/.profile          Same as vi $HOME/.profile
$ vi ~tolstoy/.profile    Edit user tolstoy's .profile file
```

In the first case, the shell replaces the ~ with $HOME, the current user's home directory. In the second case, the shell looks up user tolstoy in the system's password database, and replaces ~tolstoy with tolstoy's home directory, whatever that may be.

Tilde expansion first appeared in the Berkeley C shell, csh. It was intended primarily as an interactive feature. It proved to be very popular, and was adopted by the Korn shell, bash, and just about every other modern Bourne-style shell. It thus also found its way into the POSIX standard.

However (and there's always a "however"), many commercial Unix Bourne shell's don't support it. Thus, you should not use tilde expansion inside a shell script that has to be portable.

Tilde expansion has two advantages. First, it is a concise conceptual notation, making it clear to the reader of a shell script what's going on. Second, it avoids hardcoding pathnames into a program. Consider the following script fragment:

```
printf "Enter username: "      Print prompt
read user                      Read user
vi /home/$user/.profile        Edit user's .profile file
...
```

The preceding program assumes that all user home directories live in /home. If this ever changes (for example, by division of users into subdirectories based on department), then the script will have to be rewritten. By using tilde expansion, this can be avoided:

```
printf "Enter username: "      Print prompt
read user                      Read user
vi ~$user/.profile             Edit user's .profile file
...
```

Now the program works correctly, no matter where the user's home directory is.

Many shells, such as ksh88, ksh93, bash, and zsh, provide additional tilde expansions: see "Miscellaneous Extensions" [14.3.7], for more information.

7.5.2 Wildcarding

One of the shell's services is to look for special characters in filenames. When it finds these characters, it treats them as patterns to be matched: i.e., a specification of a set of files whose names all match the given pattern. The shell then replaces the pattern on the command line with the sorted set of filenames that match the pattern.[*]

If you've had any exposure to even the simple command-line environment available under MS-DOS, you're probably familiar with the *.* wildcard that matches all filenames in the current directory. Unix shell wildcards are similar, but much more powerful. The basic wildcards are listed in Table 7-5.

Table 7-5. Basic wildcards

Wildcard	Matches
?	Any single character
*	Any string of characters
[set]	Any character in *set*
[!set]	Any character *not* in *set*

---

[*] Since files are kept within directories in an unspecified order, the shell sorts the results of each wildcard expansion. On some systems, the sorting is subject to an ordering that is appropriate to the system's location, but that is different from the underlying machine collating order. Unix traditionalists can use export LC_ALL=C to get the behavior they're used to. This was discussed earlier, in "Internationalization and Localization" [2.8].

The ? wildcard matches any single character, so if your directory contains the files whizprog.c, whizprog.log, and whizprog.o, then the expression **whizprog.?** matches whizprog.c and whizprog.o, but not whizprog.log.

The asterisk (*) is more powerful and far more widely used; it matches any string of characters. The expression **whizprog.*** matches all three files in the previous paragraph; web designers can use the expression ***.html** to match their input files.

 MS-DOS, MS-Windows, and OpenVMS users should note that there is *nothing special* about the dot (.) in Unix filenames (aside from the leading dot, which "hides" the file); it's just another character. For example, ls * lists all files in the current directory; you don't need ***.*** as you do on other systems.

The remaining wildcard is the *set* construct. A set is a list of characters (e.g., abc), an inclusive range (e.g., a-z), or some combination of the two. If you want the dash character to be part of a list, just list it first or last. Table 7-6 (which assumes an ASCII environment) should explain things more clearly.

Table 7-6. Using the set construct wildcards

Expression	Single character matched
[abc]	a, b, or c
[.,;]	Period, comma, or semicolon
[-_]	Dash or underscore
[a-c]	a, b, or c
[a-z]	Any lowercase letter
[!0-9]	Any nondigit
[0-9!]	Any digit, or an exclamation mark
[a-zA-Z]	Any lower- or uppercase letter
[a-zA-Z0-9_-]	Any letter, any digit, underscore, or dash

In the original wildcard example, **whizprog.[co]** and **whizprog.[a-z]** both match whizprog.c and whizprog.o, but not whizprog.log.

An exclamation mark after the left bracket lets you "negate" a set. For example, **[!.;]** matches any character except period and semicolon; **[!a-zA-Z]** matches any character that isn't a letter.

The range notation is handy, but you shouldn't make too many assumptions about what characters are included in a range. It's generally safe to use a range for uppercase letters, lowercase letters, digits, or any subranges thereof (e.g., **[f-q]**, **[2-6]**). Don't use ranges on punctuation characters or mixed-case letters: e.g., **[a-Z]** and **[A-z]** should not be trusted to include all of the letters and nothing more. The problem is that such ranges are not entirely portable between different types of computers.

Another problem is that modern systems support different *locales*, which are ways of describing how the local character set works. In most countries, the default locale's character set is different from that of plain ASCII. To solve these problems, the POSIX standard introduced *bracket expressions* to denote letters, digits, punctuation, and other kinds of characters in a portable fashion. We discussed bracket expressions in "POSIX bracket expressions" [3.2.1.1]. The same elements that may appear in regular expression bracket expressions may also be used in shell wildcard patterns in POSIX-conformant shells, but should be avoided in portable shell scripts.

·7.5.2.1   Hidden files

By convention, when doing wildcard expansion, Unix shells ignore files whose names begin with a dot. Such "dot files" are typically used as program configuration or startup files. Examples include $HOME/.profile for the shell, $HOME/.exrc for the ex/vi editor, and $HOME/.inputrc for the GNU readline library used by bash and gdb (among others).

To see such files, provide an explicit period in front of the pattern. For example:

```
echo .*                  Show hidden files
```

You may use the -a (show all) option to ls to make it include hidden files in its output:

```
$ ls -la
total 4525
drwxr-xr-x   39 tolstoy   wheel        4096 Nov 19 14:44 .
drwxr-xr-x   17 root      root         1024 Aug 26 15:56 ..
-rw-------    1 tolstoy   wheel          32 Sep  9 17:14 .MCOP-random-seed
-rw-------    1 tolstoy   wheel         306 Nov 18 22:52 .Xauthority
-rw-r--r--    1 tolstoy   wheel         142 Sep 19  1995 .Xdefaults
-rw-r--r--    1 tolstoy   wheel         767 Nov 18 16:20 .article
-rw-r--r--    1 tolstoy   wheel         158 Feb 14  2002 .aumixrc
-rw-------    1 tolstoy   wheel       18828 Nov 19 11:35 .bash_history
...
```

 We cannot emphasize enough that hiding dot files is only a *convention*. It is enforced entirely in user-level software: the kernel doesn't treat dot files any differently from any other files.

7.6   Command Substitution

Command substitution is the process by which the shell runs a command and replaces the command substitution with the output of the executed command. That sounds like a mouthful, but it's pretty straightforward in practice.

There are two forms for command substitution. The first form uses so-called back-quotes, or grave accents (`` `...` ``), to enclose the command to be run:

```
for i in `cd /old/code/dir ; echo *.c`    Generate list of files in /old/code/dir
do                                          Loop over them
    diff -c /old/code/dir/$i $i | more     Compare old version to new in pager program
done
```

The shell first executes `cd /old/code/dir ; echo *.c`. The resulting output (a list of files) then becomes the list to use in the `for` loop.

The backquoted form is the historical method for command substitution, and is supported by POSIX because so many shell scripts exist that use it. However, all but the most simplest uses become complicated quickly. In particular, embedded command substitutions and/or the use of double quotes require careful escaping with the backslash character:

```
$ echo outer `echo inner1 \`echo inner2\` inner1` outer
outer inner1 inner2 inner1 outer
```

This example is contrived, but it illustrates how backquotes must be used. The commands are executed in this order:

1. `echo inner2` is executed. Its output (the word `inner2`) in placed into the next command to be executed.

2. `echo inner1 inner2 inner1` is executed. Its output (the words `inner1 inner2 inner3`) is placed into the next command to be executed.

3. Finally, `echo outer inner1 inner2 inner1 outer` is executed.

Things get worse with double-quoted strings:

```
$ echo "outer +`echo inner -\`echo \"nested quote\" here\`- inner`+ outer"
outer +inner -nested quote here- inner+ outer
```

For added clarity, the minus signs enclose the inner command substitution, and plus signs enclose the outer one. In short, it can get pretty messy.

Because nested command substitutions, with or without quoting, quickly become difficult to read, the POSIX shell adopted a feature from the Korn shell. Instead of using backquotes, enclose the command in $(...). Because this construct uses distinct opening and closing delimiters, it is *much* easier to follow. Compare the earlier examples, redone with the new syntax:

```
$ echo outer $(echo inner1 $(echo inner2) inner1) outer
outer inner1 inner2 inner1 outer
$ echo "outer +$(echo inner -$(echo "nested quote" here)- inner)+ outer"
outer +inner -nested quote here- inner+ outer
```

This is much easier to read. Note also how the embedded double quotes no longer need escaping. This style is recommended for all new development, and it is what we use in many of the examples in this book.

Here is the for loop we presented earlier that compared different versions of files from two different directories, redone with the new syntax:

```
for i in $(cd /old/code/dir ; echo *.c)    Generate list of files in /old/code/dir
do                                          Loop over them
    diff -c /old/code/dir/$i $i             Compare old version to new
done | more                                 Run all results through pager program
```

The differences here are that the example uses $(...) command substitution, and that the output of the *entire* loop is piped into the more screen-pager program.

7.6.1   Using sed for the head Command

Earlier, Example 3-1 in Chapter 3 showed a simple version of the head command that used sed to print the first *n* lines of a file. The real head command allows you to specify with an option how many lines to show; e.g., head -n 10 /etc/passwd. Traditional pre-POSIX versions of head allowed you to specify the number of lines as an option (e.g., head -10 /etc/passwd), and many longtime Unix users are used to running head that way.

Using command substitution and sed, we can provide a slightly modified shell script that works the same way as the original version of head. It is shown in Example 7-2.

Example 7-2. The head command as a script using sed, revised version

```
# head --- print first n lines
#
# usage:   head -N file

count=$(echo $1 | sed 's/^-//')    # strip leading minus
shift                              # move $1 out of the way
sed ${count}q "$@"
```

When this script is invoked as head -10 foo.xml, sed ends up being invoked as sed 10q foo.xml.

7.6.2   Creating a Mailing List

Consider the following problem. New versions of the various Unix shells appear from time to time, and at many sites users are permitted to choose their login shell from among the authorized ones listed in /etc/shells. Thus, it would be nice for system management to notify users by email when a new version of a particular shell has been installed.

To do this, we need to identify users by login shell and create a mailing list that the installer can use when preparing mail announcing the new shell version. Since the text of that message is likely to differ at each announcement, we won't make a script to send mail directly, but instead, we just want to make a list that we can mail to. Mailing-list formats differ among mail clients, so we make the reasonable assumption that ours only expects a comma-separated list of email addresses, one or more per line, and does not mind if the last address is followed by a comma.

In this case, a reasonable approach is to make one pass through the password file, creating one output file for each login shell, with one comma-terminated username per line. Here is the password file that we used in Chapter 5:

```
jones:*:32713:899:Adrian W. Jones/OSD211/555-0123:/home/jones:/bin/ksh
dorothy:*:123:30:Dorothy Gale/KNS321/555-0044:/home/dorothy:/bin/bash
toto:*:1027:18:Toto Gale/KNS322/555-0045:/home/toto:/bin/tcsh
ben:*:301:10:Ben Franklin/OSD212/555-0022:/home/ben:/bin/bash
jhancock:*:1457:57:John Hancock/SIG435/555-0099:/home/jhancock:/bin/bash
betsy:*:110:20:Betsy Ross/BMD17/555-0033:/home/betsy:/bin/ksh
tj:*:60:33:Thomas Jefferson/BMD19/555-0095:/home/tj:/bin/bash
george:*:692:42:George Washington/BST999/555-0001:/home/george:/bin/tcsh
```

The script itself combines variable and command substitution, the read command, and a while loop to get everything done in less than ten lines of executable code! See Example 7-3.

Example 7-3. Convert password file to shell mailing list

```
#! /bin/sh

# passwd-to-mailing-list
#
# Generate a mailing list of all users of a particular shell.
#
# Usage:
#    passwd-to-mailing-list < /etc/passwd
#    ypcat passwd | passwd-to-mailing-list
#    niscat passwd.org_dir | passwd-to-mailing-list

# Possibly a bit of overkill:
rm -f /tmp/*.mailing-list

# Read from standard input
while IFS=: read user passwd uid gid name home shell
do
    shell=${shell:-/bin/sh} # Empty shell field means /bin/sh
    file="/tmp/$(echo $shell | sed -e 's;^/;;' -e 's;/;-;g').mailing-list"
    echo $user, >> $file
done
```

As each password file entry is read, the program generates the filename on the fly, based on the shell's filename. The sed command removes the leading / character, and changes each subsequent / to a hyphen. This creates filenames of the form /tmp/ bin-bash.mailing-list. Each user's name and a trailing comma are then appended to the particular file, using >>. After running our script, we have the following results:

```
$ cat /tmp/bin-bash.mailing-list
dorothy,
ben,
```

```
jhancock,
tj,
$ cat /tmp/bin-tcsh.mailing-list
toto,
george,
$ cat /tmp/bin-ksh.mailing-list
jones,
betsy,
```

Being able to create mailing lists can be generally useful. For example, if process accounting is enabled, it is easy to make a mailing list for every program on the system by extracting program names and the names of the users who ran the program from the process accounting records. Note that root privileges are required to access the accounting files. Accounting software varies from vendor to vendor, but the same sort of data is accumulated by all of them, so only minor tweaks should be necessary to accommodate their differences. The GNU accounting summary utility, sa (see the manual pages for *sa*(8)), can produce a report with output lines that look like this:

```
# sa -u
...
jones       0.01 cpu      377k mem      0 io gcc
...
```

That is, we have whitespace-separated fields in which the first entry is a username and the last is a program name. This suggests that we simply filter that output to make it look like password-file data, and then pipe it into our mailing-list program:

```
sa -u | awk '{ print $1 ":::::::" $8 }' | sort -u | passwd to mailing-list
```

(The sort command sorts the data; the –u option removes duplicate lines.) The beauty of Unix filters and pipelines, and simple data markup, is readily apparent. We don't have to write a new mailing-list creation program to handle accounting data: we just need one simple awk step and a sort step to make the data look like something that we already can handle!

7.6.3   Simple Math: expr

The expr command is one of the few Unix commands that is poorly designed and hard to use. Although standardized by POSIX, its use in new programs is strongly discouraged, since there are other programs and facilities that do a better job. In shell scripting, the major use of expr is for shell arithmetic, so that is what we focus on here. Read the *expr*(1) manpage if you're curious about the rest of what it can do.

expr's syntax is picky: operands and operators must each be separate command-line arguments; thus liberal use of whitespace is highly recommended. Many of expr's operators are also shell metacharacters, so careful quoting is also required.

expr is designed to be used inside of command substitution. Thus, it "returns" values by printing them to standard output, not by using its exit code ($? in the shell).

Table 7-7 lists expr's operators, in order of increasing precedence. Operators with the same precedence are grouped together.

Table 7-7. expr operators

Expression	Meaning
e1 | *e2*	If *e1* is nonzero or non-null, its value is used. Otherwise, if *e2* is nonzero or non-null, its value is used. Otherwise, the final value is zero.
e1 & *e2*	If *e1* and *e2* are non-zero or non-null, the return value is that of *e1*. Otherwise, the final value is zero.
e1 = *e2*	Equal.
e1 != *e2*	Not equal.
e1 < *e2*	Less than.
e1 <= *e2*	Less than or equal to.
e1 > *e2*	Greater than.
e1 >= *e2*	Greater than or equal to.
	These operators cause expr to print 1 if the indicated comparison is true, 0 otherwise. If both operands are integers, the comparison is numeric; otherwise, it's a string comparison.
e1 + *e2*	The sum of *e1* and *e2*.
e1 - *e2*	The difference of *e1* and *e2*.
e1 * *e2*	The product of *e1* and *e2*.
e1 / *e2*	The integer division of *e1* by *e2* (truncates).
e1 % *e2*	The remainder of the integer division of *e1* by *e2* (truncates).
e1 : *e2*	Match of *e1* to BRE *e2*; see the *expr*(1) manpage for details.
(*expression*)	The value of *expression*; used for grouping, as in most programming languages.
integer	A number consisting only of digits, although an optional leading minus sign is allowed. Sadly, unary plus is not supported.
string	A string value that cannot be mistaken for a number or an operator.

In new code, you can do almost all of these operations using either test or $((...)). Regular-expression matching and extraction can be done with sed or the shell's case statement.

Here is an example of simple arithmetic. In a real script, the loop body would do something worthwhile, instead of just printing the loop variable's value:

```
$ i=1                          Initialize counter
$ while [ "$i" -le 5 ]         Loop test
> do
>     echo i is $i             Loop body: real code goes here
>     i=`expr $i + 1`          Increment loop counter
> done
i is 1
i is 2
i is 3
i is 4
```

```
i is 5
$ echo $i                                    Show final value
6
```

This kind of arithmetic represents 99% of the use of expr that you are likely to encounter. We've purposely shown the use of test (in its alias as [...]) and back-quotes for command substitution, since that is how expr is typically used. In new code, you should use the shell's built-in arithmetic substitution:

```
$ i=1                                        Initialize counter
$ while [ "$i" -le 5 ]                       Loop test
> do
>   echo i is $i                             Loop body: real code goes here
>   i=$((i + 1))                             Increment loop counter
> done
i is 1
i is 2
i is 3
i is 4
i is 5
$ echo $i                                    Show final value
6
```

For whatever it's worth, expr supports 32-bit arithmetic, and on many systems, 64-bit arithmetic. Thus, there is little danger of counter overflow.

7.7 Quoting

Quoting is how you prevent the shell from interpreting things differently from what you want it to. For example, if you want a command to receive an argument containing metacharacters, such as * or ?, you have to quote the metacharacters. Or, quite typically, when you want to keep something as a single argument that the shell would otherwise treat as separate arguments, you have to quote the arguments. There are three ways to quote things:

Backslash escaping

Preceding a character with a backslash (\) tells the shell to treat that character literally. This is the easiest way to quote a single character:

```
$ echo here is a real star: \* and a real question mark: \?
here is a real star: * and a real question mark: ?
```

Single quotes

Single quotes ('...') force the shell to treat everything between the pair of quotes literally. The shell strips the two quotes, and otherwise leaves the enclosed text completely alone:

```
$ echo 'here are some metacharacters: * ? [abc] ` $ \'
here are some metacharacters: * ? [abc] ` $ \
```

There is no way to embed a single quote within a single-quoted string. Even backslash is not special within single quotes. (On some systems, a command like echo 'A\tB' makes it look like the shell treats backslash specially. However, it is the echo command doing the special treatment: see Table 2-2 for more information.)

If you need to mix single and double quotes, you can do so by careful use of backslash escaping and concatenation of differently quoted strings:

```
$ echo 'He said, "How'\''s tricks?"'
He said, "How's tricks?"
$ echo "She replied, \"Movin' along\""
She replied, "Movin' along"
```

Note that no matter how you do it, though, such combinations are almost always hard to read.

Double quotes

Like single quotes, double quotes ("...") group the enclosed text as a single string. However, the shell does process the enclosed text for escaped characters and for variable, arithmetic, and command substitutions:

```
$ x="I am x"
$ echo "\$x is \"$x\". Here is some output: '$(echo Hello World)'"
$x is "I am x". Here is some output: 'Hello World'
```

Within double quotes, the characters $, ", `, and \ must be preceded by a \ if they are to be included literally. A backslash in front of any other character is not special. The sequence \-*newline* is removed completely, just as when used in the body of a script.

Note that, as shown in the example, single quotes are not special inside double quotes. They don't have to be in matching pairs, nor do they have to be escaped.

In general, use single quotes when you want no processing done at all. Otherwise, use double quotes when you want multiple words to be treated as a single string, but you need the shell to do some work for you. For example, to concatenate the value of one variable onto another, you would use something like this:

```
oldvar="$oldvar $newvar"          Append newvar's value to oldvar
```

7.8   Evaluation Order and eval

The various expansions and substitutions that we've covered are done in a defined order. The POSIX standard provides the picayune details. Here, we describe things at the level a shell programmer needs to understand things. This explanation is simplified to elide the most petty details: e.g., middles and ends of compound commands, special characters, etc.

Each line that the shell reads from the standard input or a script is called a *pipeline*; it contains one or more *commands* separated by zero or more pipe characters (|). (Actually, several special symbols separate individual commands: semicolon, ;, pipe, |, ampersand, &, logical AND, &&, and logical OR, ||.) For each pipeline it reads, the shell breaks it up into commands, sets up the I/O for the pipeline, and then does the following for each command, in the order shown:

1. Splits the command into *tokens* that are separated by the fixed set of *metacharacters*: space, tab, newline, ;, (,), <, >, |, and &. Types of tokens include *words*, *keywords*, I/O redirectors, and semicolons.

   It's a subtle point, but variable, command, and arithmetic substitution can be performed while the shell is doing token recognition. This is why the vi ~$user/ .profile example presented earlier in "Tilde Expansion" [7.5.1], actually works as expected.

2. Checks the first token of each command to see if it is a *keyword* with no quotes or backslashes. If it's an opening keyword (if and other control-structure openers, {, or ()), then the command is actually a *compound command*. The shell sets things up internally for the compound command, reads the next command, and starts the process again. If the keyword isn't a compound command opener (e.g., is a control-structure middle like then, else, or do, an end like fi or done, or a logical operator), the shell signals a syntax error.

3. Checks the first word of each command against the list of *aliases*. If a match is found, it substitutes the alias's definition and *goes back to step 1*; otherwise it goes on to step 4. (Aliases are intended for interactive shells. As such, we haven't covered them here.) The return to step 1 allows aliases for keywords to be defined: e.g., alias aslongas=while or alias procedure=function. Note that the shell does not do *recursive* alias expansion: instead, it recognizes when an alias expands to the same command, and stops the potential recursion. Alias expansion can be inhibited by quoting any part of the word to be protected.

4. Substitutes the user's home directory ($HOME) for the tilde character (~) if it is at the beginning of a word. Substitutes *user*'s home directory for *~user*.

   Tilde substitution (in shells that support it) occurs at the following places:
   - As the first unquoted character of a word on the command line
   - After the = in a variable assignment and after any : in the value of a variable assignment
   - For the *word* part of variable substitutions of the form ${*variable op word*}

5. Performs *parameter (variable) substitution* for any expression that starts with a dollar sign ($).

6. Does *command substitution* for any expression of the form $(*string*) or `*string*`.

7. Evaluates *arithmetic expressions* of the form $((*string*)).

8. Takes the parts of the line that resulted from parameter, command, and arithmetic substitution and splits them into words again. This time it uses the characters in $IFS as delimiters instead of the set of metacharacters in step 1.

Normally, successive multiple input occurrences of characters in IFS act as a single delimiter, which is what you would expect. This is true only for whitespace characters, such as space and tab. For nonwhitespace characters, this is not true. For example, when reading the colon-separated fields of /etc/passwd, two successive colons delimit an empty field:

```
while IFS=: read name passwd uid gid fullname homedir shell
do
    ...
done < /etc/passwd
```

9. Performs *filename generation*, a.k.a. *wildcard expansion*, for any occurrences of *, ?, and [...] pairs.

10. Uses the first word as a command following the search order described later in "Built-in Commands" [7.9]; i.e., as a special built-in command, then as a function, then as a regular built-in command, and finally as the first file found in a search of $PATH.

11. Runs the command after setting up I/O redirection and other such things.

As shown in Figure 7-1, quoting lets you bypass different parts of the evaluation process. On the flip side is the eval command, which lets you go through the process again. Performing command-line processing twice may seem strange, but it's actually quite powerful: it lets you write scripts that create command strings on the fly and then pass them to the shell for execution. This means that you can give scripts intelligence to modify their own behavior as they are running. (This is discussed further in the following section.)

The total sequence of steps shown in Figure 7-1 is pretty complicated. Each step happens inside the shell's memory as command lines are processed; it's not really possible to get the shell to show you each step as it happens. However, we can pretend to peek inside the shell's memory and see how the command line is transformed at each phase. We start with the following:

```
$ mkdir /tmp/x                                    Create temporary directory
$ cd /tmp/x                                        Change there
$ touch f1 f2                                       Create files for wildcarding
$ f=f y="a b"                                        Assign two variables
$ echo ~+/${f}[12] $y $(echo cmd subst) $((3 + 2)) > out   A busy command
```

Evaluation proceeds in the steps outlined previously:

1. The command is first split into tokens based on the shell's syntax. Most importantly, the I/O redirection > out is recognized and saved for later. Processing continues with this line, where the extent of each token is as shown on the line below the command:

```
echo ~+/${f}[12] $y $(echo cmd subst) $((3 + 2))
| 1| |--- 2 ---|  3 |------ 4 ------| |-- 5 ---|
```

2. The first word (echo) is checked to see if it's a keyword, such as if or for. In this case it's not, so processing continues with the line unchanged.

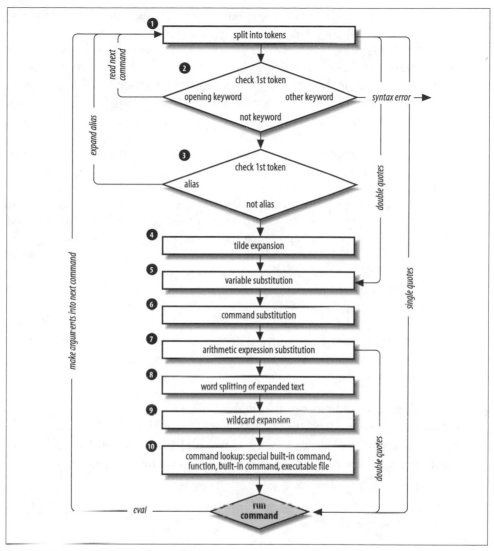

Figure 7-1. Steps in command-line processing

3. The first word (still echo) is checked to see if it's an alias. It isn't, so processing continues with the line still unchanged.

4. All words are scanned for tilde expansion. In this case, ~+ is a ksh93 and bash extension which is equivalent to $PWD, the name of the current directory. (This is described in "Miscellaneous Extensions" [14.3.7].) Token 2 is modified, and processing continues with this:

```
echo /tmp/x/${f}[12] $y $(echo cmd subst) $((3 + 2))
| 1| |----- 2 -----|  3 |------ 4 ------| |-- 5 ---|
```

5. The next step is variable expansion: tokens 2 and 3 are modified. This produces:

```
echo /tmp/x/f[12] a b $(echo cmd subst) $((3 + 2))
| 1| |---- 2 ---| |3| |------ 4 ------| |-- 5 ---|
```

6. Command substitutions are processed next. Note that this can recursively invoke all the steps in the list! In this case, since we're trying to keep things easy to follow, command substitution modifies token 4, producing:

```
echo /tmp/x/f[12] a b cmd subst $((3 + 2))
| 1| |---- 2 ---| |3| |-- 4 --| |-- 5 ---|
```

7. Arithmetic substitution is now performed. Token 5 is modified, and the result is:

```
echo /tmp/x/f[12] a b cmd subst 5
| 1| |---- 2 ---| |3| |-- 4 --| 5
```

8. The results of all the previous expansions are rescanned for the characters in $IFS. If found, they act as separators, creating additional words. For example, the two characters $y made up one word originally, but the expansion a-space-b is split at this stage into two words, a and b. The same applies for the results of the command substitution, $(echo cmd subst). The previous token 3 becomes tokens 3 and 4, and the previous token 4 becomes tokens 5 and 6. The result is:

```
echo /tmp/x/f[12] a b cmd subst 5
| 1| |---- 2 ---| 3 4 |5| | 6 | 7
```

9. The last substitution stage is wildcard expansion. Token 2 becomes tokens 2 and 3. The result is:

```
echo /tmp/x/f1 /tmp/x/f2 a b cmd subst 5
| 1| |-- 2 --| |-- 3 --| 4 5 6  | 7 | 8
```

10. The shell is now ready to run the final command. It looks up echo. It happens that in both ksh93 and bash the echo command is built into the shell.

11. The shell actually runs the command. It first performs the > out I/O redirection, and then calls its internal version of echo to print out the final arguments.

Here is the final result:

```
$ cat out
/tmp/x/f1 /tmp/x/f2 a b cmd subst 5
```

7.8.1 The eval Statement

The eval statement tells the shell to take eval's arguments and run them through the command-line processing steps all over again. Here is an example to help you understand the implications of eval.

eval ls passes the string ls to the shell to execute, so the shell prints a list of files in the current directory. This example is simplistic: nothing about the string ls needs to be sent through the command-processing steps twice. However, consider this:

```
listpage="ls | more"
$listpage
```

Instead of producing a paginated file listing, the shell treats | and more as arguments to ls, and ls complains that no files of those names exist. Why? Because the pipe character appears in step 5 when the shell evaluates the variable, *after* it has actually looked for pipe characters (in step 1). The variable's expansion isn't even parsed until step 8. As a result, the shell treats | and more as arguments to ls so that ls tries to find files called | and more in the current directory!

Now consider eval $listpage instead of just $listpage. When the shell gets to the last step, it runs the command eval with arguments ls, |, and more. This causes the shell to go back to step 1 with a line that consists of these arguments. It finds | in step 1 and splits the line into two commands, ls and more. Each command is processed in the normal (and in both cases trivial) way. The result is a paginated list of the files in your current directory.

7.8.2   Subshells and Code Blocks

Two other constructs are occasionally useful: *subshells* and *code blocks*.

A subshell is a group of commands enclosed in parentheses. The commands are run in a separate process.* This is particularly useful if you need a small group of commands to run in a different directory, without changing the directory of the main script. For example, the following pipeline, for copying a directory tree from one place to another, was in the original V7 Unix *tar*(1) manpage:

```
tar -cf - . | (cd /newdir; tar -xpf -)
```

The lefthand tar command creates a tar archive of the current directory, sending it to standard output. This archive goes down the pipe to the commands in the subshell on the right. The leading cd command first changes to the new directory where the archive is to be extracted. Then the righthand tar command extracts the files from the archive. Note that the shell (or script) running this pipeline has not changed its directory.

A code block is conceptually similar to a subshell, but it does not create a new process. Commands in a code block are enclosed in braces, and do affect the main script's state (such as its current directory). For historical reasons, the braces are treated as shell keywords: this means that they're recognized only as the first symbol in a command. Practically speaking, this means that you *must* place the closing brace after a newline or after a semicolon. For example:

```
cd /some/directory || {                          Start code block
    echo could not change to /some/directory! >&2    What went wrong
```

---

* The POSIX standard terms it a "subshell environment." This means that the commands need not actually run in a separate process; rather, they simply are forbidden to change the environment (variables, current directory, and so on) of the main script. ksh93 will avoid starting an actual process for subshell commands if it can. Most other shells do create a separate process.

```
      echo you lose! >&2                     Snide remark
      exit 1                                 Terminate whole script
}                                            End of code block
```

I/O redirection may be applied to subshells (as shown in the two-tar example) and code blocks. In that case, all the commands read their input or send their output from the redirected source. Table 7-8 summarizes the differences between subshells and code blocks.

Table 7-8. Subshell and code block summary

Construct	Delimiters	Recognized where	Separate process
Subshell	( )	Anywhere on the line	Yes
Code block	{ }	After newline, semicolon, or keyword	No

When to use a subshell versus when to use a code block is mostly a matter of taste and judgment. The primary difference is that a code block shares state with the main script. Thus, a cd command affects the main script, as do variable assignments. In particular, an exit in a code block terminates the entire script. Thus, you should use a subshell when you want the enclosed commands to run *without* affecting the main script. Otherwise, use a code block.

7.9   Built-in Commands

The shell has a number of commands that are *built-in*. This means that the shell itself executes the command, instead of running an external program in a separate process. Furthermore, POSIX distinguishes between "special" built-ins and "regular" built-ins. The built-in commands are listed in Table 7-9. Special built-ins are marked with a †. Most of the regular built-ins listed here have to be built-in for the shell to function correctly (e.g., read). Others are typically built into the shell only for efficiency (e.g., true and false). The standard allows other commands to be built-in for efficiency as well, but all regular built-ins must be accessible as separate programs that can be executed directly by other binary programs. test is a primary example of a command that often is built into the shell for efficiency reasons.

Table 7-9. POSIX shell built-in commands

Command	Summary
: (colon)[a]	Do nothing (just do expansions of arguments).
. (dot)	Read file and execute its contents in current shell.
alias	Set up shorthand for command or command line (interactive use).
bg	Put job in background (interactive use).
break[a]	Exit from surrounding for, while, or until loop.
cd	Change working directory.

Table 7-9. POSIX shell built-in commands (continued)

Command	Summary
command	Locate built-in and external commands; find a built-in command instead of an identically named function.
continue[a]	Skip to next iteration of for, while, or until loop.
eval[a]	Process arguments as a command line.
exec[a]	Replace shell with given program or change I/O for shell.
exit[a]	Exit from shell.
export[a]	Create environment variables.
false	Do nothing, unsuccessfully.
fc	Work with command history (interactive use).
fg	Put background job in foreground (interactive use).
getopts	Process command-line options.
jobs	List background jobs (interactive use).
kill	Send signals.
newgrp	Start new shell with new group ID (obsolete).
pwd	Print working directory.
read	Read a line from standard input.
readonly[a]	Make variables read-only (unassignable).
return[a]	Return from surrounding function.
set[a]	Set options or positional parameters.
shift[a]	Shift command-line arguments.
times[a]	Print accumulated user and system CPU times for the shell and its children.
trap[a]	Set up signal-catching routine.
true	Do nothing, successfully.
umask	Set/show file permission mask.
unalias	Remove alias definitions (interactive use).
unset[a]	Remove definitions of variables or functions.
wait	Wait for background job(s) to finish.

[a] The source command in bash (borrowed from the BSD C shell) is equivalent to the dot command.

The distinction between special and regular built-in commands comes into play when the shell searches for commands to execute. The command-search order is special built-ins first, then shell functions, then regular built-ins, and finally external commands found by searching the directories listed in $PATH. This search order makes it possible to define shell functions that extend or override regular shell built-ins.

This feature is used most often in interactive shells. For example, suppose that you would like the shell's prompt to contain the last component of the current directory's pathname. The easiest way to make this happen is to have the shell

change PS1 each time you change directories. You could just write your own
function:

```
# chdir --- private function to update PS1 when changing directories

chdir () {
    cd "$@"                    Actually change directory
    x=$(pwd)                   Get current directory name into variable x
    PS1="${x##*/}\$ "          Lop off leading components, assign to PS1
}
```

The problem is that you have to remember to type chdir at the shell instead of cd,
and if you accidentally forget and type cd, you'll be in the new directory, but the
prompt won't be changed. For this reason, you can write a function named cd, and
the shell will find your function *first*, since cd is a regular built-in:

```
# cd --- private version to update PS1 when changing directories
#        (won't actually work, see text)

cd () {
    cd "$@"                    Actually change directory?!?
    x=$(pwd)                   Get current directory name into variable x
    PS1="${x##*/}\$ "          Lop off leading components, assign to PS1
}
```

There is one small fly in the ointment here. How does the shell function access the
functionality of the "real" cd command? The cd "$@" shown here just calls the func-
tion again, leading to infinite recursion. What's needed is an "escape hatch" that tells
the shell to bypass the search for functions and access the real command. This is the
job of the command built-in command, whose use is shown in Example 7-4.

Example 7-4. Updating PS1 when changing directories

```
# cd --- private version to update PS1 when changing directories

cd () {
    command cd "$@"           Actually change directory
    x=$(pwd)                  Get current directory name into variable x
    PS1="${x##*/}\$ "         Lop off leading components, assign to PS1
}
```

The POSIX standard provides the following two additional special qualities for the
special built-in commands:

- A syntax error in a special built-in utility may cause a shell executing that utility
  to abort, while a syntax error in a regular built-in utility shall not cause a shell
  executing that utility to abort. [...] If a special built-in utility encountering a
  syntax error does not abort the shell, its exit value shall be nonzero.

- Variable assignments specified with special built-in utilities remain in effect after
  the built-in completes; this shall not be the case with a regular built-in or other
  utility.

---

command

Usage

command [-p] *program* [*arguments* ...]

Purpose

To bypass the shell's inclusion of functions in the search for commands to run. This allows access to built-in versions of commands from functions with the same name as the built-in command.

Major options

-p

When searching for commands, use a default value of $PATH that is guaranteed to find the system's utilities.

Behavior

command finds the named *program* by looking for special and regular built-ins, and then searching along $PATH. With the -p option, it uses a default value for $PATH, instead of the current setting.

When *program* is a special built-in command, any syntax errors do not abort the shell, and any preceding variable assignments do not remain in effect after the command has finished.

Caveats

The command built-in command is *not* a special built-in command. Woe be to the shell programmer who defines a function named command!

The second item needs some explanation. As mentioned earlier in "Variable Assignment and the Environment" [6.1.1], you can specify a variable assignment at the front of a command, and the variable will have that value in the environment of the executed command only, without affecting the variable in the current shell or subsequent commands:

```
PATH=/bin:/usr/bin:/usr/ucb awk '...'
```

However, when such an assignment is used with a special built-in command, the assignment stays in effect from then on, even after the special built-in completes.

Table 7-9 lists several commands not otherwise described in this chapter. Most of them are either specialized, or irrelevant for shell scripting, but to be complete here's a brief description of what they do and when to use them:

alias, unalias

These are used to define and remove aliases, respectively. The shell expands alias definitions when commands are read. Aliases are primarily useful for interactive shells; e.g., alias 'rm=rm -i' to force rm to ask for confirmation. The shell does not do recursive alias expansion, thus this definition is valid.

`bg`, `fg`, `jobs`, `kill`

> These commands are used for *job control*, an operating system facility by which jobs may be moved in and out of the background.

`fc`

> Short for "fix command," this command is also intended for interactive use. It manages the shell's saved history of previously executed commands, allowing the interactive user to recall a previous command, edit it, and then re-execute it.
>
> This command was originally developed in `ksh` to provide a feature comparable to the "!-history" mechanism in the BSD C shell, `csh`. `fc` is now largely superseded by the interactive command-line editing features of `ksh`, `bash`, and `zsh`.

`times`

> This command prints the CPU time accumulated by the shell and all child processes that it has run so far. It is not particularly useful for day-to-day scripting.

`umask`

> This sets the file permission creation mask, and is discussed in "Default permissions" in Appendix B.

Two remaining commands are useful in scripts. The first is `wait`, which waits for background programs to finish. With no arguments, `wait` waits for *all* background jobs to finish. Otherwise, each argument is either the process ID (see "Process Listing" [13.2]) of a background job, or a job-control job specification.

Finally, the . (dot) command is important. It is used to read and execute commands contained in a separate file. For example, if you have a number of shell functions that you would like to use in multiple scripts, the right way to do this is to place them in a separate "library" file, and then read them with the dot command:

```
. my_funcs          # read in functions
```

If the named file does not contain a slash, then the shell searches the directories in `$PATH` in order to find the file. The file does not need to be executable, just readable.

 Everything in the read-in file is executed *in the current shell*. Thus, variable assignments, function definitions, and directory changes with `cd` all take effect. This is very different from simply running a separate shell script, which runs in a separate process and does not affect the current shell.

7.9.1   The set Command

The `set` command serves several conceptually distinct purposes.[*] It also uses an unusual option syntax, which the POSIX standard retains for historical compatibility. As a result, it is somewhat hard to learn.

---

[*] It thus violates the "do one thing well" Software Tools principle. The reason for this is that Steven Bourne wished to avoid having lots of reserved commands built into the shell.

---

set

Usage

```
set
set -- [ arguments ... ]
set [ -short-options ] [ -o long-option ] [ arguments ... ]
set [ +short-options ] [ +o long-option ] [ arguments ... ]
set -o
set +o
```

Purpose

To print the names and values of all current shell variables; to set or unset the value of shell *options* (which change the way that the shell behaves); and to change the values of the positional parameters.

Major options

See text.

Behavior

- With no options or arguments, print the names and values of all shell variables in a form that can later be reread by the shell.

- With -- and arguments, replace the positional parameters with the supplied arguments.

- With short-form options that begin with a -, or long-form options that begin with -o, enable particular shell options. Additional nonoption arguments set the positional parameters. See text for details.

- With short-form options that begin with a +, or long-form options that begin with +o, disable particular shell options. See text for details.

- A single -o prints the current settings of the shell options "in an unspecified format." ksh93 and bash both print a sorted list, where each line is an option name and the word on or off:

  ```
  $ set -o              From bash
  allexport    off
  ...
  ```

- A single +o prints the current settings of the shell options in a way that they may be later reread by the shell to achieve the same set of option settings.

Caveats

Real shells have additional short and long options, above and beyond the ones described in Table 7-10. Details are given in Chapter 14. Don't use them if portability is a major concern.

Some versions of /bin/sh don't recognize set -o at all.

The simplest job of the set command is to print the names and values of all shell variables in sorted order. This is what it does when invoked with no options or arguments. The output is in a form that may later be reread by the shell, including quoting as appropriate. The idea is that it should be possible for a shell script to save its state, and then restore it later via the . (dot) command.

The next job for set is to change the positional parameters ($1, $2, etc.). By using a first argument of -- to end options to set itself, all following arguments replace the positional parameters, even if they start with a minus or plus sign.

Finally, set is used to enable or disable *shell options*, which are internal settings that change the way the shell behaves. Here's where the complexity comes in: historically, shell options were described with single letters, enabled with a minus sign and disabled with a plus sign. POSIX added long-name options, enabled or disabled with -o or +o. Each single-letter option has a corresponding long-name option. Table 7-10 lists the options, along with a brief description of what they do.

Table 7-10. POSIX shell options

Short option	−o form	Description
-a	allexport	Export all subsequently defined variables.
-b	notify	Print job-completion messages right away, instead of waiting for next prompt. Intended for interactive use.
-C	noclobber	Don't allow > redirection to existing files. The > | operator overrides the setting of this option. Intended for interactive use.
-e	errexit	Exit the shell when a command exits with nonzero status.
-f	noglob	Disable wildcard expansion.
-h		Locate and remember the location of commands called from function bodies when the function is defined, instead of when the function is executed (XSI).
-m	monitor	Enable job control (on by default). Intended for interactive use.
-n	noexec	Read commands and check for syntax errors, but don't execute them. Interactive shells are allowed to ignore this option.
-u	nounset	Treat undefined variables as errors, not as null.
-v	verbose	Print commands (verbatim) before running them.
-x	xtrace	Print commands (after expansions) before running them.
	ignoreeof	Disallow Ctrl-D to exit the shell.
	nolog	Disable command history for function definitions.
	vi	Use vi-style command-line editing. Intended for interactive use.

Perhaps surprisingly, set does *not* set shell variables (unlike the same command in the BSD C shell). That task is accomplished with simple *variable=value* assignments.

Although not part of POSIX, the command `set -o emacs` is widely implemented (ksh88, ksh93, bash, zsh). If you're already comfortable with emacs, using this command gives you a one-line mini-screen editor that accepts emacs commands for working with your shell history.

The special variable `$-` is a string representing the currently enabled shell options. Each option's short option letter appears in the string if that option is enabled. This can be used to test option settings, like so:

```
case $- in
*C*)    ...         The noclobber option is enabled
        ;;
esac
```

Interestingly enough, while the POSIX standard goes to some lengths to make it possible to save and restore the state of shell variables and traps, there is no defined way to save a list of function definitions for later reuse. This appears to be a simple oversight in the standard. We will show how to do this in "Gotchas" [14.1].

7.10 Summary

The `read` command reads lines and splits the data into fields, for assigning to named shell variables. The `-r` option provides some control over how data is read.

I/O redirection allows you to change the source or destination of one program, or multiple programs running together in a subshell or code block. Besides redirecting to or from files, pipelines let you hook multiple programs together. Here documents provide inline input.

File descriptor manipulation, particularly of file descriptors 1 and 2, is a fundamental operation, used repeatedly in everyday scripting.

`printf` is a flexible, albeit somewhat complicated, command for generating output. Most of the time, it can be used in a simple manner, but its power is occasionally needed and valuable.

The shell performs a number of expansions (or substitutions) on the text of each command line: tilde expansion (if supported) and wildcards; variable expansion; arithmetic expansion; and command substitution. Wildcarding now includes POSIX character classes for locale-dependent matching of characters in filenames. By convention, "dot files" are not included in wildcard expansions. Variable and arithmetic expansion were described in Chapter 6. Command substitution has two forms: `` `...` `` is the original form, and `$(...)` is the newer, easier-to-write form.

Quoting protects different source-code elements from special treatment by the shell. Individual characters may be quoted by preceding them with a backslash. Single quotes protect all enclosed characters; no processing is done on the quoted text, and it's impossible to embed a single quote into single-quoted text. Double quotes group the enclosed items into a single word or argument, but variable, arithmetic, and command substitutions are still applied to the contents.

The eval command exists to supersede the normal command-line substitution and evaluation order, making it possible for a shell script to build up commands dynamically. This is a powerful facility, but it must be used carefully. Because the shell does so many different kinds of substitutions, it pays to understand the order in which the shell evaluates input lines.

Subshells and code blocks give you two choices for grouping commands. They have different semantics, so you should use them appropriately.

Built-in commands exist either because they change the shell's internal state and must be built-in (such as cd), or for efficiency (such as test). The command search order that allows functions to be found before regular built-ins, combined with the command command, make it possible to write shell functions that override built-in commands. This has its uses. Of the built-in commands, the set command is the most complicated.

## CHAPTER 8

Production Scripts

In this chapter, we move on to some more-complex processing tasks. The examples that we consider are each of general utility, yet they are completely different from one another, and are absent from most Unix toolboxes.

The programs in this chapter include examples of command-line argument parsing, computing on remote hosts, environment variables, job logging, parallel processing, runtime statement evaluation with eval, scratch files, shell functions, user-defined initialization files, and consideration of security issues. The programs exercise most of the important statements in the shell language, and give a flavor of how typical Unix shell scripts are written. We developed them for this book, and they have proved to be solid production tools that we use, and rely on, in our daily work.

8.1   Path Searching

Some programs support searching for input files on directory paths, much like the Unix shell searches the colon-separated directory list in PATH for executable programs. This makes it easier for users, who can refer to files by shorter names and need not be aware of exactly where in the filesystem they are found. Unix doesn't provide any special commands or system calls for finding a file in a search path, even though there is historical precedent in other operating systems for such support. Fortunately, it isn't hard to implement a path search, given the right tools.

Rather than implement a path search for one particular program, let's write a new tool that takes as arguments an environment variable name whose expansion is the desired search path, followed by zero or more file patterns, and have it report the locations of matching files. Our program will then be of general utility in all other software that needs path-search support. (This is an example of the "Detour to build specialized tools" principle that we mentioned in Chapter 1.)

It is sometimes useful to know whether a file is found more than once in the path because you might want to adjust the path to control which version is found, when differing versions exist in the path. Our program should offer the user a command-line option to choose between reporting just the first one found, and reporting all of them. Also, it is becoming standard practice for software to provide an identifying version number on request, and to offer brief help so that the user often need not reread the program's manual pages to get a reminder about an option name. Our program provides those features too.

The complete program is shown later in Example 8-1, but because of its length, we present it here first as a *semiliterate program*, a sequence of fragments of descriptive prose and shell code.

We begin with the usual introductory comment block. It starts with the magic line that identifies the program, /bin/sh, to be used to execute the script. The comment block then continues with a brief statement of what the program does, and how it is used:

```
#! /bin/sh -
#
# Search for one or more ordinary files or file patterns on a search
# path defined by a specified environment variable.
#
# The output on standard output is normally either the full path
# to the first instance of each file found on the search path,
# or "filename: not found" on standard error.
#
# The exit code is 0 if all files are found, and otherwise a
# nonzero value equal to the number of files not found (subject
# to the shell exit code limit of 125).
#
# Usage:
#       pathfind [--all] [--?] [--help] [--version] envvar pattern(s)
#
# With the --all option, every directory in the path is
# searched, instead of stopping with the first one found.
```

In a networked environment, security has to be given serious consideration. One of the insidious ways that shell scripts can be attacked is by manipulating the input field separator, IFS, which influences how the shell subsequently interprets its input. To prevent this kind of attack, some shells simply reset IFS to a standard value before executing any script; others happily import an external setting of that variable. We prevent that by doing the job ourselves as the first action in our script:

```
IFS='
 '
```

It is hard to see on a screen or a printed page what appears inside the quotes: it is the three-character string consisting of a newline, a space, and a tab. The default value of IFS is space, tab, newline, but if we write it that way, a whitespace-trimming editor might eliminate trailing spaces, reducing the string's value to just a newline. It would be better to be able to write it with explicit escape characters, such as IFS="\040\t\n", but regrettably, the Bourne shell does not support those escape sequences.

There is one subtle point that we need to be aware of when redefining IFS. When "$*" is expanded to recover the command line, the first character of the value of IFS is used as the field separator. We don't use $* in this script, so our rearrangement of characters in IFS does not matter.

Another common way to break security is to trick software into executing unintended commands. To discourage this, we want programs that we invoke to be trusted versions, rather than imposters that might be lurking in a user-provided search path. We therefore reset PATH to a minimal value, saving the original value for later use:

```
OLDPATH="$PATH"

PATH=/bin:/usr/bin
export PATH
```

The export statement is crucial: it ensures that our secure search path is inherited by all subprocesses.

The program code continues with five short functions, ordered alphabetically for reader convenience.

The first function, error( ), prints its arguments on standard error, and then calls a function, to be described shortly, that does not return:

```
error( )
{
    echo "$@" 1>&2
    usage_and_exit 1
}
```

The second function, usage( ), writes a brief message showing the expected way to use the program, and returns to its caller. Notice that the function needs the program name, but doesn't hardcode it: it gets it from the variable PROGRAM, which will shortly be set to the name by which the program was invoked. This permits an installer to rename the program without modifying the program code, in the event that there is a collision with an already-installed program with an identical name but different purpose. The function itself is simple:

```
usage( )
{
    echo "Usage: $PROGRAM [--all] [--?] [--help] [--version] envvar pattern(s)"
}
```

The third function, usage_and_exit( ), produces the usage message, and then exits with a status code given by its single argument:

```
usage_and_exit( )
{
    usage
    exit $1
}
```

The fourth function, version( ), displays the program version number on standard output, and returns to its caller. Like usage( ), it uses PROGRAM to obtain the program name:

```
version( )
{
    echo "$PROGRAM version $VERSION"
}
```

The fifth and last function, warning( ), prints its arguments on standard error, increments the variable EXITCODE by one to track the number of warnings issued, and returns to its caller:

```
warning( )
{
    echo "$@" 1>&2
    EXITCODE=`expr $EXITCODE + 1`
}
```

We discussed expr in more detail in "Simple Math: expr" [7.6.3]. Its usage here is a common shell idiom for incrementing a variable. Newer shells permit the simpler form EXITCODE=$((EXITCODE + 1)), but there are still plenty of systems where that POSIX-ism is not yet recognized.

Even though this program is short enough that we don't really need functions, except for avoiding code duplication, it is good programming practice to hide irrelevant details: tell what we're doing, but not how we do it.

We have now reached the point where the first statement is executed at runtime. We initialize five variables to record an option choice, the user-provided environment variable name, the exit code, the program name, and the program version number:

```
all=no
envvar=
EXITCODE=0
PROGRAM=`basename $0`
VERSION=1.0
```

In our program, we follow the convention that lowercase variables are local to functions or to the main code body, whereas uppercase ones are shared globally by the entire program. We use a string value, instead of a number, for the variable all because it makes the program clearer, with negligible runtime cost.

The basename command is the traditional tool for extracting the filename part of a complete pathname: it strips all leading characters of its first argument up to and including the final slash, and reports the remainder on standard output:

```
$ basename resolv.conf                Report the bare filename
resolv.conf
$ basename /etc/resolv.conf           Report the bare filename
resolv.conf
```

Descendants of the Bourne shell offer the pattern-matching operators shown in Table 6-2 in Chapter 6 for this purpose, but basename is an ordinary command, and thus works with all shells.

With a second argument representing a filename suffix, basename strips any matching suffix from its result:

```
$ basename /etc/resolv.conf .conf     Report the suffixless filename
resolv
$ basename /etc/resolv.conf .pid      Report the bare filename
resolv.conf
```

Although basename's first argument is normally a pathname, basename simply treats it as a text string, and does not require, or check, that it corresponds to a real file.

If the argument is omitted, or is an empty string, basename's behavior is implementation-defined.

The big block of code that follows is typical of command-line argument parsing in all Unix programs: while we have an argument (determined by the argument count, $#, being greater than zero), process that argument in a case statement that selects a code block according to the string value of the argument:

```
while test $# -gt 0
do
    case $1 in
```

The case selectors bear some explanation. GNU programming style encourages long, descriptive option names, rather than the old cryptic, single-character options historically used in Unix. Such brevity is acceptable when the option count is small and the program is used frequently. Otherwise, descriptive names are better, provided that we permit the user to specify just enough of them to guarantee uniqueness. However, such abbreviations should be avoided when these options are supplied from other programs, since that makes the code clearer to a human, and guards against surprises when new options are added to later versions of the program.

There isn't any simple way in the shell language to specify that a long name can be matched by a leading unambiguous prefix of that name, so we just have to supply all of the alternatives.

Long option names retrofitted into older programs are sometimes distinguished from the original options by a leading double hyphen. For new code, we therefore allow either one or two hyphens, which is easily accommodated by duplicating the abbreviations in the case selectors and adding an extra hyphen.

We *could* write the case selectors with wildcard matching: --a* | -a*). However, we view that as unacceptably sloppy practice, since it allows matches against completely different names than those documented.

For the --all option, we simply record the fact that the option was found by resetting the variable all to yes:

```
--all | --al | --a | -all | -al | -a )
    all=yes
    ;;
```

The doubled semicolons are mandatory after each case block, except for the last. We could have written this block more compactly:

```
--all | --al | --a | -all | -al | -a ) all=yes ;;
```

However, it is easier to verify that all cases are properly terminated when the semicolons appear on their own lines, and it also facilitates adding extra statements to the block. Careful use of indentation helps to clarify and emphasize logical structure in almost any programming language.

The GNU convention is to respond to a --help request with a brief summary on standard output of how to use the program, and then to exit immediately with a success status code (0 in POSIX and Unix). For larger programs, that summary would include a short description of each of the options, but ours is simple enough that extra explanation is not necessary. Since the question mark, ?, is a shell wildcard character, we must quote its use in the case selector:

```
--help | --hel | --he | --h | '--?' | -help | -hel | -he | -h | '-?' )
    usage_and_exit 0
    ;;
```

Similarly, the GNU convention is that a --version option should produce a (usually) one-line report on standard output and an immediate successful exit. The same applies to other kinds of status-request options that might be offered by a larger program: --author, --bug-reports, --copyright, --license, --where-from, and so on:

```
--version | --versio | --versi | --vers | --ver | --ve | --v | \
-version | -versio | -versi | -vers | -ver | -ve | -v )
    version
    exit 0
    ;;
```

The case selector -*) matches any other option: we report the illegal option on standard error, call the usage( ) function to remind the user what was expected, and exit immediately with a failure status code (1):

```
    -*)
        error "Unrecognized option: $1"
        ;;
```

The distinction between standard error and standard output is not always obeyed by software, and when commands are used interactively, the user won't see a difference, since both streams go to the same display device. If the program is a filter, then both errors and status reports, like the output from the --help and --version options, should go to standard error so as not to contaminate a pipeline; otherwise, status reports can go to standard output. Since status reports are a relatively recent contribution from the GNU world, programming practice is still evolving, and standards have yet to be issued. Neither POSIX nor traditional Unix documentation seems to address this issue.

The final case selector *) matches everything else. It is analogous to the default selector in the switch statement of the C, C++, and Java languages, and it is always a good idea to include it, even if its body is empty, to demonstrate to the reader that all alternatives have been considered. Here, a match indicates that we have processed all of the options, so we can exit the loop. Since we have now handled all of the possible cases, we end the case statement with the terminating keyword:

```
    *)
        break
        ;;
    esac
```

We are now at the end of the option loop. Just before its final statement, we use shift to discard the first argument, which has now been processed, and to move the remaining ones down in the argument list. This guarantees eventual loop termination when the argument count, $#, reaches zero:

```
    shift
done
```

On exit from the loop, all options have been handled, and what remain in the argument list are the environment variable name and the files to find. We save the variable name in envvar and if at least one argument remains, we discard the first argument:

```
envvar="$1"
test $# -gt 0 && shift
```

The remaining arguments are available as "$@". We avoid storing them in a variable, such as with files="$@", because filenames with spaces would be handled incorrectly: the embedded spaces would become argument separators.

Since it is possible that the user-supplied environment variable is PATH, which we reset on entry for security reasons, we check for this, and update envvar accordingly:

```
test "x$envvar" = "xPATH" && envvar=OLDPATH
```

The leading x is commonly seen: here, it prevents the expansion of the variable from being confused with a test option, if that expansion starts with a hyphen.

All arguments have now been handled, and we come to the tricky part: the use of the shell eval statement. We have the *name* of the environment variable in envvar, available as "$envvar", but we want its expansion. We also want to turn the colon separators into normal whitespace separators. We therefore construct the argument string '${'"$envvar"'}', which the shell expands to the equivalent of '${MYPATH}', if MYPATH were the name supplied by the user. The surrounding single quotes protect it from further expansion. That string is then given to eval, which sees two arguments: echo and ${MYPATH}. eval looks up MYPATH in the environment, finding, say, /bin:/usr/bin:/home/jones/bin, and then evaluates the expanded command echo /bin:/usr/bin:/home/jones/bin, which in turn sends /bin:/usr/bin:/home/jones/bin down the pipe to the tr command, which converts colons to spaces, producing /bin /usr/bin /home/jones/bin. The surrounding backquotes (or $(...) in modern shells) turn that into the value assigned to dirpath. We silence any errors from eval by the usual technique of sending them to /dev/null:

```
dirpath=`eval echo '${'"$envvar"'}' 2>/dev/null | tr : ' '`
```

It took a long paragraph to explain the single short statement that sets dirpath, so you can see that it is tricky. Clearly, eval adds significant power to the language.

After eval, understanding the rest of the program is pretty easy. First there are some sanity checks to handle any unusual conditions that would cause problems later on: *every* good program should make such checks, to avoid the infamous garbage-in, garbage-out syndrome. Notice that the last sanity check, for an empty file list, does *not* cause an error report. The reason is that any program that processes a list should always handle an empty list gracefully: if there is nothing to do, there is nothing to report but success:

```
# sanity checks for error conditions
if test -z "$envvar"
then
    error Environment variable missing or empty
elif test "x$dirpath" = "x$envvar"
then
    error "Broken sh on this platform: cannot expand $envvar"
elif test -z "$dirpath"
then
    error Empty directory search path
elif test $# -eq 0
then
    exit 0
fi
```

We then have three nested loops: the outer one over the argument files or patterns, the middle one over the directories in the search path, and the inner one over matching files in a single directory. We want the loops in that order so that each file is dealt with completely before moving on to the next one. The reverse loop order would just prove confusing to the user, since the file reports would be mixed up. Before starting the middle loop, we set result to the empty string, since we use that later to determine whether anything was found:

```
for pattern in "$@"
do
    result=
    for dir in $dirpath
    do
        for file in $dir/$pattern
        do
```

In the body of the innermost loop, test -f tells us whether $file exists and is a regular file. (It is also true if it is a symbolic link that ultimately points to a regular file.) If it does, we record it in result, report it on standard output with an echo command, and if the default of reporting only the first one applies, we break out of the innermost and middle loops. Otherwise, the loop continues over the remaining matching files, possibly producing more reports:

```
            if test -f "$file"
            then
                result="$file"
                echo $result
                test "$all" = "no" && break 2
            fi
        done
    done
```

In this program, there is no need in the middle loop to test whether $dir itself exists as a valid directory because that is subsumed by the existence check in the innermost loop for $file. However, with a more complex loop body, such a test would be desirable, and can be easily done with a single statement: test -d $dir || continue.

At the completion of the middle loop, we have searched all of the directories in the search path for $pattern, and result either holds the name of the last match found or is still empty, if no matches were found.

We test whether the expansion $result is empty, and if so, we report the missing file on standard error, increment the error count in EXITCODE (inside the warning function), and then continue the outer loop with the next file:

```
    test -z "$result" && warning "$pattern: not found"
done
```

At the completion of the outer loop, we have looked for every requested match in every directory in the search path, and we are ready to return to the invoking program. There is only one small problem left to deal with: user exit-code values are limited to the range 0 through 125, as shown in Table 6-5 in Chapter 6, so we cap the EXITCODE value at 125:

```
test $EXITCODE -gt 125 && EXITCODE=125
```

Our program is almost complete: its last statement returns to the parent process with an explicit exit status, as all well-behaved Unix programs should. That way, the parent can test the exit status to determine whether the child process succeeded or failed:

```
exit $EXITCODE
```

In Example 8-1, we present the complete text of pathfind, without our commentary, so that you can see it as the shell sees it. The total length is about 90 lines, ignoring comments and empty lines.

Example 8-1. Searching a path for input files

```
#! /bin/sh -
#
# Search for one or more ordinary files or file patterns on a search
# path defined by a specified environment variable.
#
# The output on standard output is normally either the full path
# to the first instance of each file found on the search path,
# or "filename: not found" on standard error.
#
# The exit code is 0 if all files are found, and otherwise a
# nonzero value equal to the number of files not found (subject
# to the shell exit code limit of 125).
#
# Usage:
#       pathfind [--all] [--?] [--help] [--version] envvar pattern(s)
#
# With the --all option, every directory in the path is
# searched, instead of stopping with the first one found.

IFS='
        '

OLDPATH="$PATH"

PATH=/bin:/usr/bin
export PATH

error()
{
    echo "$@" 1>&2
    usage_and_exit 1
}

usage()
{
    echo "Usage: $PROGRAM [--all] [--?] [--help] [--version] envvar pattern(s)"
}

usage_and_exit()
{
```

Example 8-1. Searching a path for input files (continued)

```
    usage
    exit $1
}

version()
{
    echo "$PROGRAM version $VERSION"
}

warning()
{
    echo "$@" 1>&2
    EXITCODE=`expr $EXITCODE + 1`
}

all=no
envvar=
EXITCODE=0
PROGRAM=`basename $0`
VERSION=1.0

while test $# -gt 0
do
    case $1 in
    --all | --al | --a | -all | -al | -a )
        all=yes
        ;;
    --help | --hel | --he | --h | '--?' | -help | -hel | -he | -h | '-?' )
        usage_and_exit 0
        ;;
    --version | --versio | --versi | --vers | --ver | --ve | --v | \
    -version | -versio | -versi | -vers | -ver | -ve | -v )
        version
        exit 0
        ;;
    -*)
        error "Unrecognized option: $1"
        ;;
    *)
        break
        ;;
    esac
    shift
done

envvar="$1"
test $# -gt 0 && shift

test "x$envvar" = "xPATH" && envvar=OLDPATH

dirpath=`eval echo '${'"$envvar"'}' 2>/dev/null | tr : ' ' `
```

Example 8-1. Searching a path for input files (continued)

```
# sanity checks for error conditions
if test -z "$envvar"
then
    error Environment variable missing or empty
elif test "x$dirpath" = "x$envvar"
then
    error "Broken sh on this platform: cannot expand $envvar"
elif test -z "$dirpath"
then
    error Empty directory search path
elif test $# -eq 0
then
    exit 0
fi

for pattern in "$@"
do
    result=
    for dir in $dirpath
    do
        for file in $dir/$pattern
        do
            if test -f "$file"
            then
                result="$file"
                echo $result
                test "$all" = "no" && break 2
            fi
        done
    done
    test -z "$result" && warning "$pattern: not found"
done

# Limit exit status to common Unix practice
test $EXITCODE -gt 125 && EXITCODE=125

exit $EXITCODE
```

Let's wrap up this section with some simple tests of our program, using a search path, PATH, that Unix systems always have. Each test includes a display of the exit code, $?, so that we can verify the error handling. First, we check the help and version options:

```
$ pathfind -h
Usage: pathfind [--all] [--?] [--help] [--version] envvar pattern(s)
$ echo $?
0

$ pathfind --version
pathfind version 1.0
$ echo $?
```

Next, we provoke some error reports with bad options, and missing arguments:

```
$ pathfind --help-me-out
Unrecognized option: --help-me-out
Usage: pathfind [--all] [--?] [--help] [--version] envvar pattern(s)
$ echo $?
1

$ pathfind
Environment variable missing or empty
Usage: pathfind [--all] [--?] [--help] [--version] envvar pattern(s)
$ echo $?
1

$ pathfind NOSUCHPATH ls
Empty directory search path
Usage: pathfind [--all] [--?] [--help] [--version] envvar pattern(s)
$ echo $?
1
```

Then we supply some nonsense filenames:

```
$ pathfind -a PATH foobar
foobar: not found
$ echo $?
1

$ pathfind -a PATH "name with spaces"
name with spaces: not found
$ echo $?
1
```

The empty filename list test is next:

```
$ pathfind PATH
$ echo $?
0
```

Here's what happens when a quickly typed Ctrl-C interrupts the running program:

```
$ pathfind PATH foo
^C
$ echo $?
130
```

The exit code is 128 + 2, indicating that signal number 2 was caught and terminated the program. On this particular system, it is the INT signal, corresponding to interactive input of the keyboard interrupt character.

So far, error reporting is exactly as we intended. Now let's search for files that we know exist, and exercise the -a option:

```
$ pathfind PATH ls
/usr/local/bin/ls
$ echo $?
0
```

```
$ pathfind -a PATH ls
/usr/local/bin/ls
/bin/ls
$ echo $?
```

Next, we check the handling of a quoted wildcard pattern that must match files that we know exist:

```
$ pathfind -a PATH '?sh'
/usr/local/bin/ksh
/usr/local/bin/zsh
/bin/csh
/usr/bin/rsh
/usr/bin/ssh
```

Then we do the same for a pattern that should not match anything:

```
$ pathfind -a PATH '*junk*'
*junk*: not found
```

Now for a big test: find some C and C++ compilers on this system:

```
$ pathfind -a PATH c89 c99 cc c++ CC gcc g++ icc lcc pgcc pgCC
c89: not found
c99: not found
/usr/bin/cc
/usr/local/bin/c++
/usr/bin/c++
CC: not found
/usr/local/bin/gcc
/usr/bin/gcc
/usr/local/gnat/bin/gcc
/usr/local/bin/g++
/usr/bin/g++
/opt/intel_cc_80/bin/icc
/usr/local/sys/intel/compiler70/ia32/bin/icc
/usr/local/bin/lcc
/usr/local/sys/pgi/pgi/linux86/bin/pgcc
/usr/local/sys/pgi/pgi/linux86/bin/pgCC
$ echo $?
3
```

An awk one-liner lets us verify that the exit-code counter logic works as intended. We try 150 nonexistent files, but the exit code correctly caps at 125:

```
$ pathfind PATH $(awk 'BEGIN { while (n < 150) printf("x.%d ", ++n) }' )
x.1: not found
...
x.150: not found

$ echo $?
125
```

Our final test verifies that standard error and standard output are handled as promised, by capturing the two streams in separate files, and then showing their contents:

```
$ pathfind -a PATH c89 gcc g++ >foo.out 2>foo.err
$ echo $?
1

$ cat foo.out
/usr/local/bin/gcc
/usr/bin/gcc
/usr/local/gnat/bin/gcc
/usr/local/bin/g++
/usr/bin/g++

$ cat foo.err
c89: not found
```

At this point, we can probably declare our `pathfind` command a success, although some shell wizard might still be able to spot a hole[*] in it, and there is no substitute for extensive testing, particularly with unexpected input, such as from the fuzz tests cited in a footnote in "What's in a Unix File?" in Appendix B. Ideally, testing should exercise every combination of legal, and at least one illegal, argument. Since we have three main option choices, each with several abbreviations, there are $(6 + 1) \times (10 + 1) \times (14 + 1) = 1155$ option combinations, and each of these needs to be tested with zero, one, two, and at least three remaining arguments. We know from our implementation that the option abbreviations are handled the same way so that many fewer tests are necessary. However, when we put on our testing hat, we must first view the program as a black box whose contents are unknown, but which is documented to behave a certain way. Later, we should put on a different testing hat, sneak inside the program, and then knowing how it works, try hard to figure out how to break it. Also, test data needs to be devised that can be shown to exercise every single line of the program. Exhaustive testing is tedious!

Because undocumented software is likely to be unusable software, and because few books describe how to write manual pages, we develop a manual page for `pathfind` in Appendix A.

`pathfind` has proved a valuable exercise. Besides being a handy new tool that isn't available in the standard GNU, POSIX, and Unix toolboxes, it has all the major elements of most Unix programs: argument parsing, option handling, error reporting, and data processing. We have also shown three steps that can be taken to eliminate some notorious security holes, by terminating the initial shell command line with the – option, and immediately setting IFS and PATH. Serendipitously, a good bit of the

---

[*] Notable security holes include altering the input field separator (IFS); substituting rogue commands for trusted ones by altering the search path; sneaking backquoted commands, shell metacharacters, and control characters (including NUL and newline) into arguments; causing unexpected runtime interrupts; and passing arguments that are too long for various internal shell resource limits.

code can be reused, with minor modifications, for the next shell script that you write: the leading comment banner, the assignments of IFS and PATH, the five helper functions, the while and case statements for argument processing, and at least the outer loop over the files collected from the command line.

As an exercise, you might consider what needs to be changed for these extensions to pathfind:

- To save redirections of standard output and standard error to /dev/null, add a --quiet option to suppress all output so that the only indication of whether a match was found is the exit code. There is precedence for this programming convenience in cmp's -s option and grep's -q option.

- Add a --trace option to echo on standard error the full path for every file tested.

- Add a --test x option to allow the test option -f to be replaced by some other one, such as -h (file is a symbolic link), -r (file is readable), -x (file is executable), and so on.

- Make pathfind act like a filter: when no files are named on the command line, it should read a list of files from standard input. How does this affect the program's structure and organization?

- Patch any security holes that you can find, such as those listed in the most recent footnote.

8.2 Automating Software Builds

Because Unix runs on so many different platforms, it is common practice to build software packages from source code, rather than installing binary distributions. Large Unix sites often have multiple platforms, so their managers have the tedious job of installing packages on several systems. This is clearly a case for automation.

Many software developers now adopt software-packaging conventions developed within the GNU Project. Among them are:

- Packages that are distributed in compressed archive files named package-x.y.z.tar.gz (or package-x.y.z.tar.bz2) that unbundle into a directory named package-x.y.z.

- A top-level configure script, usually generated automatically by the GNU autoconf command from a list of rules in the configure.in or configure.ac file. Executing that script, sometimes with command-line options, produces a customized C/C++ header file, usually called config.h, a customized Makefile, derived from the template file Makefile.in, and sometimes, a few other files.

- A standard set of Makefile targets that is documented in *The GNU Coding Standards*, among them all (build everything), check (run validation tests), clean (remove unneeded intermediate files), distclean (restore the directory to its original distribution), and install (install all needed files on the local system).

- Installed files that reside in directories under a default tree defined by the variable `prefix` in the `Makefile` and is settable at configure time with the `--prefix=`*dir* command-line option, or supplied via a local system-wide customization file. The default prefix is `/usr/local`, but an unprivileged user could use something like `$HOME/local`, or better, `$HOME/`` `arch` ``/local`, where `arch` is a command that prints a short phrase that defines the platform uniquely. GNU/Linux and Sun Solaris provide `/bin/arch`. On other platforms, we install our own implementations, usually just a simple shell-script wrapper around a suitable `echo` command.

The task is then to make a script that, given a list of packages, finds their source distributions in one of several standard places in the current system, copies them to each of a list of remote hosts, unbundles them there, and builds and validates them. We have found it unwise to automate the installation step: the build logs first need to be examined carefully.

This script must be usable by any user at any Unix site, so we cannot embed information about particular hosts in it. Instead, we assume that the user has provided two customization files: `directories` to list places to look for the package distribution files, and `userhosts` to list usernames, remote hostnames, remote build directories, and special environment variables. We place these, and other related files, in a hidden directory, `$HOME/.build`, to reduce clutter. However, since the list of source directories is likely to be similar for all users at a given site, we include a reasonable default list so that the `directories` file may not be needed.

A build should sometimes be done on only a subset of the normal build hosts, or with archive files in unusual locations, so the script should make it possible to set those values on the command line.

The script that we develop here can be invoked like this:

```
$ build-all coreutils-5.2.1 gawk-3.1.4            Build two packages everywhere

$ build-all --on loaner.example.com gnupg-1.2.4   Build one package on a specific host

$ build-all --source $HOME/work butter-0.3.7      Build package from nonstandard location
```

These commands do a *lot* of work. Here is an outline of the steps that they carry out for each specified software package and each of the default, or selected, build hosts:

1. Find the package distribution in the local filesystem.
2. Copy the distribution to the remote build host.
3. Initiate login connections on the remote host.
4. Change to the remote build directory and unbundle the distribution file.
5. Change to the package build directory and configure, build, and test the package.
6. Record all of the output on the initiating host in separate log files for each package and build environment.

The builds on the remote hosts proceed in parallel, so the total wall-clock time required is that for the slowest machine, rather than the sum of the individual times. Thanks to build-all, builds in up to 100 environments are routine for us, and provide a challenging workout for package developers.

The build-all script is long, so we present it in parts, with surrounding commentary, and then for reader convenience we show the complete program later in this chapter, in Example 8-2.

We begin with the usual introductory comment header:

```
#! /bin/sh -
# Build one or more packages in parallel on one or more build hosts.
#
# Usage:
#        build-all [ --? ]
#                  [ --all "..." ]
#                  [ --cd "..." ]
#                  [ --check "..." ]
#                  [ --configure "..." ]
#                  [ --environment "..." ]
#                  [ --help ]
#                  [ --logdirectory dir ]
#                  [ --on "[user@]host[:dir][,envfile] ..." ]
#                  [ --source "dir ..." ]
#                  [ --userhosts "file(s)" ]
#                  [ --version ]
#                  package(s)
#
# Optional initialization files:
#        $HOME/.build/directories        list of source directories
#        $HOME/.build/userhosts          list of [user@]host[:dir][,envfile]
```

We initialize the input field separator, IFS, to newline-space-tab:

```
IFS='
       '
```

Next, we set the search path to a limited list and make it global with export, so that all subprocesses on the initiating host use it:

```
PATH=/usr/local/bin:/bin:/usr/bin
export PATH
```

We set the permission mask (see "Default permissions" in Appendix B) to allow full access for user and group, and read access for other. The group is given full access because, on some of our systems, more than one system manager handles software installations, and the managers all belong to a common trusted group. The same mask is needed later on the remote systems, so we follow our programming convention by giving it an uppercase name:

```
UMASK=002
umask $UMASK
```

It proves convenient to delegate part of the work to separate functions, so that we can limit code blocks to a comfortable size. Nine such functions are defined at this point in the program. However, for tutorial purposes, we delay their presentation until we have discussed the main body of the program.

We need a few variables, most initially empty, to collect command-line settings:

```
ALLTARGETS=                      Programs or make targets to build
altlogdir=                       Alternative location for log files
altsrcdirs=                      Alternative location for source files
ALTUSERHOSTS=                    File with list of additional hosts
CHECKTARGETS=check               Make target name to run package test suite
CONFIGUREDIR=.                   Subdirectory with configure script
CONFIGUREFLAGS=                  Special flags for configure program
LOGDIR=                          Local directory to hold log files
userhosts=                       Additional build hosts named on command line
```

We also need to refer a few times to the directory where build-all's initialization files are found, so we give it a name:

```
BUILDHOME=$HOME/.build
```

Two scripts, executed on the remote host in the context of the login shell at the beginning and end of the build, provide for further customization and log-file reports. They overcome a secure-shell (ssh) problem with login shells of ksh or sh: those shells do not read $HOME/.profile unless they are started as login shells, and the secure shell doesn't arrange for that to happen if it is invoked with command arguments, as build-all does:

```
BUILDBEGIN=./.build/begin
BUILDEND=./.build/end
```

As in pathfind in Example 8-1, warnings contribute to a final exit code:

```
EXITCODE=0
```

There are no default extra environment variables:

```
EXTRAENVIRONMENT=               Any extra environment variables to pass in
```

The program name is needed later, so we save its value and its version number:

```
PROGRAM=`basename $0`            Remember program name
VERSION=1.0                      Record program version number
```

We include timestamps in the build-log filenames, using the odometer style requested by the date format in DATEFLAGS to obtain filenames that sort in time order. Apart from punctuation, this is the format recommended in ISO 8601:2000.* We

---

* *Data elements and interchange formats—Information interchange—Representation of dates and times*, available at *http://www.iso.ch/cate/d26780.html*. That standard writes dates in the form YYYY-MM-DDThh:mm: ss or YYYYMMDDThhmmss. The colons in the first form are undesirable in filenames for portability reasons, and the second form is hard for humans to read.

invoke date the same way later on the remote hosts, so we want the complex date format to be defined in just one place:

```
DATEFLAGS="+%Y.%m.%d.%H.%M.%S"
```

At our sites, we communicate with remote hosts using the secure shell, and we need both scp and ssh. Sites that still use the old insecure *remote shell* could change them to rcp and rsh. During development, we set these variables to "echo scp" and "echo ssh" so that the logs record what would have been done, without actually doing it:

```
SCP=scp
SSH=ssh
```

Depending on user and system configuration file settings, ssh may create a separate encrypted channel for X Window System traffic. We almost never require that feature in software builds, so we reduce startup overhead by turning it off with the -x option, unless a setting of the SSHFLAGS environment variable supplies a different set of options:

```
SSHFLAGS=${SSHFLAGS--x}
```

It proves useful to permit shell-style comments in initialization files. STRIPCOMMENTS provides a simple way to remove them, assuming that the comment character does not otherwise appear in the files:

```
STRIPCOMMENTS='sed -e s/#.*$//'
```

We also need a filter to indent a data stream (for better-looking output), and another to replace newlines by spaces:

```
INDENT="awk '{ print \"\t\t\t\" \$0 }'"
JOINLINES="tr '\n' '\040'"
```

Definitions of the two optional initialization files come next:

```
defaultdirectories=$BUILDHOME/directories
defaultuserhosts=$BUILDHOME/userhosts
```

The final initialization sets the list of source directories:

```
SRCDIRS="`$STRIPCOMMENTS $defaultdirectories 2> /dev/null`"
```

Since command substitution replaces newlines by spaces and collapses runs of whitespace, directories in the initialization file can be written one or more per line.

If the user customization file does not exist, STRIPCOMMENTS produces an empty string in SRCDIRS, so we test for that condition and reset SRCDIRS to a reasonable default list honed by years of experience:

```
test -z "$SRCDIRS" && \
    SRCDIRS="

            .
            /usr/local/src
            /usr/local/gnu/src
            $HOME/src
            $HOME/gnu/src
```

```
              /tmp
              /usr/tmp
              /var/tmp
         "
```

A backslash following the || and && operators at end-of-line is required for the C-shell family, and is harmless for the Bourne-shell family. The current directory (.) is a member of this list because we might have just downloaded to an arbitrary location a package that we want to try to build.

Now that initializations have been taken care of, we are ready to process the command-line options. This is done in much the same way in all shell scripts: while an argument remains, select a suitable branch of a case statement to process the argument, then shift the argument list down, and continue the loop. Any branch that needs to consume another argument first does a shift. As we have done before, we permit both single- and double-hyphen forms of options, and we allow them to be abbreviated to any unique prefix:

```
while test $# -gt 0
do
     case $1 in
```

The --all, --cd, --check, and --configure cases save the following argument, discarding any previously saved value:

```
         --all | --al | --a | -all | -al | -a )
             shift
             ALLTARGETS="$1"
             ;;

         --cd | -cd )
             shift
             CONFIGUREDIR="$1"
             ;;

         --check | chec | --che | --ch | -check | -chec | -chc | -ch )
             shift
             CHECKTARGETS="$1"
             ;;

         --configure | --configur | --configu | --config | --confi | \
         --conf | --con | --co | \
         -configure | -configur | -configu | -config | -confi | \
         -conf | -con | -co )
             shift
             CONFIGUREFLAGS="$1"
             ;;
```

The --environment option provides a way to supply one-time settings of configure-time environment variables on the build host, without having to change build configuration files:

```
         --environment | --environmen | --environme | --environm | --environ | \
         --enviro | --envir | --envi | --env | --en | --e | \
```

```
-environment | -environmen | -environme | -environm | -environ | \
-enviro | -envir | -envi | -env | -en | -e )
    shift
    EXTRAENVIRONMENT="$1"
    ;;
```

The --help case calls one of our yet-to-be-shown functions, and terminates the program:

```
--help | --hel | --he | --h | '--?' | -help | -hel | -he | -h | '-?' )
    usage_and_exit 0
    ;;
```

The --logdirectory case also saves the following argument, discarding any saved value:

```
--logdirectory | --logdirector | --logdirecto | --logdirect | \
--logdirec | --logdire | --logdir | --logdi | --logd | --log | \
--lo | --l | \
-logdirectory | -logdirector | -logdirecto | -logdirect | \
-logdirec | -logdire | -logdir | -logdi | -logd | -log | -lo | -l )
    shift
    altlogdir="$1"
    ;;
```

The altlogdir variable names the directory where all of the build log files are written, if the default location is not desired.

The --on and --source cases merely accumulate arguments, so the user can write -s "/this/dir /that/dir" or -s /this/dir -s /that/dir:

```
--on | --o | -on | -o )
    shift
    userhosts="$userhosts $1"
    ;;

--source | --sourc | --sour | --sou | --so | --s | \
-source | -sourc | -sour | -sou | -so | -s )
    shift
    altsrcdirs="$altsrcdirs $1"
    ;;
```

Because altsrcdirs separates list elements with a space, directories with spaces in their names will not be handled properly; avoid such names.

The --userhosts case also accumulates arguments, but with the additional convenience of checking an alternate directory location, so we relegate the work to a function:

```
--userhosts | --userhost | --userhos | --userho | --userh | \
--user | --use | --us | --u | \
-userhosts | -userhost | -userhos | -userho | -userh | \
-user | -use | -us | -u )
    shift
    set_userhosts $1
    ;;
```

The --version case displays a version number and exits with a success status code:

```
--version | --versio | --versi | --vers | --ver | --ve | --v | \
-version | -versio | -versi | -vers | -ver | -ve | -v )
    version
    exit 0
    ;;
```

The next-to-last case catches any unrecognized options and terminates with an error:

```
-*)
    error "Unrecognized option: $1"
    ;;
```

The last case matches anything but an option name, so it must be a package name, and we leave the option loop:

```
*)
    break
    ;;

esac
```

A shift discards the just-processed argument, and we continue with the next loop iteration:

```
    shift
done
```

We need a mail-client program to report log-file locations. Unfortunately, some systems have a low-level mail command that does not accept a subject line, but have a mailx command that does. Other systems lack mailx, but have subject-line support in mail. Still others have both, with one of them a link to the other. Because build-all must run on any flavor of Unix without changes, we cannot hardcode the preferred mail-client name. Instead, we have to search for it dynamically using a list that we found by examining about two dozen flavors of Unix:

```
for MAIL in /bin/mailx /usr/bin/mailx /usr/sbin/mailx /usr/ucb/mailx \
            /bin/mail /usr/bin/mail
do
    test -x $MAIL && break
done
test -x $MAIL || error "Cannot find mail client"
```

If the user supplied additional source directories, we put them at the front of the default list. The possibility of replacing the default list does not appear to have any value, so we don't provide a way to do so:

```
SRCDIRS="$altsrcdirs $SRCDIRS"
```

Correct setting of the final userhosts list is complex, and requires explanation. We have three potential sources of data for the list:

- Command-line --on options added their arguments to the userhosts variable.
- Command-line --userhosts options added files, each containing zero or more build-host specifications, to the ALTUSERHOSTS variable.

- The `defaultuserhosts` variable contains the name of a file that supplies default build-host specifications, to be used only when no command-line options provide them. For most invocations of `build-all`, this file supplies the complete build list.

If the userhosts variable contains data, then the contents of any files recorded in ALTUSERHOSTS must be added to it to obtain the final list:

```
if test -n "$userhosts"
then
    test -n "$ALTUSERHOSTS" &&
        userhosts="$userhosts `$STRIPCOMMENTS $ALTUSERHOSTS 2> /dev/null`"
```

Otherwise, the userhosts variable is empty, and there are still two possibilities. If ALTUSERHOSTS was set, we leave it untouched. If it was not set, we set it to the default file. Then we assign the contents of the files in ALTUSERHOSTS to the userhosts variable for the final list:

```
else
    test -z "$ALTUSERHOSTS" && ALTUSERHOSTS="$defaultuserhosts"
    userhosts="`$STRIPCOMMENTS $ALTUSERHOSTS 2> /dev/null`"
fi
```

Before we begin the real work, a sanity check is essential to ensure that we have at least one host. Although the inner loop would not be executed in such a case, we want to avoid unnecessary directory and log-file creation. If userhosts is empty, it was probably user error, so a reminder of how to use the program is called for:

```
test -z "$userhosts" && usage_and_exit 1
```

Here at last is the outer loop of the program, a loop over packages. The shell does not execute the loop body if the argument list is empty, which is exactly what we want. The loop is large enough that we present only a few lines at a time:

```
for p in "$@"
do
```

The work of locating the package archive in the source directory list is delegated to the find_package function, which leaves its results in global variables—among them, PARFILE (package archive file):

```
    find_package "$p"
```

If PARFILE is empty, we issue a complaint on standard error and continue with the next package:

```
    if test -z "$PARFILE"
    then
        warning "Cannot find package file $p"
        continue
    fi
```

Otherwise, if a log directory was not supplied, or was but is not a directory or is not writable, we attempt to create a subdirectory named logs underneath the directory where the package archive was found. If that directory cannot be found, or is not writable, then we try to put the logs under the user's `$HOME/.build/logs` directory, or else in a temporary directory. We prefer the less-volatile temporary directories over `/tmp`, which is usually lost at a reboot, so we use it only as a last resort:

```
LOGDIR="$altlogdir"
if test -z "$LOGDIR" -o ! -d "$LOGDIR" -o ! -w "$LOGDIR"
then
    for LOGDIR in "`dirname $PARFILE`/logs/$p" $BUILDHOME/logs/$p \
                    /usr/tmp /var/tmp /tmp
    do
        test -d "$LOGDIR" || mkdir -p "$LOGDIR" 2> /dev/null
        test -d "$LOGDIR" -a -w "$LOGDIR" && break
    done
fi
```

The `dirname` command is the companion to the `basename` command that we introduced in "Path Searching" [8.1]. `dirname` strips all characters in its argument from the final slash onward, recovering a directory path from a full pathname, and reports the result on standard output:

```
$ dirname /usr/local/bin/nawk          Report the directory path
/usr/local/bin
```

If the argument does not contain a slash, `dirname` produces a dot representing the current directory:

```
$ dirname whimsical-name               Report the directory path
.
```

Like `basename`, `dirname` treats its argument as a simple text string, without checking for its existence in the filesystem.

If the argument is omitted, `dirname`'s behavior is implementation-defined.

We tell the user where the logs are created, and record that location in email as well, because the user might forget the log location before the build of a large package completes:

```
msg="Check build logs for $p in `hostname`:$LOGDIR"
echo "$msg"
echo "$msg" | $MAIL -s "$msg" $USER 2> /dev/null
```

The final step in the main loop is a nested loop over the remote hosts to start building the current package on each of them in parallel. Once again, most of the work is relegated to a function. This also ends the outer loop:

```
for u in $userhosts
do
    build_one $u
done
done
```

The build_one invocations are done sequentially so we can more easily identify communications problems. However, the work that they start on the remote build hosts runs in the background on those systems, so build_one actually completes comparatively quickly.

At this point, the program has done its work. The last statements cap the cumulative status code at the limit of 125 and return the status code to the caller:

```
test $EXITCODE -gt 125 && EXITCODE=125
exit $EXITCODE
```

We have left several build processes running in the background, with their output accumulating in associated log files. We chose to exit anyway so that build-all runs quickly.

Some people might prefer an alternate design that does not return until all of the background processes have completed. The change is simple: immediately before the final exit statement, insert this statement:

```
wait
```

We don't find that approach useful because it either ties up a terminal window until all builds are complete, or if build-all is run in the background, its completion notice is likely to be mixed in with other output, and thus missed, when it appears much later.

Now that we have a general picture of how the program works, it is time to examine the details that are hidden inside the functions. We present them in order of use.

usage is a simple function: it prints a short help message on standard output, using a here document instead of a series of echo statements:

```
usage( )
{
    cat <<EOF
Usage:
        $PROGRAM [ --? ]
                        [ --all "..." ]
                        [ --cd "..." ]
                        [ --check "..." ]
                        [ --configure "..." ]
                        [ --environment "..." ]
                        [ --help ]
                        [ --logdirectory dir ]
                        [ --on "[user@]host[:dir][,envfile] ..." ]
                        [ --source "dir ..." ]
                        [ --userhosts "file(s)" ]
                        [ --version ]
                        package(s)
    EOF
}
```

usage_and_exit calls usage, and then exits with the status code supplied as its argument:

```
usage_and_exit()
{
    usage
    exit $1
}
```

version displays the version number on standard output:

```
version()
{
    echo "$PROGRAM version $VERSION"
}
```

error displays its arguments on standard error, follows them with the usage message, and then terminates the program with a failure status code:

```
error()
{
    echo "$@" 1>&2
    usage_and_exit 1
}
```

warning displays its arguments on standard error, increments the warning count in EXITCODE, and returns:

```
warning()
{
    echo "$@" 1>&2
    EXITCODE=`expr $EXITCODE + 1`
}
```

The outer loop in the main body began with a call to find_package. That function loops over the source directories, looking for the package, and handles details that we haven't discussed yet:

```
find_package()
{
    # Usage: find_package package-x.y.z
    base=`echo "$1" | sed -e 's/[-_][.]*[0-9].*$//'`
    PAR=
    PARFILE=
    for srcdir in $SRCDIRS
    do
        test "$srcdir" = "." && srcdir="`pwd`"

        for subdir in "$base" ""
        do
            # NB: update package setting in build_one() if this list changes
            find_file $srcdir/$subdir/$1.tar.gz  "tar xfz"    && return
            find_file $srcdir/$subdir/$1.tar.Z   "tar xfz"    && return
            find_file $srcdir/$subdir/$1.tar     "tar xf"     && return
            find_file $srcdir/$subdir/$1.tar.bz2 "tar xfj"    && return
            find_file $srcdir/$subdir/$1.tgz     "tar xfz"    && return
```

```
                find_file $srcdir/$subdir/$1.zip    "unzip -q"    && return
                find_file $srcdir/$subdir/$1.jar    "jar xf"      && return
        done
    done
}
```

It is evident from the inner loop body that find_package recognizes multiple archive formats, and that another function, find_file, is called upon to do the real work: when it succeeds, we can immediately return. In the second iteration of the inner loop, subdir is empty, and the pathnames have two consecutive slashes—but that is harmless, as discussed in "Filesystem Structure" in Appendix B. While this code has superficial similarity to the pathfind command in Example 8-1, here we need to look for several files in each directory, and do different things for each one.

We noted at the beginning of this section that the .tar.gz archive format is common. However, other compression and naming schemes are also found. tar is primarily a Unix command, and although implementations for other operating systems exist, they aren't included in standard distributions. The InfoZip format* was developed collaboratively with the goal of supporting compressed archives that can be used on any operating system, and Java jar† files also use the InfoZip format. The loop body in find_package handles all of them.

At a small site, it may be reasonable to store package archives in a single directory, such as /usr/local/src. However, as the archive collection grows, that organization soon becomes unwieldy. At our sites, each package is given its own source directory so, for example, the archive for Version 3.1.4 of gawk is stored in /usr/local/gnu/src/gawk/gawk-3.1.4.tar.gz, and the build logs for that version are stored in /usr/local/gnu/src/gawk/logs/gawk-3.1.4. A WHERE-FROM file in each package directory records the package's Internet master archive location, making it easy to check for newer releases. We generally keep the last few versions of each archive around, because they might be necessary someday to rebuild a package when the network is not available or the remote master archive site is not reachable. Thus, the loop body in find_package strips the version number from the package name, storing the result in base, and it first tries to find packages in $srcdir/$base before falling back to looking in $srcdir.

We have found it quite useful to retain build logs, since investigation of a bug that shows up long after installation may need details of which compiler and options were used. Also, with less-portable packages, it is often necessary to make minor tweaks to the build process, or even to source files, to get a build to complete. If that information is recorded in log files, it can save the installer time later when newer versions of those packages need to be built and installed.

---

* See *http://www.info-zip.org/*.

† jar files can contain checksums and digital signatures that can be used to detect file corruption and tampering, so they may become popular for general software distribution.

The find_file function is essentially just a readability and existence test for the package archive file, the recording of its arguments in two global variables, and the return of a status result. It simplifies the code in find_package considerably:

```
find_file()
{
    # Usage:
    #       find_file file program-and-args
    # Return 0 (success) if found, 1 (failure) if not found

    if test -r "$1"
    then
        PAR="$2"                          Program and arguments to use for extraction
        PARFILE="$1"                      Actual file to extract source from
        return 0
    else
        return 1
    fi
}
```

The set_userhosts function provides the convenience of allowing userhosts files to be specified with explicit paths, possibly relative to the current directory, or found in the $BUILDHOME initialization directory. This makes it convenient to create sets of build hosts grouped by compiler, platform, or package, in order to accommodate packages that are known to build only in certain limited environments. Any number of userhosts files can be provided, so we simply accumulate their names in ALTUSERHOSTS:

```
set_userhosts()
{
    # Usage: set_userhosts file(s)
    for u in "$@"
    do
        if test -r "$u"
        then
            ALTUSERHOSTS="$ALTUSERHOSTS $u"
        elif test -r "$BUILDHOME/$u"
        then
            ALTUSERHOSTS="$ALTUSERHOSTS $BUILDHOME/$u"
        else
            error "File not found: $u"
        fi
    done
}
```

The last function, build_one, is where the work for one package on one remote host is handled. It is long enough that we present it in parts:

```
build_one()
{
    # Usage:
    #       build_one [user@]host[:build-directory][,envfile]
```

Until now, apart from a brief mention in the comment banner, we have not precisely specified what is in the `$HOME/.build/userhosts` initialization file. We require up to four pieces of information: the username on the remote host (if different from that on the initiating host), the hostname itself, the name of the *existing* directory on the remote host where the build should take place, and possibly additional environment variable settings specific to this build. It isn't convenient in a shell script to maintain those pieces in separate lists, so we simply borrow syntax from the remote and secure shells and jam them together with separator characters, like this:

```
jones@freebsd.example.com:/local/build,$HOME/.build/c99
```

Only the hostname component is mandatory.

We need the parts as well, so we use `echo` and `sed` to split the argument apart. Passing the argument through `eval` expands any environment variables in the name (like `HOME` in `$HOME/.build/c99`), avoiding the need to hardcode system-specific login directory paths in the userhosts files. For convenience, we provide a default build directory of `/tmp` if one was not specified:

```
arg="`eval echo $1`"                                    Expand env vars

userhost="`echo $arg | sed -e 's/:.*$//'`"              Remove colon and
                                                        everything after it

user="`echo $userhost | sed -e s'/@.*$//'`"             Extract username
test "$user" = "$userhost" && user=$USER                Use $USER if empty

host="`echo $userhost | sed -e s'/^[^@]*@//'`"          Extract host part

envfile="`echo $arg | sed -e 's/^[^,]*,//'`"            Name of env vars file
test "$envfile" = "$arg" && envfile=/dev/null

builddir="`echo $arg | sed -e 's/^.*://' -e 's/,.*//'`"  Build directory
test "$builddir" = "$arg" && builddir=/tmp
```

We would prefer one of the nonvolatile temporary directories for `builddir`, but Unix vendors disagree on what they are called. A few extra lines of code could make a suitable test, but we assume that most users will specify a sensible build directory. Besides the fact that `/tmp` is usually cleared upon a reboot, there are other reasons why `/tmp` is *not* a good choice for `builddir`:

- On many systems, `/tmp` is a separate filesystem that is too small to hold the build tree for a large package.

- On some systems, `/tmp` is mounted without permission to execute programs in it: that may cause `configure` tests and validation checks to fail.

- Under several releases of Sun Solaris, for unknown reasons native compilers could not compile code in `/tmp`.

The `envfile` facility is essential: it allows us to override defaults chosen by `configure`. Software developers should test their code with as many compilers as possible to verify portability and ferret out bugs. By choosing different build directories and envfile values, we can do multiple simultaneous builds on the same host with different compilers. The envfile files are quite simple: they just set environment variables, like this:

```
$ cat $HOME/.build/c99
CC=c99
CXX=CC
```

The next step in our program is to save the bare filename (e.g., gawk-3.1.4.tar.gz) in the variable parbase:

```
parbase=`basename $PARFILE`
```

The package name (e.g., gawk-3.1.4) is saved in the variable package:

```
package="`echo $parbase | \
        sed     -e 's/[.]jar$//' \
                -e 's/[.]tar[.]bz2$//' \
                -e 's/[.]tar[.]gz$//' \
                -e 's/[.]tar[.]Z$//' \
                -e 's/[.]tar$//' \
                -e 's/[.]tgz$//' \
                -e 's/[.]zip$//'`"
```

We use explicit sed patterns to strip the suffixes: there are too many dots in the name to make a simpler pattern reliable. To ensure that they work with older sed implementations, we specify them in separate substitution commands, instead of in a single extended regular expression. Should support for new archive formats ever be added to find_package, these editor patterns need to be updated as well.

The next step is to copy the archive file to the build directory on the remote host, unless it can already be seen on that system, perhaps via filesystem mounting or mirroring. That is common at our sites, so the check saves time and disk space.

Although we usually avoid writing chatty programs, the echo command before each communication with a remote system is intentional: it gives the user essential feedback. The remote copy can be time-consuming and can fail or hang: without that feedback, the user has no simple way to tell why the script is taking unexpectedly long, or what host is responsible for the failure. The parbaselocal variable serves to distinguish between a temporary copy of the archive file and a preexisting one:

```
echo $SSH $SSHFLAGS $userhost "test -f $PARFILE"
if $SSH $SSHFLAGS $userhost "test -f $PARFILE"
then
    parbaselocal=$PARFILE
else
    parbaselocal=$parbase
    echo $SCP $PARFILE $userhost:$builddir
    $SCP $PARFILE $userhost:$builddir
fi
```

Ideally, we should use a pipeline to do the unbundling, since that halves the amount of input/output, and also the disk space requirements. Alas, only jar and tar can read their archives that way: unzip requires an actual file. In principle, jar can read an InfoZip file, allowing us to replace unzip with jar and use the pipeline. Unfortunately, at the time of this writing, jar is still immature, and we have found at least one implementation that chokes on a .zip file.

Observe that the remote copies are done sequentially, rather than in parallel. The latter would be possible, but at the expense of extra complexity in the main body, which would have to first find and distribute packages, wait for their distribution to complete, and then build them. However, the build time is usually much longer than the remote copy time, so sequential copies do not contribute much to the total runtime.

Our log files are named with the package, remote host, and a timestamp with one-second resolution. If multiple builds are done on a single remote host, then we risk a filename collision. Using the process ID variable, $$, in the log filenames does not provide a solution because it is constant within the single invocation of build-all. We could use $$ to initialize a counter that is incremented with each build and used in the log filenames, but that would simply clutter the filenames with a meaningless number. The solution is to guarantee that at least one second elapses between the creation of two successive log files: sleep is just what we need. GNU date offers a %N (nanoseconds) format item that should suffice to generate unique filenames, allowing us to do away with sleep, but POSIX and older date implementations lack that format item. In the interests of maximal portability, we rest for a second:

```
sleep 1
now="`date $DATEFLAGS`"
logfile="$package.$host.$now.log"
```

We have now come to the last part of this exposition: the lengthy commands to carry out the build on the remote host. $SSH is prefixed with the nice command to lower its priority, reducing competition with interactive jobs on the system. Even though most of the work happens on the remote system, build logs are sometimes large, giving $SSH more to do.

Notice that the second argument to $SSH is a long string delimited with double quotes. Inside that string, variables prefixed with a dollar sign are expanded *in the context of the script*, and need *not* be known on the remote host.

The command syntax that we need in the $SSH argument string depends on the user's login shell on the remote host. We carefully restrict the syntax to work in all common Unix shells so that build-all works for any user, including users with different login shells on different hosts. We cannot demand the same login shell everywhere, because on many systems, users cannot choose their login shells. The alternative would be to pipe the command stream into the Bourne shell on each host, but that would start yet another process for each build, and get us into an even deeper quoting mess: dealing with three shells at a time is already hard enough.

```
nice $SSH $SSHFLAGS $userhost "
    echo '=======================================================' ;
```

The $BUILDBEGIN script is executed, if it exists, on the remote system in the context of the login shell early in the command sequence. It can provide login customizations, such as augmenting PATH when shell startup files cannot do this (e.g., for ksh and sh). It can also write additional information to standard error or standard output, and thus, to the build-log file. Shells in the Bourne-shell family use the dot command to execute commands in the current shell, whereas shells in the C-shell family use the source command. The bash and zsh shells support both commands.

Unfortunately, some shells, including the POSIX one, abort execution of the dot command if the specified file does not exist. This makes simple code like . $BUILDBEGIN || true fail, despite the use of the true command at the end of the conditional. We therefore also need a file-existence test, and we have to handle the source command as well. Because two shells recognize both the dot command and the source command, we must do this in a single complex command that relies on the equal precedence of the Boolean operators:

```
test -f $BUILDBEGIN && . $BUILDBEGIN || \
    test -f $BUILDBEGIN && source $BUILDBEGIN || \
        true ;
```

We are not happy with the complexity of this statement, but the severe design requirement that build-all must work for all login shells forces it upon us, and we could find no acceptable simpler solution.

We assume that the startup script has been debugged before build-all is used. Otherwise, if execution of the $BUILDBEGIN script terminates with an error, there may be two attempts to execute it.

Based on long experience, we find it useful to record extra information in the build logs, so there are a score of echo commands for that purpose, carefully formatted for better log-file readability:

```
echo 'Package:                $package' ;
echo 'Archive:                $PARFILE' ;
echo 'Date:                   $now' ;
echo 'Local user:             $USER' ;
echo 'Local host:             `hostname`' ;
echo 'Local log directory:    $LOGDIR' ;
echo 'Local log file:         $logfile' ;
echo 'Remote user:            $user' ;
echo 'Remote host:            $host' ;
echo 'Remote directory:       $builddir' ;
```

It is also sometimes useful to know how long a build takes (on one of our older systems, the GNU C compiler build takes nearly a day), so the script reports before and after dates. These are obtained on the remote host, which might be in a different time zone, or suffer from clock skew, and it may be important later to match timestamps of installed files with entries in the build logs. There is no portable way to use echo to generate a partial line, so we use printf:

```
printf 'Remote date:           ' ;
date $DATEFLAGS ;
```

Similarly, we record system and GNU compiler version information, since that may be needed in bug reports:

```
printf 'Remote uname:           ' ;
uname -a || true ;
printf 'Remote gcc version:      ' ;
gcc --version | head -n 1 || echo ;
printf 'Remote g++ version:      ' ;
g++ --version | head -n 1 || echo ;
```

There is no common way with other compilers to get version information, so we cannot handle that task in build-all. Instead, we can produce any desired reports from suitable commands in the $BUILDBEGIN script. Our script continues, providing additional information:

```
echo 'Configure environment:  `$STRIPCOMMENTS $envfile | $JOINLINES`' ;
echo 'Extra environment:      $EXTRAENVIRONMENT' ;
echo 'Configure directory:    $CONFIGUREDIR' ;
echo 'Configure flags:        $CONFIGUREFLAGS' ;
echo 'Make all targets:       $ALLTARGETS' ;
echo 'Make check targets:     $CHECKTARGETS' ;
```

Running out of disk space has proven to be a common cause of failures, so we use df to report on the available space before and after the build:

```
echo 'Disk free report for $builddir/$package:' ;
df $builddir | $INDENT ;
```

configure and make can be influenced by environment variables, so we finish off the log-file header with a sorted list of them:

```
echo 'Environment:' ;
env | env LC_ALL=C sort | $INDENT ;
echo '=====================================================' ;
```

The env command in the middle stage of the pipeline ensures that the script works properly with all shells, including the C-shell family.

We set the permission mask on the remote system, as we did on the local one, to allow full access for the group and read access for other:

```
umask $UMASK ;
```

The package archive file is already resident in the build directory, so we change to that directory, exiting with an error if cd fails:

```
cd $builddir || exit 1 ;
```

Next, we remove any old archive tree. We use an absolute path for rm because these commands are executed in the context of an interactive shell, and some sites have that command aliased to include the interactive option, -i:

```
/bin/rm -rf $builddir/$package ;
```

Builds sometimes have to be redone with changes to compilers and/or compilation options, so the recursive removal is essential to ensure that we start with a clean distribution. The -f option on the rm command silences any complaints about a nonexistent directory tree.

A recursive file-tree removal is a dangerous action and a target for attack. Because package was obtained from a trusted basename command, we can be confident that it contains no slashes, and thus, can refer only to the current directory. Adding $builddir/ to the argument of rm offers a small margin of safety, but not much, since either builddir or package could still be set to a dot, meaning the current directory.

The situation really reduces to a matter of trust, and there does not appear to be much else that we can do to protect you, other than warn of the danger. Certainly, this program should *never* be executed by the root user. That could be discouraged by statements like this near the start of the script:

```
test "`id -u`" -eq 0 && \
    error For security reasons, this program must NOT be run by root
```

Among all of our systems, only Sun Solaris id lacks support for the –u option, but we set PATH to find the GNU *coreutils* version of id first.

 You should generally ignore package installation instructions that tell you to build and install software under the root account: there are *extremely few* packages that require such privileges, and even then, only the installation step should need root access.

Next, we unpack the archive:

```
$PAR $parbaselocal ;
```

It is important to realize that $PAR is expanded on the initiating host, but run on the remote host. In particular, we have assumed that tar is the GNU version that supports the –j and –z options, and that unzip and jar are available. Each user of this script is expected to have shell startup files appropriately set on each remote host to ensure that these programs can be found. We cannot supply fixed paths to these programs because the paths may be different on each remote host.

If the archive was copied to the remote host, then parbaselocal and parbase have identical values, and since the package archive file is no longer needed on the remote host, we remove it:

```
test "$parbase" = "$parbaselocal" && /bin/rm -f $parbase ;
```

We are ready to change to the package directory and start the build. For software packages that follow the widely used GNU Project conventions, that directory is the top-level package directory. Unfortunately, some packages bury the build directory deeper in the file-tree, among them, the widely used Tcl and Tk tools for scripting and fast window-system interface construction. The command-line --cd option supplies a relative path to the build directory that is saved in CONFIGUREDIR, overriding its default value of dot (the current directory). We therefore need both the package variable and the CONFIGUREDIR variable to change to the build directory, and if that fails, we exit with an error:

```
cd $package/$CONFIGUREDIR || exit 1 ;
```

Many packages now come with configure scripts, so we test for one, and if it is found, we execute it with any additional environment variables supplied by envfile. We also pass on any additional flags supplied by a --configure option. Most packages do not require such flags, but some of the more complex ones often do:

```
test -f configure && \
    chmod a+x configure && \
        env `$STRIPCOMMENTS $envfile | $JOINLINES` \
            $EXTRAENVIRONMENT \
                nice time ./configure $CONFIGUREFLAGS ;
```

The chmod command to add execute permission is there for two reasons: first, because we have occasionally encountered package archives where that permission is lacking, and second, because current implementations of the Java jar archive format neglect to record that permission.[*] The nice command prefix lowers the job priority so that it has minimal impact on the remote system. The time command prefix reports the time for configure to run. We have seen some monster configuration scripts, so it is helpful to record their runtimes to allow estimation of build times for later versions.

We now come to where most of the work happens: the actual build and validation of the package, again with a nice time prefix, and make arguments supplied by --all and --check options (or their defaults):

```
nice time make $ALLTARGETS && nice time make $CHECKTARGETS ;
```

The make commands hide a lot of work, but the rules for carrying out that work have already been written down by the developers in the Makefile, so end installers usually need not be concerned with it.

What we expect to see in the log files on completion of a successful build is a report like All tests passed!, or some other easily understood report that all is well. The validation tests are *exceedingly important*, and should never be skipped. Even if the package worked correctly at its development sites, there is no reason to believe that it

---

[*] That certainly seems like a design flaw, since the underlying InfoZip format supports it.

will at ours because there are so many things that can go wrong: differences in architectures, compilers, environment variables, filesystems, local customizations and tuning; operating system releases; search paths; shared libraries; system header files; X Window System defaults; and so on, can all contribute to failures.

We are now ready to wrap up the remote commands, with just a few extra lines of final reports for the log files:

```
echo '=====================================================' ;
echo 'Disk free report for $builddir/$package:' ;
df $builddir | $INDENT ;
printf 'Remote date:              ' ;
date $DATEFLAGS ;
```

As with the $BUILDBEGIN script, the $BUILDEND script under the home directory provides for any final additional log-file reporting, but true ensures success:

```
cd ;
test -f $BUILDEND && . $BUILDEND || \
    test -f $BUILDEND && source $BUILDEND || \
        true ;
echo '=====================================================' ;
```

The last two lines of the build_one function close off the list of remote commands and the function body, redirect both standard output and standard error to the log file, and importantly, run the remote commands in the background so that execution can immediately continue in the inner loop of the main body. The remote shell's input is redirected to the null device so it does not hang waiting for user input:

```
    " < /dev/null > "$LOGDIR/$logfile" 2>&1 &
}
```

A program of this size and power certainly requires online documentation. Space does not permit us to present the manual pages for build-all here, but both the script and its manual-page file are available at this book's web site.

The complete script, with a few comments that we omitted in our piecewise presentation, and reordering to put the functions in alphabetical order near the beginning, is collected in Example 8-2. Although it is about 320 lines long (ignoring comments and blank lines), the payoff for our programming investment is substantial. Once a new distribution of a package has been fetched to the local system, a one-line command starts the build and validation on all of the build hosts in parallel. After a suitable wait, the installer can then check the build logs for their success or failure and decide on which machines it is safe to run make install to install the software on the system, after which the build directory can be removed from the remote system.

Build failures that are not attributable to local errors can, and should, be reported to the package developers. Few developers have access to a wide range of platforms, so it is only from installer feedback that they can make their packages more portable and more robust. Before doing so, however, it is always a good idea to check the release notes for the package (typically in files named BUGS, FAQ, INSTALL, PROBLEMS, or README) to find out whether the problem that you discovered has already been reported, but is just not fixed yet. The software model where developers get rapid installer feedback has proven to be extremely productive, and Eric Raymond has written about it in an interesting extended essay in book form.[*]

Example 8-2. The build-all program

```
#! /bin/sh -
# Build one or more packages in parallel on one or more build hosts.
#
# Usage:
#       build-all [ --? ]
#                 [ --all "..." ]
#                 [ --check "..." ]
#                 [ --configure "..." ]
#                 [ --environment "..." ]
#                 [ --help ]
#                 [ --logdirectory dir ]
#                 [ --on "[user@]host[:dir][,envfile] ..." ]
#                 [ --source "dir ..." ]
#                 [ --userhosts "file(s)" ]
#                 [ --version ]
#                 package(s)
#
# Optional initialization files:
#       $HOME/.build/directories    list of source directories
#       $HOME/.build/userhosts      list of [user@]host[:dir][,envfile]

IFS='
'

PATH=/usr/local/bin:/bin:/usr/bin
export PATH

UMASK=002
umask $UMASK

build_one()
{
    # Usage:
    #       build_one [user@]host[:build-directory][,envfile]
```

---

[*] *The Cathedral and the Bazaar: Musings on Linux and Open Source by an Accidental Revolutionary* (O'Reilly).

Example 8-2. The build-all program (continued)

```
arg="`eval echo $1`"

userhost="`echo $arg | sed -e 's/:.*$//'`"

user="`echo $userhost | sed -e s'/@.*$//'`"
test "$user" = "$userhost" && user=$USER

host="`echo $userhost | sed -e s'/^[^@]*@//'`"

envfile="`echo $arg | sed -e 's/^[^,]*,//'`"
test "$envfile" = "$arg" && envfile=/dev/null

builddir="`echo $arg | sed -e s'/^.*://' -e 's/,.*//'`"
test "$builddir" = "$arg" && builddir=/tmp

parbase=`basename $PARFILE`

# NB: update find_package( ) if these patterns are changed
package="`echo $parbase | \
        sed     -e 's/[.]jar$//' \
                -e 's/[.]tar[.]bz2$//' \
                -e 's/[.]tar[.]gz$//' \
                -e 's/[.]tar[.]Z$//' \
                -e 's/[.]tar$//' \
                -e 's/[.]tgz$//' \
                -e 's/[.]zip$//'`"

# Copy the package file if we cannot see it on the remote host
echo $SSH $SSHFLAGS $userhost "test -f $PARFILE"
if $SSH $SSHFLAGS $userhost "test -f $PARFILE"
then
    parbaselocal=$PARFILE
else
    parbaselocal=$parbase
    echo $SCP $PARFILE $userhost:$builddir
    $SCP $PARFILE $userhost:$builddir
fi

# Unbundle the archive file on the remote host, build, and
# check it, running in the background

sleep 1         # to guarantee unique log filename
now="`date $DATEFLAGS`"
logfile="$package.$host.$now.log"
nice $SSH $SSHFLAGS $userhost "
    echo '====================================================' ;
    test -f $BUILDBEGIN && . $BUILDBEGIN || \
        test -f $BUILDBEGIN && source $BUILDBEGIN || \
            true ;
    echo 'Package:                $package' ;
    echo 'Archive:                $PARFILE' ;
```

Example 8-2. The build-all program (continued)

```
        echo 'Date:                    $now' ;
        echo 'Local user:              $USER' ;
        echo 'Local host:              `hostname`' ;
        echo 'Local log directory:     $LOGDIR' ;
        echo 'Local log file:          $logfile' ;
        echo 'Remote user:             $user' ;
        echo 'Remote host:             $host' ;
        echo 'Remote directory:        $builddir' ;
        printf 'Remote date:             ' ;
        date $DATEFLAGS ;
        printf 'Remote uname:            ' ;
        uname -a || true ;
        printf 'Remote gcc version:      ' ;
        gcc --version | head -n 1 || echo ;
        printf 'Remote g++ version:      ' ;
        g++ --version | head -n 1 || echo ;
        echo 'Configure environment:  `$STRIPCOMMENTS $envfile | $JOINLINES`' ;
        echo 'Extra environment:       $EXTRAENVIRONMENT' ;
        echo 'Configure directory:     $CONFIGUREDIR' ;
        echo 'Configure flags:         $CONFIGUREFLAGS' ;
        echo 'Make all targets:        $ALLTARGETS' ;
        echo 'Make check targets:      $CHECKTARGETS' ;
        echo 'Disk free report for $builddir/$package:' ;
        df $builddir | $INDENT ;
        echo 'Environment:' ;
        env | env LC_ALL=C sort | $INDENT ;
        echo '=======================================================' ;
        umask $UMASK ;
        cd $builddir || exit 1 ;
        /bin/rm -rf $builddir/$package ;
        $PAR $parbaselocal ;
        test "$parbase" = "$parbaselocal" && /bin/rm -f $parbase ;
        cd $package/$CONFIGUREDIR || exit 1 ;
        test -f configure && \
            chmod a+x configure && \
                env `$STRIPCOMMENTS $envfile | $JOINLINES` \
                    $EXTRAENVIRONMENT \
                        nice time ./configure $CONFIGUREFLAGS ;
        nice time make $ALLTARGETS && nice time make $CHECKTARGETS ;
        echo '=======================================================' ;
        echo 'Disk free report for $builddir/$package:' ;
        df $builddir | $INDENT ;
        printf 'Remote date:             ' ;
        date $DATEFLAGS ;
        cd ;
        test -f $BUILDEND && . $BUILDEND || \
            test -f $BUILDEND && source $BUILDEND || \
                true ;
        echo '=======================================================' ;
    " < /dev/null > "$LOGDIR/$logfile" 2>&1 &
}
```

Example 8-2. The build-all program (continued)

```
error( )
{
    echo "$@" 1>&2
    usage_and_exit 1
}

find_file( )
{
    # Usage:
    #      find_file file program-and-args
    # Return 0 (success) if found, 1 (failure) if not found

    if test -r "$1"
    then
        PAR="$2"
        PARFILE="$1"
        return 0
    else
        return 1
    fi
}

find_package( )
{
    # Usage: find_package package-x.y.z
    base=`echo "$1" | sed -e 's/[-_][.]*[0-9].*$//'`
    PAR=
    PARFILE=
    for srcdir in $SRCDIRS
    do
        test "$srcdir" = "." && srcdir-"`pwd`"

        for subdir in "$base" ""
        do
            # NB: update package setting in build_one( ) if this list changes
            find_file $srcdir/$subdir/$1.tar.gz  "tar xfz"   && return
            find_file $srcdir/$subdir/$1.tar.Z   "tar xfz"   && return
            find_file $srcdir/$subdir/$1.tar     "tar xf"    && return
            find_file $srcdir/$subdir/$1.tar.bz2 "tar xfj"   && return
            find_file $srcdir/$subdir/$1.tgz     "tar xfz"   && return
            find_file $srcdir/$subdir/$1.zip     "unzip -q"  && return
            find_file $srcdir/$subdir/$1.jar     "jar xf"    && return
        done
    done
}

set_userhosts( )
{
    # Usage: set_userhosts file(s)
    for u in "$@"
    do
        if test -r "$u"
```

Example 8-2. The build-all program (continued)

```
        then
            ALTUSERHOSTS="$ALTUSERHOSTS $u"
        elif test -r "$BUILDHOME/$u"
        then
            ALTUSERHOSTS="$ALTUSERHOSTS $BUILDHOME/$u"
        else
            error "File not found: $u"
        fi
    done
}

usage()
{
    cat <<EOF
Usage:
        $PROGRAM [ --? ]
                        [ --all "..." ]
                        [ --check "..." ]
                        [ --configure "..." ]
                        [ --environment "..." ]
                        [ --help ]
                        [ --logdirectory dir ]
                        [ --on "[user@]host[:dir][,envfile] ..." ]
                        [ --source "dir ..." ]
                        [ --userhosts "file(s)" ]
                        [ --version ]
                        package(s)
EOF
}

usage_and_exit()
{
    usage
    exit $1
}

version()
{
    echo "$PROGRAM version $VERSION"
}

warning()
{
    echo "$@" 1>&2
    EXITCODE=`expr $EXITCODE + 1`
}

ALLTARGETS=
altlogdir=
altsrcdirs=
ALTUSERHOSTS=
BUILDBEGIN=./.build/begin
```

Example 8-2. The build-all program (continued)

```
BUILDEND=./.build/end
BUILDHOME=$HOME/.build
CHECKTARGETS=check
CONFIGUREDIR=.
CONFIGUREFLAGS=
DATEFLAGS="+%Y.%m.%d.%H.%M.%S"
EXITCODE=0
EXTRAENVIRONMENT=
INDENT="awk '{ print \"\t\t\t\" \$0 }'"
JOINLINES="tr '\n' '\040'"
LOGDIR=
PROGRAM=`basename $0`
SCP=scp
SSH=ssh
SSHFLAGS=${SSHFLAGS--x}
STRIPCOMMENTS='sed -e s/#.*$//'
userhosts=
VERSION=1.0

# Default initialization files
defaultdirectories=$BUILDHOME/directories
defaultuserhosts=$BUILDHOME/userhosts

# List of places to find package distributions, with a default
# list if the user has no personalized list:
SRCDIRS="`$STRIPCOMMENTS $defaultdirectories 2> /dev/null`"
test -z "$SRCDIRS" && \
    SRCDIRS="
            .
            /usr/local/src
            /usr/local/gnu/src
            $HOME/src
            $HOME/gnu/src
            /tmp
            /usr/tmp
            /var/tmp
        "

while test $# -gt 0
do
    case $1 in

    --all | --al | --a | -all | -al | -a )
        shift
        ALLTARGETS="$1"
        ;;

    --cd | -cd )
        shift
        CONFIGUREDIR="$1"
        ;;
```

Example 8-2. The build-all program (continued)

```
--check | --chec | --che | --ch | -check | -chec | -che | -ch )
    shift
    CHECKTARGETS="$1"
    ;;

--configure | --configur | --configu | --config | --confi | \
--conf | --con | --co | \
-configure | -configur | -configu | -config | -confi | \
-conf | -con | -co )
    shift
    CONFIGUREFLAGS="$1"
    ;;

--environment | --environmen | --environme | --environm | --environ | \
--enviro | --envir | --envi | --env | --en | --e | \
-environment | -environmen | -environme | -environm | -environ | \
-enviro | -envir | -envi | -env | -en | -e )
    shift
    EXTRAENVIRONMENT="$1"
    ;;

--help | --hel | --he | --h | '--?' | -help | -hel | -he | -h | '-?' )
    usage_and_exit 0
    ;;

--logdirectory | --logdirector | --logdirecto | --logdirect | \
--logdirec | --logdire | --logdir | --logdi | --logd | --log | \
--lo | --l | \
-logdirectory | -logdirector | -logdirecto | -logdirect | \
-logdirec | -logdire | -logdir | -logdi | -logd | -log | -lo | -l )
    shift
    altlogdir="$1"
    ;;

--on | --o | -on | -o )
    shift
    userhosts="$userhosts $1"
    ;;

--source | --sourc | --sour | --sou | --so | --s | \
-source | -sourc | -sour | -sou | -so | -s )
    shift
    altsrcdirs="$altsrcdirs $1"
    ;;

--userhosts | --userhost | --userhos | --userho | --userh | \
--user | --use | --us | --u | \
-userhosts | -userhost | -userhos | -userho | -userh | \
-user | -use | -us | -u )
    shift
    set_userhosts $1
    ;;
```

Example 8-2. The build-all program (continued)

```
    --version | --versio | --versi | --vers | --ver | --ve | --v | \
    -version | -versio | -versi | -vers | -ver | -ve | -v )
        version
        exit 0
        ;;

    -*)
        error "Unrecognized option: $1"
        ;;

    *)
        break
        ;;

    esac
    shift
done

# Find a suitable mail client
for MAIL in /bin/mailx /usr/bin/mailx /usr/sbin/mailx /usr/ucb/mailx \
            /bin/mail /usr/bin/mail
do
    test -x $MAIL && break
done
test -x $MAIL || error "Cannot find mail client"

# Command-line source directories precede defaults
SRCDIRS="$altsrcdirs $SRCDIRS"

if      test -n "$userhosts"
then
    test -n "$ALTUSERHOSTS" &&
        userhosts="$userhosts `$STRIPCOMMENTS $ALTUSERHOSTS 2> /dev/null`"
else
    test -z "$ALTUSERHOSTS" && ALTUSERHOSTS="$defaultuserhosts"
    userhosts="`$STRIPCOMMENTS $ALTUSERHOSTS 2> /dev/null`"
fi

# Check for something to do
test -z "$userhosts" && usage_and_exit 1

for p in "$@"
do
    find_package "$p"

    if test -z "$PARFILE"
    then
        warning "Cannot find package file $p"
        continue
    fi

    LOGDIR="$altlogdir"
```

Example 8-2. The build-all program (continued)

```
        if test -z "$LOGDIR" -o ! -d "$LOGDIR" -o ! -w "$LOGDIR"
        then
            for LOGDIR in "`dirname $PARFILE`/logs/$p" $BUILDHOME/logs/$p \
                            /usr/tmp /var/tmp /tmp
            do
                test -d "$LOGDIR" || mkdir -p "$LOGDIR" 2> /dev/null
                test -d "$LOGDIR" -a -w "$LOGDIR" && break
            done
        fi

        msg="Check build logs for $p in `hostname`:$LOGDIR"
        echo "$msg"
        echo "$msg" | $MAIL -s "$msg" $USER 2> /dev/null

        for u in $userhosts
        do
            build_one $u
        done
    done

# Limit exit status to common Unix practice
test $EXITCODE -gt 125 && EXITCODE=125

exit $EXITCODE
```

8.3   Summary

In this chapter, we have written two useful tools that do not already exist on Unix systems, using shell statements and existing standard tools to carry out the task. Neither of them is particularly time-consuming to run, so there is little temptation to rewrite them in a programming language like C or C++. As shell scripts, they can be run without change on almost any modern Unix platform.

Both programs support command-line options, cleanly processed by while and case statements. Both use shell functions to simplify processing and prevent unnecessary code duplication. Both pay attention to security issues and perform sanity checks on their arguments and variables.

## CHAPTER 9

Enough awk to Be Dangerous

The awk programming language was designed to simplify many common text processing tasks. In this chapter, we present a subset that suffices for most of the shell scripts that we use in this book.

For an extended treatment of the awk language, consult any of the books on awk listed in the Bibliography. If GNU gawk is installed on your system, then its manual should be available in the online info system.[*]

All Unix systems have at least one awk implementation. When the language was significantly extended in the mid-1980s, some vendors kept the old implementation as awk, and sometimes also as oawk, and then named the new one nawk. IBM AIX and Sun Solaris both continue that practice, but most others now provide only the new one. Solaris has a POSIX-compliant version in /usr/xpg4/bin/awk. In this book, we consider only the extended language and refer to it as awk, even though you might have to use nawk, gawk, or mawk on your system.

We must confess here to a strong bias about awk. We like it. A lot. We have implemented, maintained, ported, written about, and used the language for many years. Even though many awk programs are short, some of our larger awk programs are thousands of lines long. The simplicity and power of awk often make it just the right tool for the job, and we seldom encounter a text processing task in which we need a feature that is not already in the language, or cannot be readily implemented. When we have on occasion rewritten an awk program in a conventional programming language like C or C++, the result was usually much longer, and much harder to debug, even if it did run somewhat faster.

Unlike most other scripting languages, awk enjoys multiple implementations, a healthy situation that encourages adherence to a common language base and that

---

[*] The GNU documentation reader, info, is part of the *texinfo* package available at *ftp://ftp.gnu.org/gnu/texinfo/*. The emacs text editor also can be used to access the same documentation: type Ctrl-H i in an emacs session to get started.

permits users to switch freely from one to another. Also, unlike other scripting languages, awk is part of POSIX, and there are implementations for non-Unix operating systems.

If your local version of awk is substandard, get one of the free implementations listed in Table 9-1. All of these programs are very portable and easy to install. gawk has served as a testbed for several interesting new built-in functions and language features, including network I/O, and also for profiling, internationalization, and portability checking.

Table 9-1. Freely available awk versions

Program	Location
Bell Labs awk	*http://cm.bell-labs.com/who/bwk/awk.tar.gz*
gawk	*ftp://ftp.gnu.org/gnu/gawk/*
mawk	*ftp://ftp.whidbey.net/pub/brennan/mawk-1.3.3.tar.gz*
awka	*http://awka.sourceforge.net/* (awk-to-C translator)

9.1   The awk Command Line

An awk invocation can define variables, supply the program, and name the input files:

```
awk [ -F fs ] [ -v var=value ... ] 'program' [ -- ] \
    [ var=value ... ] [ file(s) ]

awk [ -F fs ] [ -v var=value ... ] -f programfile [ -- ] \
    [ var=value ... ] [ file(s) ]
```

Short programs are usually provided directly on the command line, whereas longer ones are relegated to files selected by the -f option. That option may be repeated, in which case the complete program is the concatenation of the specified program files. This is a convenient way to include libraries of shared awk code. Another approach to library inclusion is to use the igawk program, which is part of the gawk distribution. Options must precede filenames and ordinary *var=value* assignments.

If no filenames are specified on the command line, awk reads from standard input.

The -- option is special: it indicates that there are no further command-line options for awk itself. Any following options are then available to your program.

The -F option redefines the default field separator, and it is conventional to make it the first command-line option. Its *fs* argument is a regular expression that immediately follows the -F, or is supplied as the next argument. The field separator can also be set with an assignment to the built-in variable FS (see Table 9-3 in "Scalar Variables," later in this chapter):

```
awk -F '\t' '{ ... }' files FS="[\f\v]" files
```

Here, the value set with the -F option applies to the first group of files, and the value assigned to FS applies to the second group.

Initializations with -v options must precede any program given directly on the command line; they take effect before the program is started, and before any files are processed. A -v option after a command-line program is interpreted as a (probably nonexistent) filename.

Initializations elsewhere on the command line are done as the arguments are processed, and may be interspersed with filenames. For example:

```
awk '{...}' Pass=1 *.tex Pass=2 *.tex
```

processes the list of files twice, once with Pass set to one and a second time with it set to two.

Initializations with string values need not be quoted unless the shell requires such quoting to protect special characters or whitespace.

The special filename - (hyphen) represents standard input. Most modern awk implementations, but not POSIX, also recognize the special name /dev/stdin for standard input, even when the host operating system does not support that filename. Similarly, /dev/stderr and /dev/stdout are available for use within awk programs to refer to standard error and standard output.

9.2 The awk Programming Model

awk views an input stream as a collection of *records*, each of which can be further subdivided into *fields*. Normally, a record is a line, and a field is a word of one or more nonwhitespace characters. However, what constitutes a record and a field is entirely under the control of the programmer, and their definitions can even be changed during processing.

An awk program consists of pairs of patterns and braced actions, possibly supplemented by functions that implement the details of the actions. For each pattern that matches the input, the action is executed, and all patterns are examined for every input record.

Either part of a pattern/action pair may be omitted. If the pattern is omitted, the action is applied to every input record. If the action is omitted, the default action is to print the matching record on standard output. Here is the typical layout of an awk program:

```
pattern  { action }              Run action if pattern matches
pattern                          Print record if pattern matches
         { action }              Run action for every record
```

Input is switched automatically from one input file to the next, and awk itself normally handles the opening, reading, and closing of each input file, allowing the user program to concentrate on record processing. The code details are presented later in "Patterns and Actions" [9.5].

Although the patterns are often numeric or string expressions, awk also provides two special patterns with the reserved words BEGIN and END.

The action associated with BEGIN is performed just once, *before* any command-line files or ordinary command-line assignments are processed, but *after* any leading -v option assignments have been done. It is normally used to handle any special initialization tasks required by the program.

The END action is performed just once, *after* all of the input data has been processed. It is normally used to produce summary reports or to perform cleanup actions.

BEGIN and END patterns may occur in any order, anywhere in the awk program. However, it is conventional to make the BEGIN pattern the first one in the program, and to make the END pattern the last one.

When multiple BEGIN or END patterns are specified, they are processed in their order in the awk program. This allows library code included with extra -f options to have startup and cleanup actions.

9.3   Program Elements

Like most scripting languages, awk deals with numbers and strings. It provides *scalar* and *array* variables to hold data, numeric and string expressions, and a handful of statement types to process data: assignments, comments, conditionals, functions, input, loops, and output. Many features of awk expressions and statements are purposely similar to ones in the C programming language.

9.3.1   Comments and Whitespace

Comments in awk run from sharp (#) to end-of-line, just like comments in the shell. Blank lines are equivalent to empty comments.

Wherever whitespace is permitted in the language, any number of whitespace characters may be used, so blank lines and indentation can be used for improved readability. However, single statements usually cannot be split across multiple lines, unless the line breaks are immediately preceded with a backslash.

9.3.2   Strings and String Expressions

String constants in awk are delimited by quotation marks: "This is a string constant". Character strings may contain any 8-bit character *except* the control character NUL (character value 0), which serves as a string terminator in the underlying implementation language, C. The GNU implementation, gawk, removes that restriction, so gawk can safely process arbitrary binary files.

awk strings contain zero or more characters, and there is no limit, other than available memory, on the length of a string. Assignment of a string expression to a variable automatically creates a string, and the memory occupied by any previous string value of the variable is automatically reclaimed.

Backslash escape sequences allow representation of unprintable characters, just like those for the echo command shown in "Simple Output with echo" [2.5.3]. "A\tZ" contains the characters A, tab, and Z, and "\001" and "\x01" each contain just the character Ctrl-A.

Hexadecimal escape sequences are not supported by echo, but were added to awk implementations after they were introduced in the 1989 ISO C Standard. Unlike octal escape sequences, which use at most three digits, the hexadecimal escape consumes all following hexadecimal digits. gawk and nawk follow the C Standard, but mawk does not: it collects at most two hexadecimal digits, reducing "\x404142" to "@4142" instead of to the 8-bit value $0x42 = 66$, which is the position of "B" in the ASCII character set. POSIX awk does not support hexadecimal escapes at all.

awk provides several convenient built-in functions for operating on strings; we treat them in detail in "String Functions" [9.9]. For now, we mention only the string-length function: length(*string*) returns the number of characters in *string*.

Strings are compared with the conventional relational operators: == (equality), != (inequality), < (less than), <= (less than or equal to), > (greater than), and >= (greater than or equal to). Comparison returns 0 for false and 1 for true. When strings of different lengths are compared and one string is an initial substring of the other, the shorter is defined to be less than the longer: thus, "A" < "AA" evaluates to true.

Unlike most programming languages with string datatypes, awk has no special string concatenation operator. Instead, two strings in succession are automatically concatenated. Each of these assignments sets the scalar variable s to the same four-character string:

```
s = "ABCD"
s = "AB" "CD"
s = "A" "BC" "D"
s = "A" "B" "C" "D"
```

The strings need not be constants: if we follow the last assignment with:

```
t = s s s
```

then t has the value "ABCDABCDABCD".

Conversion of a number to a string is done implicitly by concatenating the number to an empty string: n = 123, followed by s = "" n, assigns the value "123" to s. Some caution is called for when the number is not exactly representable: we address that later when we show how to do formatted number-to-string conversions in "String Formatting" [9.9.8].

Much of the power of awk comes from its support of regular expressions. Two operators, ~ (matches) and !~ (does not match), make it easy to use regular expressions: "ABC" ~ "^[A-Z]+$" is true, because the left string contains only uppercase letters, and the right regular expression matches any string of (ASCII) uppercase letters. awk supports Extended Regular Expressions (EREs), as described in "Extended Regular Expressions" [3.2.3].

Regular expression constants can be delimited by either quotes or slashes: "ABC" ~ /^[A-Z]+$/ is equivalent to the last example. Which of them to use is largely a matter of programmer taste, although the slashed form is usually preferred, since it emphasizes that the enclosed material is a regular expression, rather than an arbitrary string. However, in the rare cases where a slash delimiter might be confused with a division operator, use the quoted form.

Just as a literal quote in a quoted string must be protected by a backslash ("...\"..."), so must a literal slash in a slash-delimited regular expression (/...\/.../). When a literal backslash is needed in a regular expression, it too must be protected, but the quoted form requires an extra level of protection: "\\\\TeX" and /\\TeX/ are regular expressions that each match a string containing \TeX.

9.3.3   Numbers and Numeric Expressions

All numbers in awk are represented as double-precision floating-point values, and we provide some of the details in the nearby sidebar. Although you do not have to become an expert in floating-point arithmetic, it is important to be aware of the limitations of computer arithmetic so that you do not expect more than the computer can deliver, and so that you can avoid some of the pitfalls.

Floating-point numbers may include a trailing power-of-10 exponent represented by the letter e (or E) and an optionally signed integer. For example, 0.03125, 3.125e-2, 3125e-5, and 0.003125E1 are equivalent representations of the value 1/32. Because all arithmetic in awk is floating-point arithmetic, the expression 1/32 can be written that way without fear that it will evaluate to zero, as happens in programming languages with integer datatypes.

There is no function for explicit conversion of a string to a number, but the awk idiom is simple: just add zero to the string. For example, s = "123", followed by n = 0 + s, assigns the number 123 to n.

Non-numeric strings are coerced to numbers by converting as much of the string that looks like a number: "+123ABC" converts to 123, and "ABC", "ABC123", and "" all convert to 0.

More on Floating-Point Arithmetic

Virtually all platforms today conform to the 1985 *IEEE 754 Standard for Binary Float-ing-Point Arithmetic*. That standard defines a 32-bit single-precision format, a 64-bit double-precision format, and an optional extended-precision format, which is usually implemented in 80 or 128 bits. awk implementations use the 64-bit format (correspond-ing to the C datatype double), although in the interests of portability, the awk language specification is intentionally vague about the details. The POSIX awk specification says only that the arithmetic shall follow the ISO C Standard, which does not require any particular floating-point architecture.

IEEE 754 64-bit double-precision values have a sign bit, an 11-bit biased exponent, and a 53-bit significand whose leading bit is not stored. This permits representing numbers with up to about 16 decimal digits. The largest finite magnitude is about 10^{+308}, and the smallest normalized nonzero magnitude is about 10^{-308}. Most IEEE 754 implementa-tions also support subnormal numbers, which extend the range down to about 10^{-324}, but with a loss of precision: this *gradual underflow* to zero has several desirable numerical properties, but is usually irrelevant to nonnumerical software.

Because the sign bit is explicitly represented, IEEE 754 arithmetic supports both posi-tive and negative zero. Many programming languages get this wrong, however, and awk is no exception: some implementations print a negative zero without its minus sign.

IEEE 754 arithmetic also includes two special values, Infinity and not-a-number (NaN). Both can be signed, but the sign of NaN is not significant. They are intended to allow nonstop computation on high-performance computers while still being able to record the occurrence of exceptional conditions. When a value is too big to repre-sent, it is said to *overflow*, and the result is Infinity. When a value is not well-defined, such as Infinity − Infinity, or 0/0, the result is a NaN.

Infinity and NaN propagate in computations: Infinity + Infinity and Infinity * Infinity produce Infinity, and NaN combined with anything produces NaN.

Infinities of the same sign compare equal. NaN compares unequal to itself: the test (x != x) is true only if x is a NaN.

awk was developed before IEEE 754 arithmetic became widely available, so the lan-guage does not fully support Infinity and NaN. In particular, current awk implementa-tions trap attempts to divide by zero, even though that operation is perfectly well-defined in IEEE 754 arithmetic.

The limited precision of floating-point numbers means that some values cannot be represented exactly: the order of evaluation is significant (floating-point arithmetic is not associative), and computed results are normally rounded to the nearest repre-sentable number.

The limited range of floating-point numbers means that very small or very large numbers are not representable. On modern systems, such values are converted to zero and infinity.

Even though all numeric computations in awk are done in floating-point arithmetic, integer values can be represented exactly, provided that they are not too large. With IEEE 754 arithmetic, the 53-bit significand limits integers to at most 2^{53} = 9,007,199,254,740,992. That number is large enough that few text processing applications that involve counting things are likely to reach it.

Numeric operators in awk are similar to those in several other programming languages. We collect them in Table 9-2.

Table 9-2. Numeric operators in awk (in decreasing precedence)

Operator	Description
++ --	Increment and decrement (either prefix or postfix)
^ **	Exponentiate (right-associative)
! + -	Not, unary plus, unary minus
* / %	Multiply, divide, remainder
+ -	Add, subtract
< <= == <= != > >=	Compare
&&	Logical AND (short-circuit)
||	Logical OR (short-circuit)
? :	Ternary conditional
= += -= *= /= %= ^= **=	Assign (right-associative)

Like most programming languages, awk allows parentheses to control evaluation order. Few people can reliably remember operator precedence, especially if they work with multiple languages: when in doubt, parenthesize!

The increment and decrement operators work like those in the shell, described in "Arithmetic Expansion" [6.1.3]. In isolation, n++ and ++n are equivalent. However, because they have the *side effect* of updating the variable as well as returning a value, ambiguities in evaluation order can arise when they are used more than once in the same statement. For example, the result of an expression like n++ + ++n is implementation defined. Despite such ambiguities, the increment and decrement operators receive wide use in programming languages that have them.

Exponentiation raises the left operand to the power given by the right operand. Thus, n^3 and n**3 both mean the cube of n. The two operator names are equivalent, but come from different ancestor languages. C programmers should note that awk's ^ operator is different from C's, despite the similarity of major parts of awk and C.

Exponentiation and assignment are the only operators in awk that are *right-associative*: thus, a^b^c^d means a^(b^(c^d)), whereas a/b/c/d means ((a/b)/c)/d. These associativity rules are common to most other programming languages, and are conventional in mathematics.

In the original awk specification, the result of the remainder operator is implementation-defined when either operand is negative. POSIX awk requires that it behave like the ISO Standard C function fmod( ). This in turn requires that if x % y is representable, then the expression has the sign of x, and magnitude less than y. All awk implementations that we tested follow the POSIX mandate.

Just as in the shell, the logical operators && and || are short-circuiting forms of AND and OR: they evaluate their righthand operand only if needed.

The operator in the next-to-last row in the table is the ternary short-circuiting conditional operator. If the first operand is nonzero (true), the result is the second operand; otherwise, it is the third operand. Only one of the second and third operands is evaluated. Thus, in awk, you can write a compact assignment a = (u > w) ? x^3 : y^7 that in other programming languages might require something like this:

```
if (u > w) then
    a = x^3
else
    a = y^7
endif
```

The assignment operators are perhaps unusual for two reasons. First, the compound ones, like /=, use the left operand as the first operand on the right: n /= 3 is simply shorthand for n = n / 3. Second, the result of an assignment is an expression that may be used as part of another expression: a = b = c = 123 first assigns 123 to c (because the assignment operator is right-associative), then assigns the value of c to b, and finally, assigns the value of b to a. The result, as expected, is that a, b, and c all receive the value 123. Similarly, x = (y = 123) + (z = 321) sets x, y, and z to 444, 123, and 321, respectively.

The ** and **= operators are not part of POSIX awk and are not recognized by mawk. They should therefore be avoided in new code: use ^ and ^= instead.

 Be sure to note the difference between assignment with =, and equality test with ==. Because assignments are valid expressions, the expression (r = s) ? t : u is syntactically correct, but is probably not what you intended. It assigns s to r, and then if that value is nonzero, it returns t, and otherwise returns u. This warning also applies to C, C++, Java, and other languages with = and == operators.

The built-in function int( ) returns the integer part of its argument: int(-3.14159) evaluates to –3.

awk provides some of the common elementary mathematical functions that may be familiar to you from calculators and from other programming languages: sqrt( ), sin( ), cos( ), log( ), exp( ), and so on. They are summarized in "Numeric Functions" [9.10]."

9.3.4 Scalar Variables

Variables that hold a single value are called scalar variables. In awk, as in most scripting languages, variables are not explicitly declared. Instead, they are created automatically at their first use in the program, usually by assignment of a value, which can be either a number or a string. When a variable is used, the context makes it clear whether a number or a string is expected, and the value is automatically converted from one to the other as needed.

All awk variables are created with an initial empty string value that is treated as zero when a numeric value is required.

awk variable names begin with an ASCII letter or underscore, and optionally continue with letters, underscores, and digits. Thus, variable names match the regular expression **[A-Za-z_][A-Za-z_0-9]***. There is no practical limit on the length of a variable name.

awk variable names are case-sensitive: foo, Foo, and FOO are distinct names. A common, and recommended, convention is to name local variables in lowercase, global variables with an initial uppercase letter, and built-in variables in uppercase.

awk provides several built-in variables, all spelled in uppercase. The important ones that we often need for simple programs are shown in Table 9-3.

Table 9-3. Commonly used built-in scalar variables in awk

Variable	Description
FILENAME	Name of the current input file
FNR	Record number in the current input file
FS	Field separator (regular expression) (default: " ")
NF	Number of fields in current record
NR	Record number in the job
OFS	Output field separator (default: " ")
ORS	Output record separator (default: "\n")
RS	Input record separator (regular expression in gawk and mawk only) (default: "\n")

9.3.5 Array Variables

Array variables in awk follow the same naming conventions as scalar variables, but contain zero or more data items, selected by an array index following the name.

Most programming languages require arrays to be indexed by simple integer expressions, but awk allows array indices to be arbitrary numeric or string expressions, enclosed in square brackets after the array name. If you have not encountered such arrays before, they may seem rather curious, but awk code like this fragment of an office-directory program makes their utility obvious:

```
telephone["Alice"] = "555-0134"
telephone["Bob"]   = "555-0135"
telephone["Carol"] = "555-0136"
telephone["Don"]   = "555-0141"
```

Arrays with arbitrary indices are called *associative arrays* because they associate names with values, much like humans do. Importantly, the technique that awk uses to implement these arrays allows *find*, *insert*, and *remove* operations to be done in essentially constant time, independent of the number of items stored.

Arrays in awk require neither declaration nor allocation: array storage grows automatically as new elements are referenced. Array storage is *sparse*: only those elements that are explicitly referenced are allocated. This means that you can follow x[1] = 3.14159 with x[10000000] = "ten million", without filling in elements 2 through 9999999. Most programming languages with arrays require all elements to be of the same type, but that is not the case with awk arrays.

Storage can be reclaimed when elements are no longer needed. delete *array[index]* removes an element from an array, and recent awk implementations allow delete *array* to delete all elements. We describe another way to delete array elements at the end of "String Splitting" [9.9.6].

A variable cannot be used as both a scalar and an array at the same time. Applying the delete statement removes *elements* of an array, but not its *name*: therefore, code like this:

```
x[1] = 123
delete x
x = 789
```

causes awk to complain that you cannot assign a value to an array name.

Sometimes, multiple indices are needed to uniquely locate tabular data. For example, the post office uses house number, street, and postal code to identify mail-delivery locations. A row/column pair suffices to identify a position in a two-dimensional grid, such as a chessboard. Bibliographies usually record author, title, edition, publisher, and year to identify a particular book. A clerk needs a manufacturer, style, color, and size to retrieve the correct pair of shoes from a stockroom.

awk simulates arrays with multiple indices by treating a *comma-separated list of indices* as a single string. However, because commas might well occur in the index values themselves, awk replaces the index-separator commas by an unprintable string stored in the built-in variable SUBSEP. POSIX says that its value is implementation-defined; generally, its default value is "\034" (the ASCII field-separator control character, FS), but you can change it if you need that string in the index values. Thus, when you write maildrop[53, "Oak Lane", "T4Q 7XV"], awk converts the index list to the string expression "53" SUBSEP "Oak Lane" SUBSEP "T4Q 7XV", and uses its string value as the index. This scheme can be subverted, although we do not recommend that you do so—these statements all print the same item:

```
print maildrop[53, "Oak Lane", "T4Q 7XV"]
print maildrop["53" SUBSEP "Oak Lane" SUBSEP "T4Q 7XV"]
print maildrop["53\034Oak Lane", "T4Q 7XV"]
print maildrop["53\034Oak Lane\034T4Q 7XV"]
```

Clearly, if you later change the value of SUBSEP, you will invalidate the indices of already-stored data, so SUBSEP really should be set just once per program, in the BEGIN action.

You can solve an astonishingly large number of data processing problems with associative arrays, once you rearrange your thinking appropriately. For a simple programming language like awk, they have shown themselves to be a superb design choice.

9.3.6   Command-Line Arguments

awk's automated handling of the command line means that few awk programs need concern themselves with it. This is quite different from the C, C++, Java, and shell worlds, where programmers are used to handling command-line arguments explicitly.

awk makes the command-line arguments available via the built-in variables ARGC (argument count) and ARGV (argument vector, or argument values). Here is a short program to illustrate their use:

```
$ cat showargs.awk
BEGIN {
    print "ARGC =", ARGC
    for (k = 0; k < ARGC; k++)
        print "ARGV[" k "] = [" ARGV[k] "]"
}
```

Here is what it produces for the general awk command line:

```
$ awk -v One=1 -v Two=2 -f showargs.awk Three=3 file1 Four=4 file2 file3
ARGC = 6
ARGV[0] = [awk]
ARGV[1] = [Three=3]
ARGV[2] = [file1]
ARGV[3] = [Four=4]
ARGV[4] = [file2]
```

```
ARGV[5] = [file3]
```

As in C and C++, the arguments are stored in array entries 0, 1, ..., ARGC − 1, and the zeroth entry is the name of the awk program itself. However, arguments associated with the –f and –v options are not available. Similarly, any command-line program is not available:

```
$ awk 'BEGIN { for (k = 0; k < ARGC; k++)
>       print "ARGV[" k "] = [" ARGV[k] "]" }' a b c
ARGV[0] = [awk]
ARGV[1] = [a]
ARGV[2] = [b]
ARGV[3] = [c]
```

Whether a directory path in the program name is visible or not is implementation-dependent:

```
$ /usr/local/bin/gawk 'BEGIN { print ARGV[0] }'
gawk

$ /usr/local/bin/mawk 'BEGIN { print ARGV[0] }'
mawk

$ /usr/local/bin/nawk 'BEGIN { print ARGV[0] }'
/usr/local/bin/nawk
```

The awk program can modify ARGC and ARGV, although it is rarely necessary to do so. If an element of ARGV is (re)set to an empty string, or deleted, awk ignores it, instead of treating it as a filename. If you eliminate trailing entries of ARGV, be sure to decrement ARGC accordingly.

awk stops interpreting arguments as options as soon as it has seen either an argument containing the program text, or the special –– option. Any following arguments that look like options must be handled by your program and then deleted from ARGV, or set to an empty string.

It is often convenient to wrap the awk invocation in a shell script. To keep the script more readable, store a lengthy program in a shell variable. You can also generalize the script to allow the awk implementation to be chosen at runtime by an environment variable with a default of nawk:

```
#! /bin/sh -
AWK=${AWK:-nawk}
AWKPROG='
    ... long program here ...
'
$AWK "$AWKPROG" "$@"
```

Single quotes protect the program text from shell interpretation, but more care is needed if the program itself contains single quotes. A useful alternative to storing the program in a shell variable is to put it in a separate file in a shared library directory that is found relative to the directory where the script is stored:

```
#! /bin/sh -
AWK=${AWK:-nawk}
$AWK -f `dirname $0`/../share/lib/myprog.awk -- "$@"
```

The dirname command was described in "Automating Software Builds" [8.2]. For example, if the script is in /usr/local/bin, then the program is in /usr/local/share/lib. The use of dirname here ensures that the script will work as long as the relative location of the two files is preserved.

9.3.7   Environment Variables

awk provides access to all of the environment variables as entries in the built-in array ENVIRON:

```
$ awk 'BEGIN { print ENVIRON["HOME"]; print ENVIRON["USER"] }'
/home/jones
jones
```

There is nothing special about the ENVIRON array: you can add, delete, and modify entries as needed. However, POSIX requires that subprocesses inherit the environment in effect when awk was started, and we found no current implementations that propagate changes to the ENVIRON array to either subprocesses or built-in functions. In particular, this means that you cannot control the possibly locale-dependent behavior of string functions, like tolower( ), with changes to ENVIRON["LC_ALL"]. You should therefore consider ENVIRON to be a read-only array.

If you need to control the locale of a subprocess, you can do so by setting a suitable environment variable in the command string. For example, you can sort a file in a Spanish locale like this:

```
system("env LC_ALL=es_ES sort infile > outfile")
```

The system( ) function is described later, in "Running External Programs" [9.7.8].

9.4   Records and Fields

Each iteration of the implicit loop over the input files in awk's programming model processes a single *record*, typically a line of text. Records are further divided into smaller strings, called *fields*.

9.4.1   Record Separators

Although records are normally text lines separated by newline characters, awk allows more generality through the record-separator built-in variable, RS.

In traditional and POSIX awk, RS must be either a single literal character, such as newline (its default value), or an empty string. The latter is treated specially: records are then paragraphs separated by one or more blank lines, and empty lines at the start or end of a file are ignored. Fields are then separated by newlines or whatever FS is set to.

gawk and mawk provide an important extension: RS may be a regular expression, provided that it is longer than a single character. Thus, RS = "+" matches a literal plus, whereas RS = ":+" matches one or more colons. This provides much more powerful record specification, which we exploit in some of the examples in "One-Line Programs in awk" [9.6].

With a regular expression record separator, the text that matches the separator can no longer be determined from the value of RS. gawk provides it as a language extension in the built-in variable RT, but mawk does not.

Without the extension of RS to regular expressions, it can be hard to simulate regular expressions as record separators, if they can match across line boundaries, because most Unix text processing tools deal with a line at a time. Sometimes, you can use tr to convert newline into an otherwise unused character, making the data stream one giant line. However, that often runs afoul of buffer-size limits in other tools. gawk, mawk, and emacs are unusual in freeing you from the limiting view of line-oriented data.

9.4.2   Field Separators

Fields are separated from each other by strings that match the current value of the field-separator regular expression, available in the built-in variable FS.

The default value of FS, a single space, receives special interpretation: it means one or more whitespace characters (space or tab), and leading and trailing whitespace on the line is ignored. Thus, the input lines:

```
alpha beta gamma
     alpha      beta        gamma
```

both look the same to an awk program with the default setting of FS: three fields with values "alpha", "beta", and "gamma". This is particularly convenient for input prepared by humans.

For those rare occasions when a single space separates fields, simply set FS = "[ ]" to match exactly one space. With that setting, leading and trailing whitespace is no longer ignored. These two examples report different numbers of fields (two spaces begin and end the input record):

```
$ echo '  un deux trois  ' | awk -F' ' '{ print NF ":" $0 }'
3:  un deux trois
```

```
$ echo '  un deux trois  ' | awk -F'[ ]' '{ print NF ":" $0 }'
7:  un deux trois
```

The second example sees seven fields: "", "", "un", "deux", "trois", "", and "".

FS is treated as a regular expression only when it contains more than one character. FS = "." uses a period as the field separator; it is *not* a regular expression that matches any single character.

Modern awk implementations also permit FS to be an empty string. Each *character* is then a separate field, but in older implementations, each record then has only one field. POSIX says only that the behavior for an empty field separator is unspecified.

9.4.3 Fields

Fields are available to the awk program as the special names $1, $2, $3, ..., $NF. Field references need not be constant, and they are converted (by truncation) to integer values if necessary: assuming that k is 3, the values $k, $(1+2), $(27/9), $3.14159, $"3.14159", and $3 all refer to the third field.

The special field name $0 refers to the current record, initially exactly as read from the input stream, and the record separator is not part of the record. References to field numbers above the range 0 to NF are *not* erroneous: they return empty strings and do not create new fields, unless you assign them a value. References to fractional, or non-numeric, field numbers are implementation-defined. References to negative field numbers are fatal errors in all implementations that we tested. POSIX says only that references to anything other than non-negative integer field numbers are unspecified.

Fields can be assigned too, just like normal variables. For example, $1 = "alef" is legal, but has an important side effect: if the complete record is subsequently referenced, it is reassembled from the current values of the fields, but separated by the string given by the output-field-separator built-in variable, OFS, which defaults to a single space.

9.5   Patterns and Actions

Patterns and actions form the heart of awk programming. It is awk's unconventional *data-driven* programming model that makes it so attractive and contributes to the brevity of many awk programs.

9.5.1   Patterns

Patterns are constructed from string and/or numeric expressions: when they evaluate to nonzero (true) for the current input record, the associated action is carried out. If a pattern is a bare regular expression, then it means to match the entire input record against that expression, as if you had written $0 ~ /regexp/ instead of just /regexp/. Here are some examples to give the general flavor of selection patterns:

```
NF == 0                    Select empty records
NF > 3                     Select records with more than 3 fields
NR < 5                     Select records 1 through 4
```

```
(FNR == 3) && (FILENAME ~ /[.][ch]$/)        Select record 3 in C source files
$1 ~ /jones/                                 Select records with "jones" in field 1
/[Xx][Mm][Ll]/                               Select records containing "XML", ignoring lettercase
$0 ~ /[Xx][Mm][Ll]/                          Same as preceding selection
```

awk adds even more power to the matching by permitting *range expressions*. Two expressions separated by a comma select records from one matching the left expression up to, and including, the record that matches the right expression. If both range expressions match a record, the selection consists of that single record. This behavior is different from that of sed, which looks for the range end only in records that follow the start-of-range record. Here are some examples:

```
(FNR == 3), (FNR == 10)                    Select records 3 through 10 in each input file
/<[Hh][Tt][Mm][Ll]>/, /<\/[Hh][Tt][Mm][Ll]>/   Select body of an HTML document
/[aeiouy][aeiouy]/, /[^aeiouy][^aeiouy]/   Select from two vowels to two nonvowels
```

In the BEGIN action, FILENAME, FNR, NF, and NR are initially undefined; references to them return a null string or zero.

If a program consists only of actions with BEGIN patterns, awk exits after completing the last action, without reading any files.

On entry to the first END action, FILENAME is the name of the last input file processed, and FNR, NF, and NR retain their values from the last input record. The value of $0 in the END action is unreliable: gawk and mawk retain it, nawk does not, and POSIX is silent.

9.5.2   Actions

We have now covered most of the awk language elements needed to select records. The action section that optionally follows a pattern is, well, where the action is: it specifies how to process the record.

awk has several statement types that allow construction of arbitrary programs. However, we delay presentation of most of them until "Statements" [9.7]. For now, apart from the assignment statement, we consider only the simple print statement.

In its simplest form, a bare print means to print the current input record ($0) on standard output, followed by the value of the output record separator, ORS, which is by default a single newline character. These programs are therefore equivalent:

```
1                         Pattern is true, default action is to print
NR > 0  { print }         Print when have records, is always true
1       { print }         Pattern is true, explicit print, default value
        { print }         No pattern is treated as true, explicit print, default value
        { print $0 }      Same, but with explicit value to print
```

A one-line awk program that contained any of those lines would simply copy the input stream to standard output.

More generally, a print statement can contain zero or more comma-separated expressions. Each is evaluated, converted to a string if necessary, and output on standard output, separated by the value of the output field separator, OFS. The last item is followed by the value of the output record separator, ORS.

The argument lists for print and its companions printf and sprintf (see "String Formatting" [9.9.8]) may optionally be parenthesized. The parentheses eliminate a parsing ambiguity when the argument list contains a relational operator, since < and > are also used in I/O redirection, as described in "User-Controlled Input" [9.7.6] and "Output Redirection" [9.7.7].

Here are some complete awk program examples. In each, we print just the first three input fields, and by omitting the selection pattern, we select all records. Semicolons separate awk program statements, and we vary the action code slightly to change the output field separators:

```
$ echo 'one two three four' | awk '{ print $1, $2, $3 }'
one two three

$ echo 'one two three four' | awk '{ OFS = "..."; print $1, $2, $3 }'
one...two...three

$ echo 'one two three four' | awk '{ OFS = "\n"; print $1, $2, $3 }'
one
two
three
```

Changing the output field separator without assigning any field does *not* alter $0:

```
$ echo 'one two three four' | awk '{ OFS = "\n"; print $0 }'
one two three four
```

However, if we change the output field separator, and we assign at least one of the fields (even if we do not change its value), then we force reassembly of the record with the new field separator:

```
$ echo 'one two three four' | awk '{ OFS = "\n"; $1 = $1; print $0 }'
one
two
three
four
```

9.6 One-Line Programs in awk

We have now covered enough awk to do useful things with as little as one line of code; few other programming languages can do so much with so little. In this section, we present some examples of these one-liners, although page-width limitations sometimes force us to wrap them onto more than one line. In some of the examples, we show multiple ways to program a solution in awk, or with other Unix tools:

• We start with a simple implementation in awk of the Unix word-count utility, wc:

```
awk '{ C += length($0) + 1; W += NF } END { print NR, W, C }'
```

Notice that pattern/action groups need not be separated by newlines, even though we usually do that for readability. Although we could have included an initialization block of the form BEGIN { C = W = 0 }, awk's guaranteed default initializations make it unnecessary. The character count in C is updated at each record to count the record length, plus the newline that is the default record separator. The word count in W accumulates the number of fields. We do not need to keep a line-count variable because the built-in record count, NR, automatically tracks that information for us. The END action handles the printing of the one-line report that wc produces.

- awk exits immediately without reading any input if its program is empty, so it can match cat as an efficient data sink:

```
$ time cat *.xml > /dev/null
0.035u 0.121s 0:00.21 71.4%      0+0k 0+0io 99pf+0w
$ time awk '' *.xml
0.136u 0.051s 0:00.21 85.7%      0+0k 0+0io 140pf+0w
```

Apart from issues with NUL characters, awk can easily emulate cat—these two examples produce identical output:

```
cat *.xml
awk 1 *.xml
```

- To print original data values and their logarithms for one-column datafiles, use this:

```
awk '{ print $1, log($1) }' file(s)
```

- To print a random sample of about 5 percent of the lines from text files, use the pseudorandom-number generator function (see "Numeric Functions" [9.10]), which produces a result uniformly distributed between zero and one:

```
awk 'rand() < 0.05' file(s)
```

- Reporting the sum of the n-th column in tables with whitespace-separated columns is easy:

```
awk -v COLUMN=n '{ sum += $COLUMN } END { print sum }' file(s)
```

- A minor tweak instead reports the average of column n:

```
awk -v COLUMN=n '{ sum += $COLUMN } END { print sum / NR }' file(s)
```

- To print the running total for expense files whose records contain a description and an amount in the last field, use the built-in variable NF in the computation of the total:

```
awk '{ sum += $NF; print $0, sum }' file(s)
```

- Here are three ways to search for text in files:

```
egrep 'pattern|pattern' file(s)
awk '/pattern|pattern/' file(s)
awk '/pattern|pattern/ { print FILENAME ":" FNR ":" $0 }' file(s)
```

- If you want to restrict the search to just lines 100–150, you can use two tools and a pipeline, albeit with loss of location information:

```
sed -n -e 100,150p -s file(s) | egrep 'pattern'
```

We need GNU sed here for its –s option, which restarts line numbering for each file. Alternatively, you can use awk with a fancier pattern:

```
awk '(100 <= FNR) && (FNR <= 150) && /pattern/ \
        { print FILENAME ":" FNR ":" $0 }' file(s)
```

- To swap the second and third columns in a four-column table, assuming tab separators, use any of these:

```
awk -F'\t' -v OFS='\t' '{ print $1, $3, $2, $4 }' old > new
awk 'BEGIN { FS = OFS = "\t" } { print $1, $3, $2, $4 }' old > new
awk -F'\t' '{ print $1 "\t" $3 "\t" $2 "\t" $4 }' old > new
```

- To convert column separators from tab (shown here as •) to ampersand, use either of these:

```
sed -e 's/•/\&/g' file(s)
awk 'BEGIN { FS = "\t"; OFS = "&" } { $1 = $1; print }' file(s)
```

- Both of these pipelines eliminate duplicate lines from a sorted stream:

```
sort file(s) | uniq
sort file(s) | awk 'Last != $0 { print } { Last = $0 }'
```

- To convert carriage-return/newline line terminators to newline terminators, use one of these:

```
sed -e 's/\r$//' file(s)
sed -e 's/^M$//' file(s)
mawk 'BEGIN { RS = "\r\n" } { print }' file(s)
```

The first sed example needs a modern version that recognizes escape sequences. In the second example, ^M represents a literal Ctrl-M (carriage return) character. For the third example, we need either gawk or mawk because nawk and POSIX awk do not support more than a single character in RS.

- To convert single-spaced text lines to double-spaced lines, use any of these:

```
sed -e 's/$/\n/' file(s)
awk 'BEGIN { ORS = "\n\n" } { print }' file(s)
awk 'BEGIN { ORS = "\n\n" } 1' file(s)
awk '{ print $0 "\n" }' file(s)
awk '{ print; print "" }' file(s)
```

As before, we need a modern sed version. Notice how a simple change to the output record separator, ORS, in the first awk example solves the problem: the rest of the program just prints each record. The two other awk solutions require more processing for each record, and usually are slower than the first one.

- Conversion of double-spaced lines to single spacing is equally easy:

```
gawk 'BEGIN { RS="\n *\n" } { print }' file(s)
```

- To locate lines in Fortran 77 programs that exceed the 72-character line-length limit,* either of these does the job:

```
egrep -n '^.{73,}' *.f
awk 'length($0) > 72 { print FILENAME ":" FNR ":" $0 }' *.f
```

We need a POSIX-compliant egrep for the extended regular expression that matches 73 or more of any character.

- To extract properly hyphenated International Standard Book Number (ISBN) values from documents, we need a lengthy, but straightforward, regular expression, with the record separator set to match all characters that cannot be part of an ISBN:

```
gawk 'BEGIN { RS = "[^-0-9Xx]" }
/[0-9][-0-9][-0-9][-0-9][-0-9][-0-9][-0-9][-0-9][-0-9][-0-9][-0-9]-[0-9Xx]/' \
    file(s)
```

With a POSIX-conformant awk, that long regular expression can be shortened to /[0-9][-0-9]{10}-[-0-9Xx]/. Our tests found that gawk --posix, HP/Compaq/DEC OSF/1 awk, Hewlett-Packard HP-UX awk, IBM AIX awk, and Sun Solaris /usr/xpg4/bin/awk are the only ones that support the POSIX extension of braced interval expressions in regular expressions.

- To strip angle-bracketed markup tags from HTML documents, treat the tags as record separators, like this:

```
mawk 'BEGIN { ORS = " "; RS = "<[^<>]*>" } { print }' *.html
```

By setting ORS to a space, HTML markup gets converted to a space, and all input line breaks are preserved.

- Here is how we can extract all of the titles from a collection of XML documents, such as the files for this book, and print them, one title per line, with surrounding markup. This program works correctly even when the titles span multiple lines, and handles the uncommon, but legal, case of spaces between the tag word and the closing angle bracket:

```
$ mawk -v ORS=' ' -v RS='[ \n]' '/<title */, /<\/title */' *.xml |
>       sed -e 's@</title *> *@&\n@g'
...
<title>Enough awk to Be Dangerous</title>
<title>Freely available awk versions</title>
<title>The awk Command Line</title>
...
```

The awk program produces a single line of output, so the modern sed filter supplies the needed line breaks. We could eliminate sed here, but to do so, we need some awk statements discussed in the next section.

---

* The Fortran line-length limit was not a problem in the old days of punched cards, but once screen-based editing became common, it became a source of nasty bugs caused by the compiler's silently ignoring statement text beyond column 72.

9.7 Statements

Programming languages need to support sequential, conditional, and iterative execution. awk provides these features with statements borrowed largely from the C programming language. This section also covers the different statement types that are specific to awk.

9.7.1 Sequential Execution

Sequential execution is provided by lists of statements, written one per line, or separated by semicolons. The three lines:

```
n = 123
s = "ABC"
t = s n
```

can also be written like this:

```
n = 123; s = "ABC"; t = s n
```

In one-liners, we often need the semicolon form, but in awk programs supplied from files, we usually put each statement on its own line, and we rarely need a semicolon.

Wherever a single statement is expected, a *compound statement* consisting of a braced group of statements can be used instead. Thus, the actions associated with awk patterns are just compound statements.

9.7.2 Conditional Execution

awk provides for conditional execution with the if statement:

```
if (expression)
    statement1

if (expression)
    statement1
else
    statement2
```

If the *expression* is nonzero (true), then execute *statement1*. Otherwise, if there is an else part, execute *statement2*. Each of these statements may themselves be if statements, so the general form of a multibranch conditional statement is usually written like this:

```
if (expression1)
    statement1
else if (expression2)
    statement2
else if (expression3)
    statement3

...
```

```
else if (expressionk)
    statementk
else
    statementk+1
```

The optional final else is always associated with the closest preceding if at the same level.

In a multibranch if statement, the conditional expressions are tested in order: the first one that matches selects the associated statement for execution, after which control continues with the statement following the complete if statement, without evaluating conditional expressions in the remainder of the statement. If no expressions match, then the final else branch, if present, is selected.

9.7.3 Iterative Execution

awk provides four kinds of iterative statements (loops):

- Loop with a termination test at the beginning:
  ```
  while (expression)
      statement
  ```
- Loop with a termination test at the end:
  ```
  do
      statement
  while (expression)
  ```
- Loop a countable number of times:
  ```
  for (expr1; expr2; expr3)
      statement
  ```
- Loop over elements of an associative array:
  ```
  for (key in array)
      statement
  ```

The while loop satisfies many iteration needs, typified by *while we have data, process it*. The do loop is much less common: it appears, for example, in optimization problems that reduce to *compute an error estimate, and repeat while the error is too big*. Both loop while the expression is nonzero (true). If the expression is initially zero, then the while loop body is not executed at all, whereas the do loop body is executed just once.

The first form of the for loop contains three semicolon-separated expressions, any or all of which may be empty. The first expression is evaluated before the loop begins. The second is evaluated at the start of each iteration, and while it is nonzero (true), the loop continues. The third is evaluated at the end of each iteration. The traditional loop from 1 to n is written like this:

```
for (k = 1; k <= n; k++)
    statement
```

However, the index need not increase by one each iteration. The loop can be run backward like this:

```
for (k = n; k >= 1; k--)
    statement
```

 Because floating-point arithmetic is usually inexact, avoid for-statement expressions that evaluate to nonintegral values. For example, the loop:

```
$ awk 'BEGIN { for (x = 0; x <= 1; x += 0.05) print x }'
...
0.85
0.9
0.95
```

does not print 1 in its last iteration because the additions of the inexactly represented value 0.05 produce a final x value that is slightly larger than 1.0.

C programmers should note that awk lacks a comma operator, so the three for loop expressions cannot be comma-separated lists of expressions.

The second form of the for loop is used for iterating over the elements of an array when the number of elements is not known, or do not form a computable integer sequence. The elements are selected in arbitrary order, so the output of:

```
for (name in telephone)
    print name "\t" telephone[name]
```

is unlikely to be in the order that you want. We show how to solve that problem in "Output Redirection" [9.7.7]. The split( ) function, described in "String Splitting" [9.9.6], handles the case of multiply-indexed arrays.

As in the shell, the break statement exits the innermost loop prematurely:

```
for (name in telephone)
    if (telephone[name] == "555-0136")
        break
print name, "has telephone number 555-0136"
```

However, the shell-style multilevel break *n* statement is not supported.

Just like in the shell, the continue statement jumps to the end of the loop body, ready for the next iteration. awk does not recognize the shell's multilevel continue *n* statement. To illustrate the continue statement, the program in Example 9-1 determines by brute-force testing of divisors whether a number is composite or prime (recall that a prime number is any whole number larger than one that has no integral divisors other than one and itself), and prints any factorization that it can find.

Example 9-1. Integer factorization

```
# Compute integer factorizations of integers supplied one per line.
# Usage:
```

Example 9-1. Integer factorization (continued)

```
#          awk -f factorize.awk
{
    n = int($1)
    m = n = (n >= 2) ? n : 2
    factors = ""
    for (k = 2; (m > 1) && (k^2 <= n); )
    {
        if (int(m % k) != 0)
        {
            k++
            continue
        }
        m /= k
        factors = (factors == "") ? ("" k) : (factors " * " k)
    }
    if ((1 < m) && (m < n))
        factors = factors " * " m
    print n, (factors == "") ? "is prime" : ("= " factors)
}
```

Notice that the loop variable k is incremented, and the continue statement executed, only when we find that k is *not* a divisor of m, so the third expression in the for statement is empty.

If we run it with suitable test input, we get this output:

```
$ awk -f factorize.awk test.dat
2147483540 = 2 * 2 * 5 * 107374177
2147483541 = 3 * 7 * 102261121
2147483542 = 2 * 3137 * 342283
2147483543 is prime
2147483544 = 2 * 2 * 2 * 3 * 79 * 1132639
2147483545 = 5 * 429496709
2147483546 = 2 * 13 * 8969 * 9209
2147483547 = 3 * 3 * 11 * 21691753
2147483548 = 2 * 2 * 7 * 76695841
2147483549 is prime
2147483550 = 2 * 3 * 5 * 5 * 19 * 23 * 181 * 181
```

9.7.4 Array Membership Testing

The membership test *key* in *array* is an expression that evaluates to 1 (true) if *key* is an index element of *array*. The test can be inverted with the *not* operator: !(*key* in *array*) is 1 if *key* is not an index element of *array*; the parentheses are mandatory.

For arrays with multiple subscripts, use a parenthesized comma-separated list of subscripts in the test: (i, j, …, n) in *array*.

A membership test never creates an array element, whereas referencing an element always creates it, if it does not already exist. Thus, you should write:

```
if ("Sally" in telephone)
    print "Sally is in the directory"
```

rather than:

```
if (telephone["Sally"] != "")
    print "Sally is in the directory"
```

because the second form installs her in the directory with an empty telephone number, if she is not already there.

It is important to distinguish finding an *index* from finding a particular *value*. The index membership test requires constant time, whereas a search for a value takes time proportional to the number of elements in the array, illustrated by the `for` loop in the `break` statement example in the previous section. If you need to do both of these operations frequently, it is worthwhile to construct an inverted-index array:

```
for (name in telephone)
    name_by_telephone[telephone[name]] = name
```

You can then use `name_by_telephone["555-0136"]` to find "Carol" in constant time. Of course, this assumes that all values are unique: if two people share a telephone, the `name_by_telephone` array records only the last name stored. You can solve that problem with just a bit more code:

```
for (name in telephone)
{
    if (telephone[name] in name_by_telephone)
        name_by_telephone[telephone[name]] = \
            name_by_telephone[telephone[name]] "\t" name
    else
        name_by_telephone[telephone[name]] = name
}
```

Now `name_by_telephone` contains tab-separated lists of people with the same telephone number.

9.7.5   Other Control Flow Statements

We have already discussed the `break` and `continue` statements for interrupting the control flow in iterative statements. Sometimes, you need to alter the control flow in awk's matching of input records against the patterns in the list of pattern/action pairs. There are three cases to handle:

Skip further pattern checking for this record only
> Use the `next` statement. Some implementations do not permit `next` in user-defined functions (described in "User-Defined Functions" [9.8]).

Skip further pattern checking for the current input file
> gawk and recent releases of nawk provide the `nextfile` statement. It causes the current input file to be closed immediately, and pattern matching restarts with records from the next file on the command line.

You can easily simulate the nextfile statement in older awk implementation, with some loss of efficiency. Replace the nextfile statement with SKIPFILE = FILENAME; next, and then add these new pattern/action pairs at the beginning of the program:

```
FNR == 1                { SKIPFILE = "" }
FILENAME == SKIPFILE    { next }
```

The first pattern/action pair resets SKIPFILE to an empty string at the start of each file so that the program works properly if the same filename appears as two successive arguments. Even though records continue to be read from the current file, they are immediately ignored by the next statement. When end-of-file is reached and the next input file is opened, the second pattern no longer matches, so the next statement in its action is not executed.

Skip further execution of the entire job, and return a status code to the shell
Use the exit *n* statement.

9.7.6 User-Controlled Input

awk's transparent handling of input files specified on the command line means that most awk programs never have to open and process files themselves. It is quite possible to do so, however, through awk's getline statement. For example, a spellchecker usually needs to load in one or more dictionaries before it can do its work.

getline returns a value and can be used like a function, even though it is actually a statement, and one with somewhat unconventional syntax. The return value is +1 when input has been successfully read, 0 at end-of-file, and −1 on error. It can be used in several different ways that are summarized in Table 9-4.

Table 9-4. getline variations

Syntax	Description
getline	Read the next record from the current input file into $0, and update NF, NR, and FNR.
getline *var*	Read the next record from the current input file into *var*, and update NR and FNR.
getline < *file*	Read the next record from *file* into $0, and update NF.
getline *var* < *file*	Read the next record from *file* into *var*.
cmd	getline	Read the next record from the external command, *cmd*, into $0, and update NF.
cmd	getline *var*	Read the next record from the external command, *cmd*, into *var*.

Let's look at some of these uses of getline. First, we pose a question, and then read and check the answer:

```
print "What is the square root of 625?"
getline answer
print "Your reply, ", answer ", is", (answer == 25) ? "right." : "wrong."
```

If we wanted to ensure that input came from the controlling terminal, rather than standard input, we instead could have used:

```
getline answer < "/dev/tty"
```

Next, we load a list of words from a dictionary:

```
nwords = 1
while ((getline words[nwords] < "/usr/dict/words") > 0)
    nwords++
```

Command pipelines are a powerful feature in awk. The pipeline is specified in a character string, and can contain arbitrary shell commands. It is used with getline like this:

```
"date" | getline now
close("date")
print "The current time is", now
```

Most systems limit the number of open files, so when we are through with the pipeline, we use the close( ) function to close the pipeline file. In older awk implementations, close was a statement, so there is no portable way to use it like a function and get a reliable return code back.

Here is how you can use a command pipeline in a loop:

```
command = "head -n 15 /etc/hosts"
while ((command | getline s) > 0)
    print s
close(command)
```

We used a variable to hold the pipeline to avoid repetition of a possibly complicated string, and to ensure that all uses of the command match exactly. In command strings, every character is significant, and even an inadvertent difference of a single space would refer to a different command.

9.7.7   Output Redirection

The print and printf statements (see "String Formatting" [9.9.8]) normally send their output to standard output. However, the output can be sent to a file instead:

```
print "Hello, world" > file
printf("The tenth power of %d is %d\n", 2, 2^10) > "/dev/tty"
```

To append to an existing file (or create a new one if it does not yet exist), use >> output redirection:

```
print "Hello, world" >> file
```

You can use output redirection to the same file on any number of output statements. When you are finished writing output, use close(file) to close the file and free its resources.

Avoid mixing > and >> for the same file without an intervening close( ). In awk, these operators tell how the output file should be opened. Once open, the file remains open until it is explicitly closed, or until the program terminates. Contrast that behavior with the shell, where redirection requires the file to be opened and closed at each command.

Alternatively, you can send output to a pipeline:

```
for (name in telephone)
    print name "\t" telephone[name] | "sort"
close("sort")
```

As with input from a pipeline, close an output pipeline as soon as you are through with it. This is particularly important if you need to read the output in the same program. For example, you can direct the output to a temporary file, and then read it after it is complete:

```
tmpfile = "/tmp/telephone.tmp"
command = "sort > " tmpfile
for (name in telephone)
    print name "\t" telephone[name] | command
close(command)
while ((getline < tmpfile) > 0)
    print
close(tmpfile)
```

Pipelines in awk put the entire Unix toolbox at our disposal, eliminating the need for much of the library support offered in other programming languages, and helping to keep the language small. For example, awk does not provide a built-in function for sorting because it would just duplicate functionality already available in the powerful sort command described in "Sorting Text" [4.1].

Recent awk implementations, but not POSIX, provide a function to flush buffered data to the output stream: fflush(*file*). Notice the doubled initial ff (for *file flush*). It returns 0 on success and −1 on failure. The behavior of calls to fflush( ) (omitted argument) and fflush("") (empty string argument) is implementation-dependent: avoid such uses in portable programs.

9.7.8   Running External Programs

We showed earlier how the getline statement and output redirection in awk pipelines can communicate with external programs. The system(*command*) function provides a third way: its return value is the exit status code of the command. It first flushes any buffered output, then starts an instance of /bin/sh, and sends it the command. The shell's standard error and standard output are the same as that of the awk program, so unless the command's I/O is redirected, output from both the awk program and the shell command appears in the expected order.

Here is a shorter solution to the telephone-directory sorting problem, using a tempo-rary file and system( ) instead of an awk pipeline:

```
tmpfile = "/tmp/telephone.tmp"
for (name in telephone)
    print name "\t" telephone[name] > tmpfile
close(tmpfile)
system("sort < " tmpfile)
```

The temporary file must be closed before the call to system( ) to ensure that any buff-ered output is properly recorded in the file.

There is no need to call close( ) for commands run by system( ), because close( ) is only for files or pipes opened with the I/O redirection operators and getline, print, or printf.

The system( ) function provides an easy way to remove the script's temporary file:

```
system("rm -f " tmpfile)
```

The command passed to system( ) can contain multiple lines:

```
system("cat <<EOFILE\nuno\ndos\ntres\nEOFILE")
```

It produces the output expected when copying the here document to standard output:

```
uno
dos
tres
```

Because each call to system( ) starts a fresh shell, there is no simple way to pass data between commands in separate calls to system( ), other than via intermediate files. There is an easy solution to this problem—use an output pipeline to the shell to send multiple commands:

```
shell = "/usr/local/bin/ksh"
print "export INPUTFILE=/var/tmp/myfile.in" | shell
print "export OUTPUTFILE=/var/tmp/myfile.out" | shell
print "env | grep PUTFILE" | shell
close(shell)
```

This approach has the added virtue that you get to choose the shell, but has the drawback that you cannot portably retrieve the exit-status value.

9.8   User-Defined Functions

The awk statements that we have covered so far are sufficient to write almost any data processing program. Because human programmers are poor at understanding large blocks of code, we need a way to split such blocks into manageable chunks that each perform an identifiable job. Most programming languages provide this ability, through features variously called functions, methods, modules, packages, and subroutines. For simplicity, awk provides only functions. As in C, awk functions can optionally return a scalar value. Only a function's documentation, or its code, if quite short, can make clear whether the caller should expect a returned value.

Functions can be defined anywhere in the program at top level: before, between, or after pattern/action groups. In single-file programs, it is conventional to place all functions after the pattern/action code, and it is usually most convenient to keep them in alphabetical order. awk does not care about these conventions, but people do.

A function definition looks like this:

```
function name(arg1, arg2, ..., argn)
{
    statement(s)
}
```

The named arguments are used as local variables within the function body, and they hide any global variables of the same name. The function may be used elsewhere in the program by calls of the form:

`name(expr1, expr2, ..., exprn)`	*Ignore any return value*
`result = name(expr1, expr2, ..., exprn)`	*Save return value in result*

The expressions at the point of each call provide initial values for the function-argument variables. The parenthesized argument list must immediately follow the function name, without any intervening whitespace.

Changes made to scalar arguments are not visible to the caller, but changes made to arrays *are* visible. In other words, scalars are passed *by value*, whereas arrays are passed *by reference*: the same is true of the C language.

A return *expression* statement in the function body terminates execution of the body, and returns control to the point of the call, with the value of *expression*. If *expression* is omitted, then the returned value is implementation-defined. All of the systems that we tested returned either a numeric zero, or an empty string. POSIX does not address the issue of a missing return statement or value.

All variables used in the function body that do not occur in the argument list are *global*. awk permits a function to be called with fewer arguments than declared in the function definition; the extra arguments then serve as *local* variables. Such variables are commonly needed, so it is conventional to list them in the function argument list, prefixed by some extra whitespace, as shown in Example 9-2. Like all other variables in awk, the extra arguments are initialized to an empty string at function entry.

Example 9-2. Searching an array for a value

```
function find_key(array, value,         key)
{
    # Search array[ ] for value, and return key such that
```

Example 9-2. Searching an array for a value (continued)

```
    # array[key] == value, or return "" if value is not found

    for (key in array)
        if (array[key] == value)
            return key
    return ""
}
```

Failure to list local variables as extra function arguments leads to hard-to-find bugs when they clash with variables used in calling code. gawk provides the --dump-variables option to help you check for this.

As in most programming languages, awk functions can call themselves: this is known as *recursion*. Obviously, the programmer must make some provision for eventual termination: this is usually done by making the job smaller for each successive invocation so that at some point, no further recursion is needed. Example 9-3 shows a famous example from elementary number theory that uses a method credited to the Greek mathematician Euclid (ca. 300 BCE), but probably known at least 200 years earlier, to find the greatest common denominator of two integers.

Example 9-3. Euclid's greatest common denominator algorithm

```
function gcd(x, y,          r)
{
    # return the greatest common denominator of integer x, y

    x = int(x)
    y = int(y)
    # print x, y
    r = x % y
    return (r == 0) ? y : gcd(y, r)
}
```

If we add this action

```
    { g = gcd($1, $2); print "gcd(" $1 ", " $2 ") =", g }
```

to the code in Example 9-3 and then we uncomment the print statement and run it from a file, we can see how the recursion works:

```
$ echo 25770 30972 | awk -f gcd.awk
25770 30972
30972 25770
25770 5202
5202 4962
4962 240
240 162
162 78
78 6
gcd(25770, 30972) = 6
```

Euclid's algorithm always takes relatively few steps, so there is no danger of overflowing the *call stack* inside awk that keeps track of the nested function-call history. However, that is not always the case. There is a particularly nasty function discovered by the German mathematician Wilhelm Ackermann[*] in 1926 whose value, and recursion depth, grow much faster than exponentially. It can be defined in awk with the code in Example 9-4.

Example 9-4. Ackermann's worse-than-exponential function

```
function ack(a, b)
{
    N++                          # count recursion depth
    if (a == 0)
        return (b + 1)
    else if (b == 0)
        return (ack(a - 1, 1))
    else
        return (ack(a - 1, ack(a, b - 1)))
}
```

If we augment it with a test action:

```
{ N = 0; print "ack(" $1 ", " $2 ") = ", ack($1, $2), "[" N " calls]" }
```

and run it from a test file, we find:

```
$ echo 2 2 | awk -f ackermann.awk
ack(2, 2) =  7 [27 calls]

$ echo 3 3 | awk -f ackermann.awk
ack(3, 3) =  61 [2432 calls]

$ echo 3 4 | awk -f ackermann.awk
ack(3, 4) =  125 [10307 calls]

$ echo 3 8 | awk -f ackermann.awk
ack(3, 8) =  2045 [2785999 calls]
```

ack(4, 4) is completely uncomputable.

9.9   String Functions

In "Strings and String Expressions" [9.3.2] we introduced the length(*string*) function, which returns the length of a string *string*. Other common string operations include concatenation, data formatting, lettercase conversion, matching, searching, splitting, string substitution, and substring extraction.

---

[*] See *http://mathworld.wolfram.com/AckermannFunction.html* for background and history of the Ackermann function.

9.9.1 Substring Extraction

The substring function, substr(*string, start, len*), returns a copy of the substring of *len* characters from *string* starting from character *start*. Character positions are numbered starting from one: substr("abcde", 2, 3) returns "bcd". The *len* argument can be omitted, in which case, it defaults to length(*string*) - *start* + 1, selecting the remainder of the string.

It is *not* an error for the arguments of substr( ) to be out of bounds, but the result may be implementation-dependent. For example, nawk and gawk evaluate substr("ABC", -3, 2) as "AB", whereas mawk produces the empty string "". All of them produce an empty string for substr("ABC", 4, 2) and for substr("ABC", 1, 0). gawk's --lint option diagnoses out-of-bounds arguments in substr( ) calls.

9.9.2 Lettercase Conversion

Some alphabets have uppercase and lowercase forms of each letter, and in string searching and matching, it is often desirable to ignore case differences. awk provides two functions for this purpose: tolower(*string*) returns a copy of *string* with all characters replaced by their lowercase equivalents, and toupper(*string*) returns a copy with uppercase equivalents. Thus, tolower("aBcDeF123") returns "abcdef123", and toupper("aBcDeF123") returns "ABCDEF123". These functions are fine for ASCII letters, but they do not correctly case-convert accented letters. Nor do they handle unusual situations, like the German lowercase letter ß (eszett, sharp s), whose uppercase form is two letters, SS.

9.9.3 String Searching

index(*string, find*) searches the text in *string* for the string *find*. It returns the starting position of *find* in *string*, or 0 if *find* is not found in *string*. For example, index("abcdef", "de") returns 4.

Subject to the caveats noted in "Lettercase Conversion" [9.9.2], you can make string searches ignore lettercase like this: index(tolower(*string*), tolower(*find*)). Because case insensitivity is sometimes needed in an entire program, gawk provides a useful extension: set the built-in variable IGNORECASE to nonzero to ignore lettercase in string matches, searches, and comparisons.

index( ) finds the first occurrence of a substring, but sometimes, you want to find the last occurrence. There is no standard function to do that, but we can easily write one, shown in Example 9-5.

Example 9-5. Reverse string search

```
function rindex(string, find,       k, ns, nf)
{
    # Return index of last occurrence of find in string,
```

Example 9-5. Reverse string search (continued)

```
    # or 0 if not found

    ns = length(string)
    nf = length(find)
    for (k = ns + 1 - nf; k >= 1; k--)
        if (substr(string, k, nf) == find)
            return k
    return 0
}
```

The loop starts at a k value that lines up the ends of the strings string and find, extracts a substring from string that is the same length as find, and compares that substring with find. If they match, then k is the desired index of the last occurrence, and the function returns that value. Otherwise, we back up one character, terminating the loop when k moves past the beginning of string. When that happens, find is known not to be found in string, and we return an index of 0.

9.9.4   String Matching

match(*string, regexp*) matches *string* against the regular expression *regexp*, and returns the index in *string* of the match, or 0 if there is no match. This provides more information than the expression (*string* ~ *regexp*), which evaluates to either 1 or 0. In addition, match( ) has a useful side effect: it sets the global variables RSTART to the index in *string* of the start of the match, and RLENGTH to the length of the match. The matching substring is then available as substr(*string*, RSTART, RLENGTH).

9.9.5   String Substitution

awk provides two functions for string substitution: sub(*regexp, replacement, target*) and gsub(*regexp, replacement, target*). sub( ) matches *target* against the regular expression *regexp*, and replaces the leftmost longest match by the string *replacement*. gsub( ) works similarly, but replaces all matches (the prefix g stands for *global*). Both functions return the number of substitutions. If the third argument is omitted, it defaults to the current record, $0. These functions are unusual in that they modify their scalar arguments: consequently, they cannot be written in the awk language itself. For example, a check-writing application might use gsub(/[^$-0-9.,]/, "*", amount) to replace with asterisks all characters other than those that can legally appear in the amount.

In a call to sub(*regexp, replacement, target*) or gsub(*regexp, replacement, target*), each instance of the character & in *replacement* is replaced in *target* by the text matched by *regexp*. Use \& to disable this feature, and remember to double the backslash if you use it in a quoted string. For example, gsub(/[aeiouyAEIOUY]/, "&&") doubles all vowels in the current record, $0, whereas gsub(/[aeiouyAEIOUY]/, "\\&\\&") replaces each vowel by a pair of ampersands.

gawk provides a more powerful generalized-substitution function, gensub( ); see the *gawk*(1) manual pages for details.

Substitution is often a better choice for data reduction than indexing and substring operations. Consider the problem of extracting the string value from an assignment in a file with text like this:

```
composer =       "P. D. Q. Bach"
```

With substitution, we can use:

```
value = $0
sub(/^ *[a-z]+ *= *"/, "", value)
sub(/" *$/, "", value)
```

whereas with indexing using code like this:

```
start = index($0, "\"") + 1
end = start - 1 + index(substr($0, start), "\"")
value = substr($0, start, end - start)
```

we need to count characters rather carefully, we do not match the data pattern as precisely, and we have to create two substrings.

9.9.6 String Splitting

The convenient splitting into fields $1, $2, ..., $NF that awk automatically provides for the current input record, $0, is also available as a function: split(*string, array, regexp*) breaks *string* into pieces stored in successive elements of *array*, where the pieces lie between substrings matched by the regular expression *regexp*. If *regexp* is omitted, then the current value of the built-in field-separator variable, FS, is used. The function return value is the number of elements in *array*. Example 9-6 demonstrates split( ).

Example 9-6. Test program for field splitting

```
{
    print "\nField separator = FS = \"" FS "\""
    n = split($0, parts)
    for (k = 1; k <= n; k++)
        print "parts[" k "] = \"" parts[k] "\""

    print "\nField separator = \"[ ]\""
    n = split($0, parts, "[ ]")
    for (k = 1; k <= n; k++)
        print "parts[" k "] = \"" parts[k] "\""

    print "\nField separator = \":\""
    n = split($0, parts, ":")
    for (k = 1; k <= n; k++)
        print "parts[" k "] = \"" parts[k] "\""
```

Example 9-6. Test program for field splitting (continued)

```
    print ""
}
```

If we put the test program shown in Example 9-6 into a file and run it interactively, we can see how split( ) works:

```
$ awk -f split.awk
  Harold   and Maude

Field separator = FS = " "
parts[1] = "Harold"
parts[2] = "and"
parts[3] = "Maude"

Field separator = "[ ]"
parts[1] = ""
parts[2] = ""
parts[3] = "Harold"
parts[4] = ""
parts[5] = "and"
parts[6] = "Maude"

Field separator = :
parts[1] = "  Harold   and Maude"

root:x:0:1:The Omnipotent Super User:/root:/sbin/sh

Field separator = FS = " "
parts[1] = "root:x:0:1:The"
parts[2] = "Omnipotent"
parts[3] = "Super"
parts[4] = "User:/root:/sbin/sh"

Field separator = "[ ]"
parts[1] = "root:x:0:1:The"
parts[2] = "Omnipotent"
parts[3] = "Super"
parts[4] = "User:/root:/sbin/sh"

Field separator = ":"
parts[1] = "root"
parts[2] = "x"
parts[3] = "0"
parts[4] = "1"
parts[5] = "The Omnipotent Super User"
parts[6] = "/root"
parts[7] = "/sbin/sh"
```

Notice the difference between the default field-separator value of " ", which causes leading and trailing whitespace to be ignored and runs of whitespace to be treated as a single space, and a field-separator value of "[ ]", which matches exactly one space. For most text processing applications, the first of these gives the desired behavior.

The colon field-separator example shows that split( ) produces a one-element array when the field separator is not matched, and demonstrates splitting of a record from a typical Unix administrative file, /etc/passwd.

Recent awk implementations provide a useful generalization: split(string, chars, "") breaks *string* apart into one-character elements in chars[1], chars[2], ..., chars[length(string)]. Older implementations require less efficient code like this:

```
n = length(string)
for (k = 1; k <= n; k++)
    chars[k] = substr(string, k, 1)
```

The call split("", *array*) deletes all elements in *array*: it is a faster method for array element deletion than the loop:

```
for (key in array)
    delete array[key]
```

when delete *array* is not supported by your awk implementation.

split( ) is an essential function for iterating through multiply subscripted arrays in awk. Here is an example:

```
for (triple in maildrop)
{
    split(triple, parts, SUBSEP)
    house_number = parts[1]
    street = parts[2]
    postal_code = parts[3]
    ...
}
```

9.9.7   String Reconstruction

There is no standard built-in awk function that is the inverse of split( ), but it is easy to write one, as shown in Example 9-7. join( ) ensures that the argument array is not referenced unless the index is known to be in bounds. Otherwise, a call with a zero array length might create array[1], modifying the caller's array. The inserted field separator is an ordinary string, rather than a regular expression, so for general regular expressions passed to split( ), join( ) does not reconstruct the original string exactly.

Example 9-7. Joining array elements into a string

```
function join(array, n, fs,        k, s)
{
    # Recombine array[1]...array[n] into a string, with elements
    # separated by fs

    if (n >= 1)
    {
        s = array[1]
```

Example 9-7. Joining array elements into a string (continued)

```
        for (k = 2; k <= n; k++)
            s = s fs array[k]
    }
    return (s)
}
```

9.9.8   String Formatting

The last string functions that we present format numbers and strings under user control: sprintf(*format,expression1,expression2,...*) returns the formatted string as its function value. printf( ) works the same way, except that it prints the formatted string on standard output or redirected to a file, instead of returning it as a function value. Newer programming languages replace format control strings with potentially more powerful formatting functions, but at a significant increase in code verbosity. For typical text processing applications, sprintf( ) and printf( ) are nearly always sufficient.

printf( ) and sprintf( ) format strings are similar to those of the shell printf command that we described in "The Full Story on printf" [7.4]. We summarize the awk format items in Table 9-5. These items can each be augmented by the same field width, precision, and flag modifiers discussed in Chapter 7.

The %i, %u, and %X items were not part of the 1987 language redesign, but modern implementations support them. Despite the similarity with the shell printf command, awk's handling of the %c format item differs for integer arguments, and output with %u for negative arguments may disagree because of differences in shell and awk arithmetic.

Table 9-5. printf and sprintf format specifiers

Item	Description
%c	ASCII character. Print the first character of the corresponding string argument, or the character whose number in the host character set is the corresponding integer argument, usually taken modulo 256.
%d, %i	Decimal integer.
%e	Floating-point format ([-]*d.precision*e[+-]*dd*).
%f	Floating-point format ([-]*ddd.precision*).
%g	%e or %f conversion, whichever is shorter, with trailing zeros removed.
%o	Unsigned octal value.
%s	String.
%u	Unsigned value. awk numbers are floating-point values: small negative integer values are output as large positive ones because the sign bit is interpreted as a data bit.
%x	Unsigned hexadecimal number. Letters a–f represent 10 to 15.
%X	Unsigned hexadecimal number. Letters A–F represent 10 to 15.
%%	Literal %.

Most of the format items are straightforward. However, we caution that *accurate* conversion of binary floating-point values to decimal strings, and the reverse, is a surprisingly difficult problem whose proper solution was only found in about 1990, and can require very high intermediate precision. awk implementations generally use the underlying C library for the conversions required by sprintf( ) format items, and although library quality continues to improve, there are still platforms in which the accuracy of floating-point conversions is deficient. In addition, differences in float-ing-point hardware and instruction evaluation order mean that floating-point results from almost any programming language vary slightly across different architectures.

When floating-point numbers appear in print statements, awk formats them accord-ing to the value of the built-in variable OFMT, which defaults to "%.6g". You can rede-fine OFMT as needed.

Similarly, when floating-point numbers are converted to strings by concatenation, awk formats them according to the value of another built-in variable, CONVFMT.* Its default value is also "%.6g".

The test program in Example 9-8 produces output like this with a recent nawk ver-sion on a Sun Solaris SPARC system:

```
$ nawk -f ofmt.awk
[ 1] OFMT = "%.6g"      123.457
[ 2] OFMT = "%d"        123
[ 3] OFMT = "%e"        1.234568e+02
[ 4] OFMT = "%f"        123.456789
[ 5] OFMT = "%g"        123.457
[ 6] OFMT = "%25.16e"       1.2345678901234568e+02
[ 7] OFMT = "%25.16f"         123.4567890123456806
[ 8] OFMT = "%25.16g"            123.4567890123457
[ 9] OFMT = "%25d"                            123
[10] OFMT = "%.25d"    0000000000000000000000123
[11] OFMT = "%25d"                     2147483647
[12] OFMT = "%25d"                     2147483647    Expected 2147483648
[13] OFMT = "%25d"                     2147483647    Expected 9007199254740991
[14] OFMT = "%25.0f"            9007199254740991
```

Evidently, despite the availability of 53-bit precision in floating-point values, on this platform nawk caps them at 32-bit integer limits for %d formats. Slightly different val-ues were produced by runs of the same nawk version on other architectures. Example 9-8 shows the source for ofmt.awk.

Example 9-8. Testing the effect of OFMT

```
BEGIN {
    test( 1, OFMT,     123.4567890123456789)
```

Example 9-8. Testing the effect of OFMT (continued)

```
    test( 2, "%d",       123.4567890123456789)
    test( 3, "%e",       123.4567890123456789)
    test( 4, "%f",       123.4567890123456789)
    test( 5, "%g",       123.4567890123456789)
    test( 6, "%25.16e", 123.4567890123456789)
    test( 7, "%25.16f", 123.4567890123456789)
    test( 8, "%25.16g", 123.4567890123456789)
    test( 9, "%25d",     123.4567890123456789)
    test(10, "%.25d",    123.4567890123456789)
    test(11, "%25d",     2^31 - 1)
    test(12, "%25d",     2^31)
    test(13, "%25d",     2^52 + (2^52 - 1))
    test(14, "%25.0f",  2^52 + (2^52 - 1))
}

function test(n,fmt,value,    save_fmt)
{
    save_fmt = OFMT
    OFMT = fmt
    printf("[%2d] OFMT = \"%s\"\t", n, OFMT)
    print value
    OFMT = save_fmt
}
```

We found that output for this test was quite sensitive to particular awk implementations, and even different releases of the same one. For example, with gawk, we get:

```
$ gawk -f ofmt.awk
...
[11] OFMT = "%25d"       2147483647                  Expected right-adjusted result
...
[13] OFMT - "%25d"                      9.0072e+15   Expected 9007199254740991
...
```

The informal language definition in the 1987 awk book specifies the default value of OFMT, but makes no mention of the effect of other values. Perhaps in recognition of implementation differences, POSIX says that the result of conversions is unspecified if OFMT is not a floating-point format specification, so gawk's behavior here is allowed.

With mawk, we find:

```
$ mawk -f ofmt.awk
...
[ 2] OFMT = "%d"        1079958844                  Expected 123
...
[ 9] OFMT = "%25d"                      1079958844   Expected 123
[10] OFMT = "%.25d"     0000000000000001079958844    Expected 00...00123
[11] OFMT = "%25d"      2147483647                   Expected right-adjusted result
[12] OFMT = "%25d"                      1105199104   Expected 2147483648
[13] OFMT = "%25d"                      1128267775   Expected 9007199254740991
...
```

There are evidently inconsistencies and idiosyncrasies in the handling of output of large numbers with the formats %d and, in separate tests, %i. Fortunately, you can get correct output from all awk implementations by using a %.0f format instead.

9.10 Numeric Functions

awk provides the elementary numeric functions listed in Table 9-6. Most of them are common to many programming languages, and their accuracy depends on the quality of the underlying native mathematical-function library.

Table 9-6. Elementary numeric functions

Function	Description
atan2(y, x)	Return the arctangent of y/x as a value in $-\pi$ to $+\pi$.
cos(x)	Return the cosine of x (measured in *radians*) as a value in -1 to $+1$.
exp(x)	Return the exponential of x, ex.
int(x)	Return the integer part of x, truncating toward zero.
log(x)	Return the natural logarithm of x.
rand( )	Return a uniformly distributed pseudorandom number, r, such that $0 \leq r < 1$.
sin(x)	Return the sine of x (measured in *radians*) as a value in -1 to $+1$.
sqrt(x)	Return the square root of x.
srand(x)	Set the pseudorandom-number generator seed to x, and return the current seed. If x is omitted, use the current time in seconds, relative to the system epoch. If srand( ) is not called, awk starts with the same default seed on each run; mawk does not.

The pseudorandom-number generator functions rand( ) and srand( ) are the area of largest variation in library functions in different awk implementations because some of them use native system-library functions instead of their own code, and the pseudorandom-number generating algorithms and precision vary. Most algorithms for generation of such numbers step through a sequence from a finite set without repetition, and the sequence ultimately repeats itself after a number of steps called the *period* of the generator. Library documentation sometimes does not make clear whether the unit interval endpoints, 0.0 and 1.0, are included in the range of rand( ), or what the period is.

The ambiguity in the generator's result interval endpoints makes programming harder. Suppose that you want to generate pseudorandom integers between 0 and 100 inclusive. If you use the simple expression int(rand( )*100), you will not get the value 100 at all if rand( ) never returns 1.0, and even if it does, you will get 100 much less frequently than any other integer between 0 and 100, since it is produced only once in the generator period, when the generator returns the exact value 1.0. Fudging by changing the multiplier from 100 to 101 does not work either because you might get an out-of-range result of 101 on some systems.

The irand( ) function in Example 9-9 provides a better solution to the problem of generating pseudorandom integers. irand( ) forces integer endpoints and then, if the requested range is empty or invalid, returns one endpoint. Otherwise, irand( ) samples an integer that might be one larger than the interval width, adds it to low, and then *retries* if the result is out of range. Now it does not matter whether rand( ) ever returns 1.0, and the return values from irand( ) are as uniformly distributed as the rand( ) values.

Example 9-9. Generating pseudorandom integers

```
function irand(low, high,         n)
{
    # Return a pseudorandom integer n such that low <= n <= high

    # Ensure integer endpoints
    low = int(low)
    high = int(high)

    # Sanity check on argument order
    if (low >= high)
        return (low)

    # Find a value in the required range
    do
        n = low + int(rand( ) * (high + 1 - low))
    while ((n < low) || (high < n))

    return (n)
}
```

In the absence of a call to srand(*x*), gawk and nawk use the same initial seed on each run so that runs are reproducible; mawk does not. Seeding with the current time via a call to srand( ) to get different sequences on each run is reasonable, *if the clock is precise enough*. Unfortunately, although machine speeds have increased dramatically, most time-of-day clocks used in current awk implementations still tick only once per second, so it is quite possible that successive runs of a simulation execute within the same clock tick. The solution is to avoid calling srand( ) more than once per run, and to introduce a delay of at least one second between runs:

```
$ for k in 1 2 3 4 5
> do
>     awk 'BEGIN {
>                   srand( )
>                   for (k = 1; k <= 5; k++)
>                       printf("%.5f ", rand( ))
>                   print ""
>               }'
>     sleep 1
> done
0.29994 0.00751 0.57271 0.26084 0.76031
0.81381 0.52809 0.57656 0.12040 0.60115
```

```
0.32768  0.04868  0.58040  0.98001  0.44200
0.84155  0.56929  0.58422  0.83956  0.28288
0.35539  0.08985  0.58806  0.69915  0.12372
```

Without the sleep 1 statement, the output lines are often identical.

9.11 Summary

A surprisingly large number of text processing jobs can be handled with the subset of awk that we have presented in this chapter. Once you understand awk's command line, and how it automatically handles input files, the programming job reduces to specifying record selections and their corresponding actions. This kind of minimalist *data-driven* programming can be extremely productive. By contrast, most conventional programming languages would burden you with dozens of lines of fairly routine code to loop over a list of input files, and for each file, open the file, read, select, and process records until end-of-file, and finally, close the file.

When you see how simple it is to process records and fields with awk, your view of data processing can change dramatically. You begin to divide large tasks into smaller, and more manageable, ones. For example, if you are faced with processing complex binary files, such as those used for databases, fonts, graphics, slide makers, spreadsheets, typesetters, and word processors, you might design, or find, a pair of utilities to convert between the binary format and a suitably marked-up simple text format, and then write small filters in awk or other scripting languages to manipulate the text representation.

## CHAPTER 10

Working with Files

In this chapter, we discuss some of the more common commands for working with files: how to list files, modify their timestamps, create temporary files, find files in a directory hierarchy, apply commands to a list of files, determine the amount of file-system space used, and compare files.

10.1 Listing Files

The echo command provides one simple way to list files that match a pattern:

```
$ echo /bin/*sh                        Show shells in /bin
/bin/ash /bin/bash /bin/bsh /bin/csh /bin/ksh /bin/sh /bin/tcsh /bin/zsh
```

The shell replaces the wildcard pattern with a list of matching files, and echo displays them in a space-separated list on a single line. However, echo does not interpret its arguments further, and thus does not associate them with files in the filesystem.–

The ls command can do much more because it knows that its arguments should be files. In the absence of command-line options, ls just verifies that its arguments exist, and displays them, either one per line if its output is not a terminal, or more compactly in multiple columns if it is. We can readily see the difference with three experiments:

```
$ ls /bin/*sh | cat                    Show shells in output pipe
/bin/ash
/bin/bash
/bin/bsh
/bin/csh
/bin/ksh
/bin/sh
/bin/tcsh
/bin/zsh
```

ls

Usage

    ls [*options*] [*file(s)*]

Purpose

List the contents of file directories.

Major options

1

Digit one. Force single-column output. In interactive mode, ls normally uses multiple columns of minimal width to fit the current window.

-a

Show all files, including hidden files (those whose names begin with a dot).

-d

Print information about directories themselves, rather than about files that they contain.

-F

Mark certain file types with special suffix characters.

-g

Group only: omit the owner name (implies -l (lowercase L)).

-i

List inode numbers.

-L

Follow symbolic links, listing the files that they point to.

-l

Lowercase L. List in long form, with type, protection, owner, group, byte count, last modification time, and filename.

-r

Reverse the default sort order.

-R

List recursively, descending into each subdirectory.

-S

Sort by descending file byte counts. GNU version only.

-s

List file size in (system-dependent) blocks.

-t

Sort by the last-modification timestamp.

--full-time

Show the complete timestamp. GNU version only.

(continued)

```
$ ls /bin/*sh                              Show shells in 80-character terminal window
/bin/ash  /bin/bash  /bin/bsh  /bin/csh  /bin/ksh  /bin/sh  /bin/tcsh  /bin/zsh
```

```
$ ls /bin/*sh                              Show shells in 40-character terminal window
/bin/ash    /bin/csh  /bin/tcsh
/bin/bash   /bin/ksh  /bin/zsh
/bin/bsh    /bin/sh
```

For terminal output, ls uses as many columns as will fit, ordering data by columns. This is merely for human convenience; if you really want single-column output to the terminal, you can force it with ls -1 (digit one). However, programs that process the piped output of ls can expect to find just the simple case of one filename per line.

On BSD, GNU/Linux, Mac OS X, and OSF/1 systems, ls replaces nonprintable characters in filenames with question marks in terminal output, but reports filenames to nonterminal output without changes. Consider a file with the peculiar name one\ntwo, where \n is a newline. Here is what GNU ls does with it:

```
$ ls one*two                               List peculiar filename
one?two
```

```
$ ls one*two | od -a -b                    Show the real filename
0000000    o    n    e   nl    t    w    o   nl
          157  156  145  012  164  167  157  012
0000010
```

The octal dump utility, od, reveals the true filename: the first reported newline is part of the name, and the second one ends the output line. A program downstream sees two apparently separate names; we show later in "The find Command" [10.4.3] how to deal with such aberrations.

Unlike echo, ls requires that its file arguments exist and complains if they do not:

```
$ ls this-file-does-not-exist              Try to list a nonexistent file
ls: this-file-does-not-exist: No such file or directory
```

```
$ echo $?                                  Show the ls exit code
1
```

Without an argument, echo displays only an empty line, but ls instead lists the contents of the current directory. We can demonstrate this behavior by first making a directory with three empty files:

```
$ mkdir sample          Make a new directory
$ cd sample             Change directory to it
$ touch one two three   Create empty files
```

and then applying echo and ls to its contents:

```
$ echo *                Echo matching files
one three two

$ ls *                  List matching files
one   three   two

$ echo                  Echo without arguments
                        This output line is empty

$ ls                    List current directory
one   three   two
```

Filenames that begin with a dot are hidden from normal shell pattern matching. We can see how such files are handled differently by creating a subdirectory with three hidden files:

```
$ mkdir hidden              Make a new directory
$ cd hidden                 Change directory to it
$ touch .uno .dos .tres     Create three hidden empty files
```

and then attempting to display its contents:

```
$ echo *                Echo matching files
*                       Nothing matched

$ ls                    List nonhidden files
                        This output line is empty

$ ls *                  List matching files
ls: *: No such file or directory
```

When no files match a pattern, the shell leaves the pattern as the argument: here, echo saw an asterisk and printed it, whereas ls tried to find a file named * and reported its failure to do so.

If we now supply a pattern that matches the leading dot, we can see further differences:

```
$ echo .*               Echo hidden files
. .. .dos .tres .uno

$ ls .*                 List hidden files
.dos   .tres   .uno

.:
```

```
  ..:
  hidden  one  three  two
```

Unix directories always contain the special entries .. (parent directory) and .
(current directory), and the shell passed all of the matches to both programs. echo
merely reports them, but ls does something more: when a command-line argument
is a directory, it lists the contents of that directory. In our example, the listing therefore includes the contents of the parent directory.

You can print information about a directory itself, instead of its contents, with the -d
option:

```
$ ls -d .*                         List hidden files, but without directory contents
.  ..  .dos  .tres  .uno

$ ls -d ../*                       List parent files, but without directory contents
../hidden  ../one  ../three  ../two
```

Because it is usually not of interest to list the parent directory, ls provides the -a
option to list all files in the current directory, including hidden ones:

```
$ ls -a                            List all files, including hidden ones
.  ..  .dos  .tres  .uno
```

The contents of the parent directory were not listed here because there was no argument that named it.

10.1.1 Long File Listings

Because ls knows that its arguments are files, it can report further details about
them—notably, some of the filesystem metadata. This is normally done with the -l
(lowercase L) option:

```
$ ls -l /bin/*sh                          List shells in /bin
-rwxr-xr-x  1 root root 110048 Jul 17  2002 /bin/ash
-rwxr-xr-x  1 root root 626124 Apr  9  2003 /bin/bash
lrwxrwxrwx  1 root root      3 May 11  2003 /bin/bsh -> ash
lrwxrwxrwx  1 root root      4 May 11  2003 /bin/csh -> tcsh
-rwxr-xr-x  1 root root 206642 Jun 28  2002 /bin/ksh
lrwxrwxrwx  1 root root      4 Aug  1  2003 /bin/sh -> bash
-rwxr-xr-x  1 root root 365432 Aug  8  2002 /bin/tcsh
-rwxr-xr-x  2 root root 463680 Jun 28  2002 /bin/zsh
```

While this output form is common, additional command-line options can modify its
appearance somewhat.

The first character on each line describes the filetype: - for ordinary files, d for directories, l for symbolic links, and so on.

The next nine characters report the file permissions for each of user, group, and
other: r for read, w for write, x for execute, and - if the permission is absent.

The second column contains the link counts: here, only /bin/zsh has a hard link to another file, but that other file is not shown in the output because its name does not match the argument pattern.

The third and fourth columns report the file owner and group, and the fifth column reports the file size in bytes.

The next three columns report the last-modification timestamp. In the historical form shown here, a month, day, and year are used for files older than six months, and otherwise, the year is replaced by a time of day:

```
$ ls -l /usr/local/bin/ksh              List a recent file
-rwxrwxr-x  1 jones devel 879740 Feb 23 07:33 /usr/local/bin/ksh
```

However, in modern implementations of ls, the timestamp is locale-dependent, and may take fewer columns. Here are tests with two different versions of ls on GNU/Linux:

```
$ LC_TIME=de_CH /usr/local/bin/ls -l /bin/tcsh   List timestamp in Swiss-German locale
-rwxr-xr-x  1 root root 365432 2002-08-08 02:34 /bin/tcsh
```

```
$ LC_TIME=fr_BE /bin/ls -l /bin/tcsh             List timestamp in Belgian-French locale
-rwxr-xr-x    1 root     root      365432 aoû  8  2002 /bin/tcsh
```

Although the timestamps are supposedly internationalized, this system shows its English roots with its bad French report of the date le 8 août 2002.

The GNU version permits display of full time precision; this example from an SGI IRIX system shows microsecond granularity:

```
$ /usr/local/bin/ls -l --full-time /bin/tcsh     Show high-resolution timestamp
-r-xr-xr-x  1 root sys 425756 1999-11-04 13:08:46.282188000 -0700 /bin/tcsh
```

The ls sidebar shows more than a dozen options common to ls implementations, but most have many more: the GNU version has nearly 40 of them! This diversity reflects the demands that have been put on ls over its more than three decades of existence. You will use ls often, so it is worthwhile to reread its manual pages from time to time to refresh your memory. For portable shell scripting, limit yourself to the more common options, and set the environment variable LC_TIME to reduce locale variations.

10.1.2 Listing File Metadata

Whenever computers store data in a compact binary form, it is useful to be able to present that same data in a more verbose form that is easily readable both by humans and by simple computer programs. We use the octal dump utility, od, several times in this book to turn streams of unprintable bytes into text, and we will discuss a special filesystem in "The /proc Filesystem" [13.7], that makes internal kernel data more accessible.

It is curious, however, that the metadata in filesystems, long available to the C programmer via the POSIX-standard fstat( ), lstat( ), and stat( ) library calls, remains largely inaccessible to programmers in the shell and scripting languages, except in the limited forms provided by the ls command.

In the late 1990s, SGI IRIX introduced a stat command, and around 2001, independent implementations of stat were written for BSD systems and the GNU *coreutils* package. Unfortunately, the output format of the three programs is quite different, as illustrated in "Other File Metadata" in Appendix B. Each has numerous command-line options that can provide more control over what data is output, and in what format. The GNU version is the only one that builds on every flavor of Unix, so if you standardize on it, you can use its features in your local shell scripts.

10.2 Updating Modification Times with touch

We have used the touch command a few times to create empty files. For a previously nonexistent file, here are equivalent ways of doing the same thing:

```
cat /dev/null  > some-file          Copy empty file to some-file
printf ""      > some-file          Print empty string to some-file
cat /dev/null >> some-file          Append empty file to some-file
printf ""     >> some-file          Append empty string to some-file
touch          some-file          Update timestamp of some-file
```

However, if the file exists already, the first two truncate the file to a zero size, whereas the last three effectively do nothing more than update its last-modification time. Clearly, the safe way to do that job is with touch, because typing > when you meant >> would inadvertently destroy the file contents.

touch is sometimes used in shell scripts to create empty files: their existence and possibly their timestamps, but not their contents, are significant. A common example is a lock file to indicate that a program is already running, and that a second instance should not be started. Another use is to record a file timestamp for later comparison with other files.

By default, or with the –m option, touch changes a file's last-modification time, but you can use the –a option to change the last-access time instead. The time used defaults to the current time, but you can override that with the –t option, which takes a following argument of the form [[CC]YY]MMDDhhmm[.SS], where the century, year within the century, and seconds are optional, the month of the year is in the range 01 through 12, the day of the month is in the range 01 through 31, and the time zone is your local one. Here is an example:

```
$ touch -t 197607040000.00 US-bicentennial     Create a birthday file
```

```
$ ls -l US-bicentennial                          List the file
-rw-rw-r--  1 jones devel 0 Jul  4  1976 US-bicentennial
```

touch also has the -r option to copy the timestamp of a reference file:

```
$ touch -r US-bicentennial birthday        Copy timestamp to the new birthday file

$ ls -l birthday                           List the new file
-rw-rw-r--  1 jones devel 0 Jul  4  1976 birthday
```

The touch command on older systems did not have the -r option, but all current versions support it, and POSIX requires it.

For the time-of-day clock, the Unix *epoch* starts at zero at 00:00:00 UTC[*] on January 1, 1970. Most current systems have a signed 32-bit time-of-day counter that increments once a second, and allows representation of dates from late 1901 to early 2038; when the timer overflows in 2038, it will wrap back to 1901. Fortunately, some recent systems have switched to a 64-bit counter: even with microsecond granularity, it can span more than a half-million years! Compare these attempts on systems with 32-bit and 64-bit time-of-day clocks:

```
$ touch -t 178907140000.00 first-Bastille-day     Create a file for the French Republic
touch: invalid date format `178907140000.00'      A 32-bit counter is clearly inadequate

$ touch -t 178907140000.00 first-Bastille-day     Try again on system with 64-bit counter

$ ls -l first-Bastille-day                         It worked! List the file
-rw-rw-r--  1 jones devel 0 1789-07-14 00:00 first-Bastille-day
```

Future dates on systems with 64-bit time-of-day clocks may still be artificially restricted by touch, but that is just a software limit imposed by the shortsighted POSIX requirement that the century have two digits:

```
$ touch -t 999912312359.59 end-of-9999     This works

$ ls -l end-of-9999                        List the file
-rw-rw-r--  1 jones devel 0 9999-12-31 23:59 end-of-9999

$ touch -t 1000001010000.00 start-of-10000    This fails
touch: invalid date format `1000001010000.00'
```

Fortunately, GNU touch provides another option that avoids the POSIX restriction:

```
$ touch -d '10000000-01-01 00:00:00' start-of-10000000 Into the next millionenium!

$ ls -l start-of-10000000                  List the file
-rw-rw-r--  1 jones devel 0 10000000-01-01 00:00 start-of-10000000
```

10.3   Creating and Using Temporary Files

While pipes eliminate much of the need for them, temporary files are still sometimes required. Unlike some operating systems, Unix has no notion of scratch files that are

---

[*] UTC is essentially what used to be called GMT; see the glossary entry for *Coordinated Universal Time*.

somehow magically removed when they are no longer needed. Instead, it provides two special directories, /tmp and /var/tmp (/usr/tmp on older systems), where such files are normally stored so that they do not clutter ordinary directories in the event that they are not cleaned up. On most systems, /tmp is cleared when the system boots, but /var/tmp must survive reboots because some text editors place backup files there to allow data recovery after a system crash.

Because /tmp is so heavily used, some systems make it a memory-resident filesystem for faster access, as shown in this example from a Sun Solaris system:

```
$ df /tmp                          Show disk free space for /tmp
Filesystem        1K-blocks    Used Available Use% Mounted on
swap              25199032   490168  24708864   2% /tmp
```

Putting the filesystem in the swap area means that it resides in memory until memory resources run low, at which point some of it may be written to swap.

The temporary-file directories are shared resources, making them subject to denial of service from other jobs that fill up the filesystem (or swap space), and to snooping or to file removal by other users. System management may therefore monitor space usage in those directories, and run cron jobs to clean out old files. In addition, the sticky permission bit is normally set on the directory so that only root and the files' owner can remove them. It is up to you to set file permissions to restrict access to files that you store in such directories. Shell scripts should normally use the umask command (see "Default permissions" in Appendix B), or else first create the needed temporary files with touch, and then run chmod to set suitable permissions.

To ensure that a temporary file is removed on job completion, programmers of compiled languages can first open the file, and then issue an unlink( ) system call. That deletes the file immediately, but because it is still open, it remains accessible until it is closed or until the job terminates, whichever happens first. The technique of unlink-after-open generally does not work on non-Unix operating systems, or in foreign filesystems mounted on directories in the Unix filesystem, and is not usable in most scripting languages.

On many systems, /tmp and /var/tmp are relatively small filesystems that are often mounted in separate *partitions* away from the root partition so that their filling up cannot interfere with, say, system logging. In particular, this means that you may not be able to create large temporary files in them, such as ones needed for a filesystem image of a CD or DVD. If /tmp fills up, you might not even be able to compile programs until your system manager fixes the problem, unless your compiler allows you to redirect temporary files to another directory.

10.3.1 The $$ Variable

Shared directories, or multiple running instances of the same program, bring the possibility of filename collisions. The traditional solution in shell scripts is to use the process ID (see "Process Listing" [13.2]), available in the shell variable $$, to form part of temporary filenames. To deal with the possibility of a full temporary filesystem, it is also conventional to allow the directory name to be overridden by an environment variable, traditionally called TMPDIR. In addition, you should use a trap command to request deletion of temporary files on job completion (see "Trapping Process Signals" [13.3.2]). A common shell-script preamble is:

```
umask 077                              Remove access for all but user

TMPFILE=${TMPDIR-/tmp}/myprog.$$       Generate a temporary filename

trap 'rm -f $TMPFILE' EXIT             Remove temporary file on completion
```

10.3.2 The mktemp Program

Filenames like /tmp/myprog.$$ have a problem: they are readily guessable. An attacker only needs to list the directory a few times while the target is running to figure out what temporary files are being used. By creating a suitably named file in advance, the attacker might be able to get your program to fail, or to read forged data, or to set the file permissions to allow the attacker to read the file.

To deal with this security issue, filenames must be unpredictable. BSD and GNU/ Linux systems have the mktemp command for creating names of temporary files that are hard to guess. While the underlying mktemp( ) library call is standardized by POSIX, the mktemp command is not. If your system lacks mktemp, we recommend that you install a portable version* derived from OpenBSD.

mktemp takes an optional filename template containing a string of trailing X characters, preferably at least a dozen of them. It replaces them with an alphanumeric string derived from random numbers and the process ID, creates the file with no access for group and other, and prints the filename on standard output.

 Here is why we recommend a dozen or more X characters. The easily guessable process ID might account for as many as six or seven of them, so the number of random letters might be as small as five: there are then 52^5 (about 380 million) random strings of letters. However, with just 10 X's (mktemp's default, and illustrated in its manual pages) and a seven-digit PID, only about 140,000 guesses are needed. We tested such an attack on our fastest machines with a 40-line C program, and found that a million guesses can be checked in less than three seconds!

---

* Available at *ftp://ftp.mktemp.org/pub/mktemp/*.

Here is an example of the use of mktemp:

```
$ TMPFILE=`mktemp /tmp/myprog.XXXXXXXXXXXX` || exit 1     Make unique temporary file

$ ls -l $TMPFILE                                          List the temporary file
-rw-------  1 jones devel 0 Mar 17 07:30 /tmp/myprog.hJmNZbq25727
```

The process ID, 25727, is visible at the end of the filename, but the rest of the suffix is unpredictable. The conditional exit command ensures that we terminate immediately with an error if the temporary file cannot be created, or if mktemp is not available.

The newest version of mktemp allows the template to be omitted; it then uses a default of /tmp/tmp.XXXXXXXXXX. However, older versions require the template, so avoid that shortcut in your shell scripts.

 HP-UX has a weak version of mktemp: it ignores any user-provided template, and constructs an easily guessable temporary filename from the username and the process ID. On HP-UX, we strongly recommend that you install the OpenBSD version mentioned earlier in this section.

To eliminate the need to hardcode a directory name, use the –t option: mktemp then uses whatever directory the environment variable TMPDIR specifies, or else /tmp.

The –d option requests the creation of a temporary directory:

```
$ SCRATCHDIR=`mktemp -d -t myprog.XXXXXXXXXXXX` || exit 1   Create temporary directory

$ ls -lFd $SCRATCHDIR                                       List the directory itself
drwx------  2 jones devel 512 Mar 17 07:38 /tmp/myprog.HStsWnFi6373/
```

Since that directory has no access for group and other, an attacker cannot even find out the names of files that you subsequently put there, but still might be able to guess them if your script is publicly readable. However, because the directory is not listable, an unprivileged attacker cannot confirm the guesses.

10.3.3 The /dev/random and /dev/urandom Special Files

Some systems provide two random *pseudodevices*: /dev/random and /dev/urandom. These are currently available only on BSD systems, GNU/Linux, IBM AIX 5.2, Mac OS X, and Sun Solaris 9, with two third-party implementations and retrofits available for earlier Solaris versions.* These devices serve as never-empty streams of random bytes: such a data source is needed in many cryptographic and security applications. While there are plenty of simple algorithms for generating streams of

---

* Available at the following: *http://www.cosy.sbg.ac.at/~andi/SUNrand/pkg/random-0.7a.tar.gz* and *http://sunrpms.maraudingpirates.org/HowTo.html*. Sun offers patches (10675[456]-01) to the SUNWski package to provide them on older Solaris releases; search for them at *http://sunsolve.sun.com/*.

pseudorandom numbers, generation of truly random data is a difficult problem: see the book *Cryptographic Security Architecture: Design and Verification.*[*]

The distinction between the two devices is that /dev/random may block until sufficient randomness has been gathered from the system so that it can guarantee high-quality random data. By contrast, /dev/urandom never blocks, but then its data may be somewhat less random (but still good enough to pass many statistical tests of randomness).

Because these devices are shared resources, it is easy to mount a denial-of-service attack against the blocking /dev/random pseudodevice simply by reading it and discarding the data. Compare these experiments on the two devices, and notice the difference in the count arguments:

```
$ time dd count=1 ibs=1024 if=/dev/random > /dev/null       Read 1KB of random bytes
0+1 records in
0+1 records out
0.000u 0.020s 0:04.62 0.4%     0+0k 0+0io 86pf+0w

$ time dd count=1024 ibs=1024 if=/dev/urandom > /dev/null   Read 1MB of random bytes
1024+0 records in
2048+0 records out
0.000u 0.660s 0:00.66 100.0%     0+0k 0+0io 86pf+0w
```

The more that /dev/random is read, the slower it responds. We experimented with these devices on several systems, and found that it could take a day or more to extract 10MB from /dev/random, and that /dev/urandom can produce that much in less than three seconds on our fastest systems.

These pseudodevices provide an alternative to mktemp for generating hard-to-guess temporary filenames:

```
$ TMPFILE=/tmp/secret.$(cat /dev/urandom | od -x | tr -d ' ' | head -n 1)

$ echo $TMPFILE                          Show the random filename
/tmp/secret.00000003024d462705664c043c04410e570492e
```

Here, we read a binary byte stream from /dev/urandom, convert it to hexadecimal with od, strip spaces with tr, and stop after collecting one line. Since od converts 16 bytes per output line, this gives us a sample of $16 \times 8 = 128$ random bits for the suffix, or 2^{128} (about 3.40×10^{38}) possible suffixes. If that filename is created in a directory that is listable only by its owner, there is effectively no chance of its being guessed by an attacker.

---

[*] By Peter Gutmann, Springer-Verlag, 2004, ISBN 0-387-95387-6.

10.4   Finding Files

Shell pattern matching is not powerful enough to match files recursively through an entire file tree, and ls and stat provide no way to select files other than by shell patterns. Fortunately, Unix provides some other tools that go beyond those commands.

10.4.1   Finding Files Quickly

locate, first introduced in Berkeley Unix, was reimplemented for the GNU *findutils* package.[*] locate uses a compressed database of all of the filenames in the filesystem to quickly find filenames that match shell-like wildcard patterns, without having to search a possibly huge directory tree. The database is created by updatedb in a suitably privileged job, usually run nightly via cron. locate can be invaluable for users, allowing them to answer questions like, Where does the system manager store the gcc distribution?:

```
$ locate gcc-3.3.tar                    Find the gcc-3.3 release
/home/gnu/src/gcc/gcc-3.3.tar-1st
/home/gnu/src/gcc/gcc-3.3.tar.gz
```

In the absence of wildcard patterns, locate reports files that contain the argument as a substring; here, two files matched.

Because locate's output can be voluminous, it is often piped into a pager, such as less, or a search filter, such as grep:

```
$ locate gcc-3.3 | fgrep .tar.gz        Find gcc-3.3, but report only its distribution archives
/home/gnu/src/gcc/gcc-3.3.tar.gz
```

Wildcard patterns must be protected from shell expansion so that locate can handle them itself:

```
$ locate '*gcc-3.3*.tar*'               Find gcc-3.3 using wildcard matching inside locate
...
/home/gnu/src/gcc/gcc-3.3.tar.gz
/home/gnu/src/gcc/gcc-3.3.1.tar.gz
/home/gnu/src/gcc/gcc-3.3.2.tar.gz
/home/gnu/src/gcc/gcc-3.3.3.tar.gz
...
```

locate may not be suitable for all sites because it reveals filenames that users might have expected to be invisible by virtue of strict directory permissions. If this is of concern, simply arrange for updatedb to be run as an unprivileged user: then no filenames are exposed that could not be found by any user by other legitimate means. Better, use the *secure locate* package, slocate;[†] it also stores file protections and ownership in the database, and only shows filenames that users have access to.

---

[*] Available at *ftp://ftp.gnu.org/gnu/findutils/*.

[†] Available at *ftp://ftp.geekreview.org/slocate/*.

updatedb has options to support creation of locate databases for selected portions of the filesystem, such as a user's home-directory tree, so locate can readily be used for personal file lookups.

10.4.2 Finding Where Commands Are Stored

Occasionally, you may want to know the filesystem location of a command that you invoke without a path. The Bourne-shell family type command does the job:

```
$ type gcc                                  Where is gcc?
gcc is /usr/local/bin/gcc

$ type type                                 What is type?
type is a shell builtin

$ type newgcc                               What is newgcc?
newgcc is an alias for /usr/local/test/bin/gcc

$ type mypwd                                What is mypwd?
mypwd is a function

$ type foobar                               What is this (nonexistent) command?
foobar not found
```

Notice that type is an internal shell command, so it knows about aliases and functions as well.

The pathfind command that we presented in Example 8-1 provides another way to search for files in *any* directory path, not just the PATH list that type searches.

10.4.3 The find Command

If you want to select, say, files larger than a certain size, or modified in the last three days, belonging to you, or having three or more hard links, you need the find command, one of the most powerful in the Unix toolbox.

Implementations of find offer as many as 60 different options, so we can discuss only a few of them. The sidebar in this section summarizes the important find options.

If you need to go swinging through the branches of directory trees looking for something, find can probably do the job for you, but you may first have to slog through its manual pages to find out how. The GNU version has an extensive manual, and we recommend it for detailed study.

10.4.3.1 Using the find command

The most unusual thing about find as a Unix command is that the files and directories to search come *first* in the argument list, and directories are (almost) always

find

Usage

> find [*files-or-directories*] [*options*]

Purpose

> Find files matching specified name patterns, or having given attributes.

Major options

> See the text for a description of the numbers *mask* and *n* that follow some of these options:

> -atime *n*
>> Select files with access times of *n* days.

> -ctime *n*
>> Select files with inode-change times of *n* days.

> -follow
>> Follow symbolic links.

> -group *g*
>> Select files in group *g* (a name or numeric group ID).

> -links *n*
>> Select files with *n* hard links.

> -ls
>> Produce a listing similar to the ls long form, rather than just filenames.

> -mtime *n*
>> Select files with modification times of *n* days.

> -name '*pattern*'
>> Select files matching the shell wildcard pattern (quoted to protect it from shell interpretation).

> -perm *mask*
>> Select files matching the specified octal permission mask.

> -prune
>> Do not descend recursively into directory trees.

> -size *n*
>> Select files of size *n*.

> -type *t*
>> Select files of type *t*, a single letter: d (directory), f (file), or l (symbolic link). There are letters for other file types, but they are not needed often.

> -user *u*
>> Select files owned by user *u* (a name or numeric user ID).

Behavior

find descends into directory trees, finding all files in those trees. It then applies selectors defined by its command-line options to choose files for further action, normally printing their names or producing an ls-like verbose listing.

Caveats

Because of find's default directory descent, it potentially can take a long time to run in a large filesystem.

find's output is *not* sorted.

find has additional options that can be used to carry out arbitrary actions on the selected files. Because this is potentially dangerous, we do not recommend their use except in tightly controlled situations.

---

descended into recursively. The options that select names for ultimate display or action come at the *end* of the command line.

Unlike ls and the shells, find has no concept of hidden files: if a dotted filename is present, find will find it.

Also unlike ls, find does *not* sort filenames. It just takes them in whatever order they are found in directories that it reads, and that order is effectively random.* Thus, you'll likely want to include a sort stage in a pipeline following the find command.

Again, unlike ls, when find has a directory to process, it dives with gusto recursively into that directory to find everything below it, unless you tell it not to with the -prune option.

When find finds a file to process, it first carries out the selection restrictions implied by the command-line options, and if those tests succeed, it hands the name off to an internal action routine. The default action is just to print the name on standard output, but the -exec option can provide a command template into which the name is substituted, and the command is then executed. Antiquated implementations of find required an explicit -print option to produce output, but fortunately, that design blunder has been fixed in every current implementation that we've tested, and in POSIX.

---

* Since users are so used to seeing sorted lists from ls and shell wildcard expansions, many assume that directories must store names in sorted order. That is not the case, but it is usually not until you write a program that uses the opendir( ), readdir( ), and closedir( ) library calls that you discover the probable need for qsort( ) as well!

Automated execution of commands on selected files is both powerful and *extremely dangerous*. If that command is destructive, it may be better to let find produce the list in a temporary file first, and then have a compctent human carefully examine that list before deciding whether to hand it off to some command for further automated processing.

Shell scripts that use find for destructive purposes must be written carefully, and then debugged with dry runs that, for example, insert the echo command at the start of the destructive command so that you can see what would have been done without actually doing it.

We are now ready for the simplest example: a bare find finds everything in the current directory tree. As before, we start with an empty directory, then populate it with a few empty files:

```
$ ls                              Verify that we have an empty directory

$ mkdir -p sub/sub1               Create a directory tree

$ touch one two .uno .dos         Create some empty top-level files

$ touch sub/three sub/sub1/four   Create some empty files deeper in the tree

$ find                            Find everything from here down
.
./sub
./sub/sub1
./sub/sub1/four
./sub/three
./one
./two
./.uno
./.dos
```

That jumbled list is easily sorted:

```
$ find | LC ALL=C sort            Sort find's output into traditional order
.
./.dos
./.uno
./one
./sub
./sub/sub1
./sub/sub1/four
./sub/three
./two
```

We set LC_ALL to get the traditional (ASCII) sort order, since modern sort implementations are locale-aware, as we described in "Sorting by Lines" [4.1.1].

find has a useful option, -ls, that gives output vaguely similar to what ls -liRs would give. However, it lacks further options to control the format of this verbose display:

```
$ find -ls                              Find files, and use ls-style output
1451550   4 drwxr-xr--  3 jones   devel   4096 Sep 26 09:40 .
1663219   4 drwxrwxr-x  3 jones   devel   4096 Sep 26 09:40 ./sub
1663220   4 drwxrwxr-x  2 jones   devel   4096 Sep 26 09:40 ./sub/sub1
1663222   0 -rw-rw-r--  1 jones   devel      0 Sep 26 09:40 ./sub/sub1/four
1663221   0 -rw-rw-r--  1 jones   devel      0 Sep 26 09:40 ./sub/three
1451546   0 -rw-rw-r--  1 jones   devel      0 Sep 26 09:40 ./one
1451547   0 -rw-rw-r--  1 jones   devel      0 Sep 26 09:40 ./two
1451548   0 -rw-rw-r--  1 jones   devel      0 Sep 26 09:40 ./.uno
1451549   0 -rw-rw-r--  1 jones   devel      0 Sep 26 09:40 ./.dos

$ find -ls | sort -k11                  Find files, and sort by filename
1451550   4 drwxr-xr--  3 jones   devel   4096 Sep 26 09:40 .
1451549   0 -rw-rw-r--  1 jones   devel      0 Sep 26 09:40 ./.dos
1451548   0 -rw-rw-r--  1 jones   devel      0 Sep 26 09:40 ./.uno
1451546   0 -rw-rw-r--  1 jones   devel      0 Sep 26 09:40 ./one
1663219   4 drwxrwxr-x  3 jones   devel   4096 Sep 26 09:40 ./sub
1663220   4 drwxrwxr-x  2 jones   devel   4096 Sep 26 09:40 ./sub/sub1
1663222   0 -rw-rw-r--  1 jones   devel      0 Sep 26 09:40 ./sub/sub1/four
1663221   0 -rw-rw-r--  1 jones   devel      0 Sep 26 09:40 ./sub/three
1451547   0 -rw-rw-r--  1 jones   devel      0 Sep 26 09:40 ./two
```

For comparison, here is how ls displays the same file metadata:

```
$ ls -liRs *                            Show ls recursive verbose output
752964   0 -rw-rw-r--  1 jones   devel      0 2003-09-26 09:40 one
752965   0 -rw-rw-r--  1 jones   devel      0 2003-09-26 09:40 two

sub:
total 4
752963   4 drwxrwxr-x  2 jones   devel   4096 2003-09-26 09:40 sub1
752968   0 -rw-rw-r--  1 jones   devel      0 2003-09-26 09:40 three

sub/sub1:
total 0
752969   0 -rw-rw-r--  1 jones   devel      0 2003-09-26 09:40 four
```

Now let's give the find command some file patterns:

```
$ find 'o*'                             Find files in this directory starting with "o"
one

$ find sub                              Find files in directory sub
sub
sub/sub1
sub/sub1/four
sub/three
```

Next, we suppress directory descent:

```
$ find -prune                           Find without looking inside this directory
.

$ find . -prune                         Another way to do the same thing
.
```

```
$ find * -prune                          Find files in this directory
one
sub
two

$ ls -d *                                List files, but not directory contents
one  sub  two
```

Notice that a missing file or directory argument is equivalent to the current directory, so the first two simply report that directory. However, the asterisk matches every nonhidden file, so the third find works like ls -d, except that it shows one file per line.

Now it is time to try out some of the more powerful selection options in find's repertoire. Let's start with owner and group selection. The options –group and –user each require a following symbolic name or numeric identifier. Thus, find / -user root starts a long-running search for files in the entire tree that are owned by root. Unless this command is run by root, directory permissions will almost certainly hide major parts of the tree.

You probably expect that all of the files in your login directory tree are owned by you. To make sure, run the command find $HOME/. ! -user $USER. The exclamation argument means *not*, so in English, this command says: start at my home directory and list all files that do not belong to me. Both HOME and USER are standard shell variables customized to your login, so this command works for everyone. We used $HOME/. rather than just $HOME so that the command also works if $HOME is a symbolic link.

The –perm option requires a following permission mask as an octal string, optionally signed. When the mask is unsigned, an exact match on the permissions is required. If it is negative, then *all* of the bits set are required to match. If it has a plus sign, then *at least one* of the bits set must match. This is pretty complex, so we present some common idioms in Table 10-1.

Table 10-1. Common permission settings for find

Option	Meaning
–perm -002	Find files writable by other.
–perm -444	Find files readable by everyone.
! –perm -444	Find files not readable by everyone.
–perm 444	Find files with exact permissions r--r--r--.
–perm +007	Find files accessible by other.
! –perm +007	Find files not accessible by other.

The –size option requires a following numeric argument. By default, the size is in 512-byte blocks, although many find implementations permit the number to be suffixed by c for characters (bytes), or k for kilobytes. If the number is unsigned, then only files of exactly that size match. If it is negative, then only files smaller than that (absolute) size match. Otherwise, with a plus sign, only files bigger than that size match. Thus, `find $HOME/. -size +1024k` finds all files in your login tree that are bigger than 1MB, and `find . -size 0` finds all files in the current directory tree that are empty.

The –type option requires a following single-letter argument to specify the file type. The important choices are d for directory, f for ordinary file, and l for symbolic link.

The –follow option asks `find` to follow symbolic links. You can use this to find broken links:

```
$ ls                              Show that we have an empty directory

$ ln -s one two                   Create a soft (symbolic) link to a nonexistent file

$ file two                        Diagnose this file
two: broken symbolic link to one

$ find .                          Find all files
.
./two

$ find . -type l                  Find soft links only
./two

$ find . -type l -follow          Find soft links and try to follow them
find: cannot follow symbolic link ./two: No such file or directory
```

The –links option requires a following integer number. If it is unsigned, it selects only files having that many hard links. If it is negative, only files with fewer than that many (in absolute value) links are selected. If it has a plus sign, then only files with more than that many links are selected. Thus, the usual way to find files with hard links is `find . -links +1`.

The –atime (access time), –ctime (inode-change time), and –mtime (modification time) options require a following integer number, measured in days. If unsigned, it means exactly that many days old. If negative, it means less than that absolute value. With a plus sign, it means more than that value. A common idiom is `find . -mtime -7` to find files modified in the last week.

 It is regrettable that `find` does not allow the number to have a fractional part or a units suffix: we've often wanted to specify units of years, months, weeks, hours, minutes, or seconds with these options. GNU `find` provides the –amin, –cmin, and –mmin options which take values in minutes, but units suffixes on the original timestamp selection options would have been more general.

A related option, –newer *filename*, selects only files modified more recently than the specified file. If you need finer granularity than a day, you can create an empty file

with touch -t *date_time* *timestampfile*, and then use that file with the –newer option. If you want to find files older than that file, negate the selector: ! –newer *timestampfile*.

The find command selector options can be combined: all must match for the action to be taken. They can be interspersed with the –a (AND) option if you wish. There is also a –o (OR) option that specifies that at least one selector of the surrounding pair must match. Here are two simple examples of the use of these Boolean operators:

```
$ find . -size +0 -a -size -10          Find nonempty files smaller than 10 blocks (5120 bytes)
...

$ find . -size 0 -o -atime +365         Find files that are empty or unread in the past year
...
```

The –a and –o operators, together with the grouping options \(and \), can be used to create complex Boolean selectors. You'll rarely need them, and when you do, you'll find them complex enough that you'll hide them in a script once they are debugged, and then just use that script happily ever after.

10.4.3.2 A simple find script

So far, we have used find just to produce lists of files matching particular selection requirements, possibly feeding them into a simple pipeline. Now let's look at a slightly more complex example. In "Substitution details" [3.2.7.1], we presented a simple sed script to (begin to) convert HTML to XHTML:

```
$ cat $HOME/html2xhtml.sed            Show sed commands for converting HTML to XHTML
s/<H1>/<h1>/g
s/<H2>/<h2>/g
...
s:</H1>:</h1>:g
s:</H2>:</h2>:g
...
s/<[Hh][Tt][Mm][Ll]>/<html>/g
s:</[Hh][Tt][Mm][Ll]>:</html>:g
s:<[Bb][Rr]>:<br/>:g
...
```

Such a script can automate a large part of the task of converting from HTML to XHTML, the standardized XML-based version of HTML. Combining sed with find and a simple loop accomplishes the task in just a few lines of code:

```
cd top level web site directory
find . -name '*.html' -type f |                    Find all HTML files
    while read file                                Read filename into variable
    do
        echo $file                                 Print progress
        mv $file $file.save                        Save a backup copy
        sed -f $HOME/html2xhtml.sed < $file.save > $file  Make the change
    done
```

10.4.3.3 A complex find script

In this section, we develop a real working example of find's virtuosity.* It is a shell script named filesdirectories that some of our local users with large home-directory trees run nightly via the crontab system (see "crontab: Rerun at Specified Times" [13.6.4]) to create several lists of files and directories, grouped by the number of days within which they have been changed. This helps remind them of their recent activities, and provides a much faster way to search their trees for particular files by searching a single list file rather than the filesystem itself.

filesdirectories requires GNU find for access to the –fprint option, which permits multiple output files to be created in one pass through the directory tree, producing a *tenfold speedup* for this script over a version that used multiple invocations of the original Unix find.

The script begins with the usual security features: specify the – option in the #! line (see "Self-Contained Scripts: The #! First Line" [2.4]):

```
#! /bin/sh -
```

set the IFS variable to newline-space-tab:

```
IFS='
'
```

and set the PATH variable to ensure that GNU find is found first:

```
PATH=/usr/local/bin:/bin:/usr/bin    # need GNU find for -fprint option
export PATH
```

It then checks for the expected single argument, and otherwise, prints a brief error message on standard error and exits with a nonzero status value:

```
if [ $# -ne 1 ]
then
        echo "Usage: $0 directory" >&2
        exit 1
fi
```

As a final security feature, the script invokes umask to limit access to the owner of the output files:

```
umask 077                            # ensure file privacy
```

filesdirectories allows the default temporary file directory to be overridden by the TMPDIR environment variable:

```
TMP=${TMPDIR:-/tmp}                  # allow alternate temporary directory
```

It then initializes TMPFILES to a long list of temporary files that collect the output:

```
TMPFILES="
```

---

* Our thanks go to Pieter J. Bowman at the University of Utah for this example.

```
    $TMP/DIRECTORIES.all.$$ $TMP/DIRECTORIES.all.$$.tmp
    $TMP/DIRECTORIES.last01.$$ $TMP/DIRECTORIES.last01.$$.tmp
    $TMP/DIRECTORIES.last02.$$ $TMP/DIRECTORIES.last02.$$.tmp
    $TMP/DIRECTORIES.last07.$$ $TMP/DIRECTORIES.last07.$$.tmp
    $TMP/DIRECTORIES.last14.$$ $TMP/DIRECTORIES.last14.$$.tmp
    $TMP/DIRECTORIES.last31.$$ $TMP/DIRECTORIES.last31.$$.tmp
    $TMP/FILES.all.$$ $TMP/FILES.all.$$.tmp
    $TMP/FILES.last01.$$ $TMP/FILES.last01.$$.tmp
    $TMP/FILES.last02.$$ $TMP/FILES.last02.$$.tmp
    $TMP/FILES.last07.$$ $TMP/FILES.last07.$$.tmp
    $TMP/FILES.last14.$$ $TMP/FILES.last14.$$.tmp
    $TMP/FILES.last31.$$ $TMP/FILES.last31.$$.tmp
    "
```

These output files contain the names of directories and files in the entire tree (*.all.*), as well as the names of those modified in the last day (*.last01.*), last two days (*.last02.*), and so on.

The WD variable saves the argument directory name for later use, and then the script changes to that directory:

```
WD=$1
cd $WD || exit 1
```

Changing the working directory before running find solves two problems:

- If the argument is not a directory, or is but lacks the needed permissions, then the cd command fails, and the script terminates immediately with a nonzero exit value.

- If the argument is a symbolic link, cd follows the link to the real location. find does not follow symbolic links unless given extra options, but there is no way to tell it to do so only for the top-level directory. In practice, we do not want filesdirectories to follow links in the directory tree, although it is straightforward to add an option to do so.

The trap commands ensure that the temporary files are removed when the script terminates:

```
trap 'exit 1'          HUP INT PIPE QUIT TERM
trap 'rm -f $TMPFILES' EXIT
```

The exit status value is preserved across the EXIT trap (see "Trapping Process Signals" [13.3.2]).

The wizardry, and all of the hard work, come next in the multiline find command. The lines with the -name option match the names of the output files from a previous run, and the -true option causes them to be ignored so that they do not clutter the output reports:

```
find . \
        -name DIRECTORIES.all -true \
    -o -name 'DIRECTORIES.last[0-9][0-9]' -true \
    -o -name FILES.all -true \
    -o -name 'FILES.last[0-9][0-9]' -true \
```

The next line matches all ordinary files, and the –fprint option writes their names to $TMP/FILES.all.$$:

```
         -o -type f          -fprint $TMP/FILES.all.$$ \
```

The next five lines select files modified in the last 31, 14, 7, 2, and 1 days (the -type f selector is still in effect), and the –fprint option writes their names to the indicated temporary files:

```
         -a          -mtime -31 -fprint $TMP/FILES.last31.$$ \
         -a          -mtime -14 -fprint $TMP/FILES.last14.$$ \
         -a          -mtime  -7 -fprint $TMP/FILES.last07.$$ \
         -a          -mtime  -2 -fprint $TMP/FILES.last02.$$ \
         -a          -mtime  -1 -fprint $TMP/FILES.last01.$$ \
```

The tests are made in order from oldest to newest because each set of files is a subset of the previous ones, reducing the work at each step. Thus, a ten-day-old file will pass the first two –mtime tests, but will fail the next three, so it will be included only in the FILES.last31.$$ and FILES.last14.$$ files.

The next line matches directories, and the –fprint option writes their names to $TMP/ DIRECTORIES.all.$$:

```
         -o -type d          -fprint $TMP/DIRECTORIES.all.$$ \
```

The final five lines of the find command match subsets of directories (the -type d selector still applies) and write their names, just as for files earlier in the command:

```
         -a          -mtime -31 -fprint $TMP/DIRECTORIES.last31.$$ \
         -a          -mtime -14 -fprint $TMP/DIRECTORIES.last14.$$ \
         -a          -mtime  -7 -fprint $TMP/DIRECTORIES.last07.$$ \
         -a          -mtime  -2 -fprint $TMP/DIRECTORIES.last02.$$ \
         -a          -mtime  -1 -fprint $TMP/DIRECTORIES.last01.$$
```

When the find command finishes, its preliminary reports are available in the temporary files, but they have not yet been sorted. The script then finishes the job with a loop over the report files:

```
for i in FILES.all FILES.last31 FILES.last14 FILES.last07 \
    FILES.last02 FILES.last01 DIRECTORIES.all \
    DIRECTORIES.last31 DIRECTORIES.last14 \
    DIRECTORIES.last07 DIRECTORIES.last02 DIRECTORIES.last01
do
```

sed replaces the prefix ./ in each report line with the user-specified directory name so that the output files contain full, rather than relative, pathnames:

```
    sed -e "s=^[.]/=$WD/=" -e "s=^[.]$=$WD=" $TMP/$i.$$ |
```

sort orders the results from sed into a temporary file named by the input filename suffixed with .tmp:

```
    LC_ALL=C sort > $TMP/$i.$$.tmp
```

Setting LC_ALL to C produces the traditional Unix sort order that we have long been used to, and avoids surprise and confusion when more modern locales are set. Using the traditional order is particularly helpful in our diverse environments because our systems differ in their default locales.

The cmp command silently checks whether the report file differs from that of a previous run, and if so, replaces the old one:

```
cmp -s $TMP/$i.$$.tmp $i || mv $TMP/$i.$$.tmp $i
```

Otherwise, the temporary file is left for cleanup by the trap handler.

The final statement of the script completes the loop over the report files:

```
done
```

At runtime, the script terminates via the EXIT trap set earlier.

The complete filesdirectories script is collected in Example 10-1. Its structure should be clear enough that you can easily modify it to add other report files, such as for files and directories modified in the last quarter, half year, and year. By changing the sign of the –mtime values, you can get reports of files that have *not* been recently modified, which might be helpful in tracking down obsolete files.

Example 10-1. A complex shell script for find

```
#! /bin/sh -
# Find all files and directories, and groups of
# recently modified ones, in a directory tree, creating
# lists in FILES.* and DIRECTORIES.* at top level.
#
# Usage:
#       filesdirectories directory

IFS='
	'

PATH=/usr/local/bin:/bin:/usr/bin    # need GNU find for -fprint option
export PATH

if [ $# -ne 1 ]
then
        echo "Usage: $0 directory" >&2
        exit 1
fi

umask 077                            # ensure file privacy
TMP=${TMPDIR:-/tmp}                  # allow alternate temporary directory
TMPFILES="
        $TMP/DIRECTORIES.all.$$ $TMP/DIRECTORIES.all.$$.tmp
        $TMP/DIRECTORIES.last01.$$ $TMP/DIRECTORIES.last01.$$.tmp
        $TMP/DIRECTORIES.last02.$$ $TMP/DIRECTORIES.last02.$$.tmp
        $TMP/DIRECTORIES.last07.$$ $TMP/DIRECTORIES.last07.$$.tmp
        $TMP/DIRECTORIES.last14.$$ $TMP/DIRECTORIES.last14.$$.tmp
        $TMP/DIRECTORIES.last31.$$ $TMP/DIRECTORIES.last31.$$.tmp
        $TMP/FILES.all.$$ $TMP/FILES.all.$$.tmp
```

Example 10-1. A complex shell script for find (continued)

```
            $TMP/FILES.last01.$$ $TMP/FILES.last01.$$.tmp
            $TMP/FILES.last02.$$ $TMP/FILES.last02.$$.tmp
            $TMP/FILES.last07.$$ $TMP/FILES.last07.$$.tmp
            $TMP/FILES.last14.$$ $TMP/FILES.last14.$$.tmp
            $TMP/FILES.last31.$$ $TMP/FILES.last31.$$.tmp
            "

WD=$1
cd $WD || exit 1

trap 'exit 1'              HUP INT PIPE QUIT TERM
trap 'rm -f $TMPFILES' EXIT

find . \
        -name DIRECTORIES.all -true \
    -o -name 'DIRECTORIES.last[0-9][0-9]' -true \
    -o -name FILES.all -true \
    -o -name 'FILES.last[0-9][0-9]' -true \
    -o -type f              -fprint $TMP/FILES.all.$$ \
    -a          -mtime -31 -fprint $TMP/FILES.last31.$$ \
    -a          -mtime -14 -fprint $TMP/FILES.last14.$$ \
    -a          -mtime  -7 -fprint $TMP/FILES.last07.$$ \
    -a          -mtime  -2 -fprint $TMP/FILES.last02.$$ \
    -a          -mtime  -1 -fprint $TMP/FILES.last01.$$ \
    -o -type d              -fprint $TMP/DIRECTORIES.all.$$ \
    -a          -mtime -31 -fprint $TMP/DIRECTORIES.last31.$$ \
    -a          -mtime -14 -fprint $TMP/DIRECTORIES.last14.$$ \
    -a          -mtime  -7 -fprint $TMP/DIRECTORIES.last07.$$ \
    -a          -mtime  -2 -fprint $TMP/DIRECTORIES.last02.$$ \
    -a          -mtime  -1 -fprint $TMP/DIRECTORIES.last01.$$

for i in FILES.all FILES.last31 FILES.last14 FILES.last07 \
        FILES.last02 FILES.last01 DIRECTORIES.all \
        DIRECTORIES.last31 DIRECTORIES.last14 \
        DIRECTORIES.last07 DIRECTORIES.last02 DIRECTORIES.last01
do
        sed -e "s=^[.]/=$WD/=" -e "s=^[.]$=$WD=" $TMP/$i.$$ |
                LC_ALL=C sort > $TMP/$i.$$.tmp
        cmp -s $TMP/$i.$$.tmp $i || mv $TMP/$i.$$.tmp $i
done
```

10.4.4 Finding Problem Files

In "Listing Files" [10.1], we noted the difficulties presented by filenames containing special characters, such as newline. GNU find has the –print0 option to display filenames as NUL-terminated strings. Since pathnames can legally contain any character *except* NUL, this option provides a way to produce lists of filenames that can be parsed unambiguously.

It is hard to parse such lists with typical Unix tools, most of which assume line-oriented text input. However, in a compiled language with byte-at-a-time input, such as

C, C++, or Java, it is straightforward to write a program to diagnose the presence of problematic filenames in your filesystem. Sometimes they get there by simple programmer error, but other times, they are put there by attackers who try to hide their presence by disguising filenames.

For example, suppose that you did a directory listing and got output like this:

```
$ ls                              List directory
.  ..
```

At first glance, this seems innocuous, since we know that empty directories always contain two special hidden dotted files for the current and parent directory. However, notice that we did not use the –a option, so we should not have seen any hidden files, and also, there appears to be a space before the first dot in the output. Something is just not right! Let's apply find and od to investigate further:

```
$ find -print0 | od -ab          Convert NUL-terminated filenames to octal and ASCII
0000000    .  nul   .   /  sp   .  nul   .   /  sp   .   .  nul   .   /   .
          056 000 056 057 040 056 000 056 057 040 056 056 000 056 057 056
0000020   nl  nul   .   /   .   .  sp   .   .  sp   .   .  sp   .  sp  nl
          012 000 056 057 056 056 040 056 056 040 056 056 040 056 040 012
0000040   nl   nl  sp  sp  nul
          012 012 040 040 000
0000045
```

We can make this somewhat more readable with the help of tr, turning spaces into S, newlines into N, and NULs into newline:

```
$ find -print0 | tr ' \n\0' 'SN\n'     Make problem characters visible as S and N
.
./S.
./S..
./.N
./..S..S..S.SNNNSS
```

Now we can see what is going on: we have the normal dot directory, then a file named space-dot, another named space-dot-dot, yet another named dot-newline, and finally one named dot-dot-space-dot-dot-space-dot-dot-space-dot-space-newline-newline-newline-space-space. Unless someone was practicing Morse code in your filesystem, these files look awfully suspicious, and you should investigate them further before you get rid of them.

10.5 Running Commands: xargs

When find produces a list of files, it is often useful to be able to supply that list as arguments to another command. Normally, this is done with the shell's command substitution feature, as in this example of searching for the symbol POSIX_OPEN_MAX in system header files:

```
$ grep POSIX_OPEN_MAX /dev/null $(find /usr/include -type f | sort)
/usr/include/limits.h:#define    _POSIX_OPEN_MAX         16
```

Whenever you write a program or a command that deals with a list of objects, you should make sure that it behaves properly if the list is empty. Because grep reads standard input when it is given no file arguments, we supplied an argument of /dev/null to ensure that it does not hang waiting for terminal input if find produces no output: that will not happen here, but it is good to develop defensive programming habits.

The output from the substituted command can sometimes be lengthy, with the result that a nasty kernel limit on the combined length of a command line and its environment variables is exceeded. When that happens, you'll see this instead:

```
$ grep POSIX_OPEN_MAX /dev/null $(find /usr/include -type f | sort)
/usr/local/bin/grep: Argument list too long.
```

That limit can be found with getconf:

```
$ getconf ARG_MAX                      Get system configuration value of ARG_MAX
131072
```

On the systems that we tested, the reported values ranged from a low of 24,576 (IBM AIX) to a high of 1,048,320 (Sun Solaris).

The solution to the ARG_MAX problem is provided by xargs: it takes a list of arguments on standard input, one per line, and feeds them in suitably sized groups (determined by the host's value of ARG_MAX) to another command given as arguments to xargs. Here is an example that eliminates the obnoxious Argument list too long error:

```
$ find /usr/include -type f | xargs grep POSIX_OPEN_MAX /dev/null
/usr/include/bits/posix1_lim.h:#define  _POSIX_OPEN_MAX       16
/usr/include/bits/posix1_lim.h:#define  _POSIX_FD_SETSIZE     _POSIX_OPEN_MAX
```

Here, the /dev/null argument ensures that grep always sees at least two file arguments, causing it to print the filename at the start of each reported match. If xargs gets no input filenames, it terminates silently without even invoking its argument program.

GNU xargs has the --null option to handle the NUL-terminated filename lists produced by GNU find's -print0 option. xargs passes each such filename as a complete argument to the command that it runs, without danger of shell (mis)interpretation or newline confusion; it is then up to that command to handle its arguments sensibly.

xargs has options to control where the arguments are substituted, and to limit the number of arguments passed to one invocation of the argument command. The GNU version can even run multiple argument processes in parallel. However, the simple form shown here suffices most of the time. Consult the *xargs*(1) manual pages for further details, and for examples of some of the wizardry possible with its fancier features.

10.6 Filesystem Space Information

With suitable options, the find and ls commands report file sizes, so with the help of a short awk program, you can report how many bytes your files occupy:

```
$ find -ls | awk '{Sum += $7} END {printf("Total: %.0f bytes\n", Sum)}'
Total: 23079017 bytes
```

However, that report underestimates the space used, because files are allocated in fixed-size blocks, and it tells us nothing about the used and available space in the entire filesystem. Two other useful tools provide better solutions: df and du.

10.6.1 The df Command

df (disk free) gives a one-line summary of used and available space on each mounted filesystem. The units are system-dependent blocks on some systems, and kilobytes on others. Most modern implementations support the –k option to force kilobyte units, and the –l (lowercase L) option to include only local filesystems, excluding network-mounted ones. Here is a typical example from one of our web servers:

```
$ df -k
Filesystem           1K-blocks     Used Available Use% Mounted on
/dev/sda5              5036284  2135488   2644964  45% /
/dev/sda2                38890     8088     28794  22% /boot
/dev/sda3             10080520  6457072   3111380  68% /export
none                    513964        0    513964   0% /dev/shm
/dev/sda8               101089     4421     91449   5% /tmp
/dev/sda9             13432904   269600  12480948   3% /var
/dev/sda6              4032092  1683824   2143444  44% /ww
```

GNU df provides the –h (human-readable) option to produce a more compact, but possibly more confusing, report:

```
$ df -h
Filesystem           Size  Used Avail Use% Mounted on
/dev/sda5            4.9G  2.1G  2.6G  45% /
/dev/sda2             38M  7.9M   29M  22% /boot
/dev/sda3            9.7G  6.2G  3.0G  68% /export
none                 502M     0  502M   0% /dev/shm
/dev/sda8             99M  4.4M   90M   5% /tmp
/dev/sda9             13G  264M   12G   3% /var
/dev/sda6            3.9G  1.7G  2.1G  44% /ww
```

The output line order may be arbitrary, but the presence of the one-line header makes it harder to apply sort while preserving that header. Fortunately, on most systems, the output is only a few lines long.

You can supply a list of one or more filesystem names or mount points to limit the output to just those:

```
$ df -lk /dev/sda6 /var
Filesystem           1K-blocks      Used Available Use% Mounted on
```

---

df

Usage

    df [*options*] [*files-or-directories*]

Purpose

    Show the inode or space usage in one or more filesystems.

Major options

    -i

        Show inode counts rather than space.

    -k

        Show space in kilobytes rather than blocks.

    -l

        Lowercase L. Show only local filesystems.

Behavior

    For each file or directory argument, or for all filesystems if there are no such arguments, df produces a one-line header that identifies the output columns, followed by a usage report for the filesystem containing that file or directory.

Caveats

    The output of df varies considerably between systems, making it hard to use reliably in portable shell scripts.

    df's output is *not* sorted.

    Space reports for remote filesystems may be inaccurate.

    Reports represent only a single snapshot that might be quite different a short time later in an active multiuser system.

```
/dev/sda6            4032092   1684660   2142608   45% /ww
/dev/sda9           13432904    269704  12480844    3% /var
```

For network-mounted filesystems, entries in the Filesystem column are prefixed by *hostname:*, making the column wide enough that some df implementations split the display into two lines, which is a nuisance for other software that parses the output. Here's an example from a Sun Solaris system:

```
$ df
Filesystem    1k-blocks      Used Available Use% Mounted on
...
/dev/sdd1      17496684  15220472   1387420  92% /export/local
fs:/export/home/0075
               35197586  33528481   1317130  97% /a/fs/export/home/0075
...
```

df's reports about the free space on remote filesystems may be inaccurate, because of software implementation inconsistencies in accounting for the space reserved for emergency use.

In "Filesystem Implementation Overview" in Appendix B, we discuss the issue that the inode table in a filesystem has an immutable size that is set when the filesystem is created. The –i (inode units) option provides a way to assess inode usage. Here is an example, from the same web server:

```
$ df -i
Filesystem           Inodes   IUsed   IFree IUse% Mounted on
/dev/sda5            640000  106991  533009   17% /
/dev/sda2             10040      35   10005    1% /boot
/dev/sda3           1281696  229304 1052392   18% /export
none                 128491       1  128490    1% /dev/shm
/dev/sda8             26104     144   25960    1% /tmp
/dev/sda9           1706880     996 1705884    1% /var
/dev/sda6            513024  218937  294087   43% /ww
```

The /ww filesystem is in excellent shape, since its inode use and filesystem space are both just over 40 percent of capacity. For a healthy computing system, system managers should routinely monitor inode usage on all local filesystems.

df is one of those commands where there is wide variation in the options and output appearance, which again is a nuisance for portable programs that want to parse its output. Hewlett-Packard's implementation on HP-UX is radically different, but fortunately, HP provides a Berkeley-style equivalent, bdf, that produces output that is similar to our example. To deal with this variation, we recommend that you install the GNU version everywhere at your site; it is part of the *coreutils* package cited in "Sort Stability" [4.1.5].

10.6.2 The du Command

df summarizes free space by filesystem, but does not tell you how much space a particular directory tree requires. That job is done by du (disk usage). Like its companion, df, du's options tend to vary substantially between systems, and its space units also may vary. Two important options are widely implemented: –k (kilobyte units) and –s (summarize). Here are examples from our web server system:

```
$ du /tmp
12        /tmp/lost+found
1         /tmp/.font-unix
24        /tmp

$ du -s /tmp
24        /tmp

$ du -s /var/log /var/spool /var/tmp
204480 /var/log
236       /var/spool
8         /var/tmp
```

The GNU version provides the –h (human-readable) option:

```
$ du -h -s /var/log /var/spool /var/tmp
200M    /var/log
236k    /var/spool
8.0k    /var/tmp
```

du does not count extra hard links to the same file, and normally ignores soft links. However, some implementations provide options to force soft links to be followed, but the option names vary: consult the manual pages for your system.

---

du

Usage
> du [*options*] [*files-or-directories*]

Purpose
> Show the space usage in one or more directory trees.

Major options
> –k
>> Show space in kilobytes rather than (system-dependent) blocks.
>
> –s
>> Show only a one-line summary for each argument.

Behavior
> For each file or directory argument, or for the current directory if no such arguments are given, du normally produces one output line containing an integer representing the usage, followed by the name of the file or directory. Unless the –s option is given, each directory argument is searched recursively, with one report line for each nested directory.

Caveats
> du's output is *not* sorted.

One common problem that du helps to solve is finding out who the big filesystem users are. Assuming that user home-directory trees reside in /home/users, root can do this:

```
# du -s -k /home/users/* | sort -k1nr | less    Find large home directory trees
```

This produces a list of the top space consumers, from largest to smallest. A find *dirs* -size +10000 command in a few of the largest directory trees can quickly locate files that might be candidates for compression or deletion, and the du output can identify user directory trees that might better be moved to larger quarters.

Some managers automate the regular processing of du reports, sending warning mail to users with unexpectedly large directory trees, such as with the script in Example 7-1 in Chapter 7. In our experience, this is much better than using the filesystem quota system (see the manual pages for *quota*(1)), since it avoids assigning magic numbers (filesystem-space limits) to users; those numbers are invariably wrong, and they inevitably prevent people from getting legitimate work done.

There is nothing magic about how du works: like any other program, it has to descend through the filesystem, and total up the space used by every file. Thus, it can be slow on large filesystems, and it can be locked out of directory trees by strict permissions; if its output contains `Permission denied` messages, its report undercounts the space usage. Generally, only root has sufficient privileges to use du everywhere in the local system.

10.7 Comparing Files

In this section, we look at four related topics that involve comparing files:

- Checking whether two files are the same, and if not, finding how they differ
- Applying the differences between two files to recover one from the other
- Using checksums to find identical files
- Using digital signatures for file verification

10.7.1 The cmp and diff Utilities

A problem that frequently arises in text processing is determining whether the *contents* of two or more files are the same, even if their names differ.

If you have just two candidates, then the file comparison utility, cmp, readily provides the answer:

```
$ cp /bin/ls /tmp                          Make a private copy of /bin/ls

$ cmp /bin/ls /tmp/ls                       Compare the original with the copy
                                            No output means that the files are identical
$ cmp /bin/cp /bin/ls                       Compare different files
/bin/cp /bin/ls differ: char 27, line 1     Output identifies the location of the first difference
```

cmp is silent when its two argument files are identical. If you are interested only in its exit status, you can suppress the warning message with the –s option:

```
$ cmp -s /bin/cp /bin/ls                    Compare different files silently

$ echo $?                                   Display the exit code
1                                           Nonzero value means that the files differ
```

If you want to know the differences between two similar files, `diff` does the job:

```
$ echo Test 1 > test.1              Create first test file

$ echo Test 2 > test.2              Create second test file

$ diff test.[12]                    Compare the two files
1c1
< Test 1
---
> Test 2
```

It is conventional in using `diff` to supply the older file as the first argument.

Difference lines prefixed by a left angle bracket correspond to the left (first) file, and those prefixed by a right angle bracket come from the right (second) file. The 1c1 preceding the differences is a compact representation of the input-file line numbers where the difference occurred, and the operation needed to make the edit: here, c means *change*. In larger examples, you will usually also find a for *add* and d for *delete*.

`diff`'s output is carefully designed so that it can be used by other programs. For example, *revision control systems* use `diff` to manage the differences between successive versions of files under their management.

There is an occasionally useful companion to `diff` that does a slightly different job. `diff3` compares *three* files, such as a base version and modified files produced by two different people, and produces an ed-command script that can be used to merge both sets of modifications back into the base version. We do not illustrate it here, but you can find examples in the *diff3*(1) manual pages.

10.7.2 The patch Utility

The `patch` utility uses the output of `diff` and either of the original files to reconstruct the other one. Because the differences are generally much smaller than the original files, software developers often exchange difference listings via email, and use `patch` to apply them. Here is how `patch` can convert the contents of test.1 to match those of test.2:

```
$ diff -c test.[12] > test.dif      Save a context difference in test.dif

$ patch < test.dif                  Apply the differences
patching file test.1

$ cat test.1                        Show the patched test.1 file
Test 2
```

`patch` applies as many of the differences as it can; it reports any failures for you to handle manually.

Although `patch` can use the ordinary output of `diff`, it is more common to use `diff`'s `-c` option to get a *context difference*. That more verbose report tells `patch` the filenames, and allows it to verify the change location and to recover from mismatches. Context differences are not essential if neither of the two files has been changed since the differences were recorded, but in software development, quite often one or the other will have evolved.

10.7.3 File Checksum Matching

If you have lots of files that you suspect have identical contents, using cmp or diff would require comparing all pairs of them, leading to an execution time that grows *quadratically* in the number of files, which is soon intolerable.

You can get nearly linear performance by using *file checksums*. There are several utilities for computing checksums of files and strings, including sum, cksum, and checksum,[*] the message-digest tools[†] md5 and md5sum, and the secure-hash algorithm[‡] tools sha, sha1sum, sha256, and sha384. Regrettably, implementations of sum differ across platforms, making its output useless for comparisons of checksums of files on different flavors of Unix. The native version of cksum on OSF/1 systems produces different checksums than versions on other systems.

Except for the old sum command, only a few of these programs are likely to be found on an out-of-the-box system, but all are easy to build and install. Their output formats differ, but here is a typical example:

```
$ md5sum /bin/l?
696a4fa5a98b81b066422a39204ffea4  /bin/ln
cd6761364e3350d010c834ce114b4779  /bin/lp
351f5eab0baa6eddae391f84d0a6c192  /bin/ls
```

The long *hexadecimal* signature string is just a many-digit integer that is computed from all of the bytes of the file in such a way as to make it unlikely that any other byte stream could produce the same value. With good algorithms, longer signatures in general mean greater likelihood of uniqueness. The md5sum output has 32 hexadecimal digits, equivalent to 128 bits. Thus, the chance[§] of having two different files with identical signatures is only about one in $2^{64} = 1.84 \times 10^{19}$, which is probably negligible. Recent cryptographic research has demonstrated that it is possible to create families of pairs of files with the same MD5 checksum. However, creating a file

---

[*] Available at *http://www.math.utah.edu/pub/checksum/*.

[†] R. Rivest, *RFC 1321: The MD5 Message-Digest Algorithm*, available at *ftp://ftp.internic.net/rfc/rfc1321.txt*. md5sum is part of the GNU *coreutils* package.

[‡] NIST, FIPS PUB 180-1: Secure Hash Standard, April 1995, available at *http://www.cerberussystems.com/ INFOSEC/stds/fip180-1.htm*, and implemented in the GNU *coreutils* package.

[§] If you randomly select an item from a collection of N items, each has a 1/N chance of being chosen. If you select M items, then of the M(M-1)/2 possible pairs, the chance of finding a pair with identical elements is (M(M-1)/2)/N. That value reaches probability 1/2 for M about the square root of N. This is called the *birthday paradox*; you can find discussions of it in books on cryptography, number theory, and probability, as well as at numerous web sites. Its glossary entry includes a short proof and numerical examples.

with similar, but not identical, contents as an existing file, both with the same checksum, is likely to remain a difficult problem.

To find matches in a set of signatures, use them as indices into a table of signature counts, and report just those cases where the counts exceed one. awk is just the tool that we need, and the program in Example 10-2 is short and clear.

Example 10-2. Finding matching file contents

```
#! /bin/sh -
# Show filenames with almost-certainly identical
# contents, based on their MD5 checksums.
#
# Usage:
#       show-identical-files files

IFS='
'

PATH=/usr/local/bin:/usr/bin:/bin
export PATH

md5sum "$@" /dev/null 2> /dev/null |
  awk '{
        count[$1]++
        if (count[$1] == 1) first[$1] = $0
        if (count[$1] == 2) print first[$1]
        if (count[$1] > 1)  print $0
     }' |
    sort |
        awk '{
                if (last != $1) print ""
                last = $1
                print
            }'
```

Here is what its output looks like on a GNU/Linux system:

```
$ show-identical-files /bin/*

2df30875121b92767259e89282dd3002   /bin/ed
2df30875121b92767259e89282dd3002   /bin/red

43252d689938f4d6a513a2f571786aa1   /bin/awk
43252d689938f4d6a513a2f571786aa1   /bin/gawk
43252d689938f4d6a513a2f571786aa1   /bin/gawk-3.1.0

...
```

We can conclude, for example, that ed and red are identical programs on this system, although they may still vary their behavior according to the name that they are invoked with.

Files with identical contents are often links to each other, especially when found in system directories. `show-identical-files` provides more useful information when applied to user directories, where it is less likely that files are links and more likely that they're unintended copies.

10.7.4 Digital Signature Verification

The various checksum utilities provide a single number that is characteristic of the file, and is unlikely to be the same as the checksum of a file with different contents. Software announcements often include checksums of the distribution files so that you have an easy way to tell whether the copy that you just downloaded matches the original. However, checksums alone do not provide *verification*: if the checksum were recorded in another file that you downloaded with the software, an attacker could have maliciously changed the software and simply revised the checksum accordingly.

The solution to this problem comes from *public-key cryptography*, where data security is obtained from the existence of two related keys: a private key, known only to its owner, and a public key, potentially known to anyone. Either key may be used for encryption; the other is then used for decryption. The security of public-key cryptography lies in the belief that knowledge of the public key, and text that is decryptable with that key, provides no practical information that can be used to recover the private key. The great breakthrough of this invention was that it solved the biggest problem in historical cryptography: secure exchange of encryption keys among the parties needing to communicate.

Here is how the private and public keys are used. If Alice wants to sign an open letter, she uses her *private* key to encrypt it. Bob uses Alice's *public* key to decrypt the signed letter, and can then be confident that only Alice could have signed it, provided that she is trusted not to divulge her private key.

If Alice wants to send a letter to Bob that only he can read, she encrypts it with Bob's *public* key, and he then uses his *private* key to decrypt it. As long as Bob keeps his private key secret, Alice can be confident that only Bob can read her letter.

It isn't necessary to encrypt the entire message: instead, if just a file checksum is encrypted, then one has a *digital signature*. This is useful if the message itself can be public, but a way is needed to verify its authenticity.

Several tools for public-key cryptography are implemented in the GNU Privacy Guard[*] (GnuPG) and Pretty Good Privacy[†] (PGP) utilities. A complete description of these packages requires an entire book; see the section "Security and Cryptography"

---

[*] Available at *ftp://ftp.gnupg.org/gcrypt/gnupg/* and *http://www.gnupg.org/*.

[†] Available at *http://web.mit.edu/network/pgp.html*.

in the Bibliography. However, it is straightforward to use them for one important task: verification of *digital signatures*. We illustrate only GnuPG here, since it is under active development and it builds more easily and on more platforms than PGP.

Because computers are increasingly under attack, many software archives now include digital signatures that incorporate information from a file checksum as well as from the signer's private key. It is therefore important to know how to verify such signatures, and if a signature file is available, you should always verify it. Here is how you can do so with GnuPG:

```
$ ls -l coreutils-5.0.tar*              Show the distribution files
-rw-rw-r--  1 jones devel 6020616 Apr  2  2003 coreutils-5.0.tar.gz
-rw-rw-r--  1 jones devel      65 Apr  2  2003 coreutils-5.0.tar.gz.sig

$ gpg coreutils-5.0.tar.gz.sig          Try to verify the signature
gpg: Signature made Wed Apr  2 14:26:58 2003 MST using DSA key ID D333CBA1
gpg: Can't check signature: public key not found
```

The signature verification failed because we have not added the signer's public key to the gpg key ring. If we knew who signed the file, then we might be able to find the public key at the signer's personal web site or ask the signer for a copy via email. However, the only information that we have here is the key ID. Fortunately, people who use digital signatures generally register their public keys with a third-party *public-key server*, and that registration is automatically shared with other key servers. Some of the major ones are listed in Table 10-2, and more can be found by web search engines. Replicated copies of public keys enhance security: if one key server is unavailable or compromised, you can easily switch to another one.

Table 10-2. Major public-key servers

Country	URL
Belgium	*http://www.keyserver.net/en/*
Germany	*http://math-www.uni-paderborn.de/pgp/*
Germany	*http://pgp.zdv.uni-mainz.de/keyserver/pks-commands.html#extract*
UK	*http://www.cl.cam.ac.uk/PGP/pks-commands.html#extract*
USA	*http://pgp.mit.edu/*

Use a web browser to visit the key server, type the key ID 0xD333CBA1 into a search box (the leading 0x is mandatory), and get a report like this:

```
Public Key Server -- Index ''0xD333CBA1 ''

Type bits /keyID   Date       User ID
pub  1024D/D333CBA1 1999/09/26 Jim Meyering <meyering@ascend.com>
...
```

Follow the link on the key ID (shown in the preceding code snippet in bold) to get a web page that looks like this:

```
Public Key Server -- Get ''0xD333CBA1 ''

-----BEGIN PGP PUBLIC KEY BLOCK-----
Version: PGP Key Server 0.9.6

mQGiBDftyYoRBACvICTt5AWe7kdbRtJ37IZ+ED5tBA/IbISfqUPO+HmL/J9JSfkV
QHbdQR5dj5mrU6BY5YOY7L4KOS6lH3AgvsZ/NhkDBraBPgnMkpDqFb7z4keCIebb
...
-----END PGP PUBLIC KEY BLOCK-----
```

Finally, save the key text in a temporary file—say, temp.key—and add it to your key ring:

```
$ gpg --import temp.key                    Add the public key to your key ring
gpg: key D333CBA1: public key "Jim Meyering <jim@meyering.net>" imported
gpg: Total number processed: 1
gpg:              imported: 1
```

Now you can verify the signature successfully:

```
$ gpg coreutils-5.0.tar.gz.sig            Verify the digital signature
gpg: Signature made Wed Apr  2 14:26:58 2003 MST using DSA key ID D333CBA1
gpg: Good signature from "Jim Meyering <jim@meyering.net>"
gpg:                 aka "Jim Meyering <meyering@na-net.ornl.gov>"
gpg:                 aka "Jim Meyering <meyering@pobox.com>"
gpg:                 aka "Jim Meyering <meycring@ascend.com>"
gpg:                 aka "Jim Meyering <meyering@lucent.com>"
gpg: checking the trustdb
gpg: checking at depth 0 signed=0 ot(-/q/n/m/f/u)=0/0/0/0/0/1
gpg: next trustdb check due at ????-??-??
gpg: WARNING: This key is not certified with a trusted signature!
gpg:          There is no indication that the signature belongs to the owner.
Primary key fingerprint: D70D 9D25 AF38 J7A5 909A  4683 FDD2 DEAC D333 CBA1
```

The warning in the successful verification simply means that you have not certified that the signer's key really does belong to him. Unless you personally know the signer and have good reason to believe that the key is valid, you should not certify keys.

An attacker could modify and repackage the distribution, but without knowledge of the signer's (secret) private key, the digital signature cannot be reproduced, and gpg detects the attack:

```
$ ls -l coreutils-5.0.tar.gz               List the maliciously modified archive file
-rw-rw-r--  1 jones devel 6074205 Apr  2 2003 coreutils-5.0.tar.gz
```

```
$ gpg coreutils-5.0.tar.gz.sig             Try to verify the digital signature
gpg: Signature made Wed Apr  2 14:26:58 2003 MST using DSA key ID D333CBA1
gpg: BAD signature from "Jim Meyering <jim@meyering.net>"
```

Digital signatures ensure that the file at your site matches the one prepared and signed at the remote site. Of course, an undetected attack on the signer's system before the software was packaged for distribution would not be revealed when the signature was verified. Security is never perfect.

You do not need to use a web browser to retrieve a public key: the GNU `wget` utility[*] can do the job once you figure out the syntax of the URL expected by a particular key server. The script in Example 10-3 makes retrieval easy and provides a reminder of how to add the public keys to your key rings.

Example 10-3. Automating public-key retrieval

```
#! /bin/sh -
# Get one or more PGP/GPG keys from a key server.
#
# Usage:
#       getpubkey key-ID-1 key-ID-2 ...

IFS='
        '

PATH=/usr/local/bin:/usr/bin:/bin
export PATH

for f in "$@"
do
  g=0x`echo $f | sed -e s'/^0x//'`                              Ensure 0x prefix
  tmpfile=/tmp/pgp-$g.tmp.$$
  wget -q -O - "http://pgp.mit.edu:11371/pks/lookup?op=get&search=$g" > $tmpfile
  ls -l $tmpfile
  echo "Try:       pgp -ka $tmpfile"
  echo "           pgpgpg -ka $tmpfile"
  echo "           rm -f $tmpfile"
done
```

Here is an example of its use:

```
$ getpubkey D333CBA1                    Get the public key for key ID D333CBA1
-rw-rw-r--  1 jones jones 4567 Apr  6 07:26 /tmp/pgp-0xD333CBA1.tmp.21649
Try:    pgp -ka /tmp/pgp-0xD333CBA1.tmp.21643
        pgpgpg -ka /tmp/pgp-0xD333CBA1.tmp.21643
        rm -f /tmp/pgp-0xD333CBA1.tmp.21643
```

Some keys can be used with both PGP and GnuPG, but others cannot, so the reminder covers both. Because the command-line options for gpg and pgp differ, and pgp was developed first, gpg comes with a wrapper program, pgpgpg, that takes the same options as pgp, but calls gpg to do the work. Here, pgpgpg -ka is the same as gpg --import.

getpubkey allows you to add retrieved keys to either, or both, of your GnuPG and PGP key rings, at the expense of a bit of cut-and-paste. gpg provides a one-step solution, but only updates your GnuPG key ring:

```
$ gpg --keyserver pgp.mit.edu --search-keys 0xD333CBA1
 gpg: searching for "0xD333CBA1" from HKP server pgp.mit.edu
Keys 1-6 of 6 for "0xD333CBA1"
```

---

[*] Available at *ftp://ftp.gnu.org/gnu/wget/*.

```
(1)      Jim Meyering <meyering@ascend.com>
            1024 bit DSA key D333CBA1, created 1999-09-26
...
Enter number(s), N)ext, or Q)uit > 1
gpg: key D333CBA1: public key "Jim Meyering <jim@meyering.net>" imported
gpg: Total number processed: 1
gpg:                 imported: 1
```

The --keyserver option is only required the first time, but you can later use it to specify a different server. Besides a key ID, the --search-keys option accepts an email address, username, or personal name.

10.8 Summary

In this chapter, we showed how to list files and file metadata with ls and stat, and how to set file timestamps with touch. The touch experiments revealed information about the time-of-day clock and its limited range in many current systems.

We showed how to create unique temporary filenames with the shell process ID variable, $$, with the mktemp utility and a do-it-yourself sampling of streams of random numbers. The computing world can be a hostile environment, so it is worth protecting your programs from attack by giving their temporary files unique and unguessable names.

We described the locate and slocate commands for fast lookup of filenames in a regularly updated database constructed by complete scans of the filesystem. When you know part or all of a filename and just want to find where it is in the filesystem, locate is generally the best way to track it down, unless it was created after the database was constructed.

The type command is a good way to find out information about shell commands, and our pathfind script from Chapter 8 provides a more general solution for locating files in a specified directory path.

We took several pages to explore the powerful find command, which uses brute-force filesystem traversal to find files that match user-specified criteria. Nevertheless, we still had to leave many of its facilities for you to discover on your own from its manual pages and the extensive manual for GNU find.

We gave a brief treatment of xargs, another powerful command for doing operations on lists of files, often produced upstream in a pipeline by find. Not only does this overcome command-line length restrictions on many systems, but it also gives you the opportunity to insert additional filters in the pipeline to further control what files are ultimately processed.

The df and du commands report the space used in filesystems and directory trees. Learn them well, because you may use them often.

We wrapped up with a description of commands for comparing files, applying patches, generating file checksums, and validating digital signatures.

## CHAPTER 11

Extended Example: Merging User Databases

By now, we've come a long way and seen a number of shell scripts. This chapter aims to tie things together by writing shell programs to solve a moderately challenging task.

11.1 The Problem

The Unix password file, /etc/passwd, has shown up in several places throughout the book. System administration tasks often revolve around manipulation of the password file (and the corresponding group file, /etc/group). The format is well known:[*]

```
tolstoy:x:2076:10:Leo Tolstoy:/home/tolstoy:/bin/bash
```

There are seven fields: username, encrypted password, user ID number (UID), group ID number (GID), full name, home directory, and login shell. It's a bad idea to leave any field empty: in particular, if the second field is empty, the user can log in without a password, and *anyone* with access to the system or a terminal on it can log in as that user. If the seventh field (the shell) is left empty, Unix defaults to the Bourne shell, /bin/sh.

As is discussed in detail in Appendix B, it is the user and group ID numbers that Unix uses for permission checking when accessing files. If two users have different names but the same UID number, then as far as Unix knows, they are *identical*. There are rare occasions when you want such a situation, but usually having two accounts with the same UID number is a mistake. In particular, NFS *requires* a uniform UID space; user number 2076 on all systems accessing each other via NFS had better be the same user (tolstoy), or else there will be serious security problems.

---

[*] BSD systems maintain an additional file, /etc/master.passwd, which has three additional fields: the user's login class, password change time, and account expiration time. These fields are placed between the GID field and the field for the full name.

Now, return with us for a moment to yesteryear (around 1986), when Sun's NFS was just beginning to become popular and available on non-Sun systems. At the time, one of us was a system administrator of two separate 4.2 BSD Unix minicomputers. These systems communicated via TCP/IP, but did not have NFS. However, a new OS vendor was scheduled to make 4.3 BSD + NFS available for these systems. There were a number of users with accounts on both systems; typically the username was the same, but the UID wasn't! These systems were soon to be sharing filesystems via NFS; it was imperative that their UID spaces be merged. The task was to write a series of scripts that would:

- Merge the /etc/passwd files of the two systems. This entailed ensuring that all users from both systems had unique UID numbers.
- Change the ownership of all files to the correct users in the case where an existing UID was to be used for a different user.

It is this task that we recreate in this chapter, from scratch. (The original scripts are long gone, and it's occasionally interesting and instructive to reinvent a useful wheel.) This problem isn't just academic, either: consider two departments in a company that have been separate but that now must merge. It's possible for there to be users with accounts on systems in multiple departments. If you're a system administrator, you may one day face this very task. In any case, we think it is an interesting problem to solve.

11.2   The Password Files

Let's call our two hypothetical Unix systems u1 and u2. Example 11-1 presents the /etc/passwd file from u1.[*]

Example 11-1. u1 /etc/passwd file

```
root:x:0:0:root:/root:/bin/bash
bin:x:1:1:bin:/bin:/sbin/nologin
daemon:x:2:2:daemon:/sbin:/sbin/nologin
adm:x:3:4:adm:/var/adm:/sbin/nologin
tolstoy:x:2076:10:Leo Tolstoy:/home/tolstoy:/bin/bash
camus:x:112:10:Albert Camus:/home/camus:/bin/bash
jhancock:x:200:10:John Hancock:/home/jhancock:/bin/bash
ben:x:201:10:Ben Franklin:/home/ben:/bin/bash
abe:x:105:10:Honest Abe Lincoln:/home/abe:/bin/bash
dorothy:x:110:10:Dorothy Gale:/home/dorothy:/bin/bash
```

And Example 11-2 presents /etc/passwd from u2.

---

[*] Any resemblance to actual users, living or dead, is purely coincidental.

Example 11-2. u2 /etc/passwd file

```
root:x:0:0:root:/root:/bin/bash
bin:x:1:1:bin:/bin:/sbin/nologin
daemon:x:2:2:daemon:/sbin:/sbin/nologin
adm:x:3:4:adm:/var/adm:/sbin/nologin
george:x:1100:10:George Washington:/home/george:/bin/bash
betsy:x:1110:10:Betsy Ross:/home/betsy:/bin/bash
jhancock:x:300:10:John Hancock:/home/jhancock:/bin/bash
ben:x:301:10:Ben Franklin:/home/ben:/bin/bash
tj:x:105:10:Thomas Jefferson:/home/tj:/bin/bash
toto:x:110:10:Toto Gale:/home/toto:/bin/bash
```

If you examine these files carefully, you'll see they represent the various possibilities that our program has to handle:

- Users for whom the username and UID are the same on both systems. This happens most typically with administrative accounts such as root and bin.

- Users for whom the username and UID exist only on one system but not the other. In this case, when the files are merged, there is no problem.

- Users for whom the username is the same on both systems, but the UIDs are different.

- Users for whom the username is different on both systems, but the UIDs are the same.

11.3 Merging Password Files

The first step is to create a merged /etc/passwd file. This involves several substeps:

1. Physically merge the files, bringing duplicate usernames together. This becomes the input for the following steps.

2. Split the merged file into three separate parts for use in later processing:

   - Users for whom the username and UID are the same go into one file, named unique1. Users with nonrepeated usernames also go into this file.

   - Users with the same username and different UIDs go into a second file, named dupusers.

   - Users with the same UID and different usernames go into a third file, named dupids.

3. Create a list of all unique UID numbers that already are in use. This will be needed so that we can find new, unused UID numbers when a conflict occurs and we need to do a UID change (e.g., users jhancock and ben).

4. Given the list of in-use UID numbers, write a separate program to find a new, unused UID number.

5. Create a list of (username, old UID, new UID) triples to be used in creating final /etc/passwd entries, and more importantly, in generating commands to change the ownership of files in the filesystem.

   At the same time, create final password file entries for the users who originally had multiple UIDs and for UIDs that had multiple users.

6. Create the final password file.

7. Create the list of commands to change file ownership, and then run the commands. As will be seen, this has some aspects that require careful planning.

In passing, we note that all the code here operates under the assumption that usernames and UID numbers are not reused more than twice. This shouldn't be a problem in practice, but it is worth being aware of in case a more complicated situation comes along one day.

11.3.1 Separating Users by Manageability

Merging the password files is easy. The files are named u1.passwd and u2.passwd, respectively. The sort command does the trick. We use tee to save the file and simultaneously print it on standard output where we can see it:

```
$ sort u1.passwd u2.passwd | tee merge1
abe:x:105:10:Honest Abe Lincoln:/home/abe:/bin/bash
adm:x:3:4:adm:/var/adm:/shin/nologin
adm:x:3:4:adm:/var/adm:/sbin/nologin
ben:x:201:10:Ben Franklin:/home/ben:/bin/bash
ben:x:301:10:Ben Franklin:/home/ben:/bin/bash
betsy:x:1110:10:Betsy Ross:/home/betsy:/bin/bash
bin:x:1:1:bin:/bin:/sbin/nologin
bin:x:1:1:bin:/bin:/sbin/nologin
camus:x:112:10:Albert Camus:/home/camus:/bin/bash
daemon:x:2:2:daemon:/sbin:/sbin/nologin
daemon:x:2:2:daemon:/sbin:/sbin/nologin
dorothy:x:110:10:Dorothy Gale:/home/dorothy:/bin/bash
george:x:1100:10:George Washington:/home/george:/bin/bash
jhancock:x:200:10:John Hancock:/home/jhancock:/bin/bash
jhancock:x:300:10:John Hancock:/home/jhancock:/bin/bash
root:x:0:0:root:/root:/bin/bash
root:x:0:0:root:/root:/bin/bash
tj:x:105:10:Thomas Jefferson:/home/tj:/bin/bash
tolstoy:x:2076:10:Leo Tolstoy:/home/tolstoy:/bin/bash
toto:x:110:10:Toto Gale:/home/toto:/bin/bash
```

Example 11-3 presents splitout.awk. This script separates the merged file into three new files, named dupusers, dupids, and unique1, respectively.

Example 11-3. The splitout.awk program

```
#! /bin/awk -f
```

Example 11-3. The splitout.awk program (continued)

```
# $1   $2    $3  $4   $5          $6       $7
# user:passwd:uid:gid:long name:homedir:shell

BEGIN { FS = ":" }

# name[ ]    --- indexed by username
# uid[ ]     --- indexed by uid

# if a duplicate appears, decide the disposition

{
    if ($1 in name) {
        if ($3 in uid)
            ;   # name and uid identical, do nothing
        else {
            print name[$1] > "dupusers"
            print $0 > "dupusers"
            delete name[$1]

            # remove saved entry with same name but different uid
            remove_uid_by_name($1)
        }
    } else if ($3 in uid) {
        # we know $1 is not in name, so save duplicate ID records
        print uid[$3] > "dupids"
        print $0 > "dupids"
        delete uid[$3]

        # remove saved entry with same uid but different name
        remove_name_by_uid($3)
    } else
        name[$1] = uid[$3] = $0     # first time this record was seen
}

END {
    for (i in name)
        print name[i] > "unique1"

    close("unique1")
    close("dupusers")
    close("dupids")
}

function remove_uid_by_name(n,      i, f)
{
    for (i in uid) {
        split(uid[i], f, ":")
        if (f[1] == n) {
            delete uid[i]
            break
        }
    }
}
```

Example 11-3. The splitout.awk program (continued)

```
function remove_name_by_uid(id,     i, f)
{
    for (i in name) {
        split(name[i], f, ":")
        if (f[3] == id) {
            delete name[i]
            break
        }
    }
}
```

The program works by keeping a copy of each input line in two arrays. The first is indexed by username, the second by UID number. The first time a record is seen, the username and UID number have not been stored in either array, so a copy of the line is saved in both.

When an exact duplicate record (the username and UID are identical) is seen, nothing is done with it, since we already have the information. If the username has been seen but the UID is new, both records are written to the dupusers file, and the copy of the first record in the uid array is removed, since we don't need it. Similar logic applies to records where the UID has been seen before but the username doesn't match.

When the END rule is executed, all the records remaining in the name array represent unique records. They are written to the unique1 file, and then all the files are closed.

remove_uid_by_name( ) and remove_name_by_uid( ) are awk functions. User-defined functions in awk were described in "User-Defined Functions" [9.8]. These two functions remove unneeded information from the uid and name arrays, respectively.

Running the program creates the files:

```
awk -f splitout.awk merge1
```

11.3.2 Managing UIDs

Now that we have separated the users by categories, the next task is to create a list of all the UID numbers in use:

```
awk -F: '{ print $3 }' merge1 | sort -n -u > unique-ids
```

We can verify that we have only the unique UID numbers by counting lines in merge1 and unique-ids:

```
$ wc -l merge1 unique-ids
    20 merge1
    14 unique-ids
    34 total
```

Continuing through our task list, the next step is to write a program that produces unused UIDs. By default, the program reads a sorted list of in-use UID numbers and prints the first available UID number. However, since we'll be working with multiple users, we'll want it to generate a batch of unused UIDs. This is done with the -c option, which provides a count of UIDs to generate. Example 11-4 presents the newuids.sh script.

Example 11-4. The newuids.sh program

```
#! /bin/sh -

# newuids --- print one or more unused uids
#
# usage:
#    newuids [-c N] list-of-ids-file
#    -c N          print N unused uids

count=1      # how many uids to print

# parse arguments, let sh issue diagnostics
# and exit if need be
while getopts "c:" opt
do
    case $opt in
    c)  count=$OPTARG ;;
    esac
done

shift $(($OPTIND - 1))

IDFILE=$1

awk -v count=$count '
    BEGIN {
        for (i = 1; getline id > 0; i++)
            uidlist[i] = id
        close(idlist)

        totalids = i

        for (i = 2; i <= totalids; i++) {
            if (uidlist[i-1] != uidlist[i]) {
                for (j = uidlist[i-1] + 1; j < uidlist[i]; j++) {
                    print j
                    if (--count == 0)
                        exit
                }
            }
        }
    }' $IDFILE
```

Most of the work is done in the inline awk program. The first part reads the list of UID numbers into the uidlist array. The for loop goes through the array. When it finds two elements whose values are not adjacent, it steps through and prints the values in between those elements. It decrements count each time so that no more than count UID numbers are printed.

In shells that have arrays and that support arithmetic more directly, such as ksh93 and bash, it's possible to let the shell do all the work. In fact, this awk script was derived from a similar one for ksh93: see *http://linux.oreillynet.com/pub/a/linux/2002/05/09/uid.html*.

11.3.3 Creating User–Old UID–New UID Triples

We now have to process the dupusers and dupids files. The output file lists the username, old UID and new UID numbers, separated by whitespace, one record per line, for further processing. For dupusers, the processing is pretty straightforward: the first entry encountered will be the old UID, and the next one will be the new chosen UID. (In other words, we arbitrarily decide to use the second, larger UID for all of the user's files.) At the same time, we can generate the final /etc/passwd records for the users listed in both files.

> This plan treats the disks of both systems equally, requiring that file ownerships (potentially) be changed on both systems. This is simpler to code, at the (possible) expense of more time spent changing file ownerships. A different option would be to leave the files on one system alone, making that system the "master" system, so to speak, and doing ownership changes only on the second system. This would be harder to code; we leave that as one of the infamous "exercises for the reader."

Here's the code:

```
rm -f old-new-list

old_ifs=$IFS
IFS=:
while read user passwd uid gid fullname homedir shell
do
    if read user2 passwd2 uid2 gid2 fullname2 homedir2 shell2
    then
        if [ $user = $user2 ]
        then
            printf "%s\t%s\t%s\n" $user $uid $uid2 >> old-new-list
            echo "$user:$passwd:$uid2:$gid:$fullname:$homedir:$shell"
        else
            echo $0: out of sync: $user and $user2 >&2
            exit 1
        fi
```

```
        else
            echo $0: no duplicate for $user >&2
            exit 1
        fi
done < dupusers > unique2
IFS=$old_ifs
```

We use the shell's read command to read pairs of lines from dupusers, sending the final password file entry to unique2. At the same time, we send the desired output to the new file old-new-list. We have to use the >> operator for this, since we add a new record each time around the loop. To ensure that the file is fresh, we remove it before the loop body.

Setting IFS to : makes it easy to read password file lines, treating each colon-separated field correctly. The original value of IFS is saved in old_ifs and restored after the loop. (We could also have used IFS=: read ..., but we would have to be careful to do so on *both* read statements.)

Similar code applies for the users for whom the UID numbers are the same but the username is different. Here too, we opt for simplicity; we give all such users a brand-new, unused UID number. (It would be possible to let, say, the first user of each pair keep the original UID number; however this would require that we do the file ownership changing only on the system where the second user's files reside. Again, in a real-life situation, this might be preferable.)

```
count=$(wc -l < dupids)      # Total duplicate ids

# This is a hack, it'd be better if POSIX sh had arrays:
set -- $(newuids.sh -c $count unique-ids)

IFS=:
while read user passwd uid gid fullname homedir shell
do
    newuid=$1
    shift

    echo "$user:$passwd:$newuid:$gid:$fullname:$homedir:$shell"

    printf "%s\t%s\t%s\n" $user $uid $newuid >> old-new-list
done < dupids > unique3
IFS=$old_ifs
```

In order to have all the new UID numbers handy, we place them into the positional parameters with set and a command substitution. Then each new UID is retrieved inside the loop by assigning from $1, and the next one is put in place with a shift. When we're done, we have three new output files:

```
$ cat unique2                                    Those who had two UIDs
ben:x:301:10:Ben Franklin:/home/ben:/bin/bash
jhancock:x:300:10:John Hancock:/home/jhancock:/bin/bash
```

```
$ cat unique3                                          Those who get new UIDs
abe:x:4:10:Honest Abe Lincoln:/home/abe:/bin/bash
tj:x:5:10:Thomas Jefferson:/home/tj:/bin/bash
dorothy:x:6:10:Dorothy Gale:/home/dorothy:/bin/bash
toto:x:7:10:Toto Gale:/home/toto:/bin/bash


$ cat old-new-list                                     List of user-old-new triples
ben      201    301
jhancock        200    300
abe      105    4
tj       105    5                                      See next section about these
dorothy  110    6
toto     110    7
```

The final password file is created by merging the three unique? files. While cat would do the trick, it'd be nice to merge them in UID order:

```
sort -k 3 -t : -n unique[123] > final.password
```

The wildcard unique[123] expands to the three filenames unique1, unique2, and unique3. Here is the final, sorted result:

```
$ cat final.password
root:x:0:0:root:/root:/bin/bash
bin:x:1:1:bin:/bin:/sbin/nologin
daemon:x:2:2:daemon:/sbin:/sbin/nologin
adm:x:3:4:adm:/var/adm:/sbin/nologin
abe:x:4:10:Honest Abe Lincoln:/home/abe:/bin/bash
tj:x:5:10:Thomas Jefferson:/home/tj:/bin/bash
dorothy:x:6:10:Dorothy Gale:/home/dorothy:/bin/bash
toto:x:7:10:Toto Gale:/home/toto:/bin/bash
camus:x:112:10:Albert Camus:/home/camus:/bin/bash
jhancock:x:300:10:John Hancock:/home/jhancock:/bin/bash
ben:x:301:10:Ben Franklin:/home/ben:/bin/bash
george:x:1100:10:George Washington:/home/george:/bin/bash
betsy:x:1110:10:Betsy Ross:/home/betsy:/bin/bash
tolstoy:x:2076:10:Leo Tolstoy:/home/tolstoy:/bin/bash
```

11.4 Changing File Ownership

At first blush, changing file ownership is pretty easy. Given the list of usernames and new UID numbers, we ought to be able to write a loop like this (to be run as root):

```
while read user old new
do
        cd /home/$user              Change to user's directory
        chown -R $new .             Recursively change ownership, see chown(1)
done < old-new-list
```

The idea is to change to the user's home directory and recursively chown everything to the new UID number. However, this isn't enough. It's possible for users to have files in places outside their home directory. For example, consider two users, ben and jhancock, working on a joint project in /home/ben/declaration:

```
$ cd /home/ben/declaration
$ ls -l draft*
-rw-r--r--    1 ben        fathers    2102 Jul  3 16:00 draft10
-rw-r--r--    1 jhancock   fathers    2191 Jul  3 17:09 draft.final
```

If we just did the recursive chown, both files would end up belonging to ben, and jhancock wouldn't be too happy upon returning to work the day after the Great Filesystem Reorganization.

Even worse, though, is the case in which users have files that live outside their home directory. /tmp is an obvious example, but consider a source code management system, such as CVS. CVS stores the master files for a project in a repository that is typically not in *any* home directory, but in a system directory somewhere. Source files in the repository belong to multiple users. The ownership of these files should also be changed over.

Thus, the only way to be sure that all files are changed correctly everywhere is to do things the hard way, using find, starting from the root directory. The most obvious way to accomplish our goal is to run chown from find, like so:

```
find / -user $user -exec chown $newuid '{}' \;
```

This runs an exhaustive file search, examining every file and directory on the system to see if it belongs to whatever user is named by $user. For each such file or directory, find runs chown on it, changing the ownership to the UID in $newuid. (The find command was covered in "The find Command" [10.4.3]. The –exec option runs the rest of the arguments, up to the semicolon, for each file that matches the given criteria. The { } in the find command means to substitute the found file's name into the command at that point.) However, using find this way is *very* expensive, since it creates a new chown process for *every* file or directory. Instead, we combine find and xargs:

```
# Regular version:
find / -user $user -print | xargs chown $newuid

# If you have the GNU utilities:
# find / -user $user -print0 | xargs --null chown $newuid
```

This runs the same exhaustive file search, this time printing the name of every file and directory on the system belonging to whatever user is named by $user. This list is then piped to xargs, which runs chown on as many files as possible, changing the ownership to the UID in $newuid.

Now, consider a case where the old-new-list file contained something like this:

```
juser       25       10
mrwizard    10       30
```

There is an ordering problem here. If we change all of juser's files to have the UID 10 *before* we change the ownership on mrwizard's files, all of juser's files will end up being owned by mrwizard!

This can be solved with the Unix tsort program, which does topological sorting. (Topological sorting imposes a complete ordering on partially ordered data.) For our purposes, we need to feed the data to tsort in the order *new UID, old UID*:

```
$ tsort << EOF
> 30 10
> 10 25
> EOF
30
10
25
```

The output tells us that 10 must be changed to 30 before 25 can be changed to 10. As you might imagine, careful scripting is required. *However*, we have managed to avoid this problem entirely! Remember the case of duplicate UID numbers with different names?

```
$ cat dupids
abe:x:105:10:Honest Abe Lincoln:/home/abe:/bin/bash
tj:x:105:10:Thomas Jefferson:/home/tj:/bin/bash
dorothy:x:110:10:Dorothy Gale:/home/dorothy:/bin/bash
toto:x:110:10:Toto Gale:/home/toto:/bin/bash
```

We gave all of these users brand-new UIDs:

```
$ cat final.passwd
...
abe:x:4:10:Honest Abe Lincoln:/home/abe:/bin/bash
tj:x:5:10:Thomas Jefferson:/home/tj:/bin/bash
dorothy:x:6:10:Dorothy Gale:/home/dorothy:/bin/bash
toto:x:7:10:Toto Gale:/home/toto:/bin/bash
...
```

By giving them UID numbers that we know are not in use anywhere, we don't have to worry about ordering our find commands.

The final part of our main program generates the list of find and xargs commands. We have chosen to write the list of commands into a file, chown-files, that can be executed separately in the background. This is because the program is likely to take a long time to run, and undoubtedly our system administrator, after spending hours developing and testing the scripts here, wants to start it running and then go home and get some sleep. Here's the script's conclusion:

```
while read user old new
do
    echo "find / -user $user -print | xargs chown $new"
done < old-new-list > chown-files

chmod +x chown-files

rm merge1 unique[123] dupusers dupids unique-ids old-new-list
```

Here is what chown-files looks like:

```
$ cat chown-files
find / -user ben -print | xargs chown 301
find / -user jhancock -print | xargs chown 300
find / -user abe -print | xargs chown 4
find / -user tj -print | xargs chown 5
find / -user dorothy -print | xargs chown 6
find / -user toto -print | xargs chown 7
```

Remember the old-new-list file?

```
$ cat old-new-list
ben      201     301
jhancock         200     300
abe      105     4
tj       105     5
dorothy  110     6
toto     110     7
```

You may have noted that both abe and tj start out with the same UID. Similarly for dorothy and toto. What happens when we run chown-files? Won't all of tj's files end up belonging to the new UID 4? Won't all of toto's files end up belonging to the new UID 6? Haven't we just created the mess that we thought we had avoided?

The answer is that we're safe, as long as we run these commands *separately* on each system, *before* we put the new /etc/passwd file in place on each system. Remember that originally, abe and dorothy were only on u1, and that tj and toto were only on u2. Thus, when chown-files runs on u1 with the original /etc/passwd in place, find will never find tj's or toto's files, since those users don't exist:

```
$ find / -user toto -print
find: invalid argument `toto' to `-user'
```

Things will fail similarly, but for the opposite pair of users, on u2. The full merge-systems.sh script is presented in Example 11-5.

Example 11-5. The merge-systems.sh program

```
#! /bin/sh

sort u1.passwd u2.passwd > merge1

awk -f splitout.awk merge1

awk -F: '{ print $3 }' merge1 | sort -n -u > unique-ids

rm -f old-new-list

old_ifs=$IFS
IFS=:
while read user passwd uid gid fullname homedir shell
do
    if read user2 passwd2 uid2 gid2 fullname2 homedir2 shell2
```

Example 11-5. The merge-systems.sh program (continued)

```
    then
        if [ $user = $user2 ]
        then
            printf "%s\t%s\t%s\n" $user $uid $uid2 >> old-new-list
            echo "$user:$passwd:$uid2:$gid:$fullname:$homedir:$shell"
        else
            echo $0: out of sync: $user and $user2 >&2
            exit 1
        fi
    else
        echo $0: no duplicate for $user >&2
        exit 1
    fi
done < dupusers > unique2
IFS=$old_ifs

count=$(wc -l < dupids)      # Total duplicate ids

# This is a hack, it'd be better if POSIX sh had arrays:
set -- $(newuids.sh -c $count unique-ids)

IFS=:
while read user passwd uid gid fullname homedir shell
do
    newuid=$1
    shift

    echo "$user:$passwd:$newuid:$gid:$fullname:$homedir:$shell"

    printf "%s\t%s\t%s\n" $user $uid $newuid >> old-new-list
done < dupids > unique3
IFS=$old_ifs

sort -k 3 -t : -n unique[123] > final.password

while read user old new
do
    echo "find / -user $user -print | xargs chown $new"
done < old-new-list > chown-files

chmod +x chown-files

rm merge1 unique[123] dupusers dupids unique-ids old-new-list
```

11.5 Other Real-World Issues

There are some other issues that are likely to come up in the Real World. For the sake of brevity we wimp out, and instead of writing code, we simply discuss them here.

First, and most obvious, is that the /etc/group file is also likely to need merging. With this file, it's necessary to:

- Make sure that all the groups from each individual system exist in the merged /etc/ group file, and with the same unique GID. This is completely analogous to the username/UID issue we just solved, only the format of the file is different.

- Do a logical merge of users in the same group on the different systems. For example:

      floppy:x:5:tolstoy,camus   In u1 /etc/group
      floppy:x:5:george,betsy   In u2 /etc/group

  When the files are merged, the entry for group floppy needs to be:

      floppy:x:5:tolstoy,camus,george,betsy   Order of users doesn't matter

- The GID of all files must be brought into sync with the new, merged /etc/group file, just as was done with the UID. If you're clever, it's possible to generate the find ... | xargs chown ... command to include the UID and GID so that they need to be run only once. This saves machine processing time at the expense of additional programming time.

Second, any large system that has been in use for some time will have files with UID or GID values that no longer (or never did) exist in /etc/passwd and /etc/group. It is possible to find such files with:

    find / '(' -nouser -o -nogroup ')' -ls

This produces a list of files in an output format similar to that of ls -dils. Such a list probably should be examined manually to determine the users and/or groups to which they should be reassigned, or new users (and/or groups) should be created for them.

In the former case, the file can be further processed to generate find ... | xargs chown ... commands to do the work.

In the latter case, it's simple to just add names for the corresponding UID and GIDs to the /etc/passwd and /etc/group files, but you should be careful that these unused UID and GID numbers don't conflict with UID and GID numbers generated for merging. This in turn implies that by creating the new user and group names on each system *before* merging, you won't have a conflict problem.

Third, the filesystems need to be absolutely *quiescent* during the operations that change the owner and group of the files. This means that there are no other activities occurring while these operations are running. It is thus best if the systems are run in *single-user mode*, whereby the super-user root is the only one allowed to log in, and then only on the system's physical console device.

Finally, there may be efficiency issues. Consider the series of commands shown earlier:

```
find / -user ben -print | xargs chown 301
find / -user jhancock -print | xargs chown 300
...
```

Each one of these pipelines traverses *every* file on the computer, for *every* user whose UID or GID needs to be changed. This is tolerable when the number of such users is small, or if the number of files on the system is reasonable (say, one disk's worth). However, if hundreds or thousands of users must have their files changed, or if the system has a nontrivial number of large drives, then another solution is needed. In such a case, it's probably better to use a pipeline similar to this:

```
find / -ls | awk -f make-commands.awk old-to-new.txt - > /tmp/commands.sh
... examine /tmp/commands.sh before running it ...
sh /tmp/commands.sh
```

Here, `make-commands.awk` would be an awk program that first reads the old-to-new UID changes from `old-to-new.txt`. (This file would be generated by modifying the scripts earlier in the chapter.) Then, for each file in the output, `make-commands.awk` looks up the owner to find if it needs to be changed. If so, it would print out a chown command line. Once all the commands are saved, you could then look them over before executing them. (We leave the actual implementation as yet another one of those famed "exercises for the reader.")

11.6 Summary

In this chapter, we have re-created and solved a "real-world" problem: merging the password files of two separate computers so that their files can be shared via NFS.

Careful study of the password files of both systems allows us to classify users into different categories: those only on the first system, those only on the second, and those with accounts on both. The problem is to ensure that when we're done, each user has an identical unique UID number on both systems, and that each user's files belong only to that user.

Solving the problem requires finding new unused UID numbers to use when there are UID conflicts, and careful ordering of the commands that change the ownership of the files. Furthermore, the entirety of both systems must be searched to be sure that every file's owner is updated correctly.

Other issues would need to be solved in a similar fashion; most notably, the merging of the group files, and assigning owners to any unowned files. For safety, the systems should be quiet while these operations are in progress, and we also outlined a different solution when efficiency is an issue.

The solution involved careful filtering of the original password files, with awk, sort, uniq, and while read ... loops being used heavily to process the data and prepare the commands to change the ownership of user files. find, xargs, and chown (of course) do the work.

The total solution represents less than 170 lines of code, including comments! A program in C that solved the same problem would take at least an order of magnitude more code, and most likely considerably longer to write, test, and debug. Furthermore, our solution, by generating commands that are executed separately, provides extra safety, since there is the opportunity for human inspection before making the commitment of changing file ownership. We think it nicely demonstrates the power of the Unix toolset and the Software Tools approach to problem solving.

## CHAPTER 12

Spellchecking

This chapter uses the task of spellchecking to demonstrate several different dimensions of shell scripting. After introducing the spell program, we show how a simple but useful spellchecker can be constructed almost entirely out of stock Unix tools. We then proceed to show how simple shell scripts can be used to modify the output of two freely available spellchecking programs to produce results similar to those of the traditional Unix spell program. Finally, we present a powerful spellchecker written in awk, which nicely demonstrates the elegance of that language.

12.1 The spell Program

The spell program does what you think it does: it checks a file for spelling errors. It reads through all the files named on the command line, producing, on standard output, a sorted list of words that are not in its dictionary or that cannot be derived from such words by the application of standard English grammatical rules (e.g., "words" from "word"). Interestingly enough, POSIX does not standardize spell. The Rationale document has this to say:

> This utility is not useful from shell scripts or typical application programs. The spell utility was considered, but was omitted because there is no known technology that can be used to make it recognize general language for user-specified input without providing a complete dictionary along with the input file.

We disagree with the first part of this statement. Consider a script for automated bug or trouble reporting: one might well want to have something along these lines:

```
#! /bin/sh -

# probreport --- simple problem reporting program

file=/tmp/report.$$
echo "Type in the problem, finish with Control-D."
cat > $file

while true
```

```
     do
          printf "[E]dit, Spell [C]heck, [S]end, or [A]bort: "
          read choice
          case $choice in
          [Ee]*)  ${EDITOR:-vi} $file
                  ;;
          [Cc]*)  spell $file
                  ;;
          [Aa]*)  exit 0
                  ;;
          [Ss]*)  break    # from loop
                  ;;
          esac
     done
     ...              Send report
```

In this chapter, we examine spellchecking from several different angles, since it's an interesting problem, and it gives us an opportunity to solve the problem in several different ways.

12.2 The Original Unix Spellchecking Prototype

Spellchecking has been the subject of more than 300 research papers and books.[*] In his book *Programming Pearls*,[†] Jon Bentley reported: Steve Johnson wrote the first version of spell in an afternoon in 1975. Bentley then sketched a reconstruction credited to Kernighan and Plauger[‡] of that program as a Unix pipeline that we can rephrase in modern terms like this:

```
prepare filename |              Remove formatting commands
    tr A-Z a-z |                Map uppercase to lowercase
      tr -c a-z '\n' |          Remove punctuation
        sort |                  Put words in alphabetical order
          uniq |                Remove duplicate words
            comm -13 dictionary -   Report words not in dictionary
```

Here, *prepare* is a filter that strips whatever document markup is present; in the simplest case, it is just cat. We assume the argument syntax for the GNU version of the tr command.

The only program in this pipeline that we have not seen before is comm: it compares two sorted files and selects, or rejects, lines common to both. Here, with the –13 option, it outputs only lines from the second file (the piped input) that are not in the first file (the dictionary). That output is the spelling-exception report.

---

[*] See *http://www.math.utah.edu/pub/tex/bib/index-table-s.html#spell* for an extensive bibliography.

[†] Jon Louis Bentley, *Programming Pearls*, Addison-Wesley, 1986, ISBN 0-201-10331-1.

[‡] Brian W. Kernighan and P. J. Plauger, *Software Tools in Pascal*, Addison-Wesley, 1981, ISBN 0-201-10342-7.

---

comm

Usage

    comm [*options* ...] *file1 file2*

Purpose

    To indicate which lines in the two input files are unique or common.

Major options

    –1

        Do *not* print column one (lines unique to *file1*).

    –2

        Do *not* print column two (lines unique to *file2*).

    –3

        Do *not* print column three (lines common to both files).

Behavior

    Read the two files line by line. The input files must be sorted. Produce three columns of output: lines that are only in *file1*, lines that are only in *file2*, and lines that are in both files. Either filename can be -, in which case comm reads standard input.

Caveats

    The options are not intuitive; it is hard to remember to *add* an option in order to *remove* an output column!

Bentley then goes on to discuss a spellchecker developed by Doug McIlroy at Bell Labs in 1981—its design and implementation; how it stores the dictionary in minimal memory; and why checking spelling is hard, especially for a language as muddled as English.

The modern spell is written in C for efficiency. However, the original pipeline was in use at Bell Labs for quite a while.

12.3   Improving ispell and aspell

Unix spell supports several options, most of which are not helpful for day-to-day use. One exception is the -b option, which causes spell to prefer British spelling: "centre" instead of "center," "colour" instead of "color," and so on.[*] See the manual page for the other options.

One nice feature is that you can provide your own local spelling list of valid words. For example, it often happens that there may be words from a particular discipline

---

[*] The *spell*(1) manual page, in the BUGS section, has long noted that "British spelling was done by an American."

that are spelled correctly, but that are not in spell's dictionary (for example, "POSIX"). You can create, and over time maintain, your own list of valid but unusual words, and then use this list when running spell. You indicate the pathname to the local spelling list by supplying it before the file to be checked, and by preceding it with a + character:

```
spell +/usr/local/lib/local.words myfile > myfile.errs
```

12.3.1 Private Spelling Dictionaries

We feel that it is an important Best Practice to have a private spelling dictionary for every document that you write: a common one for many documents is not useful because the vocabulary becomes too big and errors are likely to be hidden: "syzygy" might be correct in a math paper, but in a novel, it perhaps ought to have been "soggy." We have found, based on a several-million-line corpus of technical text with associated spelling dictionaries, that there tends to be about one spelling exception every six lines. This tells us that spelling exceptions are common and are worth the trouble of managing along with the rest of a project.

There are some nuisances with spell: only one + option is permitted, and its dictionaries must be sorted in lexicographic order, which is poor design. It also means that most versions of spell break when the locale is changed. (While one might consider this to be bad design, it is really just an unanticipated consequence of the introduction of locales. The code for spell on these systems probably has not changed in more than 20 years, and when the underlying libraries were updated to do locale-based sorting, no one realized that this would be an effect.) Here is an example:

```
$ env LC_ALL=en_GB spell +ibmsysj.sok < ibmsysj.bib | wc -l
     3674
$ env LC_ALL=en_US spell +ibmsysj.sok < ibmsysj.bib | wc -l
     3685
$ env LC_ALL=C spell +ibmsysj.sok < ibmsysj.bib | wc -l
     2163
```

However, if the sorting of the private dictionary matches that of the current locale, spell works properly:

```
$ env LC_ALL=en_GB sort ibmsysj.sok > /tmp/foo.en_GB
$ env LC_ALL=en_GB spell +/tmp/foo.en_GB < ibmsysj.bib | wc -l
     2163
```

The problem is that the default locale can change from one release of an operating system to the next. Thus, it is best to set the LC_ALL environment variable to a consistent value for private dictionary sorting, and for running spell. We provide a workaround for spell's sorted dictionary requirement in the next section.

12.3.2 ispell and aspell

There are two different, freely available spellchecking programs: ispell and aspell. ispell is an *interactive* spellchecker; it displays your file, highlighting any spelling errors and providing suggested changes. aspell is a similar program; for English it does a better job of providing suggested corrections, and its author would like it to eventually replace ispell. Both programs can be used to generate a simple list of misspelled words, and since aspell hopes to replace ispell, they both use the same options:

-l

> Print a list of misspelled words on standard output.

-p *file*

> Use *file* as a personal dictionary of correctly spelled words. This is similar to Unix spell's personal file that starts with a +.

The ispell home page is *http://ficus-www.cs.ucla.edu/geoff/ispell.html*, and the source may be found at *ftp://ftp.gnu.org/gnu/non-gnu/ispell/.** The aspell home page is *http://aspell.net/*, and the source is at *ftp://ftp.gnu.org/gnu/aspell/*.

Both programs provide basic batch spellchecking. They also share the same quirk, which is that their results are not sorted, and duplicate bad words are not suppressed. (Unix spell has neither of these problems.) Thus, one prominent GNU/Linux vendor has the following shell script in /usr/bin/spell:

```
#!/bin/sh

# aspell -l mimicks the standard unix spell program, roughly.

cat "$@" | aspell -l --mode=none | sort -u
```

The --mode option causes aspell to ignore certain kinds of markup, such as SGML and TEX. Here, --mode=none indicates that no filtering should be done. The sort -u command sorts the output and suppresses duplicates, producing output of the nature expected by an experienced Unix user. This could also be done using ispell:

```
cat "$@" | ispell -l | sort -u
```

We could enhance this script in two different ways to provide a personal dictionary the same way Unix spell does. The first replacement spell script is provided in Example 12-1.

Example 12-1. A spell replacement using ispell

```
#!/bin/sh

# Unix spell treats a first argument of `+file' as providing a
```

---

* emacs uses ispell for interactive spellchecking. This is fast, since ispell is kept running in the background.

Example 12-1. A spell replacement using ispell (continued)

```
# personal spelling list.  Let's do that too.

mydict=
case $1 in
+?*)    mydict=${1#+}   # strip off leading +
        mydict="-p $mydict"
        shift
        ;;
esac

cat "$@" | ispell -l $mydict | sort -u
```

This works by simply looking for a first argument that begins with +, saving it in a variable, stripping off the + character, and then prepending the -p option. This is then passed on to the ispell invocation.

Unfortunately, this same technique does not work with aspell: it wants its dictionaries to be in a compiled binary format. To use aspell, we instead resort to the fgrep program, which can match multiple strings provided in a file. We add the –v option, which causes fgrep to print lines that do not match. The second replacement spell script is provided in Example 12-2.

Example 12-2. A spell replacement using aspell

```
#!/bin/sh

# Unix spell treats a first argument of `+file' as providing a
# personal spelling list.  Let's do that too.

mydict=cat
case $1 in
+?*)    mydict=${1#+}   # strip off leading +
        mydict="fgrep -v -f $mydict"
        shift
        ;;
esac

# aspell -l mimics the standard Unix spell program, roughly.

cat "$@" | aspell -l --mode=none | sort -u | eval $mydict
```

This same trick of post-processing with fgrep can be used with Unix spell if you do not want to have to keep your personal dictionary sorted, or if you do not want to have to worry about different locales' sorting order.

The next section presents an awk version of spell, which provides a simple yet powerful alternative to the various spell replacements discussed here.

12.4 A Spellchecker in awk

In this section, we present a program for checking spelling. Even though all Unix systems have spell, and many also have aspell or ispell, it is instructive and useful to implement our own program. This illustrates the power of awk, and gives us a valuable program that can be used identically on every platform that has awk.

We make a strong distinction between *checking* and *correcting* spelling. The latter requires knowledge of the format of the text, and invariably requires human confirmation, making it completely unsuited to batch processing. The automatic spelling correction offered by some web browsers and word processors is even worse because it is frequently wrong, and its second-guessing your typing quickly becomes extremely annoying.

The emacs text editor offers three good solutions to spelling assistance during text entry: dynamic word completion can be invoked on demand to expand a partial word, spelling verification of the current word can be requested by a single keystroke, and the flyspell library can be used to request unobtrusive colored highlighting of suspect words.

As long as you can recognize misspellings when they are pointed out to you, it is better to have a spellchecker that reports a list of suspect words, and that allows you to provide a private list of special words not normally present in its dictionary, to reduce the size of that report. You can then use the report to identify errors, repair them, regenerate the report (which should now contain only correct words), and then add its contents to your private dictionary. Because our writing deals with technical material, which is often full of unusual words, in practice we keep a private and document-specific supplemental dictionary for every document that we write.

To guide the programming, here are the desired design goals for our spellchecker. Following the practice of ISO standards, we use *shall* to indicate a requirement and *should* to mark a desire:

- The program shall be able to read a text stream, isolate words, and report instances of words that are not in a list of known words, called the *spelling dictionary*.

- There shall be a default word list, collected from one or more system dictionaries.

- It shall be possible to replace the default word list.

- It shall be possible to augment the standard word list with entries from one or more user-provided word lists. These lists are particularly necessary for technical documents, which contain acronyms, jargon, and proper nouns, most of which would not be found in the standard list.

- Word lists shall not require sorting, unlike those for Unix spell, which behaves incorrectly when the locale is changed.

- Although the default word lists are to be in English, with suitable alternate word lists, the program shall be capable of handling text in any language that can be represented by ASCII-based character sets encoded in streams of 8-bit bytes, and in which words are separated by whitespace. This eliminates the difficult case of languages, such as Lao and Thai, that lack interword spaces, and thus require extensive linguistic analysis to identify words.

- Lettercase shall be ignored to keep the word-list sizes manageable, but exceptions shall be reported in their original lettercase.

- Punctuation and digits shall be ignored, but the apostrophe shall be considered a letter.

- The default report shall be a sorted list of unique words that are not found in the combined word lists, displayed one word per line. This is the *spelling exception list*.

- There shall be an option to augment the exception-list report with location information, such as filename and line number, to facilitate finding and correcting misspelled words. The report shall be sorted by location and, when there are multiple exceptions at one location, sorted further by exception words.

- User-specifiable suffix reduction should be supported to keep word-list sizes manageable.

In Example 12-4 near the end of this section, we present a complete program that meets all of these goals, and more. This program does quite a lot, so in the rest of this section, we describe it in detail as a semiliterate program with explanatory prose and code fragments.

With a test input file containing the first few paragraphs of the manual page for spell, a typical run might look like this:

```
$ awk -f spell.awk testfile
deroff
eqn
ier
nx
tbl
thier
```

or in verbose mode, like this:

```
$ awk -f spell.awk -- -verbose testfile
testfile:7:eqn
testfile:7:tbl
testfile:11:deroff
testfile:12:nx
testfile:19:ier
testfile:19:thier
```

12.4.1 Introductory Comments

The program begins with an extensive commentary, of which we show only the introduction and usage parts here:

```
# Implement a simple spellchecker, with user-specifiable exception
# lists.  The built-in dictionary is constructed from a list of
# standard Unix spelling dictionaries, which can be overridden on the
# command line.
#
...
#
# Usage:
#       awk [-v Dictionaries="sysdict1 sysdict2 ..."] -f spell.awk -- \
#           [=suffixfile1 =suffixfile2 ...] [+dict1 +dict2 ...] \
#           [-strip] [-verbose] [file(s)]
```

12.4.2 Main Body

The main body of the program is just three lines, typical of many awk programs that initialize, process, and report:

```
BEGIN   { initialize() }

        { spell_check_line() }

END     { report_exceptions() }
```

All of the details are relegated to functions stored in alphabetical order in the remainder of the program file, but described in logical order in the following sections.

12.4.3 initialize( )

The initialize( ) function handles program startup tasks.

The variable NonWordChars holds a regular expression that is later used to eliminate unwanted characters. Along with the ASCII letters and apostrophe, characters in the range 161 to 255 are preserved as word characters so that files in ASCII, any of the ISO 8859-n character sets, and Unicode in UTF-8 encoding all can be handled without further concern for character sets.

Characters 128 to 160 are ignored because in all of those character sets, they serve as additional control characters and a nonbreaking space. Some of those character sets have a few nonalphabetic characters above 160, but it adds undesirable character-set dependence to deal with them. The nonalphabetic ones are rare enough that their worst effect on our program may be an occasional false report of a spelling exception.

We assume that files to be spellchecked have the same character-set encoding as their associated dictionaries. If that is not the case, then use iconv to convert them to a consistent encoding.

If all awk implementations were POSIX-conformant, we would set NonWordChars like this:

```
NonWordChars = "[^'[:alpha:]]"
```

The current locale would then determine exactly which characters could be ignored. However, that assignment is not portable because many awk implementations do not yet support POSIX-style regular expressions.

Before locales were introduced to Unix, we could have assigned NonWordChars the negation of the set of word characters:

```
NonWordChars = "[^'A-Za-z\241-\377]"
```

However, in the presence of locales, character ranges in regular expressions are interpreted in a locale-dependent fashion so that value would not give consistent results across platforms. The solution is to replace the ranges by explicit enumerations of characters, writing the assignment as a concatenation of strings, neatly aligned so that a human can readily identify the characters in the negated set. We use octal representation for values above 127, since that is clearer than a jumble of accented characters.

initialize( ) then identifies and loads dictionaries, and processes command-line arguments and suffix rules.

```
function initialize( )
{
    NonWordChars = "[^" \
      "'" \
      "ABCDEFGHIJKLMNOPQRSTUVWXYZ" \
      "abcdefghijklmnopqrstuvwxyz" \
         "\241\242\243\244\245\246\247\250\251\252\253\254\255\256\257" \
      "\260\261\262\263\264\265\266\267\270\271\272\273\274\275\276\277" \
      "\300\301\302\303\304\305\306\307\310\311\312\313\314\315\316\317" \
      "\320\321\322\323\324\325\326\327\330\331\332\333\334\335\336\337" \
      "\340\341\342\343\344\345\346\347\350\351\352\353\354\355\356\357" \
      "\360\361\362\363\364\365\366\367\370\371\372\373\374\375\376\377" \
      "]"
    get_dictionaries( )
    scan_options( )
    load_dictionaries( )
    load_suffixes( )
    order_suffixes( )
}
```

12.4.4 get_dictionaries( )

get_dictionaries( ) fills in a list of default system dictionaries: we supply two convenient ones. The user can override that choice by providing a list of dictionaries as the value of the command-line variable Dictionaries, or the environment variable DICTIONARIES.

If Dictionaries is empty, we consult the environment array, ENVIRON, and use any value set there. If Dictionaries is still empty, we supply a built-in list. The selection of that list requires some care because there is considerable variation across Unix platforms and because, for small files, most of the runtime of this program is consumed by loading dictionaries. Otherwise, Dictionaries contains a whitespace-separated list of dictionary filenames, which we split and store in the global DictionaryFiles array. We chose the word list used by spell on some of our systems (about 25,000 entries), and a larger list prepared by Donald Knuth (about 110,000 words).[*]

Notice how the dictionary names are stored: they are array *indices*, rather than array *values*. There are two reasons for this design choice. First, it automatically handles the case of a dictionary that is supplied more than once: only one instance of the filename is saved. Second, it then makes it easy to iterate over the dictionary list with a for (*key* in *array*) loop. There is no need to maintain a variable with the count of the number of dictionaries.

Here is the code:

```
function get_dictionaries(          files, key)
{
    if ((Dictionaries == "") && ("DICTIONARIES" in ENVIRON))
        Dictionaries = ENVIRON["DICTIONARIES"]
    if (Dictionaries == "")       # Use default dictionary list
    {
        DictionaryFiles["/usr/dict/words"]++
        DictionaryFiles["/usr/local/share/dict/words.knuth"]++
    }
    else                # Use system dictionaries from command line
    {
        split(Dictionaries, files)
        for (key in files)
            DictionaryFiles[files[key]]++
    }
}
```

12.4.5 scan_options( )

scan_options( ) handles the command line. It expects to find options (-strip and/or -verbose), user dictionaries (indicated with a leading +, a Unix spell tradition), suffix-rule files (marked with a leading =), and files to be spellchecked. Any -v option to set the Dictionaries variable has already been handled by awk, and is not in the argument array, ARGV.

The last statement in scan_options( ) requires explanation. During testing, we found that nawk does not read standard input if empty arguments are left at the end of ARGV,

---

[*] Available at *ftp://labrea.stanford.edu/pub/dict/words.gz*.

whereas gawk and mawk do. We therefore reduce ARGC until we have a nonempty argument at the end of ARGV:

```
function scan_options(          k)
{
    for (k = 1; k < ARGC; k++)
    {
        if (ARGV[k] == "-strip")
        {
            ARGV[k] = ""
            Strip = 1
        }
        else if (ARGV[k] == "-verbose")
        {
            ARGV[k] = ""
            Verbose = 1
        }
        else if (ARGV[k] ~ /^=/)          # suffix file
        {
            NSuffixFiles++
            SuffixFiles[substr(ARGV[k], 2)]++
            ARGV[k] = ""
        }
        else if (ARGV[k] ~ /^[+]/)        # private dictionary
        {
            DictionaryFiles[substr(ARGV[k], 2)]++
            ARGV[k] = ""
        }
    }

    # Remove trailing empty arguments (for nawk)
    while ((ARGC > 0) && (ARGV[ARGC-1] == ""))
        ARGC--
}
```

12.4.6 load_dictionaries( )

load_dictionaries( ) reads the word lists from all of the dictionaries. Notice how simple the code is: an outer loop over the DictionaryFiles array, and an inner loop that uses getline to read a line at a time. Each line contains exactly one word known to be spelled correctly. The dictionaries are created once, and then used repeatedly, so we assume that lines are free of whitespace, and we make no attempt to remove it. Each word is converted to lowercase and stored as an index of the global Dictionary array. No separate count of the number of entries in this array is needed because the array is used elsewhere only in membership tests. Among all of the data structures provided by various programming languages, associative arrays are the fastest and most concise way to handle such tests:

```
function load_dictionaries(          file, word)
{
    for (file in DictionaryFiles)
```

```
        {
            while ((getline word < file) > 0)
                Dictionary[tolower(word)]++
            close(file)
        }
    }
```

12.4.7 load_suffixes( )

In many languages, words can be reduced to shorter root words by stripping suffixes. For example, in English, *jumped, jumper, jumpers, jumpier, jumpiness, jumping, jumps,* and *jumpy* all have the root word *jump*. Suffixes sometimes change the final letters of a word: *try* is the root of *triable, trial, tried,* and *trying*. Thus, the set of base words that we need to store in a dictionary is several times smaller than the set of words that includes suffixes. Since I/O is relatively slow compared to computation, we suspect that it may pay to handle suffixes in our program, to shorten dictionary size and reduce the number of false reports in the exception list.

load_suffixes( ) handles the loading of suffix rules. Unlike dictionary loading, here we have the possibility of supplying built-in rules, instead of reading them from a file. Thus, we keep a global count of the number of entries in the array that holds the suffix-rule filenames.

The suffix rules bear some explanation, and to illustrate them, we show a typical rule set for English in Example 12-3. We match suffixes with regular expressions, each of which ends with $ to anchor it to the end of a word. When a suffix is stripped, it may be necessary to supply a replacement suffix, as for the reduction *tr+ied* to *tr+y*. Furthermore, there are often several possible replacements.

Example 12-3. Suffix rules for English: english.sfx

```
'$                        # Jones' -> Jones
's$                       # it's -> it
ably$          able       # affably -> affable
ed$            "" e       # breaded -> bread, flamed -> flame
edly$          ed         # ashamedly -> ashamed
es$            "" e       # arches -> arch, blues -> blue
gged$          g          # debugged -> debug
ied$           ie y       # died -> die, cried -> cry
ies$           ie ies y   # series -> series, ties -> tie, flies -> fly
ily$           y ily      # tidily -> tidy, wily -> wily
ing$                      # jumping -> jump
ingly$         "" ing     # alarmingly -> alarming or alarm
lled$          l          # annulled -> annul
ly$            ""         # acutely -> acute
nnily$         n          # funnily -> fun
pped$          p          # handicapped -> handicap
pping$         p          # dropping -> drop
rred$          r          # deferred -> defer
```

Example 12-3. Suffix rules for English: english.sfx (continued)

```
s$                              # cats -> cat
tted$            t              # committed -> commit
```

The simplest specification of a suffix rule is therefore a regular expression to match
the suffix, followed by a whitespace-separated list of replacements. Since one of the
possible replacements may be an empty string, we represent it by "". It can be omitted if it is the only replacement. English is both highly irregular and rich in loan
words from other languages, so there are many suffix rules, and certainly far more
than we have listed in english.sfx. However, the suffix list only reduces the inci-
dence of false reports because it effectively expands the dictionary size; it does not
affect the correct operation of the program.

In order to make suffix-rule files maintainable by humans, it is essential that the rules
can be augmented with comments to give examples of their application. We follow
common Unix practice with comments that run from sharp (#) to end-of-line. load_
suffixes( ) therefore strips comments and leading and trailing whitespace, and then
discards empty lines. What remains is a regular expression and a list of zero or more
replacements that are used elsewhere in calls to the awk built-in string substitution
function, sub( ). The replacement list is stored as a space-separated string to which
we can later apply the split( ) built-in function.

Suffix replacements can use & to represent matched text, although we have no examples of that feature in english.sfx.

We considered making load_suffixes( ) supply a missing $ anchor in the regular
expression, but rejected that idea because it might limit the specification of suffix
matching required for other languages. Suffix-rule files need to be prepared with considerable care anyway, and that job needs to be done only once for each language.

In the event that no suffix files are supplied, we load a default set of suffixes with
empty replacement values. The split( ) built-in function helps to shorten the code
for this initialization:

```
function load_suffixes(          file, k, line, n, parts)
{
    if (NSuffixFiles > 0)        # load suffix regexps from files
    {
        for (file in SuffixFiles)
        {
            while ((getline line < file) > 0)
            {
                sub(" *#.*$", "", line)   # strip comments
                sub("^[ \t]+", "", line)  # strip leading whitespace
                sub("[ \t]+$", "", line)  # strip trailing whitespace
                if (line == "")
                    continue
                n = split(line, parts)
                Suffixes[parts[1]]++
                Replacement[parts[1]] = parts[2]
```

```
                for (k = 3; k <= n; k++)
                    Replacement[parts[1]] = Replacement[parts[1]] " " \
                        parts[k]
            }
            close(file)
        }
    }
    else                # load default table of English suffix regexps
    {
        split("'$ 's$ ed$ edly$ es$ ing$ ingly$ ly$ s$", parts)
        for (k in parts)
        {
            Suffixes[parts[k]] = 1
            Replacement[parts[k]] = ""
        }
    }
}
```

12.4.8 order_suffixes( )

Suffix replacement needs to be handled carefully: in particular, it should be done
with a *longest-match-first* algorithm. order_suffixes( ) takes the list of suffix rules
saved in the global Suffixes array, and copies it into the OrderedSuffix array, indexing that array by an integer that runs from one to NOrderedSuffix.

order_suffixes( ) then uses a simple bubble sort to reorder the entries in
OrderedSuffix by decreasing pattern length, using the swap( ) function in the innermost loop. swap( ) is simple: it exchanges elements i and j of its argument array. The
complexity of this sorting technique is proportional to the square of the number of
elements to be sorted, but NOrderedSuffix is not expected to be large, so this sort is
unlikely to contribute significantly to the program's runtime:

```
function order_suffixes(          i, j, key)
{
    # Order suffixes by decreasing length
    NOrderedSuffix = 0
    for (key in Suffixes)
        OrderedSuffix[++NOrderedSuffix] = key
    for (i = 1; i < NOrderedSuffix; i++)
        for (j = i + 1; j <= NOrderedSuffix; j++)
            if (length(OrderedSuffix[i]) < length(OrderedSuffix[j]))
                swap(OrderedSuffix, i, j)
}

function swap(a, i, j,          temp)
{
    temp = a[i]
    a[i] = a[j]
    a[j] = temp
}
```

12.4.9 spell_check_line( )

We have now described all of the initialization code required for the program setup. The second pattern/action pair at the start of the program calls spell_check_line( ) for each line from the input stream.

The first task is to reduce the line to a list of words. The built-in function gsub( ) does the job for us by removing nonalphanumeric characters in just one line of code. The resulting words are then available as $1, $2, ..., $NF, so it just takes a simple for loop to iterate over them, handing them off to spell_check_word( ) for individual treatment.

As a general awk programming convention, we avoid reference to anonymous numeric field names, like $1, in function bodies, preferring to restrict their use to short action-code blocks. We made an exception in this function: $k is the only such anonymous reference in the entire program. To avoid unnecessary record reassembly when it is modified, we copy it into a local variable and then strip outer apostrophes and send any nonempty result off to spell_check_word( ) for further processing:

```
function spell_check_line(        k, word)
{
    gsub(NonWordChars, " ")                  # eliminate nonword chars
    for (k = 1; k <= NF; k++)
    {
        word = $k
        sub("^'+", "", word)                 # strip leading apostrophes
        sub("'+$", "", word)                 # strip trailing apostrophes
        if (word != "")
            spell_check_word(word)
    }
}
```

It is not particularly nice to have character-specific special handling once a word has been recognized. However, the apostrophe is an overloaded character that serves both to indicate contractions in some languages, as well as provide outer quoting. Eliminating its quoting use reduces the number of false reports in the final spelling-exception list.

Apostrophe stripping poses a minor problem for Dutch, which uses it in the initial position in a small number of words: ‘n for een, ‘s for des, and ‘t for het. Those cases are trivially handled by augmenting the exception dictionary.

12.4.10 spell_check_word( )

spell_check_word( ) is where the real work happens, but in most cases, the job is done quickly. If the lowercase word is found in the global Dictionary array, it is spelled correctly, and we can immediately return.

If the word is not in the word list, it is probably a spelling exception. However, if the user requested suffix stripping, then we have more work to do. strip_suffixes() produces a list of one or more related words stored as indices of the local wordlist array. The for loop then iterates over this list, returning if it finds a word that is in the Dictionary array.

If suffix stripping is not requested, or if we did not find any replacement words in the dictionary, then the word is definitely a spelling exception. However, it is a bad idea to write a report at this point because we usually want to produce a sorted list of unique spelling exceptions. The word *awk*, for example, occurs more than 30 times in this chapter, but is not found in any of the standard Unix spelling dictionaries. Instead, we store the word in the global Exception array, and when verbose output is requested, we prefix the word with a location defined by a colon-terminated filename and line number. Reports of that form are common to many Unix tools and are readily understandable both to humans and smart text editors. Notice that the original lettercase is preserved in the report, even though it was ignored during the dictionary lookup:

```
function spell_check_word(word,          key, lc_word, location, w, wordlist)
{
    lc_word = tolower(word)
    if (lc_word in Dictionary)              # acceptable spelling
        return
    else                                    # possible exception
    {
        if (Strip)
        {
            strip_suffixes(lc_word, wordlist)
            for (w in wordlist)
                if (w in Dictionary)
                    return
        }
        location = Verbose ? (FILENAME ":" FNR ":") : ""
        if (lc_word in Exception)
            Exception[lc_word] = Exception[lc_word] "\n" location word
        else
            Exception[lc_word] = location word
    }
}
```

12.4.11 strip_suffixes( )

When a word has been found that is not in the dictionary, and the -strip option has been specified, we call strip_suffixes( ) to apply the suffix rules. It loops over the suffix regular expressions in order of decreasing suffix length. If the word matches, the suffix is removed to obtain the root word. If there are no replacement suffixes, the word is stored as an index of the wordlist array. Otherwise, we split the replacement list into its members and append each replacement in turn to the root word, adding it to the wordlist array. We need one special case in the inner loop, to check for the special two-character string "", which we replace with an empty string. If we have a match, the break statement leaves the loop, and the function returns to the caller. Otherwise, the loop continues with the next suffix regular expression.

We could have made this function do a dictionary lookup for each candidate that we store in wordlist, and return a match indication. We chose not to because it mixes lookup with suffix processing and makes it harder to extend the program to display replacement candidates (Unix spell has the -x option to do that: for every input word that can take suffixes, it produces a list of correctly spelled words with the same root).

While suffix rules suffice for many Indo-European languages, others do not need them at all, and still others have more complex changes in spelling as words change in case, number, or tense. For such languages, the simplest solution seems to be a larger dictionary that incorporates all of the common word forms.

Here is the code:

```
function strip_suffixes(word, wordlist,        ending, k, n, regexp)
{
    split("", wordlist)
    for (k = 1; k <= NOrderedSuffix; k++)
    {
        regexp = OrderedSuffix[k]
        if (match(word, regexp))
        {
            word = substr(word, 1, RSTART - 1)
            if (Replacement[regexp] == "")
                wordlist[word] = 1
            else
            {
                split(Replacement[regexp], ending)
                for (n in ending)
                {
                    if (ending[n] == "\"\"")
                        ending[n] = ""
                    wordlist[word ending[n]] = 1
                }
            }
            break
        }
    }
}
```

12.4.12 report_exceptions( )

The final job in our program is initiated by the last of the three pattern/action pairs. report_exceptions( ) sets up a pipeline to sort with command-line options that depend on whether the user requested a compact listing of unique exception words, or a verbose report with location information. In either case, we give sort the -f option to ignore lettercase, and the -u option to get unique output lines. A simple for loop outputs the exceptions to the pipeline, and the final close( ) shuts down the pipeline and completes the program.

Here is the code:

```
function report_exceptions(        key, sortpipe)
{
    sortpipe = Verbose ? "sort -f -t: -u -k1,1 -k2n,2 -k3" : \
               "sort -f -u -k1"
    for (key in Exception)
        print Exception[key] | sortpipe
    close(sortpipe)
}
```

Example 12-4 collects the complete code for our spellchecker.

Example 12-4. Spellchecker program

```
# Implement a simple spellchecker, with user-specifiable exception
# lists.  The built-in dictionary is constructed from a list of
# standard Unix spelling dictionaries, which can be overridden on the
# command line.
#
...
#
# Usage:
#       awk [-v Dictionaries="sysdict1 sysdict2 ..."] -f spell.awk -- \
#           [=suffixfile1 =suffixfile2 ...] [+dict1 +dict2 ...] \
#           [-strip] [-verbose] [file(s)]

BEGIN   { initialize() }

        { spell_check_line() }

END     { report_exceptions() }

function get_dictionaries(        files, key)
{
    if ((Dictionaries == "") && ("DICTIONARIES" in ENVIRON))
        Dictionaries = ENVIRON["DICTIONARIES"]
    if (Dictionaries == "")      # Use default dictionary list
    {
        DictionaryFiles["/usr/dict/words"]++
        DictionaryFiles["/usr/local/share/dict/words.knuth"]++
    }
    else                    # Use system dictionaries from command line
    {
        split(Dictionaries, files)
        for (key in files)
            DictionaryFiles[files[key]]++
    }
}
```

Example 12-4. Spellchecker program (continued)

```awk
function initialize( )
{
    NonWordChars = "[^" \
        "'" \
        "ABCDEFGHIJKLMNOPQRSTUVWXYZ" \
        "abcdefghijklmnopqrstuvwxyz" \
            "\241\242\243\244\245\246\247\250\251\252\253\254\255\256\257" \
        "\260\261\262\263\264\265\266\267\270\271\272\273\274\275\276\277" \
        "\300\301\302\303\304\305\306\307\310\311\312\313\314\315\316\317" \
        "\320\321\322\323\324\325\326\327\330\331\332\333\334\335\336\337" \
        "\340\341\342\343\344\345\346\347\350\351\352\353\354\355\356\357" \
        "\360\361\362\363\364\365\366\367\370\371\372\373\374\375\376\377" \
        "]"
    get_dictionaries( )
    scan_options( )
    load_dictionaries( )
    load_suffixes( )
    order_suffixes( )
}

function load_dictionaries(        file, word)
{
    for (file in DictionaryFiles)
    {
        while ((getline word < file) > 0)
            Dictionary[tolower(word)]++
        close(file)
    }
}

function load_suffixes(        file, k, line, n, parts)
{
    if (NSuffixFiles > 0)        # load suffix regexps from files
    {
        for (file in SuffixFiles)
        {
            while ((getline line < file) > 0)
            {
                sub(" *#.*$", "", line)    # strip comments
                sub("^[ \t]+", "", line)   # strip leading whitespace
                sub("[ \t]+$", "", line)   # strip trailing whitespace
                if (line == "")
                    continue
                n = split(line, parts)
                Suffixes[parts[1]]++
                Replacement[parts[1]] = parts[2]
                for (k = 3; k <= n; k++)
                    Replacement[parts[1]] = Replacement[parts[1]] " " \
                        parts[k]
            }
            close(file)
        }
```

Example 12-4. Spellchecker program (continued)

```
    }
    else                # load default table of English suffix regexps
    {
        split("'$ 's$ ed$ edly$ es$ ing$ ingly$ ly$ s$", parts)
        for (k in parts)
        {
            Suffixes[parts[k]] = 1
            Replacement[parts[k]] = ""
        }
    }
}

function order_suffixes(        i, j, key)
{
    # Order suffixes by decreasing length
    NOrderedSuffix = 0
    for (key in Suffixes)
        OrderedSuffix[++NOrderedSuffix] = key
    for (i = 1; i < NOrderedSuffix; i++)
        for (j - i + 1; j <- NOrderedSuffix; j++)
            if (length(OrderedSuffix[i]) < length(OrderedSuffix[j]))
                swap(OrderedSuffix, i, j)
}

function report_exceptions(        key, sortpipe)
{
    sortpipe = Verbose ? "sort -f -t: -u -k1,1 -k2n,2 -k3" : \
                "sort -f -u -k1"
    for (key in Exception)
        print Exception[key] | sortpipe
    close(sortpipe)
}

function scan_options(        k)
{
    for (k = 1; k < ARGC; k++)
    {
        if (ARGV[k] == "-strip")
        {
            ARGV[k] = ""
            Strip = 1
        }
        else if (ARGV[k] == "-verbose")
        {
            ARGV[k] = ""
            Verbose = 1
        }
        else if (ARGV[k] ~ /^=/)            # suffix file
        {
            NSuffixFiles++
            SuffixFiles[substr(ARGV[k], 2)]++
            ARGV[k] = ""
```

Example 12-4. Spellchecker program (continued)

```
        }
        else if (ARGV[k] ~ /^[+]/)        # private dictionary
        {
            DictionaryFiles[substr(ARGV[k], 2)]++
            ARGV[k] = ""
        }
    }

    # Remove trailing empty arguments (for nawk)
    while ((ARGC > 0) && (ARGV[ARGC-1] == ""))
        ARGC--
}

function spell_check_line(          k, word)
{
    gsub(NonWordChars, " ")                # eliminate nonword chars
    for (k = 1; k <= NF; k++)
    {
        word = $k
        sub("^'+", "", word)               # strip leading apostrophes
        sub("'+$", "", word)               # strip trailing apostrophes
        if (word != "")
            spell_check_word(word)
    }
}

function spell_check_word(word,          key, lc_word, location, w, wordlist)
{
    lc_word = tolower(word)
    if (lc_word in Dictionary)             # acceptable spelling
        return
    else                                   # possible exception
    {
        if (Strip)
        {
            strip_suffixes(lc_word, wordlist)
            for (w in wordlist)
                if (w in Dictionary)
                    return
        }
        location = Verbose ? (FILENAME ":" FNR ":") : ""
        if (lc_word in Exception)
            Exception[lc_word] = Exception[lc_word] "\n" location word
        else
            Exception[lc_word] = location word
    }
}

function strip_suffixes(word, wordlist,          ending, k, n, regexp)
{
    split("", wordlist)
    for (k = 1; k <= NOrderedSuffix; k++)
```

Example 12-4. Spellchecker program (continued)

```
        {
            regexp = OrderedSuffix[k]
            if (match(word, regexp))
            {
                word = substr(word, 1, RSTART - 1)
                if (Replacement[regexp] == "")
                    wordlist[word] = 1
                else
                {
                    split(Replacement[regexp], ending)
                    for (n in ending)
                    {
                        if (ending[n] == "\"\"")
                            ending[n] = ""
                        wordlist[word ending[n]] = 1
                    }
                }
                break
            }
        }
}

function swap(a, i, j,        temp)
{
    temp = a[i]
    a[i] = a[j]
    a[j] = temp
}
```

12.4.13 Retrospective on Our Spellchecker

The first version of a Unix spellchecker was the pipeline that we presented at the beginning of the chapter. The first Unix spelling program in C that we could find in *The Unix Heritage Society* archives[*] is the 1975 Version 6 Unix typo command; it is about 350 lines of C code. spell first appeared in the 1979 Version 7 Unix release, and took about 700 lines of C code. It was accompanied by a 940-word common English dictionary, supplemented by another 320 words each of American and British spelling variations. spell was omitted from the 1995 4.4 BSD-Lite source code release, presumably because of trade secret or copyright issues.

The modern OpenBSD spell is about 1100 lines of C code, with about 30 more words in each of its three basic dictionaries.

GNU ispell version 3.2 is about 13,500 lines of C code, and GNU aspell version 0.60 is about 29,500 lines of C++ and C code. Both have been internationalized, with

---

[*] See *http://www.tuhs.org/*.

dictionaries for 10 to 40 languages. ispell has significantly enlarged English dictionaries, with about 80,000 common words, plus 3750 or so American and British variations. The aspell dictionaries are even bigger: 142,000 English words plus about 4200 variations for each of American, British, and Canadian.

Our spellchecker, spell.awk, is a truly remarkable program, and you will appreciate it even more and understand awk even better if you reimplement the program in another programming language. Like Johnson's original 1975 spell command, its design and implementation took less than an afternoon.

In about 190 lines of code, made up of three pattern/action one-liners and 11 functions, it does most of what traditional Unix spell does, and more:

- With the -verbose option, it reports location information for the spelling exceptions.

- User control of dictionaries allows it to be readily applied to complex technical documents, and to text written in languages other than English.

- User-definable suffix lists assist in the internationalization of spelling checks, and provide user control over suffix reduction, something that few other spellcheckers on any platform provide.

- All of the associated dictionary and suffix files are simple text files that can be processed with any text editor, and with most Unix text utilities. Some spellcheckers keep their dictionaries in binary form, making the word lists hard to inspect, maintain, and update, and nearly impossible to use for other purposes.

- The major dependence on character sets is the assumption in the initialization of NonWordChars of ASCII ordering in the lower 128 slots. Although IBM mainframe EBCDIC is not supported, European 8-bit character sets pose no problem, and even the two-million-character Unicode set in the multibyte UTF-8 encoding can be handled reasonably, although proper recognition and removal of non-ASCII Unicode punctuation would require more work. Given the complexity of multibyte character sets, and the likely need for it elsewhere, that functionality would be better implemented in a separate tool used as a prefilter to spell.awk.

- Output sort order, which is a complex problem for some languages, is determined entirely by the sort command, which in turn is influenced by the locale set in the current environment. That way, a single tool localizes the sorting complexity so that other software, including our program, can remain oblivious to the difficulties. This is another example of the "Let someone else do the hard part" Software Tools principle discussed in "Software Tools Principles" [1.2].

- Despite being written in an interpreted language, our program is reasonably fast. On a 2 GHz Pentium 4 workstation, with mawk, it took just one second to check spelling in all of the files for this book, just 1.3 times longer than OpenBSD spell, and 2.0 times longer than GNU ispell.

An execution profile (see "Efficiency of awk Programs" [12.4.14]) showed that loading the dictionaries took about 5 percent of the total time, and about one word in 15 was not found in the dictionary. Adding the -strip option increased the runtime by about 25 percent, and reduced the output size by the same amount. Only about one word in 70 made it past the match( ) test inside strip_suffixes( ).

- Suffix support accounts for about 90 of the 190 lines of code, so we could have written a usable multilingual spellchecker in about 100 lines of awk.

Notably absent from this attribute list, and our program, is the stripping of document markup, a feature that some spellcheckers provide. We have intentionally not done so because it is in complete violation of the Unix tradition of one (small) tool for one job. Markup removal is useful in many other contexts, and therefore deserves to reside in separate filters, such as dehtml, deroff, desgml, detex, and dexml. Of these, only deroff is commonly found on most Unix systems, but workable implementations of the others require only a few lines of awk.

Also absent from our program, apart from three simple calls to substr( ), is handling of individual characters. The necessity for such processing in C, and many other languages, is a major source of bugs.

All that remains to be done for this program is accumulation of a suitable set of dictionaries and suffix lists for other languages, provision of a shell script wrapper to make its user interface more like conventional Unix programs, and writing a manual page. Although we do not present them here, you can find the wrapper and manual page with this book's sample programs.

12.4.14 Efficiency of awk Programs

We close this section with some observations about awk program efficiency. Like other scripting languages, awk programs are compiled into a compact internal representation, and that representation is then interpreted at runtime by a small *virtual machine*. Built-in functions are written in the underlying implementation language, currently C in all publicly available versions, and run at native software speeds.

Program efficiency is not just a question of computer time: human time matters as well. If it takes an hour to write a program in awk that runs for a few seconds, compared to several hours to write and debug the same program in a compiled language to shave a few seconds off the runtime, then human time is the only thing that matters. For many software tools, awk wins by a large measure.

With conventional compiled languages like Fortran and C, most inline code is closely related to the underlying machine language, and experienced programmers soon develop a feel for what is cheap and what is expensive. The number of arithmetic and memory operations, and the depth of loop nesting, are important, easily counted, and relate directly to runtimes. With numerical programs, a common rule of thumb is that 90 percent of the runtime is spent in 10 percent of the code: that 10 percent is called the *hot spots*. Optimizations like pulling common expressions out of innermost loops, and ordering computations to match storage layout, can sometimes make dramatic improvements in runtime. However, in higher-level languages, or languages with lots of function calls (like Lisp, where every statement is a function), or with interpreted languages, it is much harder to estimate runtimes, or to identify the hot spots.

awk programs that do a lot of pattern matching usually are limited by the complexity of that operation, which runs entirely at native speeds. Such programs can seldom be improved much by rewriting in a compiled language, like C or C++. Each of the three awk implementations that we mentioned in this chapter were written completely independently of one another, and thus may have quite different relative execution times for particular statements.

Because we have written lots of software tools in awk, some of which have been used on gigabytes of data, runtime efficiency has sometimes been important to us. A few years ago, one of us (NHFB) prepared pawk,* a profiling version of the smallest implementation, nawk. pawk reports both statement counts and times. Independently, the other (AR) added similar support with statement counts to GNU gawk so that pgawk is now standardly available from builds of releases of version 3.1.0 or later. pgawk produces an output profile in awkprof.out with a program listing annotated with statement execution counts. The counts readily identify the hot spots, and zero (or empty) counts identify code that has never been executed, so the profile also serves as a *test coverage* report. Such reports are important when test files are prepared to verify that all statements of a program are executed during testing: bugs are likely to lurk in code that is seldom, or never, executed.

Accurate execution timing has been harder to acquire because typical CPU timers have resolutions of only 60 to 100 ticks per second, which is completely inadequate in an era of GHz processors. Fortunately, some Unix systems now provide low-cost, nanosecond resolution timers, and pawk uses them on those platforms.

12.5 Summary

The original spellchecking prototype shows the elegance and power of the Unix Software Tools approach. With only one special-purpose program, an afternoon's worth of work created a usable and useful tool. As is often the case, experience with a prototype in shell was then applied to writing a production version in C.

---

* Available at *http://www.math.utah.edu/pub/pawk/*.

The use of a private dictionary is a powerful feature of Unix spell. Although the addition of locales to the Unix milieu introduced some quirks, dictionaries are still a valuable thing to use, and indeed, for each chapter of this book, we created private dictionaries to make spellchecking our work more manageable.

The freely available ispell and aspell programs are large and powerful, but lack some of the more obvious features to make their batch modes useful. We showed how with simple shell script wrappers, we could work around these deficiencies and adapt the programs to suit our needs. This is one of the most typical uses of shell scripting: to take a program that does almost what you need and modify its results slightly to do the rest of your job. This also fits in well with the "let someone else do the hard part" Software Tools principle.

Finally, the awk spellchecker nicely demonstrates the elegance and power of that language. In one afternoon, one of us (NHFB) produced a program of fewer than 200 lines that can be (and is!) used for production spellchecking.

CHAPTER 13

Processes

A *process* is an instance of a running program. New processes are started by the fork( ) and execve( ) system calls, and normally run until they issue an exit( ) system call. The details of the fork( ) and execve( ) system calls are complex and not needed for this book. Consult their manual pages if you want to learn more.

Unix systems have always supported multiple processes. Although the computer seems to be doing several things at once, in reality, this is an illusion, unless there are multiple CPUs. What really happens is that each process is permitted to run for a short interval, called a *time slice*, and then the process is temporarily suspended while another waiting process is given a chance to run. Time slices are quite short, usually only a few milliseconds, so humans seldom notice these *context switches* as control is transferred from one process to the kernel and then to another process. Processes themselves are unaware of context switches, and programs need not be written to relinquish control periodically to the operating system.

A part of the operating-system kernel, called the *scheduler*, is responsible for managing process execution. When multiple CPUs are present, the scheduler tries to use them all to handle the workload; the human user should see no difference except improved response.

Processes are assigned priorities so that time-critical processes run before less important ones. The nice and renice commands can be used to adjust process priorities.

The average number of processes awaiting execution at any instant is called the *load average*. You can display it most simply with the uptime command:

```
$ uptime                              Show uptime, user count, and load averages
  1:51pm up 298 day(s), 15:42, 32 users, load average: 3.51, 3.50, 3.55
```

Because the load average varies continually, uptime reports three time-averaged estimates, usually for the last 1, 5, and 15 minutes. When the load average continually exceeds the number of available CPUs, there is more work for the system to do than it can manage, and its response may become sluggish.

Books on operating systems treat processes and scheduling in depth. For this book, and indeed, for most users, the details are largely irrelevant. All that we need in this chapter is a description of how to create, list, and delete processes, how to send signals to them, and how to monitor their execution.

13.1 Process Creation

One of the great contributions of Unix to the computing world is that process creation is cheap and easy. This encourages the practice of writing small programs that each do a part of a larger job, and then combining them to collaborate on the completion of that task. Because programming complexity grows much faster than linearly with program size, small programs are much easier to write, debug, and understand than large ones.

Many programs are started by a shell: the first word in each command line identifies the program to be run. Each process initiated by a command shell starts with these guarantees:

- The process has a *kernel context*: data structures inside the kernel that record process-specific information to allow the kernel to manage and control process execution.

- The process has a *private*, and *protected*, virtual address space that potentially can be as large as the machine is capable of addressing. However, other resource limitations, such as the combined size of physical memory and swap space on external storage, or the size of other executing jobs, or local settings of system-tuning parameters, often impose further restrictions.

- Three file descriptors (standard input, standard output, and standard error) are already open and ready for immediate use.

- A process started from an interactive shell has a *controlling terminal*, which serves as the default source and destination for the three standard file streams. The controlling terminal is the one from which you can send signals to the process, a topic that we cover later in "Process Control and Deletion" [13.3].

- Wildcard characters in command-line arguments have been expanded.

- An environment-variable area of memory exists, containing strings with key/value assignments that can be retrieved by a library call (in C, getenv( )).

These guarantees are nondiscriminatory: all processes at the same priority level are treated equally and may be written in any convenient programming language.

The private address space ensures that processes cannot interfere with one another, or with the kernel. Operating systems that do not offer such protection are highly prone to failure.

The three already-open files suffice for many programs, which can use them without the burden of having to deal with file opening and closing, and without having to know anything about filename syntax, or filesystems.

Wildcard expansion by the shell removes a significant burden from programs and provides uniform handling of command lines.

The environment space provides another way to supply information to processes, beyond their command lines and input files.

13.2 Process Listing

The most important command for listing processes is the *process status* command, ps. For historical reasons, there are two main flavors of ps: a System V style and a BSD style. Many systems provide both, although sometimes one of them is part of an optional package. On our Sun Solaris systems, we have:

```
$ /bin/ps                         System V-style process status
   PID TTY       TIME CMD
  2659 pts/60    0:00 ps
  5026 pts/60    0:02 ksh
 12369 pts/92    0:02 bash

$ /usr/ucb/ps                     BSD-style process status
   PID TT      S  TIME COMMAND
  2660 pts/60  O  0:00 /usr/ucb/ps
  5026 pts/60  S  0:01 /bin/ksh
 12369 pts/92  S  0:02 /usr/local/bin/bash
```

Without command-line options, their output is quite similar, with the BSD style supplying a few more details. Output is limited to just those processes with the same user ID and same controlling terminal as those of the invoker.

Like the file-listing command, ls, the ps command has many options, and both have considerable variation across Unix platforms. With ls, the –l option requesting the long output form is used frequently. To get verbose ps output, we need quite different sets of options. In the System V style, we use:

```
$ ps -efl                              System V style
 F S  UID PID PPID C PRI NI ADDR  SZ WCHAN STIME TTY    TIME CMD
19 T root   0   0 0   0 SY    ?   0       Dec 27 ?     0:00 sched
 8 S root   1   0 0  41 20    ? 106     ? Dec 27 ?     9:53 /etc/init -
19 S root   2   0 0   0 SY    ?   0     ? Dec 27 ?     0:18 pageout
19 S root   3   0 0   0 SY    ?   0     ? Dec 27 ? 2852:26 fsflush
...
```

whereas in the BSD style, we use:

```
$ ps aux                          BSD style
USER     PID %CPU %MEM   SZ  RSS TT   S  START    TIME COMMAND
root       3  0.4  0.0    0    0 ?    S  Dec 27 2852:28 fsflush
smith  13680  0.1  0.2 1664 1320 pts/25 O 15:03:45  0:00 ps aux
```

```
jones 25268   0.1   2.02093619376 pts/24 S   Mar 22   29:56 emacs -bg ivory
brown 26519   0.0   0.3 5424 2944 ?        S   Apr 19    2:05 xterm -name thesis
...
```

Both styles allow option letters to be run together, and the BSD style allows the option hyphen to be dropped. In both examples, we removed excess whitespace to make the lines fit on the page.

There are some design infelicities in both styles, occasioned by the need to display a lot of information in too little space: process start dates may be abbreviated differently, commands in the last field are truncated, and column values can run together. The latter misfeature makes it hard to filter ps output reliably.

The USER and UID fields identify the owner of a process: that can be critical information if a process is hogging the system.

The PID value is the *process ID*, a number that uniquely identifies the process. In the shell, that number is available as $$: we use it in other chapters to form unique names of temporary files. Process ID assignments start out at zero, and increment for each new process throughout the run life of the system. When the maximum representable integer is reached, process numbering starts again at zero, but avoids values that are still in use for other processes. A typical single-user system might have a few dozen active processes, whereas a large multiuser system might have several thousand.

The PPID value is the *parent process ID*: the number of the process that created this one. Every process, except the first, has a parent, and each process may have zero or more child processes, so processes form a tree. Process number 0 is usually called something like kernel, sched, or swapper, and is not shown in ps output on some systems. Process number 1 is rather special; it is called init, and is described in the *init*(8) manual pages. A child process whose parent dies prematurely is assigned init as its new parent. When a system is shut down properly, processes are killed in approximate order of decreasing process IDs, until only init remains. When it exits, the system halts.

The output of ps is not guaranteed to be in any particular order, and since the list of processes is continually changing, its output usually differs on each run.

Since the process list is dynamic, many users prefer to see a continually updating ps-like text display, or a graphical representation thereof. Several utilities provide such display, but none is universally available. The most common one is top, now standard in many Unix distributions.[*] We consider it one of those critical utilities, like GNU tar, that we immediately install on any new system that does not have a native version. On most systems, top requires intimate knowledge of kernel data structures,

---

[*] Available at *ftp://ftp.groupsys.com/pub/top/*. Another implementation for GNU/Linux systems only is available at *http://procps.sourceforge.net/*.

and thus tends to require updates at each operating system upgrade. Also, top (like ps) is one of those few programs that needs to run with special privileges: on some systems, it may be setuid root.

Here's a snapshot of top output on a moderately busy multiprocessor compute server:

```
$ top                                    Show top resource consumers
load averages:  5.28,  4.74,  4.59                          15:42:00
322 processes: 295 sleeping, 4 running, 12 zombie, 9 stopped, 2 on cpu
CPU states: 0.0% idle, 95.9% user, 4.1% kernel, 0.0% iowait, 0.0% swap
Memory: 2048M real, 88M free, 1916M swap in use, 8090M swap free

  PID USERNAME THR PRI NICE  SIZE  RES STATE    TIME   CPU COMMAND
 2518 jones      1   0    0  506M 505M run     44:43 33.95% Macaulay2
 1111 owens      1   0   19   21M  21M run     87:19 24.04% ocDom
23813 smith      1   0   19  184M 184M cpu/0  768:57 20.39% mserver
25389 brown      1   1   19   30M  23M run    184:22  1.07% netscape
...
```

By default, top shows the most CPU-intensive processes at the top of the list, which is usually what you are interested in. However, it accepts keyboard input to control sort order, limit the display to certain users, and so on: type ? in a top session to see what your version offers.

Other commands useful for listing processes or showing various system loads are shown in Table 13-1.

Table 13-1. Useful system load commands

System	Commands
All	iostat, netstat, nfsstat, sar, uptime, vmstat, w, xcpustate,[a] xload, and xperfmon
Apple Mac OS X	pstat
BSD	pstat and systat
GNU/Linux	procinfo
HP Alpha OSF/1	vmubc
IBM AIX	monitor
SGI IRIX	gr_osview and osview
Sun Solaris	mpstat, perfmeter, proctool, prstat, ptree, and sdtperfmeter

[a] Available at *ftp://ftp.cs.toronto.edu/pub/jdd/xcpustate/*.

In most cases, the shell waits for a process to terminate before processing the next command. However, processes can be made to run in the background by terminating the command with an ampersand instead of a semicolon or newline: we used that feature in the build-all script in "Automating Software Builds" [8.2]. The wait command can be used to wait for a specified process to complete, or, without an argument, for completion of all background processes.

Although this book mostly ignores interactive features of the shell, we note that bg, fg, jobs, and wait are shell commands for dealing with still-running processes created under the current shell.

Four keyboard characters interrupt *foreground processes*. These characters are settable with stty command options, usually to Ctrl-C (intr: kill), Ctrl-Y (dsusp: suspend, but delay until input is flushed), Ctrl-Z (susp: suspend), and Ctrl-\ (quit: kill with *core dump*).

It is instructive to examine a simple implementation of top, shown in Example 13-1. The security issues addressed by the /bin/sh - option, and the explicit setting of IFS (to newline-space-tab) and PATH should be familiar from their treatment in "Path Searching" [8.1]. We require a BSD-style ps because it provides the %CPU column that defines the display order, so PATH must be set to find that version first. The PATH setting here works for all but one of our systems (SGI IRIX, which lacks a BSD-style ps command).

Example 13-1. A simplified version of top

```
#! /bin/sh -
# Run the ps command continuously, with a short pause after
# each redisplay.
#
# Usage:
#       simple-top

IFS='
        '

# Customize PATH to get BSD-style ps first
PATH=/usr/ucb:/usr/bin:/bin
export PATH

HEADFLAGS="-n 20"
PSFLAGS=aux
SLEEPFLAGS=5
SORTFLAGS='-k3nr -k1,1 -k2n'

HEADER="`ps $PSFLAGS | head -n 1`"

while true
do
    clear
    uptime
    echo "$HEADER"
    ps $PSFLAGS |
        sed -e 1d |
            sort $SORTFLAGS |
```

Example 13-1. A simplified version of top (continued)

```
        head $HEADFLAGS
    sleep $SLEEPFLAGS
done
```

We save command options in HEADFLAGS, PSFLAGS, SLEEPFLAGS, and SORTFLAGS to facilitate site-specific customization.

An explanatory header for the simple-top output is helpful, but since it varies somewhat between ps implementations, we do not hardcode it in the script; but instead, we just call ps once, saving it in the variable HEADER.

The remainder of the program is an infinite loop that is terminated by one of the keyboard interrupt characters mentioned earlier. The clear command at the start of each loop iteration uses the setting of the TERM environment variable to determine the escape sequences that it then sends to standard output to clear the screen, leaving the cursor in the upper-left corner. uptime reports the load average, and echo supplies the column headers. The pipeline filters ps output, using sed to remove the header line, then sorts the output by CPU usage, username, and process ID, and shows only the first 20 lines. The final sleep command in the loop body produces a short delay that is still relatively long compared to the time required for one loop iteration so that the system load imposed by the script is minor.

Sometimes, you would like to know who is using the system, and how many and what processes they are running, without all of the extra details supplied by the verbose form of ps output. The puser script in Example 13-2 produces a report that looks like this:

```
$ puser                              Show users and their processes
albert          3       -tcsh
                3       /etc/sshd
                2       /bin/sh
                1       /bin/ps
                1       /usr/bin/ssh
                1       xload
daemon          1       /usr/lib/nfs/statd
root            4       /etc/sshd
                3       /usr/lib/ssh/sshd
                3       /usr/sadm/lib/smc/bin/smcboot
                2       /usr/lib/saf/ttymon
                1       /etc/init
                1       /usr/lib/autofs/automountd
                1       /usr/lib/dmi/dmispd
                ...
victoria        4       bash
                2       /usr/bin/ssh
                2       xterm
```

The report is sorted by username, and to reduce clutter and enhance visibility, usernames are shown only when they change.

Example 13-2. The puser script

```
#! /bin/sh -
# Show a sorted list of users with their counts of active
# processes and process names, optionally limiting the
# display to a specified set of users (actually, egrep(1)
# username patterns).
#
# Usage:
#        puser [ user1 user2 ... ]

IFS='
'

PATH=/usr/local/bin:/usr/bin:/bin
export PATH

EGREPFLAGS=
while test $# -gt 0
do
    if test -z "$EGREPFLAGS"
    then
        EGREPFLAGS="$1"
    else
        EGREPFLAGS="$EGREPFLAGS|$1"
    fi
    shift
done

if test -z "$EGREPFLAGS"
then
    EGREPFLAGS="."
else
    EGREPFLAGS="^ *($EGREPFLAGS) "
fi

case "`uname -s`" in
*BSD | Darwin)      PSFLAGS=" a -e -o user,ucomm -x" ;;
*)                  PSFLAGS="-e -o user,comm" ;;
esac

ps $PSFLAGS |
  sed -e 1d |
    EGREP_OPTIONS= egrep "$EGREPFLAGS" |
      sort -b -k1,1 -k2,2 |
        uniq -c |
          sort -b -k2,2 -k1nr,1 -k3,3 |
            awk '{
                    user = (LAST == $2) ? " " : $2
                    LAST = $2
                    printf("%-15s\t%2d\t%s\n", user, $1, $3)
                  }'
```

After the familiar preamble, the puser script uses a loop to collect the optional command-line arguments into the EGREPFLAGS variable, with the vertical-bar separators that indicate alternation to egrep. The `if` statement in the loop body handles the initial case of an empty string, to avoid producing an egrep pattern with an empty alternative.

When the argument-collection loop completes, we check EGREPFLAGS: if it is empty, we reassign it a match-anything pattern. Otherwise, we augment the pattern to match only at the beginning of a line, and to require a trailing space, to prevent false matches of usernames with common prefixes, such as jon and jones.

The case statement handles implementation differences in the ps options. We want an output form that displays just two values: a username and a command name. The BSD systems and BSD-derived Mac OS X (Darwin) systems require slightly different options from all of the others that we tested.

The seven-stage pipeline handles the report preparation:

1. The output from ps contains lines like this:

   ```
   USER COMMAND
   root sched
   root /etc/init
   root /usr/lib/nfs/nfsd
   ...
      jones dtfile
      daemon /usr/lib/nfs/statd
   ...
   ```

2. The sed command deletes the initial header line.

3. The egrep command selects the usernames to be displayed. We clear the EGREP_ OPTIONS environment variable to avoid conflicts in its interpretation by different GNU versions of egrep.

4. The sort stage sorts the data by username and then by process.

5. The uniq command attaches leading counts of duplicated lines and eliminates duplicates.

6. A second sort stage sorts the data again, this time by username, then by descending count, and finally by process name.

7. The awk command formats the data into neat columns, and removes repeated usernames.

13.3   Process Control and Deletion

Well-behaved processes ultimately complete their work and terminate with an exit( ) system call. Sometimes, however, it is necessary to terminate a process prematurely, perhaps because it was started in error, requires more resources than you care to spend, or is misbehaving.

The kill command does the job, but it is misnamed. What it really does is send a *signal* to a specified running process, and with two exceptions noted later, signals can be caught by the process and dealt with: it might simply choose to ignore them. Only the owner of a process, or root, or the kernel, or the process itself, can send a signal to it. A process that receives a signal cannot tell where it came from.

ISO Standard C defines only a half-dozen signal types. POSIX adds a couple of dozen others, and most systems add more, offering 30 to 50 different ones. You can list them like this example on an SGI IRIX system:

```
$ kill -l                              List supported signal names (option lowercase L)
HUP INT QUIT ILL TRAP ABRT EMT FPE KILL BUS SEGV SYS PIPE ALRM TERM
USR1 USR2 CHLD PWR WINCH URG POLL STOP TSTP CONT TTIN TTOU VTALRM PROF
XCPU XFSZ UME RTMIN RTMIN+1 RTMIN+2 RTMIN+3 RTMAX-3 RTMAX-2 RTMAX-1
RTMAX
```

Most are rather specialized, but we've already used a few of the more common ones in trap commands in shell scripts elsewhere in this book.

Each program that handles signals is free to make its own interpretation of them. Signal names reflect *conventions*, not *requirements*, so there is some variation in exactly what a given signal means to a particular program.

Uncaught signals generally cause termination, although STOP and TSTP normally just suspend the process until a CONT signal requests that it continue execution. You might use STOP and CONT to delay execution of a legitimate process until a less-busy time, like this:

```
$ top                                  Show top resource consumers
...
  PID USERNAME  THR PRI NICE  SIZE  RES STATE   TIME   CPU COMMAND
17787 johnson     9  58    0  125M 118M cpu/3 109:49 93.67% cruncher
...

$ kill -STOP 17787                     Suspend process

$ sleep 36000 && kill -CONT 17787 &    Resume process in 10 hours
```

13.3.1 Deleting Processes

For deleting processes, it is important to know about only four signals: ABRT (abort), HUP (hangup), KILL, and TERM (terminate).

Some programs prefer to do some cleanup before they exit: they generally interpret a TERM signal to mean *clean up quickly and exit*. kill sends that signal if you do not specify one. ABRT is like TERM, but may suppress cleanup actions, and may produce a copy of the process memory image in a core, *program*.core, or core.*PID* file.

The HUP signal similarly requests termination, but with many daemons, it often means that the process should stop what it is doing, and then get ready for new work, as if it were freshly started. For example, after you make changes to a configuration file, a HUP signal makes the daemon reread that file.

The two signals that no process can catch or ignore are KILL and STOP. These two signals are always delivered immediately. For sleeping processes,* however, depending on the shell implementation and the operating system, most of the others might be delivered only when the process wakes up. For that reason, you should expect some delay in the delivery of signals.

When multiple signals are sent, the order of their delivery, and whether the same signal is delivered more than once, is unpredictable. The only guarantee that some systems provide is that at least *one* of the signals is delivered. There is such wide variation in signal handling across Unix platforms that only the simplest use of signals is portable.

We have already illustrated the STOP signal for suspending a process. The KILL signal causes immediate process termination. As a rule, you should give the process a chance to shut down gracefully by sending it a HUP signal first: if that does not cause it to exit shortly, then try the TERM signal. If that still does not cause exit, use the last-resort KILL signal. Here's an example of their use. Suppose that you experience sluggish response: run the top command to see what is happening, and get something like this:

```
$ top                                Show top resource consumers
...
  PID USERNAME THR PRI NICE SIZE  RES STATE   TIME   CPU COMMAND
25094 stevens    1  48    0 456M 414M cpu   243:58 99.64% netscape
...
```

Web browsers normally require relatively little CPU time, so this one certainly looks like a runaway process. Send it a HUP signal:

```
$ kill -HUP 25094                    Send a HUP signal to process 25094
```

Run top again, and if the runaway does not soon disappear from the display, use:

```
$ kill -TERM 25094                   Send a TERM signal to process 25094
```

or finally:

```
$ kill -KILL 25094                   Send a KILL signal to process 25094
```

Most top implementations allow the kill command to be issued from inside top itself.

Of course, you can do this only if you are stevens or root. Otherwise, you have to ask your system manager to kill the errant process.

Be cautious with the kill command. When a program terminates abnormally, it may leave remnants in the filesystem that should have been cleaned up, and besides wast-

---

* A process that is awaiting an event, such as the completion of I/O, or the expiration of a timer, is in a suspended state called a *sleep*, and the process scheduler does not consider it runnable. When the event finally happens, the process is again schedulable for execution, and is then said to be *awake*.

ing space, they might cause problems the next time the program is run. For example, daemons, mail clients, text editors, and web browsers all tend to create *locks*, which are just small files that record the fact that the program is running. If a second instance of the program is started while the first is still active, it detects the existing lock, reports that fact, and immediately terminates. Otherwise, havoc could ensue with both instances writing the same files. Unfortunately, these programs rarely tell you the name of the lock file, and seldom document it either. If that lock file is a remnant of a long-gone process, you may find that the program will not run until you find the lock and remove it. We show how to do that in "Process System-Call Tracing" [13.4].

Some systems (GNU/Linux, NetBSD, and Sun Solaris) have `pgrep` and `pkill` commands that allow you to hunt down and kill processes by name. Without extra command-line options to force it to be more selective, `pkill` sends a signal to *all* processes of the specified name. For the runaway-process example, we might have issued:

```
$ pgrep netscape                    Find process numbers of netscape jobs
25094
```

followed by:

```
$ pkill -HUP netscape               Send netscape processes a HUP signal
$ pkill -TERM netscape              Send netscape processes a TERM signal
$ pkill -KILL netscape              Send netscape processes a KILL signal
```

However, because process names are not unique, killing them by name is risky: you might zap more than the intended one.

13.3.2 Trapping Process Signals

Processes register with the kernel those signals that they wish to handle. They specify in the arguments of the `signal()` library call whether the signal should be caught, should be ignored, or should terminate the process, possibly with a core dump. To free most programs from the need to deal with signals, the kernel itself has defaults for each signal. For example, on a Sun Solaris system, we find:

```
$ man -a signal                     Look at all manual pages for signal
...
    Name        Value   Default   Event
    SIGHUP      1       Exit      Hangup (see termio(7I))
    SIGINT      2       Exit      Interrupt (see termio(7I))
    SIGQUIT     3       Core      Quit (see termio(7I))
...
    SIGABRT     6       Core      Abort
...
    SIGFPE      8       Core      Arithmetic Exception
...
    SIGPIPE     13      Exit      Broken Pipe
...
```

```
SIGUSR1          16      Exit      User Signal 1
SIGUSR2          17      Exit      User Signal 2
SIGCHLD          18      Ignore    Child Status Changed
...
```

The trap command causes the shell to register a *signal handler* to catch the specified signals. trap takes a string argument containing a list of commands to be executed when the trap is taken, followed by a list of signals for which the trap is set. In older shell scripts, you often see those signals expressed as numbers, but that is neither informative nor portable: stick with signal names.

Example 13-3 shows a small shell script, looper, that uses trap commands to illustrate caught and uncaught signals.

Example 13-3. A sleepy looping script: looper

```
#! /bin/sh -

trap 'echo Ignoring HUP ...' HUP
trap 'echo Terminating on USR1 ... ; exit 1' USR1

while true
do
    sleep 2
    date >/dev/null
done
```

looper has two trap commands. The first simply reports that the HUP signal was received, whereas the second reports a USR1 signal and exits. The program then enters an infinite loop that spends most of its time asleep. We run it in the background, and send it the two signals that it handles:

```
$ ./looper &                        Run looper in the background
[1]     24179                       The process ID is 24179

$ kill -HUP 24179                   Send looper a HUP signal
Ignoring HUP ...

$ kill -USR1 24179                  Send looper a USR1 signal
Terminating on USR1 ...
[1] + Done(1)              ./looper &
```

Now let's try some other signals:

```
$ ./looper &                        Run looper again in the background
[1]     24286

$ kill -CHLD 24286                  Send looper a CHLD signal

$ jobs                              Is looper still running?
[1] + Running              ./looper &

$ kill -FPE 24286                   Send looper an FPE signal
[1] + Arithmetic Exception(coredump)./looper &
```

```
$ ./looper &                      Run looper again in the background
[1]    24395

$ kill -PIPE 24395                Send looper a PIPE signal
[1] + Broken Pipe            ./looper &

$ ./looper &                      Run looper again in the background
[1]    24621

$ kill 24621                      Send looper the default signal, TERM
[1] + Done(208)              ./looper &
```

Notice that the CHLD signal did not terminate the process; it is one of the signals whose kernel default is to be ignored. By contrast, the floating-point exception (FPE) and broken pipe (PIPE) signals that we sent are among those that cause process termination.

As a final experiment, we add one more trap command to looper:

```
trap 'echo Child terminated ...' CHLD
```

We give the modified script a new name, and run it:

```
$ ./looper-2 &                    Run looper-2 in the background
[1]    24668
Child terminated ...
Child terminated ...
Child terminated ...
Child terminated ...

$ kill -ABRT 24668                Send looper-2 an ABRT signal
[1] + Abort(coredump)        ./looper-2 &
```

Each time the loop body sleep and date processes terminate, the CHLD trap is taken, producing a report every second or so, until we send an ABRT (abort) signal that terminates the looping process.

In addition to the standard signals listed earlier with kill -l, the shell provides one additional signal for the trap command: EXIT. That signal is always assigned the number zero, so trap '...' 0 statements in older shell scripts are equivalent to trap '...' EXIT.

The body of a trap '...' EXIT statement is invoked just before the exit( ) system call is made, either explicitly by an exit command, or implicitly by normal termination of the script. If traps are set for other signals, they are processed before the one for EXIT.

The value of the exit status $? on entry to the EXIT trap is preserved on completion of the trap, unless an exit in the trap resets its value.

bash, ksh, and zsh provide two more signals for trap: DEBUG traps at every statement, and ERR traps after statements returning a nonzero exit code.

The DEBUG trap is quite tricky, however: in ksh88, it traps *after* the statement, whereas in later shells, it traps *before*. The public-domain Korn shell implementation available on several platforms does not support the DEBUG trap at all. We can demonstrate these differences with a short test script:

```
$ cat debug-trap                          Show the test script
trap 'echo This is an EXIT trap' EXIT
trap 'echo This is a DEBUG trap' DEBUG
pwd
pwd
```

Now supply this script to several different shells on a Sun Solaris system:

```
$ /bin/sh debug-trap                      Try the Bourne shell
test-debug-trap: trap: bad trap
/tmp
/tmp
This is an EXIT trap
```

```
$ /bin/ksh debug-trap                     Try the 1988 (i) Korn shell
/tmp
This is a DEBUG trap
/tmp
This is a DEBUG trap
This is an EXIT trap
```

```
$ /usr/xpg4/bin/sh debug-trap             Try the POSIX shell (1988 (i) Korn shell)
/tmp
This is a DEBUG trap
/tmp
This is a DEBUG trap
This is an EXIT trap
```

```
$ /usr/dt/bin/dtksh debug-trap            Try the 1993 (d) Korn shell
This is a DEBUG trap
/tmp
This is a DEBUG trap
/tmp
This is a DEBUG trap
This is an EXIT trap
```

```
$ /usr/local/bin/ksh93 debug-trap         Try the 1993 (o+) Korn shell
This is a DEBUG trap
/tmp
This is a DEBUG trap
/tmp
This is a DEBUG trap
This is an EXIT trap
```

```
$ /usr/local/bin/bash debug-trap          Try the GNU Bourne-Again shell
This is a DEBUG trap
/tmp
This is a DEBUG trap
/tmp
```

```
This is a DEBUG trap
This is an EXIT trap
```

$ **/usr/local/bin/pdksh debug-trap**   *Try the public-domain Korn shell*
```
test-debug-trap[2]: trap: bad signal DEBUG
```

$ **/usr/local/bin/zsh debug-trap**   *Try the Z-shell*
```
This is a DEBUG trap
/tmp
This is a DEBUG trap
/tmp
This is a DEBUG trap
This is an EXIT trap
This is a DEBUG trap
```

We found older versions of bash and ksh that behaved differently in these tests. Clearly, this variation in behavior for the DEBUG trap is problematic, but it is unlikely that you need that trap in portable shell scripts.

The ERR trap also has a surprise: command substitutions that fail do not trap. Here's an example:

$ **cat err-trap**   *Show the test program*
```
#! /bin/ksh -
trap 'echo This is an ERR trap.' ERR
echo Try command substitution: $(ls no-such-file)
echo Try a standalone command:
ls no-such-file
```

$ **./err-trap**   *Run the test program*
```
ls: no-such-file: No such file or directory
Try command substitution:
Try a standalone command:
ls: no-such-file: No such file or directory
This is an ERR trap.
```

Both ls commands failed, but only the second caused a trap.

The most common use of signal trapping in shell scripts is for cleanup actions that are run when the script terminates, such as removal of temporary files. Code like this trap command invocation is typical near the start of many shell scripts:

```
trap 'clean up action goes here' EXIT
```

Setting a trap on the shell's EXIT signal is usually sufficient, since it is handled after all other signals. In practice, HUP, INT, QUIT, and TERM signals are often trapped as well.

To find more examples of the use of traps in shell scripts, try this on your system:

```
grep '^trap' /usr/bin/*          Find traps in system shell scripts
```

Most scripts that we found this way use old-style signal numbers. The manual pages for the signal( ) function should reveal the correspondence of numbers to names.

13.4 Process System-Call Tracing

Many systems provide *system call tracers*, programs that execute target programs, printing out each system call and its arguments as the target program executes them. It is likely you have one on your system; look for one of the following commands: ktrace, par, strace, trace, or truss. While these tools are normally not used inside shell scripts, they can be helpful for finding out what a process is doing and why it is taking so long. Also, they do not require source code access, or any changes whatsoever to the programs to be traced, so you can use them on any process that you own. They can also help your understanding of processes, so we give some small examples later in this section.

If you are unfamiliar with the names of Unix system calls, you can quickly discover many of them by examination of trace logs. Their documentation is traditionally found in Section 2 of the online manuals; e.g., *open*(2). For example, file-existence tests usually involve the access( ) or stat( ) system calls, and file deletion requires the unlink( ) system call.

Most compiled programming languages have a debugger that allows single stepping, setting of breakpoints, examination of variables, and so on. On most systems, the shells have no debugger, so you sometimes have to use the shell's –v option to get shell input lines printed, and the –x option to get commands and their arguments printed. System-call tracers can provide a useful supplement to that output, since they give a deeper view into processes that the shell invokes.

Whenever you run an unknown program, you run the risk that it will do things to your system that you do not like. Computer viruses and worms are often spread that way. Commercial software usually comes with installation programs that customers are expected to trust and run, sometimes even with root privileges. If the program is a shell script, you can inspect it, but if it is a black-box binary image, you cannot. Programs like that always give us a queasy feeling, and we usually refuse to run them as root. A system-call trace log of such an installation can be helpful in finding out exactly what the installer program has done. Even if it is too late to recover deleted or changed files, at least you have a record of what files were affected, and if your filesystem backups or snapshots* are current, you can recover from a disaster.

Most long-running processes make a substantial number of system calls, so the trace output is likely to be voluminous, and thus, best recorded in a file. If only a few system calls are of interest, you can specify them in a command-line option.

Let's follow process creation on a GNU/Linux system, tracing a short Bourne shell session. This can be a bit confusing because there is output from three sources: the

---

* Snapshots are a recent feature of some advanced filesystems: they permit freezing the state of a filesystem, usually in just a few seconds, preserving a view of it in a timestamped directory tree that can be used to recover from changes made since the snapshot.

trace, the shell, and the commands that we run. We therefore set the prompt variable, PS1, to distinguish the original and traced shells, and we annotate each line to identify its source. The trace=process argument selects a group of process-related system calls:

```
$ PS1='traced-sh$ ' strace -e trace=process /bin/sh     Trace process-related system calls
execve("/bin/sh", ["/bin/sh"], [/* 81 vars */]) = 0      This is trace output
```

Now execute a command that we know is built-in:

```
traced-sh$ pwd                                           Run a shell built-in command
/home/jones/book                                         This is command output
```

Only the expected output appeared, because no new process was created. Now use the separate program for that command:

```
traced-sh$ /bin/pwd                                      Run an external command
fork( ) = 32390                                          This is trace output
wait4(-1,                                                This is trace output
/home/jones/book                                         This is command output
 [WIFEXITED(s) && WEXITSTATUS(s) == 0], WUNTRACED, NULL) = 32390  This is trace output
--- SIGCHLD (Child exited) ---                           This is trace output
```

Finally, exit from the shell, and the trace:

```
traced-sh$ exit                                          Exit from the shell
exit                                                     This is trace output
_exit(0) = ?                                             This is trace output
```

We are now back in the original shell session:

```
$ pwd                                                    Back in original shell; check where we are
/home/jones/book                                         Working directory is unchanged
```

The shell made a fork( ) system call to start the /bin/pwd process, whose output got mixed in with the next trace report for the wait4( ) system call. The command terminated normally, and the shell received a CHLD signal, indicating completion of the child process.

Here's an example of profiling system calls on Sun Solaris; the -c option requests that a summary report be displayed after the command completes, with the normal trace output suppressed:

```
$ truss -c /usr/local/bin/pathfind -a PATH truss        Trace the pathfind command
/usr/bin/truss                                           This is output from pathfind
/bin/truss
/usr/5bin/truss
```

syscall	seconds	calls	errors	
_exit	.00	1		The truss report starts here
fork	.00	2		
read	.00	26		
write	.00	3		
open	.00	5	1	
close	.00	10	1	
brk	.00	42		
stat	.01	19	15	

```
...
stat64                    .03      33    28
open64                    .00       1
                       -------  ------  ----
sys totals:               .04     242    50
usr time:                 .01
elapsed:                  .19
```

When your program takes longer than expected, output like this can help to identify performance bottlenecks arising from system-call overhead. The `time` command can be useful in identifying candidates for system-call profiling: it reports user time, system-call time, and wall-clock time.

 One of the most common applications of system-call tracers is for monitoring file access: look for `access( )`, `open( )`, `stat( )`, and `unlink( )` call reports in the trace log. On GNU/Linux, use `strace -e trace=file` to reduce the log volume. File-access traces can be particularly helpful when newly installed software complains that it cannot find a needed configuration file, but fails to tell you the file's name.

System-call tracers are also helpful in finding the lock-file remnants that we discussed earlier. Here is an example from a Sun Solaris system that shows how to locate the lock file produced by a particular web browser:

```
$ truss -f -o foo.log mozilla          Trace browser execution
$ grep -i lock foo.log                 Search the trace for the word "lock"
...
29028:  symlink("192.168.253.187:29028",
                "/home/jones/.mozilla/jones/c7rboyyz.slt/lock") = 0
...
29028:  unlink("/home/jones/.mozilla/jones/c7rboyyz.slt/lock") = 0
```

This browser makes a lock file that is a symbolic link to a nonexistent filename containing the local machine's numeric Internet host address and the process number. Had the browser process died prematurely, the `unlink( )` system call that removed the lock file might not have been executed. Lock filenames do not always have the word lock in them, so you might have to examine the trace log more closely to identify a lock file.

Here is an abbreviated trace on an SGI IRIX system, where we test whether /bin/sh is executable:

```
$ /usr/sbin/par /bin/test -x /bin/sh       Trace the test command
...
    0mS[  0] : execve("/bin/test", 0x7ffb7e88, 0x7ffb7e98)
...
    6mS[  0] : access("/bin/sh", X_OK) OK
    6mS[  0] : stat("/bin/sh", 0x7ffb7cd0) OK
...
    6mS[  0] : prctl(PR_LASTSHEXIT) = 1
    6mS[  0] : exit(0)
```

```
System call summary :
                     Average    Total
Name         #Calls Time(ms)  Time(ms)
--------------------------------------
execve            1     3.91      3.91
open              2     0.11      0.21
access            1     0.17      0.17
stat              1     0.12      0.12
...
prctl             1     0.01      0.01
exit              1     0.00      0.00
```

Once you know what system call you are interested in, you can reduce clutter by restricting trace output to only that call:

```
$ /usr/sbin/par -n stat /bin/test -x /bin/sh          Trace only stat system calls
   0mS[  0] (5399999) : was sent signal SIGUSR1
   0mS[  3] : received signal SIGUSR1 (handler 0x100029d8)
   6mS[  3] : stat("/bin/sh", 0x7ffb7cd0) OK

System call summary :
   ...
```

The BSD and Mac OS X ktrace commands work a little differently: they write the trace to a binary file, ktrace.out. You then have to run kdump to convert it to text form. Here's a trace from a NetBSD system, testing for execute permission of /bin/sh:

```
$ ktrace test -x /bin/sh                      Trace the test command

$ ls -l ktrace.out                            List the trace log
-rw-rw-r--    1 jones     devel       8698 Jul 27 09:44 ktrace.out

$ kdump                                        Post-process the trace log
...
 19798 ktrace    EMUL  "netbsd"
 19798 ktrace    CALL  execve(0xb1b1c650,0xbfbfcb24,0xbfbfcb34)
 19798 ktrace    NAMI  "/usr/local/bin/test"
...
 19798 test      CALL  access(0xbfbfcc80,0x1)
 19798 test      NAMI  "/bin/sh"
 19798 test      RET   access 0
 19798 test      CALL  exit(0)
```

The need to post-process the trace log is unfortunate, since it prevents having a dynamic view of the system calls that a process is making. In particular, a hung system call may be hard to identify.

All of the system-call tracers can take a process ID argument instead of a command name, allowing them to trace an already-running process. Only the process owner and root can do that.

There is much more to system-call tracers than we can illustrate here. Consult your local manual pages for details.

13.5 Process Accounting

Unix systems support process accounting, although it is often disabled to reduce the administrative log-file management burden. When it is enabled, on completion of each process, the kernel writes a compact binary record in a system-dependent accounting file, such as /var/adm/pacct or /var/account/pacct. The accounting file requires further processing before it can be turned into a text stream that is amenable to processing with standard tools. For example, on Sun Solaris, root might do something like this to produce a human-readable listing:

```
# acctcom -a                            List accounting records
...
COMMAND                  START   END     REAL   CPU   MEAN
NAME      USER TTYNAME TIME    TIME    (SECS) (SECS) SIZE(K)
...
cat       jones    ? 21:33:38 21:33:38  0.07   0.04 1046.00
echo      jones    ? 21:33:38 21:33:38  0.13   0.04  884.00
make      jones    ? 21:33:38 21:33:38  0.53   0.05 1048.00
grep      jones    ? 21:33:38 21:33:38  0.14   0.03  840.00
bash      jones    ? 21:33:38 21:33:38  0.55   0.02 1592.00
....
```

Because the output format and the accounting tools differ between Unix implementations, we cannot provide portable scripts for summarizing accounting data. However, the sample output shows that the text format is relatively simple. For example, we can easily produce a list of the top ten commands and their usage counts like this:

```
# acctcom -a | cut -d ' ' -f 1 | sort | uniq -c | sort -k1nr -k2 | head -n 10
21129 bash
5538 cat
4669 rm
3538 sed
1713 acomp
1378 cc
1252 cg
1252 iropt
1172 uname
 808 gawk
```

Here, we used cut to extract the first field, then ordered that list with sort, reduced it to counts of duplicates with uniq, sorted that by descending count, and finally used head to display the first tenrecords in the list.

Use the command apropos accounting to identify accounting commands on your system. Common ones are acctcom, lastcomm, and sa: most have options to help reduce the voluminous log data to manageable reports.

13.6 Delayed Scheduling of Processes

In most cases, users want processes to start immediately and finish quickly. The shell therefore normally starts each command as soon as the previous one finishes. Command completion speed is essentially resource-limited, and beyond the shell's purview.

In interactive use, it is sometimes unnecessary to wait for one command to complete before starting another. This is so common that the shell provides a simple way to request it: any command that ends with an ampersand is started in the background, but not waited for. In those rare cases in which you need to wait for backgrounded processes to complete, simply issue the wait command, as described in "Process Listing" [13.2].

There are at least four other situations when it is desirable to delay process start until a future time; we treat them in the following subsections.

13.6.1 sleep: Delay Awhile

When a process should not be started until a certain time period has elapsed, use the sleep command to suspend execution for a specified number of seconds, then issue the delayed command. The sleep command uses few resources, and can be used without causing interference with active processes: indeed, the scheduler simply ignores the sleeping process until it finally awakes when its timer expires.

We use a short sleep in Example 13-1 and Example 13-3 to create programs that have an infinite loop, but do not consume all of the machine's resources in doing so. The short sleep in "Numeric Functions" [9.10], ensures that a new pseudorandom-number generator seed is selected for each process in a loop. The long sleep in "Process Control and Deletion" [13.3] waits until a more convenient time to resume a suspended resource-hungry job.

Most daemons do their work, and then sleep for a short while before waking to check for more work; that way, they consume few resources and run with little effect on other processes for as long as the system is operational. They usually invoke the sleep( ) or usleep( ) functions,* instead of using the sleep command directly, unless they are themselves shell scripts.

---

* Different systems vary as to which of these is a system call and which is a library function.

13.6.2 at: Delay Until Specified Time

The at command provides a simple way to run a program at a specified time. The syntax varies somewhat from system to system, but these examples give the general flavor:

```
at 21:00              < command-file   Run at 9 p.m.
at now                < command-file   Run immediately
at now + 10 minutes   < command-file   Run after 10 minutes
at now + 8 hours      < command-file   Run after 8 hours
at 0400 tomorrow      < command-file   Run at 4 a.m. tomorrow
at 14 July            < command-file   Run next Bastille Day
at noon + 15 minutes  < command-file   Run at 12:15 today
at teatime            < command-file   Run this afternoon
```

In each case, the job to be run is defined by commands in *command-file*. at has somewhat eclectic ways of specifying time, as shown by the last example, which represents 16:00.

atq lists the jobs in the at queue and atrm removes them. For further details, consult the at manual pages on your system.

 On some systems, the shell that is used to run the at commands is the Bourne shell (/bin/sh), and your login shell on other systems. You can insulate yourself from these variations by making the input to at a one-line command that names an executable script written in whatever language you find convenient, with the first line set to:

> #! */path/to/script/interpreter*

Whether the at family of commands is available to you depends on management policies. The files at.allow and at.deny control access: they are stored in /etc, /usr/lib/cron/at, /var/adm/cron, or /var/at, depending on the Unix flavor. If neither file exists, then only root can use at. If your system does not allow you to use the at commands, complain to your system manager: most sites should have little reason to forbid them.

13.6.3 batch: Delay for Resource Control

Historically, long before computers offered interactive access for humans, operating systems ran all processes in *batch mode*. A stream of jobs to be run is accumulated, and then processed in some order that might depend on the position of the job in the queue, who you are, how important you are, what resources you need and are permitted to have, how long you are prepared to wait, and how much you are willing to pay. Many mainframe computers and large compute servers still spend most of their CPU cycles this way.

All current Unix systems have a batch command that allow processes to be added to one of possibly several different batch queues. The syntax of batch varies from system to system, but all support reading commands from standard input:

```
batch < command-file          Run commands in batch
```

On some systems, this is equivalent to:

```
at -q b -m now < command-file    Run commands now under the batch queue
```

where –q b specifies the batch queue, –m requests mail to the user when the job completes, and now means that it is ready to run immediately.

The problem with batch is that it is too simplistic: it offers little control over batch processing order, and nothing in the way of batch policy. It is rarely needed on smaller systems. On larger ones, and especially on distributed systems, batch is replaced by much more sophisticated implementations, such as the ones shown in Table 13-2. Each of those packages has a collection of commands for submitting and managing batch jobs.

Table 13-2. Advanced batch queue and scheduler systems

Name	Web site
Generic Network Queueing System	http://www.gnqs.org/
IBM LoadLeveler	http://www.ibm.com/servers/eserver/pseries/library/sp_books/loadleveler.html
Maui Cluster Scheduler	http://supercluster.org/maui/
Platform LSF system	http://www.platform.com/products/LSFfamily/
Portable Batch System	http://www.openpbs.org/
Silver Grid Scheduler	http://supercluster.org/silver/
Sun GridEngine	http://gridengine.sunsource.net/

13.6.4 crontab: Rerun at Specified Times

Most computers have management tasks that need to be run repeatedly, such as file-system backup every night, log-file and temporary-directory cleanup every week, account reporting once a month, and so on. Ordinary users may need such a facility as well—for example, to synchronize files from a home computer with files on an office computer.

The facility that provides for running jobs at specified times consists of the cron daemon started at system startup, and the crontab command for management of a simple text file that records when jobs are to be run: see the manual pages for *cron*(8) and *crontab*(1). You can list your current job schedule with crontab –1 (lowercase L), and start an editor to update it with crontab –e. The editor chosen is determined by the EDITOR environment variable; depending on the system, crontab may refuse to run if that variable is not set, or it may simply start ed.

The crontab file (see the manual pages for *crontab*(5)) supports shell-style comments, so we find it helpful to start it out with comments that remind us of the expected syntax:

```
$ crontab -l                            List the current crontab schedule
#       mm    hh    dd    mon   weekday      command
#       00-59 00-23 01-31 01-12 0-6(0=Sunday)
...
```

In the first five fields, instead of a single number you can use either a hyphen-separated inclusive range (e.g., 8-17 in the second field to run hourly from 08:00 to 17:00), or a comma-separated list of numbers or ranges (e.g., 0,20,40 in the first field to run every 20 minutes), or an asterisk, meaning every possible number for that field. Here are some sample entries:

```
15   *   *   *   *   command          Run hourly at quarter past the hour
 0   2   1   *   *   command          Run at 02:00 at the start of each month
 0   8   1 1,7 *   command            Run at 08:00 on January 1 and July 1
 0   6   *   *   1   command          Run at 06:00 every Monday
 0 8-17 *   * 0,6   command           Run hourly from 08:00 to 17:00 on weekends
```

 Although POSIX says that blank lines are ignored, some commercial versions of crontab do not tolerate blank lines, actually *deleting* a crontab file that contains them! We recommend avoiding them in your own crontab files.

Commands in the crontab file run with a few environment variables already set: SHELL is /bin/sh, and HOME, LOGNAME, and sometimes, USER, are set according to values in your entry in the passwd file or database.

The PATH setting is sharply restricted, often to just /usr/bin. If you are used to a more liberal setting, you may either need to specify full paths to commands used in the crontab file, or else set the PATH explicitly:

```
0 4 * * * /usr/local/bin/updatedb              Update the GNU fast find database nightly
0 4 * * * PATH=/usr/local/bin:$PATH updatedb   Similar, but pass PATH to updatedb's children
```

Any output produced on standard error or standard output is mailed to you, or in some implementations, to the user specified by the value of the MAILTO variable. In practice, you more likely want output redirected to a log file and accumulated over successive runs. Such a crontab entry might look like this:

```
55 23 * * *    $HOME/bin/daily >> $HOME/logs/daily.log 2>&1
```

Log files like this continue to grow, so you should do an occasional cleanup, perhaps by using an editor to delete the first half of the log file, or tail -n *n* to extract the last *n* lines:

```
cd $HOME/logs                          Change to log-file directory
mv daily.log daily.tmp                 Rename the log file
tail -n 500 daily.tmp > daily.log      Recover the last 500 lines
rm daily.tmp                           Discard the old log file
```

Just be sure to do this at a time when the log file is not being updated. Obviously, this repetitive process can, and should, itself be relegated to another crontab entry.

A useful alternative to a cumulative log file is timestamped files with one cron job log per file. For a daily log, we could use a crontab entry like this:

```
55 23 * * *    $HOME/bin/daily > $HOME/logs/daily.`date +\%Y.\%m.\%d`.log 2>&1
```

cron normally changes percent characters in commands to newlines, but the backslashes prevent that unusual behavior.

You can easily compress or remove old log files with the help of the find command:

```
find $HOME/logs/*.log -ctime +31 | xargs bzip2 -9    Compress log files older than a month
```

```
find $HOME/logs/*.log -ctime +31 | xargs rm          Remove log files older than a month
```

To keep your crontab file clean and simple, put each of its commands in a separate shell script with a sensibly chosen name. You can later revise those scripts without having to tinker with your crontab file.

If it is possible that running a second instance of a cron job might be harmful (e.g., filesystem backups or log-file updates), you need to make sure to prevent that, either by using a suitable lock file, or by switching from cron to at and having the job submit its successor just before the job itself finishes. Of course, you then have to monitor its every run so that in the event of a failure, if you use lock files, you make sure to remove them, and if you use at, you reschedule the job.

You can remove your crontab file entirely with crontab -r. Like rm, this is irrevocable and unrecoverable. Caution suggests preserving a copy like this:

```
crontab -l > $HOME/.crontab.`hostname`    Save the current crontab
crontab -r                                Remove the crontab
```

so that you can later restore it with:

```
crontab $HOME/.crontab.`hostname`         Restore the saved crontab
```

Since there is potentially one crontab file per host, we include the hostname in the name of the saved file so we can readily identify which machine it belongs to.

crontab replaces any existing schedule with that in the file given on its command line, provided that no syntax errors are found; otherwise, the old schedule is preserved.

As with the at command, there are cron.allow and cron.deny files in system directories that control whether cron jobs are allowed, and who can run them. Complain to your system manager if you find yourself denied access to this useful facility.

13.7 The /proc Filesystem

Several Unix flavors have borrowed an idea developed at Bell Labs: the /proc filesystem. Instead of supplying access to kernel data via myriad system calls that need continual updating, kernel data is made available through a special device driver that implements a standard filesystem interface in the /proc directory. Each running process has a subdirectory there, named with the process number, and inside each subdirectory are various small files with kernel data. The contents of this filesystem are described in the manual pages for *proc*(4) (most systems) or *proc*(5) (GNU/Linux).

GNU/Linux has developed this idea more than most other Unix flavors, and its ps command gets all of the required process information by reading files under /proc, which you can readily verify by running a system-call trace with strace   -e trace=file ps aux.

Here's an example of the process files for a text-editor session:

```
$ ls /proc/16521                        List proc files for process 16521
cmdline  environ  fd     mem     root  statm
cwd      exe      maps   mounts  stat  status

$ ls -l /proc/16521                          List them again, verbosely
total 0
-r--r--r--    1 jones    devel    0 Oct 28 11:38 cmdline
lrwxrwxrwx    1 jones    devel    0 Oct 28 11:38 cwd -> /home/jones
-r--------    1 jones    devel    0 Oct 28 11:38 environ
lrwxrwxrwx    1 jones    devel    0 Oct 28 11:38 exe -> /usr/bin/vi
dr-x------    2 jones    devel    0 Oct 28 11:38 fd
-r--r--r--    1 jones    devel    0 Oct 28 11:38 maps
-rw-------    1 jones    devel    0 Oct 28 11:38 mem
-r--r--r--    1 jones    devel    0 Oct 28 11:38 mounts
lrwxrwxrwx    1 jones    devel    0 Oct 28 11:38 root -> /
-r--r--r--    1 jones    devel    0 Oct 28 11:38 stat
-r--r--r--    1 jones    devel    0 Oct 28 11:38 statm
-r--r--r--    1 jones    devel    0 Oct 28 11:38 status
```

Notice that the files all appear to be empty, but in fact, they contain data that is supplied by the device driver when they are read: they never really exist on a storage device. Their timestamps are suspicious as well: on GNU/Linux and OSF/1 systems, they reflect the current time, but on IRIX and Solaris, they show the time that each process started.

The zero size of /proc files confuses some utilities—among them, scp and tar. You might first have to use cp to copy them elsewhere into normal files.

Let's look at one of these files:

```
$ cat -v /proc/16521/cmdline            Display the process command line
vi^@+273^@ch13.xml^@
```

The –v option causes unprintable characters to be displayed in caret notation, where ^@ represents the NUL character. Evidently, this file contains a sequence of NUL-terminated strings, one for each argument in the command line.

Besides process-specific data, /proc may contain other useful files:

```
$ ls /proc | egrep -v '^[0-9]+$' | fmt     List all but process directories
apm bus cmdline cpuinfo devices dma driver execdomains fb
filesystems fs ide interrupts iomem ioports irq isapnp kcore kmsg
ksyms loadavg locks mdstat meminfo misc modules mounts mtrr net
partitions pci scsi self slabinfo speakup stat swaps sys sysvipc
tty uptime version
```

Here's the start of just one of them:

```
$ head -n 5 /proc/meminfo               Show first 5 lines of memory information
          total:     used:     free:  shared: buffers:  cached:
Mem:  129228800 116523008 12705792        0 2084864 59027456
Swap: 2146787328 28037120 2118750208
MemTotal:       126200 kB
MemFree:         12408 kB
```

Having process data available as files is convenient and makes the data easily available to programs written in any programming language, even those that lack a system-call interface. For example, a shell script could collect hardware details of CPU, memory, and storage devices from the /proc/*info files on all of the machines in your environment that have such files, producing reports somewhat like those from the fancy sysinfo* command. The lack of standardization of the contents of these files, however, makes the task of producing uniform reports more difficult than it ought to be.

13.8 Summary

In this chapter, we have shown how to create, list, control, schedule, and delete processes, how to send signals to them, and how to trace their system calls. Because processes run in private address spaces, they cannot interfere with one another, and no special effort needs to be made to write programs that can run at the same time.

Processes can catch all but two of several dozen signals, and either ignore them or respond to them with any desired action. The two uncatchable signals, KILL and STOP, ensure that even badly misbehaving processes can be killed or suspended. Programs that need to perform cleanup actions, such as saving active files, resetting terminal modes, or removing locks, generally catch common signals; otherwise, most uncaught signals cause process termination. The trap command makes it easy to add simple signal handling to shell scripts.

---

* Available at *http://www.magnicomp.com/sysinfo/*.

Finally, we examined several different mechanisms for delaying or controlling process execution. Of these, sleep is the most useful for shell scripting, although the others all have their uses.

## CHAPTER 14

Shell Portability Issues and Extensions

The shell language as defined by POSIX is considerably larger than the original V7 Bourne shell. However, it is considerably smaller than the languages implemented by ksh93 and bash, the two most commonly used extended versions of the Bourne shell.

It is likely that if you'll be doing heavy-duty scripting that takes advantage of shell-language extensions, you'll be using one or the other or both of these two shells. Thus, it's worthwhile to be familiar with features that the shells have in common, as well as their differences.

Over time, bash has acquired many of the extensions in ksh93, but not all of them. Thus, there is considerable functional overlap, but there are also many differences. This chapter outlines areas where bash and ksh93 differ, as well as where they have common extensions above and beyond the features of the POSIX shell.

 Many of the features described here are available only in recent versions of ksh93. Some commercial Unix systems have older versions of ksh93, particularly as a program called dtksh (the desktop Korn shell, /usr/dt/bin/dtksh), which won't have the newer features. Your best bet is to download the source for the current ksh93 and build it from scratch. For more information, see "Download Information" [14.4].

14.1 Gotchas

Here is a "laundry list" of things to watch out for:

Saving shell state
>   Example 14-1 shows how to save the shell's state into a file. An apparent oversight in the POSIX standard is that there's no defined way to save function definitions for later restoration! The example shows how to do that for both bash and ksh93.

Example 14-1. Saving shell state, indcluding functions, for bash and ksh93

```
{
    set +o                      Option settings
    (shopt -p) 2>/dev/null      bash-specific options, subshell silences ksh
    set                         Variables and values
    export -p                   Exported variables
    readonly -p                 Read-only variables
    trap                        Trap settings

    typeset -f                  Function definitions (not POSIX)
} > /tmp/shell.state
```

Note that bash and ksh93 can use different syntaxes for defining functions, so care is required if you wish to dump the state from one shell and restore it in the other!

echo *is not portable*

As described in "Simple Output with echo" [2.5.3], the echo command may only be used portably for the simplest of uses, and various options and/or escape sequences may or may not be available (the POSIX standard notwithstanding).

In ksh93, the built-in version of echo attempts to emulate whatever external version of echo would be found in $PATH. The reason behind this is compatibility: on any given Unix system, when the Korn shell executes a Bourne shell script for that system, it should behave identically to the original Bourne shell.

In bash, on the other hand, the built-in version behaves the same across Unix systems. The rationale is consistency: a bash script should behave the same, no matter what Unix variant it's running on. Thus, for complete portability, echo should be avoided, and printf is still the best bet.

OPTIND *can be a local variable*

In "shift and Option Processing" [6.4.4], we described the getopts command and the OPTIND and OPTARGS variables. ksh93 gives functions defined with the function keyword a *local* copy of OPTIND. The idea is that functions can be much more like separate scripts, using getopts to process their arguments in the same way a script does, without affecting the parent's option processing.

${var:?message} *may not exit*

The ${*variable*:?*message*} variable expansion checks if *variable* is set. If it isn't, the shell prints *message* and exits. However, when the shell is *interactive*, the behavior varies, since it's not always correct for an interactive shell to just blindly exit, possibly logging the user out. Given the following script, named x.sh:

```
echo ${somevar:?somevar is not set}
echo still running
```

bash and ksh93 show the behaviors listed in Table 14-1.

Table 14-1. Interactivity of ${var:?message} in bash and ksh93

Command	Message printed	Subsequent command run
$ `bash x.sh`	Yes	No
$ `ksh93 x.sh`	Yes	No
bash$ `. x.sh`	Yes	Yes
ksh93$ `. x.sh`	Yes	No

This implies that if you know that a script will be executed with the dot command, you should ensure that it exits after using the ${*variable*:?*message*} construct.

Missing loop items in a for *loop*

Here's a subtle point. Consider a loop such as:

```
for i in $a $b $c
do
    do something
done
```

If all three variables are empty, there are no values to loop over, so the shell silently does nothing. It's *as if* the loop had been written:

```
for i in       # nothing!
do
    do something
done
```

However, for most versions of the Bourne shell, actually writing a for loop that way would produce a syntax error. The 2001 POSIX standard made an empty loop valid when entered directly.

The current versions of both ksh93 and bash accept an empty for loop as just shown, and silently do nothing. As this is a recent feature, older versions of both shells, as well as the original Bourne shell, are likely to produce an error message.

DEBUG *traps behave differently*

Both ksh88 and ksh93 provide a special DEBUG trap for shell debugging and tracing. In ksh88, the traps on DEBUG happen *after* each command is executed. In ksh93, the DEBUG trap happens *before* each command. So far so good. More confusing is that earlier versions of bash follow the ksh88 behavior, whereas the current versions follow that of ksh93. This is illustrated in "Trapping Process Signals" [13.3.2].

Long and short options for set

The set command in both shells accepts additional short and long options. The full set of set options, for both shells, is given in Table 14-2. Items marked POSIX are available in both bash and the Korn shell.

Table 14-2. Shell options for set

Short option	−o form	Availability	Description
-a	allexport	POSIX	Export all subsequently defined variables.
-A		ksh88, ksh93	Array assignment. `set +A` does not clear the array. See "Indexed Arrays" [14.3.6] for more information.
-b	notify	POSIX	Print job completion messages right away, instead of waiting for next prompt. Intended for interactive use.
-B	braceexpand	bash	Enable brace expansion. On by default. See "Brace Expansion" [14.3.4] for more information.
-C	noclobber	POSIX	Don't allow > redirection to existing files. The > | operator overrides the setting of this option. Intended for interactive use.
-e	errexit	POSIX	Exit the shell when a command exits with nonzero status.
-f	noglob	POSIX	Disable wildcard expansion.
-h	hashall (bash) trackall (ksh)	POSIX	Locate and remember the location of commands called from function bodies when the function is defined, instead of when the function is executed (XSI).
-H	histexpand	bash	Enable !-style history expansion. On by default.[a]
-k	keyword	bash, ksh88, ksh93	Put all variable assignments into the environment, even those in the middle of a command. This is an obsolete feature and should never be used.
-m	monitor	POSIX	Enable job control (on by default). Intended for interactive use.
-n	noexec	POSIX	Read commands and check for syntax errors, but don't execute them. Interactive shells are allowed to ignore this option.
-p	privileged	bash, ksh88, ksh93	Attempt to function in a more secure mode. The details differ among the shells; see your shell's documentation.
-P	physical	bash	Use the physical directory structure for commands that change directory.
-s		ksh88, ksh93	Sort the positional parameters.
-t		bash, ksh88, ksh93	Read and execute one command and then exit. This is obsolete; it is for compatibility with the Bourne shell and should not be used.
-u	nounset	POSIX	Treat undefined variables as errors, not as null.
-v	verbose	POSIX	Print commands (verbatim) before running them.
-x	xtrace	POSIX	Print commands (after expansions) before running them.
	bgnice	ksh88, ksh93	Automatically lower the priority of all commands run in the background (with &).
	emacs	bash, ksh88, ksh93	Use emacs-style command-line editing. Intended for interactive use.

Table 14-2. Shell options for set (continued)

Short option	−o form	Availability	Description
	gmacs	ksh88, ksh93	Use GNU emacs-style command-line editing. Intended for interactive use.
	history	bash	Enable command history. On by default.
	ignoreeof	POSIX	Disallow Ctrl-D to exit the shell.
	markdirs	ksh88, ksh93	Append a / to directories when doing wildcard expansion.
	nolog	POSIX	Disable command history for function definitions.
	pipefail	ksh93	Make pipeline exit status be that of the last command that fails, or zero if all OK. ksh93n or newer.
	posix	bash	Enable full POSIX compliance.
	vi	POSIX	Use vi-style command-line editing. Intended for interactive use.
	viraw	ksh88, ksh93	Use vi-style command-line editing. Intended for interactive use. This mode can be slightly more CPU intensive than set -o vi.

ᵃ We recommend disabling this feature if you use bash.

14.2   The bash shopt Command

The bash shell, besides using the set command with long and short options, has a separate shopt command for enabling and disabling options.

The list of options for bash version 3.0 follows. For each option, we describe the behavior when the option is set (enabled):

cdable_vars

> When an argument to cd isn't a directory, bash treats it as a variable name, whose value is the target directory.

cdspell

> If a cd to a directory fails, bash attempts several minor spelling corrections to see if it can find the real directory. If it finds a correction, it prints the name and changes to the computed directory. This option works only in interactive shells.

checkhash

> As bash finds commands after a path search, it stores the path search results in a hash table, to speed up subsequent executions of the same command. The second time a command is executed, bash runs the command as stored in the hash table, on the assumption that it's still there. With this option, bash verifies that a filename stored in its hash table really exists before trying to execute it. If it's not found, bash does a regular path search.

shopt (bash)

Usage
> shopt [-pqsu] [-o] [*option-name* ...]

Purpose
> To centralize control of shell options as they're added to bash, instead of proliferating set options or shell variables.

Major options

> -o
>> Limit options to those that can be set with set -o.

> -p
>> Print output in a form suitable for rereading.

> -q
>> Quiet mode. The exit status indicates if the option is set. With multiple options, the status is zero if they are all enabled, nonzero otherwise.

> -s
>> Set (enable) the given option.

> -u
>> Unset (disable) the given option.
>> For -s and -u without named options, the display lists those options which are set or unset, respectively.

Behavior
> Control the settings of various internal shell options. With no option or -p, print the settings. Use -p to print the settings in a form that can be reread later.

Caveats
> Only in bash, not in ksh.

checkwinsize
> After each command, bash checks the window size, and updates the LINES and COLUMNS variables when the window size changes.

cmdhist
> bash stores all lines of a multiline command in the history file. This makes it possible to reedit multiline commands.

dotglob
> bash includes files whose names begin with . (dot) in the results of filename expansion.

execfail
> bash does not exit if it cannot execute the command given to the exec built-in command (see "File Descriptor Manipulation" [7.3.2]). In any case, interactive shells do not exit if exec fails.

expand_aliases
> bash expands aliases. This is the default for interactive shells.

extdebug
> bash enables behavior needed for debuggers:
>
> - `declare -F` displays the source file name and line number for each function name argument.
> - When a command run by the `DEBUG` trap fails, the next command is skipped.
> - When a command run by the `DEBUG` trap inside a shell function or script sourced with `.` (dot) or `source` fails, the shell simulates a call to `return`.
> - The array variable `BASH_ARGC` is set. Each element holds the number of arguments for the corresponding function or dot-script invocation. Similarly, the `BASH_ARGV` array variable is set. Each element is one of the arguments passed to a function or dot-script. `BASH_ARGV` functions as a stack, with values being pushed on at each call. Thus, the last element is the last argument to the most recent function or script invocation.
> - Function tracing is enabled. Command substitutions, shell functions and subshells invoked via (...) inherit the `DEBUG` and `RETURN` traps. (The `RETURN` trap is run when a `return` is executed, or a script run with `.` [dot] or `source` finishes.)
> - Error tracing is enabled. Command substitutions, shell functions, and subshells invoked via (...) inherit the `ERROR` trap.

extglob
> bash does extended pattern matching similar to that of ksh88. This is discussed in more detail in "Extended Pattern Matching" [14.3.3].

extquote
> bash allows $'...' and $"..." within ${*variable*} expansions inside double quotes.

failglob
> When a pattern does not match filenames bash produces an error.

force_fignore
> When doing completion, bash ignores words matching the list of suffixes in `FIGNORE`, even if such words are the only possible completions.

gnu_errfmt
> bash prints error messages in the standard GNU format.

histappend
> bash appends commands to the file named by the `HISTFILE` variable, instead of overwriting the file.

histreedit
> When a history substitution fails, if the `readline` library is being used, bash allows you to reedit the failed substitution.

histverify
> With readline, bash loads the result of a history substitution into the editing buffer for further changing.

hostcomplete
> bash performs hostname completion with readline on words containing an @ character. This is on by default.

huponexit
> bash sends SIGHUP to all jobs when an interactive login shell exits.

interactive_comments
> bash treats # as starting a comment for interactive shells. This is on by default.

lithist
> When used together with the cmdhist option, bash saves multiline commands in the history with embedded newlines, rather than semicolons.

login_shell
> bash sets this option when it is started as a login shell. It cannot be changed.

mailwarn
> bash prints the message "The mail in mailfile has been read" when the access time has changed on a file that bash is checking for mail.

no_empty_cmd_completion
> bash does not search $PATH when command completion is attempted on an empty line.

nocaseglob
> bash ignores case when doing filename matching.

nullglob
> bash causes patterns that don't match any files to become the null string, instead of standing for themselves. This null string is then removed from further command-line processing; in effect, a pattern that doesn't match anything disappears from the command line.

progcomp
> This option enables the programmable completion features. See the *bash*(1) manpage for details. It is on by default.

promptvars
> bash performs variable and parameter expansion on the value of the various prompt strings. This is on by default.

restricted_shell
> bash sets this to true when functioning as a restricted shell. This option cannot be changed. Startup files can query this option to decide how to behave. See "Restricted Shell" [15.2], for more information on restricted shells.

shift_verbose
> bash prints a message if the count for a shift command is more than the number of positional parameters left.

sourcepath
> bash uses $PATH to find files for the source and . (dot) commands. This is on by default. If turned off, you must use a full or relative pathname to find the file.

xpg_echo
> bash's built-in echo processes backslash escape sequences.

14.3 Common Extensions

Both bash and ksh93 support a large number of extensions over the POSIX shell. This section deals with those extensions that overlap; i.e., where both shells provide the same features, and in the same way.

14.3.1 The select Loop

bash and ksh share the select loop, which allows you to generate simple menus easily. It has concise syntax, but it does quite a lot of work. The syntax is:

```
select name [in list]
do
      statements that can use $name ...
done
```

This is the same syntax as the regular for loop except for the keyword select. And like for, you can omit the in list and it will default to "$@"; i.e., the list of quoted command-line arguments.

Here is what select does:

1. Generate a menu of each item in list, formatted with numbers for each choice
2. Print the value of PS3 as a prompt and waits for the user to enter a number
3. Store the selected choice in the variable name and the selected number in the built-in variable REPLY
4. Execute the statements in the body
5. Repeat the process forever (but see later for how to exit)

An example should help make this process clearer. Suppose you need to know how to set the TERM variable correctly for a timesharing system using different kinds of video display terminals. You don't have terminals hardwired to your computer; instead, your users communicate through a terminal server. Although the telnet protocol can pass the TERM environment variable, the terminal server isn't smart enough to do so. This means, among other things, that the tty (serial device) number does *not* determine the type of terminal.

Therefore, you have no choice but to prompt the user for a terminal type at login time. To do this, you can put the following code in /etc/profile (assume you have a fixed set of known terminal types):

```
PS3='terminal? '
select term in gl35a t2000 s531 vt99
do
    if [ -n "$term" ]
    then
        TERM=$term
        echo TERM is $TERM
        export TERM
        break
    else
        echo 'invalid.'
    fi
done
```

When you run this code, you see this menu:

```
1) gl35a
2) t2000
3) s531
4) vt99
terminal?
```

The built-in shell variable PS3 contains the prompt string that select uses; its default value is the not particularly useful "#? ". For this reason, the first line of the preceding code sets it to a more relevant value.

The select statement constructs the menu from the list of choices. If the user enters a valid number (from 1 to 4), then the variable term is set to the corresponding value; otherwise, it is null. (If the user just presses Enter, the shell prints the menu again.)

The code in the loop body checks if term is non-null. If so, it assigns $term to the environment variable TERM, exports TERM, and prints a confirmation message; then the break statement exits the select loop. If term is null, the code prints an error message and repeats the prompt (but not the menu).

The break statement is the usual way of exiting a select loop. (A user can also type Ctrl-D—for end-of-input—to get out of a select loop. This gives the interactive user a uniform way of exiting, but it doesn't help the shell programmer much.)

We can refine our solution by making the menu more user friendly so that the user doesn't have to know the terminfo name of the terminal. We do this by using quoted character strings as menu items, and then using case to determine the terminfo name. The new version is shown in Example 14-2.

Example 14-2. Combining select with more user-friendly menu items

```
echo 'Select your terminal type:'
PS3='terminal? '
select term in \
```

```
    'Givalt GL35a' \
    'Tsoris T-2000' \
    'Shande 531' \
    'Vey VT99'
do
    case $REPLY in
    1) TERM=gl35a ;;
    2) TERM=t2000 ;;
    3) TERM=s531 ;;
    4) TERM=vt99 ;;
    *) echo 'invalid.' ;;
    esac
    if [[ -n $term ]]; then
        echo TERM is $TERM
        export TERM
        break
    fi
done
```

This code looks a bit more like a menu routine in a conventional program, though select still provides the shortcut of converting the menu choices into numbers. We list each of the menu choices on its own line for reasons of readability, but we need continuation characters to keep the shell from complaining about syntax.

Here is what the user sees when this code is run:

```
Select your terminal type:
1) Givalt GL35a
2) Tsoris T-2000
3) Shande 531
4) Vey VT99
terminal?
```

This is a bit more informative than the previous code's output.

When the body of the select loop is entered, $term equals one of the four strings (or is null if the user made an invalid choice), whereas the built-in variable REPLY contains the number that the user selected. We need a case statement to assign the correct value to TERM; we use the value of REPLY as the case selector.

Once the case statement is finished, the if checks to see if a valid choice was made, as in the previous solution. If the choice was valid, then TERM has already been assigned, so the code just prints a confirmation message, exports TERM, and exits the select loop. If it wasn't valid, the select loop repeats the prompt and goes through the process again.

Within a select loop, if REPLY is set to the null string, the shell reprints the menu. This happens, as mentioned, when the user hits Enter. However, you may also explicitly set REPLY to the null string to force the shell to reprint the menu.

The variable TMOUT (time out) can affect the select statement. Before the select loop, set it to some number of seconds *n*, and if nothing is entered within that amount of time, the select will exit.

14.3.2 Extended Test Facility

ksh introduced the extended test facility, delineated by [[and]]. These are shell keywords, special to the syntax of the shell, and not a command. Recent versions of bash have adopted this special facility as well.

[[...]] differs from the regular test and [...] commands in that word expansion and pattern expansion (wildcarding) are not done. This means that quoting is much less necessary. In effect, the contents of [[...]] form a separate sublanguage, which makes it easier to use. Most of the operators are the same as for test. The full list is given in Table 14-3.

Table 14-3. Extended test operators

Operator	bash/ksh only	True if ...
-a *file*		*file* exists. (Obsolete. -e is preferred.)
-b *file*		*file* is a block device file.
-c *file*		*file* is a character device file.
-C *file*	ksh	*file* is a contiguous file. (Not for most Unix versions.)
-d *file*		*file* is a directory.
-e *file*		*file* exists.
-f *file*		*file* is a regular file.
-g *file*		*file* has its setgid bit set.
-G *file*		*file*'s group ID is the same as the effective group ID of the shell.
-h *file*		*file* is a symbolic link.
-k *file*		*file* has its sticky bit set.
-l *file*	ksh	*file* is a symbolic link. (Works only on systems where /bin/test -l tests for symbolic links.)
-L *file*		*file* is a symbolic link.
-n *string*		*string* is non-null.
-N *file*	bash	*file* was modified since it was last read.
-o *option*		*option* is set.
-O *file*		*file* is owned by the shell's effective user ID.
-p *file*		*file* is a pipe or named pipe (FIFO file).
-r *file*		*file* is readable.
-s *file*		*file* is not empty.
-S *file*		*file* is a socket.
-t *n*		File descriptor *n* points to a terminal.

Table 14-3. Extended test operators (continued)

Operator	bash/ksh only	True if ...
-u *file*		*file* has its setuid bit set.
-w *file*		*file* is writable.
-x *file*		*file* is executable, or is a directory that can be searched.
-z *string*		*string* is null.
fileA -nt *fileB*		*fileA* is newer than *fileB*, or *fileB* does not exist.
fileA -ot *fileB*		*fileA* is older than *fileB*, or *fileB* does not exist.
fileA -ef *fileB*		*fileA* and *fileB* point to the same file.
string = *pattern*	ksh	*string* matches *pattern* (which can contain wildcards). Obsolete; == is preferred.
string == *pattern*		*string* matches *pattern* (which can contain wildcards).
string != *pattern*		*string* does not match *pattern*.
stringA < *stringB*		*stringA* comes before *stringB* in dictionary order.
stringA > *stringB*		*stringA* comes after *stringB* in dictionary order.
exprA -eq *exprB*		Arithmetic expressions *exprA* and *exprB* are equal.
exprA -ne *exprB*		Arithmetic expressions *exprA* and *exprB* are not equal.
exprA -lt *exprB*		*exprA* is less than *exprB*.
exprA -gt *exprB*		*exprA* is greater than *exprB*.
exprA -le *exprB*		*exprA* is less than or equal to *exprB*.
exprA -ge *exprB*		*exprA* is greater than or equal to *exprB*.

The operators can be logically combined with && (AND) and || (OR) and grouped with parentheses. They may also be negated with !. When used with filenames of the form /dev/fd/*n*, they test the corresponding attribute of open file descriptor *n*.

The operators –eq, –ne, –lt, –le, –gt, and –ge are considered obsolete in ksh93; the let command or ((...)) should be used instead. (The let command and ((...)) are described briefly in "Miscellaneous Extensions" [14.3.7].)

14.3.3 Extended Pattern Matching

ksh88 introduced additional pattern-matching facilities that give the shell power roughly equivalent to awk and egrep extended regular expressions. (Regular expressions are described in detail in "Regular Expressions" [3.2].) With the extglob option enabled, bash also supports these operators. (They're always enabled in ksh.) Table 14-4 summarizes the additional facilities.

Table 14-4. Shell versus egrep/awk regular expression operators

ksh/bash	egrep/awk	Meaning
*(*exp*)	*exp**	0 or more occurrences of *exp*
+(*exp*)	*exp*+	1 or more occurrences of *exp*
?(*exp*)	*exp*?	0 or 1 occurrences of *exp*
@(*exp1*|*exp2*|...)	*exp1*|*exp2*|...	*exp1* or *exp2* or ...
!(*exp*)	(none)	Anything that doesn't match *exp*

The notations for shell regular expressions and standard regular expressions are very similar, but they're not identical. Because the shell would interpret an expression like dave|fred|bob as a pipeline of commands, you must use @(dave|fred|bob) for alternates by themselves.

For example:

- **@(dave|fred|bob)** matches dave, fred, or bob.
- ***(dave|fred|bob)** means 0 or more occurrences of dave, fred, or bob. This expression matches strings like the null string dave, davedave, fred, bobfred, bobbobdavefredbobfred, etc.
- **+(dave|fred|bob)** matches any of the above except the null string.
- **?(dave|fred|bob)** matches the null string dave, fred, or bob.
- **!(dave|fred|bob)** matches anything except dave, fred, or bob.

It is worth emphasizing again that shell regular expressions can still contain standard shell wildcards. Thus, the shell wildcard ? (match any single character) is the equivalent of . (dot) in egrep or awk, and the shell's character set operator [...] is the same as in those utilities.[*] For example, the expression **+([[:digit:]])** matches a number: i.e., one or more digits. The shell wildcard character * is equivalent to the shell regular expression ***(?)**. You can even nest the regular expressions: **+([[:digit:]])|!([[:upper:]]))** matches one or more digits or nonuppercase letters.

Two egrep and awk regexp operators do not have equivalents in the shell. They are:

- The beginning- and end-of-line operators ^ and $
- The beginning- and end-of-word operators \< and \>

Essentially, the ^ and $ are implied as always being there. Surround a pattern with * characters to disable this. This example illustrates the difference:

```
$ ls                                    List files
biff  bob  frederick  shishkabob
$ shopt -s extglob                      Enable extended pattern matching (Bash)
```

---

[*] And, for that matter, the same as in grep, sed, ed, vi, etc. One notable difference is that the shell uses ! inside [...] for negation, whereas the various utilities all use ^.

```
$ echo @(dave|fred|bob)                   Files that match only dave, fred, or bob
bob
$ echo *@(dave|fred|bob)*                  Add wildcard characters
bob frederick shishkabob                   More files matched
```

ksh93 supports even more pattern-matching operators. However, since the point of
this section is to cover what's common between both bash and ksh93, we stop here.
For the details, see *Learning the Korn Shell* (O'Reilly), cited in the Bibliography.

14.3.4 Brace Expansion

Brace expansion is a feature borrowed from the Berkeley C shell, csh. It is supported
by both shells. Brace expansion is a way of saving typing when you have strings that
are prefixes or suffixes of each other. For example, suppose that you have the following files:

```
$ ls
cpp-args.c  cpp-lex.c  cpp-out.c  cpp-parse.c
```

You could type vi cpp-{args,lex,parse}.c if you wished to edit three out of the four
C files, and the shell would expand this into vi cpp-args.c cpp-lex.c cpp-parse.c.
Furthermore, brace substitutions may be nested. For example:

```
$ echo cpp-{args,l{e,o}x,parse}.c
cpp-args.c cpp-lex.c cpp-lox.c cpp-parse.c
```

14.3.5 Process Substitution

Process substitution allows you to open multiple process streams and feed them into
a single program for processing. For example:

```
awk '...' <(generate_data) <(generate_more_data)
```

(Note that the parentheses are part of the syntax, you type them literally.) Here,
generate_data and *generate_more_data* represent arbitrary commands, including
pipelines, that produce streams of data. The awk program processes each stream in
turn, not realizing that the data is coming from multiple sources. This is shown
graphically in Figure 14-1.

Process substitution may also be used for output, particularly when combined with
the tee program, which sends its input to multiple output files and to standard output. For example:

```
generate_data | tee >(sort | uniq > sorted_data) \
                    >(mail -s 'raw data' joe) > raw_data
```

This command uses tee to (1) send the data to a pipeline that sorts and saves the
data, (2) send the data to the mail program for user joe, and (3) redirect the original
data into a file. This is represented graphically in Figure 14-1.b. Process substitution,
combined with tee, frees you from the straight "one input, one output" paradigm of

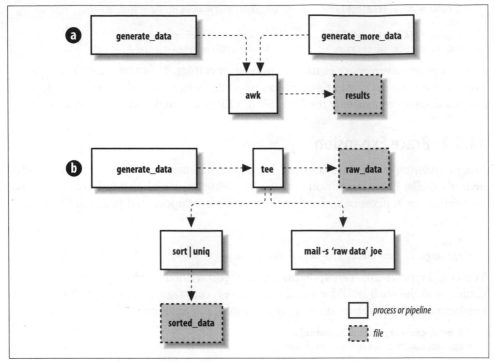

Figure 14-1. Process substitution for both input and output data streams

traditional Unix pipes, letting you split data into multiple output streams, and coalesce multiple input data streams into one.

Process substitution is available only on Unix systems that support the /dev/fd/*n* special files for named access to already open file descriptors. Most modern Unix systems, including GNU/Linux, support this feature. As with brace expansion, it is enabled by default when ksh93 is compiled from source code. bash always enables it.

14.3.6 Indexed Arrays

Both ksh93 and bash provide an indexed array facility that, while useful, is much more limited than analogous features in conventional programming languages. In particular, indexed arrays can be only one-dimensional (i.e., no arrays of arrays). Indexes start at 0. Furthermore, they may be any arithmetic expression: the shells automatically evaluate the expression to yield the index.

There are three ways to assign values to elements of an array. The first is the most intuitive: you can use the standard shell variable assignment syntax with the array index in brackets ([ ]). For example:

```
nicknames[2]=bob
nicknames[3]=ed
```

puts the values bob and ed into the elements of the array nicknames with indices 2 and 3, respectively. As with regular shell variables, values assigned to array elements are treated as character strings.

The second way to assign values to an array is with a variant of the set statement. The statement:

```
set -A aname val1 val2 val3 ...
```

creates the array *aname* (if it doesn't already exist) and assigns *val1* to aname[0], *val2* to aname[1], etc. As you would guess, this is more convenient for loading up an array with an initial set of values. This was the first mechanism added to ksh for assigning multiple array elements in one operation, and we mention it primarily so that you'll recognize it if you see it in an existing script.

 bash doesn't support set -A.

The third (recommended) way is to use the compound assignment form:

```
aname=(val1 val2 val3)
```

To extract a value from an array, use the syntax ${aname[i]}. For example, ${nicknames[2]} has the value bob. The index *i* can be an arithmetic expression. If you use * or @ in place of the index, the value will be all elements, separated by spaces. Omitting the index ($nicknames) is the same as specifying index 0 (${nicknames[0]}).

Now we come to the somewhat unusual aspect of arrays. Assume that the only values assigned to nicknames are the two that we saw earlier. If you type echo "${nicknames[*]}", you will see the output:

```
bob ed
```

In other words, nicknames[0] and nicknames[1] don't exist. Furthermore, if you were to type:

```
nicknames[9]=pete
nicknames[31]=ralph
```

and then type echo "${nicknames[*]}", the output would look like this:

```
bob ed pete ralph
```

This is why we said the elements of nicknames with indices 2 and 3 earlier, instead of the second and third elements of nicknames. Any array elements with unassigned values just don't exist; if you try to access their values, you get null strings.

You can preserve whatever whitespace you put in your array elements by using "${*aname*[@]}" (with the double quotes) rather than ${*aname*[*]}, just as you can with "$@" rather than $* or "$*".

Both shells provide an operator that tells you how many elements an array has defined: ${#*aname*[*]}. Thus, ${#nicknames[*]} has the value 4. Note that you need the [*] because the name of the array alone is interpreted as the 0th element. This means, for example, that ${#nicknames} equals the length of nicknames[0]. Since nicknames[0] doesn't exist, the value of ${#nicknames} is 0, the length of the null string.

You can think of an array as a mathematical function that takes an integer input parameter and returns a corresponding value (the element at that number). If you do so, then you can see why arrays are "number-dominated" data structures. Because shell programming tasks are much more often oriented toward character strings and text than toward numbers, the indexed array facility isn't as broadly useful as it might first appear.

Nevertheless, we can find useful things to do with indexed arrays. For example, here is a cleaner solution to the problem we presented earlier, in "The select Loop" [14.3.1]," in which a user can select a terminal type (TERM environment variable) at login time. Example 14-2 presented the user-friendly version of this code that used select and a case statement.

We can eliminate the entire case construct by taking advantage of the fact that the select construct stores the user's number choice in the variable REPLY. We just need a line of code that stores all of the possibilities for TERM in an array, in an order that corresponds to the items in the select menu. Then we can use $REPLY to index the array. The resulting code is:

```
termnames=(gl35a t2000 s531 vt99)
echo 'Select your terminal type:'
PS3='terminal? '
select term in \
    'Givalt GL35a' \
    'Tsoris T-2000' \
    'Shande 531' \
    'Vey VT99'
do
    if [[ -n $term ]]; then
        TERM=${termnames[REPLY-1]}
        echo "TERM is $TERM"
        export TERM
        break
    fi
done
```

This code sets up the array termnames so that ${termnames[0]} is gl35a, ${termnames[1]} is t2000, etc. The line TERM=${termnames[REPLY-1]} essentially replaces the entire case construct by using REPLY to index the array.

Notice that both shells know to interpret the text in an array index as an arithmetic expression, as if it were enclosed in $((and)), which in turn means that the variable need not be preceded by a dollar sign ($). We have to subtract 1 from the value of REPLY because array indices start at 0, whereas select menu item numbers start at 1.

14.3.7 Miscellaneous Extensions

Here is another laundry list, this time of small extensions to the POSIX shell supported by both bash and ksh93:

Additional tilde expansions
> POSIX specifies plain ~ as being equivalent to $HOME and *~user* as being *user*'s home directory. Both shells allow you to use ~+ as short for $PWD (the current working directory) and ~- as short for $OLDPWD (the previous working directory).

Arithmetic commands
> POSIX specifies the $((...)) notation for arithmetic expansion, and doesn't provide any other mechanism for arithmetic operations. However, both shells provide two notations for doing arithmetic directly, not as an expansion:

```
let "x = 5 + y"           The let command, requires quoting
((x = 5 + y))             No leading $, automatic quoting inside double parentheses
```

It's not clear why POSIX standardizes only arithmetic expansion. Perhaps it's because you can achieve essentially the same affect by using the : (do-nothing) command and arithmetic expansion:

```
: $((x = 5 + y))          Almost the same as let or ((...))
x=$((5 + y))              Similar, no spaces allowed around the =
```

One difference is that let and ((...)) have an exit status: zero for a true value and one for a false value. This lets you use them in if and while statements:

```
while ((x != 42))
do
    ... whatever ...
done
```

Arithmetic for *loop*
> Both shells support the *arithmetic* for loop, which is similar to the for loop in awk, C, and C++. It looks like this:

```
for ((init; condition; increment))
do
    loop body
done
```

Each one of *init*, *condition*, and *increment* can be shell arithmetic expressions, exactly the same as would appear inside $((...)). The use of ((...)) in the for loop is purposely similar to the arithmetic evaluation syntax.

Use the arithmetic `for` loop when you need to do something a fixed number of times:

```
for ((i = 1; i <= limit; i += 1))
do
      whatever needs doing
done
```

Additional arithmetic operators

POSIX specifies the list of operators that are allowed inside arithmetic expansion with $((...)). Both shells support additional operators, to provide full compatibility with C. In particular, both allow ++ and -- to increment and decrement by one. Both the prefix and postfix forms are allowed. (According to POSIX, ++ and -- are optional.) Both shells accept the comma operator, which lets you perform multiple operations in one expression. Also, as an extension over and above C, both shells accept ** for exponentiation. The full list of operators is provided in Table 14-5.

Optional matching parentheses for `case` statements

The $(...) syntax for command substitution (see "Command Substitution" [7.6]) is standardized by POSIX. It was introduced in ksh88 and is also supported in bash. ksh88 had a problem with case statements inside $(...). In particular, the closing right parenthesis used for each case pattern could terminate the entire command substitution. To get around this, ksh88 required that case patterns be enclosed in matching parentheses when inside a command substitution:

```
some command $( ...
      case $var in
      ( foo | bar )     some other command ;;
      ( stuff | junk ) something else again ;;
      esac
      ... )
```

ksh93, bash, and POSIX allow an optional open parenthesis on case selectors, but do not require it. (Thus, ksh93 is smarter than ksh88, which required the open parenthesis inside $(...).)

Printing traps with `trap -p`

According to POSIX, an unadorned `trap` command prints out the state of the shell's traps, in a form that can be reread by the shell later to restore the same traps. Both shells also allow you to use `trap -p` to print out the traps.

Here strings with `<<<`

It's common to use `echo` to generate a single line of input for further processing. For example:

```
echo $myvar1 $mvar2 | tr ... | ...
```

Both shells support a notation we term *here strings*, taken from the Unix version of the rc shell.[*] Here strings use <<< followed by a string. The string becomes the

---

[*] See *http://www.star.le.ac.uk/~tjg/rc/*.

standard input to the associated command, with the shell automatically supplying a final newline:

```
tr ... <<< "$myvar1 $myvar2" | ...
```

This potentially saves the creation of an extra process and is also notationally clear.

Extended string notation

Both bash and ksh93 support a special string notation that understands the usual set of C-like (or echo-like) escape sequences. The notation consists of a $ in front of a single-quoted string. Such strings behave like regular single-quoted strings, but the shell interprets escape sequences inside the string. For example:

```
$ echo $'A\tB'                          A, tab, B
A       B
$ echo $'A\nB'                          A, newline, B
A
B
```

Table 14-5 lists the arithmetic operators supported by both bash and ksh93.

Table 14-5. bash and ksh93 arithmetic operators

Operator	Meaning	Associativity
++ --	Increment and decrement, prefix and postfix	Left to right
+ - ! ~	Unary plus and minus; logical and bitwise negation	Right to left
**	Exponentiation[a]	Right to left
* / %	Multiplication, division, and remainder	Left to right
+ -	Addition and subtraction	Left to right
<< >>	Bit-shift left and right	Left to right
< <= > >=	Comparisons	Left to right
== !=	Equal and not equal	Left to right
&	Bitwise AND	Left to right
^	Bitwise Exclusive OR	Left to right
|	Bitwise OR	Left to right
&&	Logical AND (short-circuit)	Left to right
||	Logical OR (short-circuit)	Left to right
?:	Conditional expression	Right to left
= += -= *= /= %= &= ^= <<= >>= |=	Assignment operators	Right to left
,	Sequential evaluation	Left to right

[a] ksh93m and newer. In bash versions prior to 3.1, ** is left-associative. It will be right-associative starting with version 3.1 The ** operator is not in the C language.

Parentheses can be used to group subexpressions. The arithmetic expression syntax (like C) supports relational operators as "truth values" of 1 for true and 0 for false.

For example, $((3 > 2))$ has the value 1; $(((3 > 2) || (4 <= 1)))$ also has the value 1, since at least one of the two subexpressions is true.

14.4 Download Information

This section *briefly* describes where to find source code for bash and ksh93, and how to build each shell from source code. It assumes that you have a C compiler and the make program available on your system.

14.4.1 bash

bash is available from the Free Software Foundation GNU Project's FTP server. As of this writing, the current version is 3.0. You can use wget (if you have it) to retrieve the distribution tar file:

```
$ wget ftp://ftp.gnu.org/gnu/bash/bash-3.0.tar.gz
--17:49:21--  ftp://ftp.gnu.org/gnu/bash/bash-3.0.tar.gz
           => `bash-3.0.tar.gz'
...
```

Alternatively, you can use good old-fashioned anonymous FTP to retrieve the file:

```
$ ftp ftp.gnu.org                                    FTP to server
Connected to ftp.gnu.org (199.232.41.7).
220 GNU FTP server ready.
Name (ftp.gnu.org:tolstoy): anonymous               Anonymous login
230 Login successful.
230-Due to U.S. Export Regulations, all cryptographic software on this
230-site is subject to the following legal notice:
...
Remote system type is UNIX.
Using binary mode to transfer files.
ftp> cd /gnu/bash                                    Change to bash directory
250 Directory successfully changed.
ftp> binary                                          Ensure binary mode
200 Switching to Binary mode.
ftp> hash                                            Print # marks for feedback
Hash mark printing on (1024 bytes/hash mark).
ftp> get bash-3.0.tar.gz                             Retrieve file
local: bash-3.0.tar.gz remote: bash-3.0.tar.gz
227 Entering Passive Mode (199,232,41,7,149,247)
150 Opening BINARY mode data connection for bash-3.0.tar.gz (2418293 bytes).
#######################################################################
#######################################################################
...
226 File send OK.
2418293 bytes received in 35.9 secs (66 Kbytes/sec)
ftp> quit                                            All done
221 Goodbye.
```

Besides the bash distribution itself, you should also retrieve any patches. For Version 3.0 of bash, the patches— fixes to the source code that should be applied—must be retrieved from a different site. They're found in *ftp://ftp.cwru.edu/pub/bash/bash-3.0-patches/*. You can retrieve all of them into a temporary directory as follows:

```
$ mkdir /tmp/p          Make temporary directory
$ cd /tmp/p             Move there
$ for i in 01 02 03 04 05 06 07 08 09 10 11 12 13 14 15 16
> do wget ftp://ftp.cwru.edu/pub/bash/bash-3.0-patches/bash30-0$i
> done                  Retrieve all patches
... lots of output omitted ...
```

As of this writing, there are 16 patches. There may be more or fewer, depending upon the version of bash and what's been made available.

Now you're ready to extract the distribution and apply the patches. First, extract the source code:

```
$ gzip -d < bash-3.0.tar.gz | tar -xpvzf -          Decompress and extract
bash-3.0/
bash-3.0/CWRU/
bash-3.0/CWRU/misc/
bash-3.0/CWRU/misc/open-files.c
bash-3.0/CWRU/misc/sigs.c
... lots of output omitted ...
```

Now apply the patches:

```
$ cd bash-3.0                        Change to source directory
$ for i in /tmp/p/*                  Apply all patches
> do patch -p0 --verbose --backup < $i
> done
... lots of output omitted ...
$ find . -name '*.rej'               Check for failures
$ find . -name '*.orig' -print | xargs rm     Clean up
```

The invocation of patch just shown assumes the GNU version of patch. Beware of the older versions that are supplied on some commercial Unix systems. After applying the patches, we check for failed patches by looking for .rej (reject) files. Here, there were none, so we're OK. We then remove the .orig (original) files. Building bash follows the standard GNU recipe:

```
$ ./configure && make && make check          Configure, build, and test
checking build system type... i686-pc-linux-gnu
checking host system type... i686-pc-linux-gnu
... lots of output omitted ...
```

If all the tests pass (they should), that's it, you're all set! Use make install to install the freshly built bash executable. (You may need to do the installation step as root.)

14.4.2 ksh93

ksh93 can be downloaded in source code form from the AT&T Research web site. The URL is *http://www.research.att.com/sw/download*. Building ksh93 is relatively straightforward, but the process is somewhat more manual than for bash. We show the steps for ksh93p, from February 2004. The steps will be similar for whatever version is current. We've chosen here to just build the Korn shell, although you may wish to download and build the entire "AST Open" package, because that provides a full set of tools.

1. From the web site, download the packages INIT.2004-02-29.tgz and ast-ksh. 2004-02-29.tgz. Place them in an otherwise empty directory that you will use for building the software.

2. Make the directory lib/package/tgz and move the two files there:

   ```
   $ mkdir -p lib/package/tgz
   $ mv *.tgz lib/package/tgz
   ```

3. Extract the INIT package manually:

   ```
   $ gzip -d < lib/package/tgz/INIT.2004-02-29.tgz | tar -xvf -
   ```
   ... lots of output omitted ...

4. Start the build process using the AT&T tools by reading which packages are available:

   ```
   $ bin/package read
   package: update /home/tolstoy/ksh93/bin/execrate
   ```
   ... lots and lots of output omitted ...

5. Start the compilation, again using the AT&T tools:

   ```
   $ bin/package make
   package: initialize the /home/tolstoy/ksh93/arch/linux.i386 view
   ```
   ... lots and lots and lots of output omitted ...

   This step can take quite a while, depending upon the speed of your system and your compiler.

6. The newly built ksh93 binary is in the file arch/*ARCH*/bin/ksh, where *ARCH* represents the architecture of the machine on which you're building ksh93. For an x86 GNU/Linux system, it's linux.i386. For example:

   ```
   $ arch/linux.i386/bin/ksh          Run newly built ksh93
   $ echo ${.sh.version}              Show version
   Version M 1993-12-28 p
   ```

7. You may wish to move the newly built Korn shell to a directory in your path, such as your personal bin:

   ```
   $ cp arch/linux.i386/bin/ksh $HOME/bin/ksh93
   ```

That's it! Enjoy.

14.5 Other Extended Bourne-Style Shells

Two other shells are popular and worthy of note:

The Public Domain Korn Shell
> Many of the Open Source Unix-like systems, such as GNU/Linux, come with the Public Domain Korn Shell, pdksh. pdksh is available as source code; start at its home page: *http://web.cs.mun.ca/~michael/pdksh/*. It comes with instructions for building and installing on various Unix platforms.
>
> pdksh was originally written by Eric Gisin, who based it on Charles Forsyth's public-domain clone of the Version 7 Bourne shell. It is mostly compatible with the 1988 Korn shell and POSIX, with some extensions of its own.

The Z-Shell
> zsh is a powerful interactive shell and scripting language with many features found in ksh, bash, and tcsh, as well as several unique features. zsh has most of the features of ksh88 but few of ksh93. It is freely available and should compile and run on just about any modern version of Unix. Ports for other operating systems are also available. The zsh home page is *http://www.zsh.org/*.

Both of these shells are described in more detail in *Learning the Korn Shell* (O'Reilly), cited in the Bibliography.

14.6 Shell Versions

Our exploration of extended shells brings up the good point that it's useful occasionally to be able to find the version number of various shells. Here's how:

```
$ bash --version                              bash
GNU bash, version 3.00.16(1)-release (i686-pc-linux-gnu)
...

$ ksh --version                               Recent ksh93 only
  version         sh (AT&T Labs Research) 1993-12-28 p

$ ksh                                         Older ksh
$ ^V                                          Type ^V
$ Version 11/16/88f                           ksh shows version

$ echo 'echo $KSH_VERSION' | pdksh            pdksh
@(#)PD KSH v5.2.14 99/07/13.2

$ echo 'echo $ZSH_VERSION' | zsh              zsh
4.1.1
```

There appears to be no way to get a version number from /bin/sh. This is not surprising. Most true Bourne shells on commercial Unix systems are descended from the System V Release 3 (1987) or Release 4 (1989) Bourne shell, and have changed little or not at all since then. Commercial vendors wishing to supply a POSIX-compliant shell generally do so by adapting some version of the Korn shell for that purpose.

14.7 Shell Initialization and Termination

In order to support user customization, shells read certain specified files on startup, and for some shells, also on termination. Each shell has different conventions, so we discuss them in separate sections.

If you write shell scripts that are intended to be used by others, you *cannot* rely on startup customizations. All of the shell scripts that we develop in this book set up their own environment (e.g., the value of $PATH) so that anyone can run them.

Shell behavior depends on whether it is a *login shell*. When you sit at a terminal and enter a username and password in response to a prompt from the computer, you get a login shell. Similarly, when you use ssh *hostname*, you get a login shell. However, if you run a shell by name, or implicitly as the command interpreter named in the initial #! line in a script, or create a new workstation terminal window, or run a command in a remote shell with—for example, ssh *hostname command*—then that shell is not a login shell.

The shell determines whether it is a login shell by examining the value of $0. If the value begins with a hyphen, then the shell is a login shell; otherwise, it is not. You can tell whether you have a login shell by this simple experiment:

```
$ echo $0                        Display shell name
-ksh                             Yes, this is a login shell
```

The hyphen does *not* imply that there is a file named /bin/-ksh. It just means that the parent process set the zeroth argument that way when it ran the exec( ) system call to start the shell.

If you routinely deal with only a single shell, then the initialization and termination files described in the following sections are not much of a problem: once you get them suitably customized, you can probably leave them untouched for years. However, if you use multiple shells, you need to consider more carefully how to set up your customizations to avoid duplication and maintenance headaches. The . (dot) and test commands are your friends: use them in your customization scripts to read a small set of files that you have carefully written to be acceptable to all Bourne-family shells, and on all hosts to which you have access. System managers also need to make the system-wide customization scripts in /etc work for all users.

14.7.1 Bourne Shell (sh) Startup

When it is a login shell, the Bourne shell, sh, does the equivalent of:

```
test -r /etc/profile && . /etc/profile        Try to read /etc/profile
test -r $HOME/.profile && . $HOME/.profile    Try to read $HOME/.profile
```

That is, it potentially reads two startup files in the context of the current shell, but does not require that either exist. Notice that the home-directory file is a dot file, but the system-wide one in /etc is not.

The system shell-startup file created by local management might look something like this:

```
$ cat /etc/profile                Show system shell startup file
PATH=/usr/local/bin:$PATH         Add /usr/local/bin to start of system path
export PATH                       Make it known to child processes
umask 022                         Remove write permission for group and other
```

A typical $HOME/.profile file could then modify the local system's default login environment with commands like this:

```
$ cat $HOME/.profile              Show personal shell startup file
PATH=$PATH:$HOME/bin              Add personal bin directory to end of system path
export PATH                       Make it known to child processes
alias rm='rm -i'                  Ask for confirmation of file deletions
umask 077                         Remove all access for group and other
```

When a child shell is subsequently created, it inherits the parent's environment strings, including PATH. It also inherits the current working directory and the current file-permission mask, both of which are recorded in the process-specific data inside the kernel. However, it does *not* inherit other customizations, such as command abbreviations made with the alias command, or variables that were not exported.

The Bourne shell provides no way to automatically read a startup file when the shell is not a login shell, so aliases are of limited use. Since remote command execution also does not create a login shell, you cannot even expect PATH to be set to your accustomed value: it may be as simple as /bin:/usr/bin. We have to deal with this in the build-all script in "Automating Software Builds" [8.2].

On exit, the Bourne shell does not read a standard termination file, but you can set a trap to make it do so (we cover traps in detail in "Trapping Process Signals" [13.3.2]). For example, if you put this statement in $HOME/.profile:

```
trap '. $HOME/.logout' EXIT
```

then the $HOME/.logout script can do any cleanup actions that you need, such as wiping the screen with the clear command. However, since there can be only one trap for any given signal, the trap will be lost if it is overridden later in the session: there is thus no way to guarantee that a termination script will be executed. For nonlogin shells, each script or session that needs exit handling has to set an explicit EXIT trap, and that too cannot be guaranteed to be in effect on exit.

These limitations, the lack of support for command history,[*] and in some older implementations, job control, make the Bourne shell undesirable as a login shell for most interactive users. On most commercial Unix systems, it therefore tends to be chosen just for root and other system-administration accounts that are used interactively only for brief sessions. Nevertheless, the Bourne shell is the shell expected by portable shell scripts.

14.7.2 Korn Shell Startup

Like the Bourne shell, the Korn shell, ksh, reads /etc/profile and $HOME/.profile, if they exist and are readable, when it starts as a login shell.

When ksh93 starts as an interactive shell (either login or nonlogin), it then does the equivalent of:

```
test -n "$ENV" && eval . "$ENV"                    Try to read $ENV
```

ksh88 does the $ENV processing *unconditionally*, for all shells.

The eval command is described in "Evaluation Order and eval" [7.8]. For now, it is enough to know that it first evaluates its arguments so that any variables there are expanded, and then executes the resulting string as a command. The effect is that the file named by ENV is read and executed in the context of the current shell. The PATH directories are not searched for the file, so ENV should generally specify an absolute pathname.

The ENV feature solves the problem that the Bourne shell has in setting up private aliases for child shell sessions. However, it does not solve the customization problem for nonlogin remote sessions: their shells never read any initialization files.

Like the Bourne shell, a noninteractive ksh93 shell does not read any startup scripts, nor does it read any termination scripts just before it exits, unless you issue a suitable trap command. (As we said before, even a noninteractive ksh88 reads and executes the $ENV file at startup.)

14.7.3 Bourne-Again Shell Startup and Termination

While GNU bash is often used as a login shell in its own right, it can also masquerade as the Bourne shell when it is invoked with the name sh. It then behaves on startup largely as described in "Bourne Shell (sh) Startup" [14.7.1], in which case most of the rest of this section does not apply. On GNU/Linux systems, /bin/sh is invariably a symbolic link to /bin/bash.

---

[*] On many systems, /bin/sh is just a link to bash, in which case command history is available. However, the original Unix Bourne shell lacks command history.

The bash emulation of the Bourne shell is not perfect because bash hides only *some* of its many extensions when invoked as sh. We have occasionally found shell scripts in software packages that were developed in a GNU/Linux environment for execution by /bin/sh, but were not tested in real Bourne shell environments, where they fail because of their use of extended features.

When bash is a login shell, on startup it does the equivalent of:

```
test -r /etc/profile && . /etc/profile          Try to read /etc/profile
if test -r $HOME/.bash_profile ; then           Try three more possibilities
    . $HOME/.bash_profile
elif test -r $HOME/.bash_login ; then
    . $HOME/.bash_login
elif test -r $HOME/.profile ; then
    . $HOME/.profile
fi
```

The system-wide file is the same as for the Bourne shell, but the search order in $HOME allows you to put bash-specific initializations in either of two files. Otherwise, bash falls back to reading your personal Bourne-shell startup file.

On exit, a bash login shell effectively does this:

```
test -r $HOME/.bash_logout && . $HOME/.bash_logout   Try to read a termination script
```

Unlike the Bourne shell, bash reads an initialization file on startup when it is an interactive nonlogin shell, by steps equivalent to this:

```
test -r $HOME/.bashrc && . $HOME/.bashrc        Try to read $HOME/.bashrc
```

In this case, login-shell startup files are not read.

When bash is used noninteractively, instead of reading a .bashrc file or login-shell startup files, it reads a file defined by the BASH_ENV variable, like this:

```
test -r "$BASH_ENV" && eval . "$BASH_ENV"       Try to read $BASH_ENV
```

As with ksh, the PATH directories are not searched for this file.

Notice the difference: the Korn shell's ENV variable is used only for nonlogin *interactive* shells, whereas bash's BASH_ENV is used only for *noninteractive* shells.

To clarify the startup-file processing order, we fitted each of them with an echo command. A login session then looks like this:

```
$ login                                         Start a new login session
login: bones
Password:                                       Echo suppressed to hide password
DEBUG: This is /etc/profile
DEBUG: This is /home/bones/.bash_profile
$ exit                                          Terminate the session
logout
DEBUG: This is /home/bones/.bash_logout
```

An interactive session invokes only a single file:

```
$ bash                                          Start an interactive session
DEBUG: This is /home/bones/.bashrc
$ exit                                          Terminate the session
exit
```

A noninteractive session normally does not invoke any file:

```
$ echo pwd | bash                               Run a command under bash
/home/bones
```

However, it will if the BASH_ENV value points to a startup file:

```
$ echo pwd | BASH_ENV=$HOME/.bashenv bash       Run a command under bash
DEBUG: This is /home/bones/.bashenv
/home/bones
```

14.7.4 Z-Shell Startup and Termination

The Z-shell, zsh, can masquerade as either the Bourne shell or the Korn shell. When invoked under the names sh or ksh, or any name that begins with the letters s or k, optionally preceded by a single r (for restricted), it has the same startup behavior as those shells, and the rest of this section does not apply. (When mimicking ksh, it follows the ksh88 behavior of always processing the $ENV file.)

The Z-shell has the most complex, and most flexible, customization procedure. Every Z-shell startup, whether for a login shell, an interactive shell, or a noninteractive shell, begins by trying to read two initialization files, like this:

```
test -r /etc/zshenv && . /etc/zshenv                    Read system-wide script
if test -n "$ZDOTDIR" && test -r $ZDOTDIR/.zshenv ; then
    . $ZDOTDIR/.zshenv                                  Read this file
elif test -r $HOME/.zshenv ; then
    . $HOME/.zshenv                                     Or else this file
fi
```

The ZDOTDIR variable provides a way for system management to prevent zsh from automatically reading startup files in user home directories, and instead, to force reading them from somewhere else that is under management control. If that variable is needed, then it would be set in /etc/zshenv, so you can look there to see what your system does.

Assuming that ZDOTDIR is not set, the best place to put personal customizations that you want to be in effect for every Z-shell session is in the file $HOME/.zshenv.

If the shell is a login shell, it next does the equivalent of these commands to read two startup profiles:

```
test -r /etc/zprofile && . /etc/zprofile                    Read system-wide script
if test -n "$ZDOTDIR" && test -r $ZDOTDIR/.zprofile ; then
    . $ZDOTDIR/.zprofile                                    Read this file
elif test -r $HOME/.zprofile ; then
    . $HOME/.zprofile                                       Or else this file
fi
```

If the shell is a login shell or an interactive shell, it then tries to read two startup scripts like this:

```
test -r /etc/zshrc && . /etc/zshrc                          Read system-wide script
if test -n "$ZDOTDIR" && test -r $ZDOTDIR/.zshrc ; then
    . $ZDOTDIR/.zshrc                                       Read this file
elif test -r $HOME/.zshrc ; then
    . $HOME/.zshrc                                          Or else this file
fi
```

Finally, if the shell is a login shell, it tries to read two login scripts like this:

```
test -r /etc/zlogin && . /etc/zlogin                        Read system-wide script
if test -n "$ZDOTDIR" && test -r $ZDOTDIR/.zlogin ; then
    . $ZDOTDIR/.zlogin                                      Read this file
elif test -r $HOME/.zlogin ; then
    . $HOME/.zlogin                                         Or else this file
fi
```

When zsh exits, if it is a login shell, and it is not terminating due to exec'ing another process, it finishes by reading two termination scripts: a user one and a system one, in that order:

```
if test -n "$ZDOTDIR" && test -r $ZDOTDIR/.zlogout ; then   Read this file
    . $ZDOTDIR/.zlogout
elif test -r $HOME/.zlogout ; then                          Or else this file
    . $HOME/.zlogout
fi
test -r /etc/zlogout && . /etc/zlogout                      Read system-wide script
```

The Z-shell initialization and termination procedures are complex. To make it easier to see what is happening, we instrumented each of the files with an echo command, and we left ZDOTDIR unset so that files are looked for only in /etc and $HOME. A login session then looks likes this:

```
$ login                                 Start a new login session
login: zabriski
Password:                               Echo suppressed to hide password
DEBUG: This is /etc/zshenv
DEBUG: This is /home/zabriski/.zshenv
DEBUG: This is /etc/zprofile
DEBUG: This is /home/zabriski/.zprofile
DEBUG: This is /etc/zshrc
DEBUG: This is /home/zabriski/.zshrc
DEBUG: This is /etc/zlogin
DEBUG: This is /home/zabriski/.zlogin
$ exit                                  Terminate the session
DEBUG: This is /home/zabriski/.zlogout
DEBUG: This is /etc/zlogout
```

An interactive session invokes fewer files:

```
$ zsh                                   Start a new interactive session
DEBUG: This is /etc/zshenv
DEBUG: This is /home/zabriski/.zshenv
```

```
DEBUG: This is /etc/zshrc
DEBUG: This is /home/zabriski/.zshrc
$ exit                              Terminate the session
                                    Silence: no termination files are read
```

A noninteractive session uses only two files:

```
$ echo pwd | zsh                    Run a command under zsh
DEBUG: This is /etc/zshenv
DEBUG: This is /home/zabriski/.zshenv
/home/zabriski
```

14.8 Summary

The POSIX standard makes a yeoman effort to make portable shell scripting possible. And if you stay within the bounds of what it defines, you have a fighting chance at writing portable scripts. However, the real world remains a messy place. While bash and ksh93 provide a number of extensions above and beyond POSIX, things aren't always 100 percent compatible between the two shells. There are a large number of small "Gotchas" to watch out for, even in simple areas like set options or saving the shell's complete state.

The shopt command lets you control bash's behavior. We particularly recommend enabling the extglob option for interactive use.

bash and ksh93 share a number of common extensions that are very useful for shell programming: the select loop, the [[...]] extended test facility, extended pattern matching, brace expansion, process substitution, and indexed arrays. We also described a number of small but useful miscellaneous extensions. The arithmetic for loop and the ((...)) arithmetic command are perhaps the most notable of these.

Source code for bash and ksh93 is available for download from the Internet, and we showed how to build both shells. We also mentioned two other popular extended Bourne-style shells, pdksh and zsh.

We showed how to determine the version of the shell you're running for the popular extended Bourne-style shells. This is important for when you need to know exactly what program you're using.

Finally, different implementations of the Bourne shell language have different startup and termination customization features and files. Shell scripts intended for general use should not rely on features or variables being set by each individual user, but should instead do all required initialization on their own.

## CHAPTER 15

Secure Shell Scripts: Getting Started

Unix security is a problem of legendary notoriety. Just about every aspect of a Unix system has some security issue associated with it, and it's usually the system administrator's job to worry about this issue.

In this chapter, we first present a list of "tips" for writing shell scripts that have a better chance of avoiding security problems. Next we cover the *restricted shell*, which attempts to put a straitjacket around the user's environment. Then we present the idea of a "Trojan horse," and why such things should be avoided. Finally we discuss setuid shell scripts, including the Korn shell's *privileged mode*.

This is not a textbook on Unix system security. Be aware that this chapter merely touches the tip of the iceberg and that there are myriad other aspects to Unix system security besides how the shell is set up.

If you would like to learn more about Unix security, we recommend *Practical UNIX & Internet Security* (O'Reilly), cited in the Bibliography.

15.1 Tips for Secure Shell Scripts

Here are some tips for writing more-secure shell scripts, courtesy of Professor Eugene (Gene) Spafford, the director of Purdue University's Center for Education and Research in Information Assurance and Security:[*]

Don't put the current directory (dot) in PATH
> Executable programs should come only from standard system directories. Having the current directory (dot) in PATH opens the door wide for "Trojan horses," described in "Trojan Horses" [15.3].

---

[*] See *http://www.cerias.purdue.edu/*.

Protect bin directories

Make sure that every directory in $PATH is writable only by its owner and by no one else. The same applies to all the programs *in* the bin directories.

Design before you code

Spend some time thinking about what you want to do and how to do it. Don't just type stuff in with a text editor and keep hacking until it seems to work. Include code to handle errors and failures gracefully.

Check all input arguments for validity

If you expect a number, verify that you got a number. Check that the number is in the correct range. Do the same thing for other kinds of data; the shell's pattern-matching facilities are particularly useful for this.

Check error codes from all commands that can return errors

Things you may not expect to fail might be mischievously forced to fail to cause the script to misbehave. For instance, it is possible to cause some commands to fail even as root if the argument is an NFS-mounted disk or a character-oriented device file.

Don't trust passed-in environment variables

Check and reset them to known values if they are used by subsequent commands (e.g., TZ, PATH, IFS, etc.). ksh93 automatically resets IFS to its default upon startup, ignoring whatever was in the environment, but many other shells don't. In all cases, it's an excellent idea to explicitly set PATH to contain just the system bin directories and IFS to space-tab-newline.

Start in a known place

Explicitly cd to a known directory when the script starts so that any subsequent relative pathnames are to a known location. Be sure that the cd succeeds:

```
cd app-dir || exit 1
```

Use full pathnames for commands

Do this so that you know which version you are getting, regardless of $PATH.

Use syslog(8) to keep an audit trail

Log the date and time of invocation, username, etc.; see the manual pages for *logger*(1). If you don't have logger, create a function to keep a log file:

```
logger() {
    printf "%s\n" "$*"  >> /var/adm/logsysfile
}
logger "Run by user "  $(id -un)  "($USER) at "  $(/bin/date)
```

Always quote user input when using that input

E.g., "$1" and "$*". This prevents malicious user input from being further evaluated and executed.

Don't use eval on user input

Even after quoting user input, *don't* hand it to the shell to reprocess with eval. If the user reads your script and sees that it uses eval, it's easy to subvert the script into doing almost anything.

Quote the results of wildcard expansion

You can do several nasty things to a system administrator by creating files with spaces, semicolons, backquotes, and so on, in the filenames. If administrative scripts don't quote the filename arguments, the scripts can trash—or give away—the system.

Check user input for metacharacters

Look for metacharacters such as $ or ` (old-style command substitution) if using the input in an eval or $(...).

Test your code and read it critically

Look for assumptions and mistakes that can be exploited. Put yourself into a nasty mood, and read your code with the intent of trying to figure out how to subvert it. Then fix whatever problems you find.

Be aware of race conditions

If an attacker can execute arbitrary commands between any two commands in your script, will it compromise security? If so, find another way to do it.

Suspect symbolic links

When chmod-ing or editing a file, check it to be sure that it is a file and not a symbolic link to a critical system file. (Use [-L *file*] or [-h *file*] to test if *file* is a symbolic link.)

Have someone else review your code for mistakes

Often a fresh pair of eyes can spot things that the original author of a program missed.

Use setgid rather than setuid, if possible

These terms are discussed later in this chapter. In brief, by using setgid, you restrict the amount of damage that can be done to the group that is compromised.

Use a new user rather than root

If you must use setuid to access a group of files, consider making a new, non-root user for that purpose, and setuid to it.

Limit setuid code as much as possible

Make the amount of setuid code as small as you can. Move it into a separate program, and invoke that from within a larger script when necessary. However, be sure to code defensively as if the script can be invoked by anyone from anywhere else!

Chet Ramey, the maintainer of bash, offers the following prolog for use in shell scripts that need to be more secure:

```
# Reset IFS. Even though ksh doesn't import IFS from the environment,
# $ENV could set it.  This uses special bash and ksh93 notation,
# not in POSIX.
IFS=$' \t\n'

# Make sure unalias is not a function, since it's a regular built-in.
# unset is a special built-in, so it will be found before functions.
unset -f unalias

# Unset all aliases and quote unalias so it's not alias-expanded.
\unalias -a

# Make sure command is not a function, since it's a regular built-in.
# unset is a special built-in, so it will be found before functions.
unset -f command

# Get a reliable path prefix, handling case where getconf is not
# available.
SYSPATH="$(command -p getconf PATH 2>/dev/null)"
if [[ -z "$SYSPATH" ]]; then
        SYSPATH="/usr/bin:/bin"          # pick your poison
fi
PATH="$SYSPATH:$PATH"
```

This code uses several non-POSIX extensions, all of which are described in "Common Extensions" [14.3].

15.2 Restricted Shell

A *restricted shell* is designed to put the user into an environment where the ability to move around and write files is severely limited. It's usually used for guest accounts. POSIX does not specify that environments provide a restricted shell, "because it does not provide the level of security restriction that is implied by historical documentation." Nevertheless, both ksh93 and bash do provide this facility. We describe it here for both of them.

When invoked as rksh (or with the -r option), ksh93 acts as a restricted shell. You can make a user's login shell restricted by putting the full pathname to rksh in the user's /etc/passwd entry. The ksh93 executable file must have a link to it named rksh for this to work.

The specific constraints imposed by the restricted ksh93 disallow the user from doing the things described in the following list. Some of these features are specific to ksh93; for more information see *Learning the Korn Shell*, which is listed in the Bibliography:

- Changing working directories: cd is inoperative. If you try to use it, you will get the error message ksh: cd: restricted.

- Redirecting output to a file: the redirectors >, >|, <>, and >> are not allowed. This includes using exec.
- Assigning a new value to the environment variables ENV, FPATH, PATH, or SHELL, or trying to change their attributes with typeset.
- Specifying any pathnames of commands with slashes (/) in them. The shell only runs commands found along $PATH.
- Adding new built-in commands with the builtin command.

Similar to ksh93, when invoked as rbash, bash acts as a restricted shell, and the bash executable file must have a link to it named rbash for this to work. The list of restricted operations for bash (taken from the *bash*(1) manpage) is similar to those for ksh93. Here too, some of the features mentioned here are specific to bash and haven't been covered in this book. For more information, see the *bash*(1) manpage:

- Changing directories with cd
- Setting or unsetting the values of SHELL, PATH, ENV, or BASH_ENV
- Specifying command names containing /
- Specifying a filename containing a / as an argument to the . (dot) built-in command
- Specifying a filename containing a / as an argument to the -p option to the hash built-in command
- Importing function definitions from the shell environment at startup
- Parsing the value of SHELLOPTS from the shell environment at startup
- Redirecting output using the >, >|, <>, >&, &>, and >> redirection operators
- Using the exec built-in command to replace the shell with another command
- Adding or deleting built-in commands with the -f and -d options to the enable built-in command
- Using the enable built-in command to enable disabled shell built-in commands
- Specifying the -p option to the command built-in command
- Turning off restricted mode with set +r or set +o restricted

For both shells, these restrictions go into effect *after* the user's .profile and environment files are run. This means that the restricted shell user's entire environment is set up in .profile. This lets the system administrator configure the environment as she sees fit.

To keep the user from overwriting ~/.profile, it is not enough to make the file read-only by the user. Either the home directory should *not* be writable by the user, or the commands in ~/.profile should cd to a different directory.

Two common ways of setting up such environments are to set up a directory of "safe" commands and have that directory be the only one in PATH, and to set up a command menu from which the user can't escape without exiting the shell. In any case, make sure that there is no other shell in any directory listed in $PATH; otherwise, the user can just run that shell and avoid the restrictions listed earlier. Also make sure that there isn't any program in $PATH that allows the user to start a shell, such as a "shell escape" from the ed, ex, or vi text editors.

 Although the ability to restrict the shell has been available (if not necessarily compiled in or documented) since the original Version 7 Bourne shell, it is rarely used. Setting up a usable yet correctly restricted environment is difficult in practice. So, caveat emptor.

15.3 Trojan Horses

A *Trojan horse* is something that looks harmless, or even useful, but that contains a hidden danger.

Consider the following scenario. User John Q. Programmer (login name jprog) is an excellent programmer, and he has quite a collection of personal programs in ~jprog/ bin. This directory occurs first in the PATH variable in ~jprog/.profile. Since he is such a good programmer, management recently promoted him to system administrator.

This is a whole new field of endeavor, and John—not knowing any better—has unfortunately left his bin directory writable by other users. Along comes W.M. Badguy, who creates the following shell script, named grep, in John's bin directory:

```
/bin/grep "$@"
case $(whoami) in                    Check effective user ID name
root)   nasty stuff here             Danger Will Robinson, danger!
        rm ~/jprog/bin/grep          Hide the evidence
        ;;
esac
```

In and of itself, this script can do no damage when jprog is working *as himself*. The problem comes when jprog uses the su command. This command allows a regular user to "switch user" to a different user. By default, it allows a regular user to become root (as long as that user knows the password, of course). The problem is that normally, su uses whatever PATH it inherits.[*] In this case, $PATH includes ~jprog/ bin. Now, when jprog, working as root, runs grep, he actually executes the Trojan horse version in his bin. This version runs the real grep, so jprog gets the results he expects. More importantly, it also silently executes the *nasty stuff here* part, as root. This means that Unix will let the script do anything it wants to. *Anything*. And to

---

[*] Get in the habit of using su - *user* to switch to *user* as if the user were doing a real login. This prevents import of the existing PATH.

make things worse, by removing the Trojan horse when it's done, there's no longer any evidence.

Writable bin directories open one door for Trojan horses, as does having dot in PATH. (Consider what happens if root does a cd to a directory containing a Trojan script, and dot is in root's PATH *before* the system directories!) Having writable shell scripts in any bin directory is another door. Just as you close and lock the doors of your house at night, you should make sure that you close any doors on your system!

15.4   Setuid Shell Scripts: A Bad Idea

Many problems with Unix security hinge on a Unix file attribute called the *setuid* (set user ID) bit. This is a special permission bit: when an executable file has it turned on, the file runs with an effective user ID equal to the owner of the file. The effective user ID is distinct from the real user ID of the process, and Unix applies its permission tests to the process's effective user ID.

For example, suppose that you've written a really nifty game program that keeps a private score file showing the top 15 players on your system. You don't want to make the score file world-writable because anyone could just come along and edit the file to make themselves the high scorer. By making your game setuid to your user ID, the game program can update the file, which you own, but no one else can update it. (The game program can determine who ran it by looking at its real user ID, and using that to determine the login name.)

The setuid facility is a nice feature for games and score files, but it becomes much more dangerous when used for root. Making programs setuid root lets administrators write programs that do certain things that require root privilege (e.g., configure printers) in a controlled way. To set a file's setuid bit, type chmod u+s *filename*. Setuid is dangerous when root owns the file; thus chown root *file* followed by chmod u+s *file* is the problem.

A similar facility exists at the group level, known (not surprisingly) as *setgid* (set group ID). Use chmod g+s *filename* to turn on setgid permissions. When you do an ls –l on a setuid or setgid file, the x in the permission mode is replaced with an s; for example, -rws--s--x for a file that is readable and writable by the owner, executable by everyone, and has both the setuid and setgid bits set (octal mode 6711).

Modern system administration wisdom says that creating setuid and setgid shell scripts is a terrible idea. This has been especially true under the C shell because its .cshrc environment file introduces numerous opportunities for break-ins. In particular, there are multiple ways of tricking a setuid shell script into becoming an *interactive* shell with an effective user ID of root. This is about the best thing a *cracker* could hope for: the ability to run any command as root. Here is one example, borrowed from the discussion in *http://www.faqs.org/faqs/unix-faq/faq/part4/section-7.html*:

> ... Well, suppose that the script is called /etc/setuid_script, starting with:
>
> ```
> #!/bin/sh
> ```
>
> Now let us see what happens if we issue the following commands:
>
> ```
> $ cd /tmp
> $ ln /etc/setuid_script -i
> $ PATH=.
> $ -i
> ```
>
> We know the last command will be rearranged to:
>
> ```
> /bin/sh -i
> ```
>
> However, this command will give us an interactive shell, setuid to the owner of the script! Fortunately, this security hole can easily be closed by making the first line:
>
> ```
> #!/bin/sh -
> ```
>
> The - signals the end of the option list: the next argument -i will be taken as the name of the file to read commands from, just like it should!

Because of this, POSIX explicitly permits the single - character to end the options for /bin/sh.

> There is an important difference between a setuid shell script, and a *setuid shell*. The latter is a copy of the shell executable, which has been made to belong to root and had the setuid bit applied. In the previous section on Trojan horses, suppose that the *nasty stuff here* was this code:
>
> ```
> cp /bin/sh ~badguy/bin/myls
> chown root ~badguy/bin/myls
> chmod u+s ~badguy/bin/myls
> ```
>
> Remember, this code executes as root, so it will work. When badguy executes myls, it's a machine-code executable file, and the setuid bit *is* honored. Hello shell that runs as root. Goodbye security!

In fact, the dangers of setuid and setgid shell scripts are so great that modern Unix systems, meaning both commercial Unix systems and freeware clones (4.4 BSD-derived and GNU/Linux), disable the setuid and setgid bits on shell scripts. Even if you apply the bits to the file, the operating system does not honor them.[*]

We also note that many modern systems have options to the mount command that disable the setuid/setgid bit for entire filesystems. This can be a good idea for network-mounted filesystems, as well as for removable media such as floppy disks and CD-ROMs.

---

[*] Mac OS X and at least one version of OpenBSD that we tried seem to be notable exceptions. Be extra careful if you run one or more such systems! We found that Solaris 9 honors the setuid bit only if root is *not* the owner of the file.

15.5 ksh93 and Privileged Mode

The Korn shell's *privileged mode* was designed to protect against setuid shell scripts. This is a set –o option (set -o privileged or set -p), but the shell enters it automatically whenever it executes a script whose setuid bit is set; i.e., when the effective user ID is different from the real user ID.

In privileged mode, when a setuid Korn shell script is invoked, the shell runs the file /etc/suid_profile. This file should be written to restrict setuid shell scripts in much the same way as the restricted shell does. At a minimum, it should make PATH readonly (typeset -r PATH or readonly PATH) and set it to one or more "safe" directories. Once again, this prevents any decoys from being invoked.

Since privileged mode is an option, it is possible to turn it off with the command set +o privileged (or set +p). However, this doesn't help the potential system cracker: the shell automatically changes its effective user ID to be the same as the real user ID—i.e., if you turn off privileged mode, you also turn off setuid.

In addition to privileged mode, ksh provides a special "agent" program, /etc/suid_exec, that runs setuid shell scripts (or shell scripts that are executable but not readable).

For this to work, the script should *not* start with #! /bin/ksh. When the program is invoked, ksh attempts to run the program as a regular binary executable. When the operating system fails to run the script (because it isn't binary, and because it doesn't have the name of an interpreter specified with #!), ksh realizes that it's a script, and invokes /etc/suid_exec with the name of the script and its arguments. It also arranges to pass an authentication "token" to /etc/suid_exec, indicating the real and effective user and group IDs of the script. /etc/suid_exec verifies that it is safe to run the script and then arranges to invoke ksh with the proper real and effective user and group IDs on the script.

Although the combination of privileged mode and /etc/suid_exec allows you to avoid many of the attacks on setuid scripts, writing scripts that safely can be run setuid is a difficult art, requiring a fair amount of knowledge and experience. It should be done carefully.

Although setuid shell scripts don't work on modern systems, there are occasions when privileged mode is still useful. In particular, there is a widely used third-party program named sudo, which, to quote the web page, allows a system administrator to give certain users (or groups of users) the ability to run some (or all) commands as root or another user while logging the commands and arguments. The home page for sudo is *http://www.courtesan.com/sudo*. A system administrator could easily execute sudo /bin/ksh -p in order to get a known environment for performing administrative tasks.

15.6 Summary

Writing secure shell scripts is just one part of keeping a Unix system secure. This chapter merely scratches the surface of the issues involved, and we recommend reading up on Unix system security. (See the Bibliography.) As a beginning, we presented a list of tips for writing secure shell scripts provided by a recognized expert in the field of Unix security.

We then described restricted shells, which disable a number of potentially dangerous operations. The environment for a restricted shell should be built within the user's .profile file, which is executed when a restricted user logs in. In practice, restricted shells are difficult to set up correctly and use, and we recommend finding a different way to set up restricted environments.

Trojan horses are programs that look harmless but that actually perform an attack on your system. We looked at some of the ways that Trojan horses can be created, but there are others.

Setuid shell scripts are a bad idea, and just about all modern Unix systems disallow them, since it's very difficult to close the security holes they open up. It is worth verifying, however, that your system does indeed disallow them, and if not, to periodically search your system for such files.

Finally, we looked briefly at the Korn shell's privileged mode, which attempts to solve many of the security issues associated with shell scripts.

Writing Manual Pages

Users of programs require documentation, and the programs' authors do too, if they haven't used the software recently. Regrettably, software documentation is neglected in most computer books, so even users who want to write good documentation for their programs often don't know how, or even where, to begin. This appendix helps to remedy that deficiency.

In Unix, brief programming documentation has traditionally been supplied in the form of manual pages, written in nroff/troff[*] markup, and displayed as simple ASCII text with man, nroff -man, or groff -man, typeset for some device xxx with ditroff -man -Txxx, groff -man -Txxx, or troff -man -Txxx, or viewed in an X window in typeset form with groff -TX -man.

Longer software documentation has historically been provided as manuals or technical reports, often in troff markup, with printed pages in PostScript or PDF form. troff markup is definitely not user-friendly, however, so the GNU Project chose a different approach: the Texinfo documentation system.[†] Texinfo markup is considerably higher-level than common troff packages, and like troff, allows documents to be prepared both for viewing as simple ASCII text, as well as typeset by the TEX typesetting system.[‡] Most importantly, it supports hypertext links to allow much better navigation through online documentation.

Most documentation that you read online in Unix systems probably has been marked up for either troff[§] or Texinfo.[**] The makeinfo program from the Texinfo system can produce output in ASCII, HTML, XML, and DocBook/XML. Texinfo

---

[*] Although nroff was developed before troff, from the user's point of view, both systems are similar: ditroff and groff each emulate both of them.

[†] See Robert J. Chassell and Richard M. Stallman, *Texinfo: The GNU Documentation Format*, Free Software Foundation, 1999, ISBN 1-882114-67-1.

[‡] See Donald E. Knuth, *The TEXbook*, Addison-Wesley, 1984, ISBN 0-201-13448-9.

[§] See *http://www.troff.org/*.

[**] See *http://www.gnu.org/software/texinfo/*.

files can be typeset directly by TEX, which outputs a device-independent (DVI) file that can be translated into a wide variety of device formats by back-end programs called DVI drivers.

These are not the only markup formats, however. Sun Microsystems from Solaris 7 ships almost all of its manual pages in SGML form, and the Linux Documentation Project* promotes XML (an SGML subset) markup to facilitate its goal of translating GNU/Linux documentation into many of the world's human languages.

So, what markup system should a Unix program author adopt? Experience has definitely shown that high-level markup, even if more verbose, has great value. SGML (and thus, HTML and XML) is based on rigorous grammars, so it is possible to validate the logical structure of documents before compiling them into displayable pages. With sufficiently detailed markup, SGML documents can be translated reliably into other markup systems, and indeed, several book and journal publishers today do just that: authors submit material in any of several formats, publishers convert it to SGML, and then use troff, TEX, or some other typesetting system at the back end to produce printer-ready pages.

Unfortunately, the SGML software toolbox is still pretty deficient and not widely standardized, so the best choice for maximum software document portability is still likely to be either troff or Texinfo markup, and for manual pages, the format has to be troff, if the man command is to work everywhere.

Ultimately, one would like to be able to do reliable automated transformations between any pair of markup systems, but that goal remains elusive. What you *can* do today, however, is write manual pages in a restricted subset of troff markup, and have them converted automatically to HTML and Texinfo. To do so, you need two easily installable packages, man2html and man2texi.†

Manual Pages for pathfind

Even though complete documentation for markup systems fills one or more books, you can get by quite nicely with the easily learned troff subset that we present here. We show it step by step, as a semiliterate document to accompany the pathfind script from "Path Searching" [8.1], and then collect the pieces into the complete manual-page file shown in Example A-1.

Before we begin, some explanatory remarks about nroff/troff markup are in order. nroff built on the lessons of earlier text-formatting systems, such as DEC's runoff, and produced output for ASCII printing devices. When Bell Labs acquired a photo-typesetter, a new program, troff, was created to produce typeset pages. troff was

---

* See *http://www.tldp.org/*.

† Available at *http://www.math.utah.edu/pub/man2html/* and *http://www.math.utah.edu/pub/man2texi/*.

one of the earliest successful attempts at computer-based typesetting. Both programs accept the same input, so from now on, when we say troff, we usually also mean nroff.

Early Unix systems ran on small-memory minicomputers, and those severe constraints cramped the design of these formatters. Like many Unix commands, troff commands are short and cryptic. Most appear at the beginning of a line, in the form of a dot followed by one or two letters or digits. The font choice is limited: just roman, bold, italic, and later, fixed-width, styles in only a few sizes. Unlike later systems, in troff documents, spaces and blank lines are *significant*: two input spaces produce (approximately) two output spaces. That fact, plus the command position, prevent indentation and spacing from being used to make input more readable.

However, the simple command format makes it easy to parse troff documents, at least superficially, and several frontend processors have been developed that provide for easy specification of equations, graphs, pictures, and tables: they consume a troff data stream, and output a slightly augmented one.

While the full troff command repertoire is large, the manual-page style, selected by the –man option, has only a few commands. No frontend processors are required, so there are no equations or pictures in manual pages, and tables are rare.

A manual-page document has a simple layout, with a half-dozen standard top-level section headings, interspersed with formatted paragraphs of text, and occasionally, indented, and often labeled, blocks. You've seen that layout every time you've used the man command.

Examination of manual pages from a broad range of historical and current sources shows considerable stylistic variation, which is to be expected when the markup is visual, rather than logical. Our font choices therefore should be taken as *recommendations*, rather than as rigid requirements.

It's now time to get started writing the manual page for pathfind, which is simple enough that the text doesn't overwhelm the markup.

We begin with a comment statement, since every computer language should have one: troff comments begin with backslash-quote and continue up to, but not including, end-of-line. However, when they follow an initial dot, their line terminator disappears from the output as well:

```
.\" ==========================================================
```

Because troff input cannot be indented, it looks awfully dense. We find that a comment line of equals signs before section headings makes them much easier to spot, and we often use comparatively short input lines.

Every manual-page document starts with a *Text Header* command (.TH) containing up to four arguments: an uppercased command name, a manual section number (1 [digit one] for user commands), and optionally, a revision date and version number. These arguments are used to construct the running page headers and footers in the formatted output document:

```
.TH PATHFIND 1 "" "1.00"
```

The *Section Heading* command (.SH) takes a single argument, quoted if it contains spaces, and uppercased to follow manual-page conventions:

```
.\" =============================================================
.SH NAME
```

The body of the NAME section provides fodder for the apropos (or equivalently, man -k) command, and should be exactly one line long, without trailing punctuation. It takes the form command – description:

```
pathfind \(em find files in a directory path
```

The markup \(em is one of the few inline troff commands seen in manual pages: it stands for an em dash, a horizontal line about the width of the letter m. One space precedes and follows the em dash. Older manual pages often use \- (minus sign), or even just -, but an em dash is conventional in English-language typography.

The second section gives a brief synopsis of the command line that invokes the program. It begins with the expected heading:

```
.\" =============================================================
.SH SYNOPSIS
```

and is followed with a sometimes lengthy markup display that provides mostly font information:

```
.B pathfind
[
.B \-\^\-all
]
[
.B \-\^\-?
]
[
.B \-\^\-help
]
[
.B \-\^\-version
]
```

The option hyphen is marked with \- to get a minus sign, which looks better typeset than the shorter ordinary hyphen does. We use the half-narrow space command, \^, to prevent the hyphens from running together in troff output. The space disappears from nroff output. The program name, and options, are set in a bold font. The font-switching commands, such as .B, expect up to six arguments (quoted if they contain spaces), and then typeset them adjacent to one another. When there are multiple arguments, this means that any spacing needed must be explicitly supplied. Here, the square brackets are in the default roman font; in manual pages, they delimit optional values. Although we could have put the closing and opening brackets of consecutive options on the same line, we prefer not to because having each option complete on three consecutive lines facilitates editing. The font-pair commands to be introduced shortly could shrink them to a single line, but they are rarely used in option lists.

Despite the line breaks, troff is still typesetting in filled-paragraph mode, so everything so far fits on one line. By experiment, we find that the nroff ASCII output has a line break after the --version option, but since we are in paragraph mode, the next line continues at the left margin. That is objectionable here, so we put in a conditional statement that applies only to nroff, and is ignored by troff. It uses the *temporary indentation* command (.ti) with an argument of +9n, meaning to indent nine spaces, which is the width of the command name, plus a trailing space, in a fixed-width font:

```
.if n .ti +9n
```

The command line is short enough to fit on a single typeset line, so we don't need a similar command for troff. Here is what it would look like, but hidden inside a comment until then, in case we need it when the program is extended with more options:

```
.\" .if t .ti +\w'\fBpathfind\fP\ 'u
```

The indentation amount is more complex because with a proportional font, we don't know the width of the command name and one following space. The \w'...'u command measures the width of the material inside the single quotes. Because that text is set in a bold font, we use an inline font wrapper, \fB...\fP, meaning switch to a bold font, and then switch back to the previous font. There are similar font-switching commands for roman (\fR), italic (\fI), and fixed-width (\fC) fonts. The C stands for Courier, a widely used fixed-width font dating back to the days of manual typewriters.

The remainder of the command line comes next:

```
envvar [ files-or-patterns ]
```

The third section describes the program's options. It appears before any further description because it is the most-frequently read section of most manual pages:

```
.\" ============================================================
.SH OPTIONS
```

A few short remarks apply to the options, so they come next:

```
.B pathfind
options can be prefixed with either one or two hyphens, and
can be abbreviated to any unique prefix.  Thus,
.BR \-v ,
.BR \-ver ,
and
.B \-\^\-version
are equivalent.
```

That fragment exhibits a new feature: the font-pair command (`.BR`), which sets its arguments alternately in bold and roman text, *without* intervening space. There are similar commands `.IR` and `.RI` for the italic-roman pair, `.IB` and `.BI` for the bold-italic pair, and of course, `.RB` for the mate of the one that we used. There are no analogues for the fixed-width font because it got added later (the original Bell Labs typesetter lacked that font); you have to use `\fC...\fP` instead.

It is now time for a paragraph break:

```
.PP
```

In nroff output, a blank line and a paragraph break are identical, but troff uses less vertical space for a paragraph break. It is considered good form to use `.PP` between paragraphs; in general, manual-page input files should never contain blank lines.

The next paragraph follows:

```
To avoid confusion with options, if a filename begins with a
hyphen, it must be disguised by a leading absolute or
relative directory path, e.g.,
.I /tmp/-foo
or
.IR ./-foo .
```

We are now ready for the option descriptions. Their markup is about the most complex that is used in manual pages, but it soon becomes familiar. Essentially, we want to have labeled indented paragraphs, with the label normally set at the left of the first paragraph line. More recent markup systems would structure this as a list of items: begin-option-list, begin-option, end-option, begin-option, end-option, and so on, ending with end-option-list. The manual-page markup doesn't quite do that. It just starts the items, and they end at the next paragraph break (`.PP`) or section heading (`.SH`).

The command to start an item (`.TP`) takes an optional width argument that sets the indentation of the description paragraph from the left margin. If the argument is omitted, a default indentation is used. If a label is longer than the indentation, a new line is started immediately after the label. The paragraph indentation remains in effect for subsequent `.TP` commands, so only the first in the option list needs it. As with the indentation of a wrapped command line in the SYNOPSIS section, we use a dynamic indentation that depends on the length of the longest option name. Also, since we have several options to describe, we set them off with a comment line of dashes:

```
.\" -------------------------------------------------------
.TP \w'\fB\-\^\-version\fP'u+3n
```

The line following the `.TP` command provides the item label:

```
.B \-all
```

The label is followed by the option description:

```
Search all directories for each specified file, instead of
reporting just the first instance of each found in the
search path.
```

If the description needs a paragraph break, use the *Indented Paragraph* command (.IP) instead of the ordinary paragraph break command (.PP), so as not to terminate the list. This manual page is short enough that we don't require .IP.

The remaining option descriptions require no new markup, so here they are, completing the options section:

```
.\" ---------------------------------------------------------
.TP
.B \-?
Same as
.BR \-help .
.\" ---------------------------------------------------------
.TP
.B \-help
Display a brief help message on
.IR stdout ,
giving a usage description, and then terminate immediately
with a success return code.
.\" ---------------------------------------------------------
.TP
.B \-version
Display the program version number and release date on
.IR stdout ,
and then terminate immediately with a success return code.
```

The fourth manual-page section is the program description. It can be as long as you like: the shell's runs on for dozens of pages. Nevertheless, brevity is desirable, since manual pages are consulted often. pathfind is simple enough that just three paragraphs suffice. The first two have markup that should be familiar by now:

```
.\" =========================================================
.SH DESCRIPTION
.B pathfind
searches a colon-separated directory search path defined by
the value of the environment variable, \fIenvvar\fP, for
specified files or file patterns, reporting their full path on
.IR stdout ,
or complaining \fIfilename: not found\fP on
.I stderr
if a file cannot be found anywhere in the search path.
.PP
.BR pathfind 's
exit status is 0 on success, and otherwise is the number of
files that could not be found, possibly capped at the
exit code limit of 125.
.PP
```

The last bit of manual-page markup that we need to know shows up in the last paragraph, where we want to show indented lines in a fixed-width font indicative of computer input and output, without the normal paragraph filling. The font change is similar to what we have seen before, \fC...\fP. We prefix it with a troff no-op command, \&, when it appears at the beginning of the line, because that no-op is necessary when the text that follows begins with a period. It does not here, but general rules are easier to remember than special cases. We want the computer samples to be indented, so we put them in an indented region bounded by *Begin Right Shift* (.RS) and *End Right Shift* (.RE) commands. Furthermore, we need to stop paragraph filling, so we surround the text with *no fill* (.nf) and *fill* (.fi) commands:

```
For example,
.RS
.nf
\&\fCpathfind PATH ls\fP
.fi
.RE
reports
.RS
.nf
\&\fC/bin/ls\fP
.fi
.RE
on most Unix systems, and
.RS
.nf
\&\fCpathfind --all PATH gcc g++\fP
.fi
.RE
reports
.RS
.nf
\&\fC/usr/local/bin/gcc
/usr/bin/gcc
/usr/local/gnat/bin/gcc
/usr/local/bin/g++
/usr/bin/g++\fP
.fi
.RE
on some systems.
.PP
Wildcard patterns also work:
.RS
.nf
\&\fCpathfind --all PATH '??tex'\fP
.fi
.RE
```

```
reports
.RS
.nf
\&\fC/usr/local/bin/detex
/usr/local/bin/dotex
/usr/local/bin/latex
/usr/bin/latex\fP
.fi
.RE
on some systems.
```

The final section provides cross references to other related commands; this information can be extremely useful to readers, so it is important to do a thorough job of it.
Its format is simple: just a single paragraph of alphabetically ordered bold command
names with parenthesized manual section numbers, separated by commas, and ending with a period:

```
.\" ==========================================================
.SH "SEE ALSO"
.BR find (1),
.BR locate (1),
.BR slocate (1),
.BR type (1),
.BR whence (1),
.BR where (1),
.BR whereis (1).
.\" ==========================================================
```

We've introduced almost all of the markup that is required for virtually any manual
page. The only significant omission is the *Subsection Heading* command (.SS), but it
is comparatively rare, showing up only in long manual-page files. It works just like
the .SH command, but uses a somewhat smaller font in the typeset output. There is
no visible difference in the ASCII output from nroff. Two other inline commands
that are occasionally needed are .\|.\|. for an ellipsis (...), and \(bu for a bullet (•),
often used as the label in a list of labeled paragraphs, like this:

```
.TP \w'\(bu'u+2n
\(bu
```

We have now examined the anatomy of a manual page. The complete troff input for
our example is collected in Example A-1, and the typeset output (from groff -man,
which produces PostScript by default) is shown as a half-size page in Figure A-1.
With our description as a guide, you should be ready to document your own programs in manual pages.

NAME

    pathfind — find files in a directory path

SYNOPSIS

    pathfind [**--all**] [**--?**] [**--help**] [**--version**] envvar [file(s)]

OPTIONS

    pathfind options can be prefixed with either one or two hyphens, and can be abbreviated to any unique prefix. Thus, **−v**, **−ver**, and **−−version** are equivalent.

    To avoid confusion with options, if a filename begins with a hyphen, it must be disguised by a leading absolute or relative directory path, e.g., */tmp/-foo* or *./-foo*.

    −all   Search all directories for each specified file, instead of reporting just the first instance of each found in the search path.

    −?   Same as **−help**.

    −help   Display a brief help message on *stdout*, giving a usage description, and then terminate immediately with a success return code.

    −version Display the program version number and release date on *stdout*, and then terminate immediately with a success return code.

DESCRIPTION

    pathfind searches a colon-separated directory search path defined by the value of the environment variable, *envvar*, for specified files, reporting their full path on *stdout*, or complaining *filename: not found* on *stderr* if a file cannot be found anywhere in the search path.

    pathfind's exit status is 0 on success, and otherwise is the number of files that could not be found, possibly capped at the exit code limit of 125.

    For example,

```
        pathfind PATH ls
```

    reports

```
        /bin/ls
```

    on most Unix systems, and

```
        pathfind --all PATH gcc g++
```

    reports

```
        /usr/local/bin/gcc
        /usr/bin/gcc
        /usr/local/gnat/bin/gcc
        /usr/local/bin/g++
        /usr/bin/g++
```

    on some systems.

SEE ALSO

    find(1), **locate**(1), **slocate**(1), **type**(1), **whence**(1), **where**(1), **whereis**(1).

1.00   1

Figure A-1. Typeset manual-page markup for pathfind

Example A-1. troff manual-page markup for pathfind

```
.\" =========================================================
.TH PATHFIND 1 "" "1.00"
.\" =========================================================
.SH NAME
pathfind \(em find files in a directory path
.\" =========================================================
.SH SYNOPSIS
.B pathfind
[
.B \-\^\-all
]
[
.B \-\^\-?
]
[
.B \-\^\-help
]
[
.B \-\^\-version
]
```

Example A-1. troff manual-page markup for pathfind (continued)

```
.if n .ti +9n
.\" .if t .ti +\w'\fBpathfind\fP\ 'u
envvar [ files-or-patterns ]
.\" =========================================================
.SH OPTIONS
.B pathfind
options can be prefixed with either one or two hyphens, and
can be abbreviated to any unique prefix.  Thus,
.BR \-v ,
.BR \-ver ,
and
.B \-\^\-version
are equivalent.
.PP
To avoid confusion with options, if a filename begins with a
hyphen, it must be disguised by a leading absolute or
relative directory path, e.g.,
.I /tmp/-foo
or
.IR ./-foo .
.\" ---------------------------------------------------------
.TP \w'\fB\-\^\-version\fP'u+3n
.B \-all
Search all directories for each specified file, instead of
reporting just the first instance of each found in the
search path.
.\" ---------------------------------------------------------
.TP
.B \-?
Same as
.BR \-help .
.\" ---------------------------------------------------------
.TP
.B \-help
Display a brief help message on
.IR stdout ,
giving a usage description, and then terminate immediately
with a success return code.
.\" ---------------------------------------------------------
.TP
.B \-version
Display the program version number and release date on
.IR stdout ,
and then terminate immediately with a success return code.
.\" =========================================================
.SH DESCRIPTION
.B pathfind
searches a colon-separated directory search path defined by
the value of the environment variable, \fIenvvar\fP, for
specified files or file patterns, reporting their full path on
.IR stdout ,
or complaining \fIfilename: not found\fP on
```

Example A-1. troff manual-page markup for pathfind (continued)

```
.I stderr
if a file cannot be found anywhere in the search path.
.PP
.BR pathfind 's
exit status is 0 on success, and otherwise is the number of
files that could not be found, possibly capped at the
exit code limit of 125.
.PP
For example,
.RS
.nf
\&\fCpathfind PATH ls\fP
.fi
.RE
reports
.RS
.nf
\&\fC/bin/ls\fP
.fi
.RE
on most Unix systems, and
.RS
.nf
\&\fCpathfind --all PATH gcc g++\fP
.fi
.RE
reports
.RS
.nf
\&\fC/usr/local/bin/gcc
/usr/bin/gcc
/usr/local/gnat/bin/gcc
/usr/local/bin/g++
/usr/bin/g++\fP
.fi
.RE
on some systems.
.PP
Wildcard patterns also work:
.RS
.nf
\&\fCpathfind --all PATH '??tex'\fP
.fi
.RE
reports
.RS
.nf
\&\fC/usr/local/bin/detex
/usr/local/bin/dotex
/usr/local/bin/latex
/usr/bin/latex\fP
.fi
```

Example A-1. troff manual-page markup for pathfind (continued)

```
.RE
on some systems.
.\" ========================================================
.SH "SEE ALSO"
.BR find (1),
.BR locate (1),
.BR slocate (1),
.BR type (1),
.BR whence (1),
.BR where (1),
.BR whereis (1).
.\" ========================================================
```

Manual-Page Syntax Checking

Checking correct formatting of manual pages is usually done visually, with printed output from either of these commands:

```
groff -man -Tps pathfind.man | lp
troff -man -Tpost pathfind.man | /usr/lib/lp/postscript/dpost | lp
```

or on the screen as ASCII or typeset material, with commands like this:

```
nroff -man pathfind.man | col | more
groff -man -Tascii pathfind.man | more
groff -man -TX100 pathfind.man &
```

The col command handles certain special escape sequences that nroff generates for horizontal and vertical motion. col is not needed for groff output.

Some Unix systems have a simple-minded syntax checker, checknr; the command:

```
checknr pathfind.man
```

produces no complaints on our systems. checknr is good at catching font mismatches, but knows little about the manual-page format.

Most Unix systems have deroff, which is a simple filter that strips troff markup. You can do a spellcheck like this:

```
deroff pathfind.man | spell
```

to avoid lots of complaints from the spellchecker about troff markup. Other handy tools for catching hard-to-spot errors in documentation are a doubled-word finder[*] and a delimiter-balance checker.[†]

---

[*] Available at *http://www.math.utah.edu/pub/dw/*.

[†] Available at *http://www.math.utah.edu/pub/chkdelim/*.

Manual-Page Format Conversion

Conversion to HTML, Texinfo, Info, XML, and DVI files is simple:

```
man2html pathfind.man
man2texi --batch pathfind.man
makeinfo pathfind.texi
makeinfo --xml pathfind.texi
tex pathfind.texi
```

We don't show the output .html, .texi, .info, and .xml files here because of their length. If you are curious, make them yourself and peek inside them to get an idea of what those markup formats look like.

Manual-Page Installation

Historically, the man command expected to find manual pages in subdirectories of a search path defined by the environment variable MANPATH, typically something like /usr/man:/usr/local/man.

Some recent man versions simply assume that each directory in the program search path, PATH, can be suffixed with the string /../man to identify a companion manual-page directory, eliminating the need for MANPATH.

In each manual-page directory, it is common to find pairs of subdirectories prefixed man and cat and suffixed with the section number. Within each subdirectory, filenames are also suffixed by the section number. Thus, /usr/man/man1/ls.1 is the troff file that documents the ls command, and /usr/man/cat1/ls.1 holds nroff's formatted output. man use the latter, when it exists, to avoid rerunning the formatter unnecessarily.

While some vendors have since adopted quite different organization of the manual-page trees, their man implementations still recognize the historical practice. Thus, installation of most GNU software puts executables in $prefix/bin and manual pages in $prefix/man/man1, where prefix defaults to /usr/local, and that seems to work nicely everywhere.

System managers normally arrange to run catman or makewhatis at regular intervals to update a file containing the one-line descriptions from the manual-page NAME sections. That file is used by the apropos, man –k, and whatis commands to provide a simple index of manual pages. If that doesn't turn up what you're looking for, then you may have to resort to a full-text search with grep.

Files and Filesystems

Effective use of computers requires an understanding of files and filesystems. This appendix presents an overview of the important features of Unix filesystems: what a file is, how files are named and what they contain, how they are grouped into a filesystem hierarchy, and what properties they have.

What Is a File?

Simply put, a file is a collection of data that resides in a computer system, and that can be referenced as a single entity from a computer program. Files provide a mechanism for data storage that survives process execution, and generally, restarts of the computer.[*]

In the early days of computers, files were external to the computer system: they usually resided on magnetic tape, paper tape, or punched cards. Their management was left up to their owner, who was expected to try very hard not to drop a stack of punched cards on the floor!

Later, magnetic disks became common, and their physical size decreased sharply, from as large as the span of your arms, to some as small as the width of your thumb, while their capacity increased by several orders of magnitude, from about 5MB in the mid-1950s to about 400,000MB in 2004. Costs and access times have dropped by at least three orders of magnitude. Today, there are about as many magnetic disks in existence as there are humans.

---

[*] Some systems offer special fast filesystems that reside in central *random-access memory* (*RAM*), allowing temporary files to be shared between processes. With common RAM technologies, such filesystems require a constant electrical supply, and thus are generally created anew on system restart. However, some *embedded computer systems* use nonvolatile RAM to provide a long-term filesystem.

Optical storage devices, such as CD-ROMs and DVDs, are inexpensive and capacious: in the 1990s, CD-ROMs largely replaced removable flexible magnetic disks (floppies) and tapes for commercial software distribution.

Nonvolatile solid-state storage devices are also available; they may eventually replace devices that have moving mechanical parts, which wear out and fail. However, at the time of this writing, they remain considerably more expensive than alternatives, have lower capacity, and can be rewritten only a limited number of times.

How Are Files Named?

Early computer operating systems did not name files: files were submitted by their owners for processing, and were handled one at a time by human computer operators. It soon became evident that something better was needed if file processing was to be automated: files need names that humans can use to classify and manage them, and that computers can use to identify them.

Once we can assign names to files, we soon discover the need to handle *name collisions* that arise when the same name is assigned to two or more different files. Modern filesystems solve this problem by grouping sets of uniquely named files into logical collections called *directories*, or *folders*. We look at these in "The Unix Hierarchical Filesystem" later in this Appendix.

We name files using *characters* from the host operating system's character set. In the early days of computing, there was considerable variation in character sets, but the need to exchange data between unlike systems made it evident that standardization was desirable.

In 1963, the *American Standards Association*[*] proposed a 7-bit character set with the ponderous name *American Standard Code for Information Interchange*, thankfully known ever since by its initial letters, ASCII (pronounced *ask-ee*). Seven bits permit the representation of $2^7 = 128$ different characters, which is sufficient to handle uppercase and lowercase letters of the Latin alphabet, decimal digits, and a couple of dozen special symbols and punctuation characters, including space, with 33 left over for use as control characters. The latter have no assigned printable graphic representation. Some of them serve for marking line and page breaks, but most have only specialized uses. ASCII is supported on virtually all computer systems today. For a view of the ASCII character set, issue the command man ascii.

ASCII, however, is inadequate for representing text in most of the world's languages: its character repertoire is much too small. Since most computer systems now use 8-bit bytes as the smallest addressable unit of storage, and since that byte size permits $2^8 = 256$ different characters, systems designers acted quickly to populate the

[*] Later renamed the *American National Standards Institute (ANSI)*.

upper half of that 256-element set, leaving ASCII in the lower half. Unfortunately, they weren't guided by international standards, so hundreds of different assignments of various characters have been put into use; they are sometimes known as *code pages*. Even a single set of 128 additional character slots does not suffice for all the languages of Europe, so the *International Organization for Standardization (ISO)* has developed a family of code pages known as ISO 8859-1,[*] ISO 8859-2, ISO 8859-3, and so on.

In the 1990s, collaborative efforts were begun to develop the ultimate single universal character set, known as Unicode.[†] This will eventually require about 21 bits per character, but current implementations in several operating systems use only 16 bits. Unix systems use a variable-byte-width encoding called *UTF-8*[‡] that permits existing ASCII files to be valid Unicode files.

The point of this digression into character sets is this: with the sole exception of the IBM mainframe *EBCDIC*[§] character set, *all current ones include the ASCII characters in the lower 128 slots.* Thus, by voluntarily restricting filenames to the ASCII subset, we can make it much more likely that the names are usable everywhere. The existence of the Internet and the World Wide Web gives ample evidence that files are exchanged across unlike systems; even though they can always be renamed to match local requirements, it increases the human maintenance task to do so.

The designers of the original Unix filesystem chose to permit all but *two* characters from a 256-element set in filenames. The forbidden ones are the control character NUL (the character with all bits set to zero), which is used to mark end-of-string in several programming languages, including the ones used to write most of Unix, and forward slash (/), which is reserved for an important purpose that we describe shortly.

This choice is quite permissive, but you are strongly advised to impose further restrictions, for at least these good reasons:

- Since filenames are used by people, the names should require only visible characters: invisible control characters are not candidates.

- Filenames get used by both humans and computers: a human might well recognize a string of characters as a filename from its surrounding context, but a computer program needs more precise rules.

---

[*] Search the ISO Standards catalog at *http://www.iso.ch/iso/en/CatalogueListPage.CatalogueList*.

[†] *The Unicode Standard, Version 4.0*, Addison-Wesley, 2003, ISBN 0-321-18578-1.

[‡] See *RFC 2279: UTF-8, a transformation format of ISO 10646*, available at *ftp://ftp.internic.net/rfc/rfc2279.txt*.

[§] EBCDIC = Extended Binary-Coded Decimal Interchange Code, pronounced *eb-see-dick*, or *eb-kih-dick*, an 8-bit character set first introduced on the IBM System/360 in 1964, containing the old 6-bit IBM BCD set as a subset. System/360, and its descendants, is by far the longest-running computer architecture in history, and much of the world's business uses it. IBM supports a superb GNU/Linux implementation on it, using the ASCII character set: see *http://www.ibm.com/linux/*.

- Shell metacharacters (i.e., most punctuation characters) in filenames require special handling, and are therefore best avoided altogether.

- Initial hyphens make filenames look like Unix command options.

Some non-Unix filesystems permit both uppercase and lowercase characters to be used in filenames, but ignore lettercase differences when comparing names. Unix native filesystems do not: readme, Readme, and README are distinct filenames.*

Unix filenames are conventionally written entirely in lowercase, since that is both easier to read and easier to type. Certain common important filenames, such as AUTHORS, BUGS, ChangeLog, COPYRIGHT, INSTALL, LICENSE, Makefile, NEWS, README, and TODO, are conventionally spelled in uppercase, or occasionally, in mixed case. Because uppercase precedes lowercase in the ASCII character set, these files occur at the beginning of a directory listing, making them even more visible. However, in modern Unix systems, the sort order depends on the locale; set the environment variable LC_ALL to C to get the traditional ASCII sort order.

For portability to other operating systems, it is a good idea to limit characters in filenames to Latin letters, digits, hyphen, underscore, and at most, a single dot.

How long can a filename be? That depends on the filesystem, and on lots of software that contains fixed-size buffers that are expected to be big enough to hold filenames. Early Unix systems imposed a 14-character limit. However, Unix systems designed since the mid-1980s have generally permitted up to 255 characters. POSIX defines the constant NAME_MAX to be that length, *excluding* the terminating NUL character, and requires a minimum value of 14. The X/Open Portability Guide requires a minimum of 255. You can use the getconf† command to find out the limit on your system. Here is what most Unix systems report:

```
$ getconf NAME_MAX .                        What is longest filename in current filesystem?
255
```

The full specification of file locations has another, and larger, limit discussed in "Filesystem Structure" later in this Appendix.

---

* The old HFS-type filesystem supported on Mac OS X is case-*insensitive*, and that can lead to nasty surprises when software is ported to that environment. Mac OS X also supports normal case-sensitive Unix filesystems.

† Available on almost all Unix systems, except Mac OS X and FreeBSD (before release 5.0). Source code for getconf can be found in the glibc distribution at *ftp://ftp.gnu.org/gnu/glibc/*.

We offer a warning here about spaces in filenames. Some window-based desktop operating systems, where filenames are selected from scrolling menus, or typed into dialog boxes, have led their users to believe that spaces in filenames are just fine. They are not! Filenames get used in many other contexts outside of little boxes, and the only sensible way to recognize a filename is that it is a *word chosen from a restricted character set*. Unix shells, in particular, assume that commands can be parsed into words separated by spaces.

Because of the possibility of whitespace and other special characters in filenames, in shell scripts you should always quote the evaluation of any shell variable that might contain a filename.

What's in a Unix File?

One of the tremendous successes of Unix has been its simple view of files: Unix files are just *streams of zero or more anonymous bytes of data*.

Most other operating systems have different types of files: binary versus text data, counted-length versus fixed-length versus variable-length records, indexed versus random versus sequential access, and so on. This rapidly produces the nightmarish situation that the conceptually simple job of copying a file must be done differently depending on the file type, and since virtually all software has to deal with files, the complexity is widespread.

A Unix file-copy operation is trivial:

```
try to-get-a-byte
while (have-a-byte)
{
    put-a-byte
    try-to-get-a-byte
}
```

This sort of loop can be implemented in many programming languages, and its great beauty is that the program need not be aware of where the data is coming from: it could be from a file, or a magnetic tape device, or a pipe, or a network connection, or a kernel data structure, or any other data source that designers dream up in the future.

Ahh, you say, but I need a special file that has a trailing directory of pointers into the earlier data, and that data is itself encrypted. In Unix the answer is: Go for it! Make your application program understand your fancy file format, but don't trouble the filesystem or operating system with that complexity. They do not need to know about it.

There is, however, a mild distinction between files that Unix does admit to. Files that are created by humans usually consist of lines of text, ended by a line break, and devoid of most of the unprintable ASCII control characters. Such files can be edited, displayed on the screen, printed, sent in electronic mail, and transmitted across networks to other computing systems with considerable assurance that the integrity of the data will be maintained. Programs that expect to deal with text files, including many of the software tools that we discuss in this book, may have been designed with large, but fixed-size, buffers to hold lines of text, and they may behave unpredictably if given an input file with unexpectedly long lines, or with nonprintable characters.* A good rule of thumb in dealing with text files is to limit line lengths to something that you can read comfortably—say, 50 to 70 characters.

Text files mark line boundaries with the ASCII linefeed (LF) character, decimal value 10 in the ASCII table. This character is referred to as the newline character. Several programming languages represent this character by \n in character strings. This is simpler than the carriage-return/linefeed pair used by some other systems. The widely used C and C++ programming languages, and several others developed later, take the view that text-file lines are terminated by a single newline character; they do so because of their Unix roots.

In a mixed operating-system environment with shared filesystems, there is a frequent need to convert text files between different line-terminator conventions. The *dosmacux* package† provides a convenient suite of tools to do this, while preserving file timestamps.

All other files in Unix can be considered binary files: each of the bytes contained therein may take on any of 256 possible values. Text files are thus a subset of binary files.

Unlike some other operating systems, no character is foolishly usurped to mark end-of-file: the Unix filesystem simply keeps a count of the number of bytes in the file.

Attempts to read beyond the file byte count return an end-of-file indication, so it is not possible to see any previous contents of disk blocks.

Some operating systems forbid empty files, but Unix does not. Sometimes, it is the *existence* of a file, rather than its *contents*, that matters. Timestamps, file locks, and warnings such as THIS-PROGRAM-IS-OBSOLETE are examples of useful empty files.

The Unix files-as-byte-streams view has encouraged operating-system designers to implement file-like views of data that conventionally are not thought of as files. Several Unix flavors implement a process information pseudofilesystem: try man proc to see what your system offers. We discuss it in more detail in "The /proc Filesystem" [13.7]. Files in the /proc tree are not files on mass storage but rather, views into the

---

* See the interesting article by Barton P. Miller, Lars Fredriksen, and Bryan So, *An Empirical Study of the Reliability of UNIX Utilities*, Comm. ACM **33**(12), 32–44, December 1990, ISSN 0001-0782, and its 1995 and 2001 follow-up technical reports. Both are available, together with their associated test software, at *ftp://ftp.cs.wisc.edu/pub/paradyn/fuzz/* and *ftp://ftp.cs.wisc.edu/pub/paradyn/technical_papers/fuzz**. The 2001 work extends the testing to the various Microsoft Windows operating systems.

† Available at *http://www.math.utah.edu/pub/dosmacux/*.

---

process tables and memory space of running processes, or into information known to the operating system, such as details of the processor, network, memory, and disk systems.

For example, on one of the systems used to write this book, we can find out storage device details like this (the meaning of the slashes in the command argument is discussed in the next section):

```
$ cat /proc/scsi/scsi              Show disk device information
Attached devices:
Host: scsi0 Channel: 00 Id: 00 Lun: 00
   Vendor: IBM       Model: DMVS18V         Rev: 0077
   Type:   Direct-Access                    ANSI SCSI revision: 03
Host: scsi1 Channel: 00 Id: 01 Lun: 00
   Vendor: TOSHIBA  Model: CD-ROM XM-6401TA Rev: 1009
   Type:   CD-ROM                           ANSI SCSI revision: 02
```

The Unix Hierarchical Filesystem

Large collections of files bring the risk of filename collisions, and even with unique names, make management difficult. Unix handles this by permitting files to be grouped into *directories*: each directory forms its own little name space, independent of all other directories. Directories can also supply default attributes for files, a topic that we discuss briefly in "File Ownership and Permissions," later in this Appendix.

Filesystem Structure

Directories can be nested almost arbitrarily deep, so the Unix filesystem forms a *tree structure*. Unix avoids the synonym *folder* because paper file folders do not nest. The base of the filesystem tree is called the *root directory*, and is given a special and simple name: / (ASCII slash). The name /myfile then refers to a file named myfile in the root directory. Slash also serves another purpose: it acts as a delimiter *between* names to record directory nesting. Figure B-1 shows a tiny portion of the top-level structure of the filesystem.

Unix directories can contain arbitrary numbers of files. However, most current Unix filesystem designs, and filesystem programming interfaces, assume that directories are searched sequentially, so the time to find a file in a large directory is proportional to the number of files in that directory, even though much faster lookup schemes are known. If a directory contains more than a few hundred files, it is probably time to reorganize it into subdirectories.

The complete list of nested directories to reach a file is referred to as the *pathname*, or just the path. It may or may not include the filename itself, depending on context. How long can the complete path to a filename, including the name itself, be? Historical Unix documentation does not supply the answer, but POSIX defines the constant PATH_MAX to be that length, *including* the terminating NUL character. It requires

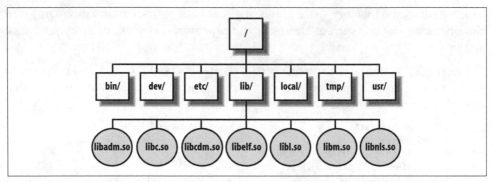

Figure B-1. Filesystem tree

a minimum value of 256, but the X/Open Portability Guide requires 1024. You can use the getconf command to find out the limit on your system. One of our systems gave this result:

```
$ getconf PATH_MAX .          What is longest pathname in current filesystem?
1023
```

Other Unix systems that we tried this on reported 1024 or 4095.

The ISO Standards for the C programming language call this value FILENAME_MAX, and require it to be defined in the standard header file stdio.h. We examined a dozen or so flavors of Unix, and found values of 255, 1024, and 4095. Hewlett-Packard HP-UX 10.20 and 11.23 have only 14, but their getconf reports 1023 and 1024.

Because Unix systems can support multiple filesystems, and filename length limits are a property of the filesystem, rather than the operating system, it really does not make sense for these limits to be defined by compile-time constants. High-level language programmers are therefore advised to use the pathconf( ) or fpathconf( ) library calls to obtain these limits: they require passing a pathname, or an open file descriptor, so that the particular filesystem can be identified. That is the reason why we passed the current directory (dot) to getconf in the previous example.

Unix directories are themselves files, albeit ones with special properties and restricted access. All Unix systems contain a top-level directory named bin that holds (often binary) executable programs, including many of the ones that we use in this book. The full pathname of this directory is /bin, and it rarely contains subdirectories.

Another universal top-level directory is usr, but it always contains other directories. The pathname of one of these is /usr/bin, which is distinct from /bin, although some magic, discussed later in this Appendix in "Filesystem Implementation Overview," can make the two bin directories look the same.*

---

* DEC/Compaq/Hewlett-Packard OSF/1 (Tru64), IBM AIX, SGI IRIX, and Sun Solaris all do this. Apple Mac OS X, BSD systems, GNU/Linux, and Hewlett-Packard HP-UX do not.

All Unix directories, even if otherwise empty, contain at least two special directories: . (dot) and .. (dot dot). The first of these refers to the directory itself: we used that earlier in the getconf example. The second refers to the parent directory: thus, in / usr/bin, .. means /usr, and ../lib/libc.a means /usr/lib/libc.a, the customary location of the C programming language runtime library.

The root directory is its own parent, so /, /.., /../.., /../../.., and so on, are equivalent.

A path that ends in a slash is of necessity a directory. If the last character is not a slash, whether the last component is a directory or some other type of file can be determined only by consulting the filesystem.

POSIX requires that consecutive slashes in a path be equivalent to a single slash. This requirement is not evident in most early Unix documentation that we consulted, but the original Version 6 source code from the mid-1970s does slash reduction.* Thus, /tmp/x, /tmp//x, and //tmp//x are the same file.

Footnotes sprinkled through this book contain World Wide Web *uniform resource locators (URLs)* whose syntax is modeled on Unix pathnames. URLs prefix a protocol† name and a hostname in the form proto://host to an absolute Unix-like pathname rooted in the host's web directory tree. Web servers are then required to map that path to whatever is appropriate for their native filesystem. The widespread use of URLs since the late 1990s in broadcast and print media has thus made the Unix pathname familiar even to people who have never used a computer.

Layered Filesystems

If slash is the root directory, and there is one in each filesystem, how does Unix support multiple filesystems without root-directory name collisions? The answer is simple: Unix permits one filesystem to be logically layered on top of an arbitrary existing directory of another filesystem. This action is called *mounting*, and the commands mount and umount, respectively, mount and unmount filesystems.

When another filesystem is mounted on top of a directory, any previous contents of that directory become invisible and inaccessible; they are exposed again when the unmount is done.

Filesystem mounting gives the illusion of a single filesystem tree that can grow without limit, simply by adding more, or larger, storage devices. The regular file-naming convention /a/b/c/d/… means that human users, and software, are completely

---

* See John Lions' book, *Lions' Commentary on UNIX 6th Edition, with Source Code*, Peer-to-Peer Communications, 1996, ISBN 1-57398-013-7. The reduction happens at kernel line 7535 (sheet 75), with the commentary on p. 19-2. "Multiple slashes are acceptable." If the code had used if instead of while, this reduction would not happen!

† The protocol is called a *scheme* in standards documents, but both terms are in wide use.

isolated from the irrelevant notion of devices, unlike several other operating systems that embed the device name in the pathname.

A fair amount of information is needed to complete a mount command, so a system manager stores the details in a special file, usually called /etc/fstab or /etc/vfstab, depending on the Unix flavor. As with most Unix configuration files, it is an ordinary text file, and its format is documented in the manual pages for *fstab*(4 or 5) or *vfstab*(4).

When shared magnetic disks were the only filesystem media available, mounting and unmounting required special privileges—normally those accorded only to system management. However, with user-owned media such as floppy disks, CD-ROMs, and DVDs, ordinary users with desktop computers need to be able to do this themselves. Many Unix systems have now been extended so that certain devices can be flagged as permitting mounts and unmounts by unprivileged users. Here are some examples from a GNU/Linux system:

```
$ grep owner /etc/fstab | sort        Which devices allow user mounts?
/dev/cdrom     /mnt/cdrom     iso9660 noauto,owner,kudzu,ro 0 0
/dev/fd0       /mnt/floppy    auto    noauto,owner,kudzu 0 0
/dev/sdb4      /mnt/zip100.0  auto    noauto,owner,kudzu 0 0
```

These make the CD-ROM, floppy disk, and Iomega Zip disk available for user mounts, which might be done like this:

```
mount /mnt/cdrom              Make the CD-ROM available
cd /mnt/cdrom                 Change to its top-level directory
ls                            List its files
...
cd                            Change to home directory
umount /mnt/cdrom             Release the CD-ROM
```

The mount command issued without arguments requires no special privileges: it simply reports all of the currently mounted filesystems. Here is an example from a standalone web server:

```
$ mount | sort               Show sorted list of mounted filesystems
/dev/sda2 on /boot type ext3 (rw)
/dev/sda3 on /export type ext3 (rw)
/dev/sda5 on / type ext3 (rw)
/dev/sda6 on /ww type ext3 (rw)
/dev/sda8 on /tmp type ext3 (rw)
/dev/sda9 on /var type ext3 (rw)
none on /dev/pts type devpts (rw,gid=5,mode=620)
none on /dev/shm type tmpfs (rw)
none on /nue/proc type proc (rw)
none on /proc/sys/fs/binfmt_misc type binfmt_misc (rw)
none on /proc type proc (rw)
```

This shows, for example, that the root filesystem is mounted on disk device /dev/sda5. Other filesystems are mounted over /boot, /export, and so on.

A system manager could unmount the /ww tree by issuing the command:

```
# umount /ww                        Here, # is the root prompt
```

The command would fail if any files in the /ww subtree were still in use. The list-open-files command, lsof,* can be used to track down processes that are preventing the unmount.

Filesystem Implementation Overview

The details of how filesystems are implemented are interesting, but are quite complex and beyond the needs of this book; for examples, see the excellent books *The Design and Implementation of the 4.4BSD Operating System*† and *UNIX Internals: The New Frontiers*.‡

There is one aspect of the filesystem implementation that is useful to know about at a higher level, however, because it is responsible for several user-visible aspects of Unix filesystems. When a filesystem is created, a table of manager-specified fixed size§ is created on disk to hold information about the files in the filesystem. Each file is associated with one entry in this table, and each entry is a filesystem data structure called an *inode* (a contraction of *index node*, and pronounced *eye node*). The contents of inodes depend on the particular filesystem design, so a single system might have different flavors. Programmers are isolated from these differences by the stat( ) and fstat( ) system calls (see the manual pages for *stat*(2)). The command man inode may reveal information about the actual structure on your system.

Since the inode structure, and other low-level details of storage devices, are system-dependent, it is generally not possible to mount a disk containing a Unix filesystem from one vendor on a system from another vendor. However, through a software layer called the *Network File System (NFS)*, across networks it is virtually always possible to share Unix filesystems between computers from different vendors.

Because the inode table has a fixed size, it is possible for a filesystem to fill up even when there is plenty of free space on the storage device: there is room for the file's data, but not for its *metadata* (data about the data).

As shown in Figure B-2, the inode entry contains everything that the system needs to know about the file, except for one thing: its filename. This might seem surprising, and indeed, several other operating systems with a similar filesystem design do include the filename in their analogues of inodes.

---

* Available at *ftp://vic.cc.purdue.edu/pub/tools/unix/lsof/*. Alternative commands available in some Unix flavors are fstat and fuser.

† By Marshall Kirk McKusick, Keith Bostic, Michael J. Karels, and John S. Quarterman, Addison-Wesley, 1996, ISBN 0-201-54979-4.

‡ By Uresh Vahalia, Prentice-Hall, 1996, ISBN 0-13-101908-2.

§ Some advanced filesystem designs permit that table to grow as needed.

Number	Type	Mode	Links	Byte count	User ID	Group ID	Disk address	Attributes
0	...	...	...	...	...	...	...	...
1	...	...	...	...	...	...	...	...
2	...	...	...	...	...	...	...	...
3	...	...	...	...	...	...	...	...
...	...	...	...	...	...	...	...	...

Figure B-2. Inode table contents

In Unix, the filename is stored in the directory, together with its inode number, and not much else, as illustrated in Figure B-3. Early Unix systems on the small computers of the 1970s allocated only 16 bytes in a directory for each file: 2 bytes gave the inode number (limiting the number of files to $2^{16} = 65,536$), and 14 bytes gave the filename, only marginally better than the 8+3 limit of some other systems.

i-Node number	Filename
2155329	.
737046	..
1294503	ch04.xml
2241988	README
3974649	Makefile
720277	ch04.ps
2945369	CVS
523023	CH-AA-SHELL-EXTENSIONS.txt
351882	ch04.xml.~1~
...etc...	...etc...

Figure B-3. Directory table contents

Modern Unix filesystems allow longer filename lengths, although there is typically a maximum length, as we showed earlier in this Appendix with the getconf example in "Filesystem Structure."

Directories can be read, but not written, by their owners, and some early Unix software opened and read directories to find filenames. When a more complex directory design was introduced in the 1980s, the opendir( ), readdir( ), and closedir( ) library calls were created to hide the structure from programmers, and those calls are now part of POSIX (see the manual pages for *opendir*(3)). To enforce library access, some current Unix implementations prohibit read operations on directory files.

Why is the filename separated from the rest of the file metadata in Unix? There are at least two good reasons:

- Users commonly list the contents of directories simply to remind themselves of what files are available. If filenames were stored in inodes, finding each filename in the directory might take one or more disk accesses. By storing the names in the directory file, many names can be retrieved from a single disk block.

- If the filename is separate from the inode, then it is possible to have multiple filenames for the same physical file, simply by having different directory entries reference the same inode. Those references need not even be in the same directory! This notion of file aliases, called *links* in Unix, is extremely convenient, and is widely used. On six different flavors of Unix, we found that 10 percent to 30 percent of the files under /usr were links.

A useful consequence of the Unix filesystem design is that renaming a file or directory, or moving it *within* the same physical Unix filesystem, is fast: only the name needs to be changed or moved, not the contents. Moving a file *between* filesystems, however, does require reading and writing all of the file's blocks.

If files can have multiple names, what does it mean to delete a file? Should all of them disappear at once, or should only one of them be removed? Both choices have been made by designers of filesystems that support aliases or links; Unix made the second choice. The Unix inode entry contains a count of the number of links to the file contents. File deletion causes the link count to be decremented, but only when it reaches zero are the file blocks finally reassigned to the list of free space.

Since the directory entry contains just an inode number, it can refer only to files within the same physical filesystem. We've already seen that Unix filesystems usually contain multiple mount points, so how can we make a link from one filesystem to another? The solution is a different kind of link, called a *soft link*, or *symbolic link*, or just *symlink*, to distinguish it from the first kind, called a *hard link*. A symbolic link is represented by a *directory entry that points to another directory entry,*[*] rather than to an inode entry. The pointed-to entry is given by its normal Unix pathname, and thus, may point anywhere in the filesystem, even across mount points.

Symbolic links make it possible to create infinite loops in the filesystem, so to prevent that, a chain of symbolic links is followed for only a few (typically, eight) steps. Here is what happens with a two-element loop:

```
$ ls -1                              Show the link loop
total 0
lrwxrwxrwx    1 jones    devel       3 2002-09-26 08:44 one -> two
lrwxrwxrwx    1 jones    devel       3 2002-09-26 08:44 two -> one
```

---

[*] The file type in the inode records that the file is a symbolic link, and in most filesystem designs, the name of the file that it points to is stored in the symbolic link's data block.

```
$ file one                          What is file one?
one: broken symbolic link to two
$ file two                          What is file two?
two: broken symbolic link to one
$ cat one                           Try to display file one
cat: one: Too many levels of symbolic links
```

For technical reasons (among them, the possibility of loops), directories normally cannot have hard links, but they *can* have symbolic links. The exceptions to this rule are the dot and dot-dot directory entries, which are created automatically when a directory is created.

Devices as Unix Files

One of the advances over earlier systems that Unix made was to extend the file notion to attached devices. All Unix systems have a top-level directory named /dev, underneath which are oddly named files like /dev/audio, /dev/sda1, and /dev/tty03. These device files are handled by special software modules, called *device drivers*, that know how to communicate with particular external devices. Although device names tend to be highly system-dependent, collectively they provide a convenient open-process-close access model similar to normal files.

The integration of devices into the hierarchical file system was the best idea in Unix.
— Rob Pike et al., *The Use of Name Spaces in Plan 9*, 1992.

Entries in the /dev tree are created by a special tool, mknod, often hidden inside a shell script, MAKEDEV, and invariably requiring system-manager privileges to run: see the manual pages for *mknod*(1) and *MAKEDEV*(8).

Most Unix users only rarely refer to members of the /dev tree, with the exception of /dev/null and /dev/tty, which we described in "Special files: /dev/null and /dev/tty" [2.5.5.2].

In the 1990s, several Unix flavors introduced a random pseudodevice, /dev/urandom, that serves as a never-empty stream of random bytes. Such a data source is needed in many cryptographic and security applications. We showed in Chapter 10 how /dev/urandom can be used to construct hard-to-guess temporary filenames.

How Big Can Unix Files Be?

The size of Unix files is normally constrained by two hard limits: the number of bits allocated in the inode entry to hold the file size in bytes, and the size of the filesystem itself. In addition, some Unix kernels have manager-settable limits on file sizes. The data structure used on most Unix filesystems to record the list of data blocks in a file imposes a limit of about 16.8 million blocks, where the block size is typically

Files Without Names

A peculiarity of the Unix operating system is that the names of files that are opened for input or output are not retained in kernel data structures. Thus, the names of files that are redirected on the command line for standard input, standard output, or standard error are unknown to the invoked process. Think of it: we have a filesystem that might contain millions of files, yet exactly three of them cannot be named! To partially remedy this deficiency, some recent Unix systems provide the names /dev/stdin, /dev/stdout, and /dev/stderr, or sometimes less mnemonically, /dev/fd/0, /dev/fd/1, and /dev/fd/2. On GNU/Linux and Sun Solaris, they are also available as /proc/*PID*/fd/0, and so on. Here is how to see whether your system supports them; you'll get either a successful run like this:

```
$ echo Hello, world > /dev/stdout
Hello, world
```

or a failure like this:

```
$ echo Hello, world > /dev/stdout
/dev/stdout: Permission denied.
```

Many Unix programs found the need for names for these redirected files, so a common convention is that a hyphen as a filename does not mean a file of that name, but rather, standard input or standard output, depending on context. We emphasize that this is merely a *convention*, and not universally implemented by Unix software. If you are stuck with such a file, just disguise its name with a directory prefix; e.g., ./--data. Some programs follow the convention (described in "Commands and Arguments" [2.5.1]) that a double hyphen option, --, means that everything that follows on the command line is a file, and not an option, but that practice is not universal either.

1024 to 65,536 bytes, settable, and fixed at filesystem-creation time. Finally, the capacity of filesystem backup devices may impose further site-dependent limits.

Most current Unix filesystems use a 32-bit integer to hold the file size, and because the file-positioning system calls can move forward or backward in the file, that integer must be signed. Thus, the largest-possible file is $2^{31} - 1$ bytes, or about 2GB.[*] Until about the early 1990s, most disks were smaller than that size, but disks containing 100GB or more became available by about 2000, and by combining multiple physical disks into a single logical disk, much larger filesystems are now feasible.

Unix vendors are gradually migrating to filesystems with 64-bit size fields, potentially supporting about 8 billion gigabytes. Just in case you think that might not be enough in the near future, consider that writing such a file once at the currently reasonable rate of 10MB/s would take more than 27,800 years! This migration is

---

[*] GB = gigabyte, approximately 1 billion (one thousand million) bytes. Despite the metric prefix, in computer use G usually means $2^{30} = 1,073,741,824$.

decidedly nontrivial because all existing software that uses random-access file-positioning system calls must be updated. To avoid the need for massive upgrades, most vendors allow the old 32-bit sizes to be used in newer systems, which works as long as the 2GB limit is not reached.

When a Unix filesystem is created, for performance reasons a certain fraction of the space, often 10 percent or so, is reserved for use by processes running as root. The filesystem itself requires space for the inode table, and in addition there may be special low-level blocks that are accessible only by the disk-controller hardware. Thus, the effective capacity of a disk is often only about 80 percent of the size quoted by the disk vendor.

Commands exist on some systems to decrease the reserved space: doing so may be advisable on large disks. Look at the manual pages for *tunefs*(8) on BSD and commercial Unix systems, and *tune2fs*(8) on GNU/Linux systems.

The ulimit built-in shell command controls system resource limits. The -a option prints the value of all resources. On our systems, we get this result concerning file sizes:

```
$ ulimit -a                          Show the current user process limits
...
file size (blocks)        unlimited
...
```

Your system might be different because of local management policies.

At some Unix sites, disk quotas are enabled (see the manual pages for *quota*(1) for details), putting further limits on the total amount of filesystem space that a single user can occupy.

Unix File Attributes

Earlier in this Appendix, in "Filesystem Implementation Overview," we described the Unix filesystem implementation, and said that the inode entries contain *metadata*: information about the file, apart from its name. It is now time to discuss some of these attributes because they can be highly relevant to users of the filesystem.

File Ownership and Permissions

Perhaps the biggest difference from single-user personal-computer filesystems is that Unix files have *ownership* and *permissions*.

Ownership

On many personal computers, any process or user can read or overwrite any file, and the term computer virus is now familiar to readers of almost any daily newspaper, even if those readers have never used a computer themselves. Because Unix users have restricted access to the filesystem, it is much harder to replace or destroy critical filesystem components: viruses are seldom a problem on Unix systems.

Unix files have two kinds of ownership: *user* and *group*, each with its own permissions. Normally, the owner of a file should have full access to it, whereas members of a work group to which the owner belongs might have limited access, and everyone else, even less access. This last category is called *other* in Unix documentation. File ownership is shown by the verbose forms of the ls command.

New files normally inherit owner and group membership from their creator, but with suitable permissions usually given only to system managers, the chown and chgrp commands can be used to change those attributes.

In the inode entry, the user and group are identified by numbers, not names. Since humans generally prefer names, system managers provide mapping tables, historically called the password file, /etc/passwd, and the group file, /etc/group. At large sites, these files are generally replaced by some sort of network-distributed database. These files, or databases, are readable by any logged-in user, although the preferred access is now via library calls to setpwent( ), getpwent( ), and endpwent( ) for the password database, and setgrent( ), getgrent( ), and endgrent( ) for the group database: see the manual pages for *getpwent*(3) and *getgrent*(3). If your site uses databases instead of files in /etc, try the shell command ypcat passwd to examine the password database, or ypmatch jones passwd to find just the entry for user jones. If your site uses NIS+ instead of NIS, the yp commands become niscat passwd.org_dir and nismatch name=jones passwd.org_dir.

The important point is that it is the *numeric values* of the user and group identifiers that control access. If a filesystem with user smith attached to user ID 100 were mounted on, or imported to, a filesystem with user ID 100 assigned to user jones, then jones would have full access to smith's files. This would be true even if another user named smith exists on the target system. Such considerations can become important as large organizations move toward globally accessible Unix filesystems: it becomes essential to have organization-wide agreement on the assignment of user and group identifiers. This is not as simple as it appears: not only are there turf wars, but there are severe limitations on the number of distinct user and group identifiers. Older Unix systems allocated only 16 bits for each, giving a total of $2^{16} = 65,536$ values. Newer Unix systems allow 32-bit identifiers, but unfortunately, many of them impose additional Draconian restrictions that sharply limit the number of identifiers to many fewer than the hundreds of thousands to millions required by large organizations.

Permissions

Unix filesystem permissions are of three types: *read*, *write*, and *execute*. Each requires only a single bit in the inode data structure, indicating the presence or absence of the permission. There is one such set for each of user, group, and other.

File permissions are shown with the verbose forms of the ls command, and are changed with the chmod command. Because each set of permissions requires only three bits, it can be represented by a single *octal* digit, and the chmod command accepts either a three or four-octal-digit argument, or a symbolic form.

---

chmod

Usage

    chmod [*options*] *mode file(s)*

Major options

    −f

        Force changes if possible (and don't complain if they fail).

    −R

        Apply changes recursively through directories.

Purpose

    Change file or directory permissions.

Behavior

    The mandatory *mode* argument is either an absolute permission mask of three or four octal digits, or a symbolic one with one or more letters a (all, same as ugo), g (group), o (other),or u (user), followed by = (set), + (add), or - (subtract), followed by one or more of r (read), w (write), or x (execute). Multiple symbolic settings may be given, provided that they are separated by commas. Thus, modes of 755 and u=rwx,go=rx and a=rx,u+w and a=rwx,go-w are equivalent.

Caveats

    The recursive form is dangerous: use it with extreme caution! It may take a file-tree restore from backup media to recover from a mistaken application of chmod -R.

Some operating systems support additional permissions. One useful permission that Unix does *not* supply is append permission:[†] it is particularly handy for log files, to ensure that data can only be added to them, but existing data can never be altered. Of course, if such a file can be deleted, it could be replaced by a copy with altered data, so append permission may only give the illusion of security.

---

* Just in case octal (base-8) and binary (base-2) number systems are unfamiliar to you, octal notation with digits 0–7 is simply a convenient way of writing the binary values 000_2, 001_2, 010_2, 011_2, 100_2, 101_2, 110_2, and 111_2. Think of an automobile odometer with only two digits on each wheel, instead of ten.

† BSD systems are an exception: they provide the *sappnd* and *uappnd* flags, settable with chflags.

Default permissions

A set of default permissions is always applied to newly created files: they are controlled by the umask command, which sets the default when given an argument, and otherwise shows the default. The umask value is three octal digits that represent permissions to be *taken away*: a common value is 077, which says that the user is given all permissions (read, write, execute), and group and other have them all taken away. The result is that access to newly created files is restricted to just the user who owns them.

It is now time for some experiments with file permissions:

```
$ umask                                     Show the current permission mask
2
$ touch foo                                 Create an empty file
$ ls -l foo                                 List information about the file
-rw-rw-r--    1 jones    devel     0 2002-09-21 16:16 foo
$ rm foo                                    Delete the file
$ ls -l foo                                 List information about the file again
ls: foo: No such file or directory
```

Initially, the permission mask is 2 (really 002), meaning that write permission should be removed for other. The touch command simply updates the last-write timestamp of a file, creating it if necessary. The ls -l command is a common idiom for asking for a verbose file listing. It reports a *file type* of - (ordinary file), and a permission string of rw-rw-r-- (that is, read-write permission for user and group, and read permission for other).

When we re-create the file after changing the mask to 023, to remove write access from the group and write and execute access from other, we see that the permission string is reported as rw-r--r--, with write permissions for group and other removed as expected:

```
$ umask 023                                 Reset the permission mask
$ touch foo                                 Create an empty file
$ ls -l foo                                 List information about the file
-rw-r--r--    1 jones    devel     0 2002-09-21 16:16 foo
```

Permissions in action

What about the execute permission? Files don't normally have that permission, unless they are intended to be executable programs or scripts. Linkers automatically add execute permission to such programs, but for scripts, you have to use chmod yourself.

When we copy a file that already has execute permissions—e.g., /bin/pwd—the permissions are preserved, unless the umask value causes them to be taken away:

```
$ umask                                     Show the current permission mask
023
$ rm -f foo                                 Delete any existing file
$ cp /bin/pwd foo                           Make a copy of a system command
```

```
$ ls -l /bin/pwd foo                          List information about the files
-rwxr-xr-x    1 root     root    10428 2001-07-23 10:23 /bin/pwd
-rwxr-xr--    1 jones    devel   10428 2002-09-21 16:37 foo
```

The resulting permission string `rwxr-xr--` reflects the loss of privileges: group lost write access, and other lost both write and execute access.

Finally, we use the symbolic form of an argument to `chmod` to add execute permission for all:

```
$ chmod a+x foo                               Add execute permission for all
$ ls -l foo                                   List verbose file information
-rwxr-xr-x    1 jones    devel   10428 2002-09-21 16:37 foo
```

The resulting permission string is then `rwxr-xr-x`, so user, group, and other have execute access. Notice that the permission mask did not affect the `chmod` operation: the mask is relevant only at file-creation time. The copied file behaves exactly like the original `pwd` command:

```
$ /bin/pwd                                    Try the system version
/tmp
$ pwd                                         And the shell built-in version
/tmp
$ ./foo                                       And our copy of the system version
/tmp
$ file foo /bin/pwd                           Ask for information about these files
foo:     ELF 32-bit LSB executable, Intel 80386, version 1,
         dynamically linked (uses shared libs), stripped
/bin/pwd: ELF 32-bit LSB executable, Intel 80386, version 1,
         dynamically linked (uses shared libs), stripped
```

Notice that we invoked `foo` with a directory prefix: for security reasons, it is *never* a good idea to include the current directory in the PATH list. If you must have it there, at least put it last!

If you try this experiment yourself, you might get a permission-denied response when you try to run commands in the /tmp directory. On systems that provide the capability, such as GNU/Linux, system managers sometimes mount that directory without execute permission anywhere in its file tree; check for the noexec option in /etc/fstab. One reason for that option to be used is that it prevents Trojan horse scripts (see Chapter 15) in a publicly writable directory like /tmp. You can still execute them by feeding them into the shell, but then you presumably know why you are doing so.

Here is what happens if you remove the execute permission, and then try to run the program:

```
$ chmod a-x foo                               Remove execute permission for all
$ ls -l foo                                   List verbose file information
-rw-r--r--    1 jones    devel   10428 2002-09-21 16:37 foo
$ ./foo                                       Try to run the program
bash: ./foo: Permission denied
```

That is, it is not the *ability* of a file to function as an executable program, but rather, its *possession of execute permission* that determines whether it can be run as a command. This is an important safety feature in Unix.

Here is what happens when you give execute permission to a file that doesn't deserve it:

```
$ umask 002                        Remove default for world write permission
$ rm -f foo                        Delete any existing file
$ echo 'Hello, world' > foo        Create a one-line file
$ chmod a+x foo                    Make it executable
$ ls -l foo                        Show our changes
-rwxrwxr-x   1 jones    devel      13 2002-09-21 16:51 foo
$ ./foo                            Try to run the program
./foo: line 1: Hello,: command not found
$ echo $?                          Display the exit status code
127
```

What happened was that the shell asked the kernel to execute ./foo, and got a failure report back, with the library error indicator set to ENOEXEC. The shell then tried to process the file itself. In the command line Hello, world, it interpreted Hello, as the name of a command to run, and world as its argument. No command by that peculiar name was found in the search path, so the shell reported that conclusion in an error message, and returned an exit status code of 127 (see "Exit Statuses" [6.2], for more on exit statuses).

When permissions are checked, the order is user, then group, then other. The first of these to which the process belongs determines which set of permission bits is used. Thus, it is possible to have a file that belongs to you, but which you cannot read, even though fellow group members, and everyone else on your system, can. Here's an example:

```
$ echo 'This is a secret' > top-secret   Create one-line file
$ chmod 044 top-secret                    Remove all but read for group and other
$ ls -l                                   Show our changes
----r--r--   1 jones    devel      17 2002-10-11 14:59 top-secret
$ cat top-secret                          Try to display file
cat: top-secret: Permission denied
$ chmod u+r top-secret                    Allow owner to read file
$ ls -l                                   Show our changes
-r--r--r--   1 jones    devel      17 2002-10-11 14:59 top-secret
$ cat top-secret                          This time, display works!
This is a secret
```

All Unix filesystems contain additional permission bits, called *set-user-ID*, *set-group-ID*, and *sticky* bits. For compatibility with older systems, and to avoid increasing the already large line length, ls does not show these permissions with three extra permission characters, but instead, changes the letter x to other letters. For the details, see the *chmod*(1), *chmod*(2), and *ls*(1) manual pages. For security reasons, shell scripts should *never* have the set-user-ID or set-group-ID permission bits set: an astonishing number of subtle security holes have been found in such scripts. We cover these permission bits and shell-script security in Chapter 15.

Execute-only permission (--x--x--x) is sometimes used for commercial software to discourage copying, debugging, and tracing, but still allow the programs to be run.

Directory permissions

So far, we have discussed permissions only of ordinary files. For directories, the permissions are given slightly different meaning. Read access for a directory means that you can list its contents with, for example, ls. Write access means that you can create or delete files in the directory, even though you cannot write the directory file yourself: that privilege is reserved for the operating system in order to preserve filesystem integrity. Execute access means that you can access files and subdirectories in the directory (subject, of course, to their own permissions); in particular, you can follow a pathname through that directory.

Since the distinction between execute and read access on a directory is subtle, here is an experiment to clarify things:

```
$ umask                          Show the current permission mask
22

$ mkdir test                     Create a subdirectory
$ ls -Fld test                   Show the directory permissions
drwxr-xr-x  2 jones devel 512 Jul 31 13:34 test/

$ touch test/the-file            Create an empty file there
$ ls -l test                     List the directory contents verbosely
-rw-r--r--  1 jones devel 0 Jul 31 13:34 test/the-file
```

So far, this is just normal behavior. Now remove read access, but leave execute access:

```
$ chmod a-r test                 Remove directory read access for all
$ ls -lFd test                   Show the directory permissions
d-wx--x--x  2 jones devel 512 Jan 31 16:39 test/

$ ls -l test                     Try to list the directory contents verbosely
ls: test: Permission denied

$ ls -l test/the-file            List the file itself
-rw-r--r--  1 jones devel 0 Jul 31 13:34 test/the-file
```

The second ls failed because of the lack of read permission, but execute permission allowed the third ls to succeed. In particular, this shows that removing read permission from a directory cannot prevent access to a file contained therein, if its filename is already known.

Here is what happens when we remove execute access, without restoring read access:

```
$ chmod a-x test                    Remove directory execute access for all
$ ls -lFd test                      List the directory
d-w-------  3 jones devel 512 Jul 31 13:34 test/

$ ls -l test                        Try to list the directory contents verbosely
ls: test: Permission denied

$ ls -l test/the-file               Try to list the file
ls: test/the-file: Permission denied

$ cd test                           Try to change to the directory
test: Permission denied.
```

The directory tree has been effectively cut off from view by any user, *except* root.

Finally, restore read access, but not execute access, and repeat the experiment:

```
$ chmod a+r test                    Add directory read access for all
$ ls -lFd test                      Show the directory permissions
drw-r--r--  2 jones devel 512 Jul 31 13:34 test/

$ ls -l test                        Try to list the directory contents
ls: test/the-file: Permission denied
total 0

$ ls -l test/the-file               Try to list the file
ls: test/the-file: Permission denied

$ cd test                           Try to change to the directory
test: Permission denied.
```

Lack of execute access on the directory has blocked attempts to see its contents, or to make it the current working directory.

When the sticky bit is set on a directory, files contained therein can be removed only by their owner, or by the owner of the directory. This feature is often used for publicly writable directories—notably, /tmp, /var/tmp (formerly called /usr/tmp), and incoming mail directories—to prevent users from deleting files that do not belong to them.

On some systems, when the set-group-ID bit is set on a directory, the group ID of newly created files is set to the group of the directory, rather than to the group of their owner. Regrettably, this permission bit is not handled the same on all systems. On some, its behavior depends on how the filesystem is mounted, so you should check the manual pages for the mount command for the details on your system. The set-group-ID bit is useful when several users share write access to a directory for a collaborative project. They are then given membership in a special group created for that project, and the group of the project directory is set to that group.

Some systems use a combination of the set-group-ID bit being set and the group-execute bit being clear to request mandatory locking, a messy topic that we do not treat in this book.

Directory Read and Execute Permissions

Why is there a distinction between reading the directory, and passing through it to a subdirectory? The answer is simple: it makes it possible for a file subtree to be visible even though its parent directories are not. A common example today is a user's web tree. The home directory might typically have permissions rwx--x--x to prevent group and other from listing its contents, or examining its files, but the web tree starting at, say, $HOME/public_html, including its subdirectories, would be given access rwxr-xr-x, and files within it would have at least rw-r--r-- permissions.

As another example, suppose that, for security reasons, a system manager wants to read-protect an entire file subtree that was not previously protected. All that needs to be done is to remove read and execute access for the *single directory* at the root of the subtree, with chmod a-rx *dirname*: all files below that point become instantly inaccessible to new open attempts (already-open files are not affected), even though their individual permissions might otherwise allow access.

Some Unix systems support a feature called *access control lists* (ACLs). These provide finer control of access permissions so that specific users or groups can be assigned nondefault permissions. Unfortunately, the tools for setting and displaying ACLs vary widely between systems, making ACLs of little use in heterogeneous environments, and too messy for further discussion in this book. If you want to learn more about them, try man -k acl or man -k 'access control list' to identify the relevant commands on your system.

File Timestamps

The inode entry for a Unix file contains three important timestamps: access time, inode-change time, and modification time. These times are normally measured in seconds since the *epoch*,[*] which for Unix systems is 00:00:00 UTC, January 1, 1970, although some Unix implementations offer finer timer granularity. Measuring in *UTC*[†] (*Coordinated Universal Time*, formerly Greenwich Mean Time, GMT) means that the timestamps are independent of the local time zone.

The access time is updated by several system calls, including those that read and write files.

---

[*] **epoch**, ep'ok, *n*. A fixed point of time from which succeeding years are numbered [*The New Webster Encyclopedic Dictionary of the English Language*].

[†] In the interests of committee harmony, UTC is a language-independent acronym; the French expansion is Temps Universel Coordonné. See *http://www.npl.co.uk/time/time_scales.html*, *http://aa.usno.navy.mil/faq/docs/UT.html*, and *http://www.boulder.nist.gov/timefreq/general/misc.htm* for some interesting history of time standards.

The inode-change time is set when the file is created, and when the inode metadata is modified.

The modification time is changed when the file blocks are altered, but not when the metadata (filename, user, group, link count, or permissions) are changed.

The touch command, or the utime( ) system call, can be used to change file access and modification times, but *not* the inode-change time. Recent GNU versions of touch provide an option to specify the time as that of a particular file. The ls -l command shows the modification time, but with the -c option displays the inode-change time, and with the -u option, the access time.

These timestamps are not optimal. The inode-change time serves two quite distinct purposes which should have been recorded separately. Consequently, it is impossible to tell when a file first came into existence in a Unix filesystem.

The access time is updated when the file is read with a read( ) system call, but might not be when the file is mapped into memory with mmap( ) and read that way.

The modification time is somewhat more reliable, but the file-copy command normally resets the output-file modification time to the current time, even though its contents were not changed; this is usually undesirable. For this reason, the copy command, cp, has a -p option for preserving file-modification times.

There is no time of last backup recorded: this means that the backup system must retain auxiliary data to track names of files that have been modified since the last incremental dump.

 Filesystem backup software is carefully written to preserve the timestamps of the files that it reads: otherwise, all files would appear to be newly read after every backup. Systems that use archive utilities, like tar, for backup update the inode-change time by necessity, making that timestamp effectively useless for other purposes.

For some purposes, one would like to have separate timestamps for read, write, renaming, change of metadata, and so on, but those distinctions are not possible in Unix.

File Links

Despite the considerable utility of the hard and soft (symbolic) filesystem links that we discussed earlier in this Appendix in "Filesystem Implementation Overview," they have been criticized on the grounds that multiple names for the same thing serve only to confuse users, since links create connections between previously isolated branches of the file tree. Moving a subtree that contains soft links can break those links, producing a filesystem inconsistency that did not exist before the move. Figure B-4 shows how a soft link can be broken by a move, and Figure B-5 shows how such a link can be preserved, depending on whether relative or absolute paths are used in the links.

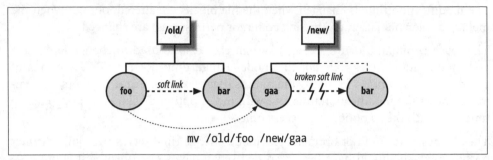

Figure B-4. Breaking relative symbolic links with moves

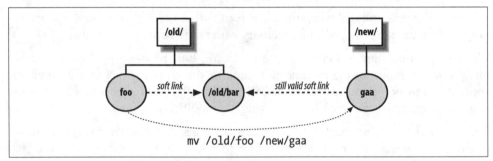

Figure B-5. Moves can preserve absolute symbolic links

There are several other problems with both hard and soft links:

- When a linked file is updated, either by replacement with a file-copy command or by a program, such as a text editor, is a hard link preserved? It depends on how the update is done. If the existing file is opened for output and rewritten, its inode number remains unchanged, and hard links are preserved. However, a system crash, or a disk-full error, during the update might result in the loss of the entire file. A cautious programmer might therefore write the new version under a temporary name, and only when the copy was safely completed would he remove the original (thus decrementing its link count by one) and rename the copy. The renaming operation is comparatively fast, so the window for failure is much smaller. The replacement file will have a new inode number and a link count of one, breaking hard links.

  We tested several text editors, and found that all seemed to use the first approach, preserving hard links. The emacs editor allows a choice of either behavior.* In contrast, if you edit or rewrite a file that is a soft link, then you are

---

* Set the variable backup-by-copying-when-linked to non-nil, and the variable backup-by-copying to nil, to preserve hard links. See the section *Copying versus Renaming* in the emacs manual.

modifying the original data, and as long as its pathname remains unchanged, all other soft links that point to it reflect the updated contents.

For hard links, the two update methods can also result in the new file having a different owner and group: update-in-place preserves owner and group, whereas copy-and-rename sets them to values for the user who performed that action. Thus, the behavior of the two kinds of links is often inconsistent after file modification.

- Consider symbolic links for directories: if you have a symbolic link from subdir to /home/jones/somedir, then that link will almost certainly be broken when you move the file tree to another filesystem where /home/jones/somedir does not exist.

- It is generally better to use relative paths in the link, and then only to directories at the same level, or below: a symbolic link from subdir to ../anotherdir is preserved if a file tree beginning at least one directory higher in the tree is moved. Otherwise, the link is broken.

- Broken symbolic links are not diagnosed at the time of the break, but are only discovered later when such a link is referenced: it may then be too late to do anything about the break. This is the same problem with personal address books: your friends can move without informing you, breaking your link to them. The find command can be used to find broken links, as shown in Chapter 10.

- Symbolic links to directories pose a problem for relative directory changes as well: changing to the parent directory of a symbolic link moves to the parent directory of the pointed-to directory, rather than to the parent of the link itself.

- Symbolic links are a problem when file archives are created: sometimes the links should be preserved, and other times, the archive should simply include a copy of the file itself in place of the link.

File Size and Timestamp Variations

The inode entry for each file includes its size in bytes, which can be zero if the file is empty. The long form of ls output displays the size in the fifth column:

```
$ ls -l /bin/ksh                          List verbose file information
-rwxr-xr-x   1 root     root    172316 2001-06-24 21:12 /bin/ksh
```

GNU versions of ls provide the -S option to sort the listing by descending file size:

```
$ ls -lS /bin | head -n 8                 Show the 8 largest, in order of descending size
total 7120
-rwxr-xr-x   1 rpm      rpm    1737960 2002-02-15 08:31 rpm
-rwxr-xr-x   1 root     root    519964 2001-07-09 06:56 bash
-rwxr-xr-x   1 root     root    472492 2001-06-24 20:08 ash.static
-rwxr-xr-x   2 root     root    404604 2001-07-30 12:46 zsh
-rwxr-xr-x   2 root     root    404604 2001-07-30 12:46 zsh-4.0.2
-rwxr-xr-x   1 root     root    387820 2002-01-28 04:10 vi
-rwxr-xr-x   1 root     root    288604 2001-06-24 21:45 tcsh
```

The -S option can be handy when you fill up a filesystem and you want to find which files are possible culprits. Of course, if your ls lacks that option, just use ls -l *files* | sort -k5nr to get the same result.

If you suspect that a currently running process has filled up the filesystem, on Sun Solaris you can find big open files like this (as root, if you want to see more than your own files):

```
# ls -lS /proc/*/fd/*                      List all open files
-rw------- 1 jones jones 111679057 Jan 29 17:23 /proc/2965/fd/4
-r--r--r-- 1 smith smith  946643 Dec  2 03:25 /proc/15993/fd/16
-r--r--r-- 1 smith smith  835284 Dec  2 03:32 /proc/15993/fd/9
...
```

In this example, killing process 2965 *might* remove that large file, but at least you know that jones is involved.

GNU/Linux has a similar /proc facility, but alas, the Solaris solution doesn't work because the reported file sizes on GNU/Linux are incorrect.

The disk-free command, df, reports the current disk usage, or with the -i option, the inode usage. The disk-usage command, du, can report the total space used for the contents of individual directories, or with the -s option, a compact summary. Examples are given in Chapter 10. The find command with the -mtime and -size options can find files that have been created recently, or are unusually large: see Chapter 10.

The -s option to ls shows an additional leading column that gives the file size in blocks:

```
$ ls -lgs /lib/lib* | head -n 4      List verbose file information for first four matching files
2220 -r-xr-xr-t  1 sys 2270300 Nov  4 1999 /lib/libc.so.1
  60 -r--r--r--  1 sys   59348 Nov  4 1999 /lib/libcpr.so
 108 -r--r--r--  1 sys  107676 Nov  4 1999 /lib/libdisk.so
  28 -r--r--r--  1 sys   27832 Nov  4 1999 /lib/libmalloc.so
```

Block sizes are operating- and filesystem-dependent: to find the block size, divide the file size in bytes by the size in blocks, and then round up to a power of two. On the system from that last example, we find 2270300/2220 = 1022.6, so the block size is 2^{10} = 1024 bytes. Storage devices are getting increasingly intelligent, so the block size that you figure out in this way may differ from what is present on the device. Also, vendor and GNU versions of ls on some systems disagree as well, so block sizes obtained in this way are probably not reliable, except for comparisons on the same system with the same ls command.

Occasionally, you may encounter files for which the block count seems too small: such a file probably contains *holes*, caused by using direct access to write bytes at specified positions. Database programs often do this, since they store sparse tables in the filesystem. The inode structure in the filesystem handles files with holes properly, but programs that simply read such a file sequentially see zero bytes from the (imaginary) disk blocks corresponding to the holes.

Copying such a file fills the holes with physical zeroed disk blocks, possibly increasing the size substantially. While this is transparent to the software that created the original file, it is a filesystem feature that well-written backup utilities need to deal with. GNU tar offers the --sparse option to request checking for such files, but most other tar implementations do not. GNU cp has the --sparse option to control the handling of files with holes.

Use of the administrative dump/restore tools may be the only way on some systems to avoid filling in the holes while copying a file tree: these utilities tend to be highly system-dependent, so we ignore them in this book.

You might have spotted another difference between the last two sample outputs: the timestamp is displayed differently. To reduce line width, ls normally displays that value as *Mmm dd hh:mm* for a timestamp within the last six months, and otherwise, as *Mmm dd yyyy* for an older one. Some people find this a nuisance, and now that windowing systems have removed the 80-character line-width limit of old style ASCII terminals,[*] there is little need for that economization. Most humans, however, find long lines hard to read, and recent GNU ls versions try harder to keep the output lines short.

Depending on the locale, GNU ls may produce something close to the *yyyy-mm-dd hh:mm:ss* format defined in *ISO 8601:2000: Data elements and interchange formats— Information interchange—Representation of dates and times*, but without the seconds field, as shown in earlier sample outputs.

The GNU ls option --full-time can be used to expose the complete timestamp recorded in the filesystem, as shown in Chapter 10.

---

[*] And they in turn got that limit from computer punched cards, which were invented by Hermann Hollerith in the 1880s to help process the 1890 U.S. Census data. His company eventually become IBM. See Geoffrey D. Austrian, *Herman Hollerith—Forgotten Giant of Information Processing*, Columbia University Press, 1982, ISBN 0-231-05146-8, and Thomas J. Watson Jr. and Peter Petre, *Father Son & Co.—My Life at IBM and Beyond*, Bantam Books, 1990, ISBN 0-553-07011-8, for interesting stories of the early days of computing.

Other File Metadata

There are a few remaining file properties recorded in inode entries that we have not yet mentioned. However, the only one visible in the output of ls -1 is the *file type*, recorded as the first character of the line, immediately before the permissions. This is - (hyphen) for an ordinary file, d for a directory, and l for a symbolic link.

Those three characters are about the only ones that you'll see in ordinary directories. However, in /dev, you'll encounter at least two more: b for block device, and c for character device. Neither of them is relevant for anything in this book.

Two other rarely seen file types are p for a named pipe, and s for socket (a special network connection). Sockets are an advanced topic that this book does not cover. Named pipes, however, are occasionally useful in programs and shell scripts: they allow for client-server communication via the filesystem namespace, and they provide a way to direct output from one process into two or more unrelated processes. They generalize ordinary pipes, which have only one writer and one reader.

The GNU stat command from the *coreutils* package displays the results of the stat( ) system call, which returns inode information about the file. Here is an example of its use with the file from SGI IRIX that we used earlier:

```
$ stat /bin/true                      Report inode information about the file
  File: `/bin/true'
  Size: 312          Blocks: 8         IO Block: 65536  regular file
Device: eeh/238d     Inode: 380        Links: 1
Access: (0755/-rwxr-xr-x) Uid: (   0/    root)  Gid: (   0/    sys)
Access: 2003-12-09 09:02:56.572619600 -0700
Modify: 1999-11-04 12:07:38.887783200 -0700
Change: 1999-11-04 12:07:38.888253600 -0700
```

The information shown more compactly by ls is just a subset of stat's more detailed report.

GNU stat supports fancy format sequences that allow you to select any subset of the data in the full report. For example, a software installation package could use them to find out whether the filesystem has sufficient free space to proceed. Consult the stat manual pages for details.

Only a few Unix flavors (FreeBSD, GNU/Linux, NetBSD, and SGI IRIX) supply a native stat command. Here are three more samples of their diverse output:

```
$ /usr/bin/stat /usr/bin/true              FreeBSD 5.0 (one long output line, wrapped here to fit)
1027 1366263 -r-xr-xr-x 1 root wheel 5464488 3120 "Dec  2 18:48:36 2003"
"Jan 16 13:29:56 2003" "Apr  4 09:14:03 2003" 16384 8 /usr/bin/true

$ stat -t /bin/true                        GNU/Linux terse inode information
/bin/true 312 8 81ed 0 0 ee 380 1 0 0 1070985776 941742458 941742458 65536

$ /sbin/stat /bin/true                      SGI IRIX system utility
    /bin/true:
      inode 380; dev 238; links 1; size 312
```

```
regular; mode is rwxr-xr-x; uid 0 (root); gid 0 (sys)
projid 0        st_fstype: xfs
change time - Thu Nov  4 12:07:38 1999 <941742458>
access time - Tue Dec  9 09:02:56 2003 <1070985776>
modify time - Thu Nov  4 12:07:38 1999 <941742458>
```

Unix File Ownership and Privacy Issues

We have made numerous mentions of file permissions, showing how they control read, write, and execute access to files and directories. By careful choice of file permissions, you can, and should, control who can access your files.

The most important tool for access control is the umask command, since it limits the permissions assigned to all files that you subsequently create. Normally, you pick a default value and set it in the file that your shell reads on startup: $HOME/.profile for sh-like shells (see "Shell Initialization and Termination" [14.7]). System managers usually pick a umask setting in a corresponding system-wide startup file, when the shell supports one. In a collaborative research environment, you might choose a mask value of 022, removing write access for group and other. In a student environment, a mask of 077 might be more appropriate, eliminating all access except for the file owner (and root).

When nondefault permissions are likely to be required, shell scripts should issue an explicit umask command near the beginning, and *before* any files are created. However, such a setting does not affect files that are redirected on the command line, since they are already open when the script starts.

The second most important tool is the chmod command: learn it well. Even in a permissive environment where read access is granted to everyone, there are still files and directories that must be more restricted. These include mail files, web browser history and cache, private correspondence, financial and personnel data, marketing plans, and so on. Mail clients and browsers generally set restrictive permissions by default, but for files that you create with a text editor, you may need to issue a chmod command yourself. If you are really paranoid, don't create the file with the text editor: instead, create an empty file with touch, run chmod, and then edit the file. That eliminates a window when there might be data in the file during initial editing that is more visible to others than you want.

You must also remember that system managers have full access to your filesystem, and can read any file. While most system managers consider it unethical to look inside user files without explicit permission from the file owners, some organizations consider all computer files, including electronic mail, their property, and subject to monitoring at any time. The legal issues on this remain fuzzy, and certainly vary around the world. Also, your site may have backups that go back a long time, and files can be recovered from them, possibly at the order of a court of law.

Encryption and Data Security

If you are really intent on storing files that (almost) no one but you can read, you need to use encryption. Because of various government export rules that classify cryptography as a weapon, most Unix vendors normally do not ship encryption software in standard distributions. Before you go off and install encryption software that you may have found on the Web, or bought commercially, we issue these caveats:

- *Security is a process, not a product.* There is a fine book that you can read to learn more about this: *Secrets and Lies: Digital Security in a Networked World* (Wiley).

- Should you ever forget your encryption key, or have an employee who leaves without passing on encryption keys, you have probably lost your data as well: good encryption methods generally cannot be broken in the time that you have available.

- Just as you might change door locks when an employee leaves, you must also accept that the ex-employee's encryption keys are compromised, and with new keys, re-encrypt all files previously secured with the no-longer-trusted keys.

- If the enhanced security of encrypted files makes life harder for users, they may simply stop using encryption. The same thing happens with complicated door locks: the doors just get propped open.

If you'd like to learn more about the fascinating history of (mostly failed) encryption algorithms, a good place to start is *The Code Book: The Evolution of Secrecy from Mary, Queen of Scots, to Quantum Cryptography* (Doubleday). If you are interested, you can then move on to the algorithmic details in *Applied Cryptography: Protocols, Algorithms, and Source Code in C* (Wiley). There are also extensive bibliographies that cover much of the literature of the field at *http://www.math.utah.edu/pub/tex/bib/index-table.html*.

Finally, in an era of networked computers, it is likely that you will at some time be separated from your filesystem, or your operating system, by a network, and unless traffic on that network is secure, your data is not safe. Wireless networks are particularly vulnerable, and software that can silently eavesdrop, and exploit weaknesses of some current wireless encryption protocols to decipher encrypted traffic, is readily available. Remote access to your electronic mail, and interactive messaging systems, are also likely to be insecure. If you are still using telnet or nonanonymous ftp to connect to your computer(s), you should immediately switch to a *secure shell* replacement.* The old-style communications software passes all data, including usernames and passwords, in clear text; a network attacker can easily recover such data. Secure-shell software uses strong public-key cryptography to accomplish a secure

---

* See, for example, *http://www.columbia.edu/kermit/*, *http://www.ssh.com/*, and *http://www.openssh.org/*. For an in-depth treatment of this important software *SSH, The Secure Shell: The Definitive Guide* (O'Reilly).

---

exchange of a randomly generated lengthy encryption key for use with any of several simpler and faster encryption algorithms. No user data is transmitted until the encrypted channel is established, and the standard encryption methods are well studied and believed to be quite secure; an attacker sees an apparently random stream of bytes in your packets, although source and destination address are still visible, and can be used for traffic analysis. Secure shell also creates a secure channel for X Window System data, protecting input keystrokes and window output from attackers. Of course, this won't help if the attacker sits between you and your computer: Internet cafes, keyboard sniffers, wireless networks, and thin clients can all open up avenues of attack that even the secure shell cannot protect against. Even the varying reflection of a monitor against a wall has been demonstrated to permit the screen image to be read by an attacker 80 meters away.[*]

Unix File Extension Conventions

Some other operating systems have filenames of the form of a base name, a dot, and a one- to three-character file type or file extension. These extensions serve an important purpose: they indicate that the file contents belong to a particular class of data. For example, an extension pas could mean that the file contains Pascal source code, and exe would identify a binary executable program.

There is no guarantee that file contents are reflected in their file extensions, but most users find them a useful custom, and follow convention.

Unix too has a substantial number of common file extensions, but Unix filenames are not forced to have at most one dot. Sometimes, the extensions are merely conventional (e.g., for most scripting languages). However, compilers generally require particular extensions, and use the base name (after stripping the extension) to form the names of other related files. Some of the more common extensions are shown in Table B-1.

Table B-1. Common Unix file extensions

Extension	Contents
1	Digit one. Manual page for section 1 (user commands)
a	Library archive file
awk	awk language source file
bz2	File compressed by bzip2
c	C language source file

---

[*] Markus Kuhn, *Optical Time-Domain Eavesdropping Risks of CRT Displays*, Proceedings: 2002 IEEE Symposium on Security and Privacy, 12–15 May, 2002, Berkeley, California, IEEE Computer Society Press, 2002, pp. 3–18, ISBN 0-7695-1543-6. Also available at *http://www.cl.cam.ac.uk/~mgk25/ieee02-optical.pdf*.

Table B-1. Common Unix file extensions (continued)

Extension	Contents
cc C cpp cxx	C++ language source file
eps ps	PostScript page-description language source file
f	Fortran 77 language source file
gz	File compressed by gzip
f90	Fortran 90/95/200x language source file
h	C language header file
html htm	HyperText Markup Language file
o	Object file (from most compiled programming languages)
pdf	Portable Document Format file
s	Assembly language source file (e.g., output by compilers in response to the symbolic code option, -S)
sh	Bourne-family shell script
so	Shared-object library (called a dynamic load library on some systems)
tar	Tape archive file (from the tar utility)
,v	cvs and rcs history file
z	Compressed file from pack (rare)
Z	Compressed file from compress

Notably absent from this table is exe. While several other operating systems use that extension for binary executable programs, and permit the extension to be omitted when using the filename as a command name, Unix does not use any particular extension for executable files (file permissions serve that purpose), and Unix software rarely permits file extensions to be dropped.

Several Unix text editors offer the user the option of creating temporary backup files so that the state of a long editing session can be safely recorded in the filesystem at suitable intervals. There are several conventions for naming these backup files: prefixes and/or suffixes of sharp (#) and tilde (~), or a suffix that includes tildes and a number, such as .~1~, .~2~, and so on. The latter mimic the file generation numbers provided by some other filesystems, a feature that Unix does not explicitly provide, but effectively permits through flexible file-naming rules.

File generation numbers used in other systems provide a way to retain multiple versions of a file, with the convention that an omitted generation number refers to the highest-numbered generation. Unix offers better ways of handling file version histories: software tools that preserve the history as differences from a base version, together with commentary that describes why the change was made. The original such package was AT&T's *Source Code Control System* (sccs), but today, the *Revision Control System* (rcs) (see "Miscellaneous Programs" in Appendix C) and the *Concurrent Versions System* (cvs) are more common.

Summary

This completes our tour of the workings of the Unix filesystem. By now, you should be familiar with its main features:

- Files are streams of zero or more 8-bit bytes, without any additional structure other than the use of newline characters to mark line boundaries in text files.

- Bytes are usually interpreted as ASCII characters, but the UTF-8 encoding and the Unicode character set permit graceful evolution of the Unix filesystem, pipes, and network communications to support millions of different characters from all of the world's writing systems, *without invalidating the majority of existing files or software.*

- Files have attributes, such as timestamps, ownership, and permissions, allowing a much greater degree of access control and privacy than is available on some other desktop operating systems, and eliminating most computer virus problems.

- Access to entire directory trees can be controlled at a single point by suitable settings of directory permissions.

- The maximum file size is large enough to rarely be a problem, and newer filesystem designs raise the maximum well beyond the limits of current technology.

- The maximum filename and pathname lengths are much longer than you are likely to need in practice.

- A clean hierarchical directory structure with slash separated path components, together with the mount command, allows logical filesystems of potentially unbounded size.

- File-like views of other data are possible, and encouraged, to simplify data processing and use by humans.

- Filenames may use any character other than NUL or slash, but practical considerations of portability, readability, and shell wildcarding sharply limit the characters that should be used.

- Filenames are case-sensitive (except in Mac OS X's non-Unix HFS filesystems).

- Although the filesystem does not impose rules on filename structure, many programs expect files to be named with particular dotted extensions, and they replace the extensions with other ones when creating related files. The shells encourage this practice through their support of wildcard patterns like ch01.* and *.xml.

- Filenames are stored in a directory file, whereas information about the file, the file *metadata*, is stored separately in an inode entry.

- Moving or renaming files and directories within the same filesystem is fast, since only their containing directory entries are updated; the file data blocks themselves are not accessed.

- Hard and soft links allow multiple names for the same physical file. Hard links are restricted to a single physical filesystem, but soft links may point anywhere in the logical filesystem.
- The inode table size is fixed when the filesystem is created, so the filesystem can be full even when plenty of storage is available for file data.

Important Unix Commands

Modern Unix systems come with hundreds and hundreds of commands. Many of them are specialized, but many are also generally useful, both in everyday interactive use and in shell scripts. It's impossible to cover every program on every system in existence, nor would that be useful. (Although books like *Unix in a Nutshell* make a valiant effort to describe a large cross section of what's out there.)

It is possible, however, to identify certain valuable commands, the ones that a Unix user or programmer should come to understand first, before moving on to the rest of the programs out there. Not surprisingly, many of these are the older commands that have been around since the early days of Unix. This appendix is our recommended list of commands that you should go out and study in order to improve your skills as a Unix developer. For brevity, we have resorted to simple, sorted, tabular lists of commands.

Shells and Built-in Commands

First and foremost, it pays to understand the Bourne shell language, particularly as codified by POSIX. Both bash and ksh93 are POSIX-compliant, and several other shells are compatible syntactically with the Bourne shell:

bash	The GNU Project's Bourne-Again Shell.
ksh	The Korn shell, either an original or clone, depending upon the operating system.
pdksh	The Public Domain Korn shell.
sh	The original Bourne shell, particularly on commercial Unix systems.
zsh	The Z-shell.

Along similar lines, you should understand the way the shell's built-in commands work:

.	Read and execute a given file, in the current shell.
break	Break out of a for, select, until, or while loop.
cd	Change the current directory.

command	Bypass the search for functions to run a regular built-in command.
continue	Start the next iteration of a for, select, until, or while loop.
eval	Evaluate given text as a shell command.
exec	With no arguments, change the shell's open files. With arguments, replace the shell with another program.
exit	Exit a shell script, optionally with a specific exit code.
export	Export a variable into the environment of subsequent programs.
false	Do nothing, unsuccessfully. For use in shell loops.
getopts	Process command-line options.
read	Read lines of input into one or more shell variables.
readonly	Mark a variable as read-only; i.e., unchangeable.
return	Return a value from a shell function.
set	Print shell variables and values; set shell options; set the command-line parameters ($1, $2, . . .).
shift	Move the command-line parameters down by one or more.
test	Evaluate expressions, which may be string-, numeric-, or file-attribute-related.
trap	Manage operating system signals.
true	Do nothing, successfully. For use in shell loops.
type	Indicate the nature of a command (keyword, built-in, external, etc.).
typeset	Declare variables and manage their type and attributes.
ulimit	Set or display various per-process system-imposed limits.
unset	Remove shell variables and functions.

The following commands are useful in day-to-day shell scripting:

basename	Print the last component of a pathname, optionally removing a suffix. Mainly used in command substitution.
dirname	Print all but the last component of a pathname. Mainly used in command substitution.
env	Manipulate the environment of a command.
id	Print user and group ID and name information.
date	Print the current date and time, optionally under control of a user-supplied format string.
who	Print a list of logged-on users.
stty	Manipulate the state of the current terminal device.

Text Manipulation

The following commands are used for text manipulation:

awk	An elegant and useful programming language in its own right, it is also an important component of many large shell scripts.
cat	Concatenate files.
cmp	Simple file comparison program.
cut	Cut out selected columns or fields.
dd	A more specialized program for blocking and unblocking data, and converting between ASCII and EBCDIC. dd is especially good for making raw copies of device files. Note that iconv is a better program for doing character set conversions.

`echo`	Print arguments to standard output.
`egrep`	Extended `grep`. Matching uses Extended Regular Expressions (EREs).
`expand`	Expand tabs to spaces.
`fgrep`	Fast `grep`. This program uses a different algorithm than `grep` for matching fixed strings. Most, but not all, Unix systems can search simultaneously for multiple fixed strings.
`fmt`	Simple tool for formatting text into paragraphs.
`grep`	From the original `ed` line editor's command `g/re/p`, "Globally match RE and Print." Matching uses Basic Regular Expressions (BREs).
`iconv`	General-purpose character-encoding conversion tool.
`join`	Join matching records from multiple files.
`less`	A sophisticated interactive *pager* program for looking at information on a terminal, one screenful (or "page") at a time. It is available from the GNU Project. The name is a pun on the `more` program.
`more`	The original BSD Unix interactive pager program.
`pr`	Format files for printing on line printers.
`printf`	A more sophisticated version of `echo` that provides control over the way each argument is printed.
`sed`	A stream editor, based on the original `ed` line editor's command set.
`sort`	Sort text files. Command-line arguments provide control over sort key specification and priority.
`spell`	A batch spellchecker. You may have `aspell` or `ispell`, with a shell script wrapper named `spell`, instead.
`tee`	Copy standard input to standard output and to one or more named output files.
`tr`	Transliterate, delete, or reduce runs of duplicate characters.
`unexpand`	Convert runs of spaces into the appropriate number of tabs.
`uniq`	Remove or count duplicate lines in sorted input.
`wc`	Count lines, words, characters, and/or bytes.

Files

The following commands work with files:

`bzip2, bunzip2`	Very high quality file compression and decompression.
`chgrp`	Change the group of files and directories.
`chmod`	Change the permissions (mode) of files and directories.
`chown`	Change the owner of files and directories.
`cksum`	Print a file checksum, POSIX standard algorithm.
`comm`	Print or omit lines that are unique or common between two sorted files.
`cp`	Copy files and directories.
`df`	Show free disk space.
`diff`	Compare files, showing differences.
`du`	Show disk block usage of files and directories.
`file`	Guess the type of data in a file by examining the first part of it.
`find`	Descend one or more directory hierarchies finding filesystem objects (files, directories, special files) that match specified criteria.
`gzip, gunzip`	High-quality file compression and decompression.

head	Print the first *n* lines of one or more files.
locate	Find a file somewhere on the system based on its name. The program uses a database of files that is usually rebuilt automatically, nightly.
ls	List files. Options control the information shown.
md5sum	Print a file checksum using the Message Digest 5 (MD5) algorithm.
mkdir	Make directories.
mktemp	Create a unique temporary file and print its name. Not universally available.
od	Octal dump; print file contents in octal, hexadecimal, or as character data.
patch	Update the contents of a given file to a newer version by reading the output of diff.
pwd	Print the current working directory. Usually built into modern shells.
rm	Remove files and directories.
rmdir	Remove just empty directories.
strings	Search binary files for printable strings and print them.
tail	Show the last *n* lines of a file. With -f, keep printing the (growing) contents of the file.
tar	Tape archiver. Now used mostly as a software distribution format.
touch	Update the modification or access time of a file.
umask	Set the default file-creation permissions mask.
zip, unzip	File archiver and compressor/decompressor. The ZIP format is portable across a broad range of operating systems.

Processes

The following commands create, remove, or manage processes:

at	Executes jobs at a specified time. at schedules jobs to be executed just once, whereas cron schedules them to be executed regularly.
batch	Executes jobs when the system is not too overloaded.
cron	Executes jobs at specified times.
crontab	Edit per-user "cron table" files that specify what commands to run, and when.
fuser	Find processes using particular files or sockets.
kill	Send a signal to one or more processes.
nice	Change the priority of a process before starting it.
ps	Process status. Print information about running processes.
renice	Change the priority of a process that has already been started.
sleep	Stop execution for the given number of seconds.
top	Interactively display the most CPU-intensive jobs on the system.
wait	Shell built-in command to wait for one or more processes to complete.
xargs	Read strings on standard input, passing as many as possible as arguments to a given command. Most often used together with find.

Miscellaneous Programs

There's always a "miscellaneous" category:

cvs	The Concurrent Versions System, a powerful source-code management program.
info	The GNU Info system for online documentation.
locale	Print information about available locales.
logger	Send messages to system logs, usually via *syslog*(3).
lp, lpr	Spool files to a printer.
lpq	Show the list of print jobs in progress and waiting in the queue.
mail	Send electronic mail.
make	Control compilation and recompilation of files.
man	Print the online manual page(s) for commands, library functions, system calls, devices, file formats, and administrative commands.
scp	Secure remote copy of files.
ssh	Secure shell. Provide an encrypted connection between machines for program execution or interactive login.
uptime	Tell how long the system has been up, and show system load information.

Also in the miscellaneous category are the commands for the Revision Control System (RCS):

ci	Check in a file to RCS.
co	Check out a file from RCS.
rcs	Manipulate a file that is under RCS control.
rcsdiff	Run diff on two different versions of a file controlled by RCS.
rlog	Print the check-in log for one or more RCS-managed files.

Bibliography

Unix Programmer's Manuals

1. *UNIX Time-sharing System: UNIX Programmers Manual*, Seventh Edition, Volumes 1, 2A, 2B. Bell Telephone Laboratories, Inc., January 1979.

   These are the reference manuals (Volume 1) and descriptive papers (Volumes 2A and 2B) for the landmark Seventh Edition Unix system, the direct ancestor of all current commercial Unix systems.

   They were reprinted by Holt Rinehart & Winston, but are now long out of print. However, they are available online from Bell Labs in troff source, PDF, and PostScript formats. See *http://plan9.bell-labs.com/7thEdMan*.

2. Your Unix programmer's manual. One of the most instructive things that you can do is to read your manual from front to back.* (This is harder than it used to be, as Unix systems have grown.) It is easier to do if your Unix vendor makes printed copies of its documentation available. Otherwise, start with the Seventh Edition manual, and then read your local documentation as needed.

Programming with the Unix Mindset

We expect that this book has helped you learn to "think Unix" in a modern context. The first two books in this list are the original presentations of the Unix "toolbox" programming methodology. The third book looks at the broader programming facilities available under Unix. The fourth and fifth are about programming in general, and also very worthwhile. We note that any book written by Brian Kernighan deserves careful reading, usually several times.

---

* One summer, while working as a contract programmer, I spent my lunchtimes reading the manual for System III (yes, that long ago), from cover to cover. I don't know that I ever learned so much in so little time. ADR.

1. *Software Tools*, Brian W. Kernighan and P. J. Plauger. Addison-Wesley, Reading, MA, U.S.A., 1976. ISBN 0-201-03669-X.

   A wonderful book* that presents the design and code for programs equivalent to Unix's grep, sort, ed, and others. The programs use Ratfor (Rational Fortran), a preprocessor for Fortran with C-like control structures.

2. *Software Tools in Pascal*, Brian W. Kernighan and P. J. Plauger. Addison-Wesley, Reading, MA, U.S.A., 1981. ISBN 0-201-10342-7.

   A translation of the previous book into Pascal. Still worth reading; Pascal provides many things that Fortran does not.

3. *The Unix Programming Environment*, Brian W. Kernighan and Rob Pike. Prentice-Hall, Englewood Cliffs, NJ, U.S.A., 1984. ISBN 0-13-937699-2 (hardcover), 0-13-937681-X (paperback).

   This books focuses explicitly on Unix, using the tools in that environment. In particular, it adds important material on the shell, awk, and the use of lex and yacc. See *http://cm.bell-labs.com/cm/cs/upe*.

4. *The Elements of Programming Style*, Second Edition, Brian W. Kernighan and P. J. Plauger. McGraw Hill, New York, NY, U.S.A., 1978. ISBN 0-07-034207-5.

   Modeled after Strunk & White's famous *The Elements of Style*, this book describes good programming practices that can be used in any environment.

5. *The Practice of Programming*, Brian W. Kernighan and Rob Pike. Addison-Wesley Longman, Reading, MA, U.S.A., 1999. ISBN 0-201 61586-X.

   Similar to the previous book, with a somewhat stronger technical focus. See *http://cm.bell-labs.com/cm/cs/tpop*.

6. *The Art of UNIX Programming*, Eric S. Raymond. Addison-Wesley, Reading, MA, U.S.A., 2003. ISBN 0-13-124085-4.

7. *Programming Pearls*, First Edition, Jon Louis Bentley. Addison-Wesley, Reading, MA, U.S.A., 1986. ISBN 0-201-10331-1.

8. *Programming Pearls*, Second Edition, Jon Louis Bentley. Addison-Wesley, Reading, MA, U.S.A., 2000. ISBN 0-201-65788-0. See *http://www.cs.bell-labs.com/cm/cs/pearls/*.

9. *More Programming Pearls: Confessions of a Coder*, Jon Louis Bentley. Addison-Wesley, Reading, MA, U.S.A., 1988. ISBN 0-201-11889-0.

   Bentley's excellent books epitomize the Unix mindset, and are wonderful examples of little languages, algorithm design, and much more. These should be on every serious programmer's bookshelf.

10. *Linux and the Unix Philosophy*, Mike Gancarz. Digital Press, Bedford, MA, U.S.A., 2003. ISBN 1-55558-273-7.

---

* One that changed my life forever. ADR.

Awk and Shell

1. *The AWK Programming Language*, Alfred V. Aho, Brian W. Kernighan, and Peter J. Weinberger. Addison-Wesley, Reading, MA, U.S.A., 1987. ISBN 0-201-07981-X.

   The original definition for the awk programming language. Extremely worthwhile. See *http://cm.bell-labs.com/cm/cs/awkbook*.

   Effective awk Programming, Third Edition, Arnold Robbins. O'Reilly, Sebastopol, CA, U.S.A., 2001. ISBN 0-596-00070-7.

   A more tutorial treatment of awk that covers the POSIX standard for awk. It also serves as the user's guide for gawk.

2. *The New KornShell Command and Programming Language*, Morris I. Bolsky and David G. Korn. Prentice-Hall, Englewood Cliffs, NJ, U.S.A., 1995. ISBN 0-13-182700-6.

   The definitive work on the Korn shell, by its author.

3. *Hands-On KornShell93 Programming*, Barry Rosenberg. Addison-Wesley Longman, Reading, MA, U.S.A., 1998. ISBN 0-201-31018-X.

Standards

Formal standards documents are important, as they represent "contracts" between implementors and users of computer systems.

1. *IEEE Standard 1003.1-2001: Standard for Information Technology—Portable Operating System Interface (POSIX®)*. IEEE, New York, NY, U.S.A., 2001.

   This is the next-to-most recent POSIX standard. It combines both the system call interface standard and the shell and utilities standard in one document. Physically, the standard consists of several volumes, available online,[*] in print,[†] electronically as PDF, and on CD-ROM:

   Base Definitions
   This provides the history of the standard, definitions of terms, and specifications for file formats and input and output formats. ISBN 0-7381-3047-8; PDF: 0-7381-3010-9/SS94956; CD-ROM: 0-7381-3129-6/SE94956.

   Rationale (Informative)
   Not a formal part of the standard, in the sense that it does not impose requirements upon implementations, this volume provides the *why* for the way things are in the POSIX standard. ISBN 0-7381-3048-6; PDF: 0-7381-3010-9/SS94956; CD-ROM: 0-7381-3129-6/SE94956.

---

[*] See *http://www.opengroup.org/onlinepubs/007904975*.

[†] See *http://www.standards.ieee.org/*.

System Interfaces

This volume describes the interface to the operating system as seen by the C or C++ programmer. ISBN 0-7381-3094-4; PDF: 0-7381-3010-9/SS94956; CD-ROM: 0-7381-3129-6/SE94956.

Shell and Utilities

This volume is more relevant for readers of this book: it describes the operating system at the level of the shell and utilities. ISBN 0-7381-3050-8; PDF: 0-7381-3010-9/SS94956; CD-ROM: 0-7381-3129-6/SE9.

2. *IEEE Standard 1003.1-2004: Standard for Information Technology—Portable Operating System Interface (POSIX®)*. IEEE, New York, NY, U.S.A., 2004.

The current POSIX standard, released as this book was going to press. It is a revision of the previous one, and is organized similarly. The standard consists of several volumes: *Base Definitions* (Volume 1), *System Interfaces* (Volume 2), *Shell and Utilities* (Volume 3), and *Rationale* (Volume 4).

The standard may be ordered from *http://www.standards.ieee.org/* on CD-ROM (Product number SE95238, ISBN 0-7381-4049-X) or as PDF (Product number SS95238, ISBN 0-7381-4048-1).

3. *The Unicode Standard, Version 4.0*, The Unicode Consortium. Addison-Wesley, Reading, MA, U.S.A., 2003. ISBN 0-321-18578-1.

4. The standard for XML, available online at *http://www.w3.org/TR/REC-xml/*.

Security and Cryptography

1. *PGP: Pretty Good Privacy*, Simson Garfinkel. O'Reilly, Sebastopol, CA, U.S.A., 1995. ISBN 1-56592-098-8.

2. *The Official PGP User's Guide*, Philip R. Zimmermann. MIT Press, Cambridge, MA, U.S.A., 1995. ISBN 0-262-74017-6.

3. *Practical UNIX & Internet Security*, Third Edition, Simson Garfinkel, Gene Spafford, and Alan Schwartz. O'Reilly, Sebastopol, CA, U.S.A., 2003. ISBN 0-596-00323-4.

4. *SSH, The Secure Shell: The Definitive Guide*, Second Edition, Daniel J. Barrett, Richard E. Silverman, and Robert G. Byrnes. O'Reilly Media, Sebastopol, CA, U.S.A., 2005. ISBN 0-596-00895-3.

5. *Secrets and Lies: Digital Security in a Networked World*, Bruce Schneier. Wiley, New York, NY, U.S.A., 2000. ISBN 0-471-25311-1.

This book is an outstanding exposition for every world citizen of the implications of computer security on their lives, their data, and their personal freedom. Bruce Schneier, like Brian Kernighan, Jon Bentley, and Donald Knuth, is one of those authors who is always worth reading.

6. *The Code Book: The Evolution of Secrecy from Mary, Queen of Scots, to Quantum Cryptography*, Simon Singh. Doubleday, New York, NY, U.S.A., 1999. ISBN 0-385-49531-5.

7. *Applied Cryptography: Protocols, Algorithms, and Source Code in C*, Second Edition, Bruce Schneier. Wiley, New York, NY, U.S.A., 1996. ISBN 0-471-12845-7 (hardcover), 0-471-11709-9 (paperback).

8. *Cryptographic Security Architecture: Design and Verification*, Peter Gutmann. Springer-Verlag, New York, NY, U.S.A., 2004. ISBN 0-387-95387-6.

Unix Internals

1. *Lions' Commentary on UNIX 6th Edition, with Source Code*, John Lions. Peer-to-Peer Communications, 1996. ISBN 1-57398-013-7.

2. *The Design and Implementation of the 4.4BSD Operating System*, Marshall Kirk McKusick, Keith Bostic, Michael J. Karels, and John S. Quarterman. Addison-Wesley, Reading, MA, U.S.A., 1996. ISBN 0-201-54979-4.

3. *UNIX Internals: The New Frontiers*, Uresh Vahalia. Prentice Hall, Englewood Cliffs, NJ, U.S.A., 1996. ISBN 0-13-101908-2.

O'Reilly Books

Here is a list of O'Reilly books. There are, of course, many other O'Reilly books relating to Unix. See *http://www.oreilly.com/catalog*.

1. *Learning the bash Shell*, Second Edition, Cameron Newham and Bill Rosenblatt. O'Reilly, Sebastopol, CA, U.S.A., 1998. ISBN 1-56592-347-2.

2. *Learning the Korn Shell*, Second Edition, Bill Rosenblatt and Arnold Robbins. O'Reilly, Sebastopol, CA, U.S.A., 2002. ISBN 0-596-00195-9.

3. *Learning the Unix Operating System*, Fifth Edition, Jerry Peek, Grace Todino, and John Strang. O'Reilly, Sebastopol, CA, U.S.A., 2001. ISBN 0-596-00261-0.

4. *Linux in a Nutshell*, Third Edition, Ellen Siever, Stephen Spainhour, Jessica P. Hekman, and Stephen Figgins. O'Reilly, Sebastopol, CA, U.S.A., 2000. ISBN 0-596-00025-1.

5. *Mastering Regular Expressions*, Second Edition, Jeffrey E. F. Friedl. O'Reilly, Sebastopol, CA, U.S.A., 2002. ISBN 0-596-00289-0.

6. *Managing Projects with GNU make*, Third Edition, Robert Mecklenburg, Andy Oram, and Steve Talbott. O'Reilly Media, Sebastopol, CA, U.S.A., 2005. ISBN: 0-596-00610-1.

7. *sed and awk*, Second Edition, Dale Dougherty and Arnold Robbins. O'Reilly, Sebastopol, CA, U.S.A., 1997. ISBN 1-56592-225-5.

8. *sed and awk Pocket Reference*, Second Edition, Arnold Robbins. O'Reilly, Sebastopol, CA, U.S.A., 2002. ISBN 0-596-00352-8.

9. *Unix in a Nutshell*, Third Edition, Arnold Robbins. O'Reilly, Sebastopol, CA, U.S.A., 1999. ISBN 1-56592-427-4.

Miscellaneous Books

1. *CUPS: Common UNIX Printing System*, Michael R. Sweet. SAMS Publishing, Indianapolis, IN, U.S.A., 2001. ISBN 0-672-32196-3.

2. *SQL in a Nutshell*, Kevin Kline and Daniel Kline. O'Reilly, Sebastopol, CA, U.S.A., 2000. ISBN 1-56592-744-3.

3. *HTML & XHTML: The Definitive Guide*, Chuck Musciano and Bill Kennedy. O'Reilly, Sebastopol, CA, U.S.A., 2002. ISBN 0-596-00026-X.

4. *The Cathedral and the Bazaar: Musings on Linux and Open Source by an Accidental Revolutionary*, Eric S. Raymond. O'Reilly, Sebastopol, CA, U.S.A., 2001. ISBN 0-596-00131-2 (hardcover), 0-596-00108-8 (paperback).

5. *Texinfo: The GNU Documentation Format*, Robert J. Chassell and Richard M. Stallman. Free Software Foundation, Cambridge, MA, U.S.A., 1999. ISBN 1-882114-67-1.

6. *The TEXbook*, Donald E. Knuth. Addison-Wesley, Reading, MA, U.S.A., 1984. ISBN 0-201-13448-9.

7. *The Art of Computer Programming, Volume 2: Seminumerical Algorithms*, Third Edition, Donald E. Knuth. Addison-Wesley, Reading, MA, U.S.A., 1997. ISBN 0-201-89684-2.

8. *Literate Programming*, Donald E. Knuth. Stanford University Center for the Study of Language and Information, Stanford, CA, U.S.A., 1992. ISBN 0-937073-80-6 (paperback) and 0-937073-81-4 (hardcover).

9. *Herman Hollerith—Forgotten Giant of Information Processing*, Geoffrey D. Austrian. Columbia University Press, New York, NY, U.S.A. 1982. ISBN 0-231-05146-8.

10. *Father Son & Co.—My Life at IBM and Beyond*, Thomas J. Watson Jr. and Peter Petre. Bantam Books, New York, NY, U.S.A., 1990. ISBN 0-553-07011-8.

11. *A Quarter Century of UNIX*, Peter H. Salus. Addison-Wesley, Reading, MA, U.S.A., 1994. ISBN 0-201-54777-5.

Glossary

access control lists (ACLs)

Extended file attributes that augment the normal user/group/other file permissions to provide finer control over file access; they typically allow binding of permissions to particular users and/or groups. More advanced filesystems might permit authentication control, such as by password or smartcard, or allow access only during certain time periods.

alternation

Another name for the vertical bar character. In regular expressions, it stands for logical OR: **apples|oranges** matches either apples or oranges.

American National Standards Institute (ANSI)

This body manages the creation and adoption of industrial standards, including many within the US computing industry. These are sometimes superseded by international standards managed by the *International Organization for Standardization* (ISO). ANSI was formerly known as the American Standards Association (ASA).

American Standard Code for Information Interchange (ASCII)

A standard assignment of human-readable characters (letters, digits, punctuation, and so on) to a 128-element table, and thus, requiring seven bits of storage per character. Today, virtually all machines have 8-bit addressable storage units called *bytes*, giving an extra bit that can be combined with the original seven to index 128 additional characters. There are many different assignments of these extra characters, only a few of which have been internationally standardized (the ISO 8859-*n* code pages). See *Unicode*.

American Standards Association (ASA)

The name of the *American National Standards Institute* from 1928 to 1966. From its founding in 1918 to 1928, it was known as the *American Engineering Standards Committee*, and from 1966 to 1969 as the *United States of America Standards Institute* (USASI).

anchors

In regular expressions, the special characters caret (^) and dollar sign

($) that bind a pattern to the beginning or end of a record.

ANSI

See *American National Standards Institute*.

arithmetic expansion

A feature of the POSIX shell that permits an arithmetic expression enclosed in $((...)) to be evaluated as the replacement value for the expression. For example, tenfact=$((10*9*8*7*6*5*4*3*2*1)) sets tenfact to 3628800. Recent Korn shell versions also allow floating-point expressions.

array variable

A program variable that is a table addressed by one or more indices provided as a comma-separated list enclosed in brackets or, in some languages, parentheses, following the variable name. See *scalar variable*.

In many programming languages, arrays must be explicitly declared with a fixed size, a fixed number of integer indices, and all elements having the same datatype. However, scripting languages generalize this by providing dynamic *associative arrays*.

ASCII

See *American Standard Code for Information Interchange*.

associative arrays

Tables indexed by comma-separated lists of arbitrary strings, rather than by simple integers in a predeclared range. Scripting languages, such as awk, provide them. In other programming languages, they are usually known as *hash tables*.

Despite the generality of the array indices, table elements can be retrieved in approximately constant time, independent of the number of elements stored.

background process

A process that is running without a controlling terminal. Such processes are started by other background processes, or by a shell command that terminates with ampersand (&). Shells with job control allow processes to be suspended with an interrupt character (usually, Ctrl-Z), and later continued by the background or foreground commands, bg and fg. See *foreground process*.

backreference

A special pattern in Basic Regular Expressions that permits reference to a subexpression matched earlier in the expression. For example, (**cat**).*\1 matches cathird catfish but not catbird cuttlefish.

basename

The last component of a *pathname*. It is also the name of a command, basename, with a companion command, dirname, for extracting all but the last component.

Basic Regular Expressions

The simple pattern-matching specifications used in ed, grep, and sed. See *Extended Regular Expressions*.

birthday paradox

The number of people required in a group before the probability is at least 50 percent that any two of them share a birthday. The surprising answer is 23, rather than the $366/2 = 183$ expected by many.

Here is the explanation. The *n*th person has a choice of 365 - (*n*-1) days to *not* share a birthday with any of the previous ones. Thus, (365 - (*n*-1))/365 is the probability that the *n*th person is *not* born on the same day as any of the previous ones, assuming that they are born on different days. If we call this probability P(*n*), we have a recursion relation P(*n*) = P(*n*-1) × (365 - (*n*-1))/365, with initial condition P(1) = 1. When we evaluate the recursion, we find P(2) = 0.00274, P(3) = 0.00820, P(4) = 0.0164, ..., P(22) = 0.476, P(23) = 0.507, ..., P(100) = 0.999999693, ..., P(200) = 0.99999999999999999999999999 9984, ..., P(366) = 1. Thus, with 23 people, the chance is slightly better than half that two share a birthday.

bracket expression

In regular expressions, a square-bracketed set of characters and/or character ranges matches any single character in that set. **[aeiouy]** matches any lowercase vowel, **[^aeiouyAEIOUY]** matches any nonvowel, and **[A-Z]** matches any uppercase letter.

built-in

In the shell, a command that is implemented by the shell itself, instead of being run as an external program. Sometimes, this is for reasons of efficiency (e.g., the `test` command), and sometimes it is because the command has a *side effect* that must be known to the shell and reported to the kernel (e.g., the `cd` command).

by reference

In function calls, arguments passed by reference are available to the function via their address in the calling program. Thus, changes made to them in the function are really made in their storage in the calling program. In `awk`, arrays are passed by reference.

by value

In function calls, arguments passed by value are available to the function only as copies of values in the calling program, and those copies are discarded on return from the function. Thus, changes to them by the function have no effect on their values in the calling program. In `awk`, scalars are passed by value.

call stack

The block of memory in which a record is made of the calling history of nested function calls. Each call typically has an entry with its return address, storage for local variables, and other administrative information. Stacks provide a clean way to support recursion, since each activation of a function gets a new record in the call stack, making local variables unique to that call instance.

code block

A set of statements enclosed in braces. The braces are shell keywords and thus must each be the first token in a shell statement. The practical effect is that the right brace must follow a newline or semicolon.

The group of statements acts as a single unit for I/O redirection. However, unlike a *subshell*, statements within the code block do affect the main script's environment, such as variables and current directory.

code page

Assignment of characters to positions in a table, so that the table index is the value of the character in storage. For example, the 256-entry ISO 8859-1 code page contains the 128-entry ASCII character set in the bottom half, and in the top half, assorted accented characters and other glyphs needed for most Western European languages.

collating

Ordering of data according to a particular set of rules. For example, the ASCII collating sequence puts 32 control characters first, then most punctuation characters and digits before uppercase letters, which in turn are followed by a few more punctuation characters, then by lowercase letters, then by the remaining punctuation characters, ending with one last control character. Use man ascii to display the ASCII character set.

command substitution

A feature of the shell in which the output of one command is substituted into the command line of another command. For example, ls -ltr $(find *.xml -prune -mtime -7) verbosely lists in reverse-time order all XML files in the current directory that have been modified within the last week. Older shells require backquotes: ls -ltr `find *.xml -prune -mtime -7`. With the old style, command nesting requires messy quoting, whereas the newer

syntax is much cleaner. Compare these two examples:

```
$ echo `echo outer \`echo middle
\\\`echo inner\\\` middle\` outer`
outer middle inner middle outer
$ echo $(echo outer $(echo middle
$(echo inner) middle) outer)
outer middle inner middle outer
```

compound statement

A group of one or more statements that can be used wherever a single statement is expected. Programming languages influenced by C delimit compound statements with braces; older languages often used distinctive reserved words, such as begin and end.

Concurrent Versions System (CVS)

A storage system that allows the maintenance of multiple versions of a set of files, with history logs, and the ability to merge in changes from multiple modified copies of any file. CVS is often used in collaborative Internet software projects when developers work at different sites. CVS is an extension of the *Revision Control System*.

context switch

The temporary transfer of control between the operating-system kernel and a process. The process runs for a brief period (typically a few milliseconds), giving the illusion of simultaneous execution of multiple processes.

controlling terminal

The I/O device from which an interactive process is started and that serves as the default for standard input, standard output, and standard error. It is also a source of user-initiated signals to a process.

Coordinated Universal Time (UTC)

The now-standard name for a worldwide time standard formerly known as Greenwich Mean Time, but based on more accurate atomic clocks, instead of the Earth's rotation. It is local mean solar time, starting at midnight, at the observatory in Greenwich, England, on the 0° meridian of longitude. Its acronym is UTC, a compromise to avoid matching its name in any of the languages of the committee members.

Unix system clocks are synchronized to UTC, and the system's local time zone is set in a configuration file, and often recorded in the TZ environment variable. The date command uses the TZ value to control its output formatting: try TZ=Canada/Newfoundland date to see the time in one of the few time zones that is not displaced by a whole number of hours from UTC.

core dump, coredump

A file containing a copy of the memory image of a running process. The name is historical, and originates with a memory technology developed in the 1950s in which each memory bit was recorded by magnetizing a tiny iron ring, called a *core*.

cracker

An attacker who attempts to crack, or break, computer-system security. See *hacker*.

current working directory

The default directory in a hierarchical filesystem that is assumed to apply to filenames without an absolute directory path.

CVS

See *Concurrent Versions System*.

daemon

A long-running process that provides a service, such as accounting, file service, login, network connection, printing, time service, and so on.

delimiter

A character or string that marks the beginning or end of a block of text. Typical examples are apostrophes, braces, brackets, parentheses, and quotation marks, or in SGML-based markup, <tagname> and </tagname>.

device driver

A software module used by the operating system kernel to communicate with a specific hardware device. In the Unix world, device drivers help to provide a uniform file-like abstraction for a wide range of peripheral hardware, simplifying access from user programs.

digital signature

An arithmetic computation performed on a data stream in such a way as to be influenced both by the individual items and their order. The result is a number that, when big enough, is extremely unlikely to be the result of any other data stream, and thus serves as an almost-unique characteristic value. It is used to guard against data modification, whether accidental or malicious. When the computation is combined in a special way with an encryption key, the resulting number can be also used to verify the source of the data.

directory

A special file in a hierarchical file-system that contains information about other files, including other directories, which are either the parent directory or subdirectories.

DocBook/XML

A document markup scheme designed for the authoring of non-mathematical technical books, as a particular instance of a document type in *XML*.

EBCDIC

Extended Binary Coded Decimal Interchange Code, an 8-bit character set introduced on the IBM System/360 in 1964. While still in use on IBM mainframe systems, it has been eclipsed by ASCII and its descendants—notably, Unicode—to which the worldwide computing industry is moving.

embedded computer system

A standalone computer environment, usually with limited connectivity and functionality, typified by computers that control automobiles, cellular (mobile) telephones, digital cameras, household devices, personal digital assistants, sprinkler systems, wristwatches, and so on. This is a surprisingly large market: in 2002, about 500 million cellular telephones were manufactured. There are now more embedded computers than people on Earth.

entity

In markup languages like HTML, SGML, and XML, a short name for a character or glyph that does not have a normal keyboard assignment. For example, the XML entity

for the Greek letter ϕ (phi) is `&phgr;`.

environment

In the shell, one or more text strings containing key/value pairs inherited by each process. Reasonable programming languages provide a mechanism to retrieve the value, given the key.

environment variable

A shell variable that has been added to the *environment* by an export command so that child processes can inherit it.

epoch

A fixed point of time from which succeeding years are numbered. Unix systems use 00:00:00 UTC, January 1, 1970 as the epoch. With a 32-bit signed counter, the timer overflows on 03:14:07 UTC, January 19, 2038, wrapping back to 20:45:52 UTC, December 13, 1901. A 64-bit signed counter with microsecond resolution spans more than a half-million years.

escape

A mechanism whereby the normal meaning of a metacharacter is suppressed in favor of its literal value, or where an unprintable character is presented in printable form. For example, many Unix programming environments recognize \n to mean newline.

execute

In filesystem permissions, an attribute that allows the file contents to be executed by the kernel on behalf of the holder of that permission, provided that execute access is present in all of the directories in the path to the file. It is a file's execute permission, and not the form of its name, that governs whether it can be run as a program.

exit status

A small integer value returned to the parent process when a child process completes. It is an 8-bit value that, for historical reasons, is further limited to the range 0 through 125, with values 126 through 255 assigned special meaning for abnormal process completion. Conventionally, a zero exit status means success, and a nonzero value, some sort of failure.

expansion

In the shell, examination of a command line for certain special characters, called *metacharacters*, and their subsequent replacement. This includes command substitution, variable replacement, and filesystem pattern matching (wildcarding). See *tilde expansion*.

Extended Regular Expressions

The advanced pattern-matching specifications supported by awk, egrep, and lex. See *Basic Regular Expressions*.

eXtensible Markup Language (XML)

A document markup scheme designed as a significantly simplified form of *SGML*. One design goal was that it should be possible for a competent programmer with a good scripting language to write a simple parser for it in an afternoon.

field

A logical subdivision of a data record, such as a word in a line of text.

FIFO

A communications structure in which the first data input is also the first data output. A pipe, whether anonymous or named, acts as a FIFO. Another name for a FIFO is a *queue*. See *named pipe*.

file checksum

See *digital signature*.

file descriptor

A small unsigned integer number that serves as an index into kernel tables describing open files.

File Transfer Protocol (FTP)

An Internet protocol built on top of *TCP/IP* that is used for transfer of files between computer systems, optionally with translation of line terminators in text files.

FTP requires a username and password on the remote host, and both are passed in the clear, as are all data transfers. For that reason, normal FTP is generally deprecated in favor of replacements like scp (secure copy) or sftp (secure FTP).

A special exception is made for the username anonymous (on Unix systems, also ftp). The connection still requires a password, but that password is usually just an email address, or any arbitrary string that looks like one. Anonymous FTP provides unrestricted global access to huge numbers of file archives. Locations of files in such archives are now generally specified in URL format, such as *ftp://ftp.example.com/pub/xml/README*.

file type

In the Unix filesystem, an attribute of a file that is displayed as the first character of the output of `ls -l`. File types include normal files, device files, directory files, named pipes, symbolic links, and so on.

filename

A name recorded in a directory file. A Unix filename may contain any byte value other than slash or NUL (the all-bits-zero byte), and all byte values are distinct (i.e., lettercase is significant).

Foreign filesystems mounted on a Unix system may impose further restrictions on filenames. See *pathname*.

filter

A program that by default reads standard input and writes standard output (and possibly, standard error). Such programs can be combined in command pipelines, each one filters its input to its output. The only interface with the neighboring programs in the pipeline is the simple standard byte stream data.

foreground process

A process that is running with a controlling terminal, and can therefore receive signals bound to keyboard interrupt characters. See *background process*.

format specifier

In I/O statements in many programming languages, a compact representation of the data-formatting requirements. For example, in the `printf` command, `%d` requests conversion of an integer to a decimal text string of minimal width, and `%8.3f` asks for the conversion of a floating-point number to a

right-justified eight-character text string with three digits after the decimal point.

FTP

See *File Transfer Protocol*.

function

A separate block of code that performs a well-defined task and is given a name, and often arguments that allow a calling program or function to communicate with it.

globbing

See *pathname expansion*.

gradual underflow

Floating-point numbers are represented by a significand of fixed precision, and a power of the base which is adjusted so that the leading significand digit is always nonzero. The number is then said to be *normalized*. When the smallest representable exponent is reached, further reduction would require the significand to underflow abruptly to zero. Gradual underflow, a feature of the IEEE 754 arithmetic system, permits the normalization requirement to be relaxed: the significand gradually loses precision until finally no bits are left, at which point it becomes zero. Gradual underflow extends the representable range of floating-point numbers, and has several desirable numerical properties that are lacking in systems with abrupt underflow to zero.

group

In file ownership, a file attribute that relates a collection of one or more users sharing a common group ID number. See *user*. Group ownership allows a useful intermediate level of access control: for example, the owner of a file would normally have read and write access, whereas group members might have only read access, and everyone else, no access at all.

hacker

A word with three quite different meanings in the computing world: (1) a clever and expert programmer; (2) a clumsy programmer (someone who works on software with a lumberjack's ax instead of a surgeon's scalpel); and (3) one who attempts to break computer security or otherwise pokes around in files that belong to others (see *cracker*).

hard link

In a Unix filesystem, each filename in a directory points to an entry in a filesystem table, called the *inode* table, which in turn points to the location of the file's data in the filesystem storage media. When more than one filename in the filesystem points to the same inode entry, the filenames are said to be *hard links* to the file.

here document

In the shell, the specification of inline data for a program, delimited by a unique user-specified word on the command line following a doubled less-than sign, and ended by the appearance of that same word at the beginning of a subsequent line. Here is an example:

```
$ cat << THATS-ALL-FOLKS
> one
> two
> three
> THATS-ALL-FOLKS
one
two
three
```

hexadecimal

A base-16 number system, with digits conventionally represented as 0–9a–f. The hexadecimal value e9 represents $14 \times 16 + 9 = 233$.

holding space

A buffer in the sed stream editor used for temporary storage of input records or matched data.

hot spots

Locations in computer programs where most of the execution time is spent. Most numerical programs spend their time in the innermost nested loops, so the most-executed statements account for only a small portion of the code, leading to the famous 90–10 rule of thumb: 90 percent of the time is spent in 10 percent of the code.

HyperText Markup Language (HTML)

One of several instances of particular document type definitions (DTDs) of the *Standard Generalized Markup Language*, SGML. HTML has achieved widespread use as the preferred markup system for text documents shared on the Internet via the World Wide Web.

HyperText Transport Protocol (HTTP)

The network protocol built on top of *TCP/IP* that supports much of the traffic on the World Wide Web. The HTTP protocol uses simple text lines with a small set of uppercase words as commands: you can try it with a telnet session on port 80 to a web server like this:

```
$ telnet www.example.com 80
  GET /
```

That should return the top-level web page, and then immediately break the connection.

implementation-defined

Left to the decision, or whim, of the programmer who writes the software. Programming language specifications sometimes declare that a feature is implementation-defined when the designers could not agree on what it should do, or when there is already widespread, but differing, use of the feature. For example, the ISO C Standard requires integer arithmetic, but does not specify the exact sizes of the various integer types.

Standards generally require that the handling of implementation-defined features be documented, whereas handling of *undefined* or *unspecified* behavior need not be documented.

inode

A Unix hierarchical filesystem table entry that contains information about a file, including its location in storage media, but not the name of the file. That information is recorded separately in directories, and permits files to have multiple names, leading to the concept of *links*.

International Organization for Standardization (ISO)

The body that coordinates worldwide standards in industry, including many that affect computers, such as character sets, data-recording media, and programming languages. Its acronym is ISO, which matches neither of its official names (the other name is French, *l'Organisation internationale de normalisation*).

Internet Protocol (IP)

The low-level networking *protocol* on which all other Internet protocols are built. The protocol defines the data packet format, which contains a version number, various flags and field lengths, a protocol identifier, source and destination addresses, and optional packet data. IP (pronounced I–P) does not provide guaranteed, or in-order, delivery. See *Transmission Control Protocol*.

interval expression

In regular expressions, a pattern that matches a string a specified number, or range of numbers, of times. For example, with Extended Regular Expressions, **vi{3}** matches viii, **vi{1,3}** matches vi, vii, and viii, and **vi{3,}** matches viii followed by zero or more i's.

I/O redirection

The process of assigning a source for standard input and destinations for standard error and standard output as alternatives to the default keyboard and display provided by the controlling terminal.

ISO

See *International Organization for Standardization*.

job control

A feature of several shells that allows an interactive user to control already-running processes, moving them between foreground and background, and to logout, leaving backgrounded processes running.

left-associative

In an expression with repeated instances of the same left-associative operator, terms are evaluated from the left. Addition, subtraction, multiplication, and division in most programming languages associate to the left, so a/b/c/d means that a is first divided by b, then that result is divided by c, and that result in turn is divided by d. Parentheses make the grouping clear: a/b/c/d is evaluated as (((a/b)/c)/d). For addition and multiplication, associativity might not seem relevant, and many programming languages leave their evaluation order unspecified. However, because of finite precision and range, computer arithmetic does not obey mathematical associativity, and intermediate overflow and/or cancellation can produce nonsensical results. See *right-associative*.

line continuation

A special marker, usually at end-of-line, to indicate that the next line is logically part of the current one. A widespread convention in the shell, many programming languages, and many program data-files, is that backslash-newline joins adjacent lines into a single logical line.

links

Multiple names for the same physical file. Unix has both *hard links* and *soft* (or *symbolic*) *links*.

load average

The average number of processes awaiting execution at any instant.

locale

A collection of attributes that affect data processing, and taken together, reflect language, country, and culture. For example, sort order differs between a Danish locale and a French-Canadian locale. The locale can be set through various shell environment variables (LANG, LC_ALL, LC_COLLATE, LC_MONETARY, LC_TIME, and others), and queried by programs, like sort, that can then adapt their behavior to the current locale. For example, the order of names in the output of ls on some systems differs when you change LC_ALL from C (meaning the historical ASCII order) to en_CA, en_US, or es_MX.

lock

A small file, or sometimes, just an agreement with the filesystem, that records the fact that a particular program is running. Programs, such as mail clients, text editors, and web browsers, use locks to prevent disasters from multiple simultaneous writes to files.

match

Selection of a text string according to a pattern.

metacharacter

A character that stands for something other than its literal meaning. For example, in filename wildcarding, the shell interprets asterisk as *match any string*, and question mark as *match any single character*.

metadata

Data about data. In a Unix filesystem, metadata in the inode includes link count, ownership, permission, size, storage media location, timestamps, and so forth.

modifier

In regular expression patterns, following characters that extend the meaning of a pattern. For example, following a character or parenthesized regular expression, question mark (**?**) means *zero or one of*, asterisk (*****) means *zero or more of*, plus (**+**) means *one or more of*, and **{3,5}** means *three, four, or five of*.

mounting

The logical layering of one filesystem on top of another, allowing filesystems to be larger than the size of any particular storage device.

named pipe

A special file created by the `mkfifo` command, permitting two unrelated processes to communicate, as if they were connected by a conventional pipe. See *FIFO*.

Network File System (NFS)

A filesystem *protocol* developed by Sun Microsystems, Inc., and widely deployed in the Unix world, that permits computers with storage systems to act as *fileservers*, making their storage available to *client* systems. Client/server filesystem designs reduce cost and enhance reliability and security, usually with some cost in performance.

null string

A string of no characters; an empty string.

octal

A base-8 number system, with digits 0 through 7. An octal digit requires three bits, and octal representation was popular in early computers with word sizes that were multiples of three: 12-, 18-, 24-, 36-, 48-, and 60-bit words were once common.

Current computer architectures are based on 8-bit bytes, and 32-bit or 64-bit word sizes, for which *hexadecimal* representation is more suitable.

Nevertheless, octal lives on in many Unix programming languages, perhaps because the first Unix machine (1969) was an 18-bit PDP-7. That early hardware was abandoned in 1970 in favor of a 16-bit PDP-11, and Unix systems since then have mostly been 32-bit or 64-bit machines. See *A Quarter Century of UNIX* in the Bibliography.

option

A command-line argument that influences a program's behavior.

ordinary character

A character that has no pattern-matching function in regular expressions: it just matches itself.

other

In Unix filesystem permissions, a catchall that includes everyone but the *user* and the *group*. The last three permission bits apply to *other*.

overflow

What happens when a number becomes too big to represent. With floating-point values in IEEE 754 arithmetic, the result is replaced by a special representation called *Infinity*. With integer values, the too-large result is simply truncated, which means that a data bit becomes a sign bit, producing the nonsensical result of a negative number for a positive overflow, and vice versa. For example, in 32-bit signed integer arithmetic, 2147483647 + 1 yields −2147483648, and 2147483648 + 2147483648 yields 0. Even worse, while floating-point Infinity propagates in calculations, and often, can be trapped if desired, on many platforms integer overflow cannot be caught, or is ignored by default.

ownership

An attribute of Unix files: each belongs to a particular *user* and a particular *group*. See also *permissions*.

parameter expansion

In the shell, the replacement of variable names by their values. For example, if variable x has the value To be or not to be, then $x is that value.

partition

A subdivision of a physical storage device in which a filesystem can be created. Historically, partitions were used to support disks that were bigger than kernel-addressing limits, and to limit filesystem size to that of backup media, usually magnetic tapes, so that a full backup could be done on a single tape. They are also used to limit filesystem growth and separate filesystems. For example, /tmp is often given its own partition because it is a public area that any process can fill up.

patch

A source-code update to a program that fixes a bug or supplies an additional feature. Patches are usually supplied as context or unified "diff" files, and are applied with the patch program.

pathname

A sequence of zero or more slash-separated filenames, where all but possibly the last filename are directory names. A Unix pathname may contain any byte value other than NUL (the all-bits-zero byte), and all byte values are distinct.

Consecutive slashes are equivalent to a single slash, although POSIX allows special interpretation of exactly two leading slashes. If the pathname starts with a slash, it is an *absolute pathname*, and otherwise, it is a *relative pathname* that starts at the *current working directory*. A pathname of slash names the root directory.

Historically, an empty pathname was interpreted as the current working directory, but modern practice is divided, with some systems treating empty pathnames as erroneous.

Foreign filesystems mounted on a Unix system may impose further restrictions on pathnames. See *filename*.

pathname expansion

Expansion of filename metacharacters to lists of files; also called *globbing* or *wildcarding*.

pattern

See *Basic Regular Expressions* and *Extended Regular Expressions*.

pattern space

A buffer in the sed stream editor used for temporary storage of input records to which editing operations are applied.

permissions

Attributes of files that associate read, write, and execute access with file ownership.

pipeline

A stream of commands separated by the pipe (|) operator, which connects standard output from the command on its left with standard input of the command on its right. All processes in a pipeline run simultaneously, and data flows through the pipeline via kernel memory buffers. This is much faster and simpler than using intermediate files, and the amount of data traversing the pipeline is not limited by filesystem size.

positional parameters

Arguments to shell scripts and shell functions. They can be referenced individually with numbered references, $1, $2, ... The special value $# contains the argument count, and the shift command discards argument $1, moves the remaining arguments down one slot, and decrements $#. The complete argument list is available as "$@"; the surrounding quotes are part of the syntax. The form "$*" is the argument list as a single string, with the arguments separated by the first character of IFS (normally a space), as if it had been written as "$1 $2 …".

print spooler

A daemon that manages all of a system's printers, ensuring that jobs are queued and sent one at a time to their requested printers. The BSD-style commands lpr, lprm, and lpq submit jobs, remove requests, and query queue status. The corre-

sponding System V commands are lp, cancel, and lpstat. Most modern Unix systems provide both flavors.

privileged mode

A Korn shell feature that is automatically enabled when any script with setuid permission is executed. It eliminates many of the security holes associated with setuid scripts.

Programmer's Workbench Unix (PWB)

A variant of Unix originally used within AT&T for telephone-switch software development, and later sold commercially to outside customers. It was developed in about 1977 from the Sixth Edition of Unix, and led to System III and System V Unix.

protocol

A formal agreement on how computer programs communicate. Most low-level network protocols use a compact binary encoding, but some higher-level protocols, such as *FTP* and *HTTP*, use simple text commands with short human-readable words, such as GET, LIST, and PUT. Protocols used on the Internet are generally described in *RFC* documents.

pseudodevice

An entry in the /dev directory that does not correspond to a physical hardware device, but nevertheless is supported by a kernel device driver that allows I/O to be performed on the pseudodevice. Typical examples are /dev/null, /dev/random, and /dev/zero.

public-key cryptography

A cryptographic system based on a pair of keys, one private and one public. Material encrypted with either key may be decrypted with the other. Although the keys are related, it is believed to be mathematically intractable to derive the private key from knowledge of the public key, and samples of known plaintext that have been encrypted with the public key.

Public-key cryptography solves the problem of key exchange for symmetric-key methods, and provides solutions to several other problems in cryptography, including secure digital signatures. Current methods for public-key cryptography are computationally much slower than symmetric-key systems, so they are often used in hybrid systems just for the initial secure exchange of symmetric keys. See *secure shell*.

Public-key cryptography was independently discovered by Ralph Merkle at the University of California, Berkeley (1974), and Whitfield Diffie and Martin E. Hellman at Stanford University (1975). The latter two began their influential 1976 paper *New Directions in Cryptography* with "We stand today on the brink of a revolution in cryptography" and ended it with "We hope this will inspire others to work in this fascinating area in which participation has been discouraged in the recent past by a nearly total government monopoly." It did: cryptographic research has exploded since the Diffie-Hellman paper appeared.

Ronald L. Rivest, Adi Shamir, and Leonard M. Adleman at MIT (1977) developed the first practical implementation of public-key cryptography, and formed RSA Data Security, Inc. (1982) to commercialize and further develop their cryptographic research.

public-key server

A networked computer system that registers public cryptographic keys and provides key-lookup services to Internet clients. Public-key servers share key data so that registration need be done only once at any one of them. See *public-key cryptography*.

quoting

A shell mechanism for protecting whitespace and metacharacters from their usual interpretation. It includes backslash (\), for protecting the following character, and single- and double-quote characters for protecting strings of zero or more characters.

random-access memory (RAM)

Central-memory storage in a computer, used for instructions and data of executing programs. Historically, it was called *core memory* (see entry for *core dump*) or just *core*, a term that remains in common use. RAM has implementations in many different technologies, with an alphabet soup of acronyms. The most important distinction is between DRAM (dynamic RAM), which must be continually refreshed to avoid data loss, and SRAM (static RAM), which retains data when power is lost. DRAM is physically denser, about 10 times slower, and about 100 times cheaper than SRAM, so DRAM is the main memory technology used in most computers, with only small amounts of SRAM used to provide a faster intermediate memory called *cache*. Most Cray supercomputers used SRAM for their entire central-memory system.

range

A feature of regular expression patterns that permits a consecutive sequence of characters to be abbreviated to the first and last, separated by a hyphen: **[0-7]** is equivalent to **[01234567]** (digits are consecutive in computer character sets).

range expression

In awk, ed, and sed, a comma-separated pair of expressions in the pattern part of a pattern/action pair. It selects a range of input records, from the first record that matches the left expression, through the next record that matches the right expression. In awk and ed, the range is a single record when both patterns match the same record, but in sed, the range always contains at least two records because the first record is not matched against the range-end pattern.

RCS

See *Revision Control System*.

read

In filesystem permissions, an attribute that permits file contents to be read by any process holding that permission, provided that exe-cute access is present in all of the directories in the path to the file.

record

In awk, a subdivision of a data stream into sequences of characters separated by text that matches the current record separator, RS. By default, records are lines of text.

recursion

The ability of a function to call itself, either directly or indirectly. Most modern programming languages provide this feature. The essential requirement is that each invocation of the function must have fresh storage for its local variables. In practice, this usually means that they are allocated on the *call stack*, instead of being statically allocated like the function's instructions.

remote shell

An insecure implementation of a facility for executing commands on a remote computer, now strongly deprecated in favor of the *secure shell*. The remote shell command family (rcp, rlogin, and rsh) provides neither strong authentication of client and server, nor session encryption, making it subject to spoofing attacks and network sniffing.

remove

Delete a filename from a directory. If there are no other hard links to the file in the filesystem, the file contents are removed as well, and their storage blocks are returned to the list of free storage for reuse.

Request for Comments (RFC)

An Internet standards and practices document, edited and archived at *ftp://ftp.isi.edu/rfc/*, and mirrored at many other Internet sites. RFC documents are assigned sequential numbers, starting with RFC 1 on April 7, 1969. About 4,000 RFCs have been written, and they serve as both the informal and the formal definition of how the Internet works.

RFCs are freely distributable simple text files written in a standardized format by technical experts on their volition, instead of being the products of national or international standardization committees, and they remain known as RFCs even after they have been formerly adopted as standards. The *rfc-index.txt* file in the archives contains a complete cross-referenced index of RFCs, including notification of earlier RFCs being superseded by later ones.

restricted shell

A shell that has had certain features removed, and others added, to enhance security. Usually, this means that there is no cd command to change directories, environment variables cannot be set, and output redirections are not permitted. The intent is to provide limited access to Unix facilities for untrusted applications or users. In practice, restricted shells are hard to set up and are not used much.

Revision Control System (RCS)

A storage system that allows the maintenance of multiple versions of a set of files, with history logs. RCS is commonly used for project files managed by a single user, or a small group of users working in the same filesystem. Most RCS users need learn only the ci (check-in), co (check out), rcsdiff (version difference), and rlog (version history) commands. A file that is checked out with write access for a single user is readable, but not writable, by other developers, and must be checked in before another user can acquire write access with a check out. For large distributed projects undergoing development at multiple independent sites, the much more complex *Concurrent Versions System* (CVS) is more suitable.

Although Bell Labs researchers had developed the related *Source Code Control System* for PWB, the general unavailability of SCCS outside Bell Labs versions of Unix led Walter Tichy to develop RCS at Purdue University in the early 1980s. RCS Version 3 (1983) was included in 4.3 BSD, and RCS was publicly described in the journal *Software—Practice and Experience* in July 1985. RCS was later contributed to the GNU Project and released under the GNU General Public License; it is available at *ftp://ftp.gnu.org/gnu/rcs/*.

RFC

See *Request for Comments*.

right-associative

In an expression with repeated instances of the same right-associative operator, terms are evaluated from the right. Exponentiation and assignment operators typically associate to the right. For example, the assignment a = b = c = d is carried out by assigning d to c, then assigning c to b, and finally, assigning b to a. Parentheses make this clear: a = b = c = d is evaluated as (a = (b = (c = d))). See *left-associative*.

root

See *superuser*.

root directory

The top-level directory in a Unix filesystem tree. The root directory is represented by /, and is its own parent: /.. is the same as /.

sappnd

An additional filesystem permission bit provided by BSD systems that, when set by root, allows data to be written to the end of the file, even when it has no write permission. The file cannot be deleted unless the sappnd permission is removed, and that can be done only if the containing directory has write permission. See *uappnd*.

scalar variable

A program variable that holds a single value. See *array variable*.

SCCS

See *Source Code Control System*.

scheduler

A component of a computer operating system that is responsible for managing the execution of all of the processes in the system.

scratch file

A temporary file that needs to survive only for the duration of a job.

secure shell

A secure implementation of the ability to execute commands on a remote computer, developed to replace the insecure *remote shell*, but from the user's viewpoint, operating in much the same way. The secure shell command family (scp, slogin, and ssh) provides strong authentication of client and server, and strong session encryption, making spoofing attacks much harder. Network sniffing attacks are still possible, but the attacker sees only an encrypted data stream that must then somehow be decrypted without knowledge of the encryption key. To make decryption even more difficult, the encryption key is changed at management-specified intervals (by default, every hour).

setgid

See *set-group-ID*.

set-group-ID

A permission in the Unix filesystem that, when set on a directory, causes files in that directory to be created with the group ID of the directory, rather than the group ID of the user who creates them. This is typically used to guarantee that files shared by multiple users in a common group remain accessible to the group members.

When set on an executable regular file, it causes the program to run as the group of the file, rather than as the group of the user who invoked the program. On some systems, this permission enables mandatory file and record locking for nonexecutable files.

setuid

See *set-user-ID*.

set-user-ID

A permission in the Unix filesystem that, when set on an executable file, causes the program to run as the owner of the file, rather than as the user who invoked the program. This allows a trusted program to be run by an ordinary user, without giving that user the special privileges needed by the program to do its job.

The set-user-ID invention by Dennis Ritchie is protected under U.S. Patent 4,135,240, filed by Bell Telephone Laboratories, Inc., on July 9, 1973, and granted on January 16, 1979. Although the intent was to collect license fees for its use, this proved impractical, and Bell Labs later assigned the patent to the public. See *http://lpf.ai.mit.edu/ Links/prep.ai.mit.edu/patent-list* and *http://patft.uspto.gov/netahtml/ srchnum.htm*.

SGML

See *Standard Generalized Markup Language*.

shadowed

Hidden. A shell function's positional parameters override, and hide, the shell script's positional parameters, almost as if the function were a separate script. The difference is that the function has access to all variables that have been defined earlier in the script's execution, and can modify any of them. Functions can also change other parts of the global state, such as signal traps and the current working directory. By contrast, a separate script inherits only exported variables through its environment string space, and cannot change the parent's global state.

shell

The command interpreter in a Unix or Unix-like operating system that users interact with, and that processes command files. The shell provides a complete programming language, and to some users, the shell *is* the computer, since that is the view of the system that they most often see.

shell options

Settings in the shell that control its behavior. They can be changed by command-line options, or by the set command.

side effect

A change in state that occurs peripherally to the execution of a block of code, such as a function or procedure. For example, a pseudorandom number generator returns a pseudorandom number, but it also updates the internal generator seed so that the next call produces a different value. By contrast, most mathematical functions, such as square root, are free of side effects, and produce the same result for the same arguments, no matter how often they are called. A function that performs I/O also has a side effect, since it changes file positions, and possibly file contents. Functions with side effects are generally deprecated in computer programming because they make it much harder to reason about what the program is doing. But as the examples indicate, side effects are also sometimes essential.

signal

An asynchronous event that happens to a running program. Signals can be initiated by hardware, software, or human users. Signal handlers can catch most signals and respond to them, possibly doing nothing, and thus ignoring them. Uncaught signals cause default actions to be taken; for most signals, this means that the process is terminated. The trap command provides signal management for shell programs.

signal handler

A set of statements that is registered with the kernel to handle one or more signals. In compiled programming languages, it is generally a function with a prescribed calling sequence, but in shell scripts, it is just a list of commands supplied as the first argument of the trap command.

Single Unix Specification

An integrated specification of Unix developed by the Open Group. It includes POSIX (IEEE Std 1003.1-2001/ISO/IEC 9945:2002) and X/Open standards. It is available at *http://www.unix.org/version3/*.

soft link

See *symbolic link*.

Source Code Control System (SCCS)

A storage system that allows the maintenance of multiple versions of a set of files, with history logs. SCCS was developed as part of the PWB Unix work at Bell Labs, but because of licensing restrictions, was not made easily available on other Unix flavors. See *Revision Control System* and *Concurrent Versions System*, which have largely eclipsed SCCS.

sparse

Occupying only a few of a set of storage locations. awk arrays are sparse tables.

special character

In regular expressions, a character that has a meaning other than its literal value; another name for it is *metacharacter*. For example, *, ?, +, [,], {, }, (,), ^, and $ are all special characters; see also *modifier*.

spelling dictionary

A list of words that are known to be correctly spelled.

spelling exception list

A list of words that are not found in a *spelling dictionary*; they may be spelling errors, or just unusual or unexpected words that are candidates for inclusion in the spelling dictionary.

spooled

Sent to a queue of jobs awaiting processing. The printing commands send a copy of the job to be printed to the *print spooler daemon*. The word *spool* derives from early mainframe computers of the 1950s. While physically large, they did not have large-capacity memories, and often not even disk storage. Instead, a job to be executed, printed, or punched was first written to a reel, or spool, of magnetic tape, and then when a suitable number of them had been collected on tape, the jobs were processed in order from the tape.

SQL

See *Structured Query Language*.

stability

A property of certain sorting algorithms that preserves the input order of records with equal keys. This makes it possible to sort records again on a secondary key without losing the order imposed by a prior sort on the primary key.

One of the best, and most popular, sorting methods for records with arbitrary keys is the famous *Quicksort* algorithm, often implemented in the C library as the function qsort( ), and discussed at length in most computer-science texts about algorithms. Quicksort is generally quick, but it is *not* stable.

Standard Generalized Markup Language (SGML)

An abstract document markup system defined in several ISO standards issued since 1986. SGML has growing interest among publishers, and a particular instance of it, called *HyperText Markup Language* (HTML), is the preferred markup system used for text documents in the World Wide Web. A more recent instance of SGML, the *eXtensible Markup Language* (XML), has attracted wide interest.

standard I/O

A fundamental concept in the Software Tools philosophy, that all programs should have a standard input source, a standard output sink, and a standard error stream to report problems.

standard input, output, and error

Three standard I/O streams guaranteed open and available to all user processes in Unix, generally directed to the controlling terminal, but easily reassignable to files or pipes. *Filters* read their normal input from standard input and write their normal output on standard output. The standard error stream is conventionally used for display of error, informational, status, and warning messages.

sticky

A permission bit in the Unix filesystem. It was originally introduced to indicate to the kernel that, after execution, the text segment of the executable should be preserved in swap space for later reuse. That practice is now deprecated. However, when set on a directory, it means that files therein can be removed only by their owner, or the directory owner. It is widely used for this purpose, with public directories like /tmp, to prevent users from deleting files that do not belong to them. (Recall that file deletion requires write access to the directory, *not* to the file itself.)

Structured Query Language (SQL)

A method for communicating with database programs in a program- and vendor-independent fashion. SQL (pronounced either S–Q–L or sequel) is defined in several ISO standards issued since 1992. Despite these standards, there are numerous incompatible, and usually unnecessary, variations in SQL implementations that force authors of books about SQL to spend time and table space discussing the deviations.

subshell

How a parenthesized list of commands is processed by the shell. It automatically runs a copy of itself to process the command list, with the result that changes made by the commands to environment variables or the current working directory have no effect outside the command list.

substitution

See *expansion*.

suffix

In Unix filenames, trailing text, usually from the last dot to the end of the name. Although the filesystem does not attribute any significance to filenames, many applications do, grouping related files with a common basename and different suffixes: myprog.c (C source file), myprog.h (C header file), myprog.i (preprocessor output), myprog.o (object code), myprog.s (assembly code), myprog (executable program), and so on.

superuser

The privileged user in a Unix system, conventionally called root, although other cute names are sometimes assigned at administrator whim. What really identifies the super user is a user ID of zero. Any username with that user ID has superuser privileges, meaning full and unrestricted access to all files in the local filesystem, including low-level device and network access, and the ability to start and stop system processes, send signals to any process, install and remove kernel modules, and gracefully shut down or abruptly halt the system. While system administrators require these privileges, they are dangerous and easily misused. Consequently, recommended practice is never to log in as the superuser, but instead, to only briefly assume superuser privileges via the su or sudo commands.

symbolic link

A filename that points to another filename, possibly even in a different filesystem. Also called a *soft link*, to distinguish it from a *hard link*.

TCP

See *Transmission Control Protocol*.

tilde expansion

A convenient feature of some shells that replaces an unprotected tilde (~) character at the start of an argument with the path to the user's home directory. The expansion of $HOME does the same thing, except that it is also recognized and expanded inside quoted strings, such as "$HOME/.profile", whereas tilde is not expanded inside a quoted string. It must be emphasized that tilde expansion is a *shell feature* that is unknown to the kernel and most programs, and is therefore best used only to speed typing in interactive shell sessions.

time slice

A small interval of time, usually a few milliseconds, that the *scheduler* allows a process to run before suspending it and giving system resources to another process for the next time slice.

Transmission Control Protocol (TCP)

One of two major networking *protocols* (the other is *Internet Protocol*, IP) on which many Internet services are built. They are usually spoken of together, TCP/IP, and pronounced T–C–P–I–P. The lower-level protocol, IP, does not provide either guaranteed or in-order delivery, but TCP does. Protocols that need reliable connections, such as FTP (*File Transfer Protocol*) and HTTP (*HyperText Transfer Protocol*), are built on top of TCP.

trap

A signal caught by the shell, causing execution of a set of commands registered by a trap command for a specified list of signals. See *signal handler*.

tree structure

A data structure, such as the Unix filesystem, possessing a root node with zero or more branches, each of which is itself a tree structure. File trees provide an excellent way to organize filesystem data, and can grow to enormous sizes. The names of the nodes starting from the root node form a *pathname* that uniquely identifies the location of any object in the tree.

Trojan horse

An imposter program that masquerades as another program, sometimes carrying out the function of the original, but also doing something nefarious or malicious.

uappnd

An additional filesystem permission bit provided by BSD systems that, when set by the user, allows data to be written to the end of the file, even when it has no write permission. The file cannot be deleted unless the uappnd permission is removed, and that can be done only if the containing directory has write permission. Unlike *sappnd*, uappnd permission can be set by the unprivileged owner of the file.

Unicode

A universal character set designed to handle all of the world's writing systems. Development by a multivendor consortium began in the early 1990s, and is expected to continue for many years. Differences with a similar effort in the ISO 10646 Standard have now been resolved, and the two character sets will remain in agreement.

Although early versions of Unicode required no more than 16 bits per character, and were implemented as such by some operating systems and at least one programming language (Java), Unicode developers now insist that 21-bit characters will ultimately be needed. Consequently, there are several encodings of Unicode, including 32-bit values (UCS-4 and UTF-32), one or two 16-bit values (UCS-2 and UTF-16), and one to four 8-bit values (UTF-8).

Importantly, Unicode includes the ASCII character set in the lower 128 positions, so all existing ASCII files are automatically valid Unicode files in UTF-8 encoding.

All computing vendors are adopting Unicode, but the transition will take many years, especially since many complex aspects of multilingual text processing and display did not exist in the simple ASCII world, and since confusion over the different data encodings will be widespread.

Production of an adequate font repertoire is also an enormous problem: tens of thousands of fonts are available for 8-bit character sets, but only a small handful for Unicode, and then only for small subsets.

uniform resource locator (URL)

An object that identifies the location of a file or resource on the World Wide Web. If you see colon-slash-slash somewhere, it is probably part of a URL (pronounced U–R–L).

user

In file ownership, a file attribute that relates a file to a particular user-identifier number, which in turn is mapped to a human-friendly username by a record in the password database. See *group*.

UTC

See *Coordinated Universal Time*.

UTF-8

An encoding of *Unicode* character values in one to four 8-bit bytes. All ASCII files are valid UTF-8 files.

virtual machine

A software program for the execution of a computer instruction set. The runtime behavior of the Java language is defined in terms of an underlying virtual-machine instruction set that is generally executed by software, rather than hardware. Most scripting languages are translated to the instruction set of a virtual machine unique to their interpreter.

whitespace

Space (ASCII 32) and/or tab (ASCII 9) characters. Sometimes called *horizontal space*, to distinguish it from *vertical space* produced by form feed (FF, ASCII 13), newline (NL or LF, ASCII 10), and vertical tab (VT, ASCII 11).

wildcard expansion

See *pathname expansion*.

word

In computer architectures, a data item that is operated on by machine instructions. Current architectures usually have 32-bit or 64-bit words, although historically, many other sizes, right down to a single bit, have been used.

word-constituent

Characters that make up words. In many applications, this means letters, digits, and underscore.

write

In filesystem permissions, an attribute that permits file contents to be overwritten by any process holding that permission, provided that execute access is present in all of the directories in the path to the file. Lack of write permission does not necessarily protect file contents, since the file may be removed by anyone with write access to the file's directory, and then replaced with the same name, but new data.

XML

See *eXtensible Markup Language*.

X/Open System Interface Extension (XSI)

A formal extension to the base POSIX standard, documenting attributes that make a system not only POSIX-compliant, but also XSI-compliant; it is informally called the *Single Unix Specification*.

Index

& (ampersand)
  &= (assignment operator), 119, 401
  && (logical AND operator), 118, 123,
    230, 401
  beginning HTML entities, 96
  bitwise AND operator, 118, 401
  expr operator, 160
  in sed replacement text, 50
  preceding file descriptor, 146
  run in background, 13
* (asterisk)
  ** (arithmetic operator), 230, 400, 401
  **= (assignment operator), 230
  *= (assignment operator), 119, 230, 401
  arithmetic operator, 118, 230, 401
  expr operator, 160
  in regular expressions, 34, 40
  variable, 117
  wildcard, 153
@ (at sign) variable, 117
` (backquote)
  `...` (command substitution), 156
\ (backslash)
  \(...\) (backreferences), 35, 39
  \\ (escape sequence), 17, 148
  \< (in regular expressions), 46
  \> (in regular expressions), 46
  \{...\} (interval expressions), 34, 40
  in bracket expressions in EREs, 42
  in regular expressions, 34
  line continuation character, 142
  line continuation character, awk, 226
  literal interpretation, 161
  preceding echo escape sequences, 16
  preceding printf escape sequences, 148

{...} (braces)
  brace expansion, 395
  code blocks, 167, 486
  compound statements, awk, 244
  in Extended Regular Expressions, 43
  in regular expressions, 35
  positional parameters greater than 9, 115
^ (caret)
  ^= (assignment operator), 119, 230, 401
  arithmetic operator, 230
  bitwise exclusive OR operator, 118, 401
  in Basic Regular Expressions, 37
  in regular expressions, 34, 41, 45, 484
: (colon)
  :+ (substitution operator), 114
  :- (substitution operator), 113
  := (substitution operator), 113
  :? (substitution operator), 114
  command, 123
  expr operator, 160
  special built-in command, 168
, (comma)
  sequential evaluation, 401
$ (dollar sign)
  $((...)) (arithmetic expansion), 118–120,
    485
  $(...) (command substitution), 156
  ${...} (parameter expansion), 113
  "$*" (variable), 116
  "$@" (variable), 116
  $# (variable), 115
  $$ (variable), 118, 276, 355
  $* (variable), 116
  $- (variable), 175
  $@ (variable), 116

We'd like to hear your suggestions for improving our indexes. Send email to *index@oreilly.com*.

$ (dollar sign) (*continued*)
  in regular expressions, 34, 41, 45, 484
  preceding field values in awk, 63
  preceding variables, 15, 113
  variable, 117
. (dot)
  command, 172, 473
  directory, 445
  hidden files preceded by, 155
  in Basic Regular Expressions, 37
  in filenames, 154
  in regular expressions, 34
  preceding hidden files, 270
  special built-in command, 168
.. (dot dot) directory, 445
"..." (double quotes)
  enclosing string constants, awk, 226
  grouping text, 162
... (ellipses), inserting in troff markup, 431
= (equal sign)
  == (comparison operator), 118, 230, 401
  == (test expression), 393
  assigning values to variables, 15
  assignment operator, 119, 230, 401
  expr operator, 160
  test expression, 125, 393
! (exclamation mark)
  != (comparison operator), 118, 230, 401
  != (expr operator), 160
  != (test expression), 125, 393
  !~ (matches operator, awk), 228
  arithmetic operator, 118, 230, 401
  in wildcard set, 153, 154
  logical NOT operator, 122
  variable, 117
(hash mark)
  ## (pattern-matching operator), 114
  #! (specifying interpreter in shell
     script), 10–12
  pattern-matching operator, 114
  preceding comments, 24
  preceding comments, awk, 226
  prefixing temporary backup file
     name, 470
  printf flag, 151
  string-length operator, 115
  variable, 117
- (hyphen)
  -- (arithmetic operator), 118, 230, 400,
     401
  -= (assignment operator), 119, 230, 401

-- (end of options), 13
  arithmetic operator, 118, 230, 401
  as bare option, 12
  expr operator, 160
  in filenames, 440
  preceding command options, 13
  preceding file type in listing, 466
  printf flag, 151
  variable, 117
< (left angle bracket)
  <!-- ... --> (HTML comments), 96
  <<= (assignment operator), 119, 401
  <= (comparison operator), 118, 230, 401
  <= (expr operator), 160
  << (here document), 98, 143
  <<- (here document, leading tabs
     removed), 144
  <<< (here strings), 400
  <> (open file for reading and
     writing), 144
  changing standard input, 19
  comparison operator, 118, 230, 401
  expr operator, 160
  test expression, 393
(...) (parentheses)
  ((...)) (arithmetic command), 399
  grouping arithmetic expressions, 119
  grouping, expr expressions, 160
  in Extended Regular Expressions, 44
  in regular expressions, 35
  subshell, 167
% (percent sign)
  %= (assignment operator), 119, 230, 401
  %% (format specifier), 149
  %% (format specifier, awk), 261
  %% (pattern-matching operator), 115
  arithmetic operator, 118, 230, 401
  expr operator, 160
  pattern-matching operator, 114
  preceding format specifications, 18
  preceding printf format specifiers, 149
+ (plus sign)
  ++ (arithmetic operator), 118, 230, 400,
     401
  += (assignment operator), 119, 230, 401
  arithmetic operator, 118, 230, 401
  expr operator, 160
  in Extended Regular Expressions, 43
  in regular expressions, 35
  in trace output, 24
  printf flag, 151

? (question mark)
  ?: (conditional expression), 119, 230, 401
  in Extended Regular Expressions, 43
  in regular expressions, 35
  variable, 117, 120
  wildcard, 153
> (right angle bracket)
  >> (appending to standard output), 19
  >> (bit-shift right operator), 118, 401
  >> (output redirection, awk), 251
  >>= (assignment operator), 119, 401
  >= (comparison operator), 118, 230, 401
  >= (expr operator), 160
  >| (redirect output overriding
      noclobber), 143, 145
  changing standard output, 19
  comparison operator, 118, 230, 401
  expr operator, 160
  output redirection, awk, 251
  test expression, 393
; (semicolon)
  ending HTML entities, 96
  separating commands, 13
  separating statements, awk, 240, 244
'...' (single quotes), literal interpretation, 161
/ (slash)
  /= (assignment operator), 119, 230, 401
  arithmetic operator, 118, 230, 401
  expr operator, 160
  forbidden in filenames, 439
  in pathname, 445
  root directory, 443
[...] (square brackets)
  [: ... :] (character classes), 36, 38
  [. .... .] (collating symbols), 36, 38
  [= ... =] (equivalence classes), 36, 38
  [...] (test command variant form), 124
  [[...]] (extended test facility), 392–393
  array indices, awk, 233
  in regular expressions, 34, 486
  wildcard set, 153
~ (tilde)
  ~- ($OLDPWD tilde expansion), 399
  ~+ ($PWD tilde expansion), 399
  arithmetic operator, 118, 401
  in temporary backup file name, 470
  matches operator, awk, 228
  tilde expansion, 152, 399, 505
| (vertical bar)
  |= (assignment operator), 119, 401
  || (logical OR operator), 118, 123, 230,
     401

alternation operator, 43, 484
bitwise OR operator, 118, 401
expr operator, 160
in regular expressions, 35
pipe symbol, 10

Symbols

< (left angle bracket)
  << (arithmetic operator), 118, 401

Numbers

$0 ... $NF field references, awk, 238
\0 escape sequence, 17, 148
0 exit status, 121
0 printf flag, 151
0 variable, 117, 406
0...9 file descriptors, 145–147
.1 file extension, 469
1–125 exit statuses, 121
126 exit status, 121
127 exit status, 121
128 exit status, 121
129 or higher exit statuses, 121
$1...$9 (see positional parameters)

A

\a escape sequence, 16, 148
.a file extension, 469
-a logical AND, test expression, 126
-a shell option, 174
-a test expression, 392
ABRT signal, 361
access control lists (ACLs), 460, 484
access time for files, 286, 460–461
accounting, process, 372
ACLs (access control lists), 460, 484
actions, awk, 225, 239
addition operator, 118, 401
Adobe PDF (Portable Document
     Format), 80, 82
Adobe PostScript, 80, 82
alert character, escape sequence for, 16, 148
alias command, 168, 171
aliases
  defining, 168, 171
  finding location of, 280
  removing, 169, 171
allexport shell option, 174
alternation operator, 43, 45, 484
American National Standards Institute
     (ANSI), 484

American Standard Code for Information
  Interchange (ASCII), 438, 484
American Standards Association (ASA), 484
ampersand (&)
  &= (assignment operator), 119, 401
  && (logical AND operator), 118, 123,
    230, 401
  beginning HTML entities, 96
  bitwise AND operator, 118, 401
  expr operator, 160
  in sed replacement text, 50
  preceding file descriptor, 146
  run in background, 13
anchors, 41, 42, 45, 484
ANSI (American National Standards
    Institute), 484
archives, InfoZip format for, 204
ARGC variable, awk, 234
ARG_MAX variable, 294
arguments
  all, representing, 116
  awk arguments, 234
  for current process, 117
  for options, 13
  function arguments, 136
  maximum length of, 294
  number of, 115, 117
  passed by reference, 486
  passed by value, 486
  shifting to the left, 116, 132, 169, 474
  validating, 414
  wildcard expansion of, 353
  (see also positional parameters)
ARGV variable, awk, 234
arithmetic commands, 399
arithmetic expansion, 109, 118–120, 485
arithmetic for loop, 399
arithmetic operators, 118, 230, 400, 401
arrays
  array variables, 485
  array variables, awk, 233–234
  associative arrays, 233, 485
  awk arrays, 247
  indexed arrays, 396–399
ASA (American Standards Association), 484
ASCII (American Standard Code for
    Information Interchange), 438, 484
aspell command, 329–330, 347
assignment operators, 119, 230, 401
associative arrays, 233, 485

asterisk (*)
  ** (arithmetic operator), 230, 400, 401
  **= (assignment operator), 230
  *= (assignment operator), 119, 230, 401
  arithmetic operator, 118, 230, 401
  expr operator, 160
  in regular expressions, 34, 40
  variable, 117
  wildcard, 153
at command, 374, 476
at sign (@) variable, 117
at.allow file, 374
atan2() function, awk, 264
at.deny file, 374
AT&T, UWIN package, xxii
audit trails, 414
.awk file extension, 469
awk interpreter, 62–65
  command line arguments, accessing, 234
  command line for, 224
  efficiency of, 349
  environment variables, accessing, 236
  examples, one-line programs, 240–243
  extracting first lines, 83
  -F option, 63, 224
  -f option, 224
  for field extraction, 89–94
  free implementations of, 224
  input from files, 224
  input from standard input, 224, 225
  interval expressions support, 48
  regular expressions support, 47, 228, 238
  tag list example using, 106
awk language, 223–226, 474
  -- option, 224
  actions, 225, 239
  array variables, 233–234
  arrays, membership testing, 247
  assignment operators, 231
  BEGIN pattern, 64, 226, 239
  built-in variables, 232
  comments, 226
  compound statements, 244
  conditional execution, 244
  control flow, 248
  END pattern, 64, 226, 239
  external programs, running, 251
  field separators, 224, 237
  fields in, 62, 225, 238
  floating-point arithmetic, 229

global variables in functions, 253
iterative execution, 245–247
line continuation character, 226
local variables in functions, 253
logical operators, 231
looping, 245–247
numbers, 228–232
numbers, converting to strings, 227
numeric functions, 264–266
numeric operators, 230
output redirection, 250
patterns, 225, 238
printing lines, 64
record separators, 72, 236
records in, 62, 225, 236
recursion, 254
spellchecking implemented
      with, 331–343, 348
statements, separation of, 244
string constants, 226
string functions, 255–264
string operators, 227
strings
    concatenating, 227
    converting to numbers, 228
user-controlled input, 249–250
user-defined functions, 252–255
-v option, 224, 225
variables, scalar, 232
whitespace, 226
awka translator, 224

B

.B command, troff, 426
\b escape sequence, 16, 148
%b format specifier, 149
b, preceding block device in listing, 466
-b shell option, 174
-b test expression, 125, 392
background processes, 485
    process ID of last background
        command, 117
    running, 356
backquote (`)
    `...` (command substitution), 156
backreferences, 35, 485
    in Basic Regular Expressions, 39
    in regular expressions, 42
    in sed program, 50
    not supported in Extended Regular
        Expressions, 42

backslash (\)
    \(...\) (backreferences), 35, 39
    \\ (escape sequence), 17, 148
    \< (in regular expressions), 46
    \> (in regular expressions), 46
    \{...\} (interval expressions), 34, 40
    in bracket expressions in EREs, 42
    in regular expressions, 34
    line continuation character, 142, 226
    literal interpretation, 161
    preceding echo escape sequences, 16
    preceding printf escape sequences, 148
backslash escaping, 161
backspace, escape sequence for, 16, 148
backup files, temporary, 470
basename, 485
basename command, 181, 474
bash (Bourne Again Shell), 473
    differences from ksh93, 381–385
    downloading, 402–403
    shopt command, 385–389
    startup and termination, 408–410
BASH_ENV variable, 409
Basic Regular Expressions (BREs), 30,
        37–42, 485
    backreferences in, 35, 39
    metacharacters for, 34
    programs using, 46–48
    (see also grep command)
batch command, 374, 476
BEGIN pattern, awk, 64, 226, 239
Bell Labs awk, 224
Bell Telephone Laboratories, 1
Bentley, Jon, word list challenge by, 102
bg command, 168, 172
.BI command, troff, 428
bin directories, 414, 444
binary files, 442
birthday paradox, 485
"bit bucket" file, 21
bit-shift left operator, 118, 401
bit-shift right operator, 118, 401
bitwise AND operator, 118, 401
bitwise exclusive OR operator, 118, 401
bitwise negation operator, 118, 401
bitwise OR operator, 118, 401
black box, 8
block device
    preceded by b in listing, 466
    test expression for, 125
block sizes, 464
BODY object, HTML, 96

Bourne-Again Shell (see bash)
Bourne shell (see sh)
.BR command, troff, 428
brace expansion, 395
braces ({...})
    brace expansion, 395
    code blocks, 167, 486
    compound statements, 244
    in Extended Regular Expressions, 43
    in regular expressions, 35
    positional parameters greater than 9, 115
bracket expressions, 34, 42, 486
    in Basic Regular Expressions, 37
    in Extended Regular Expressions, 42, 43,
        45
    internationalization and localization
        features for, 35–36
brackets (see square brackets)
break command, 131, 168, 473
break statement, awk, 246, 248
BREs (see Basic Regular Expressions)
bubble sort algorithm, 74
building software packages, automating
        procedure for, 192–222
built-in commands, 13, 168–172, 486
built-in variables, in awk, 232
bullets, inserting in troff markup, 431
bunzip2 command, 475
.bz2 file extension, 469
bzip2 command, 475

C

\c escape sequence, 16, 148
.C file extension, 470
.c file extension, 469
%c format specifier, 149, 261
c, preceding character device in listing, 466
-C shell option, 174
-C test expression, 392
-c test expression, 125, 392
call stack, 255, 486
cancel command, 79
caret (^)
    ^= (assignment operator), 119, 230, 401
    arithmetic operator, 230
    bitwise exclusive OR operator, 118, 401
    in Basic Regular Expressions), 37
    in regular expressions, 34, 41, 45, 484
carriage return, escape sequence for, 16, 148
case conversion
    awk, 256
    tr command, 20

case sensitivity, in filenames, 440
case statement, 129
    optional matching parentheses, 400
    path searching example using, 181–183
    software build example using, 197
cat command, 474
    awk implementation of, 241
    tag list example using, 105
catman program, 436
.cc file extension, 470
cd command, 168, 473
CD-ROMs, 438
character classes
    in Basic Regular Expressions, 38
    in regular expressions, 36, 42
character device
    preceded by c in listing, 466
    test expression for, 125
character sets, 438
characters
    counting, 10, 77
    transliterating, 20
    (see also metacharacters; special
        characters)
checknr command, 435
checksum command, 301
chgrp command, 453, 475
chmod command, 10, 454, 467, 475
chown command, 453, 475
ci command, 477
cksum command, 301, 475
close() function, awk, 250
closedir() function, 448
cmp command, 299, 474
co command, 477
code blocks, 167, 486
code examples in book, using, xxi
code pages, 439, 487
col command, 435
collating symbols, 487
    in Basic Regular Expressions, 38
    in regular expressions, 36, 42
colon (:)
    :+ (substitution operator), 114
    :- (substitution operator), 113
    := (substitution operator), 113
    :? (substitution operator), 114
    command, 123
    expr operator, 160
    special built-in command, 168
comm command, 326, 475
comma (,)
    sequential evaluation, 401

command command, 169, 170, 171, 474
command history
    disabling for functions, 174, 385
    enabling, 385
    interactive use of, 169
    sh shell not supporting, 408
command line arguments (see arguments)
command line options, 13, 133, 495
command substitution, 155–161, 487
    expr command and, 159–161
    mailing list example of, 157–159
    sed command and, 157
command-line editing, vi-style editing
        for, 174
commands, 12–14
    alias command, 168, 171
    aspell command, 329–330, 347
    at command, 374, 476
    basename command, 181, 474
    batch command, 374, 476
    bg command, 168, 172
    break command, 131, 168, 473
    built-in, 168–172
    bunzip2 command, 475
    bzip2 command, 475
    cancel command, 79
    cat command, 474
    cd command, 168, 473
    changing environment variable for
        duration of, 111
    checking for syntax errors, 174
    checknr command, 435
    checksum command, 301
    chgrp command, 453, 475
    chmod command, 10, 454, 467, 475
    chown command, 453, 475
    ci command, 477
    cksum command, 301, 475
    cmp command, 299, 474
    co command, 477
    col command, 435
    colon (:) command, 123, 168
    comm command, 326, 475
    command command, 169, 170, 171, 474
    continue command, 131, 169, 474
    cp command, 475
    cron command, 377, 476
    crontab command, 375–377, 476
    cut command, 58, 474
    date command, 474
    dd command, 85, 474
    deroff command, 435

df command, 295–297, 464, 475
diff command, 299, 475
diff3 command, 300
dirname command, 201, 474
dot (.) command, 168, 172
du command, 297–299, 464, 475
echo command, 15, 16, 267, 382, 475
egrep command, 5, 30, 475
env command, 111, 474
eval command, 166, 169, 415, 474
evaluation order of, 162–166
exec command, 146, 169, 474
exit command, 121, 169, 474
exit status of, 117
expand and print before executing, 174
expand command, 475
export command, 110, 474
expr command, 159–161
false command, 169, 474
fc command, 169, 172
fg command, 169, 172
fgrep command, 31, 475
file command, 85, 475
files, list of, 475
find command, 280–291, 464, 475
finding location of, in PATH, 280
fmt command, 76, 475
fuser command, 476
getconf command, 444
getopts command, 133, 169, 474
getpubkey command, 306
gpg command, 306
grep command, 5, 23, 30, 32, 475
groff command, 435
gr_osview command, 356
grouping, 167
gunzip command, 475
gzip command, 475
head command, 83, 476
iconv command, 475
id command, 474
info command, 477
iostat command, 356
ispell command, 329–330, 347
jobs command, 169, 172
join command, 60, 475
kill command, 169, 172, 360–363, 476
ktrace command, 368
less command, 475
let command, 399
list of, 473–477
locale command, 26, 477

commands (*continued*)
  locate command, 279, 476
  logger command, 414, 477
  long lists of arguments to, 293
  lp command, 79, 477
  lpq command, 79, 477
  lpr command, 79, 477
  lprm command, 79
  lpstat command, 79
  ls command, 268–272, 463, 476
  mail command, 199, 477
  mailx command, 199
  make command, 477
  man command, 477
  maximum length of, with arguments, 294
  md5 command, 301
  md5sum command, 301, 476
  mkdir command, 476
  mktemp command, 118, 276, 476
  monitor command, 356
  more command, 475
  mount command, 445
  mpstat command, 356
  netstat command, 356
  newgrp command, 169
  nfsstat command, 356
  nice command, 352, 476
  nroff command, 435
  od command, 85, 269, 476
  osview command, 356
  par command, 368
  patch command, 300, 476
  perfmeter command, 356
  pgp command, 306
  pgpgpg command, 306
  pgrep command, 363
  pkill command, 363
  pr command, 80–82, 475
  printf command, 17, 147–152, 475
  printing before executing, 174
  processes, list of, 476
  procinfo command, 356
  proctool command, 356
  prompt string for, 118
  prstat command, 356
  ps command, 354–360, 476
  pstat command, 356
  ptree command, 356
  pwd command, 169, 476
  rcp command, 196
  rcs command, 477
  rcs, list of, 477

rcsdiff command, 477
read command, 140–143, 169, 474
reading without executing, 174
readonly command, 110, 169, 474
renice command, 352, 476
return command, 136, 169, 474
rlog command, 477
rm command, 476
rmdir command, 476
rsh command, 196
running in separate process, 167
sar command, 356
scp command, 196, 477
sdtperfmeter command, 356
search path, 169
search path for, 118
section number references in, xx
sed command, 48–56, 83, 475
set command, 25, 116, 143, 169,
    172–175, 383–385, 474
setting environment variable for duration
    of, 111
shift command, 116, 132, 169, 474
shopt command, 385–389
show command, 155
sleep command, 373, 476
sort command, 67–75, 475
spell command, 325, 327, 347, 475
ssh command, 196, 477
stat command, 273, 466
strace command, 368
strings command, 85, 476
stty command, 474
su command, 418
sum command, 301
syslog command, 414
systat command, 356
tail command, 84, 476
tar command, 476
tee command, 475
test command, 124–128, 474
text manipulation, list of, 474
tgrind command, 83
times command, 169, 172
top command, 355, 357, 476
touch command, 273–274, 461, 476
tr command, 20, 475
trace command, 368
trap command, 169, 276, 364–367, 400,
    474
troff command, 82, 435
true command, 169, 474
truss command, 368

type command, 280, 474
types of, 13
typeset command, 474
typo command, 347
ulimit command, 452, 474
umask command, 169, 172, 455, 467, 476
umount command, 445
unalias command, 169, 171
unexpand command, 475
uniq command, 75, 475
unset command, 111–113, 169, 474
unsetting environment variable for duration of, 111
unzip command, 476
updatedb command, 279
uptime command, 352, 356, 477
vgrind command, 83
vmstat command, 356
vmubc command, 356
w command, 356
wait command, 169, 172, 356, 476
wc command, 10, 77, 475
wget command, 306
where shell searches for, 22
who command, 9, 474
xargs command, 293, 476
xcpustate command, 356
xload command, 356
xperfmon command, 356
ypcat command, 453
ypmatch command, 453
zip command, 476
comments, 24
    awk language, 226
    HTML, 96
    troff, 425
Common UNIX Printing System (see CUPS)
comparison operators, 118, 230, 401
compiled languages, 8
compound statements, 244, 487
compressed archive files, software packages distributed in, 192
Computing Sciences Research Center, Bell Telephone Laboratories, 1
Concurrent Versions System (cvs), 470, 477, 487
conditional execution
    awk, 244
    shell script, 121–122
conditional expression operator, 119, 230, 401

config.h file, 192
configure script, with software packages, 192
CONT signal, 361
contact information, xxiii
context switches, 352, 487
continue command, 131, 169, 474
continue statement, awk, 246, 248
controlling terminal, 353, 487
conventions used in this book, xix
Coordinated Universal Time (UTC), 460, 488
core dump, 488
coreutils package, stable sort option in, 75
cos() function, awk, 264
cp command, 475
.cpp file extension, 470
cracker, 488
cron command, 377, 476
cron.allow file, 377
cron.deny file, 377
crontab command, 375–377, 476
crossword puzzles, pattern matching dictionary for, 100–101
cryptography, public-key, 303, 498
Ctrl key, xix
Ctrl-D, disabling, 174
CUPS (Common UNIX Printing System), 80
current working directory, 118, 488
    adding to PATH, 23
    not included in PATH, 413
cut command, 58, 474
cvs (Concurrent Versions System), 470, 477, 487
.cxx file extension, 470
cygwin environment (Cygnus Consulting), xxi

D

%d format specifier, 149, 150, 261
d, preceding directory in listing, 466
-d test expression, 125, 392
daemon, 488
dash (see hyphen)
data sink (see standard output)
data source (see standard input)
databases, 95
data-driven programming model, 238
date command, 474
dd command, 85, 474
DEBUG trap, 383
decrement operator, 118, 230, 400, 401
delete statement, awk, 233

delimiter, 488
Delorie, D.J., DJGPP suite, xxii
deroff command, 435
dev directory, 450
device driver, 488
devices
    as files, 450
    block devices, 125, 466
    random pseudodevices, 277
/dev/null file, 21
/dev/random pseudodevice, 277
/dev/tty file, 21
/dev/urandom pseudodevice, 277
df command, 295–297, 464, 475
dictionary, spelling, 100
diff command, 299, 475
diff3 command, 300
digital signature, 303–307, 488
directories, 489
    adding to PATH, 22
    bin directory, 414, 444
    dev directory, 450
    dot (.) directory, 445
    dot dot (..) directory, 445
    listing, 271
    number of files in, 443
    permissions for, 458–460
    preceded by d in listing, 466
    reading and writing, 448
    root directory, 443, 501
    searchable, test expression for, 125
    test expression for, 125
    usr directory, 444
directories file for customization, 193
dirname command, 201, 474
disk quotas, 452
disk usage, determining, 464
division operator, 118, 401
DJGPP suite, xxii
do statement, awk, 245–247
DocBook/XML, 489
documentation (see manual pages)
dollar sign ($)
    $((...)) (arithmetic expansion), 118–120,
        485
    $(...) (command substitution), 156
    ${...} (parameter expansion), 113
    "$*" (variable), 116
    "$@" (variable), 116
    $# (variable), 115
    $$ (variable), 118, 276, 355
    $* (variable), 116

$- (variable), 175
$@ (variable), 116
    in regular expressions, 34, 41, 45, 484
    preceding field values in awk, 63
    preceding variables, 15, 113
    variable, 117
dosmacux package, 442
dot (.)
    command, 172, 473
    directory, 445
    hidden files preceded by, 155
    in Basic Regular Expressions, 37
    in filenames, 154
    in regular expressions, 34
    preceding hidden files, 270
    special built-in command, 168
dot dot (..) directory, 445
double quotes ("...")
    enclosing string constants, awk, 226
    grouping text, 162
du command, 297–299, 464, 475
DVDs, 438

E

%E format specifier, 149, 150
%e format specifier, 149, 150, 261
-e shell option, 174
-e test expression, 125, 392
EBCDIC (Extended Binary Coded Decimal
        Interchange Code), 439, 489
echo command, 15, 16, 267, 382, 475
ed program, regular expressions used by, 47
EDITOR variable, 375
-ef test expression, 393
egrep command, 5, 30, 475
    regular expressions used by, 47
    tag list example using, 106
ellipses (...), inserting in troff markup, 431
embedded computer systems, 437, 489
empty field, 57
empty files, 125, 273, 442
empty (null) values, 14
encryption
    of data, 468
    public-key cryptography, 303
    secure shell software using, 468
END pattern, awk, 64, 226, 239
endgrent() function, 453
endpwent() function, 453
entity, 489
env command, 111, 210, 474
ENV file, 408

ENV variable, 117
ENVIRON variable, awk, 236
environment, 489
    adding variables to, 110
    printing, 111
environment variables, 489
    accessing in awk, 236
    changing for specific program, 111
    for locale, 26–28
    setting, 110
    unsetting, 111–113
epoch, 274, 460, 489
.eps file extension, 470
-eq test expression, 125, 393
equal operator, 118, 230, 401
equal sign (=)
    == (comparison operator), 118, 230, 401
    == (test expression), 393
    assigning values to variables, 15
    assignment operator, 119, 230, 401
    expr operator, 160
    test expression, 125, 393
equivalence classes
    in Basic Regular Expressions, 38
    in regular expressions, 36, 42
EREs (see Extended Regular Expressions)
errexit shell option, 174
errors
    checking error status, 414
    (see also exit status; standard error)
escape mechanism, 489
escape sequences
    for echo command, 16
    for printf command, 148
eval command, 166, 169, 474
    not using on user input, 415
    path search example using, 184
evaluation order of commands, 162–166
examples (see code examples in book, using)
exclamation mark (!)
    != (comparison operator), 118, 230, 401
    != (expr operator), 160
    != (test expression), 125, 393
    !~ (matches operator, awk), 228
    arithmetic operator, 118, 230, 401
    in wildcard set, 153, 154
    logical NOT operator, 122
    variable, 117
.exe file extension, 470
exec command, 146, 169, 474
executable file, test expression for, 125
execute permission, 10, 453, 455–458, 489

execution tracing, 24, 118
execve() function, 352
exit command, 121, 169, 474
exit() function, 352, 360
exit statement, awk, 249
exit status, 490
    if statement and, 121–122
    logical operators and, 122
    of previous command, 117
    of test command, 124–128
    passing back to caller, 121
    values of, 120
exp() function, awk, 264
expand command, 475
expansion, 490
    arithmetic expansion, 109, 118–120, 485
    brace expansion, 395
    parameter expansion, 113–118, 496
    pathname expansion, 496
    tilde expansion, 152, 399, 505
    wildcard expansion, 174, 353, 415
expansion operators, 113
exponentiation operator, 230, 400, 401
export command, 110, 169, 474
expr command, 159–161
Extended Binary Coded Decimal Interchange
        Code (EBCDIC), 439, 489
extended pattern matching, 393
Extended Regular Expressions (EREs), 30,
        42–45, 490
    metacharacters for, 34
    operator precedence for, 45
    programs using, 46–48
    (see also egrep command)
extended test facility, 392–393
eXtensible Markup Language (XML), 490
extensions, xv
external commands, 14
extglob option, 393
ex/vi program, regular expressions used
        by, 47

F

\f escape sequence, 16, 148
.f file extension, 470
%f format specifier, 149, 150, 261
-f shell option, 174
-f test expression, 125, 392
.f90 file extension, 470
false command, 169, 474
fc command, 169, 172
fflush() function, awk, 251

fg command, 169, 172
fgrep command, 31, 475
.fi command, troff, 430
field separators, awk, 63, 237
fields, 57, 490
    awk language, 62, 225
    joining, 60
    rearranging, 62–65
    selecting, 58
    separating in text files, 57
    separator characters for, 117
    sorting based on, 70–72
FIFO (first in first out), 490
file checksums, 301
    (see also digital signature)
file command, 85, 475
file descriptors, 145–147, 490
file extensions, conventions for, 469–470
file generation numbers, 470
file sizes, total used (see filesystem space)
File Transfer Protocol (FTP), 490
file type, 286, 490
filename, 491
    containing special characters,
        finding, 292
    extracting directory path from, 201
    restrictions on, 438–441
    suffix of, 505
    wildcards in, 153–155
filename collisions, 438
FILENAME variable, awk, 232
FILENAME_MAX constant, 444
files, 437
    access time for, 286, 460–461
    appending standard output to, 19
    binary files, 442
    commands for, list of, 475
    comparing contents of, 299
    comparing file checksums, 301
    devices as, 450
    differences between, finding, 300
    differences between, reconstructing file
        from, 300
    digital signature verification for, 303–307
    empty files, 125, 273, 442
    file type of, 271, 466
    finding, 279, 280–291
    finding in a search path, 177–192
    format of contents, 441–443
    group of, listing, 272
    hidden files, 155, 270, 282
    holes in, 465

inode-change time for, 286, 460–461
line-terminator conventions for, 442
links for, 449, 461–463
listing, 267–272
metadata for, listing, 272
modification time for, 272, 273–274, 286,
    460–461
monitoring access of, 370
not overwriting with I/O redirection, 143
number of, in directory, 443
opening for both reading and writing, 144
ownership of, 272, 452, 467–469, 496
pathname for, 443
permissions for, 271, 453–458, 467–469
printing, 78–83
reading, 141
searching for text in, 241
size limits of, 450–452
size of, 272, 463
temporary, 274–278
test expressions for, 125
text files, 441
    records and fields in, 57
    structured, extracting data
        from, 87–94
    timestamps for, 460–461, 465
filesystem space
    df command for, 295–297
    du command for, 297–299
    find command for, 295
    ls command for, 295
filesystems
    hierarchical, 443–450
    implementation of, 447–450
    layered, 445–447
    mounting, 445
filters, 140, 491
find command, 280–291, 464, 475
    -a (AND) option, 287
    actions to be taken on found files, 282
    -atime option, 286
    -ctime option, 286
    -exec option, 282
    -follow option, 286
    -fprint option, 290
    -group option, 285
    hidden files found by, 282
    -links option, 286
    -ls option, 283
    -mtime option, 286
    -name option, 289
    -newer option, 286

-o (OR) option, 287
-perm option for, 285
-print option, 282
-print0 option, 292
-prune option, 282
-size option, 285
sorting results of, 282, 283
-true option, 289
-type option, 286
-user option, 285
flags for printf command, 151
floating-point arithmetic, awk, 229
fmt command, 76, 475
FNR variable, awk, 232
folders (see directories)
fonts
    changing, in HTML, 96
    in troff, 425, 427
    used in this book, xix
fonts, in troff, 428
for statement, 130
    arithmetic, 399
    awk, 245–247
foreground processes, 357, 491
fork() function, 352
format specifiers, 18, 149, 491
formfeed, escape sequence for, 16, 148
forward slash (/)
    forbidden in filenames, 139
    in pathname, 445
    root directory, 443
fpathconf() function, 444
frequency of words, creating list of, 102–104
FS variable, 62, 224, 232, 237
fstat() function, 447
FTP (File Transfer Protocol), 490
function statement, awk, 252–255
functions, 14, 135–138, 491
    arguments for, 136
    disabling command history for, 174
    finding location of, 280
    line number just ran, 118
    positional parameters in, 136
    removing from environment, 111
    user-defined, awk, 252–255
fuser command, 476

G

%G format specifier, 149, 150
%g format specifier, 149, 150, 261

-G test expression, 392
-g test expression, 125, 392
gawk interpreter, 223, 224
    (see also awk interpreter)
-ge test expression, 125, 393
Generic Network Queueing System, 375
getconf command, 444
get_dictionaries() function, awk
            spellchecker, 334
getgrent() function, 453
getline statement, awk, 249–250
getopts command, 133, 169, 474
getpubkey command, 306
getpwent() function, 453
gettext package, 28
global variables, case of, 180
globbing (see pathname expansion)
GMT (Greenwich Mean Time), 460
GNU General Public License (GPL), xxi
GNU Info system (see info command)
GNU Privacy Guard (GnuPG), 303
GnuPG (GNU Privacy Guard), 303
gpg command, 306
GPL (GNU General Public License), xxi
gradual underflow, 491
Greenwich Mean Time (GMT), 460
grep command, 5, 23, 30, 32, 175
    constant strings, searching for, 31
    -F option, 31
    regular expressions for, 33–36
    regular expressions used by, 47
    solving word puzzles using, 100–101
groff command, 435
gr_osview command, 356
group, 285, 491
group files, 322, 453
group ownership, 453
grouping, in Extended Regular
            Expressions, 44, 45
gsub() function, 73, 257
-gt test expression, 125, 393
gunzip command, 475
.gz file extension, 470
gzip command, 475

H

.h file extension, 470
-h shell option, 174
-h test expression, 125, 392
hacker, 492

hard links, 286, 449, 461–463, 492
hash mark (#)
    ## (pattern-matching operator), 114
    #! (specifying interpreter in shell
        script), 10–12
    pattern-matching operator, 114
    preceding comments, 24
    preceding comments, awk, 226
    prefixing temporary backup file
        name, 470
    printf flag, 151
    string-length operator, 115
    variable, 117
head command, 83, 157, 476
HEAD object, HTML, 96
--help option, 182
here documents, 98, 143, 144, 492
here strings, 400
Hewlett-Packard PCL (Printer Command
    Language), 80
hexadecimal, 492
hidden files, 155
    finding, 282
    listing, 270
hierarchical filesystem, 443–450
history of Unix, 1–4
holding space, 35, 492
holes in files, 465
home (login) directory, 117, 152
HOME variable, 117
horizontal tab, escape sequence for, 16, 148
hot spots, 492
HPGL (HP Graphics Language), 80
.htm file extension, 470
.html file extension, 470
HTML (HyperText Markup Language), 492
    converting troff markup to, 436
    formatting text as, 94–100
    syntax for, 95–97
    tag lists, creating, 105–107
HTTP (HyperText Transport Protocol), 492
HUP signal, 361, 362
HyperText Markup Language (see HTML)
HyperText Transport Protocol (see HTTP)
hyphen (-)
    -- (arithmetic operator), 118, 230, 400,
        401
    -= (assignment operator), 119, 230, 401
    -- (end of options), 13
    arithmetic operator, 118, 230, 401
    as bare option, 12

expr operator, 160
in filenames, 440
preceding command options, 13
preceding file type in listing, 466
printf flag, 151
variable, 117

I

%i format specifier, 149, 150, 261
i18n (see internationalization)
.IB command, troff, 428
IBM LoadLeveler, 375
icons used in this book, xx
iconv command, 475
id command, 474
IEEE 754 Standard for Binary Floating-Point
    Arithmetic, 229
IEEE Std. 1003.1 - 2001 standard, xv, 3
if statement
    awk, 244
    exit status and, 121–122
IFS variable, 117, 141, 178
IGNORECASE variable, awk, 256
ignoreeof shell option, 174
implementation-defined, 17, 493
in Basic Regular Expressions, 35
increment operator, 118, 230, 400, 401
index() function, awk, 256
index node (inode), 447
indexed arrays, 396–399
Infinity, in floating-point arithmetic, 229
info command, 477
InfoZip format, 204
initialize() function, awk spellchecker, 333
inline input, 143
inode (index node), 447, 493
inode-change time for files, 286, 460–461
input redirection (see I/O redirection)
insertion sort algorithm, 74
int() function, awk, 231, 264
integers, numeric tests for, 125, 128
International Organization for
    Standardization (see ISO)
internationalization, 25–28
    regular expressions features for, 33,
        35–36, 38
    sorting conventions and, 69
Internet Protocol (IP), 493
interpreted languages, 9
interpreter, 9, 10–12
interval expressions, 34, 40, 43, 493

I/O redirection, 19–22, 143–147, 493
  awk, 250
  exec command for, 146
  file descriptors for, 145–147
  preventing overwriting of existing
      files, 174
iostat command, 356
.IP command, troff, 429
IP (Internet Protocol), 493
.IR command, troff, 428
ISO (International Organization for
      Standardization), 493
  code pages, 439
  superseding ANSI, 484
ispell command, 329–330, 347
iterative execution (see looping)

J

job control, 174, 493
jobs command, 169, 172
join command, 60, 89, 91, 475
join() function, awk, 260

K

-k test expression, 392
kernel context, 353
kill command, 169, 172, 360–363, 476
KILL signal, 361, 362
Korn, David, UWIN package, xxii
Korn shell (see ksh)
ksh (Korn shell), 408, 473
ksh88 shell
  extended pattern matching in, 393
  startup, 408
ksh93 shell
  differences from bash, 381–385
  downloading, 404
  privileged mode, 421
  startup, 408
ktrace command, 368

L

l, preceding link in listing, 466
-L test expression, 125, 392
-l test expression, 392
l10n (see localization)
LANG variable, 26, 117
language
  for output messages, 118
  (see also internationalization; localization)

layered filesystems, 445–447
LC_ALL variable, 26, 117
LC_COLLATE variable, 26, 117
LC_CTYPE variable, 26, 118
LC_MESSAGES variable, 26, 118
LC_MONETARY variable, 26
LC_NUMERIC variable, 26
LC_TIME variable, 26
-le test expression, 125, 393
left angle bracket (<)
  <!-- ... --> (HTML comments), 96
  <<= (assignment operator), 119, 401
  <= (comparison operator), 118, 230, 401
  <= (expr operator), 160
  << (arithmetic operator), 118, 401
  << (here document), 98, 143
  <<- (here document, leading tabs
      removed), 144
  <<< (here strings), 400
  <> (open file for reading and
      writing), 144
  changing standard input, 19
  comparison operator, 118, 230, 401
  expr operator, 160
  test expression, 393
left-associative, 494
length() function, awk, 227
less command, 475
let command, 399
lettercase conversion, awk, 256
lex program, regular expressions used by, 47
line continuation character, 142, 226, 494
line number of script or function, 118
LINENO variable, 118
lines
  changing line breaks, 76
  counting, 10, 77
  extracting first and last lines from
      text, 83–86
line-terminator conventions in files, 442
LINK object, HTML, 96
links, 449, 461–463, 494
  count of, in file listing, 272
  hard links, 286, 492
  preceded by l in listing, 466
  symbolic links, 125, 286, 415, 505
load average, 352, 494
load_dictionaries() function, awk
      spellchecker, 336
load_suffixes() function, awk
      spellchecker, 337
local variables, case of, 180

locale, 494
environment variables for, 26–28
name of, 117
locale command, 26, 477
localization, 25–28
regular expressions features for, 33,
35–36, 38
sorting conventions and, 69
locate command, 279, 476
lock for running program, 494
log() function, awk, 264
logger command, 414, 477
logical AND operator, 118, 122, 401
logical NOT operator, 118, 122, 401
logical OR operator, 118, 122, 401
login directory (see home directory)
login shell, 406
looping, 130–135
arithmetic for loop, 399
awk language, 245–247
portability of, 383
select statement, 389–392
lp command, 79, 477
LPDEST variable, 79
lpq command, 79, 477
lpr command, 79, 477
lprm command, 79
LPRng (lpr next generation), 80
lpstat command, 79
ls command, 268–272, 463, 476
-lt test expression, 125, 393

M

-m shell option, 174
magnetic disks, 437
mail command, 199, 477
mailing list, implementing with command
substitution, 157–159
mailx command, 199
make command, 212, 477
Makefile file, 192
makeinfo program, 423
makewhatis program, 436
man command, 477
MANPATH environment variable, 436
manual pages
converting to other output formats, 436
creating, 424–431
formats for, 423
installing, 436
output forms of, 423
syntax checking for, 435

markup removal, 349
match, 494
match() function, awk, 257
Maui Cluster Scheduler, 375
mawk interpreter, 223, 224
(see also awk interpreter)
McIlroy, Doug, word list solution by, 102
md5 command, 301
md5sum command, 301, 476
message catalogs, location of, 118
messages
language for, 118
printing right away, 174
Software Tools principles for, 5
metacharacters, 494
avoiding in filenames, 440
escaping, 37, 45
in regular expressions, 34, 40
metadata, 447, 494
minus sign (see hyphen)
mkdir command, 476
MKS Toolkit, xxii
mktemp command, 118, 276, 476
modification time for files, 272, 273–274,
286, 460–461
modifier, 495
modifier metacharacters, in regular
expressions, 40
monitor command, 356
monitor shell option, 174
more command, 47, 475
Mortice Kern Systems, MKS Toolkit, xxii
mount command, 445
mounting, 495
mpstat command, 356
Multics operating system, 1
multiplication operator, 118, 401

N

\n escape sequence, 16, 148
-n shell option, 174
-N test expression, 392
-n test expression, 125, 392
named pipe, 125, 466, 495
NaN (not-a-number), in floating-point
arithmetic, 229
nawk interpreter, 223
(see also awk interpreter)
-ne test expression, 125, 393
netstat command, 356
Network File System (NFS), 447, 495

networks
    accessing with secure shell software, 468
    security and, 468
newgrp command, 169
newline
    escape sequence for, 16, 148
    suppressing, escape sequence for, 16, 148
next statement, awk, 248
nextfile statement, awk, 248
.nf command, troff, 430
NF variable, 62, 232
NFS (Network File System), 447, 495
nfsstat command, 356
nice command, 352, 476
NLSPATH variable, 118
noclobber shell option, 143, 174
noexec shell option, 174
noglob shell option, 174
nolog shell option, 174
not equal operator, 118, 230, 401
not-a-number (NaN), in floating-point
        arithmetic, 229
notify shell option, 174
nounset shell option, 174
NR variable, awk, 232
nroff command, 435
nroff markup format, 423, 424
-nt test expression, 393
NUL character, 439
    in Basic Regular Expressions, 39
    matching, 46
null string, 495
null values, 14
numbers, in awk, 228–232
numeric functions, awk, 264–266

O

.o file extension, 470
%o format specifier, 149, 150, 261
-o logical OR, test expression, 126
-O test expression, 392
-o test expression, 392
oawk interpreter, 223
    (see also awk interpreter)
object code, 8
octal, 495
octal value, escape sequence for, 17, 148
od command, 85, 269, 476
OFS variable, awk, 232
OLDPWD variable, 399
opendir() function, 448

operator precedence
    in Basic Regular Expressions, 42
    in Extended Regular Expressions, 45
OPTARG variable, 133
optical storage devices, 438
OPTIND variable, 133, 135, 382
options, command line, 13, 133, 495
order_suffixes() function, awk
        spellchecker, 339
ordinary character, 495
O'Reilly Media, Inc., contact
        information, xxiii
ORS variable, awk, 232, 239
osview command, 356
-ot test expression, 393
other ownership, 453, 495
output redirection (see I/O redirection)
output, Software Tools principles for, 5
overflow, 495
ownership, 496
    finding files based on, 285
    of files, 272, 452, 467–469
    of groups, 453
    of other users, 453, 495
    of processes, 355

P

p, preceding named pipe in listing, 466
-p test expression, 125, 392
par command, 368
parameter expansion, 113–118, 496
    length of variable's value, 115
    pattern-matching operators for, 114
    substitution operators for, 113
parent process ID (PPID), 118, 355
parentheses ((...))
    ((...)) (arithmetic command), 399
    grouping arithmetic expressions, 119
    grouping, expr expressions, 160
    in Extended Regular Expressions, 44
    in regular expressions, 35
    subshell, 167
partition, 496
pass by reference, 486
pass by value, 486
passwd file, 453
    extracting data from, 88–94
    history of, 309
    merging two password files, 309–320
    problems with, 308
    structure of, 87

password file (see passwd file)
patch, 496
patch command, 300, 476
path searching, 177–192
PATH variable, 118
  adding current directory to, 23
  adding directories to, 22
  commands searched with, 22
  current directory in, avoiding, 413
  default value for, 22
  finding commands in, 280
  protecting directories in, 414
  resetting in script, for security, 179
pathconf() function, 444
PATH_MAX constant, 443
pathname, 443, 496
  basename component of, 485
  extracting directory path from, 201
  extracting filename from, 181
pathname expansion, 496
pattern matching (see regular expressions)
pattern space, 52, 496
pattern-matching operators, 114
patterns, awk, 225, 238
PCL (Printer Command Language), 80
.pdf file extension, 470
PDF (Portable Document Format), 80, 82
pdksh (Public Domain Korn Shell), 405, 473
percent sign (%)
  %= (assignment operator), 119, 230, 401
  %% (format specifier), 149
  %% (format specifier, awk), 261
  %% (pattern-matching operator), 115
  arithmetic operator, 118, 230, 401
  expr operator, 160
  pattern-matching operator, 114
  preceding format specifications, 18
  preceding printf format specifiers, 149
perfmeter command, 356
permissions, 497
  changing, 454
  default, 455
  displaying, 454
  finding files based on, 285
  for directories, 458–460
  for files, 271, 453–458, 467–469
pgp command, 306
PGP (Pretty Good Privacy), 303
pgpgpg command, 306
pgrep command, 363
PID (process ID), 355

pipelines, 10, 497
  creating, 19
  extracting data from text using, 87–94
  formatting text as HTML using, 94–100
  named pipe, 125, 466, 495
  performance of, 21
  solving word puzzles using, 100–101
  tag lists using, 105–107
  word frequency lists using, 102–104
pkill command, 363
Platform LSF system, 375
plus sign (+)
  ++ (arithmetic operator), 118, 230, 400, 401
  += (assignment operator), 119, 230, 401
  arithmetic operator, 118, 230, 401
  expr operator, 160
  in Extended Regular Expressions, 43
  in regular expressions, 35
  in trace output, 24
  printf flag, 151
portability
  of #! line in shell script, 11
  of shell scripts, xiii, 9
  shell, 381–385
Portable Batch System, 375
Portable Document Format (see PDF)
positional parameters, 23, 109, 115–117, 497
  changing, 174
  in functions, 136
  removing one at a time, from the left, 116
  setting explicitly, 116
POSIX standards, xv, 3
postfix operator, 119
PostScript, Adobe, 80, 82
pound sign (see hash mark)
.PP command, troff, 428
PPID (parent process ID), 355
PPID variable, 118
pr command, 80–82, 475
prefix operator, 119
Pretty Good Privacy (PGP), 303
print daemon, 78
print queue
  name of, 79
  removing files from, 79
  sending files to, 79
  status of, reporting, 79
print spooler, 497
print statement, awk, 64, 239, 250

Printer Command Language (see PCL)
printer, default, setting, 79
PRINTER variable, 79
printf command, 17, 147–152, 475
    escape sequences for, 148
    flags for, 151
    format specifiers for, 149
    precision modifier, 150
    width modifier, 150
printf() function, awk, 261–264
printf statement, awk, 64, 250
printing, 78–83
privileged mode, 497
/proc filesystem, 378–379
process ID (PID), 117, 355
    of last background command, 117
    of parent process, 118
process substitution, 395–396
processes, 352
    accounting of, 372
    background process, 485
    commands for, list of, 476
    controlling terminal for, 353, 487
    current, arguments for, 117
    delayed scheduling of, 373–377
    deleting, 361–363
    ending, 352, 360
    foreground process, 491
    interrupting foreground processes, 357
    kernel context for, 353
    listing, 354–360
    owner of, 355
    PID (process ID), 355
    PPID (parent process ID), 355
    priority of, 352
    running commands in a separate
        process, 167
    running in background, 356
    scheduler managing, 352
    starting, 352, 353
    system-call tracing for, 368–371
    terminating prematurely, 360
    trapping signals, 363–367
    virtual address space for, 353
procinfo command, 356
proctool command, 356
.profile file, adding to PATH in, 22
Programmer's Workbench Unix (PWB), 497
prompt string, 118
protocol, 497
prstat command, 356
ps command, 354–360, 476

.ps file extension, 470
PS1 variable, 118
PS2 variable, 118
PS4 variable, 118
pseudodevices, 497
    random, 277, 450
pstat command, 356
ptree command, 356
Public Domain Korn Shell (see pdksh)
public-key cryptography, 303, 498
public-key servers, 304, 498
punctuation characters, avoiding in
        filenames, 440
PWB (Programmer's Workbench Unix), 497
pwd command, 169, 476
PWD variable, 118, 399

Q

question mark (?)
    ?: (conditional expression), 119, 230, 401
    in Extended Regular Expressions, 43
    in regular expressions, 35
    variable, 117, 120
    wildcard, 153
quoting, 161, 498
    of shell variables containing
        filenames, 441
    results of wildcard expansion, 415
    user input, 414

R

\r escape sequence, 16, 148
-r test expression, 125, 392
race condition, 415
RAM (random-access memory), 498
    filesystems residing in, 437
Ramey, Chet (bash maintainer), prolog for
        making shell scripts secure, 416
rand() function, awk, 264
random pseudodevices, 277, 450
random-access memory (see RAM)
range expressions, 239, 499
ranges, 37, 499
.RB command, troff, 428
rbash (restricted bash), 417
rcp command, 196
rcs command, 477
rcs (Revision Control System), 470, 477, 500
rcsdiff command, 477
.RE command, troff, 430
read command, 140–143, 169, 474

read permission, 453, 458, 499
readable file, test expression for, 125
readdir() function, 448
readonly command, 110, 169, 474
records, 56, 499
    as lines in text files, 57
    awk language, 62, 225, 236
    changing line breaks, 76
    duplicate, removing, 75
    multiline, sorting, 72
    sorting, 67–72
    unique key for, 94
recursion, 254, 499
redirection (see I/O redirection)
regular built-in commands, 168
regular expressions, 33–36
    awk support for, 228, 238
    Basic Regular Expressions, 30, 37–42,
        485
      character classes in, 36
      collating symbols in, 36
      commands using, 33
      equivalence classes in, 36
      extended pattern matching in ksh
        for, 393
      Extended Regular Expressions, 30,
        42–45, 490
      extensions to, 45
      in sed program, 53
      internationalization and localization
        features for, 33, 35–36, 38
      locale for pattern matching, 118
      metacharacters in, 34
      programs using, 46–48
      Software Tools principles for, 5
      solving word puzzles using, 100–101
relational databases, 95
remainder operator, 118, 401
remote shell, 196, 499
remove, 499
renice command, 352, 476
report_exceptions() functions, awk
    spellchecker, 342
Request for Comments (RFC), 500
restricted shell, 416–418, 500
return command, 136, 169, 474
return statement, awk, 253
Revision Control System (rcs), 470, 477, 500
RFC (Request for Comments), 500
.RI command, troff, 428
right angle bracket (>)
    >> (appending to standard output), 19

>> (arithmetic operator), 118, 401
>> (output redirection, awk), 251
>>= (assignment operator), 119, 401
>= (comparison operator), 118, 230, 401
>= (expr operator), 160
>| (redirect output overriding
    noclobber), 143, 145
    changing standard output, 19
    comparison operator, 118, 230, 401
    expr operator, 160
    output redirection, awk, 251
    test expression, 393
right-associative, 500
rksh (restricted ksh93), 416
RLENGTH variable, awk, 257
rlog command, 477
rm command, 476
rmdir command, 476
root directory, 443, 501
root user
    package installations by, 211
    security and, 415
.RS command, troff, 430
RS variable, awk, 232, 236
rsh command, 196
RSTART variable, awk, 257
RT variable, awk, 237
runoff markup format, 424

S

.s file extension, 470
%s format specifier, 149, 150, 261
s, preceding socket in listing, 466
-S test expression, 125, 392
-s test expression, 125, 392
sappnd permission, 501
sar command, 356
scalar variables, 232, 501
scan_options() function, awk
    spellchecker, 335
sccs (Source Code Control System), 470, 503
scheduler, 352, 501
scp command, 196, 477
scratch file, 501
scripts (see shell scripts)
sdtperfmeter command, 356
search path
    for commands, 118
    script implementing, 177–192
    special vs. regular built-in commands
        affecting, 169
    (see also PATH variable)

searching for text (see grep command)
secure shell, 196, 468, 501
security
    bare option in #! line, 12
    current directory in PATH, 23
    data encryption, 468
    digital signature verification, 303–307
    file ownership and permissions, 467–469
    guidelines for secure shell
        scripts, 413–416
    IFS variable and, 178
    monitoring of files by system
        managers, 467
    of locate command, 279
    of networked computers, 468
    of temporary files, 275, 276
    package installations by root user, 211
    PATH variable and, 179
    restricted shell, 416–418
    secure shell access to network, 468
    setuid and setgid bits, 415, 419
    Trojan horses, 418
sed command, 48–56, 475
    command substitution and, 157
    extracting first lines, 83
    regular expressions used by, 47
    tag list example using, 106
    word frequency example using, 102
select statement, 389–392
semicolon (;)
    ending HTML entities, 96
    separating commands, 13
    separating statements, awk, 240, 244
set command, 116, 169, 172–175, 474
    -C option, 143
    noclobber option, 143
    portability of, 383–385
    shopt command as alternative
        to, 385–389
    -x option, 25
setgid bit
    security and, 415, 419
    test expression for, 125
setgrent() function, 453
set-group-ID bit, 457, 459, 501
setpwent() function, 453
setuid bit
    privileged mode and, 421
    security and, 415, 419
    test expression for, 125
set-user-ID bit, 457, 502

SGML (Standard Generalized Markup
        Language), 94, 424, 504
sh (Bourne shell), 407, 473
.SH command, troff, 426
.sh file extension, 470
shadowed, 502
Shakespeare, word frequency lists of, 103
sharp sign (see hash mark)
shell, 502
    bash (Bourne Again Shell), 381–389,
        402–403, 408–410, 473
    evaluation of commands, 162–166
    exiting, disabling Ctrl-D for, 174
    exiting on error, 174
    interactive, file to be executed at
        startup, 117
    ksh (Korn shell), 408, 473
    login shell, 406
    name of, 117
    pdksh (Public Domain Korn Shell), 405,
        473
    process ID for, 117
    replacing with specific program, 146
    restricted, 416–418, 500
    secure, 196, 468, 501
    sh (Bourne shell), 407, 473
    startup and termination of, 406–412
    subshells, 167, 505
    version number of, finding, 405
    zsh (Z-Shell), 405, 410–412, 473
shell functions (see functions)
shell options, 502
    list of, 174
    setting, 172–175
    variable containing enabled options, 117,
        175
shell portability, 381–385
shell scripts, xiii
    creating, 9
    evaluation order of, 162–166
    interpreter for, specifying, 10–12
    knowledge requirements for, xvi
    line number just ran, 118
    portability of, xiii, 9, 11
    reasons to use, 9
    security guidelines for, 413–416
    Software Tools principles for, xiii, 4–6
    tracing, 24, 118
    uses of, 8
shell state, saving, 381
shell variables (see variables)

shift command, 116, 132, 169, 474
   path search example using, 183
   software build example using, 197, 199
shopt command, 385–389
short-circuit operators, 123
show command, 155
side effect, 502
signal() function, 363
signal handler, 364, 503
signals, 503
   for deleting processes, 361–363
   sending to processes, 360
   trapping, 363–367
Silver Grid Scheduler, 375
sin() function, awk, 264
single quotes ('...'), literal interpretation, 161
Single UNIX Specification, xv, 4, 503
slash (/)
   /= (assignment operator), 119, 230, 401
   arithmetic operator, 118, 230, 401
   expr operator, 160
   forbidden in filenames, 439
   in pathname, 445
   root directory, 443
sleep command, 373, 476
.so file extension, 470
sockets
   preceded by s in listing, 466
   test expression for, 125
soft links, 449, 461–463
software builds, automating, 192–222
Software Tools philosophy, xiii, 4–6
software-packaging conventions, 192
sort command, 67–75, 475
   duplicate records, removing, 75
   efficiency of, 74
   field to sort on, 70–72
   -k option, 70–72
   stability of, 74
   -t option, 70–72
   tag list example using, 106
   -u option, 75
   with multiline records, 72
   word frequency example using, 102
sorting algorithms, 74, 504
sorting, locale to use for, 117
source code, 8, 192–222
Source Code Control System (sccs), 470, 503
space used by filesystem (see filesystem
     space)
spaces (see whitespace)
sparse, 503
special built-in commands, 168

special characters, xix, 503
   in filenames, 292, 439, 441
   (see also metacharacters)
spell command, 325, 327, 347, 475
spellchecking
   aspell command, 329–330
   history of, 347
   implementing in awk, 331–343, 348
   ispell command, 329–330
   original prototype for, 326
   private spelling dictionaries for, 328
   spell command for, 325
spell_check_line() function, awk
     spellchecker, 340
spell_check_word() function, awk
     spellchecker, 340
spelling dictionary, 100, 328, 503
spelling exception list, 503
split() function, awk, 258–260
spoofing attacks, preventing, 12
spooled, 503
sprintf() function, awk, 261–264
SQL (Structured Query Language), 95, 504
sqrt() function, awk, 264
square brackets ([...])
   [: ... :] (character classes), 36, 38
   [. .... .] (collating symbols), 36, 38
   [= ... =] (equivalence classes), 36, 38
   [...] (test command variant form), 124
   [[...]] (extended test facility), 392–393
   array indices, awk, 233
   in regular expressions, 34, 486
   wildcard set, 153
srand() function, awk, 264
.SS command, troff, 431
ssh command, 196, 477
SSHFLAGS variable, 196
stability, 504
standard error, 18, 140, 504
   file descriptor for, 145
   filename of, 451
Standard Generalized Markup Language (see
     SGML)
standard input, 18, 140, 504
   changing to file, 19
   evaluation order of, 162–166
   file descriptor for, 145
   filename of, 451
   printing from, 79
   receiving from previous program in
     pipeline, 19
   receiving from terminal, 21

standard I/O, 5, 18, 140, 504
  (see also standard error; standard input; standard output)
standard output, 18, 140, 504
  appending to file, 19
  changing to file, 19
  discarding to /dev/null, 21
  file descriptor for, 145
  filename of, 451
  redirecting to next program in pipeline, 19
  writing to terminal, 21
standards
  IEEE Std. 1003.1 - 2001, xv, 3
  POSIX standards, xv, 3
  unspecified behaviors in, xv
  X/Open, 3
stat command, 273, 466
stat() function, 447
sticky bit, 457, 459, 504
STOP signal, 361, 362
strace command, 368
Stream Editor (see sed command)
string constants, awk, 226
string functions, awk, 255–264
string substitution, awk, 257
string-length operator, 115
strings
  comparing, awk, 227
  concatenating, awk, 227
  converting to numbers, awk, 228
  extended notation for, 401
  formatting, awk, 261–264
  matching, awk, 257
  reconstruction, awk, 260
  searching, in awk, 256
  splitting, awk, 258–260
  test expressions, 127
  test expressions for, 125
strings command, 85, 476
strip_suffixes() function, awk spellchecker, 341
Structured Query Language (SQL), 95, 504
stty command, 357, 474
su command, 418
sub() function, awk, 257
SUBSEP variable, awk, 234
subshells, 167, 505
substitution operators, 113
substitution (see expansion)
substr() function, awk, 256
substring extraction, awk, 256

subtraction operator, 118, 401
sudo program, 421
suffix, 505
suid_profile file, 421
sum command, 301
Sun GridEngine, 375
superuser, 505
symbolic links, 449, 461–463, 505
  following to find broken links, 286
  security and, 415
  test expression for, 125
symlink, 449
syslog command, 414
systat command, 356
system call tracers, 368–371
system() function, awk, 251
system managers, monitoring file contents, 467

T

\t escape sequence, 16, 148
-t test expression, 125, 392
TABLE environment, HTML, 97
tabs, escape sequence for, 16, 148
tag lists
  creating, 105–107
  processing, 137
tags, HTML, 96
tail command, 84, 476
tar command, 476
.tar file extension, 470
TCP (Transmission Control Protocol), 506
tee command, 475
temporary files, 274–278
TERM signal, 361, 362
terminal
  redirecting to, 21
  test expression for, 125
test command, 124–128, 474
test facility, extended, 392–393
TEX, 82
Texinfo markup format, 423, 436
text
  characters
    counting, 10, 77
    transliterating, 20
  commands for, list of, 474
  counting lines, words, characters in, 77
  duplicate records in, removing, 75
  extracting first and last lines of, 83–86
  formatting as HTML, 94–100
  processing of, history of, 3

text (*continued*)
reformatting paragraphs in, 76
searching for (see grep command)
Software Tools principles for, 4
sorting multiline records in, 72
sorting records in, 67–72
words, 507
counting, 10, 77, 240
frequency list of, 102–104
separator characters for, 117
tags in, finding, 105–107
(see also strings)
text files, 441
(see also files)
text substitution, 48–56
tgrind command, 83
.TH command, troff, 425
.ti command, troff, 427
tilde (~)
~- ($OLDPWD tilde expansion), 399
~+ ($PWD tilde expansion), 399
arithmetic operator, 118, 401
in temporary backup file name, 470
matches operator, awk, 228
tilde expansion, 152, 399, 505
tilde expansion, 152, 399, 505
time
epoch for, 274
representation of, 274
time slice, 352, 505
times command, 169, 172
timestamps for files, 286, 460–461, 465
TITLE object, HTML, 96
/tmp directory, 206, 275
TMPDIR variable, 276
tolower() function, awk, 256
toolbox approach (see Software Tools
philosophy)
tools, xiii, xiv
top command, 355, 357, 476
touch command, 273–274, 461, 476
toupper() function, awk, 256
.TP command, troff, 428
tr command, 20, 475
tag list example using, 105–107
word frequency example using, 102
trace command, 368
tracing (see execution tracing)
Transmission Control Protocol (TCP), 506
trap, 506
trap command, 90, 169, 276, 364–367, 474
-p option, 400

tree structure of filesystem, 443, 506
troff command, 82, 435
troff markup format, 423
command syntax, 425
comments in, 425
creating manual pages using, 424–431
fonts in, 425, 427, 428
white space in, 425
Trojan horses, 418, 506
true command, 169, 474
truss command, 368
TSTP signal, 361
type command, 280, 474
typeset command, 474
typo command, 347

U

%u format specifier, 149, 150, 261
-u shell option, 174
-u test expression, 125, 393
uappnd permission, 506
ulimit command, 452, 474
umask command, 169, 172, 455, 467, 476
umount command, 445
unalias command, 169, 171
unary minus operator, 118, 401
unary plus operator, 118, 401
unexpand command, 475
Unicode character set, 25, 35, 99, 333, 348,
439, 471, 506
uniform resource locator (URL), 445, 507
uniq command, 75, 475
tag list example using, 106
word frequency example using, 102
unique key, 94
Unix, history of, 1–4
Unix spelling dictionary, 100
Unix User's Manual, references to, xx
unlink() function, 275
unset command, 111–113, 169, 474
until statement, 130
unzip command, 476
updatedb command, 279
uptime command, 352, 356, 477
urandom device, 450
URL (uniform resource locator), 445, 507
user, 507
user input
checking for metacharacters, 415
quoting, 414
running eval command on, 415
user ownership, 453

user-controlled input, awk, 249–250
user-defined functions, awk, 252–255
userhosts file for customization, 193
usr directory, 444
/usr/tmp directory, 275
UTC (Coordinated Universal Time), 460,
    488
UTF-8 encoding, 78, 333, 348, 439, 471, 507
utime() function, 461
UWIN package, xxii

V

\v escape sequence, 16, 148
,v file extension, 470
-v shell option, 174
variables, 14
    array variables, 233–234, 485
    assigning values to, 15
    built-in, in awk, 232
    changing for program environment, 111
    exporting all subsequently defined, 174
    global, case of, 180
    in format specifiers, 151
    in functions, awk, 253
    length of value of, 115
    local, case of, 180
    naming conventions for, 180
    passed in to scripts, security of, 414
    printing all values of, 174
    putting in program environment, 111
    putting into environment, 110
    reading data into, 140–143
    read-only, setting, 110
    removing from environment, 111–113
    removing from program
        environment, 111
    retrieving values from, 15, 113–118
    scalar, in awk, 232
    undefined, treating as errors, 174
/var/tmp directory, 275
verbose shell option, 174
--version option, 182
vertical bar (|)
    |= (assignment operator), 119, 401
    || (logical OR operator), 118, 123, 230,
        401
    alternation operator, 43, 484
    bitwise OR operator, 118, 401
    expr operator, 160
    in regular expressions, 35
    pipe symbol, 10
vertical tab, escape sequence for, 16, 148

vgrind command, 83
vi shell option, 174
vi, using for command-line editing, 174
virtual machine, 507
vmstat command, 356
vmubc command, 356

W

w command, 356
-w test expression, 125, 393
wait command, 169, 172, 356, 476
wc command, 10, 77, 240, 475
websites
    awk interpreter, free implementations
        of, 224
    batch queue and scheduler systems, 375
    code examples, xxi
    cygwin environment, xxi
    DJGPP suite, xxii
    MKS Toolkit, xxii
    O'Reilly Media, Inc., xxiii
    public-key servers, 304
    Single UNIX Specification, xv
    sudo program, 421
    Unix history, 1
    Unix-related standards, xv
    UWIN package, xxiii
wget command, 306
while statement, 130
    awk, 245–247
    path search example using, 181
    read file example using, 141
    software build example using, 197
whitespace, 507
    awk language, 226
    in command line, 13
    in filenames, 441
    in HTML, 96
who command, 9, 474
wildcard expansion
    disabling, 174
    of command-line arguments, 353
    quoting results of, 415
    (see also pathname expansion)
wildcards
    in filenames, 153–155
    in parameter expansion, 114
Windows operating system, Unix tools
        for, xxi–xxiii
wireless networks, security and, 468
word matching, in regular expressions, 46

word puzzles, pattern matching dictionary for, 100–101
word-constituent characters, 46, 507
words, 507
    counting, 10, 77, 240
    frequency list of, 102–104
    separator characters for, 117
    tags in, finding, 105–107
working directory (see current working directory)
writable file, test expression for, 125
write permission, 453, 458, 507

X

%X format specifier, 149, 150, 261
%x format specifier, 149, 150, 261
-x shell option, 174
-x test expression, 125, 393
xargs command, 293, 476
xcpustate command, 356
xload command, 356
XML (eXtensible Markup Language), 490
    converting troff markup to, 436
    defining multiline records with, 74
    for manual pages, 424
X/Open Portability Guide, Fourth Edition (XPG4), 3

X/Open standards, 3
X/Open System Interface Extension (XSI), 4, 508
X/Open System Interface (XSI) specification, xv
xperfmon command, 356
XPG4 (X/Open Portability Guide, Fourth Edition), 3
XSI (X/Open System Interface Extension), 4, 508
XSI (X/Open System Interface) specification, xv
xtrace shell option, 174

Y

ypcat command, 453
ypmatch command, 453

Z

.Z file extension, 470
.z file extension, 470
-z test expression, 125, 393
ZDOTDIR variable, 410
zip command, 476
zsh (Z-Shell), 405, 410–412, 473
Z-shell (see zsh)

About the Authors

Arnold Robbins, an Atlanta native, is a professional programmer and technical author. He is also a happy husband, the father of four very cute children, and an amateur Talmudist (Babylonian and Jerusalem). Since late 1997, he and his family have been living in Israel.

Arnold has been working with Unix systems since 1980, when he was introduced to a PDP-11 running a version of Sixth Edition Unix. He has been doing serious shell scripting since 1984, when he started enhancing the Bourne shell and then later moved to using the Korn shell and bash.

Arnold has also been a heavy awk user since 1987, when he became involved with gawk, the GNU project's version of awk. As a member of the POSIX 1003.2 balloting group, he helped shape the POSIX standard for awk. He is currently the maintainer of gawk and its documentation.

In previous incarnations, he has been a systems administrator and a teacher of Unix and networking continuing education classes. He has also had more than one poor experience with start-up software companies, which he prefers not to think about anymore. One day he hopes to put up his own web site at *http://www.skeeve.com*.

O'Reilly has been keeping him busy. He is author and/or coauthor of the bestselling titles *Learning the vi Editor*, *Effective awk Programming*, *sed and awk*, *Learning the Korn Shell*, *Unix in a Nutshell*, and several pocket references.

Nelson H. F. Beebe is Research Professor of Mathematics at the University of Utah with a background in chemistry, physics, mathematics, computer science, and computing facility management. He has worked on computers from most of the major manufacturers for longer than he likes to admit. He keeps a score of Unix flavors on his desktop at all times, along with some vintage systems that now run only in simulators. He is an expert in several programming languages (including awk), floating-point arithmetic, software portability, scientific software, and computer graphics, and has had a long involvement with electronic document production and typography dating back to the early days of Unix.

Colophon

Our look is the result of reader comments, our own experimentation, and feedback from distribution channels. Distinctive covers complement our distinctive approach to technical topics, breathing personality and life into potentially dry subjects.

The animal on the cover of *Classic Shell Scripting* is the knobby geometric or African tent tortoise (*Psammobates tentorius*). The genus *Psammobates* literally means "sand-loving," so it isn't surprising that the tent tortoise is found only in the steppes and outer desert zones of southern Africa. All species in this genus are small, ranging in size from five to ten inches, and have yellow radiating marks on their carapace. The tent tortoise is particularly striking, with arched scutes that look like tents.

Tortoises are known for their long lifespan, and turtles and tortoises are also among the most ancient animal species alive today. They existed in the era of dinosaurs some 200 million years ago. All tortoises are temperature dependent, which means they eat only when the temperature is not too extreme. During hot summer and cold winter days, tortoises go into a torpor and stop feeding altogether. In the spring, the tent tortoise's diet consists of succulent, fibrous plants and grasses.

In captivity, this species may hibernate from June to September, and will sometimes dig itself into a burrow and remain there for quite a long time. All "sand-loving" tortoises are very difficult to maintain in captivity. They are highly susceptible to shell disease and respiratory problems brought on by cold or damp environments, so their enclosures must be extremely sunny and dry. The popularity of these species among tortoise enthusiasts and commercial traders, along with the continued destruction of their natural habitat, has made the African tent tortoise among the top twenty-five most endangered tortoises in the world.

Adam Witwer was the production editor and Audrey Doyle was the copyeditor for *Classic Shell Scripting*. Ann Schirmer proofread the text. Colleen Gorman and Claire Cloutier provided quality control. Angela Howard wrote the index.

Emma Colby designed the cover of this book, based on a series design by Edie Freedman. The cover image is a 19th-century engraving from the Dover Pictorial Archive. Karen Montgomery produced the cover layout with Adobe InDesign CS using Adobe's ITC Garamond font.

David Futato designed the interior layout. This book was converted by Keith Fahlgren to FrameMaker 5.5.6 with a format conversion tool created by Erik Ray, Jason McIntosh, Neil Walls, and Mike Sierra that uses Perl and XML technologies. The text font is Linotype Birka; the heading font is Adobe Myriad Condensed; and the code font is LucasFont's TheSans Mono Condensed. The illustrations that appear in the book were produced by Robert Romano, Jessamyn Read, and Lesley Borash using Macromedia FreeHand MX and Adobe Photoshop CS. The tip and warning icons were drawn by Christopher Bing. This colophon was written by Lydia Onofrei.

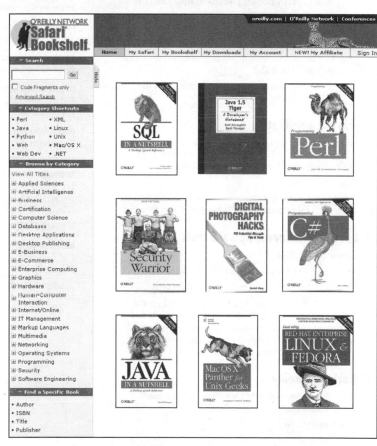
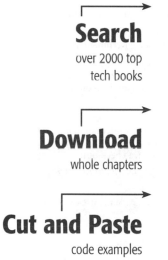
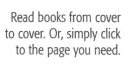

Keep in touch with O'Reilly

1. Download examples from our books

To find example files for a book, go to:

www.oreilly.com/catalog

select the book, and follow the "Examples" link.

2. Register your O'Reilly books

Register your book at *register.oreilly.com*

Why register your books?
Once you've registered your O'Reilly books you can:

- Win O'Reilly books, T-shirts or discount coupons in our monthly drawing.
- Get special offers available only to registered O'Reilly customers.
- Get catalogs announcing new books (US and UK only).
- Get email notification of new editions of the O'Reilly books you own.

3. Join our email lists

Sign up to get topic-specific email announcements of new books and conferences, special offers, and O'Reilly Network technology newsletters at:

elists.oreilly.com

It's easy to customize your free elists subscription so you'll get exactly the O'Reilly news you want.

4. Get the latest news, tips, and tools

www.oreilly.com

- "Top 100 Sites on the Web"—PC Magazine
- CIO Magazine's Web Business 50 Awards

Our web site contains a library of comprehensive product information (including book excerpts and tables of contents), downloadable software, background articles, interviews with technology leaders, links to relevant sites, book cover art, and more.

5. Work for O'Reilly

Check out our web site for current employment opportunities:

jobs.oreilly.com

6. Contact us

O'Reilly & Associates
1005 Gravenstein Hwy North
Sebastopol, CA 95472 USA

TEL: 707-827-7000 or 800-998-9938
         (6am to 5pm PST)

FAX: 707-829-0104

order@oreilly.com
For answers to problems regarding your order or our products. To place a book order online, visit:

www.oreilly.com/order_new

catalog@oreilly.com
To request a copy of our latest catalog.

booktech@oreilly.com
For book content technical questions or corrections.

corporate@oreilly.com
For educational, library, government, and corporate sales.

proposals@oreilly.com
To submit new book proposals to our editors and product managers.

international@oreilly.com
For information about our international distributors or translation queries. For a list of our distributors outside of North America check out:

international.oreilly.com/distributors.html

adoption@oreilly.com
For information about academic use of O'Reilly books, visit:

academic.oreilly.com